MASS MEDIA LAW

A SURVEY OF CONTENT AND CULTURE

MASS MEDIA LAW

A SURVEY OF CONTENT AND CULTURE

MICHAEL M. EPSTEIN

Mass Media Law: A Survey of Content and Culture

Epstein, Michael M.

Third Edition

Published by:

Vandeplas Publishing, LLC
801 International Pkwy., 5th Floor
Lake Mary, FL 32746
US

www.vandeplaspublishing.com

ISBN 978-1-60042-291-1

For Molly and Max – 143.

PREFACE TO THE THIRD EDITION

As we approach the third decade of the 21st century, mass media is in a period of rapid, far-reaching change. New technologies of production, distribution and exhibition mean that many of the business models and legal structures of television and film entertainment, journalism, and the Internet are converging. With the advent of the Trump Administration in Washington, laws relating to privacy, journalist privilege, net neutrality, and consolidation are in play. Despite this change, mass media law remains multifaceted, with different regulations applying to different technologies, and legacy companies seeking to adapt to, and exert control over, expanding channels of discourse.

To address the old and the new, I have culled the reading materials in this book to their essential core. In addition to explanatory text in each chapter, I have edited court decisions and statutory provisions, where possible, to let them speak for themselves. Most of the longer cases already offer the type of descriptive history that can set the stage for greater understanding of the current law. Keeping the text lean also underscores another main goal of this course—to teach concepts and critical thinking that will help students and practitioners. My objective is to enable you to flag potential problems and recognize solutions out in the "real world." Now that searchable legal databases are available to all of us at the touch of a button, creative thinking and critical problem-solving are skills that good lawyers need to have.

For the Third Edition, my thanks go to the faculty and staff of Southwestern Law School, and to my former research assistants Melissa A. Agnetti, Addison J. Martinez, and Julie L. Bedigian.

Michael M. Epstein
Los Angeles, July 2017

TABLE OF CONTENTS

CHAPTER 1

GENERAL APPROACHES TO SPEECH

Introduction—Mass Media Defined

Mass media is where the action is. By its very nature, mass media is about movement, the movement of information from one to many or many to many. To understand mass media is to understand the technologies and economics of communication on a scale that is greater than one-to-one, or even one to a few. Mass media is about creating and delivering content to the masses through the use of communication and distribution technologies. Broadcast airwaves, cable wires, newsprint, and broadband are just a few examples of the pathways over which communication technologies operate. These pathways—also called conduits—allow content to flow from a transmission point to a reception point. Since the conduit is in between the beginning and end point of the communication, it is referred to as "media"—from the Latin for "in between." To be "mass media," technologies of distribution must also be in place so that many can receive the communication. The dawn of the mass media age came with the development of the printing press in the fifteenth century, which, for the first time, allowed multiple copies of a book to be printed and distributed to a large audience. In the ensuing 500 years, new technologies of communication and distribution have enabled content to be transmitted and received more efficiently, and over greater distances. The use of electricity, for example, in broadcasting, cable, satellite, and the Internet, allows transmissions to travel very long distances as signals that can be received by many people far from the source—and far from each other. Think about it as communication on steroids. These electronically assisted conduits are called telecommunications, since they travel far.

This book looks specifically at the law relating to mass media. In some respect, the laws of mass media are the laws of content. Laws relating generally to speech, such as defamation, privacy, obscenity, and incitement, comprise a significant portion of this text. But mass media is also about the law of the conduit. This type of law or regulation may relate to the structure of a specific conduit (for example, broadcasting or cable) or it may relate to the content that flows over the conduit (such as broadcast indecency). For those of you who have a basic understanding of the American legal system and its sources of law, you may want to skip ahead to the next section.

Sources of Law

The American legal system is really fifty-one different legal systems—each of the fifty states independently enacts laws and maintains courts to adjudicate those laws. In addition, the United States enacts its own laws and maintains a separate court system. Under the United States Constitution, U.S. laws—federal laws—may take precedence over state laws, or they may operate independently of state laws. In some cases, a federal law will preempt a state from acting to regulate in a specific area or industry. Nearly all the structural laws relating to telecommunications conduits are handled exclusively by the federal government. Federal law, for example, precludes state governments from regulating television or radio broadcasting. On the other hand, states have a wide range of authority over speech that is unrelated to electronic telecommunications. Cases involving speech torts such as defamation and privacy, obscenity, incitement, or journalistic privilege are commonly heard in state court under state law. State laws include statutes passed by state legislatures or local entities and laws that evolved from English legal traditions known as the common law. The final say on the law in a state lies generally in that state's highest court, which is usually but not always known as a supreme court. In cases, however, that implicate federal law or rights enshrined in the U.S. Constitution, the decision of the state's highest court is subject to review and reversal by the U.S. Supreme Court, which is the highest court in the land.

While the governing structure of each state may vary, the U.S. Constitution sets out a clear division of authority between the three branches of the federal government: the executive, the legislature, and the judiciary. In addition to the U.S. Supreme Court, the federal judiciary consists of twelve circuit courts of appeal, which impanel judges to decide cases on appeal from trials conducted in district courts within that circuit. Only cases that involve highly contentious legal questions or conflicting decisions in different circuit courts will be considered by the U.S. Supreme Court, generally under what is known as a writ of certiorari. The U.S. Supreme Court is the final word in interpreting federal statutes, which are enacted by the U.S. Congress and, in most cases, signed by the U.S. President. The Court is also charged with interpreting the U.S. Constitution itself; it can enunciate rights under the document, and invalidate federal laws by declaring them unconstitutional.

Though Congress has the sole power to pass legislation, many federal statutes cannot address the complex and specialized nature of the subject it seeks to regulate. For that reason, Congress routinely delegates its authority to agencies that function as part of the executive branch. These agencies have administrative powers to issue federal regulations in their specialized areas and to enforce those regulations, subject to review by the federal courts. Judicial review of agency regulations may seek to determine if a regulation is an abuse of the agency's discretion, not authorized by a statute, or unconstitutional. In the United States, the agency charged with regulating civilian telecommunications is the Federal Communications Commission (FCC). FCC rules and regulations are subject to federal court review to determine if they exceed the agency's authority under the Communications Act of 1934. The Communications Act of 1934 is the statute that governs telecommunications—including mass media like cable, broadcasting, and satellite, and point-to-point "common carrier" technologies like telephony. Later communications statutes are codified as amendments to the Communications Act of 1934, so even though the statute sounds old, much of it is quite new.

The Communications Act is the main statute governing electronic forms of mass media law, but an attorney with a broad mass media practice would expect to encounter a number of other federal and state laws along the way. Federal examples include the Federal Trade Commission Act of 1914, which created the Federal Trade Commission (FTC) to regulate advertising standards and handle complaints, the Food, Drug, and Cosmetic Act, which authorized the Food and Drug Administration (FDA) to regulate prescription drug commercials, and the Freedom of Information Act, which allows conditional access to government records. At the state level, state statutes and common-law precedents relating to speech are relevant to the media lawyer, including the defamation and privacy torts, right of publicity protections, pornography restrictions, and reporter's privilege.

All of the above sources of mass media law, whether federal, state, or common law, are ultimately subject to court scrutiny under the U.S. Constitution, which in most cases, means those provisions relating to free speech under the First Amendment to the U.S. Constitution.

HOW TO FIND AND READ A CASE

Locating published court decisions can be counterintuitive to the uninitiated. Unlike most citation formats, case citations do not use descriptors to denote volume or page numbers. As a rule of thumb, volume numbers go first, followed by the court (or a work's title). Numbers representing the first page of the decision come third, along with the year in parentheses. Thus, New York Times v. Sullivan is cited as 376 U.S. 254 (1964). That tells a reader that the case can be found on page 254 of volume 367 of the U.S. Supreme Court's official reporter. Some citations include another number for a pinpoint citation, to identify the page from which a particular excerpt is quoted. Of course, in this age, one can find many well-known decisions by simply typing the case name into an Internet search engine.

The best way to understand a case is to write while reading it. Whether it is a stand-alone outline of the case, called a brief, or annotations in the margins, it is important to focus on the following: the parties, the court, the issue(s) in dispute, the holding, and dicta. The first three of these are usually easy to spot. Finding a decision's holding and dicta, if any, can be more elusive. The holding describes the court's resolution of a case and often includes its reasoning. Dicta refer to conclusions expressed by the court that do not contribute directly to a case's outcome. In most cases, a court's holding has precedent value under the principle of stare decisis, which means that judges on the same court must take the holding into account when rendering a later decision in a similar case, unless they decide to overrule that earlier decision's holding. If a higher court decides to reject the holding of a lower court in a particular case, the decision is said to be "reversed" on appeal. The court's holding is found in the opinion ascribed to the majority of judges and, in some cases, a single trial judge. A concurrence is written by a judge who agrees with the outcome but disagrees with all or some of the majority opinion's reasoning. A dissent is prepared by a judge or judges who disagree with the decision made by the majority. Concurrences and dissents are an important part of any case outline as they may develop persuasive value for later courts tasked to decide cases with the same or similar issues in dispute.

The First Amendment: Speech and Press Clauses

"Congress shall make no law . . . abridging the freedom of speech, or of the press . . . ."

The First Amendment to the U.S. Constitution was ratified as part of the Bill of Rights in 1791, three years after the drafting of the Constitution itself. Despite this delay, freedom of speech was no afterthought for the Framers. A long history of British laws restricting speech and press freedom played a large role in fomenting the unrest among colonists that led to the American Revolution. By the time of the Declaration of Independence in 1776, and in the years following under the Articles of Confederation, freedom of speech was regarded as a state issue, enshrined to varying degrees in state constitutions. The First Amendment was not intended to upend state free speech guarantees. Like much of the Bill of Rights, it was ratified to place a limitation on the powers of the newly created federal government over citizens. This is reflected in the language of the First Amendment, which is framed as a negation of Congress' authority, as opposed to the declaration of an affirmative right.

In an 1833 case, Barron v. Baltimore, the Supreme Court considered—and rejected—arguments that the Bill of Rights should apply to protect citizens against state power. It is only after World War I, in the case of Gitlow v. New York, that the Supreme Court decided that the First Amendment can apply against the states, through the Due Process Clause of the Fourteenth Amendment, ratified in 1868. It is now widely accepted that the First Amendment applies against all branches and appendages of both state and federal government, and the courts have developed a rich and varied First Amendment jurisprudence since the 1930s.

Why Do We Care About Free Speech?

With the onset of First Amendment cases following World War I, many jurists and legal scholars began opining about the value of free speech to society. In Abrams v. United States, (excerpted infra), Supreme Court Justice Oliver Wendell Holmes, Jr. dissents eloquently from a decision to jail anti-war activists, citing the value of criticizing Congress in the absence of a "clear and present danger" that imminent harm would result. Justice Louis D. Brandeis, concurring in Whitney v. California, 274 U.S. 357 (1927), places the value of free speech in an historical context:

> Those who won our independence believed that the final end of the State was to make men free to develop their faculties; and that in its government the deliberative forces should prevail over the arbitrary. They valued liberty both as an end and as a means. They believed liberty to be the secret of happiness and courage to be the secret of liberty. They believed that freedom to think as you will and to speak as you think are means indispensable to the discovery and spread of political truth; that without free speech and assembly discussion would be futile; that with them, discussion affords ordinarily adequate protection against the dissemination of noxious doctrine; that the greatest menace to freedom is an inert people; that public discussion is a political duty; and that this should be a fundamental principle of the American government. They recognized the risks to which all human institutions are subject. But they knew that order cannot be secured merely through fear of punishment for its infraction; that it is hazardous to discourage thought, hope and imagination; that fear breeds repression; that repression breeds hate; that hate menaces stable government; that the path of safety lies in the opportunity to discuss freely supposed grievances and proposed remedies; and that the fitting remedy for evil counsels is good ones. Believing in the power of reason as applied through public discussion, they eschewed silence coerced by law—the argument of force in its worst form. Recognizing the occasional tyrannies of governing majorities, they amended the Constitution so that free speech and assembly should be guaranteed.

These reasons are also present in the work of elite legal scholars in the middle part of the twentieth century, which was also a time when television and radio were maturing as powerful influences on society. Professor Thomas I. Emerson, writing in 1970, described a number of values that free speech brings to the individual and society. For Emerson, free speech: (1) facilitates self-fulfillment, (2) is essential for advancing knowledge and discovering truth, (3) fosters a more stable and adaptable community, (4) encourages people to become involved in democratic decision-making, and (5) promotes rational debate that allows disagreeing factions to blow off steam. In the 1940s, Zachariah Chafee and Alexander Meiklejohn, both eminent professors, debated differing views of the "marketplace of ideas," a free market ideal embraced by Justice Holmes that suggests that speech flourishes in the absence of regulation.

Chafee expressed concern that media companies operating in a free market might accumulate too much market power, becoming monopolies that would restrict access to media by others. Meiklejohn envisioned a marketplace of ideas in which the First Amendment would bar any regulation of political speech. Other speech, including art, would be regulated under the Fifth Amendment's Due Process Clause, which permits greater government intervention. In the 1960s, the Marxist philosopher Herbert Marcuse critiqued the very premise that a free market for speech would foster rationale debate, and allow for dissent. Concerned that the concentration of economic power engendered by monopolistic media suppresses "effective dissent" instead of fostering it, Marcuse proposed suspending free speech in favor of a system that would privilege leftist movements over those of the right.

In the second decade of the twenty-first century, one has to wonder who among these scholars from yesterday has the better argument. Have the benefits of free speech to society come to pass? This is an age, after all, when candidates can be "swift-boated" by false political ads and government officials replace substantive debate with television-friendly sound bites. Does free speech always lead us to truth? And is the free "marketplace of ideas" really free when media access is controlled by conglomerates? In the United States, market power in media is dominated by a relative few—mainly corporations seeking to provide a profitable return to shareholders. Although, as we will see later, a right of reply, if it existed, would be constitutional in broadcasting, there is currently no such right; moreover, the First Amendment prohibits government from mandating a right of reply or access to non-broadcast media. As a result, whether you can get your idea heard through mass media largely depends on whether you can get a media company to disseminate your message. To a small extent, the Internet may be changing this—some homegrown messages get wide dissemination via YouTube as memes, which then get repeated prominently on television, radio, and in newspapers. But even the possibility of access via the Internet is limited, as many of the most popular Web sites are owned by the same conglomerates who dominate in traditional media.

For all its failings in practice, free speech is the best system for a democratic society. With every freedom comes responsibility, and it is our responsibility to use speech wisely, even though we may not have to by law. In short, free speech can do all the good for society that Holmes, Brandeis, Emerson, Chafee, and Meiklejohn believed. It can also be abused, as Chafee worried and Marcuse declared. Whether freedom of speech lives up to its potential depends ultimately on us—and the courts.

Limits on Free Speech

Some readers might agree with Alexander Meiklejohn that people should be absolutely free to engage in political speech without government interference. A few of you may go even farther and argue that government should be absolutely barred from restricting any type of speech, a position that would make you a free speech absolutist. The First Amendment does enunciate an absolute bar on government absolutists argue that the words "shall make no law" should be given their plain meaning. Most people today—and virtually all courts—subscribe to the view that government can restrict certain speech content and regulate the way in which speech is disseminated. Few would argue, for example, that a speaker is free to display child pornography, incite a riot, or utter a true threat without the government taking action. And it is unlikely that anyone would doubt the ability of government to enact legislation that prohibited protestors from holding rallies with bullhorns on a residential street after midnight.

Over the last ninety years, the courts have developed a First Amendment jurisprudence that allows the government to regulate different types of speech content with different levels of scrutiny from the courts. This categorical approach to the First Amendment classifies speech content as either protected or unprotected. Examples of protected speech content are political speech, literary and scientific speech, and artistic expression. To the extent that government wants to impose restraints based on the substance of speech content, the law will be subject to strict judicial scrutiny, which means that the government must have a compelling interest for the law and demonstrate that the restraint is the least restrictive means.

While the First Amendment presumes to protect most speech, the second category of unprotected speech applies to speech that the courts have determined to be of little or no value to society. Obscenity, "fighting words," incitements to violence, and defamation can be regulated by the government as long as there is a rational basis for the restriction. It may be easy to spot extreme examples of protected or unprotected speech, but some speech may be harder to classify. Is a political tract that uses obscene illustrations protected or unprotected? Under the test currently used by the courts, such speech would likely be protected. Even so, it is hard cases such as this that courts often adjudicate today under the First Amendment's categorical approach.

Content-Neutral Regulations

Regulations that seek to restrict protected speech content are subject to strict scrutiny by the courts; but what of regulations that seek to regulate the time, place, or manner of speech? If the time, place, or manner regulation restricts all speech equally—regardless of the message or viewpoint—then it will be deemed content-neutral. Content-neutral regulations are subject to intermediate scrutiny, a less rigorous form of court review that greatly improves the chances that a speech restraint will be upheld under the First Amendment. Whether a regulation is content-neutral can sometimes be tricky; a city ordinance that denies parade permits to racist groups at night will not qualify, as it discriminates on the basis of viewpoint. For the regulation to be content-neutral, the nighttime restriction would have to apply to all parade groups, without regard to viewpoint.

The test used for content neutrality comes from the 1968 Supreme Court case United States v. O'Brien. O'Brien, who opposed the Vietnam War, destroyed his draft card in front of cameras on the steps of a Boston courthouse. Convicted under a federal law that prohibited mutilation of a draft card, O'Brien argued before the Court that the regulation infringed his free speech rights. While the Court conceded that some regulations might have an impact on speech content, the justices ruled against O'Brien. According to the Court, a government regulation will be constitutional if: (1) it is within the Constitutional power of the government, (2) it furthers an important or substantial interest, (3) the interest is unrelated to the free speech event, and (4) the resulting suppression is no greater than essential. As you review the case excerpt infra, consider how the Court applied this test to David O'Brien.

UNITED STATES V. O'BRIEN
391 U.S. 367 (1968)

Mr. Chief Justice WARREN delivered the opinion of the Court.
On the morning of March 31, 1966, David Paul O'Brien and three companions burned their Selective Service registration certificates on the steps of the South Boston Courthouse. A sizable crowd, including several agents of the Federal Bureau of Investigation, witnessed the event. Immediately after the burning, members of the crowd began attacking O'Brien and his companions. An FBI agent ushered O'Brien to safety inside the courthouse. After he was advised of his right to counsel and to silence, O'Brien stated to FBI agents that he had burned his registration

certificate because of his beliefs, knowing that he was violating federal law. He produced the charred remains of the certificate, which, with his consent, were photographed.

Burning draft card, 1967.

For this act, O'Brien was indicted, tried, convicted, and sentenced in the United States District Court for the District of Massachusetts. He did not contest the fact that he had burned the certificate. He stated in argument to the jury that he burned the certificate publicly to influence others to adopt his antiwar beliefs, as he put it, "so that other people would reevaluate their positions with Selective Service, with the armed forces, and reevaluate their place in the culture of today, to hopefully consider my position."

The indictment upon which he was tried charged that he "willfully and knowingly did mutilate, destroy, and change by burning . . . [his] Registration Certificate (Selective Service System Form No. 2); in violation of Title 50, App., United States Code, Section 462(b)." Section 462(b) is part of the Universal Military Training and Service Act of 1948. Section 462(b)(3), one of six numbered subdivisions of § 462(b), was amended by Congress in 1965, 79 Stat. 586 (adding the words italicized below), so that at the time O'Brien burned his certificate an offense was committed by any person, "who forges, alters, *knowingly destroys, knowingly mutilates*, or in any manner changes any such certificate . . . ." (Italics supplied.)

. . .

O'Brien nonetheless argues that the 1965 Amendment is unconstitutional in its application to him, and is unconstitutional as enacted because what he calls the "purpose" of Congress was "to suppress freedom of speech." We consider these arguments separately.

II.

O'Brien first argues that the 1965 Amendment is unconstitutional as applied to him because his act of burning his registration certificate was protected "symbolic speech" within the First Amendment. His argument is that the freedom of expression which the First Amendment guarantees includes all modes of "communication of ideas by conduct," and that his conduct is within this definition because he did it in "demonstration against the war and against the draft."

We cannot accept the view that an apparently limitless variety of conduct can be labeled "speech" whenever the person engaging in the conduct intends thereby to express an idea. However, even on the assumption that the alleged communicative element in O'Brien's conduct is sufficient to bring into play the First Amendment, it does not necessarily follow that the destruction of a registration certificate is constitutionally protected activity. This Court has held that when "speech" and "nonspeech" elements are combined in the same course of conduct, a sufficiently important governmental interest in regulating the nonspeech element can justify incidental limitations on First Amendment freedoms. To characterize the quality of the governmental interest which must appear, the Court has employed a variety of descriptive terms: compelling; substantial; subordinating; paramount; cogent; strong. Whatever imprecision inheres in these terms, we think it clear that a government regulation is sufficiently justified if it is within the constitutional power of the Government; if it furthers an important or substantial governmental interest; if the governmental interest is unrelated to the suppression of free expression; and if the incidental restriction on alleged First Amendment freedoms is no greater than is essential to the furtherance of that interest. We find that the 1965 Amendment to § 12(b)(3) of the Universal Military Training and Service Act meets all of these requirements, and consequently that O'Brien can be constitutionally convicted for violating it.

. . .

The many functions performed by Selective Service certificates establish beyond doubt that Congress has a legitimate and substantial interest in preventing their wanton and unrestrained destruction and assuring their continuing availability by punishing people who knowingly and wilfully [sic] destroy or mutilate them. And we are unpersuaded that the pre-existence of the nonpossession regulations in any way negates this interest.

. . .

In conclusion, we find that because of the Government's substantial interest in assuring the continuing availability of issued Selective Service certificates, because amended § 462(b) is an appropriately narrow means of protecting this interest and condemns only the independent noncommunicative impact of conduct within its reach, and because the noncommunicative impact of O'Brien's act of burning his registration certificate frustrated the Government's interest, a sufficient governmental interest has been shown to justify O'Brien's conviction.

III.

O'Brien finally argues that the 1965 Amendment is unconstitutional as enacted because what he calls the "purpose" of Congress was "to suppress freedom of speech." We reject this argument because under settled principles the purpose of Congress, as O'Brien uses that term, is not a basis for declaring this legislation unconstitutional.

. . .

IV.

Since the 1965 Amendment to § 12(b)(3) of the Universal Military Training and Service Act is constitutional as enacted and as applied, the Court of Appeals should have affirmed the judgment of conviction entered by the District Court. Accordingly, we vacate the judgment of the Court of Appeals, and reinstate the judgment and sentence of the District Court. This disposition makes unnecessary consideration of O'Brien's claim that the Court of Appeals erred in affirming his conviction on the basis of the nonpossession regulation.

It is so ordered.

. . .

Mr. Justice HARLAN, concurring.

The crux of the Court's opinion, which I join, is of course its general statement, *ante*, at 1679, that:

> "a government regulation is sufficiently justified if it is within the constitutional power of the Government; if it furthers an important or substantial governmental interest; if the governmental interest is unrelated to the suppression of free expression; and if the incidental restriction on alleged First Amendment freedoms is no greater than is essential to the furtherance of that interest."

I wish to make explicit my understanding that this passage does not foreclose consideration of First Amendment claims in those rare instances when an "incidental" restriction upon expression, imposed by a regulation which furthers an "important or substantial" governmental interest and satisfies the Court's other criteria, in practice has the effect of entirely preventing a "speaker" from reaching a significant audience with whom he could not otherwise lawfully communicate. This is not such a case, since O'Brien manifestly could have conveyed his message in many ways other than by burning his draft card.

—

The *O'Brien* test thus provides courts with an intermediate level of scrutiny when the regulation is content-neutral. Content neutrality, however, is a concept that is not limited to time, place, and manner regulations. *O'Brien*, for example, is commonly used when a regulation that purports to outlaw conduct also has an impact on speech. A regulation that may appear to have nothing to do with speech may be ruled unconstitutional because the state's interest in not unrelated to the speech, or the burden on the speaker is too great. It is for this reason that the Supreme Court, in cases such as Turner v. FCC (1997) infra, uses the *O'Brien* test to determine if a structural regulation of a medium will pass muster under the First Amendment. If, for example, a regulation designed to curb the cable industry's market power is determined to be unrelated to speech, the regulation will be constitutional, unless the court finds that the law is too burdensome on the speaker.

O'Brien is useful to courts because some laws that appear to be regulating conduct may actual be content regulations in disguise. That is because some conduct is actually symbolic speech—which would require strict scrutiny under the categorical approach. The speech value of some conduct is readily apparent to anyone who has been on the receiving end of a raised middle finger. No words were spoken, but the action has the same impact as words. Symbolic speech restraints are different than time, place, and manner regulations because the conduct is the speech—which makes it difficult to be content-neutral. Consider, in contrast, the next U.S. Supreme Court case infra, Cohen v. California, in which a citizen's carefully choreographed anti-war protest inside a courthouse led to a state court conviction for "offensive conduct."

COHEN V. CALIFORNIA
403 U.S. 15 (1971)

Mr. Justice HARLAN delivered the opinion of the Court.
This case may seem at first blush too inconsequential to find its way into our books, but the issue it presents is of no small constitutional significance.

Appellant Paul Robert Cohen was convicted in the Los Angeles Municipal Court of violating that part of California Penal Code § 415 which prohibits "maliciously and willfully disturb[ing] the peace or quiet of any neighborhood or person . . . by . . . offensive conduct . . . ." He was given 30 days' imprisonment. . . .

"On April 26, 1968, the defendant was observed in the Los Angeles County Courthouse in the corridor outside of division 20 of the municipal court wearing a jacket bearing the words 'Fuck the Draft' which were plainly visible. There were women and children present in the corridor. The defendant was arrested. The defendant testified that he wore the jacket knowing that the words were on the jacket as a means of informing the public of the depth of his feelings against the Vietnam War and the draft.

"The defendant did not engage in, nor threaten to engage in, nor did anyone as the result of his conduct in fact commit or threaten to commit any act of violence. The defendant did not make any loud or unusual noise, nor was there any evidence that he uttered any sound prior to his arrest." 81 Cal. Rptr. 503, 505 (1969).

. . .

Against this background, the issue flushed by this case stands out in bold relief. It is whether California can excise, as "offensive conduct," one particular scurrilous epithet from the public discourse, either upon the theory of the court below that its use is inherently likely to cause violent reaction or upon a more general assertion that the States, acting as guardians of public morality, may properly remove this offensive word from the public vocabulary.

The rationale of the California court is plainly untenable. At most it reflects an "undifferentiated fear or apprehension of disturbance [which] is not enough to overcome the right to freedom of expression." Tinker v. Des Moines Indep. Community School Dist., 393 U.S. 503, 508 (1969). We have been shown no evidence that substantial numbers of citizens are standing ready to strike out physically at whoever may assault their sensibilities with execrations like that uttered by Cohen. There may be some persons about with such lawless and violent proclivities, but that is an insufficient base upon which to erect, consistently with constitutional values, a governmental power to force persons who wish to ventilate their dissident views into avoiding particular forms of expression. The argument amounts to little more than the self-defeating proposition that to avoid physical censorship of one who has not sought to provoke such a response by a hypothetical coterie of the violent and lawless, the States may more appropriately effectuate that censorship themselves. . . .

Admittedly, it is not so obvious that the First and Fourteenth Amendments must be taken to disable the States from punishing public utterance of this unseemly expletive in order to maintain what they regard as a suitable level of discourse within the body politic. We think, however, that examination and reflection will reveal the shortcomings of a contrary viewpoint.

At the outset, we cannot overemphasize that, in our judgment, most situations where the State has a justifiable interest in regulating speech will fall within one or more of the various established exceptions, discussed above but not applicable here, to the usual rule that governmental bodies may not prescribe the form or content of individual expression. Equally important to our conclusion is the constitutional backdrop against which our decision must be made. The constitutional right of free expression is powerful medicine in a society as diverse and populous as ours. It is designed and intended to remove governmental restraints from the arena of public discussion, putting the decision as to what views shall be voiced largely into the hands of each of us, in the hope that use of such freedom will ultimately produce a more capable citizenry and more perfect polity and in the belief that no other approach would comport with the premise of individual dignity and choice upon which our political system rests. See Whitney v. California, 274 U.S. 357, 375-377, (1927) (Brandeis, J., concurring).

How is one to distinguish this from any other offensive word? Surely the State has no right to cleanse public debate to the point where it is grammatically palatable to the most squeamish among us. Yet no readily ascertainable general principle exists for stopping short of that result were we to affirm the judgment below. For, while the particular four-letter word being litigated here is perhaps more distasteful than most others of its genre, it is nevertheless often true that one man's vulgarity is another's lyric. Indeed, we think it is largely because governmental officials cannot make principled distinctions in this area that the Constitution leaves matters of taste and style so largely to the individual.

Additionally, we cannot overlook the fact, because it is well illustrated by the episode involved here, that much linguistic expression serves a dual communicative function: it conveys not only ideas capable of relatively precise, detached explication, but otherwise inexpressible emotions as well. In fact, words are often chosen as much for their emotive as their cognitive force. We cannot sanction the view that the Constitution, while solicitous of the cognitive content of individual speech has little or no regard for that emotive function which practically speaking, may often be the more important element of the overall message sought to be communicated. . . .

Finally, and in the same vein, we cannot indulge the facile assumption that one can forbid particular words without also running a substantial risk of suppressing ideas in the process. Indeed, governments might soon seize upon the censorship of particular words as a convenient guise for banning the expression of unpopular views. We have been able, as noted above, to discern little social benefit that might result from running the risk of opening the door to such grave results.

It is, in sum, our judgment that, absent a more particularized and compelling reason for its actions, the State may not, consistently with the First and Fourteenth Amendments, make the simple public display here involved of this single four-letter expletive a criminal offense. Because that is the only arguably sustainable rationale for the conviction here at issue, the judgment below must be reversed.

Reversed.

Mr. Justice BLACKMUN, with whom THE CHIEF JUSTICE and Mr. Justice BLACK join.

I dissent. . . .Cohen's absurd and immature antic, in my view, was mainly conduct and little speech. . . .

Prior Restraint

As we examine the cases to follow in this chapter, it is useful to determine how the cases fit into the categorical approach of the First Amendment.

In later chapters, we will see some speech that gets exceptional treatment—outside of the categorical approach—such as child pornography and commercial speech. The first case infra, Near v. Minnesota, has to do with prior restraint—the increasingly rare case when the government can restrain a speaker from speaking. *Near* is also the first case to use the Fourteenth Amendment's due process clause to apply the First Amendment against state law under the doctrine of incorporation.

NEAR v. STATE OF MINNESOTA EX REL. OLSON

283 U.S. 697 (1931)

Mr. Chief Justice HUGHES delivered the opinion of the Court.

Chapter 285 of the Session Laws of Minnesota for the year 1925 provides for the abatement, as a public nuisance, of a "malicious, scandalous and defamatory newspaper, magazine or other periodical." Section 1 of the act is as follows:

"Section 1. Any person who, as an individual, or as a member or employee of a firm, or association or organization, or as an officer, director, member or employee of a corporation, shall be engaged in the business of regularly or customarily producing, publishing or circulating, having in possession, selling or giving away.

"(a) an obscene, lewd and lascivious newspaper, magazine, or other periodical, or

"(b) a malicious, scandalous and defamatory newspaper, magazine or other periodical,

"is guilty of a nuisance, and all persons guilty of such nuisance may be enjoined, as hereinafter provided.

"Participation in such business shall constitute a commission of such nuisance and render the participant liable and subject to the proceedings, orders and judgments provided for in this Act. Ownership, in whole or in part, directly or indirectly, of any such periodical, or of any stock of interest in any corporation or organization which owns the same in whole or in part, or which publishes the same, shall constitute such participation.

"In actions brought under (b) above, there shall be available the defense that the truth was published with good motives and for justifiable ends and in such actions the plaintiff shall not have the right to report [sic] to issues or editions or periodicals taking place more than three months before the commencement of the action."

Section 2 provides that, whenever any such nuisance is committed or exists, the county attorney of any county where any such periodical is published or circulated, or, in case of his failure or refusal to proceed upon written request in good faith of a reputable citizen, the Attorney General, or, upon like failure or refusal of the latter, any citizen of the county, may maintain an action in the district court of the county in the name of the state to enjoin perpetually the persons committing or maintaining any such nuisance from further committing or maintaining it. Upon such evidence as the court shall deem sufficient, a temporary injunction may be granted. The defendants have the right to plead by demurrer or answer, and the plaintiff may demur or reply as in other cases.

The action, by section 3, is to be "governed by the practice and procedure applicable to civil actions for injunctions," and after trial the court may enter judgment permanently enjoining the defendants found guilty of violating the act from continuing the violation, and, "in and by such judgment, such nuisance may be wholly abated." The court is empowered, as in other cases of contempt, to punish disobedience to a temporary or permanent injunction by fine of not more than $1,000 or by imprisonment in the county jail for not more than twelve months.

Under this statute (section 1, clause (b)), the county attorney of Hennepin county brought this action to enjoin the publication of what was described as a "malicious, scandalous and defamatory newspaper, magazine or other periodical," known as The Saturday Press, published by the defendants in the city of Minneapolis. The complaint alleged that the defendants, on September 24, 1927, and on eight subsequent dates in October and November, 1927, published and circulated editions of that periodical which were "largely devoted to malicious, scandalous and defamatory articles" concerning Charles G. Davis, Frank W. Brunskill, the Minneapolis Tribune, the Minneapolis Journal, Melvin C. Passolt, George E. Leach, the Jewish Race, the members of the grand jury of Hennepin county impaneled in November, 1927, and then holding office, and other persons, as more fully appeared in exhibits annexed to the complaint, consisting of copies of the articles described and constituting 327 pages of the record. While the complaint did not so allege, it appears from the briefs of both parties that Charles G. Davis was a special law enforcement officer employed by a civic organization, that George E. Leach was mayor of Minneapolis, that Frank W. Brunskill was its chief of police, and that Floyd B. Olson, the relator in this action, was county attorney.

Without attempting to summarize the contents of the voluminous exhibits attached to the complaint, we deem it sufficient to say that the articles charged, in substance, that a Jewish gangster was in control of gambling, bootlegging, and racketeering in Minneapolis, and that law enforcing officers and agencies were not energetically performing their duties. Most of the charges were directed against the chief of police; he was charged with gross neglect of duty, illicit relations with gangsters, and with participation in graft. The county attorney was charged with knowing the existing conditions and with failure to take adequate measures to remedy them. The mayor was accused of inefficiency and dereliction. One member of the grand jury was stated to be in sympathy with the gangsters. A special grand jury and a special prosecutor were demanded to deal with the situation in general, and, in particular, to investigate an attempt to assassinate one Guilford, one of the original defendants, who, it appears from the articles, was shot by gangsters after the first issue of the periodical had been published. There is no question but that the articles made serious accusations against the public officers named and others in connection with the prevalence of crimes and the failure to expose and punish them.

At the beginning of the action on November 22, 1927, and upon the verified complaint, an order was made directing the defendants to show cause why a temporary injunction should not issue and meanwhile forbidding the defendants to publish, circulate, or have in their possession any editions of the periodical from September 24, 1927, to November 19, 1927, inclusive, and from publishing, circulating or having in their possession, "any future editions of said The Saturday Press" and "any publication, known by any other name whatsoever containing malicious, scandalous and defamatory matter of the kind alleged in plaintiff's complaint herein or otherwise."

The defendants demurred to the complaint upon the ground that it did not state facts sufficient to constitute a cause of action, and on this demurrer challenged the constitutionality of the statute. The district court overruled the demurrer and certified the question of constitutionality to the Supreme Court of the state. The Supreme Court sustained the statute (219 N.W. 770), and it is conceded by the appellee that the act was thus held to be valid over the objection that it violated not only the State Constitution, but also the Fourteenth Amendment of the Constitution of the United States.

Thereupon the defendant Near, the present appellant, answered the complaint. He averred that he was the sole owner and proprietor of the publication in question. He admitted the publication of the articles in the issues described in the complaint, but denied that they were malicious, scandalous, or defamatory as alleged. He expressly invoked the protection of the due process clause of the Fourteenth Amendment. . . .

The question is whether a statute authorizing such proceedings in restraint of publication is consistent with the conception of the liberty of the press as historically conceived and guaranteed. In determining the extent of the constitutional protection, it has been generally, if not universally, considered that it is the chief purpose of the guaranty to prevent previous restraints upon publication. The struggle in England, directed against the legislative power of the licenser, resulted in renunciation of the censorship of the press. The liberty deemed to be established was thus described by Blackstone: "The liberty of the press is indeed essential to the nature of a free state; but this consists in laying no previous restraints upon publications, and not in freedom from censure for criminal matter when published. Every freeman has an undoubted right to lay what sentiments he pleases before the public; to forbid this, is to destroy the freedom of the press; but if he publishes what is improper, mischievous or illegal, he must take the consequence of his own temerity." 4 Bl. Com. 151, 152; see Story on the Constitution, §§ 1884, 1889. The distinction was early pointed out between the extent of the freedom with respect to censorship under our constitutional system and that enjoyed in England. Here, as Madison said, "the great and essential rights of the people are secured against legislative as well as against executive ambition. They are secured, not by laws paramount to prerogative, but by constitutions paramount to laws. This security of the freedom of the press requires that it should be exempt not only from previous restraint by the Executive, as in Great Britain, but from legislative restraint also."

. . .

The objection has also been made that the principle as to immunity from previous restraint is stated too broadly, if every such restraint is deemed to be prohibited. That is undoubtedly true; the protection even as to previous restraint is not absolutely unlimited. But the limitation has been recognized only in exceptional cases. "When a nation is at war many things that might be said in time of peace are such a hindrance to its effort that their utterance will not be endured so long as men fight and that no Court could regard them as protected by any constitutional right."

Schenck v. United States, 249 U.S. 47. No one would question but that a government might prevent actual obstruction to its recruiting service or the publication of the sailing dates of transports or the number and location of troops. On similar grounds, the primary requirements of decency may be enforced against obscene publications. The security of the community life may be protected against incitements to acts of violence and the overthrow by force of orderly government. The constitutional guaranty of free speech does not "protect a man from an injunction against uttering words that may have all the effect of force. Gompers v. Buck's Stove & Range Co., 221 U.S. 418." Schenck v. United States, supra. These limitations are not applicable here. Nor are we now concerned with questions as to the extent of authority to prevent publications in order to protect private rights according to the principles governing the exercise of the jurisdiction of courts of equity.

The exceptional nature of its limitations places in a strong light the general conception that liberty of the press, historically considered and taken up by the Federal Constitution, has meant, principally although not exclusively, immunity from previous restraints or censorship. The conception of the liberty of the press in this country had broadened with the exigencies of the colonial period and with the efforts to secure freedom from oppressive administration. That liberty was especially cherished for the immunity it afforded from previous restraint of the publication of censure of public officers and charges of official misconduct. As was said by Chief Justice Parker, in Commonwealth v. Blanding, 20 Mass. 304, 313, with respect to the Constitution of Massachusetts: "Besides, it is well understood and received as a commentary on this provision for the liberty of the press, that it was intended to prevent all such previous restraints upon publications as had been practiced by other governments, and in early times here, to stifle the efforts of patriots towards enlightening their fellow subjects upon their rights and the duties of rulers. The liberty of the press was to be unrestrained, but he who used it was to be responsible in case of its abuse." In the letter sent by the Continental Congress (October 26, 1774) to the Inhabitants of Quebec, referring to the "five great rights" it was said: "The last right we shall mention, regards the freedom of the press. The importance of this consists, besides the advancement of truth, science, morality, and arts in general, in its diffusion of liberal sentiments on the administration of Government, its ready communication of thoughts between subjects, and its consequential promotion of union among them, whereby oppressive officers are shamed or intimidated, into more honourable and just modes of conducting affairs." Madison, who was the leading spirit in the preparation of the First Amendment of the Federal Constitution, thus described the practice and sentiment which led to the guaranties of liberty of the press in State Constitutions.

. . .

The fact that for approximately one hundred and fifty years there has been almost an entire absence of attempts to impose previous restraints upon publications relating to the malfeasance of public officers is significant of the deep-seated conviction that such restraints would violate constitutional right. Public officers, whose character and conduct remain open to debate and free discussion in the press, find their remedies for false accusations in actions under libel laws providing for redress and punishment, and not in proceedings to restrain the publication of newspapers and periodicals. The general principle that the constitutional guaranty of the liberty of the press gives immunity from previous restraints has been approved in many decisions under the provisions of state constitutions.

The importance of this immunity has not lessened. . . . The fact that the liberty of the press may be abused by miscreant purveyors of scandal does not make any the less necessary the immunity of the press from previous restraint in dealing with official misconduct. Subsequent punishment for such abuses as may exist is the appropriate remedy, consistent with constitutional privilege.

In attempted justification of the statute, it is said that it deals not with publication per se, but with the "business" of publishing defamation. If, however, the publisher has a constitutional right to publish, without previous restraint, an edition of his newspaper charging official derelictions, it cannot be denied that he may publish subsequent editions for the same purpose. He does not lose his right by exercising it. If his right exists, it may be exercised in publishing nine editions, as in this case, as well as in one edition. If previous restraint is permissible, it may be imposed at once; indeed, the wrong may be as serious in one publication as in several. Characterizing the publication as a business, and the business as a nuisance, does not permit an invasion of the constitutional immunity against restraint. Similarly, it does not matter that the newspaper or periodical is found to be "largely" or "chiefly" devoted to the publication of such derelictions. If the publisher has a right, without previous restraint, to publish them, his right cannot be deemed to be dependent upon his publishing something else, more or less, with the matter to which objection is made.

Nor can it be said that the constitutional freedom from previous restraint is lost because charges are made of derelictions which constitute crimes.

. . .

Equally unavailing is the insistence that the statute is designed to prevent the circulation of scandal which tends to disturb the public peace and to provoke assaults and the commission of crime. Charges of reprehensible conduct, and in particular of official malfeasance, unquestionably create a public scandal, but the theory of the constitutional guaranty is that even a more serious public evil would be caused by authority to prevent publication. "To prohibit the intent to excite those unfavorable sentiments against those who administer the Government, is equivalent to a prohibition of the actual excitement of them; and to prohibit the actual excitement of them is equivalent to a prohibition of discussions having that tendency and effect; which, again, is equivalent to a protection of those who administer the Government, if they should at any time deserve the contempt or hatred of the people, against being exposed to it by free animadversions on their characters and conduct." There is nothing new in the fact that charges of reprehensible conduct may create resentment and the disposition to resort to violent means of redress, but this well-understood tendency did not alter the determination to protect the press against censorship and restrain upon publication. As was said in New Yorker Staats-Zeitung v. Nolan, 105 A. 72, 72: "If the township may prevent the circulation of a newspaper for no reason other than that some of its inhabitants may violently disagree with it, and resent its circulation by resorting to physical violence, there is no limit to what may be prohibited." The danger of violent reactions becomes greater with effective organization of defiant groups resenting exposure, and, if this consideration warranted legislative interference with the initial freedom of publication, the constitutional protection would be reduced to a mere form of words.

For these reasons we hold the statute, so far as it authorized the proceedings in this action under clause (b) of section 1, to be an infringement of the liberty of the press guaranteed by the Fourteenth Amendment. We should add that this decision rests upon the operation and effect of the statute, without regard to the question of the truth of the charges contained in the particular periodical. The fact that the public officers named in this case, and those associated with the charges of official dereliction, may be deemed to be impeccable, cannot affect the conclusion that the statute imposes an unconstitutional restraint upon publication.

Judgment reversed.

Incitement

The incitement cases infra deal with subsequent punishments—cases in which the government typically holds speakers accountable for speech after it is uttered. Incitement cases test the limits of government restraints on provocative speech that the government fears will result in violence. Schenck v. United States and Abrams v. United States, two World War I-era U.S. Supreme Court decisions, show how Justice Oliver Wendell Holmes went from being a proponent of his own "clear and present danger" test to becoming an opponent of it, and the reasons for his change of heart. In Brandenburg v. Ohio, the Court moves beyond its "clear and present danger" precedents to enunciate a modern two-part test for incitement. After *Brandenburg*, mere advocacy of imminent lawless conduct is no longer sufficient for punishment by the government.

Supreme Court Justice Oliver Wendell Holmes, Jr.

SCHENCK V. UNITED STATES

249 U.S. 47 (1919)

Mr. Justice HOLMES delivered the opinion of the Court.

This is an indictment in three counts. The first charges a conspiracy to violate the Espionage Act of June 15, 1917, c. 30, tit. 1, § 3, 40 Stat. 217, 219 (Comp. St. 1918, § 10212c), by causing and attempting to cause insubordination, &c., in the military and naval forces of the United States, and to obstruct the recruiting and enlistment service of the United States, when the United States was at war with the German Empire, to-wit, that the defendant wilfully conspired to have printed and circulated to men who had been called and accepted for military service under the Act of May 18, 1917, c. 15, 40 Stat. 76 (Comp. St. 1918, §§ 2044a-2044k), a document set forth and alleged to be calculated to cause such insubordination and obstruction. The count alleges overt acts in pursuance of the conspiracy, ending in the distribution of the document set forth. The second count alleges a conspiracy to commit an offense against the United States, to-wit, to use the mails for the transmission of matter declared to be non-mailable by title 12, § 2, of the Act of June 15, 1917 (Comp. St. 1918, § 10401b), to-wit, the above mentioned document, with an averment of the same overt acts. The third count charges an unlawful use of the mails for the transmission of the same matter and otherwise as above. The defendants were found guilty on all the counts. They set up the First Amendment to the Constitution forbidding Congress to make any law abridging the freedom of speech, or of the press, and bringing the case here on that ground have argued some other points also of which we must dispose.

It is argued that the evidence, if admissible, was not sufficient to prove that the defendant Schenck was concerned in sending the documents. According to the testimony Schenck said he was general secretary of the Socialist party and had charge of the Socialist headquarters from which the documents were sent. He identified a book found there as the minutes of the Executive Committee of the party. The book showed a resolution of August 13, 1917, that 15,000 leaflets should be printed on the other side of one of them in use, to be mailed to men who had passed exemption boards, and for distribution. Schenck personally attended to the printing. On August 20 the general secretary's report said "Obtained new leaflets from printer and started work addressing envelopes" &c.; and there was a resolve that Comrade Schenck be allowed $125 for sending leaflets through the mail. He said that he had about fifteen or sixteen thousand printed. There were files of the circular in question in the inner office which he said were printed on the other side of the one sided circular and were there for distribution. Other copies were proved to have been sent through the mails to drafted men. Without going into confirmatory details that were proved, no reasonable man could doubt that the defendant Schenck was largely instrumental in sending the circulars about. As to the defendant Baer there was evidence that she was a member of the Executive Board and that the minutes of its transactions were hers. The argument as to the sufficiency of the evidence that the defendants conspired to send the documents only impairs the seriousness of the real defence.

...

The document in question upon its first printed side recited the first section of the Thirteenth Amendment, said that the idea embodied in it was violated by the conscription act and that a conscript is little better than a convict. In impassioned language it intimated that conscription was despotism in its worst form and a monstrous wrong against humanity in the interest of Wall Street's chosen few. It said, "Do not submit to intimidation," but in form at least confined itself to peaceful measures such as a petition for the repeal of the act. The other and later printed side of the sheet was headed "Assert Your Rights." It stated reasons for alleging that any one violated the Constitution when he refused to recognize "your right to assert your opposition to the draft," and went on, "If you do not assert and support your rights, you are helping to deny or disparage rights which it is the solemn duty of all citizens and residents of the United States to retain." It described the arguments on the other side as coming from cunning politicians and a mercenary capitalist press, and even silent consent to the conscription law as helping to support an infamous conspiracy. It denied the power to send our citizens away to foreign shores to shoot up the people of other lands, and added that words could not express the condemnation such cold-blooded ruthlessness deserves, &c., &c., winding up, "You must do your share to maintain, support and uphold the rights of the people of this country." Of course the document would not have been sent unless it had been intended to have some effect, and we do not see what effect it could be expected to have upon persons subject to the draft except to influence them to obstruct the carrying of it out. The defendants do not deny that the jury might find against them on this point.

But it is said, suppose that that was the tendency of this circular, it is protected by the First Amendment to the Constitution. Two of the strongest expressions are said to be quoted respectively from well-known public men. It well may be that the prohibition of laws abridging the freedom of speech is not confined to previous restraints, although to prevent them may have been the main purpose, as intimated in Patterson v. Colorado, 205 U.S. 454, 462. We admit that in many places and in ordinary times the defendants in saying all that was said in the circular would have been within their constitutional rights. But the character of every act depends upon the circumstances in which it is done. Aikens v. Wisconsin, 195 U.S. 194, 205, 206. The most stringent protection of free speech would not protect a man in falsely shouting fire in a theatre and causing a panic. It does not even protect a man from an injunction against uttering words that may have all the effect of force. Gompers v. Buck's Stove & Range Co., 221 U.S. 418, 439. The question in every case is whether the words used are used in such circumstances and are of such a nature as to create a clear and present danger that they will bring about the substantive evils that Congress has a right to prevent. It is a question of proximity and degree. When a nation is at war many things that might be said in time of peace are such a hindrance to its effort that their utterance will not be endured so long as men fight and that no Court could regard them as protected by any constitutional right. It seems to be admitted that if an actual obstruction of the recruiting service were proved, liability for words that produced that effect might be enforced. The statute of 1917 in section 4 (Comp. St. 1918, § 10212d) punishes conspiracies to obstruct as well as actual obstruction. If the act, (speaking, or circulating a paper,) its tendency and the intent with which it is done are the same, we perceive no ground for saying that success alone warrants making the act a crime....

Judgments affirmed.

ABRAMS V. UNITED STATES
250 U.S. 616 (1919)

Mr. Justice CLARKE delivered the opinion of the Court.
On a single indictment, containing four counts, the five plaintiffs in error, hereinafter designated the defendants, were convicted of conspiring to violate provisions of the Espionage Act of Congress (section 3, title I, of Act June 15, 1917, c. 30, 40 Stat. 219, as amended by Act May 16, 1918, c. 75, 40 Stat. 553 [Comp. St. 1918, § 10212c]).

Each of the first three counts charged the defendants with conspiring, when the United States was at war with the Imperial Government of Germany, to unlawfully utter, print, write and publish: In the first count, "disloyal, scurrilous and abusive language about the form of government of the United States;" in the second count, language "intended to bring the form of government of the United States into contempt, scorn, contumely, and disrepute;" and in the third count, language "intended to incite, provoke and encourage resistance to the United States in said war." The charge in the fourth count was that the defendants conspired "when the United States was at war with the Imperial German Government, . . . unlawfully and willfully, by utterance, writing, printing and publication to urge, incite and advocate curtailment of production of things and products, to wit, ordnance and ammunition, necessary and essential to the prosecution of the war." The offenses were charged in the language of the act of Congress.

It was charged in each count of the indictment that it was a part of the conspiracy that the defendants would attempt to accomplish their unlawful purpose by printing, writing and distributing in the city of New York many copies of a leaflet or circular, printed in the English language, and of another printed in the Yiddish language, copies of which, properly identified, were attached to the indictment.

All of the five defendants were born in Russia. They were intelligent, had considerable schooling, and at the time they were arrested they had lived in the United States terms varying from five to ten years, but none of them had applied for naturalization. Four of them testified as witnesses in their own behalf, and of these three frankly avowed that they were "rebels," "revolutionists," "anarchists," that they did not believe in government in any form, and they declared that they had no interest whatever in the government of the United States. The fourth defendant testified that he was a "Socialist" and believed in "a proper kind of government, not capitalistic," but in his classification the government of the United States was "capitalistic."

. . .

The defendants pleaded "not guilty," and the case of the government consisted in showing the facts we have stated, and in introducing in evidence copies of the two printed circulars attached to the indictment, a sheet entitled "Revolutionists Unite for Action," written by the defendant Lipman, and found on him when he was arrested, and another paper, found at the headquarters of the group, and for which Abrams assumed responsibility.

Thus the conspiracy and the doing of the overt acts charged were largely admitted and were fully established.

. . .

This is not an attempt to bring about a change of administration by candid discussion, for no matter what may have incited the outbreak on the part of the defendant anarchists, the manifest purpose of such a publication was to create an attempt to defeat the war plans of the government of the United States, by bringing upon the country the paralysis of a general strike, thereby arresting the production of all munitions and other things essential to the conduct of the war.

. . .

These excerpts sufficiently show, that while the immediate occasion for this particular outbreak of lawlessness, on the part of the defendant alien anarchists, may have been resentment caused by our government sending troops into Russia as a strategic operation against the Germans on the eastern battle front, yet the plain purpose of their propaganda was to excite, at the supreme crisis of the war, disaffection, sedition, riots, and, as they hoped, revolution, in this country for the purpose of embarrassing and if possible defeating the military plans of the government in Europe. A technical distinction may perhaps be taken between disloyal and abusive language applied to the *form* of our government or language intended to bring the *form* of our government into contempt and disrepute, and language of like character and intended to produce like results directed against the President and Congress, the agencies through which that form of government must function in time of war. But it is not necessary to a decision of this case to consider whether such distinction is vital or merely formal, for the language of these circulars was obviously intended to provoke and to encourage resistance to the United States in the war, as the third count runs, and, the defendants, in terms, plainly urged and advocated a resort to a general strike of workers in ammunition factories for the purpose of curtailing the production of ordnance and munitions necessary and essential to the prosecution of the war as is charged in the fourth count. Thus it is clear not only that some evidence but that much persuasive evidence was before the jury tending to prove that the defendants were guilty as charged in both the third and fourth counts of the indictment and under the long established rule of law hereinbefore stated the judgment of the District Court must be

Affirmed.

Mr. Justice HOLMES, dissenting.
This indictment is founded wholly upon the publication of two leaflets which I shall describe in a moment. The first count charges a conspiracy pending the war with Germany to publish abusive language about the form of government of the United States, laying the preparation and publishing of the first leaflet as overt acts. The second count charges a conspiracy pending the war to publish language intended to bring the form of government into contempt, laying the preparation and publishing of the two leaflets as overt acts. The third count alleges a conspiracy to encourage resistance to the United States in the same war and to attempt to effectuate the purpose by publishing the same leaflets. The fourth count lays a conspiracy to incite curtailment of production of things necessary to the prosecution of the war and to attempt to accomplish it by publishing the second leaflet to which I have referred.

The first of these leaflets says that the President's cowardly silence about the intervention in Russia reveals the hypocrisy of the plutocratic gang in Washington. It intimates that "German militarism combined with allied capitalism to crush the Russian revolution" – goes on that the tyrants of the world fight each other until they see a common enemy – working class enlightenment, when they combine to crush it; and that now militarism and capitalism combined, though not openly, to crush the Russian revolution. It says that there is only one enemy of the workers of the world and that is capitalism; that it is a crime for workers of America, etc., to fight the workers' republic of Russia, and ends "Awake! Awake, you workers of the world! Revolutionists." A note adds "It is absurd to call us pro-German. We hate and despise German militarism more than do you hypocritical tyrants. We have more reason for denouncing German militarism than has the coward of the White House."

The other leaflet, headed "Workers – Wake Up," with abusive language says that America together with the Allies will march for Russia to help the Czecko-Slovaks in their struggle against the Bolsheviki, and that this time the hypocrites shall not fool the Russian emigrants and friends of Russia in America. It tells the Russian emigrants that they now must spit in the face of the false military propaganda by which their sympathy and help to the prosecution of the war have been called forth and says that with the money they have lent or are going to lend "they will make bullets not only for the Germans but also for the Workers Soviets of Russia," and further, "Workers in the ammunition factories, you are producing bullets, bayonets, cannon to murder not only the Germans, but also your dearest, best, who are in Russia fighting for freedom." It then appeals to the same Russian emigrants at some length not to consent to the "inquisitionary expedition in Russia," and says that the destruction of the Russian revolution is "the politics of the march on Russia." The leaflet winds up by saying "Workers, our reply to this barbaric intervention has to be a general strike!" and after a few words on the spirit of revolution, exhortations not to be afraid, and some usual tall talk ends "Woe unto those who will be in the way of progress. Let solidarity live! The Rebels."

No argument seems to be necessary to show that these pronunciamentos in no way attack the form of government of the United States, or that they do not support either of the first two counts. What little I have to say about the third count may be postponed until I have considered the fourth. With regard to that it seems too plain to be denied that the suggestion to workers in the ammunition factories that they are producing bullets to murder their dearest, and the further advocacy of a general strike, both in the second leaflet, do urge curtailment of production of things necessary to the prosecution of the war within the meaning of the Act of May 16, 1918, c. 75, 40 Stat. 553, amending section 3 of the earlier Act of 1917 (Comp. St. § 10212c). But to make the conduct criminal that statute requires that it should be "with intent by such curtailment to cripple or hinder the United States in the prosecution of the war." It seems to me that no such intent is proved.

I am aware of course that the word "intent" as vaguely used in ordinary legal discussion means no more than knowledge at the time of the act that the consequences said to be intended will ensue. Even less than that will satisfy the general principle of civil and criminal liability. A man may have to pay damages, may be sent to prison, at common law might be hanged, if at the time of his act he knew facts from which common experience showed that the consequences would follow, whether he individually could foresee them or not. But, when words are used exactly, a deed is not done with intent to produce a consequence unless that consequence is the aim of the deed. It may be obvious, and obvious to the actor, that the consequence will follow, and he may be liable for it even if he regrets it, but he does not do the act with intent to produce it unless the aim to produce it is the proximate motive of the specific act, although there may be some deeper motive behind.

It seems to me that this statute must be taken to use its words in a strict and accurate sense. They would be absurd in any other. A patriot might think that we were wasting money on aeroplanes, or making more cannon of a certain kind than we needed, and might advocate curtailment with success, yet even if it turned out that the curtailment hindered and was thought by other minds to have been obviously likely to hinder the United States in the prosecution of the war, no one would hold such conduct a crime. I admit that my illustration does not answer all that might be said but it is enough to show what I think and to let me pass to a more important aspect of the case. I refer to the First Amendment to the Constitution that Congress shall make no law abridging the freedom of speech.

I never have seen any reason to doubt that the questions of law that alone were before this Court in the Cases of Schenck (249 U.S. 47) Frohwerk (249 U.S. 204), and Debs (249 U.S. 211), were rightly decided. I do not doubt for a moment that by the same reasoning that would justify punishing persuasion to murder, the United States constitutionally may punish speech that produces or is intended to produce a clear and imminent danger that it will bring about forthwith certain substantive evils that the United States constitutionally may seek to prevent. The power undoubtedly is greater in time of war than in time of peace because war opens dangers that do not exist at other times.

But as against dangers peculiar to war, as against others, the principle of the right to free speech is always the same. It is only the present danger of immediate evil or an intent to bring it about that warrants Congress in setting a limit to the expression of opinion where private rights are not concerned. Congress certainly cannot forbid all effort to change the mind of the country. Now nobody can suppose that the surreptitious publishing of a silly leaflet by an unknown man, without more, would present any immediate danger that its opinions would hinder the success of the government arms or have any appreciable tendency to do so. Publishing those opinions for the very purpose of obstructing, however, might indicate a greater danger and at any rate would have the quality of an attempt. So I assume that the second leaflet if published for the purposes alleged in the fourth count might be punishable. But it seems pretty clear to me that nothing less than that would bring these papers within the scope of this law. An actual intent in the sense that I have explained is necessary to constitute an attempt, where a further act of the same individual is required to complete the substantive crime, for reasons given in Swift & Co. v. United States, 196 U.S. 375, 396. It is necessary where the success of the attempt depends upon others because if that intent is not present the actor's aim may be accomplished without bringing about the evils sought to be checked. An intent to prevent interference with the revolution in Russia might have been satisfied without any hindrance to carrying on the war in which we were engaged.

I do not see how anyone can find the intent required by the statute in any of the defendant's words. The second leaflet is the only one that affords even a foundation for the charge, and there, without invoking the hatred of German militarism expressed in the former one, it is evident from the beginning to the end that the only object of the paper is to help Russia and stop American intervention there against the popular government—not to impede the United States in the war that it was carrying on. To say that two phrases taken literally might import a suggestion of conduct that would have interference with the war as an indirect and probably undesired effect seems to me by no means enough to show an attempt to produce that effect.

I return for a moment to the third count. That charges an intent to provoke resistance to the United States in its war with Germany. Taking the clause in the statute that deals with that in connection with the other elaborate provisions of the Act, I think that resistance to the United States means some forcible act of opposition to some proceeding of the United States in pursuance of the war. I think the intent must be the specific intent that I have described and for the reasons that I have given I think that no such intent was proved or existed in fact. I also think that there is no hint at resistance to the United States as I construe the phrase.

In this case sentences of twenty years imprisonment have been imposed for the publishing of two leaflets that I believe the defendants had as much right to publish as the Government has to publish the Constitution of the United States now vainly invoked by them. Even if I am technically wrong and enough can be squeezed from these poor and puny anonymities to turn the color of legal litmus paper; I will add, even if what I think the necessary intent were shown; the most nominal punishment seems to me all that possibly could be inflicted, unless the defendants are to be made to suffer not for what the indictment alleges but for the creed that they avow—a creed that I believe to be the creed of ignorance and immaturity when honestly held, as I see no reason to doubt that it was held here but which, although made the subject of examination at the trial, no one has a right even to consider in dealing with the charges before the Court.

Persecution for the expression of opinions seems to me perfectly logical. If you have no doubt of your premises or your power and want a certain result with all your heart you naturally express your wishes in law and sweep away all opposition. To allow opposition by speech seems to indicate that you think the speech impotent, as when a man says that he has squared the circle, or that you do not care whole heartedly for the result, or that you doubt either your power or your premises. But when men have realized that time has upset many fighting faiths, they may come to believe even more than they believe the very foundations of their own conduct that the ultimate good desired is better reached by free trade in ideas—that the best test of truth is the power of the thought to get itself accepted in the competition of the market, and that truth is the only ground upon which their wishes safely can be carried out. That at any rate is the theory of our Constitution. . . I wholly disagree with the argument of the Government that the First Amendment left the common law as to seditious libel in force. History seems to me against the notion. I had conceived that the United States through many years had shown its repentance for the Sedition Act of 1798 (Act July 14, 1798, c. 73, 1 Stat. 596), by repaying fines that it imposed. Only the emergency that makes it immediately dangerous to leave the correction of evil counsels to time warrants making any exception to the sweeping command, "Congress shall make no law abridging the freedom of speech." Of course I am speaking only of expressions of opinion and exhortations, which were all that were uttered here, but I regret that I cannot put into more impressive words my belief that in their conviction upon this indictment the defendants were deprived of their rights under the Constitution of the United States.

Mr. Justice BRANDEIS concurs with the foregoing opinion.

BRANDENBURG V. OHIO
395 U.S. 444 (1969)

PER CURIAM.
The appellant, a leader of a Ku Klux Klan group, was convicted under the Ohio Criminal Syndicalism statute for "advocat(ing) . . . the duty, necessity, or propriety of crime, sabotage, violence, or unlawful methods of terrorism as a means of accomplishing industrial or political reform" and for "voluntarily assembl(ing) with any society, group, or assemblage of persons formed to teach or advocate the doctrines of criminal syndicalism." Ohio Rev. Code Ann. § 2923.13. He was fined $1,000 and sentenced to one to 10 years' imprisonment. The appellant challenged the constitutionality of the criminal syndicalism statute under the First and Fourteenth Amendments to the United States Constitution, but the intermediate appellate court of Ohio affirmed his conviction without opinion. The Supreme Court of Ohio dismissed his appeal, *sua sponte*, "for the reason that no substantial constitutional question exists herein." It did not file an opinion or explain its conclusions. Appeal was taken to this Court, and we noted probable jurisdiction. 393 U.S. 948 (1968). We reverse.

The record shows that a man, identified at trial as the appellant, telephoned an announcer-reporter on the staff of a Cincinnati television station and invited him to come to a Ku Klux Klan "rally" to be held at a farm in Hamilton County. With the cooperation of the organizers, the reporter and a cameraman attended the meeting and filmed the events. Portions of the films were later broadcast on the local station and on a national network.

The prosecution's case rested on the films and on testimony identifying the appellant as the person who communicated with the reporter and who spoke at the rally. The State also introduced into evidence several articles appearing in the film, including a pistol, a rifle, a shotgun, ammunition, a Bible, and a red hood worn by the speaker in the films.

One film showed 12 hooded figures, some of whom carried firearms. They were gathered around a large wooden cross, which they burned. No one was present other than the participants and the newsmen who made the film. Most of the words uttered during the scene were incomprehensible when the film was projected, but scattered phrases could be understood that were derogatory of Negroes and, in one instance, of Jews.

The second film showed six hooded figures one of whom, later identified as the appellant, repeated a speech very similar to that recorded on the first film. The reference to the possibility of "revengeance" was omitted, and one sentence was added: "Personally, I believe the nigger should be returned to Africa, the Jew returned to Israel." Though some of the figures in the films carried weapons, the speaker did not.

The Ohio Criminal Syndicalism Statute was enacted in 1919. From 1917 to 1920, identical or quite similar laws were adopted by 20 States and two territories. E. Dowell, A History of Criminal Syndicalism Legislation in the United States 21 (1939). In 1927, this Court sustained the constitutionality of California's Criminal Syndicalism Act, Cal. Penal Code §§ 11400-11402, the text of which is quite similar to that of the laws of Ohio. Whitney v. California, 274 U.S. 357 (1927). The Court upheld the statute on the ground that, without more, "advocating" violent means to effect political and economic change involves such danger to the security of the State that the State may outlaw it. Cf. Fiske v. Kansas, 274 U.S. 380 (1927). But *Whitney* has been thoroughly discredited by later decisions. See Dennis v. United States, 341 U.S. 494, at 507 (1951). These later decisions have fashioned the principle that the constitutional guarantees of free speech and free press do not permit a State to forbid or proscribe advocacy of the use of force or of law violation except where such advocacy is directed to inciting or producing imminent lawless action and is likely to incite or produce such action. As we said in Noto v. United States, 367 U.S. 290, 297-298 (1961), "the mere abstract teaching . . . of the moral propriety or even moral necessity for a resort to force and violence, is not the same as preparing a group for violent action and steeling it to such action." See also Herndon v. Lowry, 301 U.S. 242, 259-261 (1937); Bond v. Floyd, 385 U.S. 116, 134 (1966). A statute which fails to draw this distinction impermissibly intrudes upon the freedoms guaranteed by the First and Fourteenth Amendments. It sweeps within its condemnation speech which our Constitution has immunized from governmental control. . . .

Measured by this test, Ohio's Criminal Syndicalism Act cannot be sustained. The Act punishes persons who "advocate or teach the duty, necessity, or propriety" of violence "as a means of accomplishing industrial or political reform"; or who publish or circulate or display any book or paper containing such advocacy; or who "justify" the commission of violent acts "with intent to exemplify, spread or advocate the propriety of the doctrines of criminal syndicalism"; or who "voluntarily assemble" with a group formed "to teach or advocate the doctrines of criminal syndicalism." Neither the indictment nor the trial judge's instructions to the jury in any way refined the statute's bald definition of the crime in terms of mere advocacy not distinguished from incitement to imminent lawless action.

Accordingly, we are here confronted with a statute which, by its own words and as applied, purports to punish mere advocacy and to forbid, on pain of criminal punishment, assembly with others merely to advocate the described type of action.

Mr. Justice BLACK, concurring.
I agree with the views expressed by Mr. Justice DOUGLAS in his concurring opinion in this case that the "clear and present danger" doctrine should have no place in the interpretation of the First Amendment. I join the Court's opinion, which, as I understand it, simply cites Dennis v. United States, 341 U.S. 494 (1951), but does not indicate any agreement on the Court's part with the "clear and present danger" doctrine on which Dennis purported to rely.

Mr. Justice DOUGLAS, concurring.
While I join the opinion of the Court, I desire to enter a *caveat*.

The "clear and present danger" test was adumbrated by Mr. Justice Holmes in a case arising during World War I—a war "declared" by the Congress, not by the Chief Executive. The case was Schenck v. United States, 249 U.S. 47, 52, where the defendant was charged with attempts to cause insubordination in the military and obstruction of enlistment. The pamphlets that were distributed urged resistance to the draft, denounced conscription, and impugned the motives of those backing the war effort. The First Amendment was tendered as a defense. Mr. Justice Holmes in rejecting that defense said:

> "The question in every case is whether the words used are used in such circumstances and are of such a nature as to create a clear and present danger that they will bring about

> the substantive evils that Congress has a right to prevent. It is a question of proximity and degree."

. . .

In the 1919 Term, the Court applied the Schenck doctrine to affirm the convictions of other dissidents in World War I. Abrams v. United States, 250 U.S. 616, was one instance. Mr. Justice Holmes, with whom Mr. Justice Brandeis concurred, dissented. While adhering to Schenck, he did not think that on the facts a case for overriding the First Amendment had been made out:

> "It is only the present danger of immediate evil or an intent to bring it about that warrants Congress in setting a limit to the expression of opinion where private rights are not concerned. Congress certainly cannot forbid all effort to change the mind of the country." 250 U.S., at 628.

Those, then, were the World War I cases that put the gloss of "clear and present danger" on the First Amendment. Whether the war power—the greatest leveler of them all—is adequate to sustain that doctrine is debatable. The dissents in Abrams, Schaefer, and Pierce show how easily "clear and present danger" is manipulated to crush what Brandeis called "(t)he fundamental right of free men to strive for better conditions through new legislation and new institutions" by argument and discourse (Pierce v. United States, supra, at 273) even in time of war. Though I doubt if the "clear and present danger" test is congenial to the First Amendment in time of a declared war, I am certain it is not reconcilable with the First Amendment in days of peace.

The Court quite properly overrules Whitney v. California, 274 U.S. 357, which involved advocacy of ideas which the majority of the Court deemed unsound and dangerous.

Mr. Justice Holmes, though never formally abandoning the "clear and present danger" test, moved closer to the First Amendment ideal when he said in dissent in Gitlow (Gitlow v. People of State of New York, 268 U.S. 652):

> "Every idea is an incitement. It offers itself for belief and if believed it is acted on unless some other belief outweighs it or some failure of energy stifles the movement at its birth. The only difference between the expression of an

> opinion and an incitement in the narrower sense is the speaker's enthusiasm for the result. Eloquence may set fire to reason. But whatever may be thought of the redundant discourse before us it had no chance of starting a present conflagration. If in the long run the beliefs expressed in proletarian dictatorship are destined to be accepted by the dominant forces of the community, the only meaning of free speech is that they should be given their chance and have their way."

We have never been faithful to the philosophy of that dissent.

. . .

NOTES AND QUESTIONS

1. If you believe in the old aphorism "sticks and stones may break my bones, but words will never harm me," you may be a free speech absolutist. But before you accept that label, consider that even so-called absolutists like Justices William O. Douglas and Hugo Black believed in laws that limited speech. Ask yourself—and perhaps people you know well—under what circumstances laws should punish or censor speech? Hate speech against a racial or religious minority? Incitement to violence? Explicit or suggested sexual depictions to minors? Political speech amplified by an excessively loud sound truck?
2. Near v. Minnesota allows the government to place a prior restraint on speech in very limited circumstances, such as to safeguard troops during wartime or to protect national security. But is prior restraint even possible in an age where information is transmitted and repeated instantly and constantly from locations around the world via new media? Have we moved to a system that effectively relies on subsequent sanctions to punish those who have already spoken, assuming we can locate them?
3. In 2012, the U.S. Supreme Court held that an individual has a First Amendment right to lie about military awards and honors, unless the lie was used in a commercial context. U.S. v. Alvarez, 132 S. Ct. 2537 (2012). Should the First Amendment protect fabrications? In the 2004 presidential election, a group of Vietnam War veterans, backed by Republican operative Karl Rove, aired a political commercial accusing Democrat candidate John Kerry of lying about his heroism aboard a "swift boat" in Vietnam. While the accusations turned out to be de-

liberate falsehoods, the timing of the commercial, just weeks before the election, may have contributed to Kerry's defeat. Because the speech was in a non-commercial context, there were no legal consequences for politically motivated lying, now known as "swift-boating." Should there be consequences?

4. Are you skeptical of the First Amendment's benefits to our society, as described by Alexander Meiklejohn, Zachariah Chafee and other eminent professors of the mid-twentieth century? Does the "marketplace of ideas" foster free and fair debate of differing perspectives and opinions if some speakers, like Rupert Murdoch or Stephen Colbert, have much more power to promote their ideas than ordinary folks like you and I do? If you are skeptical about the First Amendment, can you think of a better free-speech alternative?
5. In his *Abrams* dissent supra, Justice Holmes states that a defendant must act with a specific intent to bring about the unlawful consequence; it must be the "aim of the deed." How does the Court in *Brandenburg* address the issue of intent?

CHAPTER 2

DEFAMATION

Defamation is a topic that many law students have studied before in Torts or Constitutional Law. Torts, of course, allow plaintiffs to sue civilly for personal injuries caused by a defendant. Defamation is the first of two torts examined in this book where the injury is the result of speech—the second, privacy, is covered in the next chapter. Defamation is also taught in Constitutional Law because, as we will see later, the First Amendment limits defamation suits under certain circumstances. Any speaker or writer can be liable for defamation, though journalists are most likely to be sued because speech is their stock-in-trade.

There are four elements of the defamation tort. A defendant must (1) utter a (2) false statement, (3) of and concerning the plaintiff, that (4) harms the plaintiff's reputation in his or her community.

Utterances: Libel and Slander

For something to be an utterance, it must be communicated to a third party. Defamation does not permit recovery for lowered self-esteem—the damage has to be to one's reputation among people other than the plaintiff and the defendant. So if someone says something false about you to your face but not to anyone else, you would not be able to sue for your hurt feelings.

The general rule is that spoken utterances are considered slander; if they are written they are considered libel. Plaintiffs have an easier time collecting damages for libel, since they can sue for general or presumed damages, without providing evidence of specific damages. In slander cases, plaintiffs have to show specific or "special" damages in order to recover. The reason for this distinction is logical, since libel has a permanence that slander generally does not have. The spoken word is, after all, ephemeral. In most cases, the harm from someone's slander decreases over time. The permanence of a written record, however, is the speech equivalent of a "gift that keeps on giving." With every subsequent repetition of the utterance, the injury can begin anew. In most states, any type of recordation—including sound or video recordings of spoken words—is considered libel. An important exception to this rule is California, which treats recordings as slander. The prevailing rule, even in California, is that utterances on the Internet are libel.

Utterances also include repeating someone else's libel or slander. If I utter a falsity about the defendant to you, and you relate it to others, then you will also be liable for my utterance. Under the common law you did not even have to know or believe that my statement was false. A journalist who in good faith repeated a defamatory statement uttered by a source would have been equally liable for damages. This strict liability for repetition libel no longer exists, thanks to the First Amendment.

Falsity

Even with respect to original utterances, all that mattered under the common law was that the utterance was false. A journalist who did careful research and thorough fact-checking in reporting a story could be held liable for an innocent utterance that turned out to be false. Intent, in effect, was irrelevant under the common law. A defendant could have had the purest of motives—mistakenly identifying someone as a rehabilitated ex-convict in laudatory remarks, for example. If damage resulted to the plaintiff, it did not matter what the defendant was thinking or why the comment was made. Today, the constitution requires some degree of fault on the part of a defendant—which can vary depending on circumstances addressed in New York Times Co. v. Sullivan and Gertz v. Robert Welch, Inc. infra.

Of and Concerning Plaintiff

For a plaintiff to prevail, the plaintiff must show that the defamatory statement was somehow connected to him or her. The simplest cases, of course, are when the plaintiff is named or otherwise clearly identified. In some situations, however, the reference to the plaintiff may be ambiguous or indirect. In such cases, courts may require the plaintiff to make a three-part showing of "colloquium, inducement, and innuendo" to show the defamatory impact of an ambiguous statement on plaintiff. Colloquium identifies the plaintiff: "Jim is the only member of the team who is left-handed." Inducement alleges facts to show the defamatory context:

"Only team members were allowed near the bus last night." Innuendo shows that the context has a defamatory impact on the plaintiff: "Jim is the only player who uses left-handed equipment." It does not take a Perry Mason to realize that Jim is being accused of vandalism, even though no one ever actually says it.

Groups presented a particularly challenging issue for the "of and concerning" element. If a false comment is directed toward a large group such as Philadelphia lawyers or Walmart employees, the general rule is that an individual in that group cannot sue. This is true even if the member was prominent in the group or believed that the comment was directed to him or her. Members of smaller groups—or subgroups—can sue for defamation directed toward the small group or subgroup. The reason for this is that it is reasonable to assume that the defamation directed to the group would also apply to the individual. If you say that the five-person city council conspired to steal money from taxpayers, the defamatory impact would clearly devolve unto any one of the five. It would not be reasonable for an individual lawyer to claim that a statement about "all Philadelphia lawyers" would reasonably be understood to refer to him or her. Corporations are persons under the law—not groups. They can sue just as an individual can.

The Nature of the Harm

The false utterance must lower the plaintiff's reputation in the community. This includes insular communities like church groups. Falsely alleging that a pastor questions the existence of God to members of a church group may result in damages, even though such an allegation may not lower the pastor's standing in the greater community. As discussed supra, the general rule is that if it is libel, plaintiff needs only to show general, presumed damage to her reputation. If it is slander, the plaintiff has the additional requirement of itemizing special damages. This general rule for slander, however, does not apply to four common law categories of slander, known as slander per se (or sometimes libel per se). False statements concerning (1) the imputation of a loathsome disease, (2) a crime of moral turpitude, (3) professional incompetency, or (4) the unchastity of a woman, are treated as libel with respect to damages. This means that a plaintiff needs only to show general, presumed damages even though the defamation is spoken. Despite the archaic nature of the categories, the exceptional treatment makes sense. While most spoken defamation loses its impact over time, these are more likely to be repeated as gossip—which gives it the more lasting defamatory impact that libel has.

In addition to general and special damages, there are two other types of damages available in defamation suits: nominal and punitive. Nominal damages are token damages awarded by juries in cases where there is technically defamation but little damage to reputation. For a plaintiff, this can be the equivalent of a slap in the face. For attorneys working on a contingency fee basis, this is a Pyrrhic victory at best, and an economic loss. Punitive damages, designed to punish a defendant for willful or egregious conduct, are offered in excess of the compensatory damages that reimburse plaintiff for her injury. Punitive damages, when appropriate, are the damages that plaintiffs and their attorneys often seek. Under the First Amendment, punitive damages are only available under limited circumstances, as discussed infra in the *Gertz* case.

Opinion Libel

Is there such a thing as a false opinion? In effect, couching certain statements as opinions may have the same defamatory impact as a declarative statement. There is little difference between calling someone a "serial liar," and saying that "in my opinion," that person is a serial liar. Other opinions seem much more subjective—assessing a performer as "untalented" or "second-rate," for instance. While there had been some debate on how to treat the defamatory impact of false opinion, the Supreme Court settled the question in Milkovich v. Lorain Journal Co.

MILKOVICH V. LORAIN JOURNAL CO.
497 U.S. 1 (1990)

Chief Justice REHNQUIST delivered the opinion of the Court.
Respondent J. Theodore Diadiun authored an article in an Ohio newspaper implying that petitioner Michael Milkovich, a local high school wrestling coach, lied under oath in a judicial proceeding about an incident involving petitioner and his team which occurred at a wrestling match. Petitioner sued Diadiun and the newspaper for libel, and the Ohio Court of Appeals affirmed a lower court entry of summary judgment against petitioner. This judgment was based in part on the grounds

that the article constituted an "opinion" protected from the reach of state defamation law by the First Amendment to the United States Constitution. We hold that the First Amendment does not prohibit the application of Ohio's libel laws to the alleged defamations contained in the article.

. . .

Respondents would have us recognize, in addition to the established safeguards discussed above, still another First-Amendment-based protection for defamatory statements which are categorized as "opinion" as opposed to "fact." For this proposition they rely principally on the following dictum from our opinion in *Gertz*:

> "Under the First Amendment there is no such thing as a false idea. However pernicious an opinion may seem, we depend for its correction not on the conscience of judges and juries but on the competition of other ideas. But there is no constitutional value in false statements of fact." 418 U.S., at 339-340 (footnote omitted).

Judge Friendly appropriately observed that this passage "has become the opening salvo in all arguments for protection from defamation actions on the ground of opinion, even though the case did not remotely concern the question." *Cianci v. New Times Publishing Co.,* 639 F.2d 54, 61 (2d Cir. 1980). Read in context, though, the fair meaning of the passage is to equate the word "opinion" in the second sentence with the word "idea" in the first sentence. Under this view, the language was merely a reiteration of Justice Holmes' classic "marketplace of ideas" concept. See *Abrams v. United States,* 250 U.S. 616, 630 (1919) (dissenting opinion) ("[T]he ultimate good desired is better reached by free trade in ideas— . . . the best test of truth is the power of the thought to get itself accepted in the competition of the market").

Thus, we do not think this passage from *Gertz* was intended to create a wholesale defamation exemption for anything that might be labeled "opinion." See *Cianci, supra,* at 62, n. 10 (The "marketplace of ideas" origin of this passage "points strongly to the view that the 'opinions' held to be constitutionally protected were the sort of thing that could be corrected by discussion"). Not only would such an interpretation be contrary to the tenor and context of the passage, but it would also ignore the fact that expressions of "opinion" may often imply an assertion of objective fact.

If a speaker says, "In my opinion John Jones is a liar," he implies a knowledge of facts which lead to the conclusion that Jones told an untruth. Even if the speaker states the facts upon which he bases his opinion, if those facts are either incorrect or incomplete, or if his assessment of them is erroneous, the statement may still imply a false assertion of fact. Simply couching such statements in terms of opinion does not dispel these implications; and the statement, "In my opinion Jones is a liar," can cause as much damage to reputation as the statement, "Jones is a liar." As Judge Friendly aptly stated: "[It] would be destructive of the law of libel if a writer could escape liability for accusations of [defamatory conduct] simply by using, explicitly or implicitly, the words 'I think.'" See *Cianci, supra,* at 64. It is worthy of note that at common law, even the privilege of fair comment did not extend to "a false statement of fact, whether it was expressly stated or implied from an expression of opinion." Restatement (Second) of Torts, § 566, Comment *a* (1977).

Apart from their reliance on the *Gertz* dictum, respondents do not really contend that a statement such as, "In my opinion John Jones is a liar," should be protected by a separate privilege for "opinion" under the First Amendment. But they do contend that in every defamation case the First Amendment mandates an inquiry into whether a statement is "opinion" or "fact," and that only the latter statements may be actionable. They propose that a number of factors developed by the lower courts (in what we hold was a mistaken reliance on the *Gertz* dictum) be considered in deciding which is which. But we think the "'breathing space'" which "'[f]reedoms of expression require in order to survive,'" *Hepps,* 475 U.S., at 772 (quoting *New York Times, supra,* 376 U.S., at 272), is adequately secured by existing constitutional doctrine without the creation of an artificial dichotomy between "opinion" and fact.

Foremost, we think *Hepps* stands for the proposition that a statement on matters of public concern must be provable as false before there can be liability under state defamation law, at least in situations, like the present, where a media defendant is involved. Thus, unlike the statement, "In my opinion Mayor Jones is a liar," the statement, "In my opinion Mayor Jones shows his abysmal ignorance by accepting the teachings of Marx and Lenin," would not be actionable. *Hepps* ensures that a statement of opinion relating to matters of public concern which does not contain a provably false factual connotation will receive full constitutional protection.

. . .

The *New York Times-Butts-Gertz* culpability requirements further ensure that debate on public issues remains "uninhibited, robust, and wide-open." *New York Times,* 376 U.S., at 270. Thus, where a statement of "opinion" on a matter of public concern reasonably implies false and defamatory facts regarding public figures or officials, those individuals must show that such statements were made with knowledge of their false implications or with reckless disregard of their truth. Similarly, where such a statement involves a private figure on a matter of public concern, a plaintiff must show that the false connotations were made with some level of fault as required by *Gertz.* Finally, the enhanced appellate review required by *Bose Corp.* provides assurance that the foregoing determinations will be made in a manner so as not to "constitute a forbidden intrusion of the field of free expression." *Bose Corp.,* 466 U.S., at 499 (quotation omitted).

We are not persuaded that, in addition to these protections, an additional separate constitutional privilege for "opinion" is required to ensure the freedom of expression guaranteed by the First Amendment. The dispositive question in the present case then becomes whether a reasonable factfinder could conclude that the statements in the Diadiun column imply an assertion that petitioner Milkovich perjured himself in a judicial proceeding. We think this question must be answered in the affirmative. As the Ohio Supreme Court itself observed: "[T]he clear impact in some nine sentences and a caption is that [Milkovich] 'lied at the hearing after . . . having given his solemn oath to tell the truth.'" *Scott,* 496 N.E.2d, at 707. This is not the sort of loose, figurative, or hyperbolic language which would negate the impression that the writer was seriously maintaining that petitioner committed the crime of perjury. Nor does the general tenor of the article negate this impression.

We also think the connotation that petitioner committed perjury is sufficiently factual to be susceptible of being proved true or false. . . .

Defenses to Defamation

The simplest defense to defamation is to prove the truth of the statement, since defamation requires falsity. But proving the truth can be very costly in a trial, since it may require investigation and expert testimony. To the extent that you can assert truth, you need only to prove substantial truth, or the truth in spirit. If you allege that a bank robber stole a million dollars, but can prove that he only stole $980,000, you would likely prevail. In addition to the defense of truth, there are a number of absolute and conditional privileges available to defendants.

The best-known absolute privileges are those pertaining to defamatory statements made by legislators in floor debate, and by the participants in a court trial. For public policy reasons, legislators need to be free from the fear of legal liability. Similarly, we privilege defamatory statements made by lawyers, witnesses, and judges. If a witness, for example, thought that her statement would result in a lawsuit by a defendant for defamation, she would likely refrain from making the statement, even if her allegation against the defendant were true. This is an example of the so-called chilling effect because nothing stops someone from claiming falsity even when a statement is, in fact, true. A lesser-known absolute privilege, important for broadcasters, is for speech aired by political candidates under the "equal opportunities" provisions of the Communications Act. We will address these provisions more fully in Chapter 9 infra.

Conditional privileges apply in certain situations. If reporters fairly report a statement from law enforcement that turns out to be defamatory, the privilege of record libel will apply, but the journalists must report the statements without embellishment or bias. Another form of conditional privilege is constitutional privilege, available under the First Amendment, which can greatly limit defamation suits under certain circumstances.

Constitutional Privilege

In 1964, the Supreme Court determined that the First Amendment may protect defendants from liability for defamation when the plaintiff is a public official who was acting in an official capacity. The case, New York Times Co. v. Sullivan, arose out of a 'Times' advertisement in support of Dr. Martin Luther King, Jr. that contained false statements upon which a police commissioner in Alabama alleged defamation. As you review Justice Brennan's opinion below, consider the justifications offered for curtailing public official defamation suits. The case that follows, Curtis Publishing v. Butts, extends the public official concept to public figures such as celebrities. Are the justifications the same as in *New York TImes*? As you consider the final two cases, Rosenblatt v. Baer and the landmark

Gertz v. Robert Welch, Inc., ask yourself whether the cases are more consistent with the reasoning of *New Yok Times* or *Butts*.

NEW YORK TIMES CO. V. SULLIVAN

376 U.S. 254 (1964)

Mr. Justice BRENNAN delivered the opinion of the Court.

We are required in this case to determine for the first time the extent to which the constitutional protections for speech and press limit a State's power to award damages in a libel action brought by a public official against critics of his official conduct.

Heed Their Rising Voices, New York Times, March 29, 1960.

Respondent L. B. Sullivan is one of the three elected Commissioners of the City of Montgomery, Alabama. He testified that he was "Commissioner of Public Affairs and the duties are supervision of the Police Department, Fire Department, Department of Cemetery and Department of Scales." He brought this civil libel action against the four individual petitioners, who are Negroes and Alabama clergymen, and against petitioner the New York Times Company, a New York corporation which publishes the New York Times, a daily newspaper. A jury in the Circuit Court of Montgomery County awarded him damages of $500,000, the full amount claimed, against all the petitioners, and the Supreme Court of Alabama affirmed. 144 So.2d 25.Respondent's complaint alleged that he had been libeled by statements in a full-page advertisement that was carried in the New York Times on March 29, 1960. Entitled "Heed Their Rising Voices," the advertisement began by stating that "As the whole world knows by now, thousands of Southern Negro students are engaged in widespread non-violent demonstrations in positive affirmation of the right to live in human dignity as guaranteed by the U.S. Constitution and the Bill of Rights." It went on to charge that "in their efforts to uphold these guarantees, they are being met by an unprecedented wave of terror by those who would deny and negate that document which the whole world looks upon as setting the pattern for modern freedom. . . ." Succeeding paragraphs purported to illustrate the "wave of terror" by describing certain alleged events. The text concluded with an appeal for funds for three purposes: support of the student movement, "the struggle for the right-to-vote," and the legal defense of Dr. Martin Luther King, Jr., leader of the movement, against a perjury indictment then pending in Montgomery.

. . .

It is uncontroverted that some of the statements contained in the two paragraphs were not accurate descriptions of events which occurred in Montgomery. Although Negro students staged a demonstration on the State Capital steps, they sang the National Anthem and not "My Country, 'Tis of Thee." Although nine students were expelled by the State Board of Education, this was not for leading the demonstration at the Capitol, but for demanding service at a lunch counter in the Montgomery County Courthouse on another day. Not the entire student body, but most of it, had protested the expulsion, not by refusing to register, but by boycotting classes on a single day; virtually all the students did register for the ensuing semester. The campus dining hall was not padlocked on any occasion, and the only students who may have been barred from eating there were the few who had neither signed a preregistration application nor requested temporary meal tickets. Although the police were deployed near the campus in large numbers on three occasions, they did not at any time "ring" the campus, and they were not called to the campus in connection with the demonstration on the State Capitol steps, as the third paragraph implied. Dr. King had not been arrested seven times, but only four; and although he claimed to have been assaulted some years earlier in connection with his arrest for loitering outside a courtroom, one of the officers who made the arrest denied that there was such an assault.

. . .

Because of the importance of the constitutional issues involved, we granted the separate petitions for certiorari of the individual petitioners and of the Times. 371 U.S. 946. We reverse the judgment. We hold that the rule of law applied by the Alabama courts is constitutionally deficient for failure to provide the safeguards for freedom of speech and of the press that are required by the First and Fourteenth Amendments in a libel action brought by a public official against critics of his official conduct. We further hold that under the proper safeguards the evidence presented in this case is constitutionally insufficient to support the judgment for respondent.

. . .

II.

Under Alabama law as applied in this case, a publication is "libelous per se" if the words "tend to injure a person . . . in his reputation" or to "bring [him] into public contempt"; the trial court stated that the standard was met if the words are such as to "injure him in his public office, or impute misconduct to him in his office, or want of official integrity, or want of fidelity to a public trust . . . ." The jury must find that the words were published "of and concerning" the plaintiff, but where the plaintiff is a public official his place in the governmental hierarchy is sufficient evidence to support a finding that his reputation has been affected by statements that reflect upon the agency of which he is in charge. Once "libel per se" has been established, the defendant has no defense as to stated facts unless he can persuade the jury that they were true in all their particulars. Alabama Ride Co. v. Vance, 178 So. 438 (Ala. 1938); Johnson Publishing Co. v. Davis, 124 So.2d 441, 457-458 (Ala. 1960). His privilege of "fair comment" for expressions of opinion depends on the truth of the facts upon which the comment is based. Parsons v. Age-Herald Publishing Co., 61 So. 345, 350 (1913). Unless he can discharge the burden of proving truth, general damages are presumed, and may be awarded without proof of pecuniary injury. A showing of actual malice is apparently a prerequisite to recovery of punitive damages, and the defendant may in any event forestall a punitive award by a retraction meeting the statutory requirements. Good motives and belief in truth do not negate an inference of malice, but are relevant only in mitigation of punitive damages if the jury chooses to accord them weight. . . .

The question before us is whether this rule of liability, as applied to an action brought by a public official against critics of his official conduct, abridges the freedom of speech and of the press that is guaranteed by the First and Fourteenth Amendments.

. . .

The general proposition that freedom of expression upon public questions is secured by the First Amendment has long been settled by our decisions. The constitutional safeguard, we have said, "was fashioned to assure unfettered interchange of ideas for the bringing about of political and social changes desired by the people." Roth v. United States, 354 U.S. 476, 484. "The maintenance of the opportunity for free political discussion to the end that government may be responsive to the will of the people and that changes may be obtained by lawful means, an opportunity essential to the security of the Republic, is a fundamental principle of our constitutional system." Stromberg v. California, 283 U.S. 359, 369. . . .

Thus we consider this case against the background of a profound national commitment to the principle that debate on public issues should be uninhibited, robust, and wide-open, and that it may well include vehement, caustic, and sometimes unpleasantly sharp attacks on government and public officials. See Terminiello v. Chicago, 337 U.S. 1, 4; De Jonge v. Oregon, 299 U.S. 353, 365. The present advertisement, as an expression of grievance and protest on one of the major public issues of our time, would seem clearly to qualify for the constitutional protection. The question is whether it forfeits that protection by the falsity of some of its factual statements and by its alleged defamation of respondent.

Authoritative interpretations of the First Amendment guarantees have consistently refused to recognize an exception for any test of truth—whether administered by judges, juries, or administrative officials—and especially one that puts the burden of proving truth on the speaker. Cf. Speiser v. Randall, 357 U.S. 513, 525-526. The constitutional protection does not turn upon "the truth, popularity, or social utility of the ideas and beliefs which are offered." N.A.A.C.P. v. Button, 371 U.S. 415, 445. As Madison said, "Some degree of abuse is inseparable from the proper use of every thing; and in no instance is this more true than in that of the press." 4 Elliot's Debates on the Federal Constitution (1876), p. 571. . . .

That erroneous statement is inevitable in free debate, and that it must be protected if the freedoms of expression are to have the "breathing space" that they "need . . . to survive," N.A.A.C.P. v. Button, 371 U.S. 415, 433, was also recognized by the Court of Appeals for the District of Columbia

Circuit in Sweeney v. Patterson, 128 F.2d 457, 458 (D.C. Cir. 1942), cert. denied, 317 U.S. 678. Judge Edgerton spoke for a unanimous court which affirmed the dismissal of a Congressman's libel suit based upon a newspaper article charging him with anti-Semitism in opposing a judicial appointment. . . .

Injury to official reputation error affords no more warrant for repressing speech that would otherwise be free than does factual error. Where judicial officers are involved, this Court has held that concern for the dignity and reputation of the courts does not justify the punishment as criminal contempt of criticism of the judge or his decision. Bridges v. California, 314 U.S. 252. This is true even though the utterance contains "half-truths" and "misinformation." Pennekamp v. Florida, 328 U.S. 331, 342, 343, n. 5, 345. Such repression can be justified, if at all, only by a clear and present danger of the obstruction of justice. . . . Criticism of their official conduct does not lose its constitutional protection merely because it is effective criticism and hence diminishes their official reputations.

If neither factual error nor defamatory content suffices to remove the constitutional shield from criticism of official conduct, the combination of the two elements is no less inadequate. . . .

What a State may not constitutionally bring about by means of a criminal statute is likewise beyond the reach of its civil law of libel. The fear of damage awards under a rule such as that invoked by the Alabama courts here may be markedly more inhibiting than the fear of prosecution under a criminal statute. See City of Chicago v. Tribune Co., 139 N.E. 86, 90 (Ill. 1923). Alabama, for example, has a criminal libel law which subjects to prosecution "any person who speaks, writes, or prints of and concerning another any accusation falsely and maliciously importing the commission by such person of a felony, or any other indictable offense involving moral turpitude," and which allows as punishment upon conviction a fine not exceeding $500 and a prison sentence of six months. Alabama Code, Tit. 14, § 350. Presumably a person charged with violation of this statute enjoys ordinary criminal-law safeguards such as the requirements of an indictment and of proof beyond a reasonable doubt. These safeguards are not available to the defendant in a civil action. The judgment awarded in this case—without the need for any proof of actual pecuniary loss—was one thousand times greater than the maximum fine provided by the Alabama criminal statute, and one hundred times greater than that provided by the Sedition Act. And since there is no double-jeopardy limitation applicable to civil lawsuits, this is not the only judgment that may be awarded against petitioners for the same publication.

Whether or not a newspaper can survive a succession of such judgments, the pall of fear and timidity imposed upon those who would give voice to public criticism is an atmosphere in which the First Amendment freedoms cannot survive. Plainly the Alabama law of civil libel is "a form of regulation that creates hazards to protected freedoms markedly greater than those that attend reliance upon the criminal law." Bantam Books, Inc. v. Sullivan, 372 U.S. 58, 70.

The state rule of law is not saved by its allowance of the defense of truth. A defense for erroneous statements honestly made is no less essential here than was the requirement of proof of guilty knowledge which, in Smith v. California, 361 U.S. 147, we held indispensable to a valid conviction of a bookseller for possessing obscene writings for sale. We said:

> "For if the bookseller is criminally liable without knowledge of the contents, . . . he will tend to restrict the books he sells to those he has inspected; and thus the State will have imposed a restriction upon the distribution of constitutionally protected as well as obscene literature. . . . And the bookseller's burden would become the public's burden, for by restricting him the public's access to reading matter would be restricted. . . . [H]is timidity in the face of his absolute criminal liability, thus would tend to restrict the public's access to forms of the printed word which the State could not constitutionally suppress directly. The bookseller's self-censorship, compelled by the State, would be a censorship affecting the whole public, hardly less virulent for being privately administered. Through it, the distribution of all books, both obscene and not obscene, would be impeded." (361 U.S. 147, 153-154.)

A rule compelling the critic of official conduct to guarantee the truth of all his factual assertions—and to do so on pain of libel judgments virtually unlimited in amount—leads to a comparable "self-censorship." Allowance of the defense of truth, with the burden of proving it on the defendant, does not mean that only false speech will be deterred. Even courts accepting this defense as an adequate safeguard have recognized the difficulties of adducing legal proofs that the alleged libel was true in all its factual particulars. . . . Under such a rule, would-be critics of official conduct may be deterred from voicing their criticism, even though it is believed to be true and even though it is in fact true, because of doubt whether it can be proved in court or fear of the expense of having to do so. They tend to make only statements which "steer far wider of the unlawful zone." Speiser v. Randall, supra, 357 U.S., at 526. The rule thus dampens the vigor and limits the variety of public debate. It is inconsistent with the First and Fourteenth Amendments.

The constitutional guarantees require, we think, a federal rule that prohibits a public official from recovering damages for a defamatory falsehood relating to his official conduct unless he proves that the statement was made with "actual malice"—that is, with knowledge that it was false or with reckless disregard of whether it was false or not. . . .

Such a privilege for criticism of official conduct is appropriately analogous to the protection accorded a public official when he is sued for libel by a private citizen. In Barr v. Matteo, 360 U.S. 564, 575, this Court held the utterance of a federal official to be absolutely privileged if made "within the outer perimeter" of his duties. The States accord the same immunity to statements of their highest officers, although some differentiate their lesser officials and qualify the privilege they enjoy. But all hold that all officials are protected unless actual malice can be proved. The reason for the official privilege is said to be that the threat of damage suits would otherwise "inhibit the fearless, vigorous, and effective administration of policies of government" and "dampen the ardor of all but the most resolute, or the most irresponsible, in the unflinching discharge of their duties." Barr v. Matteo, supra, 360 U.S., at 571. Analogous considerations support the privilege for the citizen-critic of government. It is as much his duty to criticize as it is the official's duty to administer. See Whitney v. California, 274 U.S. 357, 375 (concurring opinion of Mr. Justice Brandeis), quoted supra, pp. 720, 721. As Madison said, see supra, p. 723, "the censorial power is in the people over the Government, and not in the Government over the people." It would give public servants an unjustified preference over the public they serve, if critics of official conduct did not have a fair equivalent of the immunity granted to the officials themselves.

We conclude that such a privilege is required by the First and Fourteenth Amendments.

III.

We hold today that the Constitution delimits a State's power to award damages for libel in actions brought by public officials against critics of their official conduct. Since this is such an action, the rule requiring proof of actual malice is applicable. While Alabama law apparently requires proof of actual malice for an award of punitive damages, where general damages are concerned malice is "presumed." Such a presumption is inconsistent with the federal rule. "The power to create presumptions is not a means of escape from constitutional restrictions," Bailey v. Alabama, 219 U.S. 219, 239; "[t]he showing of malice required for the forfeiture of the privilege is not presumed but is a matter for proof by the plaintiff . . . ." Lawrence v. Fox, 97 N.W.2d 719, 725 (Mich. 1959). Since the trial judge did not instruct the jury to differentiate between general and punitive damages, it may be that the verdict was wholly an award of one or the other. But it is impossible to know, in view of the general verdict returned. Because of this uncertainty, the judgment must be reversed and the case remanded. . . .

> "We think it common knowledge that the average person knows that municipal agents, such as police and firemen, and others, are under the control and direction of the city governing body, and more particularly under the direction and control of a single commissioner. In measuring the performance or deficiencies of such groups, praise or criticism is usually attached to the official in complete control of the body." . . .

This proposition has disquieting implications for criticism of governmental conduct. For good reason, "no court of last resort in this country has ever held, or even suggested, that prosecutions for libel on government have any place in the American system of jurisprudence." City of Chicago v. Tribune Co., 139 N.E. 86, 88 (1923). The present proposition would sidestep this obstacle by transmuting criticism of government, however impersonal it may seem on its face, into personal criticism, and hence potential libel, of the officials of whom the government is composed. There is no legal alchemy by which a State may thus create the cause of action that would otherwise be denied for a publication which, as respondent himself said of the advertisement, "reflects not only on me but on the other Commissioners and the community." Raising as it does the possibility that a good-faith critic of government will be penalized for his criticism, the proposition relied on by the Alabama courts strikes at the very center of the constitutionally protected area of free expression. We hold that such a proposition may not constitutionally be utilized to establish that an otherwise impersonal attack on governmental operations was a libel of an official responsible for those operations. Since it was relied on exclusively here, and there was no other evidence to connect the statements with respondent, the evidence was constitutionally insufficient to support a finding that the statements referred to respondent.

The judgment of the Supreme Court of Alabama is reversed and the case is remanded to that court for further proceedings not inconsistent with this opinion.

Reversed and remanded.

CURTIS PUBLISHING CO. V. BUTTS
388 U.S. 130 (1967)

Mr. Justice HARLAN announced the judgments of the Court and delivered an opinion in which Mr. Justice CLARK, Mr. Justice STEWART, and Mr. Justice FORTAS join.

. . .

In the cases we decide today none of the particular considerations involved in *New York Times* is present. These actions cannot be analogized to prosecutions for seditious libel. Neither plaintiff has any position in government which would permit a recovery by him to be viewed as a vindication of governmental policy. Neither was entitled to a special privilege protecting his utterances against accountability in libel. We are prompted, therefore, to seek guidance from the rules of liability which prevail in our society with respect to compensation of persons injured by the improper performance of a legitimate activity by another. Under these rules, a departure from the kind of care society may expect from a reasonable man performing such activity leaves the actor open to a judicial shifting of loss. In defining these rules, and especially in formulating the standards for determining the degree of care to be expected in the circumstances, courts have consistently given much attention to the importance of defendants' activities. Prosser, The Law of Torts § 31, at 151. The courts have also, especially in libel cases, investigated the plaintiff's position to determine whether he has a legitimate call upon the court for protection in light of his prior activities and means of self-defense. See Brewer v. Hearst Publishing Co., 7 Cir., 185 F.2d 846; Flanagan v. Nicholson Publishing Co., 68 So. 964. We note that the public interest in the circulation of the materials here involved, and the publisher's interest in circulating them, is not less than that involved in *New York Times*. And both Butts and Walker commanded a substantial amount of independent public interest at the time of the publications; both, in our opinion, would have been labeled "public figures" under ordinary tort rules. See Spahn v. Julian Messner, Inc., 221 N.E.2d 543, remanded on other grounds, 387 U.S. 239. Butts may have attained that status by position alone and Walker by his purposeful activity amounting to a thrusting of his personality into the "vortex" of an important public controversy, but both commanded sufficient continuing public interest and had sufficient access to the means of counterargument to be able "to expose through discussion the falsehood and fallacies" of the defamatory statements. Whitney v. People of State of California, 274 U.S. 357, 377 (Brandeis, J., dissenting).

These similarities and differences between libel actions involving persons who are public officials and libel actions involving those circumstanced as were Butts and Walker, viewed in light of the principles of liability which are of general applicability in our society, lead us to the conclusion that libel actions of the present kind cannot be left entirely to state libel laws, unlimited by any overriding constitutional safeguard, but that the rigorous federal requirements of *New York Times* are not the only appropriate accommodation of the conflicting interests at stake. We consider and would hold that a "public figure" who is not a public official may also recover damages for a defamatory falsehood . . . .

ROSENBLATT V. BAER

383 U.S. 75 (1966)

A jury in New Hampshire Superior Court awarded respondent damages in this civil libel action based on one of petitioner's columns in the Laconia Evening Citizen. Respondent alleged that the column contained defamatory falsehoods concerning his performance as Supervisor of the Belknap County Recreation Area, a facility owned and operated by Belknap County. . . .

The Recreation Area was used principally as a ski resort but also for other recreational activities. Respondent was employed by and directly responsible to the Belknap County Commissioners, three elected officials in charge of the county government. During the 1950's, a public controversy developed over the way respondent and the Commissioners operated the Area; some protested that respondent and the Commissioners had not developed the Area's full potential, either as a resort for local residents or as a tourist attraction that might contribute to the county's taxes. The discussion culminated in 1959, when the New Hampshire Legislature enacted a law transferring control of the Area to a special five-man commission. At least in part to give this new regime a fresh start, respondent was discharged.

Petitioner regularly contributed an unpaid column to the Laconia Evening Citizen. In it he frequently commented on political matters. As an outspoken proponent of the change in operations at the Recreation Area, petitioner's views were often sharply stated, and he had indicated disagreement with the actions taken by respondent and the County Commissioners. In January 1960, during the first ski season under the new management, some six months after respondent's discharge, petitioner published the column that respondent alleges libeled him. . . .

Turning, then, to the question whether respondent was a "public official" within *New York Times* we reject at the outset his suggestion that it should be answered by reference to state-law standards. States have developed definitions of "public official" for local administrative purposes, not the purposes of a national constitutional protection. If existing state-law standards reflect the purposes of *New York Times*, this is at best accidental. Our decision in *New York Times*, moreover, draws its force from the constitutional protections afforded free expression. The standards that set the scope of its principles cannot therefore be such that "the constitutional limits of free expression in the Nation would vary with state lines." Pennekamp v. State of Florida, 328 U.S. 331, 335.

We remarked in *New York Times* that we had no occasion "to determine how far down into the lower ranks of government employees the 'public official' designation would extend for purposes of this rule, or otherwise to specify categories of persons who would or would not be included." 376 U.S., at 283, n. 23. No precise lines need be drawn for the purposes of this case. The motivating force for the decision in New York Times was twofold. We expressed "a profound national commitment to the principle that debate on public issue should be uninhibited, robust, and wide-open, and that [such debate] may well include vehement, caustic, and sometimes unpleasantly sharp attacks on government and public officials." 376 U.S., at 270. (Emphasis supplied.) There is, first, a strong interest in debate on public issues, and, second, a strong interest in debate about those persons who are in a position significantly to influence the resolution of those issues. Criticism of government is at the very center of the constitutionally protected area of free discussion. Criticism of those responsible for government operations must be free, lest criticism of government itself be penalized. It is clear, therefore, that the "public official" designation applies at the very least to those among the hierarchy of government employees who have, or appear to the public to have, substantial responsibility for or control over the conduct of governmental affairs.

This conclusion does not ignore the important social values which underlie the law of defamation. Society has a pervasive and strong interest in preventing and redressing attacks upon reputation. But in cases like the present, there is tension between this interest and the values nurtured by the First and Fourteenth Amendments. The thrust of *New York Times* is that when interests in public discussion are particularly strong, as they were in that case, the Constitution limits the protections afforded by the law of defamation. Where a position in government has such apparent importance that the public has an independent interest in the qualifications and performance of the person who holds it, beyond the general public interest in the qualifications and performance of all government employees, both elements we identified in *New York Times* are present and the *New York Times* malice standards apply.

. . .

GERTZ V. ROBERT WELCH INC.

418 U.S. 323 (1974)

Mr. Justice POWELL delivered the opinion of the Court.

This Court has struggled for nearly a decade to define the proper accommodation between the law of defamation and the freedoms of speech and press protected by the First Amendment. With this decision we return to that effort. We granted certiorari to reconsider the extent of a publisher's constitutional privilege against liability for defamation of a private citizen. 410 U.S. 925 (1973).

I.

In 1968 a Chicago policeman named Nuccio shot and killed a youth named Nelson. The state authorities prosecuted Nuccio for the homicide and ultimately obtained a conviction for murder in the second degree. The Nelson family retained petitioner Elmer Gertz, a reputable attorney, to represent them in civil litigation against Nuccio.

Respondent publishes American Opinion, a monthly outlet for the views of the John Birch Society. Early in the 1960's the magazine began to warn of a nationwide conspiracy to discredit local law enforcement agencies and create in their stead a national police force capable of supporting a Communist dictatorship. As part of the continuing effort to alert the public to this assumed danger, the managing editor of American Opinion commissioned an article on the murder trial of Officer Nuccio. For this purpose he engaged a regular contributor to the magazine. In March

1969 respondent published the resulting article under the title "FRAME-UP: Richard Nuccio And The War On Police." The article purports to demonstrate that the testimony against Nuccio at his criminal trial was false and that his prosecution was part of the Communist campaign against the police.

In his capacity as counsel for the Nelson family in the civil litigation, petitioner attended the coroner's inquest into the boy's death and initiated actions for damages, but he neither discussed Officer Nuccio with the press nor played any part in the criminal proceeding. Notwithstanding petitioner's remote connection with the prosecution of Nuccio, respondent's magazine portrayed him as an architect of the "frame-up." According to the article, the police file on petitioner took "a big, Irish cop to lift." The article stated that petitioner had been an official of the "Marxist League for Industrial Democracy, originally known as the Intercollegiate Socialist Society, which has advocated the violent seizure of our government." It labeled Gertz a "Leninist" and a "Communist-fronter." It also stated that Gertz had been an officer of the National Lawyers Guild, described as a Communist organization that "probably did more than any other outfit to plan the Communist attack on the Chicago police during the 1968 Democratic Convention."

These statements contained serious inaccuracies. The implication that petitioner had a criminal record was false. Petitioner had been a member and officer of the National Lawyers Guild some 15 years earlier, but there was no evidence that he or that organization had taken any part in planning the 1968 demonstrations in Chicago. There was also no basis for the charge that petitioner was a "Leninist" or a "Communist-fronter." And he had never been a member of the "Marxist League for Industrial Democracy" or the "Intercollegiate Socialist Society."

The managing editor of American Opinion made no effort to verify or substantiate the charges against petitioner. Instead, he appended an editorial introduction stating that the author had "conducted extensive research into the Richard Nuccio Case." And he included in the article a photograph of petitioner and wrote the caption that appeared under it: "Elmer Gertz of Red Guild harasses Nuccio." Respondent placed the issue of American Opinion containing the article on sale at newsstands throughout the country and distributed reprints of the article on the streets of Chicago.

. . .

II.

The principal issue in this case is whether a newspaper or broadcaster that publishes defamatory falsehoods about an individual who is neither a public official nor a public figure may claim a constitutional privilege against liability for the injury inflicted by those statements. The Court considered this question on the rather different set of facts presented in Rosenbloom v. Metromedia, Inc., 403 U.S. 29 (1971). Rosenbloom, a distributor of nudist magazines, was arrested for selling allegedly obscene material while making a delivery to a retail dealer. The police obtained a warrant and seized his entire inventory of 3,000 books and magazines. He sought and obtained an injunction prohibiting further police interference with his business. He then sued a local radio station for failing to note in two of its newscasts that the 3,000 items seized were only "reportedly" or "allegedly" obscene and for broadcasting references to "the smut literature racket" and to "girlie-book peddlers" in its coverage of the court proceeding for injunctive relief. He obtained a judgment against the radio station, but the Court of Appeals for the Third Circuit held the New York Times privilege applicable to the broadcast and reversed. 415 F.2d 892 (3d Cir. 1969).

. . .

In his opinion for the plurality in Rosenbloom v. Metromedia, Inc., 403 U.S. 29 (1971), Mr. Justice Brennan took the New York Times privilege one step further. He concluded that its protection should extend to defamatory falsehoods relating to private persons if the statements concerned matters of general or public interest. He abjured the suggested distinction between public officials and public figures on the one hand and private individuals on the other. He focused instead on society's interest in learning about certain issues: "If a matter is a subject of public or general interest, it cannot suddenly become less so merely because a private individual is involved, or because in some sense the individual did not 'voluntarily' choose to become involved." Id., at 4. Thus, under the plurality opinion, a private citizen involuntarily associated with a matter of general interest has no recourse for injury to his reputation unless he can satisfy the demanding requirements of the New York Times test.

. . .

III.

We begin with the common ground. Under the First Amendment there is no such thing as a false idea. However pernicious an opinion may seem, we depend for its correction not on the conscience of judges and juries but on the competition of other ideas. But there is no constitutional value in false statements of fact. Neither the intentional lie nor the careless error materially advances society's interest in "uninhibited, robust, and wide-open" debate on public issues. New York Times Co. v. Sullivan, 376 U.S., at 270. They belong to that category of utterances which "are no essential part of any exposition of ideas, and are of such slight social value as a step to truth that any benefit that may be derived from them is clearly outweighed by the social interest in order and morality." Chaplinsky v. New Hampshire, 315 U.S. 568, 572 (1942).

Although the erroneous statement of fact is not worthy of constitutional protection, it is nevertheless inevitable in free debate. As James Madison pointed out in the Report on the Virginia Resolutions of 1798: "Some degree of abuse is inseparable from the proper use of every thing; and in no instance is this more true than in that of the press." 4 J. Elliot, Debates on the Federal Constitution of 1787, p. 571 (1876). And punishment of error runs the risk of inducing a cautious and restrictive exercise of the constitutionally guaranteed freedoms of speech and press. Our decisions recognize that a rule of strict liability that compels a publisher or broadcaster to guarantee the accuracy of his factual assertions may lead to intolerable self-censorship. Allowing the media to avoid liability only by proving the truth of all injurious statements does not accord adequate protection to First Amendment liberties. As the Court stated in New York Times Co. v. Sullivan, supra, 376 U.S., at 279: "Allowance of the defense of truth, with the burden of proving it on the defendant, does not mean that only false speech will be deterred." The First Amendment requires that we protect some falsehood in order to protect speech that matters.

The need to avoid self-censorship by the news media is, however, not the only societal value at issue. If it were, this Court would have embraced long ago the view that publishers and broadcasters enjoy an unconditional and indefeasible immunity from liability for defamation.... Such a rule would, indeed, obviate the fear that the prospect of civil liability for injurious falsehood might dissuade a timorous press from the effective exercise of First Amendment freedoms. Yet absolute protection for the communications media requires a total sacrifice of the competing value served by the law of defamation.

The legitimate state interest underlying the law of libel is the compensation of individuals for the harm inflicted on them by defamatory falsehood. We would not lightly require the State to abandon this purpose, for, as Mr. Justice Stewart has reminded us, the individual's right to the protection of his own good name

> "reflects no more than our basic concept of the essential dignity and worth of every human being—a concept at the root of any decent system of ordered liberty. The protection of private personality, like the protection of life itself, is left primarily to the individual States under the Ninth and Tenth Amendments. But this does not mean that the right is entitled to any less recognition by this Court as a basic of our constitutional system." Rosenblatt v. Baer, 383 U.S. 75, 92 (1966) (concurring opinion).

Some tension necessarily exists between the need for a vigorous and uninhibited press and the legitimate interest in redressing wrongful injury. As Mr. Justice Harlan stated, "some antithesis between freedom of speech and press and libel actions persists, for libel remains premised on the content of speech and limits the freedom of the publisher to express certain sentiments, at least without guaranteeing legal proof of their substantial accuracy." Curtis Publishing Co. v. Butts, supra, 388 U.S., at 152. In our continuing effort to define the proper accommodation between these competing concerns, we have been especially anxious to assure to the freedoms of speech and press that "breathing space" essential to their fruitful exercise. NAACP v. Button, 371 U.S. 415, 433 (1963). To that end this Court has extended a measure of strategic protection to defamatory falsehood.

The New York Times standard defines the level of constitutional protection appropriate to the context of defamation of a public person. Those who, by reason of the notoriety of their achievements or the vigor and success with which they seek the public's attention, are properly classed as public figures and those who hold governmental office may recover for injury to reputation only on clear and convincing proof that the defamatory falsehood was made with knowledge of its falsity or with reckless disregard for the truth. This standard administers an extremely powerful antidote to the inducement to media self-censorship of the common-law rule of strict liability for libel and slander. And it exacts a correspondingly high price from the victims of defamatory falsehood. Plainly many deserving plaintiffs, including some intentionally subjected to injury, will be unable to surmount the barrier of the New York Times test. Despite this substantial abridgment of the state law right to compensation for wrongful hurt to one's reputation, the Court has concluded that the protection of the New York Times privilege should be available to publishers and broadcasters of defamatory falsehood concerning public officials and public figures. New York Times Co. v. Sullivan, supra; Curtis Publishing Co. v. Butts, supra. We think that these decisions are correct, but we do not find their holdings justified solely by reference to the interest of the press and broadcast media in immunity from liability. Rather, we believe that the New York Times rule states an accommodation between this concern and the limited state interest present in the context of libel actions brought by public persons. For the reasons stated below, we conclude that the state interest in compensating injury to the reputation of private individuals requires that a different rule should obtain with respect to them.

. . .

[W]e have no difficulty in distinguishing among defamation plaintiffs. The first remedy of any victim of defamation is self-help—using available opportunities to contradict the lie or correct the error and thereby to minimize its adverse impact on reputation. Public officials and public figures usually enjoy significantly greater access to the channels of effective communication and hence have a more realistic opportunity to counteract false statements then private individuals normally enjoy. Private individuals are therefore more vulnerable to injury, and the state interest in protecting them is correspondingly greater.

More important than the likelihood that private individuals will lack effective opportunities for rebuttal, there is a compelling normative consideration underlying the distinction between public and private defamation plaintiffs. An individual who decides to seek governmental office must accept certain necessary consequences of that involvement in public affairs. He runs the risk of closer public scrutiny than might otherwise be the case. And society's interest in the officers of government is not strictly limited to the formal discharge of official duties. As the Court pointed out in Garrison v. Louisiana, 379 U.S., at 77 the public's interest extends to "anything which might touch on an official's fitness for office. . . . Few personal attributes are more germane to fitness for office than dishonesty, malfeasance, or improper motivation, even though these characteristics may also affect the official's private character."

Those classed as public figures stand in a similar position. Hypothetically, it may be possible for someone to become a public figure through no purposeful action of his own, but the instances of truly involuntary public figures must be exceedingly rare. For the most part those who attain this status have assumed roles of especial prominence in the affairs of society.

Some occupy positions of such persuasive power and influence that they are deemed public figures for all purposes. More commonly, those classed as public figures have thrust themselves to the forefront of particular public controversies in order to influence the resolution of the issues involved. In either event, they invite attention and comment.

Even if the foregoing generalities do not obtain in every instance, the communications media are entitled to act on the assumption that public officials and public figures have voluntarily exposed themselves to increased risk of injury from defamatory falsehood concerning them. No such assumption is justified with respect to a private individual. He has not accepted public office or assumed an "influential role in ordering society." Curtis Publishing Co. v. Butts, 388 U.S., at 164 (Warren, C.J., concurring in result). He has relinquished no part of his interest in the protection of his own good name, and consequently he has a more compelling call on the courts for redress of injury inflicted by defamatory falsehood. Thus, private individuals are not only more vulnerable to injury than public officials and public figures; they are also more deserving of recovery.

For these reasons we conclude that the States should retain substantial latitude in their efforts to enforce a legal remedy for defamatory falsehood injurious to the reputation of a private individual. The extension of the New York Times test proposed by the Rosenbloom plurality would abridge this legitimate state interest to a degree that we find unacceptable. And it would occasion the additional difficulty of forcing state and federal judges to decide on an ad hoc basis which publications address issues of "general or public interest" and which do not—to determine, in the words of Mr. Justice Marshall, "what information is relevant to self-government." Rosenbloom v. Metromedia, Inc., 403 U.S., at 79. We doubt the wisdom of committing this task to the conscience of judges. Nor does the Constitution require us to draw so thin a line between the drastic alternatives of the New York Times privilege and the common law of strict liability for defamatory error. The "public or general interest" test for determining the applicability of the New York Times standard to private defamation actions inadequately serves both of the competing values at stake. On the one hand, a private individual whose reputation is injured by defamatory falsehood that does concern an issue of public or general interest has no recourse unless he can meet the rigorous requirements of New York Times. This is true despite the factors that distinguish the state interest in compensating private individuals from the analogous interest involved in the context of public persons. On the other hand, a publisher or broadcaster of a defamatory error which a court deems unrelated to an issue of public or general interest may be held liable in damages even if it took every reasonable precaution to ensure the accuracy of its assertions. And liability may far exceed compensation for any actual injury to the plaintiff, for the jury may be permitted to presume damages without proof of loss and even to award punitive damages.

We hold that, so long as they do not impose liability without fault, the States may define for themselves the appropriate standard of liability for a publisher or broadcaster of defamatory falsehood injurious to a private individual. This approach provides a more equitable boundary between the competing concerns involved here. It recognizes the strength of the legitimate state interest in compensating private individuals for wrongful injury to reputation, yet shields the press and broadcast media from the rigors of strict liability for defamation. At least this conclusion obtains where, as here, the substance of the defamatory statement "makes substantial danger to reputation apparent." This phrase places in perspective the conclusion we announce today. Our inquiry would involve considerations somewhat different from those discussed above if a State purported to condition civil liability on a factual misstatement whose content did not warn a reasonably prudent editor or broadcaster of its defamatory potential. Cf. Time, Inc. v. Hill, 385 U.S. 374 (1967). Such a case is not now before us, and we intimate no view as to its proper resolution.

IV.

Our accommodation of the competing values at stake in defamation suits by private individuals allows the States to impose liability on the publisher or broadcaster of defamatory falsehood on a less demanding showing than that required by New York Times. This conclusion is not based on a belief that the considerations which prompted the adoption of the New York Times privilege for defamation of public officials and its extension to public figures are wholly inapplicable to the context of private individuals. Rather, we endorse this approach in recognition of the strong and legitimate state interest in compensating private individuals for injury to reputation. But this countervailing state interest extends no further than compensation for actual injury. For the reasons stated below, we hold that the States may not permit recovery of presumed or punitive damages, at least when liability is not based on a showing of knowledge of falsity or reckless disregard for the truth.

The common law of defamation is an oddity of tort law, for it allows recovery of purportedly compensatory damages without evidence of actual loss. Under the traditional rules pertaining to actions for libel, the existence of injury is presumed from the fact of publication. Juries may award substantial sums as compensation for supposed damage to reputation without any proof that such harm actually occurred. The largely uncontrolled discretion of juries to award damages where there is no loss unnecessarily compounds the potential of any system of liability for defamatory falsehood to inhibit the vigorous exercise of First Amendment freedoms. Additionally, the doctrine of presumed damages invites juries to punish unpopular opinion rather than to compensate individuals for injury sustained by the publication of a false fact. More to the point, the States have no substantial interest in securing for plaintiffs such as this petitioner gratuitous awards of money damages far in excess of any actual injury.

We would not, of course, invalidate state law simply because we doubt its wisdom, but here we are attempting to reconcile state law with a competing interest grounded in the constitutional command of the First Amendment. It is therefore appropriate to require that state remedies for defamatory falsehood reach no farther than is necessary to protect the legitimate interest involved. It is necessary to restrict defamation plaintiffs who do not prove knowledge of falsity or reckless disregard for the truth to compensation for actual injury. We need not define "actual injury," as trial courts have wide experience in framing appropriate jury instructions in tort actions. Suffice it to say that actual injury is not limited to out-of-pocket loss. Indeed, the more customary types of actual harm inflicted by defamatory falsehood include impairment of reputation and standing in the community, personal humiliation, and mental anguish and suffering. Of course, juries must be limited by appropriate instructions, and all awards must be supported by competent evidence concerning the injury, although there need be no evidence which assigns an actual dollar value to the injury.

We also find no justification for allowing awards of punitive damages against publishers and broadcasters held liable under state-defined standards of liability for defamation. In most jurisdictions jury discretion over the amounts awarded is limited only by the gentle rule that they not be excessive. Consequently, juries assess punitive damages in wholly unpredictable amounts bearing no necessary relation to the actual harm caused. And they remain free to use their discretion selectively to punish expressions of unpopular views. Like the doctrine of presumed damages, jury discretion to award punitive damages unnecessarily exacerbates the danger of media self-censorship, but, unlike the former rule, punitive damages are wholly irrelevant to the state interest that justifies a negligence standard for private defamation actions. They are not compensation for injury. Instead, they are private fines levied by civil juries to punish reprehensible conduct and to deter its future occurrence. In short, the private defamation plaintiff who establishes liability under a less demanding standard than that stated by New York Times may recover only such damages as are sufficient to compensate him for actual injury.

V.
Notwithstanding our refusal to extend the New York Times privilege to defamation of private individuals, respondent contends that we should affirm the judgment below on the ground that petitioner is either a public official or a public figure. There is little basis for the former assertion. Several years prior to the present incident, petitioner had served briefly on housing committees appointed by the mayor of Chicago, but at the time of publication he had never held any remunerative governmental position. Respondent admits this but argues that petitioner's appearance at the coroner's inquest rendered him a "de facto public official." Our cases recognized no such concept. Respondent's suggestion would sweep all lawyers under the New York Times rule as officers of the court and distort the plain meaning of the "public official" category beyond all recognition. We decline to follow it.

NOTES AND QUESTIONS

1. As a speech tort, defamation allows a plaintiff to recover damages after-the-fact for reputational injury. It is rare that plaintiffs will seek a preliminary injunction from a court. Why is that? Would it be better for litigants to use a prior restraint to stop potentially injurious speech before it is disseminated and repeated? Does Justice Brennan consider this issue in New York Times v. Sullivan?
2. What is the "chilling effect"? Is that a good enough reason to require actual malice for public officials? Does the same reasoning justify requiring actual malice in cases involving public figures like celebrities and athletes?
3. Do wealthy corporations and individuals have an advantage over people with modest or low incomes? Consider a controversial church group or a sports team owner who puts the world on notice that any alleged falsity will be aggressively litigated by a first-rate legal team. Would you hesitate to post a truthful criticism online if you believed the subject of your criticism would threaten court action against you? Would you have the same hesitation if you were posting about an indigent person?

4. **Anti-SLAPP laws.** Many states have procedural laws in place designed to thwart Strategic Lawsuits Against Public Participation (SLAPP), cases in which plaintiffs use the courts to chill a defendant's right to have a voice in matters of public significance. California Code of Civil Procedure §425.16, for example, permits the complaining defendant to file an anti-SLAPP motion at the outset of litigation, immediately stopping discovery. Once the defendant demonstrates that the plaintiff's lawsuit curtails rights protected by the statute, the burden shifts to the plaintiff to present evidence that it would likely prevail at trial, with a right of immediate appeal by the defendant. If the plaintiff fails to meet its burden, the suit will be dismissed with reasonable attorney fees awarded to the defendant.
5. In the weeks before he was elected president, Donald Trump declared that he would sue women whom he claimed had fabricated accusations of sexual misconduct. Trump did not sue, but if he had, would the women have benefited from an anti-SLAPP motion? Is just the threat of litigation too burdensome on persons of modest means?
6. Defamation law makes no distinction between the press and others, nor do the constitutional privilege cases. Should special rules apply only to the press, given its Fourth Estate function as a source of information and watchdog against abuse?
7. Does actual malice go far enough to protect whistleblowers? Should journalists be concerned that their good-faith behavior may later be determined to meet the scienter requirements of actual malice?
8. In an age when Internet postings and tweets can instantly go viral, has *Gertz's* distinction between public and private speech become antiquated? Can new media thrust you into the vortex of public debate?

CHAPTER 3

PRIVACY

Contrary to popular belief, the right of privacy is not enshrined in a long history of common law tradition. In fact, it is a modern tort first articulated in an 1890 law review article co-authored by Louis Brandeis, who would later serve on the Supreme Court. In the article, excerpted infra, the authors draw from existing common law traditions to construct a multifaceted tort. Today, that multifaceted tort is represented by four distinct prongs of the privacy action: (1) intrusion into physical solitude, (2) false light, (3) embarrassing disclosure of private facts, and (4) appropriation. While each of these prongs are independent of the other—with different elements and defenses—they are all designed to provide a remedy for the harm that Brandeis and his co-author recognized in their article: unwanted attention or humiliation. In this chapter, we will review the first three prongs of the privacy tort and the constitutional limitations on privacy actions under the First Amendment. Appropriation privacy is discussed in the next chapter.

"THE RIGHT TO PRIVACY"
BY SAMUEL WARREN AND LOUIS BRANDEIS

4 Harv. L. Rev. 193 (Dec. 15, 1890)

"It could be done only on principles of private justice, moral fitness, and public convenience, which, when applied to a new subject, make common law without a precedent; much more when received and approved by usage." — Willes, J., in Millar v. Taylor, 4 Burr. 2303, 2312

That the individual shall have full protection in person and in property is a principle as old as the common law; but it has been found necessary from time to time to define anew the exact nature and extent of such protection. Political, social, and economic changes entail the recognition of new rights, and the common law, in its eternal youth, grows to meet the new demands of society. Thus, in very early times, the law gave a remedy only for physical interference with life and property, for trespasses vi et armis. Then the "right to life" served only to protect the subject from battery in its various forms; liberty meant freedom from actual restraint; and the right to property secured to the individual his lands and his cattle. Later, there came a recognition of man's spiritual nature, of his feelings and his intellect. Gradually the scope of these legal rights broadened; and now the right to life has come to mean the right to enjoy life,—the right to be let alone; the right to liberty secures the exercise of extensive civil privileges; and the term "property" has grown to comprise every form of possession—intangible, as well as tangible.

Thus, with the recognition of the legal value of sensations, the protection against actual bodily injury was extended to prohibit mere attempts to do such injury; that is, the putting another in fear of such injury. From the action of battery grew that of assault. Much later there came a qualified protection of the individual against offensive noises and odors, against dust and smoke, and excessive vibration. The law of nuisance was developed. So regard for human emotions soon extended the scope of personal immunity beyond the body of the individual. His reputation, the standing among his fellow-men, was considered, and the law of slander and libel arose. Man's family relations became a part of the legal conception of his life, and the alienation of a wife's affections was held remediable. Occasionally the law halted, as in its refusal to recognize the intrusion by seduction upon the honor of the family. But even here the demands of society were met. A mean fiction, the action per quod servitium amisit, was resorted to, and by allowing damages for injury to the parents' feelings, an adequate remedy was ordinarily afforded. Similar to the expansion of the right to life was the growth of the legal conception of property. From corporeal property arose the incorporeal rights issuing out of it; and then there opened the wide realm of intangible property, in the products and processes of the mind, as works of literature and art, goodwill, trade secrets, and trademarks.

This development of the law was inevitable. The intense intellectual and emotional life, and the heightening of sensations which came with the advance of civilization, made it clear to men that only a part of the pain, pleasure, and profit of life lay in physical things. Thoughts, emotions, and sensations demanded legal recognition, and the beautiful capacity for growth which characterizes the common law enabled the judges to afford the requisite protection, without the interposition of the legislature.

Recent inventions and business methods call attention to the next step which must be taken for the protection of the person, and for securing to the individual what Judge Cooley calls the right "to be let alone" Instantaneous photographs and newspaper enterprise have invaded the sacred precincts of private and domestic life; and numerous mechanical devices threaten to make good the prediction that "what is whispered in the closet shall be proclaimed from the house-tops." For years there has been a feeling that the law must afford some remedy for the unauthorized circulation of portraits of private persons; and the evil of invasion of privacy by the newspapers, long keenly felt, has been but recently discussed by an able writer. The alleged facts of a somewhat notorious case brought before an inferior tribunal in New York a few months ago, directly involved the consideration of the right of circulating portraits; and the question whether our law will recognize and protect the right to privacy in this and in other respects must soon come before our courts for consideration.

Of the desirability—indeed of the necessity—of some such protection, there can, it is believed, be no doubt. The press is overstepping in every direction the obvious bounds of propriety and of decency. Gossip is no longer the resource of the idle and of the vicious, but has become a trade, which is pursued with industry as well as effrontery. To satisfy a prurient taste the details of sexual relations are spread broadcast in the columns of the daily papers. To occupy the indolent, column upon column is filled with idle gossip, which can only be procured by intrusion upon the domestic circle. The intensity and complexity of life, attendant upon advancing civilization, have rendered necessary some retreat from the world, and man, under the refining influence of culture, has become more sensitive to publicity, so that solitude and privacy have become more essential to the individual; but modern enterprise and invention have, through invasions upon his privacy, subjected him to mental pain and distress, far greater than could be inflicted by mere bodily injury. Nor is the harm wrought by such invasions confined to the suffering of those who may be the subjects of journalistic or other enterprise. In this, as in other branches of commerce, the supply creates the demand. Each crop of unseemly gossip, thus harvested, becomes the seed of more, and, in direct proportion to its circulation, results in the lowering of social standards and of morality. Even gossip apparently harmless, when widely and persistently circulated, is potent for evil. It both belittles and perverts. It belittles by inverting the relative importance of things, thus dwarfing the thoughts and aspirations of a people. When personal gossip attains the dignity of print, and crowds the space available for matters of real interest to the community, what wonder that the ignorant and thoughtless mistake its relative importance. Easy of comprehension, appealing to that weak side of human nature which is never wholly cast down by the misfortunes and frailties of our neighbors, no one can be surprised that it usurps the place of interest in brains capable of other things. Triviality destroys at once robustness of thought and delicacy of feeling. No enthusiasm can flourish, no generous impulse can survive under its blighting influence.

It is our purpose to consider whether the existing law affords a principle which can properly be invoked to protect the privacy of the individual; and, if it does, what the nature and extent of such protection is.

Owing to the nature of the instruments by which privacy is invaded, the injury inflicted bears a superficial resemblance to the wrongs dealt with by the law of slander and of libel, while a legal remedy for such injury seems to involve the treatment of mere wounded feelings, as a substantive cause of action. The principle on which the law of defamation rests, covers, however, a radically different class of effects from those for which attention is now asked. It deals only with damage to reputation, with the injury done to the individual in his external relations to the community, by lowering him in the estimation of his fellows. The matter published of him, however widely circulated, and however unsuited to publicity, must, in order to be actionable, have a direct tendency to injure him in his intercourse with others, and even if in writing or in print, must subject him to the hatred, ridicule, or contempt of his fellowmen,—the effect of the publication upon his estimate of himself and upon his own feelings nor forming an essential element in the cause of action. In short, the wrongs and correlative rights recognized by the law of slander and libel are in their nature material rather than spiritual. That branch of the law simply extends the protection surrounding physical property to certain of the conditions necessary or helpful to worldly prosperity. On the other hand, our law recognizes no principle upon which compensation can be granted for mere injury to the feelings. However painful the mental effects upon another of an act, though purely wanton or even malicious, yet if the act itself is otherwise lawful, the suffering inflicted is dannum absque injuria. Injury of feelings may indeed be taken account of in ascertaining the amount of damages when attending what is recognized as a legal injury; but our system, unlike the Roman law, does not afford a remedy even for mental suffering which results from mere contumely and insult, but from an intentional and unwarranted violation of the "honor" of another.

It is not however necessary, in order to sustain the view that the common law recognizes and upholds a principle applicable to cases of invasion of privacy, to invoke the analogy, which is but superficial, to injuries sustained, either by an attack upon reputation or by what the civilians called a violation of honor; for the legal doctrines relating to infractions of what is ordinarily termed the common-law right to intellectual and artistic property are, it is believed, but instances and applications of a general right to privacy, which properly understood afford a remedy for the evils under consideration.

The common law secures to each individual the right of determining, ordinarily, to what extent his thoughts, sentiments, and emotions shall be communicated to others. Under our system of government, he can never be compelled to express them (except when upon the witness stand); and even if he has chosen to give them expression, he generally retains the power to fix the limits of the publicity which shall be given them. The existence of this right does not depend upon the particular method of expression adopted. It is immaterial whether it be by word or by signs, in painting, by sculpture, or in music. Neither does the existence of the right depend upon the nature or value of the thought or emotions, nor upon the excellence of the means of expression. The same protection is accorded to a casual letter or an entry in a diary and to the most valuable poem or essay, to a botch or daub and to a masterpiece. In every such case the individual is entitled to decide whether that which is his shall be given to the public. No other has the right to publish his productions in any form, without his consent. This right is wholly independent of the material on which, the thought, sentiment, or emotions is expressed. It may exist independently of any corporeal being, as in words spoken, a song sung, a drama acted. Or if expressed on any material, as in a poem in writing, the author may have parted with the paper, without forfeiting any proprietary right in the composition itself. The right is lost only when the author himself communicates his production to the public,—in other words, publishes it. It is entirely independent of the copyright laws, and their extension into the domain of art. The aim of those statutes is to secure to the author, composer, or artist the entire profits arising from publication; but the common-law protection enables him to control absolutely the act of publication, and in the exercise of his own discretion, to decide whether there shall be any publication at all. The statutory right is of no value, unless there is a publication; the common-law right is lost as soon as there is a publication.

What is the nature, the basis, of this right to prevent the publication of manuscripts or works of art? It is stated to be the enforcement of a right of property; and no difficulty arises in accepting this view, so long as we have only to deal with the reproduction of literary and artistic compositions. They certainly possess many of the attributes of ordinary property; they are transferable; they have a value; and publication or reproduction is a use by which that value is realized. But where the value of the production is found not in the right to take the profits arising from publication, but in the peace of mind or the relief afforded by the ability to prevent any publication at all, it is difficult to regard the right as one of property, in the common acceptation of that term. A man records in a letter to his son, or in his diary, that he did not dine with his wife on a certain day. No one into whose hands those papers fall could publish them to the world, even if possession of the documents had been obtained rightfully; and the prohibition would not be confined to the publication of a copy of the letter itself, or of the diary entry; the restraint extends also to a publication of the contents. What is the thing which is protected? Surely, not the intellectual act of recording the fact that the husband did not dine with his wife, but that fact itself. It is not the intellectual product, but the domestic occurrence. A man writes a dozen letters to different people. No person would be permitted to publish a list of the letters written. If the letters or the contents of the diary were protected as literary compositions, the scope of the protection afforded should be the same secured to a published writing under the copyright law. But the copyright law would not prevent an enumeration of the letters, or the publication of some of the facts contained therein. The copyright of a series of paintings or etchings would prevent a reproduction of the paintings as pictures; but it would not prevent a publication of list or even a description of them. Yet in the famous case of Prince Albert v. Strange, the court held that the common-law rule prohibited not merely the reproduction of the etchings which the plaintiff and Queen Victoria had made for their own pleasure, but also "the publishing (at least by printing or writing), though not by copy or resemblance, a description of them, whether more or less limited or summary, whether in the form of a catalogue or otherwise." Likewise, an unpublished collection of news possessing no element of a literary nature is protected from privacy. That this protection cannot rest upon the right to literary or artistic property in any exact sense, appears the more clearly when the subject-matter for which protection is invoked is not even in the form of intellectual property, but has the attributes of ordinary tangible property. Suppose a man has a collection of gems or curiosities which he keeps private : it would hardly be contended that any person could publish a catalogue of them, and yet the articles enumerated are certainly not intellectual property in the legal sense, any more than a collection of stoves or of chairs.

. . .

These considerations lead to the conclusion that the protection afforded to thoughts, sentiments, and emotions, expressed through the medium of writing or of the arts, so far as it consists in preventing publication, is merely an instance of the enforcement of the more general right of the individual to be let alone. It is like the right not be assaulted or beaten, the right not be imprisoned, the right not to be maliciously prosecuted, the right not to be defamed. In each of these rights, as indeed in all other rights recognized by the law, there inheres the quality of being owned or possessed—and (as that is the distinguishing attribute of property) there may some propriety in speaking of those rights as property. But, obviously, they bear little resemblance to what is ordinarily comprehended under that term. The principle which protects personal writings and all other personal productions, not against theft and physical appropriation, but against publication in any form, is in reality not the principle of private property, but that of an inviolate personality.

If we are correct in this conclusion, the existing law affords a principle from which may be invoked to protect the privacy of the individual from invasion either by the too enterprising press, the photographer, or the possessor of any other modern device for rewording or reproducing scenes or sounds. For the protection afforded is not confined by the authorities to those cases where any particular medium or form of expression has been adopted, not to products of the intellect. The same protection is afforded to emotions and sensations expressed in a musical composition or other work of art as to a literary composition; and words spoken, a pantomime acted, a sonata performed, is no less entitled to protection than if each had been reduced to writing. The circumstance that a thought or emotion has been recorded in a permanent form renders its identification easier, and hence may be important from the point of view of evidence, but it has no significance as a matter of substantive right. If, then, the decisions indicate a general right to privacy for thoughts, emotions, and sensations, these should receive the same protection, whether expressed in writing, or in conduct, in conversation, in attitudes, or in facial expression.

It may be urged that a distinction should be taken between the deliberate expression of thoughts and emotions in literary or artistic compositions and the casual and often involuntary expression given to them in the ordinary conduct of life. In other words, it may be contended that the protection afforded is granted to the conscious products of labor, perhaps as an encouragement to effort. This contention, however plausible, has, in fact, little to recommend it. If the amount of labor involved be adopted as the test, we might well find that the effort to conduct one's self properly in business and in domestic relations had been far greater than that involved in painting a picture or writing a book; one would find that it was far easier to express lofty sentiments in a diary than in the conduct of a noble life. If the test of deliberateness of the act be adopted, much casual correspondence which is now accorded full protection would be excluded from the beneficent operation of existing rules. After the decisions denying the distinction attempted to be made between those literary productions which it was intended to publish and those which it was not, all considerations of the amount of labor involved, the degree of deliberation, the value of the product, and the intention of publishing must be abandoned, and no basis is discerned upon which the right to restrain publication and reproduction of such so-called literary and artistic works can be rested, except the right to privacy, as a part of the more general right to the immunity of the person,—the right to one's personality.

It should be stated that, in some instances where protection has been afforded against wrongful publication, the jurisdiction has been asserted, not on the ground of property, or at least not wholly on that ground, but upon the ground of an alleged breach of an implied contract or of a trust or confidence.

. . .

This process of implying a term in a contract, or of implying a trust (particularly where a contract is written, and where these is no established usage or custom), is nothing more nor less than a judicial declaration that public morality, private justice, and general convenience demand the recognition of such a rule, and that the publication under similar circumstances would be considered an intolerable abuse. So long as these circumstances happen to present a contract upon which such a term can be engrafted by the judicial mind, or to supply relations upon which a trust or confidence can be erected, there may be no objection to working out the desired protection though the doctrines of contract or of trust. But the court can hardly stop there. The narrower doctrine may have satisfied the demands of society at a time when the abuse to be guarded against could rarely have arisen without violating a contract or a special confidence; but now that modern devices afford abundant opportunities for the perpetration of such wrongs without any participation by the injured party, the protection granted by the law must be placed upon a broader foundation. While, for instance, the state of the photographic art was such that one's picture could seldom be taken without his consciously "sitting" for the purpose, the law of contract or of trust might afford the prudent man sufficient safeguards against the improper circulation of his portrait; but since the latest advances in photographic art have rendered it possible to take pictures surreptitiously, the doctrines of contract and of trust are inadequate to support the required protection, and the law of tort must be resorted to. The right of property in its widest sense, including all possession, including all rights and privileges, and hence embracing the right to an inviolate personality, affords alone that broad basis upon which the protection which the individual demands can be rested.

Thus, the courts, in searching for some principle upon which the publication of private letters could be enjoined, naturally came upon the ideas of a breach of confidence, and of an implied contract; but it required little consideration to discern that this doctrine could not afford all the protection required, since it would not support the court in granting a remedy against a stranger; and so the theory of property in the contents of letters was adopted. Indeed, it is difficult to conceive on what theory of the law the casual recipient of a letter, who proceeds to publish it, is guilty of a breach of contract, express or implied, or of any breach of trust, in the ordinary acceptation of that term. Suppose a letter has been addressed to him without his solicitation. He opens it, and reads. Surely, he has not made any contract; he has not accepted any trust. He cannot, by opening and reading the letter, have come under any obligation save what the law declares; and, however expressed, that obligation is simply to observe the legal right of the sender, whatever it may be, and whether it be called his right or property in the contents of the letter, or his right to privacy.

A similar groping for the principle upon which a wrongful publication can be enjoined is found in the law of trade secrets. There, injunctions have generally been granted on the theory of a breach of contract, or of an abuse of confidence. It would, of course, rarely happen that any one would be in possession of a secret unless confidence had been reposed in him. But can it be supposed that the court would hesitate to grant relief against one who had obtained his knowledge by an ordinary trespass,—for instance, by wrongfully looking into a book in which the secret was recorded, or by eavesdropping? Indeed, in Yovatt v. Winyard, I J.&W. 394 (1820), where an injunction was granted against making any use or of communicating certain recipes for veterinary medicine, it appeared that the defendant while in the plaintiff's employ, had surreptitiously got access to his book of recipes, and copied them. Lord Eldon "granted the injunction, upon the ground of there having been a breach of trust and confidence;" but it would seem difficult to draw any sound legal distinction between such a case and one where a mere stranger wrongfully obtained access to the book.

We must therefore conclude that the rights, so protected, whatever their exact nature, are not rights arising from contract or from special trust, but are rights as against the world; and, as above stated, the principle which has been applied to protect these rights is in reality not the principle of private property, unless that word be used in an extended and unusual sense. The principle which protects personal writings and any other productions of the intellect of or the emotions, is the right to privacy, and the law has no new principle to formulate when it extends this protection to the personal appearance, sayings, acts, and to personal relation, domestic or otherwise.

If the invasion of privacy constitutes a legal injuria, the elements for demanding redress exist, since already the value of mental suffering, caused by an act wrongful in itself, is recognized as a basis for compensation.

The right of one who has remained a private individual, to prevent his public portraiture, presents the simplest case for such extension; the right to protect one's self from pen portraiture, from a discussion by the press of one's private affairs, would be a more important and far-reaching one. If casual and unimportant statements in a letter, if handiwork, however inartistic and valueless, if possessions of all sorts are protected not only against reproduction, but also against description and enumeration, how much more should the acts and sayings of a man in his social and domestic relations be guarded from ruthless publicity. If you may not reproduce a woman's face photographically without her consent, how much less should be tolerated the reproduction of her face, her form, and her actions, by graphic descriptions colored to suit a gross and depraved imagination.

The right to privacy, limited as such right must necessarily be, has already found expression in the law of France.

It remains to consider what are the limitations of this right to privacy, and what remedies may be granted for the enforcement of the right. To determine in advance of experience the exact line at which the dignity and convenience of the individual must yield to the demands of the public welfare or of private justice would be a difficult task; but the more general rules are furnished by the legal analogies already developed in the law of slander and libel, and in the law of literary and artistic property.

1. The right to privacy does not prohibit any publication of matter which is of public or general interest. In determining the scope of this rule, aid would be afforded by the analogy, in the law of libel and slander, of cases which deal with the qualified privilege of comment and criticism on

matters of public and general interest. There are of course difficulties in applying such a rule; but they are inherent in the subject-matter, and are certainly no greater than those which exist in many other branches of the law,—for instance, in that large class of cases in which the reasonableness or unreasonableness of an act is made the test of liability. The design of the law must be to protect those persons with whose affairs the community has no legitimate concern, from being dragged into an undesirable and undesired publicity and to protect all persons, whatsoever; their position or station, from having matters which they may properly prefer to keep private, made public against their will. It is the unwarranted invasion of individual privacy which is reprehended, and to be, so far as possible, prevented. The distinction, however, noted in the above statement is obvious and fundamental. There are persons who may reasonably claim as a right, protection from the notoriety entailed by being made the victims of journalistic enterprise. There are others who, in varying degrees, have renounced the right to live their lives screened from public observation. Matters which men of the first class may justly contend, concern themselves alone, may in those of the second be the subject of legitimate interest to their fellow-citizens. Peculiarities of manner and person, which in the ordinary individual should be free from comment, may acquire a public importance, if found in a candidate for public office. Some further discrimination is necessary, therefore, than to class facts or deeds as public or private according to a standard to be applied to the fact or deed per se. To publish of a modest and retiring individual that he suffers from an impediment in his speech or that he cannot spell correctly, is an unwarranted, if not an unexampled, infringement of his rights, while to state and comment on the same characteristics found in a would-be congressman could not be regarded as beyond the pale of propriety.

The general object in view is to protect the privacy of private life, and to whatever degree and in whatever connection a man's life has ceased to be private, before the publication under consideration has been made, to that extent the protection is likely to be withdrawn. Since, then, the propriety of publishing the very same facts may depend wholly upon the person concerning whom they are published, no fixed formula can be used to prohibit obnoxious publications. Any rule of liability adopted must have in it an elasticity which shall take account of the varying circumstances of each case,—a necessity which unfortunately renders such a doctrine not only more difficult of application, but also to a certain extent uncertain in its operation and easily rendered abortive. Besides, it is only the more flagrant breaches of decency and propriety that could in practice be reached, and it is not perhaps desirable even to attempt to repress everything which the nicest taste and keenest sense of the respect due to private life would condemn.

In general, then, the matters of which the publication should be repressed may be described as those which concern the private life, habits, acts, and relations of an individual, and have no legitimate connection with his fitness for a public office which he seeks or for which he is suggested, or for any public or quasi public position which he seeks or for which he is suggested, and have no legitimate relation to or bearing upon any act done by him in a public or quasi public capacity. The foregoing is not designed as a wholly accurate or exhaustive definition, since that which must ultimately in a vast number of cases become a question of individual judgment and opinion is incapable of such definition; but it is an attempt to indicate broadly the class of matters referred to. Some things all men alike are entitled to keep from popular curiosity, whether in public life or not, while others are only private because the persons concerned have not assumed a position which makes their doings legitimate matters of public investigation.

2. The right to privacy does not prohibit the communication of any matter, though in its nature private, when the publication is made under circumstances which would render it a privileged communication according to the law of slander and libel. Under this rule, the right to privacy is not invaded by any publication made in a court of justice, in legislative bodies, or the committees of those bodies; in municipal assemblies, or the committees of such assemblies, or practically by any communication in any other public body, municipal or parochial, or in any body quasi public, like the large voluntary associations formed for almost every purpose of benevolence, business, or other general interest; and (at least in many jurisdictions) reports of any such proceedings would in some measure be accorded a like privilege. Nor would the rule prohibit any publication made by one in the discharge of some public or private duty, whether legal or moral, or in conduct of one's own affairs, in matters where his own interest is concerned.

3. The law would probably not grant any redress for the invasion of privacy by oral publication in the absence of special damage. The same reasons exist for distinguishing between oral and written publications of private matters, as is afforded in the law of defamation by the restricted liability for slander as compared with the liability for libel. The injury resulting from such oral communications would ordinarily be so trifling that the law might well, in the interest of free speech, disregard it altogether.

4. The right to privacy ceases upon the publication of the facts by the individual, or with his consent.

This is but another application of the rule which has become familiar in the law of literary and artistic property. The cases there decided establish also what should be deemed a publication,—the important principle in this connection being that a private communication of circulation for a restricted purpose is not a publication within the meaning of the law.

5. The truth of the matter published does not afford a defence. Obviously this branch of the law should have no concern with the truth or falsehood of the matters published. It is not for injury to the individual's character that redress or prevention is sought, but for injury to the right of privacy. For the former, the law of slander and libel provides perhaps a sufficient safeguard. The latter implies the right not merely to prevent inaccurate portrayal of private life, but to prevent its being depicted at all.

6. The absence of "malice" in the publisher does not afford a defence. Personal ill-will is not an ingredient of the offence, any more than in an ordinary case of trespass to person or to property. Such malice is never necessary to be shown in an action for libel or slander at common law, except in rebuttal of some defence, e.g., that the occasion rendered the communication privileged, or, under the statutes in this State and elsewhere, that the statement complained of was true. The invasion of the privacy that is to be protected is equally complete and equally injurious, whether the motives by which the speaker or writer was actuated are taken by themselves, culpable or not; just as the damage to character, and to some extent the tendency to provoke a breach of the peace, is equally the result of defamation without regard to motives leading to its publication. Viewed as a wrong to the individual, this rule is the same pervading the whole law of torts, by which one is held responsible for his intentional acts, even though they care committed with no sinister intent; and viewed as a wrong to society, it is the same principle adopted in a large category of statutory offences.

. . .

The common law has always recognized a man's house as his castle, impregnable, often, even to his own officers engaged in the execution of its command. Shall the courts thus close the front entrance to constituted authority, and open wide the back door to idle or prurient curiosity?

Intrusion into Physical Solitude

Intrusion into physical solitude is less about speech than the law of trespass. Typically, invasion into physical solitude is an issue in the newsgathering process. If, in the course, of investigating and reporting a news story, a journalist intrudes upon the private domain of a plaintiff who has a reasonable expectation of privacy, then the plaintiff can sue for the harm caused by the intrusion. There must be a reasonable expectation of privacy, so if defendant photographs a naked couple through an open bay window abutting a busy street, recovery under this tort would be less likely. As with trespassing, granting consent to enter the premises is a defense. Some consents, however, may be ruled invalid if the grantor was not competent to give it (such as minors), or if there was a misunderstanding or misrepresentation. In some cases, a court may rule that consent was implied, even if no express consent was given. A person whose house is on fire, for example, has granted implied consent for firefighters to enter the home to save an animal or douse flames.

Jacqueline Kennedy and her children, 1962.

Although intrusion into physical solitude historically required a physical domain, the concept has been extended to include what we would describe today as our personal space. As you review the following case, note that the judge does not rule that the photographer, Don Galella, does not have a First Amendment right to photograph Jacqueline Kennedy Onassis in public. The issue is about how Galella takes his photos.

GALELLA V. ONASSIS
487 F.2d 986 (2d Cir. 1973)

J. JOSEPH SMITH, Circuit Judge.
Donald Galella, a free-lance photographer, appeals from a summary

judgment dismissing his complaint against three Secret Service agents for false arrest, malicious prosecution and interference with trade (S.D.N.Y., Edward C. McLean, Judge), the dismissal after trial of his identical complaint against Jacqueline Onassis and the grant of injunctive relief to defendant Onassis on her counterclaim and to the intervenor, the United States, on its intervening complaint and a third judgment retaxing transcript costs to plaintiff (S.D.N.Y., Irving Ben Cooper, Judge), 353 F.Supp. 196 (1972). In addition to numerous alleged procedural errors, Galella raises the First Amendment as an absolute shield against liability to any sanctions. The judgments dismissing the complaints are affirmed, the grant of injunctive relief is affirmed as herein modified. Taxation of costs against the plaintiff is affirmed in part, reversed in part.

. . .

Galella is a free-lance photographer specializing in the making and sale of photographs of well-known persons. Defendant Onassis is the widow of the late President, John F. Kennedy, mother of the two Kennedy children, John and Caroline, and is the wife of Aristotle Onassis, widely known shipping figure and reputed multimillionaire. John Walsh, James Kalafatis and John Connelly are U.S. Secret Service agents assigned to the duty of protecting the Kennedy children under 18 U.S.C. § 3056, which provides for protection of the children of deceased presidents up to the age of 16.

Galella fancies himself as a "paparazzo" (literally a kind of annoying insect, perhaps roughly equivalent to the English "gadfly.") Paparazzi make themselves as visible to the public and obnoxious to their photographic subjects as possible to aid in the advertisement and wide sale of their works.

Some examples of Galella's conduct brought out at trial are illustrative. Galella took pictures of John Kennedy riding his bicycle in Central Park across the way from his home. He jumped out into the boy's path, causing the agents concern for John's safety. The agents' reaction and interrogation of Galella led to Galella's arrest and his action against the agents; Galella on other occasions interrupted Caroline at tennis, and invaded the children's private schools. At one time he came uncomfortably close in a power boat to Mrs. Onassis swimming. He often jumped and postured around while taking pictures of her party notably at a theater opening but also on numerous other occasions. He followed a practice of bribing apartment house, restaurant and nightclub doormen as well as romancing a family servant to keep him advised of the movements of the family.

After detention and arrest following complaint by the Secret Service agents protecting Mrs. Onassis' son and his acquittal in the state court, Galella filed suit in state court against the agents and Mrs. Onassis. Galella claimed that under orders from Mrs. Onassis, the three agents had falsely arrested and maliciously prosecuted him, and that this incident in addition to several others described in the complaint constituted an unlawful interference with his trade.

Mrs. Onassis answered denying any role in the arrest or any part in the claimed interference with his attempts to photograph her, and counterclaimed for damages and injunctive relief, charging that Galella had invaded her privacy, assaulted and battered her, intentionally inflicted emotional distress and engaged in a campaign of harassment.

The action was removed under 28 U.S.C. § 1442(a) to the United States District Court. On a motion for summary judgment, Galella's claim against the Secret Service agents was dismissed, the court finding that the agents were acting within the scope of their authority and thus were immune from prosecution. At the same time, the government intervened requesting injunctive relief from the activities of Galella which obstructed the Secret Service's ability to protect Mrs. Onassis' children. Galella's motion to remand the case to state court, just prior to trial, was denied.

Certain incidents of photographic coverage by Galella, subsequent to an agreement among the parties for Galella not to so engage, resulted in the issuance of a temporary restraining order to prevent further harassment of Mrs. Onassis and the children. Galella was enjoined from "harassing, alarming, startling, tormenting, touching the person of the defendant . . . or her children . . . and from blocking their movements in the public places and thoroughfares, invading their immediate zone of privacy by means of physical movements, gestures or with photographic equipment and from performing any act reasonably calculated to place the lives and safety of the defendant . . . and her children in jeopardy." Within two months, Galella was charged with violation of the temporary restraining order; a new order was signed which required that the photographer keep 100 yards from the Onassis apartment and 50 yards from the person of the defendant and her children. Surveillance was also prohibited.

Upon notice of consolidation of the preliminary injunction hearing and trial for permanent injunction, plaintiff moved for a jury trial-nine months after answer was served, and to remand to state court. The first motion was denied as untimely, the second on grounds of judicial economy. Just prior to trial Galella deposed Mrs. Onassis. Under protective order of this court, the defendant was allowed to testify at the office of the U.S. Attorney and outside the presence of Galella.

After a six-week trial the court dismissed Galella's claim and granted relief to both the defendant and the intervenor. Galella was enjoined from (1) keeping the defendant and her children under surveillance or following any of them; (2) approaching within 100 yards of the home of defendant or her children, or within 100 yards of either child's school or within 75 yards of either child or 50 yards of defendant; (3) using the name, portrait or picture of defendant or her children for advertising; (4) attempting to communicate with defendant or her children except through her attorney.

We conclude that grant of summary judgment and dismissal of Galella's claim against the Secret Service agents was proper. Federal agents when charged with duties which require the exercise of discretion are immune from liability for actions within the scope of their authority. Ordinarily enforcement agents charged with the duty of arrest are not so immune. Bivens v. Six Unknown Named Agents of Fed. Bur. of Narc., 456 F.2d 1339 (2d Cir. 1972). The protective duties assigned the agents under this statute, however, require the instant exercise of judgment which should be protected. The agents saw Galella jump into the path of John Kennedy who was forced to swerve his bike dangerously as he left Central Park and was about to enter Fifth Avenue, whereupon the agents gave chase to the photographer. Galella indicated that he was a press photographer listed with the New York City Police; he and the agents went to the police station to check on the story, where one of the agents made the complaint on which the state court charges were based. Certainly it was reasonable that the agents "check out" an individual who has endangered their charge, and seek prosecution for apparent violation of state law which interferes with them in the discharge of their duties.

If an officer is acting within his role as a government officer his conduct is at least within the outer perimeter of his authority. *Bivens, supra,* 456 F.2d at 1345. The Secret Service agents were charged under 18 U.S.C. § 3056 with "guarding against and preventing any activity by any individual which could create a risk to the safety and well being of the . . . children or result in their physical injury." It was undisputed that the agents were on duty at the time, and there was evidence that they believed John Kennedy to be endangered by Galella's actions. Unquestionably the agents were acting within the scope of their authority.

To be sure, even where acting within their authority, not all federal agents are immune from liability. Immunity is accorded officials whose decisions involve an element of discretion so that the decisions may be made without fear or threat of vexatious or fictitious suits and alleged personal liability. Ove Gustavsson Contracting Co. v. Floete, 299 F.2d 655, 659 (2d Cir. 1962), cert. denied, 374 U.S. 827 (1963). The issue in each case is whether the public interest in a particular official's unfettered judgments outweighs the private rights that may be violated. *See Bivens, supra,* 456 F.2d at 1346. The protective duties of the agents on assignments similar to this warrant this protection. See Scherer v. Brennan, 379 F.2d 609 (7th Cir.), cert. denied, 389 U.S. 1021 (1967).

Discrediting all of Galella's testimony the court found the photographer guilty of harassment, intentional infliction of emotional distress, assault and battery, commercial exploitation of defendant's personality, and invasion of privacy. Fully crediting defendant's testimony, the court found no liability on Galella's claim. Evidence offered by the defense showed that Galella had on occasion intentionally physically touched Mrs. Onassis and her daughter, caused fear of physical contact in his frenzied attempts to get their pictures, followed defendant and her children too closely in an automobile, endangered the safety of the children while they were swimming, water skiing and horseback riding. Galella cannot successfully challenge the court's finding of tortious conduct.

Finding that Galella had "insinuated himself into the very fabric of Mrs. Onassis' life . . ." the court framed its relief in part on the need to prevent further invasion of the defendant's privacy. Whether or not this accords with present New York law, there is no doubt that it is sustainable under New York's proscription of harassment.

Although the New York courts have not yet recognized a common law right of privacy, if we were required to reach the question, we would be inclined to agree with the court below that when again faced with the issue the Court of Appeals may well modify or distinguish its 1902 holding in Roberson v. Rochester Folding-Box Co., 64 N.E. 442 (N.Y. 1902), that "The so-called right of privacy has not as yet found an abiding place in our jurisprudence." There is substantive support today for the proposition that privacy is a "basic right" entitled to legal protection, Time v. Hill, 385 U.S. 374, 415 (1967) (Fortas, J., dissenting), nor can the "power of a State to control and remedy such intrusion [even] for news gathering purposes . . . be denied." *Id.* at 404, 87 S.Ct. at 550 (Harlan, J., concurring and dissenting). Privacy essential to individual dignity and personal liberty underlies the fundamental rights guaranteed in the Bill of Rights... There is an emerging recognition of privacy as a distinct, constitutionally protected right. Roe v. Ingraham, 480 F.2d 102 (2d Cir., 1973), (Friendly, J.) While the Constitution provides protection for specific manifestations of privacy ". . . the protection of a person's general right to privacy-his right to be let alone by other people is like the protection of his property and his very life left largely to the law of the individual states. . . ." *Katz, supra,* 389 U.S. at 350-351, citing Warren & Brandeis, Right to Privacy, 4 Harv. L.Rev. 193 (1890). The vast majority of states have now recognized and protect a right to privacy. Restatement of Torts 2d § 652(a), comment *a* (Tent. Draft No. 13, 1967). Statutory protection has been afforded the right in New York through imposition of criminal sanctions for invasion of privacy through the use of mechanical devices for wiretap and eavesdropping and for tampering with certain private communications. New York Penal Code §§ 250.00-250.35 (McKinney, 1967). Although not recognizing a right to privacy as such except as defined by statute, the New York courts have softened this rule in many cases by recognizing and liberally applying freedom from emotional distress as a protectable interest. . . .

Of course legitimate countervailing social needs may warrant some intrusion despite an individual's reasonable expectation of privacy and freedom from harassment. However the interference allowed may be no greater than that necessary to protect the overriding public interest. Mrs. Onassis was properly found to be a public figure and thus subject to news coverage. *See* Sidis v. F. R. Publishing Corp., 113 F.2d 806 (2d Cir.), cert. denied, 311 U.S. 711 (1940). Nonetheless, Galella's action went far beyond the reasonable bounds of news gathering. When weighed against the *de minimis* public importance of the daily activities of the defendant, Galella's constant surveillance, his obtrusive and intruding presence, was unwarranted and unreasonable. If there were any doubt in our minds, Galella's inexcusable conduct toward defendant's minor children would resolve it.

Galella does not seriously dispute the court's finding of tortious conduct. Rather, he sets up the First Amendment as a wall of immunity protecting newsmen from any liability for their conduct while gathering news. There is no such scope to the First Amendment right. Crimes and torts committed in news gathering are not protected... There is no threat to a free press in requiring its agents to act within the law.

. . .

Injunctive relief is appropriate. Galella has stated his intention to continue his coverage of defendant so long as she is newsworthy, and his continued harassment even while the temporary restraining orders were in effect indicate that no voluntary change in his technique can be expected. New York courts have found similar conduct sufficient to support a claim for injunctive relief. Flamm v. Van Nierop, 291 N.Y.S.2d 189 (1968).

The injunction, however, is broader than is required to protect the defendant. Relief must be tailored to protect Mrs. Onassis from the "paparazzo" attack which distinguishes Galella's behavior from that of other photographers; it should not unnecessarily infringe on reasonable efforts to "cover" defendant. Therefore, we modify the court's order to prohibit only (1) any approach within twenty-five (25) feet of defendant or any touching of the person of the defendant Jacqueline Onassis; (2) any blocking of her movement in public places and thoroughfares; (3) any act foreseeably or reasonably calculated to place the life and safety of defendant in jeopardy; and (4) any conduct which would reasonably be foreseen to harass, alarm or frighten the defendant.

Any further restriction on Galella's taking and selling pictures of defendant for news coverage is, however, improper and unwarranted by the evidence. . . .

Likewise, we affirm the grant of injunctive relief to the government modified to prohibit any action interfering with Secret Service agents' protective duties. Galella thus may be enjoined from (a) entering the children's schools or play areas; (b) engaging in action calculated or reasonably foreseen to place the children's safety or well being in jeopardy, or which would threaten or create physical injury; (c) taking any action which could reasonably be foreseen to harass, alarm, or frighten the children; and (d) from approaching within thirty (30) feet of the children.

. . .

As modified, the relief granted fully allows Galella the opportunity to photograph and report on Mrs. Onassis' public activities. Any prior restraint on news gathering is miniscule and fully supported by the findings.

Affirmed in part, reversed in part and remanded for modification of the judgment in accordance with this opinion. Costs on appeal to be taxed in favor of appellees.

TIMBERS, Circuit Judge (concurring in part and dissenting in part).

. . .

In light of Galella's repeated misbehavior, it is clear that only a strong restraint-an injunction which will clearly protect Mrs. Onassis' rights and leave no room for quibbling about compliance and no room for evasion or circumvention-is appropriate in this case.

. . .

As for the actual distance to be proscribed, we must bear in mind that plaintiff never moved to modify the distances heretofore imposed by our restraining order, even after the Court had clearly and explicitly invited him to do so if he could prove it was too harsh. (Minutes, Proceedings January 19, 1972, p. 31)." 353 F.Supp. at 237.

But here is what the majority's modification of the critical distance provisions of the injunction has done:

DISTANCES GALELLA IS REQUIRED TO MAINTAIN	AS PROVIDED IN DISTRICT COUT INJUNCTION	AS MODIFIED BY COURT OF APPEALS MAJORITY
From Home of Mrs. Onassis & her Children	100 yards	No restriction
From Children's Schools	100 yards	Restrict only from entering schools or play areas
From Mrs. Onassis Personally	50 yards	25 feet and not to touch her
From Children Person-ally	75 yards	30 feet

False Light

False light, in most respects, is like "defamation-lite." To recover in a false-light action, a plaintiff must show that defendant uttered a false statement of and concerning the plaintiff that caused injury. The main difference is that the injury is not reputational; as with all privacy claims, the injury is unwanted attention or humiliation. False light also has the same defenses and privileges of defamation, including truth and courtroom immunity. In Time Inc. v Hill infra, the Supreme Court extended *New York Times'* actual malice requirements to false light claims involving public figures. In Cantrell v. Forest City Publishing Co., the Court applied the distinctions between public and private figures from *Gertz*, but left unanswered the issue of whether a private figure must show actual malice to recover punitive damages for false light.

TIME, INC. V. HILL
385 U.S. 374 (1967)

Mr. Justice BRENNAN delivered the opinion of the Court.
The question in this case is whether appellant, publisher of Life Magazine, was denied constitutional protections of speech and press by the application by the New York courts of §§ 50-51 of the New York Civil Rights Law, McKinney's Consol. Laws, c. 6 to award appellee damages on allegations that Life falsely reported that a new play portrayed an experience suffered by appellee and his family.

The article appeared in Life in February 1955. It was entitled "True Crime Inspires Tense Play," with the subtitle, "The ordeal of a family trapped by convicts gives Broadway a new thriller, 'The Desperate Hours.'" The text of the article reads as follows:

"Three years ago Americans all over the country read about the desperate ordeal of the James Hill family, who were held prisoners in their home outside Philadelphia by three escaped convicts. Later they read about it in Joseph Hayes's novel, The Desperate Hours, inspired by the family's experience. Now they can see the story re-enacted in Hayes's Broadway play based on the book, and next year will see it in his movie, which has been filmed but is being held up until the play has a chance to pay off.

"The play, directed by Robert Montgomery and expertly acted, is a heart-stopping account of how a family rose to heroism in a crisis. LIFE photographed the play during its Philadelphia tryout, transported some of the actors to the actual house where the Hills were besieged. On the next page scenes from the play are re-enacted on the site of the crime."

The pictures on the ensuing two pages included an enactment of the son being "roughed up" by one of the convicts, entitled "brutish convict," a picture of the daughter biting the hand of a convict to make him drop a gun, entitled "daring daughter," and one of the father throwing his gun through the door after a "brave try" to save his family is foiled.

The James Hill referred to in the article is the appellee. He and his wife and five children involuntarily became the subjects of a front-page news story after being held hostage by three escaped convicts in their suburban, Whitemarsh, Pennsylvania, home for 19 hours on September 11-12, 1952. The family was released unharmed. In an interview with newsmen after the convicts departed, appellee stressed that the convicts had treated the family courteously, had not molested them, and had not been at all violent. The convicts were thereafter apprehended in a widely publicized encounter with the police which resulted in the killing of two of the convicts. Shortly thereafter the family moved to Connecticut. The appellee discouraged all efforts to keep them in the public spotlight through magazine articles or appearances on television.

. . .

In New York Times Co. v. Sullivan, 376 U.S. 254, we held that the Constitution delimits a State's power to award damages for libel in actions brought by public officials against critics of their official conduct. Factual error, content defamatory of official reputation, or both, are insufficient for an award of damages for false statements unless actual malice-knowledge that the statements are false or in reckless disregard of the truth-is alleged and proved. The Spahn opinion reveals that the defendant in that case relied on New York Times as the basis of an argument that application of the statute to the publication of a substantially fictitious biography would run afoul of the constitutional guarantees. The Court of Appeals held that New York Times had no application. The court, after distinguishing the cases on the ground that Spahn did not deal with public officials or official conduct, then says, "The free speech which is encouraged and essential to the operation of a healthy government is something quite different from an individual's attempt to enjoin the publication of a fictitious biography of him. No public interest is served by protecting the dissemination of the latter. We perceive no constitutional infirmities in this respect." 221 N.E.2d, at 546.

If this is meant to imply that proof of knowing or reckless falsity is not essential to a constitutional application of the statute in these cases, we disagree with the Court of Appeals. We hold that the constitutional protections for speech and press preclude the application of the New

York statute to redress false reports of matters of public interest in the absence of proof that the defendant published the report with knowledge of its falsity or in reckless disregard of the truth.

The guarantees for speech and press are not the preserve of political expression or comment upon public affairs, essential as those are to healthy government. One need only pick up any newspaper or magazine to comprehend the vast range of published matter which exposes persons to public view, both private citizens and public officials. Exposure of the self to others in varying degrees is a concomitant of life in a civilized community. The risk of this exposure is an essential incident of life in a society which places a primary value on freedom of speech and of press. . . .

CANTRELL V. FOREST CITY PUBLISHING. CO.

419 U.S. 245 (1974)

In December 1967, Margaret Cantrell's husband Melvin was killed along with 43 other people when the Silver Bridge across the Ohio River at Point Pleasant, W.Va., collapsed. The respondent [Joe] Eszterhas was assigned by the Plain Dealer to cover the story of the disaster. He wrote a "news feature" story focusing on the funeral of Melvin Cantrell and the impact of his death on the Cantrell family.

Five months later, after conferring with the Sunday Magazine editor of the Plain Dealer, Eszterhas and photographer Conway returned to the Point Pleasant area to write a follow-up feature. The two men went to the Cantrell residence, where Eszterhas talked with the children and Conway took 50 pictures. Mrs. Cantrell was not at home at any time during the 60 to 90 minutes that the men were at the Cantrell residence.

Eszterhas' story appeared as the lead feature in the August 4, 1968, edition of the Plain Dealer Sunday Magazine. The article stressed the family's abject poverty; the children's old, ill-fitting clothes and the deteriorating condition of their home were detailed in both the text and accompanying photographs. As he had done in his original, prize-winning article on the Silver Bridge disaster, Eszterhas used the Cantrell family to illustrate the impact of the bridge collapse on the lives of the people in the Point Pleasant area.

It is conceded that the story contained a number of inaccuracies and false statements. Most conspicuously, although Mrs. Cantrell was not present at any time during the reporter's visit to her home, Eszterhas wrote, 'Margaret Cantrell will talk neither about what happened nor about how they are doing. She wears the same mask of non-expression she wore at the funeral. She is a proud woman. Her world has changed. She says that after it happened, the people in town offered to help them out with money and they refused to take it.' Other significant misrepresentations were contained in details of Eszterhas' descriptions of the poverty in which the Cantrells were living and the dirty and dilapidated conditions of the Cantrell home.

The case went to the jury on a so-called 'false light' theory of invasion of privacy. In essence, the theory of the case was that by publishing the false feature story about the Cantrells and thereby making them the objects of pity and ridicule, the respondents damaged Mrs. Cantrell and her son William by causing them to suffer outrage, mental distress, shame, and humiliation.

. . .

The District Judge in the case before us, in contrast to the trial judge in Time, Inc. v. Hill, did instruct the jury that liability could be imposed only if it concluded that the false statements in the Sunday Magazine feature article on the Cantrells had been made with knowledge of their falsity or in reckless disregard of the truth. No objection was made by any of the parties to this knowing-or-reckless-falsehood instruction. Consequently, this case presents no occasion to consider whether a State may constitutionally apply a more relaxed standard of liability for a publisher or broadcaster of false statements injurious to a private individual under a false-light theory of invasion of privacy, or whether the constitutional standard announced in Time, Inc. v. Hill applies to all false-light cases. Cf. Gertz v. Robert Welch, Inc., 418 U.S. 323. Rather, the sole question that we need decide is whether the Court of Appeals erred in setting aside the jury's verdict.

III.

At the close of the petitioners' case-in-chief, the District Judge struck the demand for punitive damages. He found that Mrs. Cantrell had failed to present any evidence to support the charges that the invasion of privacy "was done maliciously within the legal definition of that term." The Court of Appeals interpreted this finding to be a determination by the District Judge that there was no evidence of knowing falsity or reckless disregard of the truth introduced at the trial. Having made such a determination, the Court of Appeals held that the District Judge should have granted the motion for a directed verdict for respondents as to all the Cantrells' claims. 484 F.2d, at 155.

The Court of Appeals appears to have assumed that the District Judge's finding of no malice "within the legal definition of that term" was a finding based on the definition of "actual malice" established by this Court in New York Times Co. v. Sullivan, 376 U.S., at 280: "with knowledge that (a defamatory statement) was false or with reckless disregard of whether it was false or not." As so defined, of course, 'actual malice' is a term of art, created to provide a convenient shorthand expression for the standard of liability that must be established before a State may constitutionally permit public officials to recover for libel in actions brought against publishers. As such, it is quite different from the common-law standard of 'malice' generally required under state tort law to support an award of punitive damages. In a false-light case, common-law malice-frequently expressed in terms of either personal ill will toward the plaintiff or reckless or wanton disregard of the plaintiff's rights-would focus on the defendant's attitude toward the plaintiff's privacy, not toward the truth or falsity of the material published. See Time, Inc. v. Hill, 385 U.S., at 396 n. 12. See generally W. Prosser, Law of Torts 9-10 (4th ed.).

Although the verbal record of the District Court proceedings is not entirely unambiguous, the conclusion is inescapable that the District Judge was referring to the common-law standard of malice rather than to the New York Times "actual malice" standard when he dismissed the punitive damages claims. For at the same time that he dismissed the demands for punitive damages, the District Judge refused to grant the respondents' motion for directed verdicts as to Mrs. Cantrell's and William's claims for compensatory damages. And, as his instructions to the jury made clear, the District Judge was fully aware that the Time, Inc. v. Hill meaning of the New York Times "actual malice" standard had to be satisfied for the Cantrells to recover actual damages. Thus, the only way to harmonize these two virtually simultaneous rulings by the District Judge is to conclude, contrary to the decision of the Court of Appeals, that in dismissing the punitive damages claims he was not determining that Mrs. Cantrell had failed to introduce any evidence of knowing falsity or reckless disregard of the truth. This conclusion is further fortified by the District Judge's subsequent denial of the respondents' motion for judgment n.o.v. and alternative motion for a new trial.

Moreover, the District Judge was clearly correct in believing that the evidence introduced at trial was sufficient to support a jury finding that the respondents Joseph Eszterhas and Forest City Publishing Co. had published knowing or reckless falsehoods about the Cantrells. There was no dispute during the trial that Eszterhas, who did not testify, must have known that a number of the statements in the feature story were untrue. In particular, his article plainly implied that Mrs. Cantrell had been present during his visit to her home and that Eszterhas had observed her "wear(ing) the same mask of nonexpression she wore (at her husband's) funeral." These were "calculated falsehoods," and the jury was plainly justified in finding that Eszterhas had portrayed the Cantrells in a false light through knowing or reckless untruth.

Embarrassing Disclosure of Private Facts

Embarrassing disclosure of private facts is a privacy action that plaintiffs only rarely win. This prong of the privacy tort allows a plaintiff to recover damages for the harm caused by the public disclosure of something truthful, which often places the tort squarely in conflict with the First Amendment. To overcome First Amendment concerns, a plaintiff must prove the following elements: (1) public disclosure, (2) of a private fact, (3) which would be offensive and objectionable to the reasonable person, and (4) which is not of legitimate public concern.

Legitimate public concern is not always the same as newsworthy, and the passage of time may make some formerly public facts private, as the case of Melvin v. Reid suggests. Disclosure of objectionable facts in a public record that are obtained by the press through legal means are generally protected by the First Amendment. According to the Supreme Court in Cox Broadcasting v. Cohn, journalists are permitted under the First Amendment to publish the name, for example, of a rape victim taken from publicly available sources such as court transcripts or police reports. The fact that many in the press do not identify these victims is a matter of policy and ethics; in cases in which an accuser's story is cast in doubt, news organizations as respected as the New York Times and NBC News have exercised their First Amendment rights to identify the accuser.

MELVIN V. REID

297 P. 91 (4th Cir. 1931)

Appellant filed her complaint in the court below seeking judgment against defendants for money. The complaint contains four causes of action separately stated. The first is based upon the violation of what has become known as the "right of privacy." . . .

It is alleged that appellant's maiden name was Gabrielle Darley; that a number of years ago she was a prostitute and was tried for murder, the trial resulting in her acquittal; that during the year 1918, and after her acquittal, she abandoned her life of shame and became entirely rehabilitated; that during the year 1919 she married Bernard Melvin and commenced the duties of caring for their home, and thereafter at all times lived an exemplary, virtuous, honorable, and righteous life; that she assumed a place in respectable society, and made many friends who were not aware of the incidents of her earlier life; that during the month of July, 1925, the defendants, without her permission, knowledge, or consent, made, photographed, produced, and released a moving picture film entitled "The Red Kimono," and thereafter exhibited it in moving picture houses in California, Arizona, and throughout many other states; that this moving picture was based upon the true story of the past life of appellant, and that her maiden name, Gabrielle Darley, was used therein; that defendants featured and advertised that the plot of the film was the true story of the unsavory incidents in the life of appellant; that Gabrielle Darley was the true name of the principal character; and that Gabrielle Darley was appellant; that by the production and showing of the picture, friends of appellant learned for the first time of the unsavory incidents of her early life. This caused them to scorn and abandon her, and exposed her to obloquy, contempt, and ridicule, causing her grievous mental and physical suffering to her damage in the sum of $50,000. These allegations were set forth in the first cause of action. It will not be necessary to detail the other three causes of action which are based upon an invasion of a supposed property right.

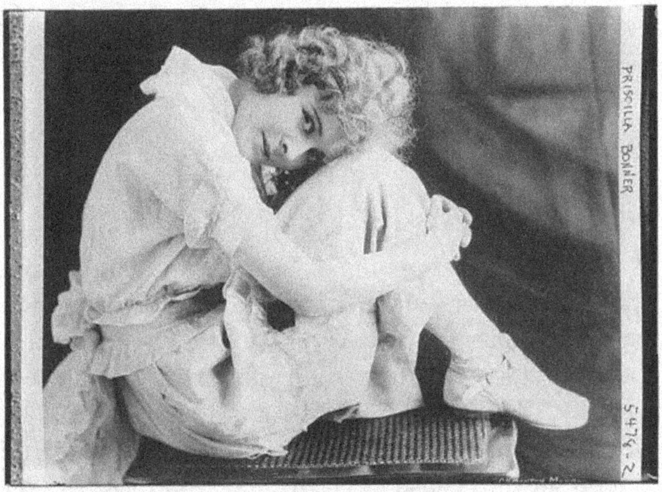

Priscilla Bonner played prostitute Gabrielle Darley, using Mrs. Melvin's real unmarried name.

The law of privacy is of recent origin. It was first discussed in an essay published in a law journal in 1860. It did not gain prominence or notice of the bench or bar until an article appeared in 4 Harvard Law Review, p. 193, written by the Honorable Louis D. Brandeis in collaboration with Samuel D. Warren. Since the publication of this article, a number of cases have arisen in various states involving the so-called doctrine of the right of privacy.

. . .

The question is a new one in California.

. . .

The right of privacy as recognized in a number of states has been defined as follows: "The right of privacy may be defined as the right to live one's life in seclusion, without being subjected to unwarranted and undesired publicity. In short, it is the right to be let alone. There are times, however, when one, whether willingly or not, becomes an actor in an occurrence of public or general interest. When this takes place, he emerges from his seclusion, and it is not an invasion of his right of privacy to publish his photograph with an account of such occurrence." Jones v. Herald Post Co., supra.

. . .

[T]the use of the incidents from the life of appellant in the moving picture is in itself not actionable. These incidents appeared in the records of her trial for murder, which is a public record, open to the perusal of all. The very fact that they were contained in a public record is sufficient to negative the idea that their publication was a violation of a right of privacy. When the incidents of a life are so public as to be spread upon a public record, they come within the knowledge and into the possession of the public and cease to be private. Had respondents, in the story of "The Red Kimono," stopped with the use of those incidents from the life of appellant which were spread upon the record of her trial, no right of action would have accrued. They went further, and in the formation of the plot used the true maiden name of appellant. If any right of action exists, it arises from the use of this true name in connection with the true incidents from her life together with their advertisements in which they stated that the story of the picture was taken from true incidents in the life of Gabrielle Darley, who was Gabrielle Darley Melvin.

In the absence of any provision of law, we would be loath to conclude that the right of privacy as the foundation for an action in tort, in the form known and recognized in other jurisdictions, exists in California. We find, however, that the fundamental law of our state contains provisions which, we believe, permit us to recognize the right to pursue and obtain safety and happiness without improper infringements thereon by others. Section 1 of article 1 of the Constitution of California provides as follows: "All men are by nature free and independent, and have certain inalienable rights, among which are those of enjoying and defending life and liberty; acquiring, possessing, and protecting property; and pursuing and obtaining safety and happiness."

The right to pursue and obtain happiness is guaranteed to all by the fundamental law of our state. This right by its very nature includes the right to live free from the unwarranted attack of others upon one's liberty, property, and reputation. Any person living a life of rectitude has that right to happiness which includes a freedom from unnecessary attacks on his character, social standing, or reputation.

The use of appellant's true name in connection with the incidents of her former life in the plot and advertisements was unnecessary and indelicate, and a willful and wanton disregard of that charity which should actuate us in our social intercourse, and which should keep us from unnecessarily holding another up to the scorn and contempt of upright members of society.

Upon demurrer, the allegations of the complaint must be taken as true. We must therefore conclude that eight years before the production of "The Red Kimono" appellant had abandoned her life of shame, had rehabilitated herself, and had taken her place as a respected and honored member of society. This change having occurred in her life, she should have been permitted to continue its course without having her reputation and social standing destroyed by the publication of the story of her former depravity with no other excuse than the expectation of private gain by the publishers. . . .

We believe that the publication by respondents of the unsavory incidents in the past life of appellant after she had reformed, coupled with her true name, was not justified by any standard of morals or ethics known to us, and was a direct invasion of her inalienable right guaranteed to her by our Constitution, to pursue and obtain happiness. Whether we call this a right of privacy or give it any other name is immaterial, because it is a right guaranteed by our Constitution that must not be ruthlessly and needlessly invaded by others. We are of the opinion that the first cause of action of appellant's complaint states facts sufficient to constitute a cause of action against respondents . . . .

COX BROADCASTING CORP. V. COHN

420 U.S. 469 (1975)

Mr. Justice WHITE delivered the opinion of the Court.

The issue before us in this case is whether, consistently with the First and Fourteenth Amendments, a State may extend a cause of action for damages for invasion of privacy caused by the publication of the name of a deceased rape victim which was publicly revealed in connection with the prosecution of the crime.

I.

In August 1971, appellee's 17-year-old daughter was the victim of a rape and did not survive the incident. Six youths were soon indicted for murder and rape. Although there was substantial press coverage of the crime and of subsequent developments, the identity of the victim was not disclosed pending trial, perhaps because of Ga. Code Ann. § 26-9901 (1972), which makes it a misdemeanor to publish or broadcast the name or identity of a rape victim. In April 1972, some eight months later, the six defendants appeared in court. Five pleaded guilty to rape or attempted rape, the charge of murder having been dropped. The guilty pleas were accepted by the court, and the trial of the defendant pleading not guilty was set for a later date.

In the course of the proceedings that day, appellant Wasell, a reporter covering the incident for his employer, learned the name of the victim from an examination of the indictments which were made available for his inspection in the courtroom. That the name of the victim appears in the indictments and that the indictments were public records available for inspection are not disputed. Later that day, Wassell broadcast over the facilities of station WSB-TV, a television station owned by appellant Cox Broadcasting Corp., a news report concerning the court proceedings. The report named the victim of the crime and was repeated the following day.

. . .

In May 1972, appellee brought an action for money damages against appellants, relying on § 26-9901 and claiming that his right to privacy had been invaded by the television broadcasts giving the name of his deceased daughter. Appellants admitted the broadcasts but claimed that they were privileged under both state law and the First and Fourteenth Amendments. The trial court, rejecting appellants' constitutional claims and holding that the Georgia statute gave a civil remedy to those injured by its violation, granted summary judgment to appellee as to liability, with the determination of damages to await trial by jury.

On appeal, the Georgia Supreme Court, in its initial opinion, held that the trial court had erred in construing § 26-9901 to extend a civil cause of action for invasion of privacy and thus found it unnecessary to consider the constitutionality of the statute. 200 S.E.2d 127 (Ga. 1973). The court went on to rule, however, that the complaint stated a cause of action "for the invasion of the appellee's right of privacy, or for the tort of public disclosure"—a "common law tort exist[ing] in this jurisdiction without the help of the statute that the trial judge in this case relied on." Id., at 130. Although the privacy invaded was not that of the deceased victim, the father was held to have stated a claim for invasion of his own privacy by reason of the publication of his daughter's name. The court explained, however, that liability did not follow as a matter of law and that summary judgment was improper; whether the public disclosure of the name actually invaded appellee's "zone of privacy," and if so, to what extent, were issues to be determined by the trier of fact. Also, "in formulating such an issue for determination by the fact-finder, it is reasonable to require the appellee to prove that the appellants invaded his privacy with willful or negligent disregard for the fact that reasonable men would find the invasion highly offensive." Id., at 131. The Georgia Supreme Court did agree with the trial court, however, that the First and Fourteenth Amendments did not, as a matter of law, require judgment for appellants. The court concurred with the statement in Briscoe v. Reader's Digest Assn., Inc., 483 P.2d 34, 42 (1971), that "the rights guaranteed by the First Amendment do not require total abrogation of the right to privacy. The goals sought by each may be achieved with a minimum of intrusion upon the other."

Upon motion for rehearing the Georgia court countered the argument that the victim's name was a matter of public interest and could be published with impunity by relying on § 26-9901 as an authoritative declaration of state policy that the name of a rape victim was not a matter of public concern. This time the court felt compelled to determine the constitutionality of the statute and sustained it as a "legitimate limitation on the right of freedom of expression contained in the First Amendment." The court could discern "no public interest or general concern about the identity of the victim of such a crime as will make the right to disclose the identity of the victim rise to the level of First Amendment protection." 200 S.E.2d, at 134.

We postponed decision as to our jurisdiction over this appeal to the hearing on the merits. 415 U.S. 912 (1974). We conclude that the Court has jurisdiction, and reverse the judgment of the Georgia Supreme Court.

II.

. . .

III.

Georgia stoutly defends both § 26-9901 and the State's common-law privacy action challenged here. Its claims are not without force, for powerful arguments can be made, and have been made, that however it may be ultimately defined, there is a zone of privacy surrounding every individual, a zone within which the State may protect him from intrusion by the press, with all its attendant publicity. Indeed, the central thesis of the root article by Warren and Brandeis, The Right to Privacy, 4 Harv. L. Rev. 193, 196 (1890), was that the press was overstepping its prerogatives by publishing essentially private information and that there should be a remedy for the alleged abuses.

. . .

More compellingly, the century has experienced a strong tide running in favor of the so-called right of privacy. In 1967, we noted that "[i]t has been said that a 'right of privacy' has been recognized at common law in 30 States plus the District of Columbia and by statute in four States." Time, Inc. v. Hill, 385 U.S. 374, 383 n. 7. We there cited the 1964 edition of Prosser's Law of Torts. The 1971 edition of that same source states that "[i]n one form or another, the right of privacy is by this time recognized and accepted in all but a very few jurisdictions." W. Prosser, Law of Torts 804 (4th ed.) (footnote omitted). Nor is it irrelevant here that the right of privacy is no recent arrival in the jurisprudence of Georgia, which has embraced the right in some form since 1905 when the Georgia Supreme Court decided the leading case of Pavesich v. New England Life Ins. Co., 50 S.E. 68 (Ga.).

These are impressive credentials for a right of privacy, but we should recognize that we do not have at issue here an action for the invasion of privacy involving the appropriation of one's name or photograph, a physical or other tangible intrusion into a private area, or a publication of otherwise private information that is also false although perhaps not defamatory. The version of the privacy tort now before us-termed in Georgia "the tort of public disclosure," 200 S.E.2d, at 130—is that in which the plaintiff claims the right to be free from unwanted publicity about his private affairs, which, although wholly true, would be offensive to a person of ordinary sensibilities. Because the gravamen of the claimed injury is the publication of information, whether true or not, the dissemination of which is embarrassing or otherwise painful to an individual, it is here that claims of privacy most directly confront the constitutional freedoms of speech and press. The face-off is apparent, and the appellants urge upon us the broad holding that the press may not be made criminally or civilly liable for publishing information that is neither false nor misleading but absolutely accurate, however damaging it may be to reputation or individual sensibilities.

. . .

In this sphere of collision between claims of privacy and those of the free press, the interests on both sides are plainly rooted in the traditions and significant concerns of our society. Rather than address the broader question whether truthful publications may ever be subjected to civil or criminal liability consistently with the First and Fourteenth Amendments, or to put it another way, whether the State may ever define and protect an area of privacy free from unwanted publicity in the press, it is appropriate to focus on the narrower interface between press and privacy that this case presents, namely, whether the State may impose sanctions on the accurate publication of the name of a rape victim obtained from public records-more specifically, from judicial records which are maintained in connection with a public prosecution and which themselves are open to public inspection. We are convinced that the State may not do so.

In the first place, in a society in which each individual has but limited time and resources with which to observe at first hand the operations of his government, he relies necessarily upon the press to bring to him in convenient form the facts of those operations. Great responsibility is accordingly placed upon the news media to report fully and accurately the proceedings of government, and official records and documents open to the public are the basic data of governmental operations. Without the information provided by the press most of us and many of our representatives would be unable to vote intelligently or to register opinions on the administration of government generally. With respect to judicial proceedings in particular, the function of the press serves to guarantee the fairness of trials and to bring to bear the beneficial effects of public scrutiny upon the administration of justice. See Sheppard v. Maxwell, 384 U.S. 333, 350 (1966).

Appellee has claimed in this litigation that the efforts of the press have infringed his right to privacy by broadcasting to the world the fact that his daughter was a rape victim. The commission of crime, prosecutions resulting from it, and judicial proceedings arising from the prosecutions, however, are without question events of legitimate concern to the public and consequently fall within the responsibility of the press to report the operations of government.

The special protected nature of accurate reports of judicial proceedings has repeatedly been recognized. This Court, in an opinion written by Mr. Justice Douglas, has said:

> "A trial is a public event. What transpires in the court room is public property. If a transcript of the court proceedings had been published, we suppose none would claim that the judge could punish the publisher for contempt. And we can see no difference though the conduct of the attorneys, of the jury, or even of the judge himself, may have reflected on the court. Those who see and hear what transpired can report it with impunity. There is no special perquisite of the judiciary which enables it, as distinguished from other institutions of democratic government, to suppress, edit, or censor events which transpire in proceedings before it." Craig v. Harney, 331 U.S. 367, 374 (1947) (emphasis added).

. . .

The developing law surrounding the tort of invasion of privacy recognizes a privilege in the press to report the events of judicial proceedings. The Warren and Brandeis article, supra, noted that the proposed new right would be limited in the same manner as actions for libel and slander where such a publication was a privileged communication: "the right to privacy is not invaded by any publication made in a court of justice . . . and (at least in many jurisdictions) reports of any such proceedings would in some measure be accorded a like privilege."

The Restatement of Torts, § 867, embraced an action for privacy. Tentative Draft No. 13 of the Second Restatement of Torts, §§ 652A-652E, divides the privacy tort into four branches; and with respect to the wrong of giving unwanted publicity about private life, the commentary to § 652D states: "There is no liability when the defendant merely gives further publicity to information about the plaintiff which is already public. Thus there is no liability for giving publicity to facts about the plaintiff's life which are matters of public record . . . ." The same is true of the separate tort of physically or otherwise intruding upon the seclusion or private affairs of another. Section 652B, Comment c, provides that "there is no liability for the examination of a public record concerning the plaintiff, or of documents which the plaintiff is required to keep and make available for public inspection." According to this draft, ascertaining and publishing the contents of public records are simply not within the reach of these kinds of privacy actions.

. . .

Thus even the prevailing law of invasion of privacy generally recognizes that the interests in privacy fade when the information involved already appears on the public record. The conclusion is compelling when viewed in terms of the First and Fourteenth Amendments and in light of the public interest in a vigorous press. The Georgia cause of action for invasion of privacy through public disclosure of the name of a rape victim imposes sanctions on pure expression—the content of a publication-and not conduct or a combination of speech and nonspeech elements that might otherwise be open to regulation or prohibition. See United States v. O'Brien, 391 U.S. 367, 376-377 (1968). The publication of truthful information available on the public record contains none of the indicia of those limited categories of expression, such as "fighting" words, which "are no essential part of any exposition of ideas, and are of such slight social value as a step to truth that any benefit that may be derived from them is clearly outweighed by the social interest in order and morality." Chaplinsky v. New Hampshire, 315 U.S. 568, 572 (1942).

By placing the information in the public domain on official court records, the State must be presumed to have concluded that the public interest was thereby being served. Public records by their very nature are of interest to those concerned with the administration of government, and a public benefit is performed by the reporting of the true contents of the records by the media. The freedom of the press to publish that information appears to us to be of critical importance to our type of government in which the citizenry is the final judge of the proper conduct of public business. In preserving that form of government the First and Fourteenth Amendments command nothing less than that the States may not impose sanctions on the publication of truthful information contained in official court records open to public inspection.

We are reluctant to embark on a course that would make public records generally available to the media but forbid their publication if offensive to the sensibilities of the supposed reasonable man. Such a rule would make it very difficult for the media to inform citizens about the public business and yet stay within the law. The rule would invite timidity and self-censorship and very likely lead to the suppression of many items that would otherwise be published and that should be made available to the public. At the very least, the First and Fourteenth Amendments will not allow exposing the press to liability for truthfully publishing information released to the public in official court records. If there are privacy interests to be protected in judicial proceedings, the States must respond by means which avoid public documentation or other exposure of private information. Their political institutions must weigh the interests in privacy with the interests of the public to know and of the press to publish. Once true information is disclosed in public court documents open to public inspection, the press cannot be sanctioned for publishing it. In this instance as in others reliance must rest upon the judgment of those who decide what to publish or broadcast. See Miami Herald Publishing Co. v. Tornillo, 418 U.S., at 258.

Appellant Wassell based his televised report upon notes taken during the court proceedings and obtained the name of the victim from the indictments handed to him at his request during a recess in the hearing. Appellee has not contended that the name was obtained in an improper fashion or that it was not on an official court document open to public inspection. Under these circumstances, the protection of freedom of the press provided by the First and Fourteenth Amendments bars the State of Georgia from making appellants' broadcast the basis of civil liability.

Reversed . . . .

Notes and Questions

1. **Donald Sterling and Jay-Z.** In 2014, National Basketball Association (NBA) team owner Sterling was publicly vilified after a surreptitious recording of his racist comments in a private conversation was subsequently made public. A security video of an elevator altercation between rapper and businessman Jay-Z and his sister-in-law Solange

Knowles was also made public and quickly went viral. Should the proliferation of portable eavesdropping and surveillance devices and security cameras change one's expectation of privacy?

2. **Shower cams in Sochi.** Is it intrusion into physical solitude if there is a clearly visible notice advising that your activities and statements are subject to surveillance in an area where you would otherwise have an expectation of privacy?
3. In 2013, California passed a law that punishes paparazzi who attempt to photograph or video record a celebrity's children in a harassing manner. In the United States, however, there is no special privacy protection that attaches to these minors. Should there be?
4. In Melvin v. Reid, the plaintiff sued for unwanted attention and humiliation because a film publicized events from her past that had long ago fallen out of the public eye. Today, search engines and databases make it difficult for people to forget their pasts. An individual's misdeeds or salacious history can be easily and permanently accessed by the public and retransmitted to others. In the digital age, is an action for embarrassing disclosure no longer viable?
5. As a matter of public policy, should private figures have to show actual malice to collect punitive damages in a false light suit? While private-figure plaintiffs seeking punitive damages for defamation must show actual malice, the issue was left open by the U.S. Supreme Court in Cantrell v. Forest City Publishing. Can you think of any reason for treating false light cases differently from defamation cases?
6. Since privacy is a personal right that dies with an individual, will future generations be able to access the volumes of private data collected during one's lifetime, including Internet searches, diaries, health records, purchasing history, and the like?
7. In 2014, the U.S. Supreme Court ruled unanimously that the Fourth Amendment requires police to get a warrant before a routine search of a smartphone. Riley v. California, 573 U.S. __ (2014). Chief Justice Roberts concluded that, while portable, smartphones contain the type of personal data about citizen's lives that makes it akin to a virtual home. What implications might this ruling have on press investigations that access digital information?

CHAPTER 4

APPROPRIATION & PUBLICITY

Appropriation privacy, the fourth prong of the privacy tort, allows plaintiffs to recover for the misappropriation of a name or likeness by a defendant for commercial purposes. As is the case with the other three privacy actions, the harm is unwanted attention or humiliation. Imagine if the maker of a paper products company decided to use your image to sell bathroom tissue. The harm here is that the company has taken away your right to be let alone, free from people recognizing you as the "toilet-paper lady," or from those who think they know you because you look familiar. With appropriation privacy, the harm is not the value of an endorsement; appropriation plaintiffs are generally private people without a marketable public image to exploit.

Celebrities who sell their names, likenesses, or endorsements for profit do not make good plaintiffs in appropriation actions because they court the attention that the private person wants to avoid. Some public figures, however, have an intellectual property interest in the use of their names or likenesses to sell products and services. This commercial interest, known as the right of publicity, can be transferred like other intellectual property rights, and in a number of states (including California), it can "descend" to the heirs of a celebrity. The owner of a right of publicity can control the commercial use of a star's identity—including image, likeness, signature, and name—although commercial uses that transform the original content into something culturally, politically, or artistically significant are considered acceptable "fair uses."

Consent is a defense to both appropriation privacy and the right of publicity.

ZACCHINI V. SCRIPPS-HOWARD BROADCASTING CO.

433 U.S. 562 (1977)

Mr. Justice WHITE delivered the opinion of the Court.
Petitioner, Hugo Zacchini, is an entertainer. He performs a "human cannonball" act in which he is shot from a cannon into a net some 200 feet away. Each performance occupies some 15 seconds. In August and September 1972, petitioner was engaged to perform his act on a regular

basis at the Geauga County Fair in Burton, Ohio. He performed in a fenced area, surrounded by grandstands, at the fair grounds. Members of the public attending the fair were not charged a separate admission fee to observe his act.

On August 30, a freelance reporter for Scripps-Howard Broadcasting Co., the operator of a television broadcasting station and respondent in this case, attended the fair. He carried a small movie camera. Petitioner noticed the reporter and asked him not to film the performance. The reporter did not do so on that day; but on the instructions of the producer of respondent's daily newscast, he returned the following day and videotaped the entire act. This film clip approximately 15 seconds in length, was shown on the 11 o'clock news program that night, together with favorable commentary.

This "cannon," mounted on a truck, was used by Hugo Zacchini. © Roger Wollstadt. Used under license: https://creativecommons.org/licenses/by-sa/2.0/legalcode.

Petitioner then brought this action for damages, alleging that he is "engaged in the entertainment business," that the act he performs is one "invented by his father and . . . performed only by his family for the last fifty years," that respondent "showed and commercialized the film of his act without his consent," and that such conduct was an "unlawful appropriation of plaintiff's professional property." . . .

We granted certiorari, 429 U.S. 1037 (1977), to consider an issue unresolved by this Court: whether the First and Fourteenth Amendments immunized respondent from damages for its alleged infringement of petitioner's state law "right of publicity." Pet. for Cert. 2. Insofar as the Ohio Supreme Court held that the First and Fourteenth Amendments of the United States Constitution required judgment for respondent, we reverse the judgment of that court. . . .

II.

The Ohio Supreme Court held that respondent is constitutionally privileged to include in its newscasts matters of public interest that would otherwise be protected by the right of publicity, absent an intent to injure or to appropriate for some nonprivileged purpose. If under this standard respondent had merely reported that petitioner was performing at the fair and described or commented on his act, with or without showing his picture on television, we would have a very different case. But petitioner is not contending that his appearance at the fair and his performance could not be reported by the press as newsworthy items. His complaint is that respondent filmed his entire act and displayed that film on television for the public to see and enjoy. This, he claimed, was an appropriation of his professional property. The Ohio Supreme Court agreed that petitioner had "a right of publicity" that gave him "personal control over commercial display and exploitation of his personality and the exercise of his talents." This right of "exclusive control over the publicity given to his performances" was said to be such a "valuable part of the benefit which may be attained by his talents and efforts" that it was entitled to legal protection. It was also observed, or at least expressly assumed, that petitioner had not abandoned his rights by performing under the circumstances present at the Geauga County Fair Grounds.

The Ohio Supreme Court nevertheless held that the challenged invasion was privileged, saying that the press "must be accorded broad latitude in its choice of how much it presents of each story or incident, and of the emphasis to be given to such presentation. No fixed standard which would bar the press from reporting or depicting either an entire occurrence or an entire discrete part of a public performance can be formulated which would not unduly restrict the 'breathing room' in reporting which freedom of the press requires." 351 N.E.2d, at 461. Under this view, respondent was thus constitutionally free to film and display petitioner's entire act.

The Ohio Supreme Court relied heavily on Time, Inc. v. Hill, 385 U.S. 374 (1967), but that case does not mandate a media privilege to televise a performer's entire act without his consent. Involved in Time, Inc. v. Hill was a claim under the New York "Right of Privacy" statute that Life Magazine, in the course of reviewing a new play, had connected the play with a long-past incident involving petitioner and his family and had falsely described their experience and conduct at that time. The complaint sought damages for humiliation and suffering flowing from these nondefamatory falsehoods that allegedly invaded Hill's privacy. The Court held, however, that the opening of a new play linked to an actual incident was a matter of public interest and that Hill could not recover without showing that the Life report was knowingly false or was published with reckless disregard for the truth the same rigorous standard that had been applied in New York Times Co. v. Sullivan, 376 U.S. 25 (1964).

Time, Inc. v. Hill, which was hotly contested and decided by a divided Court, involved an entirely different tort from the "right of publicity" recognized by the Ohio Supreme Court. As the opinion reveals in Time, Inc. v. Hill, the Court was steeped in the literature of privacy law and was aware of the developing distinctions and nuances in this branch of the law. The Court, for example, cited W. Prosser, Law of Torts 831-832 (3d ed. 1964), and the same author's well-known article, Privacy, 48 Calif.L.Rev. 383 (1960), both of which divided privacy into four distinct branches. The Court was aware that it was adjudicating a "false light" privacy case involving a matter of public interest, not a case involving "intrusion," 385 U.S., at 384-385, n. 9, "appropriation" of a name or likeness for the purposes of trade, id., at 381, or "private details" about a non-newsworthy person or event, id., at 383 n. 7. It is also abundantly clear that Time, Inc. v. Hill did not involve a performer, a person with a name having commercial value, or any claim to a "right of publicity." This discrete kind of 'appropriation' case was plainly identified in the literature cited by the Court and had been adjudicated in the reported cases.

> Ettore v. Philco Television Broadcasting Corp., supra, involved a challenge to television exhibition of a film made of a prize fight that had occurred some time ago. Judge Biggs, writing for the Court of Appeals, said:
>
> "There are, speaking very generally, two polar types of cases. One arises when some accidental occurrence rends the veil of obscurity surrounding an average person and makes him, arguably, newsworthy. The other type involves the appropriation of the performance or production of a professional performer or entrepreneur. Between the two extremes are many gradations, most involving strictly commercial exploitation of some aspect of an individual's personality, such as his name or picture." 229 F.2d, at 486.
>
> . . .
>
> "The fact is that, if a performer performs for hire, a cur-

> tailment, without consideration, of his right to control his performance is a wrong to him. Such a wrong vitally affects his livelihood, precisely as a trade libel, for example, affects the earnings of a corporation. If the artistry of the performance be used as a criterion, every judge perforce must turn himself into a literary, theatrical or sports critic." Id., at 490.

The differences between these two torts are important. First, the State's interests in providing a cause of action in each instance are different. "The interest protected' in permitting recovery for placing the plaintiff in a false light "is clearly that of reputation, with the same overtones of mental distress as in defamation." Prosser, supra, 48 Calif.L.Rev., at 400. By contrast, the State's interest in permitting a "right of publicity" is in protecting the proprietary interest of the individual in his act in part to encourage such entertainment. As we later note, the State's interest is closely analogous to the goals of patent and copyright law, focusing on the right of the individual to reap the reward of his endeavors and having little to do with protecting feelings or reputation. Second, the two torts differ in the degree to which they intrude on dissemination of information to the public. In "false light" cases the only way to protect the interests involved is to attempt to minimize publication of the damaging matter, while in "right of publicity" cases the only question is who gets to do the publishing. An entertainer such as petitioner usually has no objection to the widespread publication of his act as long as the gets the commercial benefit of such publication. Indeed, in the present case petitioner did not seek to enjoin the broadcast of his act; he simply sought compensation for the broadcast in the form of damages.

. . .

It is evident, and there is no claim here to the contrary, that petitioner's state-law right of publicity would not serve to prevent respondent from reporting the newsworthy facts about petitioner's act. Wherever the line in particular situations is to be drawn between media reports that are protected and those that are not, we are quite sure that the First and Fourteenth Amendments do not immunize the media when they broadcast a performer's entire act without his consent. The Constitution no more prevents a State from requiring respondent to compensate petitioner for broadcasting his act on television than it would privilege respondent to film and broadcast a copyrighted dramatic work without liability to the copyright owner. . . .

The broadcast of a film of petitioner's entire act poses a substantial threat to the economic value of that performance. As the Ohio court recognized, this act is the product of petitioner's own talents and energy, the end result of much time, effort, and expense. Much of its economic value lies in the "right of exclusive control over the publicity given to his performance"; if the public can see the act free on television, it will be less willing to pay to see it at the fair. . . . Moreover, the broadcast of petitioner's entire performance, unlike the unauthorized use of another's name for purposes of trade or the incidental use of a name or picture by the press, goes to the heart of petitioner's ability to earn a living as an entertainer. Thus, in this case, Ohio has recognized what may be the strongest case for a "right of publicity" involving, not the appropriation of an entertainer's reputation to enhance the attractiveness of a commercial product, but the appropriation of the very activity by which the entertainer acquired his reputation in the first place.

Of course, Ohio's decision to protect petitioner's right of publicity here rests on more than a desire to compensate the performer for the time and effort invested in his act; the protection provides an economic incentive for him to make the investment required to produce a performance of interest to the public. . . .

There is no doubt that entertainment, as well as news, enjoys First Amendment protection. It is also true that entertainment itself can be important news. Time, Inc. v. Hill. But it is important to note that neither the public nor respondent will be deprived of the benefit of petitioner's performance as long as his commercial stake in his act is appropriately recognized. Petitioner does not seek to enjoin the broadcast of his performance; he simply wants to be paid for it. Nor do we think that a state-law damages remedy against respondent would represent a species of liability without fault contrary to the letter or spirit of Gertz v. Robert Welch, Inc., 418 U.S. 323 (1974). Respondent knew that petitioner objected to televising his act, but nevertheless displayed the entire film.

We conclude that although the State of Ohio may as a matter of its own law privilege the press in the circumstances of this case, the First and Fourteenth Amendments do not require it to do so.

Reversed.

Mr. Justice POWELL, with whom Mr. Justice BRENNAN and Mr. Justice MARSHALL join, dissenting.
Disclaiming any attempt to do more than decide the narrow case before

us, the Court reverses the decision of the Supreme Court of Ohio based on repeated incantation of a single formula: "a performer's entire act." The holding today is summed up in one sentence:

"Wherever the line in particular situations is to be drawn between media reports that are protected and those that are not, we are quite sure that the First and Fourteenth Amendments do not immunize the media when they broadcast a performer's entire act without his consent." Ante, at 2856.

I doubt that this formula provides a standard clear enough even for resolution of this case. In any event, I am not persuaded that the Court's opinion is appropriately sensitive to the First Amendment values at stake, and I therefore dissent. . . .

In my view the First Amendment commands a different analytical starting point from the one selected by the Court. Rather than begin with a quantitative analysis of the performer's behavior - is this or is this not his entire act? - we should direct initial attention to the actions of the news media: what use did the station make of the film footage? When a film is used, as here, for a routine portion of a regular news program, I would hold that the First Amendment protects the station from a "right of publicity" or "appropriation" suit, absent a strong showing by the plaintiff that the news broadcast was a subterfuge or cover for private or commercial exploitation. . . .

Since the film clip here was undeniably treated as news and since there is no claim that the use was subterfuge, respondent's actions were constitutionally privileged. I would affirm.

. . .

Before moving on to the next page, please pause and look at this photograph.

Does it remind you of anyone famous? If so, whom?

WHITE V. SAMSUNG ELECTRONICS AMERICA, INC.
971 F.2d 1395 (9th Cir. 1992)

Before: GOODWIN, PREGERSON, and ALARCON, Circuit Judges. GOODWIN, Senior Circuit Judge.
Plaintiff Vanna White is the hostess of "Wheel of Fortune," one of the most popular game shows in television history. An estimated forty million people watch the program daily. Capitalizing on the fame which her participation in the show has bestowed on her, White markets her identity to various advertisers.

The dispute in this case arose out of a series of advertisements prepared for Samsung by Deutsch. The series ran in at least half a dozen publications with widespread, and in some cases national, circulation. Each of the advertisements in the series followed the same theme. Each depicted a current item from popular culture and a Samsung electronic product. Each was set in the twenty-first century and conveyed the message that the Samsung product would still be in use by that time. By hypothesizing outrageous future outcomes for the cultural items, the ads created humorous effects. For example, one lampooned current popular notions of an unhealthy diet by depicting a raw steak with the caption: "Revealed to be health food. 2010 A.D." Another depicted irreverent "news"-show host Morton Downey Jr. in front of an American flag with the caption: "Presidential candidate. 2008 A.D."

The non-robotic Vanna White.

The advertisement which prompted the current dispute was for Samsung video-cassette recorders (VCRs). The ad depicted a robot, dressed in a wig, gown, and jewelry which Deutsch consciously selected to resemble White's hair and dress. The robot was posed next to a game board which is instantly recognizable as the Wheel of Fortune game show set, in a stance for which White is famous. The caption of the ad read: "Longest-running game show. 2012 A.D." Defendants referred to the ad as the "Vanna White" ad. Unlike the other celebrities used in the campaign, White neither consented to the ads nor was she paid.

Following the circulation of the robot ad, White sued Samsung and Deutsch in federal district court under: (1) California Civil Code § 3344; (2) the California common law right of publicity; and (3) § 43(a) of the Lanham Act, 15 U.S.C. § 1125(a). The district court granted summary judgment against White on each of her claims. White now appeals.

I. *Section 3344*

White first argues that the district court erred in rejecting her claim under section 3344. Section 3344(a) provides, in pertinent part, that "[a]ny person who knowingly uses another's name, voice, signature, photograph, or likeness, in any manner, ... for purposes of advertising or selling, ... without such person's prior consent ... shall be liable for any damages sustained by the person or persons injured as a result thereof."

White argues that the Samsung advertisement used her "likeness" in contravention of section 3344. In *Midler v. Ford Motor Co.*, 849 F.2d 460 (9th Cir. 1988), this court rejected Bette Midler's section 3344 claim concerning a Ford television commercial in which a Midler "sound-alike" sang a song which Midler had made famous. In rejecting Midler's claim, this court noted that "[t]he defendants did not use Midler's name or anything else whose use is prohibited by the statute. The voice they used was [another person's], not hers. The term 'likeness' refers to a visual image not a vocal imitation." *Id.* at 463.

In this case, Samsung and Deutsch used a robot with mechanical features, and not, for example, a manikin molded to White's precise features. Without deciding for all purposes when a caricature or impressionistic resemblance might become a "likeness," we agree with the district court that the robot at issue here was not White's "likeness" within the meaning of section 3344. Accordingly, we affirm the court's dismissal of White's section 3344 claim.

II. *Right of Publicity*

White next argues that the district court erred in granting summary judgment to defendants on White's common law right of publicity claim. In *Eastwood v. Superior Court*, 198 Cal.Rptr. 342 (1983), the California court of appeal stated that the common law right of publicity cause of action "may be pleaded by alleging (1) the defendant's use of the plaintiff's identity; (2) the appropriation of plaintiff's name or likeness to defendant's advantage, commercially or otherwise; (3) lack of consent; and (4) resulting injury." *Id.* at 417, 198 Cal.Rptr. 342 (citing Prosser, Law of Torts (4th ed. 1971) § 117, pp. 804-807). The district court dismissed White's claim for failure to satisfy *Eastwood's* second prong, reasoning that defendants had not appropriated White's "name or likeness" with their robot ad. We agree that the robot ad did not make use of White's name or likeness. However, the common law right of publicity is not so confined.

The *Eastwood* court did not hold that the right of publicity cause of action could be pleaded only by alleging an appropriation of name or likeness. *Eastwood* involved an unauthorized use of photographs of Clint Eastwood and of his name. Accordingly, the *Eastwood* court had no occasion to consider the extent beyond the use of name or likeness to which the right of publicity reaches. That court held only that the right of publicity cause of action "may be" pleaded by alleging, *inter alia,* appropriation of name or likeness, not that the action may be pleaded *only* in those terms.

The "name or likeness" formulation referred to in *Eastwood* originated not as an element of the right of publicity cause of action, but as a description of the types of cases in which the cause of action had been recognized. The source of this formulation is Prosser, *Privacy,* 48 Cal.L.Rev. 383, 401-07 (1960), one of the earliest and most enduring articulations of the common law right of publicity cause of action. In looking at the case law to that point, Prosser recognized that right of publicity cases involved one of two basic factual scenarios: name appropriation, and picture or other likeness appropriation. *Id.* at 401-02, nn. 156-57.

Even though Prosser focused on appropriations of name or likeness in discussing the right of publicity, he noted that "[i]t is not impossible that there might be appropriation of the plaintiff's identity, as by impersonation, without the use of either his name or his likeness, and that this would be an invasion of his right of privacy." *Id.* at 401, n. 155. At the time Prosser wrote, he noted however, that "[n]o such case appears to have arisen." *Id.*

Since Prosser's early formulation, the case law has borne out his insight that the right of publicity is not limited to the appropriation of name or likeness. In *Motschenbacher v. R.J. Reynolds Tobacco Co.,* 498 F.2d 821 (9th Cir. 1974), the defendant had used a photograph of the plaintiff's race car in a television commercial. Although the plaintiff appeared driving the car in the photograph, his features were not visible. Even though the defendant had not appropriated the plaintiff's name or likeness, this court held that plaintiff's California right of publicity claim should reach the jury.

In *Midler,* this court held that, even though the defendants had not used Midler's name or likeness, Midler had stated a claim for violation of her California common law right of publicity because "the defendants . . . for their own profit in selling their product did appropriate part of her identity" by using a Midler sound-alike. *Id.* at 463-64.

In *Carson v. Here's Johnny Portable Toilets, Inc.,* 698 F.2d 831 (6th Cir. 1983), the defendant had marketed portable toilets under the brand name "Here's Johnny"—Johnny Carson's signature "Tonight Show" introduction—without Carson's permission. The district court had dismissed Carson's Michigan common law right of publicity claim because the defendants had not used Carson's "name or likeness." *Id.* at 835. In reversing the district court, the sixth circuit found "the district court's conception of the right of publicity . . . too narrow" and held that the right was implicated because the defendant had appropriated Carson's identity by using, *inter alia,* the phrase "Here's Johnny." *Id.* at 835-37.

These cases teach not only that the common law right of publicity reaches means of appropriation other than name or likeness, but that the specific means of appropriation are relevant only for determining whether the defendant has in fact appropriated the plaintiff's identity. The right of publicity does not require that appropriations of identity be accomplished through particular means to be actionable. It is noteworthy that the *Midler* and *Carson* defendants not only avoided using the plaintiff's name or likeness, but they also avoided appropriating the celebrity's voice, signature, and photograph. The photograph in *Motschenbacher* did include the plaintiff, but because the plaintiff was not visible the driver could have been an actor or dummy and the analysis in the case would have been the same.

Although the defendants in these cases avoided the most obvious means of appropriating the plaintiffs' identities, each of their actions directly implicated the commercial interests which the right of publicity is designed to protect. As the *Carson* court explained:

> [t]he right of publicity has developed to protect the commercial interest of celebrities in their identities. The theory

> of the right is that a celebrity's identity can be valuable in the promotion of products, and the celebrity has an interest that may be protected from the unauthorized commercial exploitation of that identity. . . . If the celebrity's identity is commercially exploited, there has been an invasion of his right whether or not his "name or likeness" is used.

Carson, 698 F.2d at 835. It is not important *how* the defendant has appropriated the plaintiff's identity, but *whether* the defendant has done so. *Motschenbacher*, *Midler*, and *Carson* teach the impossibility of treating the right of publicity as guarding only against a laundry list of specific means of appropriating identity. A rule which says that the right of publicity can be infringed only through the use of nine different methods of appropriating identity merely challenges the clever advertising strategist to come up with the tenth.

Indeed, if we treated the means of appropriation as dispositive in our analysis of the right of publicity, we would not only weaken the right but effectively eviscerate it. The right would fail to protect those plaintiffs most in need of its protection. Advertisers use celebrities to promote their products. The more popular the celebrity, the greater the number of people who recognize her, and the greater the visibility for the product. The identities of the most popular celebrities are not only the most attractive for advertisers, but also the easiest to evoke without resorting to obvious means such as name, likeness, or voice.

Consider a hypothetical advertisement which depicts a mechanical robot with male features, an African-American complexion, and a bald head. The robot is wearing black hightop Air Jordan basketball sneakers, and a red basketball uniform with black trim, baggy shorts, and the number 23 (though not revealing "Bulls" or "Jordan" lettering). The ad depicts the robot dunking a basketball one-handed, stiff-armed, legs extended like open scissors, and tongue hanging out. Now envision that this ad is run on television during professional basketball games. Considered individually, the robot's physical attributes, its dress, and its stance tell us little. Taken together, they lead to the only conclusion that any sports viewer who has registered a discernible pulse in the past five years would reach: the ad is about Michael Jordan.

Viewed separately, the individual aspects of the advertisement in the present case say little. Viewed together, they leave little doubt about the celebrity the ad is meant to depict. The female-shaped robot is wearing a long gown, blond wig, and large jewelry. Vanna White dresses exactly like this at times, but so do many other women. The robot is in the process of turning a block letter on a game-board. Vanna White dresses like this while turning letters on a game-board but perhaps similarly attired Scrabble-playing women do this as well. The robot is standing on what looks to be the Wheel of Fortune game show set. Vanna White dresses like this, turns letters, and does this on the Wheel of Fortune game show. She is the only one. Indeed, defendants themselves referred to their ad as the "Vanna White" ad. We are not surprised.

Television and other media create marketable celebrity identity value. Considerable energy and ingenuity are expended by those who have achieved celebrity value to exploit it for profit. The law protects the celebrity's sole right to exploit this value whether the celebrity has achieved her fame out of rare ability, dumb luck, or a combination thereof. We decline Samsung and Deutch's invitation to permit the evisceration of the common law right of publicity through means as facile as those in this case. Because White has alleged facts showing that Samsung and Deutsch had appropriated her identity, the district court erred by rejecting, on summary judgment, White's common law right of publicity claim.

III. *The Lanham Act*

White's final argument is that the district court erred in denying her claim under § 43(a) of the Lanham Act, 15 U.S.C. § 1125(a). The version of section 43(a) applicable to this case provides, in pertinent part, that "[a]ny person who shall . . . use, in connection with any goods or services . . . any false description or representation . . . shall be liable to a civil action . . . by any person who believes that he is or is likely to be damaged by the use of any such false description or designation." 15 U.S.C. § 1125(a).

To prevail on her Lanham Act claim, White is required to show that in running the robot ad, Samsung and Deutsch created a likelihood of confusion, *Academy of Motion Picture Arts v. Creative House,* 944 F.2d 1446, 1454 (9th Cir. 1991); *Toho Co. Ltd. v. Sears Roebuck & Co.,* 645 F.2d 788, 790 (9th Cir. 1981) *New West Corp. v. NYM Co. of California,* 595 F.2d 1194, 1201 (9th Cir. 1979), over whether White was endorsing Samsung's VCRs. *HMH Publishing Co. v. Brincat,* 504 F.2d 713 (9th Cir. 1974); *Allen v. National Video, Inc.,* 610 F.Supp. 612 (D.C.N.Y.1985).

This circuit recognizes several different multi-factor tests for determining whether a likelihood of confusion exists. *See Academy,* 944 F.2d at 1454, n. 3. None of these tests is correct to the exclusion of the others. *Eclipse*

Associates Ltd. v. Data General Corp., 894 F.2d 1114, 1118 (9th Cir. 1990). Normally, in reviewing the district court's decision, this court will look to the particular test that the district court used. *Academy*, 944 F.2d at 1454, n. 3; *Eclipse*, 894 F.2d at 1117-1118. However, because the district court in this case apparently did not use any of the multi-factor tests in making its likelihood of confusion determination, and because this case involves an appeal from summary judgment and we review de novo the district court's determination, we will look for guidance to the 8-factor test enunciated in *AMF, Inc. v. Sleekcraft Boats*, 599 F.2d 341 (9th Cir. 1979). According to *AMF*, factors relevant to a likelihood of confusion include:

(1) strength of the plaintiff's mark;
(2) relatedness of the goods;
(3) similarity of the marks;
(4) evidence of actual confusion;
(5) marketing channels used;
(6) likely degree of purchaser care;
(7) defendant's intent in selecting the mark;
(8) likelihood of expansion of the product lines.

599 F.2d at 348-49. We turn now to consider White's claim in light of each factor.

In cases involving confusion over endorsement by a celebrity plaintiff, "mark" means the celebrity's persona. *See Allen*, 610 F.Supp. at 627. The "strength" of the mark refers to the level of recognition the celebrity enjoys among members of society. *See Academy*, 944 F.2d at 1455. If Vanna White is unknown to the segment of the public at whom Samsung's robot ad was directed, then that segment could not be confused as to whether she was endorsing Samsung VCRs. Conversely, if White is well-known, this would allow the possibility of a likelihood of confusion. For the purposes of the *Sleekcraft* test, White's "mark," or celebrity identity, is strong.

In cases concerning confusion over celebrity endorsement, the plaintiff's "goods" concern the reasons for or source of the plaintiff's fame. Because White's fame is based on her televised performances, her "goods" are closely related to Samsung's VCRs. Indeed, the ad itself reinforced the relationship by informing its readers that they would be taping the "longest-running game show" on Samsung's VCRs well into the future.

The third factor, "similarity of the marks," both supports and contradicts a finding of likelihood of confusion. On the one hand, all of the aspects of the robot ad identify White; on the other, the figure is quite clearly a robot, not a human. This ambiguity means that we must look to the other factors for resolution.

The fourth factor does not favor White's claim because she has presented no evidence of actual confusion.

Fifth, however, White has appeared in the same stance as the robot from the ad in numerous magazines, including the covers of some. Magazines were used as the marketing channels for the robot ad. This factor cuts toward a likelihood of confusion.
Sixth, consumers are not likely to be particularly careful in determining who endorses VCRs, making confusion as to their endorsement more likely.

Concerning the seventh factor, "defendant's intent," the district court found that, in running the robot ad, the defendants had intended a spoof of the "Wheel of Fortune." The relevant question is whether the defendants "intended to profit by confusing consumers" concerning the endorsement of Samsung VCRs. *Toho,* 645 F.2d 788. We do not disagree that defendants intended to spoof Vanna White and "Wheel of Fortune." That does not preclude, however, the possibility that defendants also intended to confuse consumers regarding endorsement. The robot ad was one of a series of ads run by defendants which followed the same theme. Another ad in the series depicted Morton Downey Jr. as a presidential candidate in the year 2008. Doubtless, defendants intended to spoof presidential elections and Mr. Downey through this ad. Consumers, however, would likely believe, and would be correct in so believing, that Mr. Downey was paid for his permission and was endorsing Samsung products. Looking at the series of advertisements as a whole, a jury could reasonably conclude that beneath the surface humor of the series lay an intent to persuade consumers that celebrity Vanna White, like celebrity Downey, was endorsing Samsung products.

Finally, the eighth factor, "likelihood of expansion of the product lines," does not appear apposite to a celebrity endorsement case such as this.

Application of the *Sleekcraft* factors to this case indicates that the district court erred in rejecting White's Lanham Act claim at the summary judgment stage. In so concluding, we emphasize two facts, however. First, construing the motion papers in White's favor, as we must, we hold only that White has raised a genuine issue of material fact concerning a likelihood of confusion as to her endorsement. *Cohen v. Paramount*

Pictures Corp., 845 F.2d 851, 852-53 (9th Cir. 1988). Whether White's Lanham Act claim should succeed is a matter for the jury. Second, we stress that we reach this conclusion in light of the peculiar facts of this case. In particular, we note that the robot ad identifies White and was part of a series of ads in which other celebrities participated and were paid for their endorsement of Samsung's products.

IV. *The Parody Defense*

In defense, defendants cite a number of cases for the proposition that their robot ad constituted protected speech. The only cases they cite which are even remotely relevant to this case are *Hustler Magazine v. Falwell*, 485 U.S. 46, 108 S.Ct. 876, 99 L.Ed.2d 41 (1988) and *L.L. Bean, Inc. v. Drake Publishers, Inc.*, 811 F.2d 26 (1st Cir. 1987). Those cases involved parodies of advertisements run for the purpose of poking fun at Jerry Falwell and L.L. Bean, respectively. This case involves a true advertisement run for the purpose of selling Samsung VCRs. The ad's spoof of Vanna White and Wheel of Fortune is subservient and only tangentially related to the ad's primary message: "buy Samsung VCRs." Defendants' parody arguments are better addressed to non-commercial parodies. The difference between a "parody" and a "knock-off" is the difference between fun and profit.

V. *Conclusion*

In remanding this case, we hold only that White has pleaded claims which can go to the jury for its decision.

AFFIRMED IN PART, REVERSED IN PART, and REMANDED.

ALARCON, Circuit Judge, concurring in part, dissenting in part.
Vanna White seeks recovery from Samsung based on three theories: the right to privacy, the right to publicity, and the Lanham Act. I concur in the majority's conclusions on the right to privacy. I respectfully dissent from its holdings on the right to publicity and the Lanham Act claims.

. . .

The case before this court is distinguishable from the factual showing made in *Motschenbacher, Midler*, and *Carson*. It is patently clear to anyone viewing the commercial advertisement that Vanna White was not being depicted. No reasonable juror could confuse a metal robot with Vanna White.

The majority contends that "the individual aspects of the advertisement . . . [v]iewed together leave little doubt about the celebrity the ad is meant to depict." Majority Opinion at p. 1399. It derives this conclusion from the fact that Vanna White is "the only one" who "dresses like this, turns letters, and does this on the Wheel of Fortune game show." *Id.* In reaching this conclusion, the majority confuses Vanna White, the person, with the role she has assumed as the current hostess on the "Wheel of Fortune" television game show. A recognition of the distinction between a performer and the part he or she plays is essential for a proper analysis of the facts of this case. As is discussed below, those things which Vanna White claims identify her are not unique to her. They are, instead, attributes of the *role* she plays. The representation of those attributes, therefore, does not constitute a representation of Vanna White. *See Nurmi v. Peterson,* 10 U.S.P.Q.2d 1775 (C.D.Cal.1989) (distinguishing between performer and role).

Vanna White is a one-role celebrity. She is famous solely for appearing as the hostess on the "Wheel of Fortune" television show. There is nothing unique about Vanna White or the attributes which she claims identify her. Although she appears to be an attractive woman, her face and figure are no more distinctive than that of other equally comely women. She performs her role as hostess on "Wheel of Fortune" in a simple and straight-forward manner. Her work does not require her to display whatever artistic talent she may possess.

The majority appears to argue that because Samsung created a robot with the physical proportions of an attractive woman, posed it gracefully, dressed it in a blond wig, an evening gown, and jewelry, and placed it on a set that resembles the Wheel of Fortune layout, it thereby appropriated Vanna White's identity. But an attractive appearance, a graceful pose, blond hair, an evening gown, and jewelry are attributes shared by many women, especially in Southern California. These common attributes are particularly evident among game-show hostesses, models, actresses, singers, and other women in the entertainment field. They are not unique attributes of Vanna White's identity. Accordingly, I cannot join in the majority's conclusion that, even if viewed together, these attributes identify Vanna White and, therefore, raise a triable issue as to the appropriation of her identity.

The only characteristic in the commercial advertisement that is not common to many female performers or celebrities is the imitation of the "Wheel of Fortune" set. This set is the only thing which might possibly lead a viewer to think of Vanna White. The Wheel of Fortune set, however, is not an attribute of Vanna White's identity. It is an identifying characteristic of a television game show, a prop with which Vanna White interacts in her role as the current hostess. To say that Vanna White may bring an action when another blond female performer or robot appears on such a set as a hostess will, I am sure, be a surprise to the owners of the show.

. . .

COMEDY III PRODUCTIONS, INC. v. SADERUP, INC.

21 P.3d 797 (Cal. 2001)

MOSK, J.

. . .

II. Facts

Plaintiff Comedy III Productions, Inc. (hereafter Comedy III), brought this action against defendants Gary Saderup and Gary Saderup, Inc. (hereafter collectively Saderup), seeking damages and injunctive relief for violation of section 990 and related business torts. The parties waived the right to jury trial and the right to put on evidence, and submitted the case for decision on the following stipulated facts:

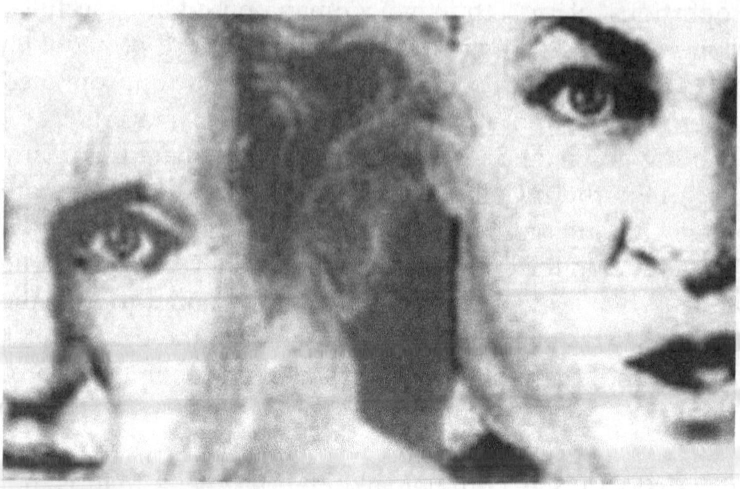

Gary Saderup's Three Stooges (detail). From Appendix 1, Comedy III Productions, Inc. v. Gary Saderup, Inc., 25 Cal. 4th 387 (2001).

Comedy III is the registered owner of all rights to the former comedy act known as The Three Stooges, who are deceased personalities within the meaning of the statute.

Saderup is an artist with over 25 years' experience in making charcoal drawings of celebrities. These drawings are used to create lithographic and silkscreen masters, which in turn are used to produce multiple reproductions in the form, respectively, of lithographic prints and silk-screened images on T-shirts. Saderup creates the original drawings and is actively involved in the ensuing lithographic and silkscreening processes.

Without securing Comedy III's consent, Saderup sold lithographs and T-shirts bearing a likeness of The Three Stooges reproduced from a charcoal drawing he had made. These lithographs and T-shirts did not constitute an advertisement, endorsement, or sponsorship of any product.
Saderup's profits from the sale of unlicensed lithographs and T-shirts bearing a likeness of The Three Stooges was $75,000 and Comedy III's reasonable attorney fees were $150,000.

On these stipulated facts the court found for Comedy III and entered judgment against Saderup awarding damages of $75,000 and attorney fees of $150,000 plus costs. The court also issued a permanent injunction restraining Saderup from violating the statute by use of any likeness of The Three Stooges in lithographs, T-shirts, "or any other medium by which [Saderup's] art work may be sold or marketed." The injunction further prohibited Saderup from "Creating, producing, reproducing, copying, distributing, selling or exhibiting any lithographs, prints, posters, t-shirts, buttons, or other goods, products or merchandise of any kind, bearing the photograph, image, face, symbols, trademarks, likeness, name, voice or signature of The Three Stooges or any of the individual members of The Three Stooges." The sole exception to this broad prohibition was Saderup's original charcoal drawing from which the reproductions at issue were made.

Saderup appealed. The Court of Appeal modified the judgment by striking the injunction. The court reasoned that Comedy III had not proved a likelihood of continued violation of the statute, and that the wording of the injunction was overbroad because it exceeded the terms of the statute and because it "could extend to matters and conduct protected by the First Amendment. . . ."

The Court of Appeal affirmed the judgment as thus modified, however, upholding the award of damages, attorney fees, and costs. In so doing, it rejected Saderup's contentions that his conduct (1) did not violate the terms of the statute, and (2) in any event was protected by the constitutional guaranty of freedom of speech. We granted review to address these two issues.

III. Discussion

A. The Statutory Issue

. . .

B. The Constitutional Issue
Saderup next contends that enforcement of the judgment against him violates his right of free speech and expression under the First Amendment. He raises a difficult issue, which we address below.

The right of publicity is often invoked in the context of commercial speech when the appropriation of a celebrity likeness creates a false and misleading impression that the celebrity is endorsing a product. (See *Waits v. Frito-Lay, Inc.* (9th Cir. 1992) 978 F.2d 1093; *Midler v. Ford Motor Co.* (9th Cir. 1988) 849 F.2d 460.) Because the First Amendment does not protect false and misleading commercial speech (*Central Hudson Gas & Elec. Corp. v. Public Serv. Com'n* (1980) 447 U.S. 557, 563-564), and because even nonmisleading commercial speech is generally subject to somewhat lesser First Amendment protection (*Central Hudson,* at p. 566), the right of publicity may often trump the right of advertisers to make use of celebrity figures.

But the present case does not concern commercial speech. As the trial court found, Saderup's portraits of The Three Stooges are expressive works and not an advertisement for or endorsement of a product. Although his work was done for financial gain, "[t]he First Amendment is not limited to those who publish without charge. . . . [An expressive activity] does not lose its constitutional protection because it is undertaken for profit." (*Guglielmi v. Spelling-Goldberg Productions* (1979) 603 P.2d 454 (conc. opn. of Bird, C.J.) (*Guglielmi*).)

The tension between the right of publicity and the First Amendment is highlighted by recalling the two distinct, commonly acknowledged purposes of the latter. First, "'to preserve an uninhibited marketplace of ideas' and to repel efforts to limit the '"uninhibited, robust and wide-open" debate on public issues.'" (*Guglielmi, supra,* 603 P.2d at 458.) Second, to foster a "fundamental respect for individual development and self-realization. The right to self-expression is inherent in any political system which respects individual dignity. Each speaker must be free of government restraint regardless of the nature or manner of the views expressed unless there is a compelling reason to the contrary." (*Ibid.,* fn.

omitted; see also Emerson, The System of Freedom of Expression (1970) pp. 6-7.)

The right of publicity has a potential for frustrating the fulfillment of both these purposes. Because celebrities take on public meaning, the appropriation of their likenesses may have important uses in uninhibited debate on public issues, particularly debates about culture and values. And because celebrities take on personal meanings to many individuals in the society, the creative appropriation of celebrity images can be an important avenue of individual expression. As one commentator has stated: "Entertainment and sports celebrities are the leading players in our Public Drama. We tell tales, both tall and cautionary, about them. We monitor their comings and goings, their missteps and heartbreaks. We copy their mannerisms, their styles, their modes of conversation and of consumption. Whether or not celebrities are 'the chief agents of moral change in the United States,' they certainly are widely used—far more than are institutionally anchored elites—to symbolize individual aspirations, group identities, and cultural values. . . ."

But having recognized the high degree of First Amendment protection for noncommercial speech about celebrities, we need not conclude that all expression that trenches on the right of publicity receives such protection. The right of publicity, like copyright, protects a form of intellectual property that society deems to have some social utility. "Often considerable money, time and energy are needed to develop one's prominence in a particular field. Years of labor may be required before one's skill, reputation, notoriety or virtues are sufficiently developed to permit an economic return through some medium of commercial promotion. [Citations.] For some, the investment may eventually create considerable commercial value in one's identity." (*Lugosi, supra,* 603 P.2d at p. 438 (dis. opn. of Bird, C. J.)).

The present case exemplifies this kind of creative labor. Moe and Jerome (Curly) Howard and Larry Fein fashioned personae collectively known as The Three Stooges, first in vaudeville and later in movie shorts, over a period extending from the 1920's to the 1940's. (See Fleming, The Three Stooges: Amalgamated Morons to American Icons (1999) pp. 10-46.) The three comic characters they created and whose names they shared—Larry, Moe, and Curly—possess a kind of mythic status in our culture. Their journey from ordinary vaudeville performers to the heights (or depths) of slapstick comic celebrity was long and arduous. (*Ibid.*) Their brand of physical humor—the nimble, comically stylized violence, the "nyuk-nyuks" and "whoop-whoop-whoops," eye-pokes, slaps and head conks (see, e.g., Three Little Pigskins (Columbia Pictures 1934), Hoi Polloi

(Columbia Pictures 1935), A Gem of a Jam (Columbia Pictures 1943), Micro Phonies (Columbia Pictures 1945))—created a distinct comedic trademark. Through their talent and labor, they joined the relatively small group of actors who constructed identifiable, recurrent comic personalities that they brought to the many parts they were scripted to play. "Groucho Marx just being Groucho Marx, with his moustache, cigar, slouch and leer, cannot be exploited by others. Red Skelton's variety of self-devised roles would appear to be protectible, as would the unique personal creations of Abbott and Costello, Laurel and Hardy and others of that genre. . . . '[W]e deal here with actors portraying themselves and developing their own characters.'" (*Lugosi, supra,* 603 P.2d at 432 (conc. opn. of Mosk, J.).)

In sum, society may recognize, as the Legislature has done here, that a celebrity's heirs and assigns have a legitimate protectable interest in exploiting the value to be obtained from merchandising the celebrity's image, whether that interest be conceived as a kind of natural property right or as an incentive for encouraging creative work. (See 1 McCarthy, The Rights of Publicity and Privacy (2d ed.2000) §§ 2.2-2.7, pp. 2-1 to 2-22 (McCarthy).) Although critics have questioned whether the right of publicity truly serves any social purpose (see, e.g., Madow, *supra,* 81 Cal. L.Rev. at pp. 178-238), there is no question that the Legislature has a rational basis for permitting celebrities and their heirs to control the commercial exploitation of the celebrity's likeness.

Although surprisingly few courts have considered in any depth the means of reconciling the right of publicity and the First Amendment, we follow those that have in concluding that depictions of celebrities amounting to little more than the appropriation of the celebrity's economic value are not protected expression under the First Amendment. . . .

It is admittedly not a simple matter to develop a test that will unerringly distinguish between forms of artistic expression protected by the First Amendment and those that must give way to the right of publicity. Certainly, any such test must incorporate the principle that the right of publicity cannot, consistent with the First Amendment, be a right to control the celebrity's image by censoring disagreeable portrayals. Once the celebrity thrusts himself or herself forward into the limelight, the First Amendment dictates that the right to comment on, parody, lampoon, and make other expressive uses of the celebrity image must be given broad scope. The necessary implication of this observation is that the right of publicity is essentially an economic right. What the right of publicity holder possesses is not a right of censorship, but a right to prevent others from misappropriating the economic value generated by the celebrity's fame through the merchandising of the "name, voice, signature, photograph, or likeness" of the celebrity. (§ 990.)

Beyond this precept, how may courts distinguish between protected and unprotected expression? Some commentators have proposed importing the fair use defense from copyright law (17 U.S.C. § 107), which has the advantage of employing an established doctrine developed from a related area of the law. (See Barnett, *First Amendment Limits on the Right of Publicity* (1995) 30 Tort & Ins. L.J. 635, 650-657; Coyne, *Toward a Modified Fair Use Defense in Right of Publicity Cases* (1988) 29 Wm. & Mary L.Rev. 781, 812- 820.) Others disagree, pointing to the murkiness of the fair use doctrine and arguing that the idea/expression dichotomy, rather than fair use, is the principal means of reconciling copyright protection and First Amendment rights. (2 McCarthy, *supra,* § 8.38, pp. 8-358 to 8-360; see also Kwall, *The Right of Publicity vs. The First Amendment: A Property and Liability Rule Analysis* (1994) 70 Ind. L.J. 47, 58, fn. 54.)

We conclude that a wholesale importation of the fair use doctrine into right of publicity law would not be advisable. At least two of the factors employed in the fair use test, "the nature of the copyrighted work" and "the amount and substantiality of the portion used" (17 U.S.C. § 107(2), (3)), seem particularly designed to be applied to the partial copying of works of authorship "fixed in [a] tangible medium of expression" (17 U.S.C. § 102); it is difficult to understand why these factors would be especially useful for determining whether the depiction of a celebrity likeness is protected by the First Amendment.

Nonetheless, the first fair use factor—"the purpose and character of the use" (17 U.S.C. § 107(1))—does seem particularly pertinent to the task of reconciling the rights of free expression and publicity. As the Supreme Court has stated, the central purpose of the inquiry into this fair use factor "is to see, in Justice Story's words, whether the new work merely 'supersede[s] the objects' of the original creation, or instead adds something new, with a further purpose or different character, altering the first with new expression, meaning, or message; it asks, in other words, whether and to what extent the new work is 'transformative.' Although such transformative use is not absolutely necessary for a finding of fair use, the goal of copyright, to promote science and the arts, is generally furthered by the creation of transformative works." (*Campbell v. Acuff-Rose Music, Inc.* (1994) 510 U.S. 569, 579, fn. omitted.)

This inquiry into whether a work is "transformative" appears to us to be necessarily at the heart of any judicial attempt to square the right of publicity with the First Amendment. As the above quotation suggests, both the First Amendment and copyright law have a common goal of encouragement of free expression and creativity, the former by protecting such expression from government interference, the latter by protecting the creative fruits of intellectual and artistic labor. (See 1 Nimmer on Copyright (2000 ed.) § 1.10, pp. 1-66.43 to 1-66.44 (Nimmer).) The right of publicity, at least theoretically, shares this goal with copyright law. (1 McCarthy, *supra,* § 2.6, pp. 2-14 to 2-19.) When artistic expression takes the form of a literal depiction or imitation of a celebrity for commercial gain, directly trespassing on the right of publicity without adding significant expression beyond that trespass, the state law interest in protecting the fruits of artistic labor outweighs the expressive interests of the imitative artist. (See *Zacchini, supra,* 433 U.S. at pp. 575-576, 97 S.Ct. 2849.)

On the other hand, when a work contains significant transformative elements, it is not only especially worthy of First Amendment protection, but it is also less likely to interfere with the economic interest protected by the right of publicity. As has been observed, works of parody or other distortions of the celebrity figure are not, from the celebrity fan's viewpoint, good substitutes for conventional depictions of the celebrity and therefore do not generally threaten markets for celebrity memorabilia that the right of publicity is designed to protect. (See *Cardtoons, L.C. v. Major League Baseball Players Association* (10th Cir. 1996) 95 F.3d 959, 974 (*Cardtoons*).) Accordingly, First Amendment protection of such works outweighs whatever interest the state may have in enforcing the right of publicity. The right-of-publicity holder continues to enforce the right to monopolize the production of conventional, more or less fungible, images of the celebrity.

Cardtoons, supra, 95 F.3d 959, cited by Saderup, is consistent with this "transformative" test. There, the court held that the First Amendment protected a company that produced trading cards caricaturing and parodying well-known major league baseball players against a claim brought under the Oklahoma right of publicity statute. The court concluded that "[t]he cards provide social commentary on public figures, major league baseball players, who are involved in a significant commercial enterprise, major league baseball," and that "[t]he cards are no less protected because they provide humorous rather than serious commentary." (*Cardtoons,* at p. 969.) The *Cardtoons* court weighed these First Amendment rights against what it concluded was the less-than-compelling interests advanced by the right of publicity outside the advertising context—especially in light of the reality that parody would not likely substantially impact the economic interests of celebrities—and found the cards to be a form of protected expression. (*Cardtoons,* at pp.

973-976.) While *Cardtoons* contained dicta calling into question the social value of the right of publicity, its conclusion that works parodying and caricaturing celebrities are protected by the First Amendment appears unassailable in light of the test articulated above.

We emphasize that the transformative elements or creative contributions that require First Amendment protection are not confined to parody and can take many forms, from factual reporting (see, e.g., *Rosemont Enterprises, Inc. v. Random House, Inc.* (1968) (N.Y.S.2d 122, 129, affd. mem. (1969) 301 N.Y.S.2d 948) to fictionalized portrayal (*Guglielmi, supra,* 603 P.2d 461; see also *Parks v. LaFace Records* (E.D.Mich.1999) 76 F.Supp.2d 775, 779-782 [use of civil rights figure Rosa Parks in song title is protected expression]), from heavy-handed lampooning (see *Hustler Magazine v. Falwell* (1988) 485 U.S. 46) to subtle social criticism (see Coplans et al., Andy Warhol (1970) pp. 50-52 [explaining Warhol's celebrity portraits as a critique of the celebrity phenomenon]).

Another way of stating the inquiry is whether the celebrity likeness is one of the "raw materials" from which an original work is synthesized, or whether the depiction or imitation of the celebrity is the very sum and substance of the work in question. We ask, in other words, whether a product containing a celebrity's likeness is so transformed that it has become primarily the defendant's own expression rather than the celebrity's likeness. And when we use the word "expression," we mean expression of something other than the likeness of the celebrity. We further emphasize that in determining whether the work is transformative, courts are not to be concerned with the quality of the artistic contribution—vulgar forms of expression fully qualify for First Amendment protection. (See, e.g., *Hustler Magazine v. Falwell, supra,* 485 U.S. 46; see also *Campbell v. Acuff-Rose Music, Inc., supra,* 510 U.S. at p. 582.) On the other hand, a literal depiction of a celebrity, even if accomplished with great skill, may still be subject to a right of publicity challenge. The inquiry is in a sense more quantitative than qualitative, asking whether the literal and imitative or the creative elements predominate in the work.

Furthermore, in determining whether a work is sufficiently transformative, courts may find useful a subsidiary inquiry, particularly in close cases: does the marketability and economic value of the challenged work derive primarily from the fame of the celebrity depicted? If this question is answered in the negative, then there would generally be no actionable right of publicity. When the value of the work comes principally from some source other than the fame of the celebrity—from the creativity, skill, and reputation of the artist—it may be presumed that sufficient transformative elements are present to warrant First Amendment protection. If the question is answered in the affirmative, however, it does not necessarily follow that the work is without First Amendment protection—it may still be a transformative work.

In sum, when an artist is faced with a right of publicity challenge to his or her work, he or she may raise as affirmative defense that the work is protected by the First Amendment inasmuch as it contains significant transformative elements or that the value of the work does not derive primarily from the celebrity's fame.

Although not entirely clear, the trial court seemed to be holding that *reproductions* of celebrity images are categorically outside First Amendment protection. The Court of Appeal was more explicit in adopting this rationale: "Simply put, although the First Amendment protects speech that is sold [citation], reproductions of an image, made to be sold for profit do not per se constitute speech." But this position has no basis in logic or authority. No one would claim that a published book, because it is one of many copies, receives less First Amendment protection than the original manuscript. It is true that the statute at issue here makes a distinction between a single and original work of fine art and a reproduction. . . .
Rather, the inquiry is into whether Saderup's work is sufficiently transformative. Correctly anticipating this inquiry, he argues that all portraiture involves creative decisions, that therefore no portrait portrays a mere literal likeness, and that accordingly all portraiture, including reproductions, is protected by the First Amendment. We reject any such categorical position. Without denying that all portraiture involves the making of artistic choices, we find it equally undeniable, under the test formulated above, that when an artist's skill and talent is manifestly subordinated to the overall goal of creating a conventional portrait of a celebrity so as to commercially exploit his or her fame, then the artist's right of free expression is outweighed by the right of publicity. As is the case with fair use in the area of copyright law, an artist depicting a celebrity must contribute something more than a "'"merely trivial"' variation, [but must create] something recognizably '"his own"'" (*L. Batlin & Son, Inc. v. Snyder* (2d Cir. 1976) 536 F.2d 486, 490), in order to qualify for legal protection.

On the other hand, we do not hold that all reproductions of celebrity portraits are unprotected by the First Amendment. The silkscreens of Andy Warhol, for example, have as their subjects the images of such celebrities as Marilyn Monroe, Elizabeth Taylor, and Elvis Presley. Through distortion and the careful manipulation of context, Warhol was able to convey a message that went beyond the commercial exploitation of celebrity images and became a form of ironic social comment on the dehumanization of celebrity itself. (See Coplans et al., *supra,* at p. 52.) Such expression may well be entitled to First Amendment protection. Although the distinction between protected and unprotected expression will sometimes be subtle, it is no more so than other distinctions triers of fact are called on to make in First Amendment jurisprudence. (See, e.g., *Miller v. California* (1973) 413 U.S. 15, 24 [requiring determination, in the context of work alleged to be obscene, of "whether the work, taken as a whole, lacks serious literary, artistic, political, or scientific value"].)

Turning to Saderup's work, we can discern no significant transformative or creative contribution. His undeniable skill is manifestly subordinated to the overall goal of creating literal, conventional depictions of The Three Stooges so as to exploit their fame. Indeed, were we to decide that Saderup's depictions were protected by the First Amendment, we cannot perceive how the right of publicity would remain a viable right other than in cases of falsified celebrity endorsements.

Moreover, the marketability and economic value of Saderup's work derives primarily from the fame of the celebrities depicted. While that fact alone does not necessarily mean the work receives no First Amendment protection, we can perceive no transformative elements in Saderup's works that would require such protection.

Saderup argues that it would be incongruous and unjust to protect parodies and other distortions of celebrity figures but not wholesome, reverential portraits of such celebrities. The test we articulate today, however, does not express a value judgment or preference for one type of depiction over another. Rather, it reflects a recognition that the Legislature has granted to the heirs and assigns of celebrities the property right to exploit the celebrities' images, and that certain forms of expressive activity protected by the First Amendment fall outside the boundaries of that right. Stated another way, we are concerned not with whether conventional celebrity images should be produced but with who produces them and, more pertinently, who appropriates the value from their production. Thus, under section 990, if Saderup wishes to continue to depict The Three Stooges as he has done, he may do so only with the consent of the right of publicity holder.

IV. Disposition

The judgment of the Court of Appeal is affirmed.

GEORGE, C.J., KENNARD, J., BAXTER, J., WERDEGAR, J., CHIN, J., BROWN, J., concur.

Notes and Questions

1. Zacchini v. Scripps-Howard Broadcasting is both an appropriation and right-of-publicity case. Why?
2. If Zacchini had missed his mark and crashed, would the news reporter have a First Amendment right to air the footage? What if the reporter caught an image of a crime occurring in the background, unrelated to Zacchini's act?
3. Why are Andy Warhol's silkscreen portraits transformative, but Gary Saderup's rendering of the Three Stooges is not? If Saderup had made a similar Warhol-style image of the Stooges, would the California Supreme Court accept that as a "fair use"?
4. Is the California Supreme Court's *Saderup* decision consistent with the Ninth Circuit's opinion in White v. Samsung Electronics? Isn't an image of a bejeweled robot in front of letters sufficiently transformative of Vanna White to constitute "fair use"? Does it matter that the robot appeared in a purely commercial advertisement?
5. What would it take to make an image of the Three Stooges transformative? Would it be enough to add macabre elements to their image to make them appear like Halloween ghouls? What if an artist decided to depict them as uniformed Nazis?
6. Privacy rights die with the individual, but the right of publicity, in some jurisdictions, can potentially extend forever. Should there be a time limit after which a famous dead person's image falls into the public domain? Does it make sense that you can sell shirts emblazoned with an image of Thomas Edison, but not one depicting Albert Einstein?

CHAPTER 5

REPRESENTING JOURNALISTS

Lawyers who represent news organizations or reporters typically encounter a number of challenging issues. Under the common law, for example, journalists do not enjoy a privilege in court that would permit them to conceal the identity of a confidential source. The reasons for this are fundamental to the way we understand press freedoms. In the United States, anyone can be a journalist. You do not need to go to school, work for a news organization, or even publish. And you certainly do not need to be licensed, as a doctor or lawyer needs to be. Journalists do not have clients like these other professionals—they have sources—and the relationship with their sources is not trust-based. Thus, unlike doctors and lawyers, who do enjoy a confidentiality privilege with respect to clients, journalists can be compelled to testify or face fines or jail for contempt of court.

Some states have enacted "shield laws" that protect journalists (and sources) from punishment under certain circumstances or placed protections in their state constitutions. There is, however, no federal shield law. In the first case infra, Branzburg v. Hayes, the Supreme Court took up the issue of whether the First Amendment privileged journalists from compelled testimony. While a plurality of four justices said that no privilege existed, a dissenting plurality of four said that a qualified privilege exists under certain circumstances. Although the final justice, Lewis Powell, concurred that no privilege existed under *Branzburg's* facts, he left open the possibility that a privilege would be appropriate in cases where the media is being abused by government. As a result, courts have begun to cite Justice Potter Stewart's dissent in *Branzburg* to justify a qualified privilege, especially in civil cases where the state's interest is less compelling.

Press lawyers are often asked to assess the potential for liability for news stories published by clients. Liability may occur when a journalist unfairly uses a copyrighted work's expression in a story. In Harper and Row v. Nation Enterprises, infra, "fair use" of copyrighted content is not merely a matter of how much of a work was used; the Supreme Court employs a broader four-fold inquiry into the substantiality of the use and the nature, purpose, and market of the work. In Food Lion, Inc. v. Capital Cities/ABC, Inc., a supermarket chain argued that it was entitled to damages for an expose that aired on ABC because the networks' reporters committed torts during newsgathering. Using Supreme Court speech precedents, the Fourth Circuit Court of Appeals ruled that Food Lion could not recover damages for the exposé's publication unless actual malice was present.

Reporter's Privilege

Should the law protect a journalist from disclosing the identity of a confidential source in court? If one asked most journalists and the media outlets they work for, the answer would be an unequivocal yes. Journalists who are compelled to reveal sources after promising secrecy risk not only their own credibility, but also their profession's credibility. If a whistleblower or other at-risk source cannot rely on a reporter's promise of confidentiality, how likely is it that the source will emerge from the shadows, especially if identification could place the source or the source's family in jeopardy? On the other hand, courts may need access to information to assure parties a speedy and fair trial. If a confidential source—or a journalist's private notes or outtakes—possesses knowledge or evidence that could exonerate the innocent or justly punish a wrongdoer, should the dictates of justice outweigh the professional concerns of journalists?

Judy Garland was a CBS star in the 1950s.

While there is no common-law reporter's privilege, forty states and the District of Columbia have enacted shield laws—statutes that, in one way or another, provide journalists with the type of protections against compelled testimony that doctors, lawyers, and clergy enjoy under the common law. But, in jurisdictions that do not have a shield law, journalists often risk jail if they refuse to comply with a court order to testify. In 1958, Marie Torre, a reporter for a New York daily newspaper, found herself in precisely that predicament. Torre had reported that an unidentified CBS executive made disparaging remarks about Judy Garland, who, at that time, had a show on that television network. Torre's source, who had heard the remarks firsthand, informed Torre of the statement on condition of confidentiality. When Garland subsequently sued for defamation, a court ordered Torre to identify her source. Faced with the prospect of jail time, Torre argued that the First Amendment protected her from compelled disclosure, a position that has reverberated in the courts ever since. While Torre ended up spending ten days in jail for contempt of court, the point was made. The U.S. Supreme Court addressed the issue in 1972, in Branzburg v. Hayes.

In the years since *Branzburg*, many journalists have chosen to go to jail in contempt of a court order to testify. *New York Times* reporter Myron Farber spent ten days in a New Jersey jail for refusing to identify a serial killer known as Dr. X. In 2005, *New York Times* reporter Judith Miller entered a Washington, DC-area jail to serve eighty-five days of her stayed eighteen-month sentence after she lost her appeal to the U.S. Supreme Court. She agreed to testify after her source, I. Lewis "Scooter" Libby, directly released Miller from her confidentiality promise. Libby was a White House staffer who illegally leaked the identity of a CIA operative.

While the case excerpts following *Branzburg* suggest that a qualified privilege may exist in civil cases, other courts, like the Fourth Circuit in the *Sterling* case infra, may be questioning the validity of using Justice Stewart's *Branzburg* dissent as the basis for a qualified reporter's privilege. The issue is interesting because, while Justice Powell provided the crucial fifth vote in *Branzburg*'s majority opinion, his concurring opinion contains dictum that suggests that he might have swung over to Stewart's dissent under different facts.

In *Sterling*, Pulitzer Prize-winning journalist James Risen appealed a court order to identify a national security source he interviewed for his book *State of War: The Secret History of the CIA and the Bush Administration*. While the Fourth Circuit rejected his appeal, Judge Gregory wrote a compelling dissent in which he argued that this is precisely the type of circumstance that the First Amendment should protect against. In June 2014, the U.S. Supreme Court dismissed Risen's appeal without argument. At that point, the only thing that stood between Risen and jail time was then-U.S. Attorney General Eric Holder. President Obama also publicly announced that he would support the enactment of a federal shield law. Such a law would help keep reporters like Risen out of jail when faced with a subpoena to testify in federal court. In 2015, Holder decided not to subpoena Risen, ending the threat of his incarceration.

Sterling was subsequently convicted on all counts, without the need for Risen's testimony.

BRANZBURG V. HAYES
408 U.S. 665 (1972)

Opinion of the Court by Mr. Justice WHITE, announced by THE CHIEF JUSTICE.

The issue in these cases is whether requiring newsmen to appear and testify before state or federal grand juries abridges the freedom of speech and press guaranteed by the First Amendment. We hold that it does not.

I.

. . . On November 15, 1969, the Courier-Journal carried a story under petitioner's by-line describing in detail his observations of two young residents of Jefferson County synthesizing hashish from marihuana, an activity which, they asserted, earned them about $5,000 in three weeks. The article included a photograph of a pair of hands working above a laboratory table on which was a substance identified by the caption as hashish. The article stated that petitioner had promised not to reveal the identity of the two hashish makers. Petitioner was shortly subpoenaed by the Jefferson County grand jury; he appeared, but refused to identify the individuals he had seen possessing marihuana or the persons he had seen making hashish from marihuana. A state trial court judge ordered petitioner to answer these questions and rejected his contention that the Kentucky reporters' privilege statute, Ky.Rev.Stat. § 421.100 (1962), the First Amendment of the United States Constitution, or §§ 1, 2 and 8 of the Kentucky Constitution authorized his refusal to answer. Petitioner then sought prohibition and mandamus in the Kentucky Court of Appeals on the same grounds, but the Court of Appeals denied the petition. Branzburg v. Pound, 461 S.W.2d 345 (1970), as modified on denial of rehearing, Jan. 22, 1971. It held that petitioner had abandoned his First Amendment argument in a supplemental memorandum he had filed and tacitly rejected his argument based on the Kentucky Constitution. It also construed Ky.Rev.Stat. § 421.100 as affording a newsman the privilege of refusing to divulge the identity of an informant who supplied him with information, but held that the statute did not permit a reporter to refuse to testify about events he had observed personally, including the identities of those persons he had observed.

The second case involving petitioner Branzburg arose out of his later story published on January 10, 1971, which described in detail the use of drugs in Frankfort, Kentucky. The article reported that in order to provide a comprehensive survey of the "drug scene" in Frankfort, petitioner had "spent two weeks interviewing several dozen drug users in the capital city" and had seen some of them smoking marihuana. A number of conversations with and observations of several unnamed drug users were recounted. Subpoenaed to appear before a Franklin County grand jury "to testify in the matter of violation of statutes concerning use and sale of drugs," petitioner Branzburg moved to quash the summons; the motion was denied, although an order was issued protecting Branzburg from revealing "confidential associations, sources or information" but requiring that he "answer any questions which concern or pertain to any criminal act, the commission of which was actually observed by (him)." Prior to the time he was slated to appear before the grand jury, petitioner sought mandamus and prohibition from the Kentucky Court of Appeals, arguing that if he were forced to go before the grand jury or to answer questions regarding the identity of informants or disclose information given to him in confidence, his effectiveness as a reporter would be greatly damaged. The Court of Appeals once again denied the requested writs, reaffirming its construction of Ky.Rev.Stat. § 421.100, and rejecting petitioner's claim of a First Amendment privilege. It distinguished Caldwell v. United States, 434 F.2d 1081 (CA9 1970), and it also announced its "misgivings" about that decision, asserting that it represented "a drastic departure from the generally recognized rule that the sources of information of a newspaper reporter are not privileged under the First Amendment." It characterized petitioner's fear that his ability to obtain news would be destroyed as "so tenuous that it does not, in the opinion of this court, present an issue of abridgement of the freedom of the press within the meaning of that term as used in the Constitution of the United States."

. . .

"Thus, the controversy continues as to whether a newsman's source of information should be privileged. However, that question is not before the Court in this case. The Legislature of Kentucky has settled the issue, having decided that a newsman's source of information is to be privileged. Because of this there is no point in citing Professor Wigmore and other authorities who speak against the grant of such a privilege. The question has been many times debated, and the Legislature has spoken. The only question before the Court is the construction of the term 'source of information' as it was intended by the Legislature."

. . .

II.

Petitioners Branzburg and Pappas and respondent Caldwell press First Amendment claims that may be simply put: that to gather news it is often necessary to agree either not to identify the source of information published or to publish only part of the facts revealed, or both; that if the reporter is nevertheless forced to reveal these confidences to a grand jury, the source so identified and other confidential sources of other reporters will be measurably deterred from furnishing publishable information, all to the detriment of the free flow of information protected by the First Amendment. Although the newsmen in these cases do not claim an absolute privilege against official interrogation in all circumstances, they assert that the reporter should not be forced either to appear or to testify before a grand jury or at trial until and unless sufficient grounds are shown for believing that the reporter possesses information relevant to a crime the grand jury is investigating, that the information the reporter has is unavailable from other sources, and that the need for the information is sufficiently compelling to override the claimed invasion of First Amendment interests occasioned by the disclosure. Principally relied upon are prior cases emphasizing the importance of the First Amendment guarantees to individual development and to our system of representative government, decisions requiring that official action with adverse impact on First Amendment rights be justified by a public interest that is "compelling" or "paramount," and those precedents establishing the principle that justifiable governmental goals may not be achieved by unduly broad means having an unnecessary impact on protected rights of speech, press, or association. The heart of the claim is that the burden on news gathering resulting from compelling reporters to disclose confidential information outweighs any public interest in obtaining the information.

We do not question the significance of free speech, press, or assembly to the country's welfare. Nor is it suggested that news gathering does not qualify for First Amendment protection; without some protection for seeking out the news, freedom of the press could be eviscerated. But these cases involve no intrusions upon speech or assembly, no prior restraint or restriction on what the press may publish, and no express or implied command that the press publish what it prefers to withhold. No exaction or tax for the privilege of publishing, and no penalty, civil or criminal, related to the content of published material is at issue here. The use of confidential sources by the press is not forbidden or restricted; reporters remain free to seek news from any source by means within the law. No attempt is made to require the press to publish its sources of information or indiscriminately to disclose them on request.

The sole issue before us is the obligation of reporters to respond to grand jury subpoenas as other citizens do and to answer questions relevant to an investigation into the commission of crime. Citizens generally are not constitutionally immune from grand jury subpoenas; and neither the First Amendment nor any other constitutional provision protects the average citizen from disclosing to a grand jury information that he has received in confidence. The claim is, however, that reporters are exempt from these obligations because if forced to respond to subpoenas and identify their sources or disclose other confidences, their informants will refuse or be reluctant to furnish newsworthy information in the future. This asserted burden on news gathering is said to make compelled testimony from newsmen constitutionally suspect and to require a privileged position for them.

It is clear that the First Amendment does not invalidate every incidental burdening of the press that may result from the enforcement of civil or criminal statutes of general applicability. Under prior cases, otherwise valid laws serving substantial public interests may be enforced against the press as against others, despite the possible burden that may be imposed. The Court has emphasized that "(t)he publisher of a newspaper has no special immunity from the application of general laws. He has no special privilege to invade the rights and liberties of others." Associated Press v. NLRB, 301 U.S. 103, 132-133 (1937). . . .

The prevailing view is that the press is not free to publish with impunity everything and anything it desires to publish. Although it may deter or regulate what is said or published, the press may not circulate knowing or reckless falsehoods damaging to private reputation without subjecting itself to liability for damages, including punitive damages, or even criminal prosecution. . . . A newspaper or a journalist may also be punished for contempt of court, in appropriate circumstances. Craig v. Harney, 331 U.S. 367, 377-378 (1947).

It has generally been held that the First Amendment does not guarantee the press a constitutional right of special access to information not available to the public generally. . . .

Despite the fact that news gathering may be hampered, the press is regularly excluded from grand jury proceedings, our own conferences, the meetings of other official bodies gathered in executive session, and the meetings of private organizations. Newsmen have no constitutional right of access to the scenes of crime or disaster when the general public is excluded, and they may be prohibited from attending or publishing information about trials if such restrictions are necessary to assure a defendant a fair trial before an impartial tribunal. . . .

It is thus not surprising that the great weight of authority is that newsmen are not exempt from the normal duty of appearing before a grand jury and answering questions relevant to a criminal investigation. At common law, courts consistently refused to recognize the existence of any privilege authorizing a newsman to refuse to reveal confidential information to a grand jury. . . . In 1958, a news gatherer asserted for the first time that the First Amendment exempted confidential information from public disclosure pursuant to a subpoena issued in a civil suit, Garland v. Torre, 259 F.2d 545 (*2D CIR.*), cert. denied, 358 U.S. 910 (1958), but the claim was denied, and this argument has been almost uniformly rejected since then although there are occasional dicta that, in circumstances not presented here, a newsman might be excused. . . . These courts have applied the presumption against the existence of an asserted testimonial privilege, United States v. Bryan, 339 U.S. 323, 331 (1950), and have concluded that the First Amendment interest asserted by the newsman was outweighed by the general obligation of a citizen to appear before a grand jury or at trial, pursuant to a subpoena, and give what information he possesses. The opinions of the state courts in Branzburg and Pappas are typical of the prevailing view, although a few recent cases, such as Caldwell, have recognized and given effect to some form of constitutional newsman's privilege. . . .

. . .

A number of States have provided newsmen a statutory privilege of varying breadth, but the majority have not done so, and none has been provided by federal statute. Until now the only testimonial privilege for unofficial witnesses that is rooted in the Federal Constitution is the Fifth Amendment privilege against compelled self-incrimination. We are asked to create another by interpreting the First Amendment to grant newsmen a testimonial privilege that other citizens do not enjoy. This we decline to do. Fair and effective law enforcement aimed at providing security for the person and property of the individual is a fundamental function of government, and the grand jury plays an important, constitutionally mandated role in this process. On the records now before us, we perceive no basis for holding that the public interest in law enforcement and in ensuring effective grand jury proceedings is insufficient to override the consequential, but uncertain, burden on news gathering that is said to result from insisting that reporters, like other citizens, respond to relevant questions put to them in the course of a valid grand jury investigation or criminal trial.

. . .

The argument for such a constitutional privilege rests heavily on those cases holding that the infringement of protected First Amendment rights must be no broader than necessary to achieve a permissible governmental purpose, see cases cited at n. 19, supra. We do not deal, however, with a governmental institution that has abused its proper function, as a legislative committee does when it "expose(s) for the sake of exposure." Watkins v. United States, 354 U.S. 178, 200 (1957). Nothing in the record indicates that these grand juries were "prob(ing) at will and without relation to existing need." DeGregory v. Attorney General of New Hampshire, 383 U.S. 825, 829 (1966). Nor did the grand juries attempt to invade protected First Amendment rights by forcing wholesale disclosure of names and organizational affiliations for a purpose that was not germane to the determination of whether crime has been committed ... and the characteristic secrecy of grand jury proceedings is a further protection against the undue invasion of such rights. See Fed. Rule Crim. Proc. 6(e). The investigative power of the grand jury is necessarily broad if its public responsibility is to be adequately discharged. Costello v. United States, 350 U.S. 359, at 364 (1956).

The requirements of those cases, see n. 18, supra, which hold that a State's interest must be "compelling" or "paramount" to justify even an indirect burden on First Amendment rights, are also met here. As we have indicated, the investigation of crime by the grand jury implements a fundamental governmental role of securing the safety of the person and property of the citizen, and it appears to us that calling reporters to give testimony in the manner and for the reasons that other citizens are called "bears a reasonable relationship to the achievement of the governmental purpose asserted as its justification." Bates v. Little Rock, supra, 361 U.S. at 525. If the test is that the government "convincingly show a substantial relation between the information sought and a subject of overriding and compelling state interest," ... it is quite apparent (1) that the State has the necessary interest in extirpating the traffic in illegal drugs, in forestalling assassination attempts on the President, and in preventing the community from being disrupted by violent disorders endangering both persons and property; and (2) that, based on the stories Branzburg and Caldwell wrote and Pappas' admitted conduct, the grand jury called these reporters as they would others—because it was likely that they could supply information to help the government determine whether illegal conduct had occurred and, if it had, whether there was sufficient evidence to return an indictment.

. . .

III.

We turn, therefore, to the disposition of the cases before us. From what we have said, it necessarily follows that the decision in United States v. Caldwell, No. 70-57, must be reversed. If there is no First Amendment privilege to refuse to answer the relevant and material questions asked during a good-faith grand jury investigation, then it is a fortiori true that there is no privilege to refuse to appear before such a grand jury until the Government demonstrates some "compelling need" for a newsman's testimony. Other issues were urged upon us, but since they were not passed upon by the Court of Appeals, we decline to address them in the first instance.

The decisions in No. 70-85, Branzburg v. Hayes and Branzburg v. Meigs, must be affirmed. Here, petitioner refused to answer questions that directly related to criminal conduct that he had observed and written about. The Kentucky Court of Appeals noted that marihuana is defined as a narcotic drug by statute, Ky.Rev.Stat. § 218.010(14) (1962), and that unlicensed possession or compounding of it is a felony punishable by both fine and imprisonment. Ky.Rev.Stat. § 218.210 (1962). It held that petitioner "saw the commission of the statutory felonies of unlawful possession of marijuana and the unlawful conversion of it into hashish," in Branzburg v. Pound, 461 S.W.2d, at 346. Petitioner may be presumed to have observed similar violations of the state narcotics laws during the research he did for the story that forms the basis of the subpoena in Branzburg v. Meigs. In both cases, if what petitioner wrote was true, he had direct information to provide the grand jury concerning the omission of serious crimes.

The only question presented at the present time in In re Pappas, No. 70-94, is whether petitioner Pappas must appear before the grand jury to testify pursuant to subpoena. The Massachusetts Supreme Judicial Court characterized the record in this case as "meager," and it is not clear what petitioner will be asked by the grand jury. It is not even clear that he will be asked to divulge information received in confidence. We affirm the decision of the Massachusetts Supreme Judicial Court and hold that petitioner must appear before the grand jury to answer the questions put to him, subject, of course, to the supervision of the presiding judge as to "the propriety, purposes, and scope of the grand jury inquiry and the pertinence of the probable testimony."

So ordered.

Mr. Justice POWELL, concurring.
I add this brief statement to emphasize what seems to me to be the limited nature of the Court's holding. The Court does not hold that newsmen, subpoenaed to testify before a grand jury, are without constitutional rights with respect to the gathering of news or in safeguarding their sources. Certainly, we do not hold, as suggested in Mr. Justice STEWART's dissenting opinion, that state and federal authorities are free to "annex" the news media as "an investigative arm of government." The solicitude repeatedly shown by this Court for First Amendment freedoms should be sufficient assurance against any such effort, even if one seriously believed that the media-properly free and untrammeled in the fullest sense of these terms-were not able to protect themselves.

As indicated in the concluding portion of the opinion, the Court states that no harassment of newsmen will be tolerated. If a newsman believes that the grand jury investigation is not being conducted in good faith he is not without remedy. Indeed, if the newsman is called upon to give information bearing only a remote and tenuous relationship to the subject of the investigation, or if he has some other reason to believe that his testimony implicates confidential source relationship without a legitimate need of law enforcement, he will have access to the court on a motion to quash and an appropriate protective order may be entered. The asserted claim to privilege should be judged on its facts by the striking of a proper balance between freedom of the press and the obligation of all citizens to give relevant testimony with respect to criminal conduct. The balance of these vital constitutional and societal interests on a case-by-case basis accords with the tried and traditional way of adjudicating such questions.

In short, the courts will be available to newsmen under circumstances where legitimate First Amendment interests require protection.

. . .

Mr. Justice STEWART, with whom Mr. Justice BRENNAN and Mr. Justice MARSHALL join, dissenting.
The Court's crabbed view of the First Amendment reflects a disturbing insensitivity to the critical role of an independent press in our society. The question whether a reporter has a constitutional right to a confidential relationship with his source is of first impression here, but the principles that should guide our decision are as basic as any to be found in the

Constitution. While Mr. Justice POWELL'S enigmatic concurring opinion gives some hope of a more flexible view in the future, the Court in these cases holds that a newsman has no First Amendment right to protect his sources when called before a grand jury. . . .

II.

. . .

In striking the proper balance between the public interest in the efficient administration of justice and the First Amendment guarantee of the fullest flow of information, we must begin with the basic proposition that because of their "delicate and vulnerable" nature, NAACP v. Button, 371 U.S., at 433, and their transcendent importance for the just functioning of our society, First Amendment rights require special safeguards.

. . .

This Court has erected such safeguards when government, by legislative investigation or other investigative means, has attempted to pierce the shield of privacy inherent in freedom of association. In no previous case have we considered the extent to which the First Amendment limits the grand jury subpoena power. . . .

Thus, when an investigation impinges on First Amendment rights, the government must not only show that the inquiry is of "compelling and overriding importance" but it must also "convincingly" demonstrate that the investigation is "substantially related" to the information sought.

Governmental officials must, therefore, demonstrate that the information sought is clearly relevant to a precisely defined subject of governmental inquiry. Watkins, supra; Sweezy, supra. They must demonstrate that it is reasonable to think the witness in question has that information. Sweezy, supra; Gibson, supra. And they must show that there is not any means of obtaining the information less destructive of First Amendment liberties. . . .

These requirements, which we have recognized in decisions involving legislative and executive investigations, serve established policies reflected in numerous First Amendment decisions arising in other contexts. The requirements militate against vague investigations that, like vague laws, create uncertainty and needlessly discourage First Amendment activity. . . .

This is not to say that a grand jury could not issue a subpoena until such a showing were made, and it is not to say that a newsman would be in any way privileged to ignore any subpoena that was issued. Obviously, before the government's burden to make such a showing were triggered, the reporter would have to move to quash the subpoena, asserting the basis on which he considered the particular relationship a confidential one.

. . .

C.B.S., INC. V. SUPERIOR COURT

149 Cal. Rptr. 421 (Ct. App. 1978)

SUMMARY

In a prosecution of defendants charged with selling a controlled substance, PCP, commonly known as "Angel Dust," defendants caused a subpoena duces tecum to be issued and served on a television broadcasting company's custodian of records to discover certain videotapes, tape recordings and motion pictures of meetings between defendants and narcotics officers of a sheriff's department. These materials had been compiled by the broadcasting company for broadcast as a television segment regarding the dangers and increase in the use of "Angel Dust." The broadcasting company moved to quash the subpoena on grounds that no showing of good cause had been made; that Evid. Code, § 1070, made the subpoena unenforceable; and that its enforcement would violate the company's First Amendment rights under the United States Constitution, as well as its rights under Cal. Const., art. I, § 2. After a hearing, the court denied the company's motion, holding that defendants had made the requisite showing of good cause, and that, in weighing defendants' right to a fair trial against the company's rights, the interests of defendants should prevail.

The Court of Appeal denied the broadcasting company's petition for a writ of prohibition commanding the superior court to set aside its order denying its motion to quash the subpoena. The court held that Evid. Code, § 1070, which protects unpublished material gathered for a newspaper or magazine and information obtained for radio or television reporting, was not applicable to the video and audio tapes sought by defendants. Since the three undercover agents, whose identity the broadcasting company had agreed with the sheriff's department to protect, had revealed their identities and roles when called as witnesses at the hearing on the broadcasting company's motion to quash the subpoena, the underlying purpose of the confidentiality was lost. The court held that to deny discovery would directly impair defendant's right to a fair trial, and that in balancing defendants interest in a fair trial against the tenuous restraint on the broadcasting company's right to gather information, which affirmance of the trial court's order would entail, the necessity of permitting discovery became clear. The court held that the trial court's discovery order was impermissibly broad and that the infringement upon the broadcasting company's First Amendment rights must be no greater than essential to guarantee the defendants' constitutional rights; and that to protect those First Amendment rights, an examination in camera of the subpoenaed materials must be made to determine how discovery might be limited. (Opinion by Newsom, J., with Racanelli, P. J., and Elkington, J., Concurring.)

PEOPLE V. KORKALA
472 N.Y.S.2d 310 (App. Div. 1984)

PER CURIAM.
. . . An order denying a motion by CBS, Inc., to quash a subpoena duces tecum issued by the District Attorney for the production of video and audio tapes, including unpublished outtakes of interviews with the defendant in a pending criminal prosecution conducted by a CBS news correspondent, is modified. The privilege against disclosure provided by the Shield Law (Civil Rights Law, § 79-h) is not absolute, and may be invoked only after there has been established an express or implied agreement of confidentiality; no such understanding or expectation of confidentiality existed in regard to interviews conducted for the purpose of television broadcast. Moreover, the qualified privilege against compelled disclosure of a news reporter's material or source provided by the First Amendment may not be invoked; the unbroadcast material is relevant to the subject of the prosecution and is not obtainable from any other source; however, since it is not apparent that said material is necessary to the prosecution, the subpoenaed material should be delivered to the trial court for an *in camera* inspection and a determination as to the necessity for use of any of such material in respect to any defense offered by defendant during the course of the trial.

HERBERT V. LANDO
441 U.S. 153 (1979)

In a defamation action brought by a "public figure," plaintiff sought order compelling discovery. The United States District Court for the Southern District of New York, 73 F.R.D. 387, granted discovery motion, and defendants filed interlocutory appeal. The Court of Appeals for the Second Circuit, 568 F.2d 974, remanded with directions, and petition for certiorari was granted. The Supreme Court, Mr. Justice White, held that where member of the press is alleged to have circulated damaging falsehoods and is sued for injury to reputation of a "public figure" plaintiff, who is required to prove "actual malice," First Amendment does not bar plaintiff from inquiring into editorial process and state of mind of those responsible for publication.

Reversed.

DEMOCRATIC NATIONAL COMMITTEE V. MCCORD
356 F. Supp 1394 (D.D.C. 1973)

CHARLES R. RICHEY, District Judge.
The Court is well aware that other courts in "civil" and "criminal" cases, and the Supreme Court of the United States in a landmark case involving a newsman's testimony before a grand jury, have been reluctant in the absence of a statute to recognize even a qualified newsman's privilege from disclosure of confidential news sources. In view of the decisions and circumstances present in the above-cited cases, it is instructive to note what is *not* present in the instant cases. These cases are not "criminal" cases, and even though they are primarily actions for money damages, their importance transcends anything yet encountered in the annals of American judicial history. Moreover, Movants are not parties to the actions, but have merely been called to testify and produce documents at deposition. The parties on whose behalf the subpoenas were issued have not demonstrated that the testimony and materials sought go to the "heart of [their] claim," as was found to be true in the case of Garland v. Torre. What *is* ultimately involved in these cases between the major political parties is the very integrity of the judicial and executive branches of our government and our political processes, for without information concerning the workings of the government, the public's confidence in that integrity will inevitably suffer. This is especially true where, as here, strong allegations have been made of corruption within the highest circles of government, and in a campaign for the Presidency

itself. This Court cannot blind itself to the possible "chilling effect" the enforcement of these broad subpoenas would have on the flow of information to the press, and so to the public. This Court stands convinced that if it allows the discouragement of investigative reporting into the highest levels of government no amount of legal theorizing could allay the public suspicions engendered by its actions and by the matters alleged in these lawsuits.

It is of critical importance in these cases to note and bear in mind that the main purpose of the judicial system-a search for the truth-must be flexible in order to accommodate itself to the needs of our times and the needs of an individual case. The cases at bar are unprecedented in the annals of legal history and have raised more than one issue of first impression. In such circumstances, the Court is called upon to fashion a remedy consistent with the ends of justice. In proceeding to fashion a remedy in the instant cases, the Court remains in full accord with the language of Mr. Justice Powell's concurring opinion in Branzburg v. Hayes, in which he stated:

"The asserted claim to privilege should be judged on its facts by the striking of a proper balance between freedom of the press and the obligation of all citizens to give relevant testimony. . . . The balance of these vital constitutional and societal interests on a case-by-case basis accords with the tried and traditional way of adjudicating such questions."

The Court has noted the above constitutional interest-an interest which translates into nothing less than the problem of maintaining "an informed public capable of conducting its own affairs. . . ." Against this interest must be balanced the interests of the parties to receive evidence going to the substance of their claims. Yet there has been no showing by the parties that alternative sources of evidence have been exhausted or even approached as to the possible gleaning of facts alternatively available from the Movants herein. Nor has there been any positive showing of the materiality of the documents and other materials sought by the subpoenas. In the face of these considerations the parties still insist that Movants in effect open their doors for inspection. The scales, however, are heavily weighted in the Movant's favor.

The recognition that Movants are entitled to a qualified privilege from having to testify under the circumstances of these cases is not totally without legal precedent. Thus, in Baker v. F. & F. Investment, the Second Circuit held that a reporter could not be compelled by civil discovery to reveal a confidential source who had informed him of discriminatory practices by sellers of homes in the City of Chicago. The Court stated:

"[T]he [Supreme] Court's concern with the integrity of the grand jury as an investigating arm of the criminal justice system distinguishes *Branzburg* from the case presently before us. If, as Mr. Justice Powell noted in that case, instances will arise in which First Amendment values outweigh the duty of a journalist to testify even in the context of a criminal investigation, surely in civil cases, courts must recognize that the public interest in non-disclosure of journalists' confidential news sources will often be weightier than the private interest in compelled disclosure."

U.S. v. STERLING
724 F.3d 482 (4th Cir. 2013)

Before TRAXLER, Chief Judge, and GREGORY and DIAZ, Circuit Judges.
Affirmed in part, reversed in part, and remanded by published opinion. Chief Judge TRAXLER wrote the opinion for the court in Part I, in which Judge GREGORY and Judge DIAZ joined. Chief Judge TRAXLER wrote the opinion for the court in Parts II–V, in which Judge DIAZ joined. Judge GREGORY wrote the opinion for the court in Part VI, in which Chief Judge TRAXLER and Judge DIAZ joined. Judge GREGORY wrote the opinion for the court in Part VII, in which Judge DIAZ joined. Chief Judge TRAXLER wrote an opinion concurring in part and dissenting in part as to Part VII. Judge GREGORY wrote an opinion dissenting as to Parts II–V.

TRAXLER, Chief Judge:
Jeffrey Sterling is a former CIA agent who has been indicted for, inter alia, the unauthorized retention and disclosure of national defense information, in violation of the Espionage Act, 18 U.S.C. § 793(d) & (e). The indictment followed the grand jury's probable cause determination that Sterling illegally disclosed classified information about a covert CIA operation pertaining to the Iranian nuclear weapons operation to James Risen, for publication in a book written by Risen, and that he may have done so in retaliation for the CIA's decision to terminate his employment and to interfere with his efforts to publish such classified information in his personal memoirs. Prior to trial, the district court made three evidentiary rulings that are the subject of this appeal. We affirm in part, reverse in part, and remand for further proceedings.

I. Background

A.

According to the indictment, Defendant Jeffrey Sterling was hired as a CIA case officer in 1993, and granted a top secret security clearance. As a condition of his hire, and on several occasions thereafter, Sterling signed agreements with the CIA explicitly acknowledging that he was not permitted to retain or disclose classified information that he obtained in the course of his employment, without prior authorization from the CIA, and that doing so could be a criminal offense.

In November 1998, the CIA assigned Sterling to a highly classified program intended to impede Iran's efforts to acquire or develop nuclear weapons ("Classified Program No. 1"). Sterling also served as the case officer for a covert asset ("Human Asset No. 1") who was assisting the CIA with this program. In May 2000, Sterling was reassigned and his involvement with Classified Program No. 1 ended.

In August 2000, shortly after Sterling's reassignment and after being told that he had not met performance targets, Sterling filed an equal opportunity complaint alleging that the CIA had denied him certain assignments because he was African American. The EEO office of the CIA investigated Sterling's complaint and determined that it was without merit. In August 2001, Sterling filed a federal lawsuit against the CIA alleging that he had been the victim of racial discrimination, and seeking monetary compensation. Several settlement demands were rejected, and the lawsuit was dismissed in March 2004, following the government's invocation of the state secrets doctrine. We affirmed the dismissal. *See* Sterling v. Tenet, 416 F.3d 338, 341 (4th Cir. 2005).

Sterling was officially terminated from the CIA on January 31, 2002, but he had been "outprocessed" and effectively removed from service in October 2001. As part of his termination, Sterling was asked to sign a final acknowledgment of his continuing legal obligation not to disclose classified information. Sterling refused.

On November 4, 2001, James Risen published an article in The New York Times, under the headline "Secret C.I.A. Site in New York Was Destroyed on Sept. 11." J.A. 655. A "former agency official" was cited as a source. J.A. 655. In March 2002, Risen published an article about Sterling's discrimination suit in The New York Times, under the headline "Fired by C.I.A., He Says Agency Practiced Bias." J.A. 156, 725. The article states that Sterling provided Risen with a copy of one of his CIA performance evaluations, which is identified as a classified document. The article also states that Sterling "relished his secret assignment to recruit Iranians as spies." J.A. 156.

. . .

On April 3, 2003, Risen informed the CIA and the National Security Council that he had classified information concerning Classified Program No. 1 and that he intended to publish a story about it in The New York Times. In response, senior administration officials, including National Security Advisor Condoleezza Rice and Director of the CIA George Tenet, met with Risen and Jill Abramson, then Washington Bureau Chief of The New York Times, to discuss the damage that publication would cause to national security interests and the danger to the personal safety of the CIA asset involved in the operation. Several days later, Ms. Abramson advised the administration that the newspaper would not publish the story.

. . .

Although The New York Times had agreed not to publish information about Classified Program No. 1, Risen published a book, State of War: The Secret History of the CIA and the Bush Administration ("State of War "), in January 2006, which did disclose the classified information. J.A. 721. Specifically, Chapter 9 of the book, entitled "A Rogue Operation," reveals details about Classified Program No. 1. J.S.A. 219-32. In the book, Risen entitled the program "Operation Merlin" and described it as a "failed attempt by the CIA to have a former Russian scientist provide flawed nuclear weapon blueprints to Iran." J.A. 722. Risen does not reveal his sources for the classified information in Chapter 9, nor has he indicated whether he had more than one source. However, much of the chapter is told from the point of view of a CIA case officer responsible for handling Human Asset No. 1. The chapter also describes two classified meetings at which Sterling was the only common attendee.

B.

On December 22, 2010, a federal grand jury indicted Sterling on six counts . . . .

On May 23, 2011, Attorney General Eric Holder authorized the government to issue a trial subpoena seeking Risen's testimony about the identity of his source for information about Classified Program No. 1 and asking Risen to confirm that statements attributed to sources were actually made by those sources. The government also filed a motion in limine to admit Risen's testimony. Risen moved to quash the subpoena and for a protective order, asserting that he was protected from compelled testimony by the First Amendment or, in the alternative, by a federal common-law reporter's privilege.

The motions were denied in part and granted in part by the district court. The subpoena was "quashed for Risen's testimony about his reporting and source(s) except to the extent that Risen [would] be required to provide testimony that authenticates the accuracy of his journalism, subject to a protective order." United States v. Sterling, 818 F.Supp.2d 945, 947 (E.D.Va.2011). The district court held that Risen had "a qualified First Amendment reporter's privilege that may be invoked when a subpoena either seeks information about confidential sources or is issued to harass or intimidate the journalist," *id.* at 951 (emphasis added), and that the government could overcome the privilege only by meeting the three-part test that this circuit established for reporters' claims of privilege in civil cases in LaRouche v. National Broadcasting Co., 780 F.2d 1134 (4th Cir. 1986). The district court held that, while the information sought was clearly relevant under the first prong of the LaRouche test, the Government had failed to demonstrate that the information was unavailable from other means and that it had a compelling interest in presenting it to the jury.

. . .

In a majority opinion written by Chief Judge Traxler, we now reverse the district court's order holding that Risen has a reporter's privilege that entitles him to refuse to testify at trial concerning the source and scope of the classified national defense information illegally disclosed to him (Issue I). . . .

TRAXLER, Chief Judge, writing for the court on Issue I:

II. The Reporter's Privilege Claim

We begin with the government's appeal of the district court order quashing the trial subpoena issued to Risen on the basis of a First Amendment reporter's privilege, and Risen's challenge to our jurisdiction to consider this portion of the appeal.

A. Jurisdiction

Risen contends that we lack jurisdiction to consider the district court's ruling under 18 U.S.C. § 3731, because the district court stated that the limitations on Risen's testimony might be reconsidered under the LaRouche test as the testimony developed at trial. We disagree.

. . .

B. The First Amendment Claim

1.

There is no First Amendment testimonial privilege, absolute or qualified, that protects a reporter from being compelled to testify by the prosecution or the defense in criminal proceedings about criminal conduct that the reporter personally witnessed or participated in, absent a showing of bad faith, harassment, or other such non-legitimate motive, even though the reporter promised confidentiality to his source. In Branzburg v. Hayes, 408 U.S. 665 . . . .

Notwithstanding the clarity of Justice White's opinion for the Court in Branzburg, and the fact that Justice Powell joined that opinion, Risen argues that Justice Powell's concurring opinion in Branzburg should instead be interpreted as a tacit endorsement of Justice Stewart's dissenting opinion, which argued in favor of recognizing a First Amendment privilege in criminal cases that could be overcome only if the government carries the heavy burden of establishing a compelling interest or need. *See Branzburg*, 408 U.S. at 739, 743 (Stewart, J., dissenting).

We cannot accept this strained reading of Justice Powell's opinion. By his own words, Justice Powell concurred in Justice White's opinion for the majority, and he rejected the contrary view of Justice Stewart . . .

To the extent Justice Powell addressed any further inquiry that might take place in a criminal proceeding, he appeared to include within the realm of harassment a request that "implicates confidential source relationships without a legitimate need of law enforcement," *id.* at 710 (emphasis added), and he again rejected the dissent's contrary view that the heavy burdens of the three-part, compelling interest test were appropriate.

In LaRouche [v. National Broadcasting Co., 780 F.2d 1134 (4th Cir. 1986)], we considered a civil litigant's right to compel evidence from a reporter and the First Amendment claim of the press to protect its newsgathering activities. We recognized a reporter's privilege in this civil context that could only be overcome if the litigant met the three-part test that the Branzburg Court rejected in the criminal context. . . .

. . .

[W]e have continued to recognize the important distinction between enforcing subpoenas issued to reporters in criminal proceedings and enforcing subpoenas issued to reporters in civil litigation. Subpoenas in criminal cases are driven by the quite different and compelling public interest in effective criminal investigation and prosecution, an interest that simply is not present in civil cases. . . .

There is good reason for this distinction between civil and criminal cases. It has roots in both the majority and concurring opinions in Branzburg, both of which highlight the critical importance of criminal proceedings and the right to compel all available evidence in such matters. . . .

Like the Branzburg reporters, Risen has "direct information . . . concerning the commission of serious crimes." Branzburg, 408 U.S. at 709. Indeed, he can provide the only first-hand account of the commission of a most serious crime indicted by the grand jury—the illegal disclosure of classified, national security information by one who was entrusted by our government to protect national security, but who is charged with having endangered it instead. The subpoena for Risen's testimony was not issued in bad faith or for the purposes of harassment. *See id.* at 707–08; *id.* at 709–10 (Powell, J., concurring). Risen is not being "called upon to give information bearing only a remote and tenuous relationship to the subject of the investigation," and there is no "reason to believe that his testimony implicates confidential source relationships without a legitimate need of law enforcement." *Id.* at 710 (Powell, J., concurring). Nor is the government attempting to "annex" Risen as its "investigative arm." *Id.* at 709 (internal quotation marks omitted). Rather, the government seeks to compel evidence that Risen alone possesses—evidence that goes to the heart of the prosecution.

. . .

The only constitutional, testimonial privilege that Risen was entitled to invoke was the Fifth Amendment privilege against self-incrimination, but he has been granted immunity from prosecution for his potential exposure to criminal liability. Accordingly, we reverse the district court's decision granting Risen a qualified First Amendment reporter's privilege that would shield him from being compelled to testify in these criminal proceedings.

III. The Common-Law Privilege Claim

Risen next argues that, even if Branzburg prohibits our recognition of a First Amendment privilege, we should recognize a qualified, federal common-law reporter's privilege protecting confidential sources. We decline to do so.

A.

In the course of rejecting the First Amendment claim in Branzburg, the Supreme Court also plainly observed that the common law recognized no such testimonial privilege . . .

B.

Risen does not take issue with the clarity of Branzburg's statements regarding the state of the common law. Rather, he argues that Federal Rule of Evidence 501, as interpreted by the Supreme Court in Jaffee v. Redmond, 518 U.S. 1 (1996), grants us authority to reconsider the question and now grant the privilege. We disagree.

. . .

Rule 501 seems to be more notable for what it failed to do, than for what it did. The proposed Rules originally "defined [nine] specific nonconstitutional privileges which the federal courts [would have been compelled to] recognize (i.e. required reports, lawyer-client, psychotherapist-patient, husband-wife, communications to clergymen, political vote, trade secrets, secrets of state and other official information, and identity of informer)" and "provided that only those privileges set forth [therein] or in some other Act of Congress could be recognized by the federal courts." Fed. R. Evid. 501 advisory committee's note; *see* also *Jaffee*, 518 U.S. at 8 n. 7 This exclusive list of enumerated privileges was ultimately rejected. . . .

In Jaffee, the Supreme Court recognized a psychotherapist-patient privilege protecting private communications that took place during counseling sessions between a police officer and a licensed clinical social worker following a fatal shooting. Applying Rule 501, the Court weighed the competing interests and concluded that the plaintiff's interest in obtaining evidence of the confidential communications in the ensuing excessive-force action was outweighed by the patient's private interest in maintaining confidence and trust with his mental health provider and the public's interest in protecting that privacy in order to "facilitat[e] the provision of appropriate treatment for individuals suffering the effects of a mental or emotional problem." *Id.* at 11. As noted above, the Court also relied, in part, upon the fact that a psychotherapist-patient privilege was one of the nine, enumerated privileges considered when Rule 501 was adopted and had found near unanimous support in state laws as well. Contrary to Risen's claim on appeal, Rule 501 and the Supreme Court's use of it to recognize a psychotherapist-patient privilege in Jaffee does not authorize us to ignore Branzburg or support our recognition of a common-law reporter-source privilege today.

. . .

C.

Even if we were at liberty to reconsider the existence of a common-law reporter's privilege under Rule 501, we would decline to do so.

. . .

Risen contends that the public and private recognizing a reporter's privilege "are surely as significant public interest at stake in patient and psychotherapist communication." Risen's Brief at 50. But we see several critical distinctions.

1.

First, unlike in the case of the spousal, attorney-client, and psychotherapist-patient privileges that have been recognized, the reporter-source privilege does not share the same relational privacy interests or ultimate goal. The recognized privileges promote the public's interest in full and frank communications between persons in special relationships by protecting the confidentiality of their private communications. Jaffee, 518 U.S. at 10. A reporter's privilege might also promote free and full discussion between a reporter and his source, but Risen does not seek to protect from public disclosure the "confidential communications" made to him. *Id.* Risen published information conveyed to him by his source or sources. His primary goal is to protect the identity of the person or persons who communicated with him because their communications violated federal, criminal laws. . . .

We are also mindful that the Court in Branzburg considered and was unpersuaded by a virtually identical argument that a reporter's privilege was necessary to prevent a chilling effect on newsgathering.

. . .

We fail to see how these policy considerations would differ in a Rule 501 analysis. Unlike the individual privacy interests in confidential communications shared by those protected by a common-law privilege, "[t]he preference for anonymity of those confidential informants involved in actual criminal conduct . . . , while understandable, is hardly deserving of constitutional protection." *Id.* at 691. The preference is equally undeserving of protection under the common law. Indeed, even those common-law privileges that do protect confidential communications between persons in special relationships have yielded where the communication furthers or shields ongoing criminal activity. . . .

2.

Risen's reliance upon state statutes and decisions that have adopted a reporter's shield also fails to persuade us that we can or should create a federal common-law privilege.

At the time of Branzburg, "[a]number of States ha[d] provided newsmen a statutory privilege of varying breadth." *Id.* at 689. And, as Risen argues, nearly all of the remaining states have since "recognized a reporter's privilege in one context or another." Risen's Brief at 55. Generally speaking, such "policy decisions of the States bear on the question whether federal courts should recognize a new privilege or amend the coverage of an existing one." Jaffee, 518 U.S. at 12–13. However, there is still no "uniform judgment of the States" on the issue of a reporter's privilege or shield, nor was the privilege "among the nine specific privileges recommended by the Advisory Committee in its proposed privilege rules." *Id.* at 14. . . .

We decline the invitation to step in now and create a testimonial privilege under common law that the Supreme Court has said does not exist and that Congress has considered and failed to provide legislatively. If Risen is to be protected from being compelled to testify and give what evidence of crime he possesses, in contravention of every citizen's duty to do so, we believe that decision should rest with the Supreme Court, which can revisit Branzburg and the policy arguments it rejected, or with Congress, which can more effectively and comprehensively weigh the policy arguments for and against adopting a privilege and define its scope.

. . .

GREGORY, Circuit Judge, dissenting as to Issue I:

Today we consider the importance of a free press in ensuring the informed public debate critical to citizens' oversight of their democratically elected representatives. Undoubtedly, the revelation of some government secrets is too damaging to our country's national security to warrant protection by evidentiary privilege. Yet the trial by press of secret government actions can expose misguided policies, poor planning, and worse. More importantly, a free and vigorous press is an indispensable part of a system of democratic government. Our country's Founders established the First Amendment's guarantee of a free press as a recognition that a government unaccountable to public discourse renders that essential element of democracy—the vote—meaningless. The majority reads narrowly the law governing the protection of a reporter from revealing his sources, a decision that is, in my view, contrary to the will and wisdom of our Founders.

The district court ruled that under Branzburg v. Hayes, 408 U.S. 665 (1972), and subsequent precedent from this Circuit, the Government could not compel Risen to reveal his source for chapter nine of his book, *State of War*. . . .

A reporter's need for keeping sources confidential is not hypothetical. The record on appeal contains affidavits proffered by Risen detailing the integral role of confidential sources in the newsgathering process. Scott Armstrong, executive director of the Information Trust and former Washington Post reporter, points to three ways in which investigative journalism uses confidential sources: "developing factual accounts and documentation unknown to the public," "tak[ing] a mix of known facts and new information and produc[ing] an interpretation previously unavailable to the public," and "publiciz[ing] information developed in government investigations that has not been known to the public and might well be suppressed." Joint App'x (J.A.) 531. "It would be rare," Armstrong asserts, "for there not to be multiple sources—including confidential sources—for news stories on highly sensitive topics." *Id.* In turn, "[m]any sources require such guarantees of confidentiality before any extensive exchange of information is permitted." J.A. 350. Such guarantees of confidentiality enable sources to discuss "sensitive matters such as major policy debates, personnel matters, investigations of improprieties, and financial and budget matters." *Id.* Even in ordinary daily reporting, confidential sources are critical. "[O]fficial government pronouncements must be verified before they are published," and this is frequently done through discussion with officials not authorized to speak on the subject but who rely on assurances of confidentiality. J.A. 352. These discussions can often lead to "unique and relevant, contextual comments" made by the confidential source, comments that deepen the story. *Id.*

The affidavits also recount numerous instances in which the confidentiality promised to sources was integral to a reporter's development of major stories critical to informing the public of the government's actions. . . .

B.

Any consideration of the reporter's privilege must start with Branzburg, where the Supreme Court upheld, by a vote of five to four, the compulsion of confidential source information from reporters. Branzburg v. Hayes, 408 U.S. 665 (1972). The majority opinion highlighted the "longstanding principle that 'the public . . . has a right to every man's evidence,' except for those persons protected by a constitutional, common law, or statutory privilege." *Id.* at 688 (citations omitted). The opinion also stated that "news gathering is not without its First Amendment protections," *id.* at 707, but the Court did not specify exactly what those protections might encompass, although it indicated that "[o]fficial harassment of the press" and bad faith investigations might fall within the parameters of the First Amendment's protection of reporters. *Id.* at 707-08.

Further complicating matters is Justice Powell's "enigmatic concurring opinion," *id.* at 725 (Stewart, J., dissenting), which is in part at odds with the majority opinion he joined. In the concurrence, Justice Powell emphasized "the limited nature of the Court's holding," and endorsed a balancing test, according to which "if the newsman is called upon to give information bearing only a remote and tenuous relationship to the subject of the investigation," then courts should consider the applicability of the reporter's privilege on a "case-by-case basis" by "the striking of a proper balance between freedom of the press and the obligation of all citizens to give relevant testimony with respect to criminal conduct." *Id.* at 709–10 (Powell, J., concurring).

The full import of Justice Powell's concurrence continues to be debated. Some analogize the Branzburg majority opinion to a plurality opinion, and therefore assert Justice Powell's concurrence as the narrowest opinion is controlling. . . . Others, like my good friends in the majority, treat Justice Powell's concurrence as ancillary, *see* ante 22–24, and simply rejoin that "the meaning of a majority opinion is to be found within the opinion itself." McKoy, 494 U.S. at 448 n. 3 (Blackmun, J., concurring).

Given this confusion, appellate courts have subsequently hewed closer to Justice Powell's concurrence—and Justice Stewart's dissent—than to the majority opinion, and a number of courts have since recognized a qualified reporter's privilege, often utilizing a three-part balancing test. . . . In short, Justice Powell's concurrence and the subsequent appellate history have made the lessons of Branzburg about as clear as mud.

The Fourth Circuit, like our sister circuits, has applied Justice Powell's balancing test in analyzing whether to apply a reporter's privilege to quash subpoenas seeking confidential source information from reporters. We first explicitly adopted Justice Powell's balancing test in an en banc opinion in United States v. Steelhammer, 539 F.2d 373, 376 (4th Cir. 1976) (Winter, J., dissenting), adopted by the court en banc, 561 F.2d 539, 540 (4th Cir. 1977). Then in LaRouche, we applied the reporter's privilege doctrine to a civil case, again citing Justice Powell's concurrence in Branzburg for authority. 780 F.2d at 1139. Following the lead of the Fifth Circuit, we applied a three-part test to help us balance the interests at stake in determining whether the reporter's privilege should be applied; that is, we considered "(1) whether the information is relevant, (2) whether the information can be obtained by alternative means, and (3) whether there is a compelling interest in the information." *Id.* . . .

In a subsequent case in the criminal context, In re Shain, four reporters in South Carolina asserted the reporter's privilege to protect information gleaned from interviews with a state legislator. 978 F.2d 850, 851–52 (4th Cir. 1992). But applying Justice Powell's principles, we rejected the reporters' claim on the ground that none of the reporters asserted that the interviews were confidential, that there were agreements to refuse revealing the identity of the interviewee, or that the government sought to harass the reporters. *Id.* at 853. Thus, although the reporter's privilege was not recognized in "the circumstances of this case," *see id.* at 854, it is clear to me that we have acknowledged that a reporter's privilege attaches in criminal proceedings given the right circumstances.

The most recent federal appellate court decision to address the reporter's privilege at length is In re Grand Jury Subpoena, Judith Miller, 438 F.3d 1141, 1145–49 (D.C. Cir. 2006). In that case, the court rejected the reporter's privilege claim asserted by Judith Miller of *The New York Times*, stating that the *Branzburg* decision was dispositive. . . . In a thoughtful concurrence, though, Judge Tatel pointed to the ambiguities of the *Branzburg* decision, and noted that nearly every state and the District of Columbia has recognized a reporter's privilege. Nevertheless, Judge Tatel concluded that "if *Branzburg* is to be limited or distinguished in the circumstances of this case, we must leave that task to the Supreme Court." *Id.* at 1166 (Tatel, J., concurring). And although he felt constrained to deny applying a First Amendment privilege, Judge Tatel would have held that Rule 501 of the Federal Rules of Evidence provides for a reporter's privilege (though on the facts of that case, the privilege would have given way due to the extraordinary national security issue involved). *See id.* at 1177–78 (Tatel, J., concurring).

C.

On this background, I turn to the question now before the court: Are there circumstances in which a reporter may refuse to testify as to the identity of one of his confidential sources, when the government seeks this information as part of a criminal investigation, and there is no evidence of prosecutorial bad faith or harassment? Some appellate courts have used a three-part test, essentially identical to the test we announced in *LaRouche* in the civil context, to help determine whether to apply the reporter's privilege in criminal cases. . . .

I, too, would recognize a qualified reporter's privilege in the criminal context, and evaluate the privilege using the three-part test enunciated in LaRouche as an "aid" to help "balance the interests involved." 780 F.2d at 1139. I would add a caveat to this general rule, however; in cases involving questions of national security, if the three-part LaRouche test is satisfied in favor of the reporter's privilege, I would require consideration of two additional factors: the harm caused by the public dissemination of the information, and the newsworthiness of the information conveyed. . . .

D.

Whatever the limits of who may claim reporter's privilege, it is clear that Risen—a full-time reporter for a national news publication, *The New York Times*—falls into the category of people who should be eligible to invoke the privilege. . . .

Under the majority's articulation of the reporter's privilege, or lack thereof, absent a showing of bad faith by the government, a reporter can *always* be compelled against her will to reveal her confidential sources in a criminal trial. The majority exalts the interests of the government while unduly trampling those of the press, and in doing so, severely impinges on the press and the free flow of information in our society. The First Amendment was designed to counteract the very result the majority reaches today. In sum, I would affirm the district court's ruling as to Risen's assertion of a First Amendment reporter's privilege, albeit using the three-part *LaRouche* test and balancing the two additional factors identified herein: newsworthiness of the leaked information and the harm resulting from the leak.

E.

Even if I were not inclined to recognize a First Amendment privilege for a reporter in the criminal context given *Branzburg,* I would recognize a common law privilege protecting a reporter's sources pursuant to Federal Rule of Evidence 501. . . .

The Supreme Court has stated that "the policy decisions of the States bear on the question [of] whether federal courts should recognize a new privilege or amend coverage of an existing one," and "[i]t is of no consequence that recognition of the privilege in the vast majority of States is the product of legislative action rather than judicial decision." [Jaffe] at 12-13. When the *Branzburg* decision issued, only seventeen states had recognized some protection for a reporter regarding his or her confidential sources. *Branzburg,* 408 U.S. at 689 n. 27. Today, only one state, Wyoming, has not enacted or adopted a reporter's privilege. Thirty-nine states and the District of Columbia have shield laws for reporters, whether those shields are absolute or qualified. . . . A number of these jurisdictions—Alabama, Arizona, California, Delaware, the District of Columbia, Indiana, Kentucky, Maryland, Montana, Nebraska, Nevada, New York, Ohio, Oklahoma, Oregon, and Pennsylvania—make the privilege an absolute bar to compelling a reporter to divulge his sources. On the basis of "the uniform judgment of the States," the Supreme Court recognized the psychotherapist-patient privilege. Jaffee, 518 U.S. at 14. The landscape in regards to the reporter's privilege has changed drastically since *Branzburg*. The unanimity of the States compels my conclusion that Rule 501 calls for a reporter's privilege.

F.

The paramount importance of the free press guaranteed by our Constitution compels me to conclude that the First Amendment encompasses a qualified reporter's privilege. Using the factors identified herein and given the facts at hand, Risen must be protected from disclosing the identity of his confidential sources. . . .

Fair Use

The mass media industry would not function if creators and producers could not protect their content through copyrights. Under the Copyright Act of 1976, authors of content have a copyright interest in their expressive creations, an intellectual property right that can be assigned to or inherited by third parties. The copyright gives its holder the exclusive right to exploit the content—this includes the right to profit from the work, to modify it, to distribute it, and to license it for others to use. Until the copyright period expires (the duration of protection can vary greatly depending on the author and publication circumstances), those who exploit the work without a license can be sued for an infringing use. The only exception to infringement is "fair use."

Fair use is a limited use allowance—some call it an affirmative defense—that allows an unlicensed user to excerpt a work for a variety of transformative purposes, including for education, art, journalism, and criticism. Since almost everything we see or hear on television, radio, books, magazines, theaters, and the Internet is copyrighted, fair use is critical for artists, teachers, and reporters. With fair use, an individual can creatively sample one or more copyrighted works without asking for permission or paying a fee to the copyright holder.

In Harper & Row v. Nation Enterprises infra, the U.S. Supreme Court was asked to apply the fair use exception to a copyright dispute between the publishers of President Gerald Ford's memoir and a magazine that printed 300 words of the memoir without permission. In assessing the applicability of fair use, the Court balances four factors, the purpose and character of the use, the nature of the copyrighted work, the amount and substantiality of the use, and the effect of the use on the copyrighted work's potential market value. In popular culture, *Harper & Row* is sometimes referred to as "the 300 words case." But this is a misnomer, since the factors that weigh most heavily in fair-use disputes are the purpose of the use and its effect on the work's market. Indeed, it is these two factors that form the justification for the Court's later decision in Sony v. Universal City Studios Inc. infra, also known as the "Betamax Case." In that case, the U.S. Supreme Court enunciated special rules for the noncommercial recording of television shows, ushering in the VCR and the digital video recorder (DVR) era.

HARPER & ROW PUBLISHERS, INC. V. NATION ENTERPRISES

471 U.S. 539 (1985)

Justice O'CONNOR delivered the opinion of the Court.

This case requires us to consider to what extent the "fair use" provision of the Copyright Revision Act of 1976, (hereinafter the Copyright Act) 17 U.S.C. § 107, sanctions the unauthorized use of quotations from a public figure's unpublished manuscript. In March 1979, an undisclosed source provided The Nation Magazine with the unpublished manuscript of "A

Time to Heal: The Autobiography of Gerald R. Ford." Working directly from the purloined manuscript, an editor of The Nation produced a short piece entitled "The Ford Memoirs-Behind the Nixon Pardon." The piece was timed to "scoop" an article scheduled shortly to appear in Time Magazine. Time had agreed to purchase the exclusive right to print prepublication excerpts from the copyright holders, Harper & Row Publishers, Inc. (hereinafter Harper & Row), and Reader's Digest Association, Inc. (hereinafter Reader's Digest). As a result of The Nation article, Time canceled its agreement. Petitioners brought a successful copyright action against The Nation. On appeal, the Second Circuit reversed the lower court's finding of infringement, holding that The Nation's act was sanctioned as a "fair use" of the copyrighted material. We granted certiorari, 467 U.S. 1214 (1984), and we now reverse.

I.

In February 1977, shortly after leaving the White House, former President Gerald R. Ford contracted with petitioners Harper & Row and Reader's Digest, to publish his as yet unwritten memoirs. The memoirs were to contain "significant hitherto unpublished material" concerning the Watergate crisis, Mr. Ford's pardon of former President Nixon and "Mr. Ford's reflections on this period of history, and the morality and personalities involved." App. to Pet. for Cert. C-14-C-15. In addition to the right to publish the Ford memoirs in book form, the agreement gave petitioners the exclusive right to license prepublication excerpts, known in the trade as "first serial rights." Two years later, as the memoirs were nearing completion, petitioners negotiated a prepublication licensing agreement with Time, a weekly news magazine. Time agreed to pay $25,000, $12,500 in advance and an additional $12,500 at publication, in exchange for the right to excerpt 7,500 words from Mr. Ford's account of the Nixon pardon. The issue featuring the excerpts was timed to appear approximately one week before shipment of the full length book version to bookstores. Exclusivity was an important consideration; Harper & Row instituted procedures designed to maintain the confidentiality of the manuscript, and Time

President Gerald Ford appearing before Congress after pardoning former President Nixon.

retained the right to renegotiate the second payment should the material appear in print prior to its release of the excerpts.

Two to three weeks before the Time article's scheduled release, an unidentified person secretly brought a copy of the Ford manuscript to Victor Navasky, editor of The Nation, a political commentary magazine. Mr. Navasky knew that his possession of the manuscript was not authorized and that the manuscript must be returned quickly to his "source" to avoid discovery. 557 F.Supp. 1067, 1069 (SDNY 1983). He hastily put together what he believed was "a real hot news story" composed of quotes, paraphrases, and facts drawn exclusively from the manuscript. *Ibid.* Mr. Navasky attempted no independent commentary, research or criticism, in part because of the need for speed if he was to "make news" by "publish[ing] in advance of publication of the Ford book." App. 416-417. The 2,250-word article, reprinted in the Appendix to this opinion, appeared on April 3, 1979. As a result of The Nation's article, Time canceled its piece and refused to pay the remaining $12,500.

. . .

Article I, § 8, of the Constitution provides:

> "The Congress shall have Power . . . to Promote the Progress of Science and useful Arts, by securing for limited Times to Authors and Inventors the exclusive Right to their respective Writings and Discoveries."

As we noted last Term: "[This] limited grant is a means by which an important public purpose may be achieved. It is intended to motivate the creative activity of authors and inventors by the provision of a special reward, and to allow the public access to the products of their genius after the limited period of exclusive control has expired." *Sony Corp. of America v. Universal City Studios, Inc.*, 464 U.S. 417, 429 (1984). "The monopoly created by copyright thus rewards the individual author in order to benefit the public." *Id.*, at 477 (dissenting opinion). This principle applies equally to works of fiction and nonfiction. The book at issue here, for example, was two years in the making, and began with a contract giving the author's copyright to the publishers in exchange for their services in producing and marketing the work. In preparing the book, Mr. Ford drafted essays and word portraits of public figures and participated in hundreds of taped interviews that were later distilled to chronicle his personal viewpoint. It is evident that the monopoly granted by copyright actively served its intended purpose of inducing the creation of new material of potential historical value.

Section 106 of the Copyright Act confers a bundle of exclusive rights to the owner of the copyright. Under the Copyright Act, these rights-to publish, copy, and distribute the author's work-vest in the author of an original work from the time of its creation. § 106. In practice, the author commonly sells his rights to publishers who offer royalties in exchange for their services in producing and marketing the author's work. The copyright owner's rights, however, are subject to certain statutory exceptions. §§ 107-118. Among these is § 107 which codifies the traditional privilege of other authors to make "fair use" of an earlier writer's work. In addition, no author may copyright facts or ideas. § 102. The copyright is limited to those aspects of the work-termed "expression"-that display the stamp of the author's originality.

Creation of a nonfiction work, even a compilation of pure fact, entails originality. See, *e.g., Schroeder v. William Morrow* .... The copyright holders of "A Time to Heal" complied with the relevant statutory notice and registration procedures. See §§ 106, 401, 408; App. to Pet. for Cert. C-20. Thus there is no dispute that the unpublished manuscript of "A Time to Heal," as a whole, was protected by § 106 from unauthorized reproduction. Nor do respondents dispute that verbatim copying of excerpts of the manuscript's original form of expression would constitute infringement unless excused as fair use .... Yet copyright does not prevent subsequent users from copying from a prior author's work those constituent elements that are not original-for example, quotations borrowed under the rubric of fair use from other copyrighted works, facts, or materials in the public domain-as long as such use does not unfairly appropriate the author's original contributions.... Perhaps the controversy between the lower courts in this case over copyrightability is more aptly styled a dispute over whether The Nation's appropriation of unoriginal and uncopyrightable elements encroached on the originality embodied in the work as a whole. Especially in the realm of factual narrative, the law is currently unsettled regarding the ways in which uncopyrightable elements combine with the author's original contributions to form protected expression....

We need not reach these issues, however, as The Nation has admitted to lifting verbatim quotes of the author's original language totaling between 300 and 400 words and constituting some 13% of The Nation article. In using generous verbatim excerpts of Mr. Ford's unpublished manuscript to lend authenticity to its account of the forthcoming memoirs, The Nation effectively arrogated to itself the right of first publication, an important marketable subsidiary right. For the reasons set forth below, we find that this use of the copyrighted manuscript, even stripped to the verbatim quotes conceded by The Nation to be copyrightable expression, was not a fair use within the meaning of the Copyright Act.

III.

A.

Fair use was traditionally defined as "a privilege in others than the owner of the copyright to use the copyrighted material in a reasonable manner without his consent." . . . The statutory formulation of the defense of fair use in the Copyright Act reflects the intent of Congress to codify the common-law doctrine. . . . Section 107 requires a case-by-case determination whether a particular use is fair, and the statute notes four nonexclusive factors to be considered. This approach was "intended to restate the [pre-existing] judicial doctrine of fair use, not to change, narrow, or enlarge it in any way." H.R.Rep. No. 94-1476, p. 66 (1976) (hereinafter House Report). . . .

"[T]he author's consent to a reasonable use of his copyrighted works ha[d] always been implied by the courts as a necessary incident of the constitutional policy of promoting the progress of science and the useful arts, since a prohibition of such use would inhibit subsequent writers from attempting to improve upon prior works and thus . . . frustrate the very ends sought to be attained." . . .

Perhaps because the fair use doctrine was predicated on the author's implied consent to "reasonable and customary" use when he released his work for public consumption, fair use traditionally was not recognized as a defense to charges of copying from an author's as yet unpublished works. Under common-law copyright, "the property of the author . . . in his intellectual creation [was] absolute until he voluntarily part[ed] with the same." *American Tobacco Co. v. Werckmeister*, 207 U.S. 284, 299 (1907); 2 Nimmer § 8.23, at 8-273. This absolute rule, however, was tempered in practice by the equitable nature of the fair use doctrine. In a given case, factors such as implied consent through *de facto* publication on performance or dissemination of a work may tip the balance of equities in favor of prepublication use. See Copyright Law Revision-Part 2: Discussion and Comments on Report of the Register of Copyrights on General Revision of the U.S. Copyright Law, 88th Cong., 1st Sess., 27 (H.R.Comm. Print 1963) (discussion suggesting works disseminated to the public in a form not constituting a technical "publication" should nevertheless be subject to fair use); 3 Nimmer § 13.05, at 13-62, n. 2. But it has never been seriously disputed that "the fact that the plaintiff's work is unpublished

. . . is a factor tending to negate the defense of fair use." *Ibid.* Publication of an author's expression before he has authorized its dissemination seriously infringes the author's right to decide when and whether it will be made public, a factor not present in fair use of published works. Respondents contend, however, that Congress, in including first publication among the rights enumerated in § 106, which are expressly subject to fair use under § 107, intended that fair use would apply *in pari materia* to published and unpublished works. The Copyright Act does not support this proposition.

. . .

The Copyright Act represents the culmination of a major legislative reexamination of copyright doctrine... Among its other innovations, it eliminated publication "as a dividing line between common law and statutory protection," House Report, ... extending statutory protection to all works from the time of their creation. It also recognized for the first time a distinct statutory right of first publication, which had previously been an element of the common-law protections afforded unpublished works. . . .

Though the right of first publication, like the other rights enumerated in § 106, is expressly made subject to the fair use provision of § 107, fair use analysis must always be tailored to the individual case. *Id.*, at 65; 3 Nimmer § 13.05[A]. The nature of the interest at stake is highly relevant to whether a given use is fair. From the beginning, those entrusted with the task of revision recognized the "overbalancing reasons to preserve the common law protection of undisseminated works until the author or his successor chooses to disclose them." ... The right of first publication implicates a threshold decision by the author whether and in what form to release his work. First publication is inherently different from other § 106 rights in that only one person can be the first publisher; as the contract with Time illustrates, the commercial value of the right lies primarily in exclusivity. Because the potential damage to the author from judicially enforced "sharing" of the first publication right with unauthorized users of his manuscript is substantial, the balance of equities in evaluating such a claim of fair use inevitably shifts.

. . .

The author's control of first public distribution implicates not only his personal interest in creative control but his property interest in exploitation of prepublication rights, which are valuable in themselves and serve as a valuable adjunct to publicity and marketing. See *Belushi v. Woodward,* 598 F.Supp. 36 (DC 1984) (successful marketing depends on coordination of serialization and release to public); Marks, Subsidiary Rights and Permissions, in What Happens in Book Publishing 230 (C. Grannis ed. 1967) (exploitation of subsidiary rights is necessary to financial success of new books). Under ordinary circumstances, the author's right to control the first public appearance of his undisseminated expression will outweigh a claim of fair use.

B.

Respondents, however, contend that First Amendment values require a different rule under the circumstances of this case. The thrust of the decision below is that "[t]he scope of [fair use] is undoubtedly wider when the information conveyed relates to matters of high public concern." ... Respondents advance the substantial public import of the subject matter of the Ford memoirs as grounds for excusing a use that would ordinarily not pass muster as a fair use-the piracy of verbatim quotations for the purpose of "scooping" the authorized first serialization. Respondents explain their copying of Mr. Ford's expression as essential to reporting the news story it claims the book itself represents. In respondents' view, not only the facts contained in Mr. Ford's memoirs, but "the precise manner in which [he] expressed himself [were] as newsworthy as what he had to say." Brief for Respondents 38-39. Respondents argue that the public's interest in learning this news as fast as possible outweighs the right of the author to control its first publication.

The Second Circuit noted, correctly, that copyright's idea/expression dichotomy "strike[s] a definitional balance between the First Amendment and the Copyright Act by permitting free communication of facts while still protecting an author's expression." ... No author may copyright his ideas or the facts he narrates. ... As this Court long ago observed: "[T]he news element-the information respecting current events contained in the literary production-is not the creation of the writer, but is a report of matters that ordinarily are *publici juris;* it is the history of the day." *International News Service v. Associated Press* ... But copyright assures those who write and publish factual narratives such as "A Time to Heal" that they may at least enjoy the right to market the original expression contained therein as just compensation for their investment. ...

The promise of copyright would be an empty one if it could be avoided merely by dubbing the infringement a fair use "news report" of the book. ...

Nor do respondents assert any actual necessity for circumventing the copyright scheme with respect to the types of works and users at issue here. Where an author and publisher have invested extensive resources in creating an original work and are poised to release it to the public, no legitimate aim is served by pre-empting the right of first publication. . . .

In our haste to disseminate news, it should not be forgotten that the Framers intended copyright itself to be the engine of free expression. By establishing a marketable right to the use of one's expression, copyright supplies the economic incentive to create and disseminate ideas. . . .

It is fundamentally at odds with the scheme of copyright to accord lesser rights in those works that are of greatest importance to the public. Such a notion ignores the major premise of copyright and injures author and public alike. . . .

IV.

. . .

[W]hether The Nation article constitutes fair use under § 107 must be reviewed in light of the principles discussed above. The factors enumerated in the section are not meant to be exclusive: "[S]ince the doctrine is an equitable rule of reason, no generally applicable definition is possible, and each case raising the question must be decided on its own facts." . . . The four factors identified by Congress as especially relevant in determining whether the use was fair are: (1) the purpose and character of the use; (2) the nature of the copyrighted work; (3) the substantiality of the portion used in relation to the copyrighted work as a whole; (4) the effect on the potential market for or value of the copyrighted work. We address each one separately.

Purpose of the Use. The Second Circuit correctly identified news reporting as the general purpose of The Nation's use. News reporting is one of the examples enumerated in § 107 to "give some idea of the sort of activities the courts might regard as fair use under the circumstances. . . . The Nation has every right to seek to be the first to publish information. But The Nation went beyond simply reporting uncopyrightable information and actively sought to exploit the headline value of its infringement, making a "news event" out of its unauthorized first publication of a noted figure's copyrighted expression.

The fact that a publication was commercial as opposed to nonprofit is a separate factor that tends to weigh against a finding of fair use. "[E]very commercial use of copyrighted material is presumptively an unfair exploitation of the monopoly privilege that belongs to the owner of the copyright." *Sony* .... In arguing that the purpose of news reporting is not purely commercial, The Nation misses the point entirely. The crux of the profit/nonprofit distinction is not whether the sole motive of the use is monetary gain but whether the user stands to profit from exploitation of the copyrighted material without paying the customary price....

In evaluating character and purpose we cannot ignore The Nation's stated purpose of scooping the forthcoming hardcover and Time abstracts. App. to Pet. for Cert. C-27. The Nation's use had not merely the incidental effect but the *intended purpose* of supplanting the copyright holder's commercially valuable right of first publication. See *Meredith Corp. v. Harper & Row, Publishers, Inc.*, 378 F.Supp. 686, 690 (SDNY) (purpose of text was to compete with original), aff'd, 500 F.2d 1221 (2d Cir. 1974). Also relevant to the "character" of the use is "the propriety of the defendant's conduct.... The trial court found that The Nation knowingly exploited a purloined manuscript.... Unlike the typical claim of fair use, The Nation cannot offer up even the fiction of consent as justification. Like its competitor newsweekly, it was free to bid for the right of abstracting excerpts from "A Time to Heal." ...

Nature of the Copyrighted Work. Second, the Act directs attention to the nature of the copyrighted work. "A Time to Heal" may be characterized as an unpublished historical narrative or autobiography. The law generally recognizes a greater need to disseminate factual works than works of fiction or fantasy.... Some of the briefer quotes from the memoirs are arguably necessary adequately to convey the facts; for example, Mr. Ford's characterization of the White House tapes as the "smoking gun" is perhaps so integral to the idea expressed as to be inseparable from it. Cf. 1 Nimmer § 1.10[C]. But The Nation did not stop at isolated phrases and instead excerpted subjective descriptions and portraits of public figures whose power lies in the author's individualized expression. Such use, focusing on the most expressive elements of the work, exceeds that necessary to disseminate the facts.

The fact that a work is unpublished is a critical element of its "nature." ... Our prior discussion establishes that the scope of fair use is narrower with respect to unpublished works....

In the case of Mr. Ford's manuscript, the copyright holders' interest in confidentiality is irrefutable; the copyright holders had entered into a contractual undertaking to "keep the manuscript confidential" and required that all those to whom the manuscript was shown also "sign an agreement to keep the manuscript confidential." . . . While the copyright holders' contract with Time required Time to submit its proposed article seven days before publication, The Nation's clandestine publication afforded no such opportunity for creative or quality control. . . . It was hastily patched together and contained "a number of inaccuracies." . . . A use that so clearly infringes the copyright holder's interests in confidentiality and creative control is difficult to characterize as "fair."

Amount and Substantiality of the Portion Used. Next, the Act directs us to examine the amount and substantiality of the portion used in relation to the copyrighted work as a whole. In absolute terms, the words actually quoted were an insubstantial portion of "A Time to Heal." The District Court, however, found that "[T]he Nation took what was essentially the heart of the book." ... We believe the Court of Appeals erred in overruling the District Judge's evaluation of the qualitative nature of the taking. . . . A Time editor described the chapters on the pardon as "the most interesting and moving parts of the entire manuscript." . . .

As the statutory language indicates, a taking may not be excused merely because it is insubstantial with respect to the *infringing* work. As Judge Learned Hand cogently remarked, "no plagiarist can excuse the wrong by showing how much of his work he did not pirate." . . . Conversely, the fact that a substantial portion of the infringing work was copied verbatim is evidence of the qualitative value of the copied material, both to the originator and to the plagiarist who seeks to profit from marketing someone else's copyrighted expression.

Stripped to the verbatim quotes, the direct takings from the unpublished manuscript constitute at least 13% of the infringing article. See *Meeropol v. Nizer* . . . (copyrighted letters constituted less than 1% of infringing work but were prominently featured). The Nation article is structured around the quoted excerpts which serve as its dramatic focal points. . . .
Effect on the Market. Finally, the Act focuses on "the effect of the use upon the potential market for or value of the copyrighted work." This last factor is undoubtedly the single most important element of fair use. . . . "Fair use, when properly applied, is limited to copying by others which does not materially impair the marketability of the work which is copied. . . . The trial court found not merely a potential but an actual effect on the market. Time's cancellation of its projected serialization and its refusal to pay the $12,500 were the direct effect of the infringement. . . . Rarely will a case of copyright infringement present such clear-cut evidence of actual damage. Petitioners assured Time that there would be

no other authorized publication of *any* portion of the unpublished manuscript prior to April 23, 1979. *Any* publication of material from chapters 1 and 3 would permit Time to renegotiate its final payment. Time cited The Nation's article, which contained verbatim quotes from the unpublished manuscript, as a reason for its nonperformance.... [O]nce a copyright holder establishes with reasonable probability the existence of a causal connection between the infringement and a loss of revenue, the burden properly shifts to the infringer to show that this damage would have occurred had there been no taking of copyrighted expression....

It is undisputed that the factual material in the balance of The Nation's article, besides the verbatim quotes at issue here, was drawn exclusively from the chapters on the pardon. The excerpts were employed as featured episodes in a story about the Nixon pardon-precisely the use petitioners had licensed to Time. The borrowing of these verbatim quotes from the unpublished manuscript lent The Nation's piece a special air of authenticity-as Navasky expressed it, the reader would know it was Ford speaking and not The Nation.... Thus it directly competed for a share of the market for prepublication excerpts....

V.

...

In sum, the traditional doctrine of fair use, as embodied in the Copyright Act, does not sanction the use made by The Nation of these copyrighted materials. Any copyright infringer may claim to benefit the public by increasing public access to the copyrighted work.... But Congress has not designed, and we see no warrant for judicially imposing, a "compulsory license" permitting unfettered access to the unpublished copyrighted expression of public figures.

The Nation conceded that its verbatim copying of some 300 words of direct quotation from the Ford manuscript would constitute an infringement unless excused as a fair use. Because we find that The Nation's use of these verbatim excerpts from the unpublished manuscript was not a fair use, the judgment of the Court of Appeals is reversed, and the case is remanded for further proceedings consistent with this opinion.

It is so ordered.

...

Justice BRENNAN, with whom Justice WHITE and Justice MARSHALL join, dissenting.

The Court holds that The Nation's quotation of 300 words from the unpublished 200,000-word manuscript of President Gerald R. Ford infringed the copyright in that manuscript, even though the quotations related to a historical event of undoubted significance-the resignation and pardon of President Richard M. Nixon. Although the Court pursues the laudable goal of protecting "the economic incentive to create and disseminate ideas," *ante,* at 2230, this zealous defense of the copyright owner's prerogative will, I fear, stifle the broad dissemination of ideas and information copyright is intended to nurture. Protection of the copyright owner's economic interest is achieved in this case through an exceedingly narrow definition of the scope of fair use. The progress of arts and sciences and the robust public debate essential to an enlightened citizenry are ill served by this constricted reading of the fair use doctrine. See 17 U.S.C. § 107. I therefore respectfully dissent.

I.

A.

This case presents two issues. First, did The Nation's use of material from the Ford manuscript in forms other than direct quotation from that manuscript infringe Harper & Row's copyright. Second, did the quotation of approximately 300 words from the manuscript infringe the copyright because this quotation did not constitute "fair use" within the meaning of § 107 of the Copyright Act. 17 U.S.C. § 107. The Court finds no need to resolve the threshold copyrightability issue. The use of 300 words of quotation was, the Court finds, beyond the scope of fair use and thus a copyright infringement. Because I disagree with the Court's fair use holding, it is necessary for me to decide the threshold copyrightability question. . . .

The "originality" requirement now embodied in § 102 of the Copyright Act is crucial to maintenance of the appropriate balance between these competing interests. Properly interpreted in the light of the legislative history, this section extends copyright protection to an author's literary form but permits free use by others of the ideas and information the author communicates. . . .

It follows that infringement of copyright must be based on a taking of literary form, as opposed to the ideas or information contained in a copyrighted work. Deciding whether an infringing appropriation of literary form has occurred is difficult for at least two reasons. First, the distinction between literary form and information or ideas is often elusive in practice. Second, infringement must be based on a *substantial* appropriation of literary form. This determination is equally challenging. Not surprisingly, the test for infringement has defied precise formulation. In general, though, the inquiry proceeds along two axes: *how closely* has the second author tracked the first author's particular language and structure of presentation; and *how much* of the first author's language and structure has the second author appropriated.

. . .

The Language. Much of the information The Nation conveyed was not in the form of paraphrase at all, but took the form of synopsis of lengthy discussions in the Ford manuscript. In the course of this summary presentation, The Nation did use occasional sentences that closely resembled language in the original Ford manuscript. But these linguistic similarities are insufficient to constitute an infringement. . . .

The Structure of Presentation. The article does not mimic Mr. Ford's structure. The information The Nation presents is drawn from scattered sections of the Ford work and does not appear in the sequence in which Mr. Ford presented it. . . . Also, it is difficult to suggest that a 2,000-word article could bodily appropriate the structure of a 200,000-word book. Most of what Mr. Ford created, and most of the history he recounted, were simply not represented in The Nation's article.

. . .

When The Nation was not quoting Mr. Ford, therefore, its efforts to convey the historical information in the Ford manuscript did not so closely and substantially track Mr. Ford's language and structure as to constitute an appropriation of literary form.

II.

The Nation is thus liable in copyright only if the quotation of 300 words infringed any of Harper & Row's exclusive rights under § 106 of the Act. . . . The question here is whether The Nation's quotation was a noninfringing fair use within the meaning of § 107. . . .

. . .

With respect to a work of history, particularly the memoirs of a public official, the statutorily prescribed analysis cannot properly be conducted without constant attention to copyright's crucial distinction between protected literary form and unprotected information or ideas. The question must always be: Was the subsequent author's use of *literary form* a fair use within the meaning of § 107, in light of the purpose for the use, the nature of the copyrighted work, the amount of literary form used, and the effect of this use of literary form on the value of or market for the original?

Limiting the inquiry to the propriety of a subsequent author's use of the copyright owner's literary form is not easy in the case of a work of history. Protection against only substantial appropriation of literary form does not ensure historians a return commensurate with the full value of their labors. . . . Copyright thus does not protect that which is often of most value in a work of history, and courts must resist the tendency to reject the fair use defense on the basis of their feeling that an author of history has been deprived of the full value of his or her labor. A subsequent author's taking of information and ideas is in no sense piratical because copyright law simply does not create any property interest in information and ideas.

. . .

Application of the statutorily prescribed analysis with attention to the distinction between information and literary form leads to a straightforward finding of fair use within the meaning of § 107.

The Purpose of the Use. The Nation's purpose in quoting 300 words of the Ford manuscript was, as the Court acknowledges, news reporting. . . .

The Court concedes the validity of the news reporting purpose but then quickly offsets it against three purportedly countervailing considerations. First, the Court asserts that because The Nation publishes for profit, its publication of the Ford quotes is a presumptively unfair commercial use. Second, the Court claims that The Nation's stated desire to create a "news event" signaled an illegitimate purpose of supplanting the copyright owner's right of first publication. *Ante,* at 2231. Third, The Nation acted in bad faith, the Court claims, because its editor "knowingly exploited a purloined manuscript." *Ibid.*

. . .

The Court's reliance on the commercial nature of The Nation's use as "a separate factor that tends to weigh against a finding of fair use," *ante,* at 2231, is inappropriate in the present context. Many uses § 107 lists as paradigmatic examples of fair use, including criticism, comment, and *news reporting,* are generally conducted for profit in this country, a fact of which Congress was obviously aware when it enacted § 107. To negate any argument favoring fair use based on news reporting or criticism because that reporting or criticism was published for profit is to render meaningless the congressional imprimatur placed on such uses.

. . .

Nor should The Nation's intent to create a "news event" weigh against a finding of fair use. Such a rule, like the Court's automatic presumption against news reporting for profit, would undermine the congressional validation of the news reporting purpose. A news business earns its reputation, and therefore its readership, through consistent prompt publication of news-and often through "scooping" rivals. . . . Indeed the Court's reliance on this factor would seem to amount to little more than distaste for the standard journalistic practice of seeking to be the first to publish news.

The Court's reliance on The Nation's putative bad faith is equally unwarranted. No court has found that The Nation possessed the Ford manuscript illegally or in violation of any common-law interest of Harper & Row; all common-law causes of action have been abandoned or dismissed in this case. 723 F.2d, at 199-201. Even if the manuscript had been "purloined" by someone, nothing in this record imputes culpability to The Nation. On the basis of the record in this case, the most that can be said is that The Nation made use of the contents of the manuscript knowing the copyright owner would not sanction the use. . . .

The Nature of the Copyrighted Work . . .

The Court acknowledges that "[t]he law generally recognizes a greater need to disseminate factual works than works of fiction or fantasy," *ante,* at 2228, and that "[s]ome of the briefer quotations from the memoir are arguably necessary to convey the facts," *ibid.* But the Court discounts the force of this consideration, primarily on the ground that "[t]he fact that a work is unpublished is a crucial element of its 'nature.'" *Ante,* at 2228. At this point the Court introduces into analysis of this case a categorical presumption against prepublication fair use. . . .

This categorical presumption is unwarranted on its own terms and unfaithful to congressional intent. Whether a particular prepublication use will impair any interest the Court identifies as encompassed within the right of first publication, see *ante,* at 2227-2228, will depend on the nature of the copyrighted work, the timing of prepublication use, the amount of expression used and the medium in which the second author communicates. Also, certain uses might be tolerable for some purposes but not for others. . . .

The Amount and Substantiality of the Portion Used. More difficult questions arise with respect to judgments about the importance to this case of the amount and substantiality of the quotations used. . . . At least with respect to the six particular quotes of Mr. Ford's observations and reflections about President Nixon, I agree with the Court's conclusion that The Nation appropriated some literary form of substantial quality. I do not agree, however, that the substantiality of the expression taken was clearly excessive or inappropriate to The Nation's news reporting purpose.

Had these quotations been used in the context of a critical book review of the Ford work, there is little question that such a use would be fair use within the meaning of § 107 of the Act. The amount and substantiality of the use-in both quantitative and qualitative terms-would have certainly been appropriate to the purpose of such a use. It is difficult to see how the use of these quoted words in a news report is less appropriate. . . .

The Effect on the Market. The Court correctly notes that the effect on the market "is undoubtedly the single most important element of fair use." *Ante,* at 2233, citing 3 Nimmer § 13.05[A], at 13-76, and the Court properly focuses on whether The Nation's use adversely affected Harper & Row's serialization potential and not merely the market for sales of the Ford work itself. *Ante,* at 2233. Unfortunately, the Court's failure to distinguish between the use of information and the appropriation of literary form badly skews its analysis of this factor. . . .

The Nation's publication indisputably precipitated Time's eventual cancellation. But that does not mean that The Nation's use of the 300 quoted words caused this injury to Harper & Row. Wholly apart from these quoted words, The Nation published significant information and ideas from the Ford manuscript. If it was this publication of information, and not the publication of the few quotations, that caused Time to abrogate its serialization agreement, then whatever the negative effect on the serialization market, that effect was the product of wholly legitimate activity. . . .

Balancing the Interests. Once the distinction between information and literary form is made clear, the statutorily prescribed process of weighing the four statutory fair use factors discussed above leads naturally to a conclusion that The Nation's limited use of literary form was not an infringement. . . .

III.

The Court's exceedingly narrow approach to fair use permits Harper & Row to monopolize information. This holding "effect[s] an important extension of property rights and a corresponding curtailment in the free use of knowledge and of ideas." *International News Service v. Associated Press,* 248 U.S., at 263, 39 S.Ct., at 81 (Brandeis, J., dissenting). The Court has perhaps advanced the ability of the historian-or at least the public official who has recently left office-to capture the full economic value of information in his or her possession. But the Court does so only by risking the robust debate of public issues that is the "essence of self-government." *Garrison v. Louisiana,* 379 U.S., at 74-75, 85 S.Ct., at 215-216. The Nation was providing the grist for that robust debate. The Court imposes liability upon The Nation for no other reason than that The Nation succeeded in being the first to provide certain information to the public. I dissent.

SONY CORP. OF AMERICA V. UNIVERSAL CITY STUDIOS, INC.

464 U.S. 417 (1984)

Justice STEVENS delivered the opinion of the Court.

Petitioners manufacture and sell home video tape recorders. Respondents own the copyrights on some of the television programs that are broadcast on the public airwaves. Some members of the general public use video tape recorders sold by petitioners to record some of these broadcasts, as well as a large number of other broadcasts. The question presented is whether the sale of petitioners' copying equipment to the general public violates any of the rights conferred upon respondents by the Copyright Act.

Respondents commenced this copyright infringement action against petitioners in the United States District Court for the Central District of California in 1976. Respondents alleged that some individuals had used Betamax video tape recorders (VTR's) to record some of respondents' copyrighted works which had been exhibited on commercially sponsored television and contended that these individuals had thereby infringed respondents' copyrights. Respondents further maintained that petitioners were liable for the copyright infringement allegedly committed by Betamax consumers because of petitioners' marketing of the Betamax VTR's. Respondents sought no relief against any Betamax consumer.

Instead, they sought money damages and an equitable accounting of profits from petitioners, as well as an injunction against the manufacture and marketing of Betamax VTR's.

After a lengthy trial, the District Court denied respondents all the relief they sought and entered judgment for petitioners. 480 F.Supp. 429 (1979). The United States Court of Appeals for the Ninth Circuit reversed the District Court's judgment on respondent's copyright claim, holding petitioners liable for contributory infringement and ordering the District Court to fashion appropriate relief. 659 F.2d 963 (1981). We granted certiorari, 457 U.S. 1116 (1982); since we had not completed our study of the case last Term, we ordered reargument, 463 U.S. 1226 (1983). We now reverse. . . .

[A]lthough every commercial use of copyrighted material is presumptively an unfair exploitation of the monopoly privilege that belongs to the owner of the copyright, noncommercial uses are a different matter. A challenge to a noncommercial use of a copyrighted work requires proof either that the particular use is harmful, or that if it should become widespread, it would adversely affect the potential market for the copyrighted work. Actual present harm need not be shown; such a requirement would leave the copyright holder with no defense against predictable damage. Nor is it necessary to show with certainty that future harm will result. What is necessary is a showing by a preponderance of the evidence that *some* meaningful likelihood of future harm exists. If the intended use is for commercial gain, that likelihood may be presumed. But if it is for a noncommercial purpose, the likelihood must be demonstrated.

In this case, respondents failed to carry their burden with regard to home time-shifting. . . .

Reporters' Liability for Non-Speech Torts

In New York Times Co. v. Sullivan, 376 U.S. 254 (1964), the U.S. Supreme Court held that public officials must show that a defamation defendant acted with actual malice—reckless disregard or knowledge of falsity—before pursuing damages. Justice Brennan, writing for the Court, makes clear that free speech considerations outweigh the right to recover for reputational damage. In later cases, the Supreme Court extended the actual malice standard to cases involving public figures, private figures seeking punitive damages, and to privacy cases. At the center of the Court's reasoning in these cases is the "chilling effect" that speech torts like defamation and privacy may have on the press because journalism is not an exact science. Despite careful investigation and sourcing, the press may make an honest mistake—or a court may apply scrutiny after the fact to conclude that the press made mistakes. In those cases, the actual malice standard protects the press from liability even if it ends up publishing something that was false. But what about liability for actions other than defamation and privacy? Should the First Amendment protect journalists from liability if the tort at issue is not directly related to speech, such as infliction of emotional distress? That issue went to the Supreme Court in the 1988 case of Hustler Magazine, Inc. v. Falwell, 485 U.S. 46. Jerry Falwell, a celebrity evangelist, sued Larry Flint's *Hustler* over a vulgar cartoon parody that purported to quote Falwell reminiscing about a sexual encounter with his mother in an outhouse. By the time the case made it to the Supreme Court, the only issue under consideration was whether Falwell could sue for the emotional distress that the publication caused him, without regard to the First Amendment. The Court said that he could not, concluding that, "public figures and public officials may not recover . . . without showing in addition that the publication contains a false statement of fact which was made with 'actual malice' . . . ."

At the same time, journalists are not above the law. Consider, for example, Cohen v. Cowles Media Co., 501 U.S. 663 (1991). Cohen, a political operative, had uncovered damaging information about an opposing candidate for lieutenant governor. Reporters for two Minnesota newspapers promised Cohen that they would keep his identity secret, but after interviewing the candidate, the newspapers decided to identify Cohen as the source. Cohen sued for breach of contract. The Supreme Court ultimately determined that Cohen was entitled to damages, holding that "the First Amendment does not confer on the press a constitutional right to disregard promises that would otherwise be enforced under state law." The rights and liability of the press under state law is at the heart of the case of Food Lion, Inc. v. Capital Cities/ABC, Inc. infra. In this case, two ABC reporters broke state law when they used hidden cameras to document unhygienic practices at a supermarket chain. When Diane Sawyer aired the footage on *Primetime Live,* Food Lion sued ABC for damages, arguing that since the reporters acted unlawfully, the grocery chain was entitled to damages that resulted from the broadcast. The Fourth Circuit concluded that journalists are not above state law, but that plaintiffs cannot circumvent constitutional speech tort protections if the damages flowed from publication. Publication damages are speech-related and, as such, the press should be entitled to the same protections that it would otherwise have had in a defamation or privacy action. In reaching this conclusion, the circuit panel engaged a number of competing Supreme Court precedents, including *Hustler* and *Cowles*.

FOOD LION, INC. V. CAPITAL CITIES/ABC, INC.

194 F. 3d 505 (4th Cir. 1999)

MICHAEL, Circuit Judge.

Two ABC television reporters, after using false resumes to get jobs at Food Lion, Inc. supermarkets, secretly videotaped what appeared to be unwholesome food handling practices. Some of the video footage was used by ABC in a *PrimeTime Live* broadcast that was sharply critical of Food Lion. The grocery chain sued Capital Cities/ABC, Inc., American Broadcasting Companies, Inc., Richard Kaplan and Ira Rosen, producers of *PrimeTime Live,* and Lynne Dale and Susan Barnett, two reporters for the program (collectively, "ABC" or the "ABC defendants"). Food Lion did not sue for defamation, but focused on how ABC gathered its information through claims for fraud, breach of duty of loyalty, trespass, and unfair trade practices. Food Lion won at trial, and judgment for compensatory damages of $1,402 was entered on the various claims. Following a substantial (over $5 million) remittitur, the judgment provided for $315,000 in punitive damages. The ABC defendants appeal the district court's denial of their motion for judgment as a matter of law, and Food Lion appeals the court's ruling that prevented it from proving publication damages. Having considered the case, we (1) reverse the judgment that the ABC defendants committed fraud and unfair trade practices, (2) affirm the judgment that Dale and Barnett breached their duty of loyalty and committed a trespass, and (3) affirm, on First Amendment grounds, the district court's refusal to allow Food Lion to prove publication damages.

I.

In early 1992 producers of ABC's *PrimeTime Live* program received a report alleging that Food Lion stores were engaging in unsanitary meat-handling practices. The allegations were that Food Lion employees ground out-of-date beef together with new beef, bleached rank meat to remove its odor, and re-dated (and offered for sale) products not sold before their printed expiration date. The producers recognized that these allegations presented the potential for a powerful news story, and they decided to conduct an undercover investigation of Food Lion. ABC reporters Lynne Dale (Lynne Litt at the time) and Susan Barnett concluded that they would have a better chance of investigating the allegations if they could become Food Lion employees. With the approval of their superiors, they proceeded to apply for jobs with the grocery chain, submitting applications with false identities and references and fictitious local addresses. Notably, the applications failed to mention the reporters' concurrent employment with ABC and otherwise misrepresented their educational and employment experiences. Based on these applications, a South Carolina Food Lion store hired Barnett as a deli clerk in April 1992, and a North Carolina Food Lion store hired Dale as a meat wrapper trainee in May 1992.

Barnett worked for Food Lion for two weeks, and Dale for only one week. As they went about their assigned tasks for Food Lion, Dale and Barnett used tiny cameras ("lipstick" cameras, for example) and microphones concealed on their bodies to secretly record Food Lion employees treating, wrapping and labeling meat, cleaning machinery, and discussing the practices of the meat department. They gathered footage from the meat cutting room, the deli counter, the employee break room, and a manager's office. All told, in their three collective weeks as Food Lion employees, Dale and Barnett recorded approximately 45 hours of concealed camera footage.

Some of the videotape was eventually used in a November 5, 1992, broadcast of *PrimeTime Live.* ABC contends the footage confirmed many of the allegations initially leveled against Food Lion. The broadcast included, for example, videotape that appeared to show Food Lion employees repackaging and redating fish that had passed the expiration date, grinding expired beef with fresh beef, and applying barbeque sauce to chicken past its expiration date in order to mask the smell and sell it as fresh in the gourmet food section. The program included statements by former Food Lion employees alleging even more serious mishandling of meat at Food Lion stores across several states. The truth of the *PrimeTime Live* broadcast was not an issue in the litigation we now describe.

Food Lion sued ABC and the *PrimeTime Live* producers and reporters. Food Lion's suit focused not on the broadcast, as a defamation suit would, but on the methods ABC used to obtain the video footage. The grocery chain asserted claims of fraud, breach of the duty of loyalty, trespass, and unfair trade practices, seeking millions in compensatory damages. Specifically, Food Lion sought to recover (1) administrative costs and wages paid in connection with the employment of Dale and Barnett and (2) broadcast (publication) damages for matters such as loss of good will, lost sales and profits, and diminished stock value. Punitive damages were also requested by Food Lion.

The district court, in a remarkably efficient effort, tried the case with a jury in three phases. At the liability phase, the jury found all of the ABC defendants liable to Food Lion for fraud and two of them, Dale and Barnett, additionally liable for breach of the duty of loyalty and trespass . . . the district court determined that the ABC defendants had violated the North Carolina Unfair and Deceptive Trade Practices Act (UTPA). Prior to the compensatory damages phase, the district court ruled that damages allegedly incurred by Food Lion as a result of ABC's broadcast of *PrimeTime Live*—"lost profits, lost sales, diminished stock value or anything of that nature"—could not be recovered because these damages were not proximately caused by the acts (fraud, trespass, etc.) attributed to the ABC defendants in this case. *See Food Lion, Inc. v. Capital Cities/ABC, Inc.*, 964 F.Supp. 956, 958 (M.D.N.C.1997) (setting forth rationale for ruling at trial). Operating within this constraint, the jury in the second phase awarded Food Lion $1,400 in compensatory damages on its fraud claim, $1.00 each on its duty of loyalty and trespass claims, and $1,500 on its UTPA claim. (The court required Food Lion to make an election between the fraud and UTPA damages, and the grocery chain elected to take the $1,400 in fraud damages.) At the final stage the jury lowered the boom and awarded $5,545,750 in punitive damages on the fraud claim against ABC and its two producers, Kaplan and Rosen. The jury refused to award punitive damages against the reporters, Dale and Barnett. In post-trial proceedings the district court ruled that the punitive damages award was excessive, and Food Lion accepted a remittitur to a total of $315,000.

After trial the ABC defendants moved for judgment as a matter of law on all claims, the motion was denied, and the defendants now appeal. Food Lion cross-appeals, contesting the district court's ruling that the damages the grocery chain sought as a result of the *PrimeTime Live* broadcast were not recoverable in this action. We now turn to the legal issues.

II.

A.

We must first consider whether the ABC defendants can be held liable for fraud, breach of the duty of loyalty, and trespass as a matter of North Carolina and South Carolina law and whether the North Carolina UTPA applies. . . .

The district court found an UTPA violation because ABC is a business that engaged in deception. However, the deception—the misrepresentations in Dale's application—did not harm the consuming public. Presumably, ABC intended to benefit the consuming public by letting it know about Food Lion's food handling practices. Moreover, ABC was not competing with Food Lion, and it did not have any actual or potential business relationship with the grocery chain. The UTPA, therefore, cannot be used here because there is no competitive or business relationship that can be policed for the benefit of the consuming public. The North Carolina statute has not been applied to a circumstance like this, and we believe the Supreme Court of North Carolina would hold that it should not be. We therefore reverse the district court's judgment that the ABC defendants, including Dale, were liable under the North Carolina UTPA.

B.

ABC argues that even if state tort law covers some of Dale and Barnett's conduct, the district court erred in refusing to subject Food Lion's claims to any level of First Amendment scrutiny. ABC makes this argument because Dale and Barnett were engaged in newsgathering for *PrimeTime Live.* It is true that there are "First Amendment interests in newsgathering." *In re Shain,* 978 F.2d 850, 855 (4th Cir. 1992) (Wilkinson J., concurring) . . . . However, the Supreme Court has said in no uncertain terms that "generally applicable laws do not offend the First Amendment simply because their enforcement against the press has incidental effects on its ability to gather and report the news." *Cohen v. Cowles Media Co.,* 501 U.S. 663, 669 (1991) . . . .

In *Cowles,* Cohen, who was associated with a candidate for governor of Minnesota, gave damaging information about a candidate for another office to two reporters on their promise that his (Cohen's) identity would not be disclosed. Because editors at the reporters' newspapers concluded that the source was an essential part of the story, it was published with Cohen named as the origin. Cohen was fired from his job as a result, and he sued the newspapers for breaking the promise. The question in the Supreme Court was whether the First Amendment barred Cohen from recovering damages under state promissory estoppel law. The newspapers argued that absent "a need to further a state interest of the highest order," the First Amendment protected them from liability for publishing truthful information, lawfully obtained, about a matter of public concern. *Id.* at 668-69 (quoting *Smith v. Daily Mail Publ'g Co.,* 443 U.S. 97, 103 (1979)). The Supreme Court disagreed, holding that the press "has no special immunity from the application of general laws" and that the enforcement of general laws against the press "is not subject to stricter scrutiny than would be applied to enforcement against other persons or organizations." *Id.* at 670 (quoting *Associated Press v. NLRB,* 301 U.S. 103, 132 (1937)).

The key inquiry in *Cowles* was whether the law of promissory estoppel was a generally applicable law. The Court began its analysis with some examples of generally applicable laws that must be obeyed by the press, such as those relating to copyright, labor, antitrust, and tax. *Id.* at 669. More relevant to us, "[t]he press may not with impunity break and enter an office or dwelling to gather news." *Id.* In analyzing the doctrine of promissory estoppel, the Court determined that it was a law of general applicability because it "does not target or single out the press," but instead applies "to the daily transactions of all the citizens of Minnesota." *Id.* at 670. The Court concluded that "the First Amendment does not confer on the press a constitutional right to disregard promises that would otherwise be enforced under state law." *Id.* at 672. The Court thus refused to apply any heightened scrutiny to the enforcement of Minnesota's promissory estoppel law against the newspapers.

The torts Dale and Barnett committed, breach of the duty of loyalty and trespass, fit neatly into the *Cowles* framework. Neither tort targets or singles out the press. Each applies to the daily transactions of the citizens of North and South Carolina. If, for example, an employee of a competing grocery chain hired on with Food Lion and videotaped damaging information in Food Lion's non-public areas for later disclosure to the public, these tort laws would apply with the same force as they do against Dale and Barnett here. Nor do we believe that applying these laws against the media will have more than an "incidental effect" on newsgathering. *See Cowles,* 501 U.S. at 669, 671-72. We are convinced that the media can do its important job effectively without resort to the commission of run-of-the-mill torts.

ABC argues that *Cowles* is not to be applied automatically to every "generally applicable law" because the Supreme Court has since said that "the enforcement of [such a] law may or may not be subject to heightened scrutiny under the First Amendment." *Turner Broadcasting System, Inc. v. FCC,* 512 U.S. 622, 640 (1994) (contrasting *Barnes v. Glen Theatre, Inc.,* 501 U.S. 560 (1991), and *Cowles*). In *Glen Theatre* nude dancing establishments and their dancers challenged a generally applicable law prohibiting public nudity. Because the general ban on public nudity covered nude dancing, which was expressive conduct, the Supreme Court applied heightened scrutiny. *Glen Theatre,* 501 U.S. at 566. In *Cowles* a generally applicable law (promissory estoppel) was invoked against newspapers who broke their promises to a source that they would keep his name confidential in exchange for information leading to a news story. There, the Court refused to apply heightened scrutiny, concluding that application of the doctrine of promissory estoppel had "no more than [an] incidental" effect on the press's ability to gather or report news. *Cowles,* 501 U.S. at 671-72. There is arguable tension between the approaches in the two cases. The cases are consistent, however, if we view the challenged conduct in *Cowles* to be the breach of promise and not some form of expression. In *Glen Theatre,* on the other hand, an activity directly covered by the law, nude dancing, necessarily involved expression, and heightened scrutiny was applied. Here, as in *Cowles,* heightened scrutiny does not apply because the tort laws (breach of duty of loyalty and trespass) do not single out the press or have more than an incidental effect upon its work.

C.

For the foregoing reasons, we affirm the judgment that Dale and Barnett breached their duty of loyalty to Food Lion and committed trespass. We likewise affirm the damages award against them for these torts in the amount of $2.00. We have already indicated that the fraud claim against all of the ABC defendants must be reversed. Because Food Lion was awarded punitive damages only on its fraud claim, the judgment awarding punitive damages cannot stand.

III.

In its cross-appeal Food Lion argues that the district court erred in refusing to allow it to use its non-reputational tort claims (breach of duty of loyalty, trespass, etc.) to recover compensatory damages for ABC's broadcast of the *PrimeTime Live* program that targeted Food Lion. The publication damages Food Lion sought (or alleged) were for items relating to its reputation, such as loss of good will and lost sales. The district court determined that the publication damages claimed by Food Lion "were the direct result of diminished consumer confidence in the store" and that "it was [Food Lion's] food handling practices themselves—not the method by which they were recorded or published—which caused the loss of consumer confidence." *Food Lion, Inc. v. Capital Cities/ABC, Inc.,* 964 F.Supp. 956, 963 (M.D.N.C. 1997). The court therefore concluded that the publication damages were not proximately caused by the non-reputational torts committed by ABC's employees. We do not reach the matter of proximate cause because an overriding (and settled) First Amendment principle precludes the award of publication damages in this case, as ABC has argued to the district court and to us. Food Lion attempted to avoid the First Amendment limitations on defamation claims by seeking publication damages under non-reputational tort claims, while holding to the normal state law proof standards for these torts. This is precluded by *Hustler Magazine v. Falwell,* 485 U.S. 46 (1988).

Food Lion acknowledges that it did not sue for defamation because its "ability to bring an action for defamation . . . required proof that ABC acted with actual malice." Appellee's Opening Br. at 44. Food Lion thus understood that if it sued ABC for defamation it would have to prove that the *PrimeTime Live* broadcast contained a false statement of fact that was made with "actual malice," that is, with knowledge that it was false or with reckless disregard as to whether it was true or false. *See New York Times Co. v. Sullivan,* 376 U.S. 254, 279-80 (1964). It is clear that Food Lion was not prepared to offer proof meeting the *New York Times* standard under any claim that it might assert. What Food Lion sought to do, then, was to recover defamation-type damages under non-reputational tort claims, without satisfying the stricter (First Amendment) standards of a defamation claim. We believe that such an end-run around First Amendment strictures is foreclosed by *Hustler.*

In *Hustler* a popular liquor advertisement prompted the magazine to run a parody of the ad, labeled as such, that featured the Reverend Jerry Falwell "discussing" an incestuous sexual act he had undertaken while drunk in disgusting circumstances. Falwell sued the magazine and its publisher, Larry Flynt, seeking damages for libel and intentional infliction of emotional distress. At trial the jury held against Falwell on the libel claim, specifically finding that the ad parody could not reasonably be understood as describing actual facts about Falwell or actual events in which he participated. The jury, however, found for Falwell on the emotional distress claim and awarded compensatory and punitive damages.

The Rev. Jerry Falwell

It was clear that Falwell, in asserting the claim for intentional infliction of emotional distress, sought "damages for emotional harm *caused by the publication* of an ad parody offensive to him." *Hustler,* 485 U.S. at 50, 108 S.Ct. 876 (emphasis added). In the Supreme Court the question was whether Falwell had to satisfy the heightened First Amendment proof standard set forth in *New York Times.* After concluding that the ad parody was protected expression, the Court, in an opinion by Chief Justice Rehnquist, held that the constitutional libel standard applied to Falwell's emotional distress claim:

> We conclude that public figures and public officials may not recover for the tort of intentional infliction of emotional distress by reason of publications such as the one here at issue without showing in addition that the publication contains a false statement of fact which was made with "actual malice," *i.e.,* with knowledge that the statement was false or with reckless disregard as to whether or not it was true.

Hustler, 485 U.S. at 56, 108 S.Ct. 876.

Hustler confirms that when a public figure plaintiff uses a law to seek damages resulting from speech covered by the First Amendment, the plaintiff must satisfy the proof standard of *New York Times.* Here, Food Lion was not prepared to meet this standard for publication damages under any of the claims it asserted. Unless there is some way to distinguish *Hustler* (we think there is not, *see* below), Food Lion cannot sustain its request for publication damages from the ABC broadcast.

. . . Food Lion, in seeking compensation for matters such as loss of good will and lost sales, is claiming reputational damages from publication, which the *Cowles* Court distinguished by placing them in the same category as the emotional distress damages sought by Falwell in *Hustler.* In other words, according to *Cowles,* "constitutional libel standards" apply to damage claims for reputational injury from a publication such as the one here.

Food Lion also argues that because ABC obtained the videotapes through unlawful acts, that is, the torts of breach of duty of loyalty and trespass, it (Food Lion) is entitled to publication damages without meeting the *New York Times* standard. The Supreme Court has never suggested that it would dispense with the *Times* standard in this situation, and we believe *Hustler* indicates that the Court would not. In *Hustler* the magazine's conduct would have been sufficient to constitute an unlawful act, the intentional infliction of emotional distress, if state law standards of proof had applied. Indeed, the Court said, "[g]enerally speaking the law does not regard the intent to inflict emotional distress as one which should receive much solicitude." *Hustler*, 485 U.S. at 53, 108 S.Ct. 876. Notwithstanding the nature of the underlying act, the Court held that satisfying *New York Times* was a prerequisite to the recovery of publication damages. That result was "necessary," the Court concluded, in order "to give adequate 'breathing space' to the freedoms protected by the First Amendment." *Id.* at 56, 108 S.Ct. 876.

In sum, Food Lion could not bypass the *New York Times* standard if it wanted publication damages. The district court therefore reached the correct result when it disallowed these damages, although we affirm on a different ground.

IV.

To recap, we *reverse* the judgment to the extent it provides that the ABC defendants committed fraud and awards compensatory damages of $1,400 and punitive damages of $315,000 on that claim; we *affirm* the judgment to the extent it provides that Dale and Barnett breached their duty of loyalty to Food Lion and committed a trespass and awards total damages of $2.00 on those claims; we *reverse* the judgment to the extent it provides that the ABC defendants violated the North Carolina UTPA; and we *affirm* the district court's ruling that Food Lion was not entitled to prove publication damages on its claims.

AFFIRMED IN PART AND REVERSED IN PART.

NIEMEYER, Circuit Judge, concurring in part and dissenting in part.

Because I believe that ample evidence supports the jury's verdict finding that the ABC defendants acted fraudulently, I dissent from Part II.A.1. of the majority opinion. I am pleased to join the remainder. . . .

Though the Food Lion case was never heard in the U.S. Supreme Court, the justices granted certiorari in 2001 to a case involving reporters who published stories based on a surreptitious audio recording of a private telephone conversation. While the reporters knew that the recording itself was an unlawful wiretap, none of the journalists had any role in planning or creating the tape. Plaintiffs, however, argued that federal wiretapping statutes and Pennsylvania law imposed liability on the reporters since they "knew or had reason to know" that the tape was obtained by illegal means. The resulting decision, Bartnicki v. Vopper, infra, addresses a question that has become much more significant today in light of unauthorized leaks of sensitive, illegally obtained, content by WikiLeaks, Edward Snowden, and Guccifer 2.0 to major news organizations like the *New York Times*, the *Guardian*, and the *Washington Post*.

BARTNICKI V. VOPPER
413 U.S. 15 (2001)

Justice STEVENS delivered the opinion of the Court.

These cases raise an important question concerning what degree of protection, if any, the First Amendment provides to speech that discloses the contents of an illegally intercepted communication. That question is both novel and narrow. Despite the fact that federal law has prohibited such disclosures since 1934, this is the first time that we have confronted such an issue.

The suit at hand involves the repeated intentional disclosure of an illegally intercepted cellular telephone conversation about a public issue. The persons who made the disclosures did not participate in the interception, but they did know—or at least had reason to know—that the interception was unlawful. Accordingly, these cases present a conflict between interests of the highest order—on the one hand, the interest in the full and free dissemination of information concerning public issues, and, on the other hand, the interest in individual privacy and, more specifically, in fostering private speech. The Framers of the First Amendment surely did not foresee the advances in science that produced the conversation, the interception, or the conflict that gave rise to this action. It is therefore not surprising that Circuit judges, as well as the Members of this Court, have come to differing conclusions about the First Amendment's application to this issue. Nevertheless, having considered the interests at stake, we are firmly convinced that the disclosures made by respondents in this suit are protected by the First Amendment.

...

During 1992 and most of 1993, the Pennsylvania State Education Association, a union representing the teachers at the Wyoming Valley West High School, engaged in collective-bargaining negotiations with the school board. Petitioner Kane, then the president of the local union, testified that the negotiations were " 'contentious' " and received "a lot of media attention." App. 79, 92. In May 1993, petitioner Bartnicki, who was acting as the union's "chief negotiator," used the cellular phone in her car to call Kane and engage in a lengthy conversation about the status of the negotiations. An unidentified person intercepted and recorded that call.

In their conversation, Kane and Bartnicki discussed the timing of a proposed strike, *id.*, at 41–45, difficulties created by public comment on the negotiations, *id.*, at 46, and the need for a dramatic response to the board's intransigence. At one point, Kane said: " 'If they're not gonna move for three percent, we're gonna have to go to their, their homes .... To blow off their front porches, we'll have to do some work on some of those guys. (PAUSES). Really, uh, really and truthfully because this is, you know, this is bad news. (UNDECIPHERABLE).' " *Ibid.*

In the early fall of 1993, the parties accepted a nonbinding arbitration proposal that was generally favorable to the teachers. In connection with news reports about the settlement, respondent Vopper, a radio commentator who had been critical of the union in the past, played a tape of the intercepted conversation on his public affairs talk show. Another station also broadcast the tape, and local newspapers published its contents. After filing suit against Vopper and other representatives of the media, Bartnicki and Kane (hereinafter petitioners) learned through discovery that Vopper had obtained the tape from respondent Jack Yocum, the head of a local taxpayers' organization that had opposed the union's demands throughout the negotiations. Yocum, who was added as a defendant, testified that he had found the tape in his mailbox shortly after the interception and recognized the voices of Bartnicki and Kane. Yocum played the tape for some members of the school board, and later delivered the tape itself to Vopper.

...

In their amended complaint, petitioners alleged that their telephone conversation had been surreptitiously intercepted by an unknown person using an electronic device, that Yocum had obtained a tape of that conversation, and that he intentionally disclosed it to Vopper, as well as other individuals and media representatives. Thereafter, Vopper and other members of the media repeatedly published the contents of that conversation. The amended complaint alleged that each of the defendants "knew or had reason to know" that the recording of the private telephone conversation had been obtained by means of an illegal interception. *Id.*, at 27. Relying on both federal and Pennsylvania statutory provisions, petitioners sought actual damages, statutory damages, punitive damages, and attorney's fees and costs.

Thereafter, the District Court granted a motion for an interlocutory appeal, pursuant to 28 U.S.C. § 1292(b). It certified as controlling questions of law: "(1) whether the imposition of liability on the media Defendants under the [wiretapping statutes] solely for broadcasting the newsworthy tape on the Defendant [Vopper's] radio news/public affairs program, when the tape was illegally intercepted and recorded by unknown persons who were not agents of [the] Defendants, violates the First Amendment; and (2) whether imposition of liability under the aforesaid [wiretapping] statutes on Defendant Jack Yocum solely for providing the anonymously intercepted and recorded tape to the media Defendants violates the First Amendment." App. to Pet. for Cert. in No. 99-1728, p. 76a. The Court of Appeals accepted the appeal, and the United States, also a petitioner, intervened pursuant to 28 U.S.C. § 2403 in order to defend the constitutionality of the federal statute.

All three members of the panel agreed with petitioners and the Government that the federal and Pennsylvania wiretapping statutes are "content-neutral" and therefore subject to "intermediate scrutiny." 200 F.3d 109, 121 (C.A.3 1999). Applying that standard, the majority concluded that the statutes were invalid because they deterred significantly more speech than necessary to protect the privacy interests at stake. The court remanded the case with instructions to enter summary judgment for respondents. In dissent, Senior Judge Pollak expressed the view that the prohibition against disclosures was necessary in order to remove the incentive for illegal interceptions and to preclude compounding the harm caused by such interceptions through wider dissemination. In so doing, he agreed with the majority opinion in a similar case decided by the Court of Appeals for the District of Columbia, *Boehner v. McDermott,* 191 F.3d 463 (C.A.D.C.1999). See also *Peavy v. WFAA-TV, Inc.,* 221 F.3d 158 (C.A.5 2000).[5] We granted certiorari to resolve the conflict. 530 U.S. 1260, 120 S.Ct. 2716, 147 L.Ed.2d 981 (2000).

...

As we pointed out in *Berger v. New York,* 388 U.S. 41, 45-49, 87 S.Ct. 1873, 18 L.Ed.2d 1040 (1967), sophisticated (and not so sophisticated) methods of eavesdropping on oral conversations and intercepting telephone calls have been practiced for decades, primarily by law enforcement authorities. In *Berger,* we held that New York's broadly written statute authorizing the police to conduct wiretaps violated the Fourth Amendment. Largely in response to that decision, and to our holding in *Katz v. United States,* 389 U.S. 347, 88 S.Ct. 507, 19 L.Ed.2d 576 (1967), that the attachment of a listening and recording device to the outside of a telephone booth constituted a search, "Congress undertook to draft comprehensive legislation both authorizing the use of evidence obtained by electronic surveillance on specified conditions, and prohibiting its use otherwise. S.Rep. No. 1097, 90th Cong., 2d Sess., 66 (1968), U.S.Code Cong. & Admin.News 1968, pp. 2112, 2153." *Gelbard v. United States,* 408 U.S. 41, 78, 92 S.Ct. 2357, 33 L.Ed.2d 179 (1972) (REHNQUIST, J., dissenting). The ultimate result of those efforts was Title III of the Omnibus Crime Control and Safe Streets Act of 1968, 82 Stat. 211, entitled Wiretapping and Electronic Surveillance.

One of the stated purposes of that title was "to protect effectively the privacy of wire and oral communications." *Ibid.* In addition to authorizing and regulating electronic surveillance for law enforcement purposes, Title III also regulated private conduct. One part of those regulations, § 2511(1), defined five offenses punishable by a fine of not more than $10,000, by imprisonment for not more than five years, or by both. Subsection (a) applied to any person who "willfully intercepts ... any wire or oral communication." Subsection (b) applied to the intentional use of devices designed to intercept oral conversations; subsection (d) applied to the use of the contents of illegally intercepted wire or oral communications; and subsection (e) prohibited the unauthorized disclosure of the contents of interceptions that were authorized for law enforcement purposes. Subsection (c), the original version of the provision most directly at issue in this suit, applied to any person who "willfully discloses, or endeavors to disclose, to any other person the contents of any wire or oral communication, knowing or having reason to know that the information was obtained through the interception of a wire or oral communication in violation of this subsection." The oral communications protected by the Act were only those "uttered by a person exhibiting an expectation that such communication is not subject to interception under circumstances justifying such expectation." § 2510(2).

As enacted in 1968, Title III did not apply to the monitoring of radio transmissions. In the Electronic Communications Privacy Act of 1986, 100 Stat. 1848, however, Congress enlarged the coverage of Title III to prohibit the interception of "electronic" as well as oral and wire communications. By reason of that amendment, as well as a 1994 amendment which applied to cordless telephone communications, 108 Stat. 4279, Title III now applies to the interception of conversations over both cellular and cordless phones. Although a lesser criminal penalty may apply to the interception of such transmissions, the same civil remedies are available whether the communication was "oral," "wire," or "electronic," as defined by 18 U.S.C. § 2510 (1994 ed. and Supp. V).

...

The constitutional question before us concerns the validity of the statutes as applied to the specific facts of these cases. Because of the procedural posture of these cases, it is appropriate to make certain important assumptions about those facts. We accept petitioners' submission that the interception was intentional, and therefore unlawful, and that, at a minimum, respondents "had reason to know" that it was unlawful. Accordingly, the disclosure of the contents of the intercepted conversation by Yocum to school board members and to representatives of the media, as well as the subsequent disclosures by the media defendants to the public, violated the federal and state statutes. Under the provisions of the federal statute, as well as its Pennsylvania analogue, petitioners are thus entitled to recover damages from each of the respondents. The only question is whether the application of these statutes in such circumstances violates the First Amendment.

In answering that question, we accept respondents' submission on three factual matters that serve to distinguish most of the cases that have arisen under § 2511. First, respondents played no part in the illegal interception. Rather, they found out about the interception only after it occurred, and in fact never learned the identity of the person or persons who made the interception. Second, their access to the information on the tapes was obtained lawfully, even though the information itself was intercepted unlawfully by someone else. Cf. *Florida Star v. B.J.F.*, 491 U.S. 524, 536, 109 S.Ct. 2603, 105 L.Ed.2d 443 (1989) ("Even assuming the Constitution permitted a State to proscribe *receipt* of information, Florida has not taken this step"). Third, the subject matter of the conversation was a matter of public concern. If the statements about the labor negotiations had been made in a public arena—during a bargaining session, for example—they would have been newsworthy. This would also be true if a third party had inadvertently overheard Bartnicki making the same statements to Kane when the two thought they were alone.

...

As a general matter, "state action to punish the publication of truthful information seldom can satisfy constitutional standards." *Smith v. Daily Mail Publishing Co.*, 443 U.S. 97, 102, 99 S.Ct. 2667, 61 L.Ed.2d 399 (1979). More specifically, this Court has repeatedly held that "if a newspaper lawfully obtains truthful information about a matter of public significance then state officials may not constitutionally punish publication of the information, absent a need ... of the highest order." *Id.*, at 103, 99 S.Ct. 2667; see also *Florida Star v. B.J.F.*, 491 U.S. 524, 109 S.Ct. 2603, 105 L.Ed.2d 443 (1989); *Landmark Communications, Inc. v. Virginia*, 435 U.S. 829, 98 S.Ct. 1535, 56 L.Ed.2d 1 (1978).

Accordingly, in *New York Times Co. v. United States*, 403 U.S. 713, 91 S.Ct. 2140, 29 L.Ed.2d 822 (1971) *(per curiam)*, the Court upheld the right of the press to publish information of great public concern obtained from documents stolen by a third party. In so doing, that decision resolved a conflict between the basic rule against prior restraints on publication and the interest in preserving the secrecy of information that, if disclosed, might seriously impair the security of the Nation. In resolving that conflict, the attention of every Member of this Court was focused on the character of the stolen documents' contents and the consequences of public disclosure. Although the undisputed fact that the newspaper intended to publish information obtained from stolen documents was noted in Justice Harlan's dissent, *id.*, at 754, 91 S.Ct. 2140, neither the majority nor the dissenters placed any weight on that fact.

However, *New York Times v. United States* raised, but did not resolve, the question "whether, in cases where information has been acquired *unlawfully* by a newspaper or by a source, government may ever punish not only the unlawful acquisition, but the ensuing publication as well." *Florida Star,* 491 U.S., at 535, n. 8, 109 S.Ct. 2603. The question here, however, is a narrower version of that still-open question. Simply put, the issue here is this: "Where the punished publisher of information has obtained the information in question in a manner lawful in itself but from a source who has obtained it unlawfully, may the government punish the ensuing publication of that information based on the defect in a chain?" *Boehner,* 191 F.3d, at 484–485 (Sentelle, J., dissenting).

Our refusal to construe the issue presented more broadly is consistent with this Court's repeated refusal to answer categorically whether truthful publication may ever be punished consistent with the First Amendment. Rather,

> "[o]ur cases have carefully eschewed reaching this ultimate question, mindful that the future may bring scenarios which prudence counsels our not resolving anticipatorily.... We continue to believe that the sensitivity and significance of the interests presented in clashes between [the] First Amendment and privacy rights counsel relying on limited principles that sweep no more broadly than the appropriate context of the instant case." *Florida Star,* 491 U.S., at 532–533, 109 S.Ct. 2603.

See also *Landmark Communications,* 435 U.S., at 838, 98 S.Ct. 1535. Accordingly, we consider whether, given the facts of these cases, the interests served by § 2511(1)(c) can justify its restrictions on speech.

The Government identifies two interests served by the statute—first, the interest in removing an incentive for parties to intercept private conversations, and second, the interest in minimizing the harm to persons whose conversations have been illegally intercepted. We assume that those interests adequately justify the prohibition in § 2511(1)(d) against the interceptor's own use of information that he or she acquired by violating § 2511(1)(a), but it by no means follows that punishing disclosures of lawfully obtained information of public interest by one not involved in the initial illegality is an acceptable means of serving those ends.

The normal method of deterring unlawful conduct is to impose an appropriate punishment on the person who engages in it. If the sanctions that presently attach to a violation of § 2511(1)(a) do not provide sufficient deterrence, perhaps those sanctions should be made more severe. But it would be quite remarkable to hold that speech by a law-abiding possessor of information can be suppressed in order to deter conduct by a non-law-abiding third party. Although there are some rare occasions in which a law suppressing one party's speech may be justified by an interest in deterring criminal conduct by another, see, *e.g., New York v. Ferber,* 458 U.S. 747, 102 S.Ct. 3348, 73 L.Ed.2d 1113 (1982), this is not such a case.

With only a handful of exceptions, the violations of § 2511(1)(a) that have been described in litigated cases have been motivated by either financial gain or domestic disputes. In virtually all of those cases, the identity of the person or persons intercepting the communication has been known. Moreover, petitioners cite no evidence that Congress viewed the prohibition against disclosures as a response to the difficulty of identifying persons making improper use of scanners and other surveillance devices and accordingly of deterring such conduct, and there is no empirical evidence to support the assumption that the prohibition against disclosures reduces the number of illegal interceptions.

Although this suit demonstrates that there may be an occasional situation in which an anonymous scanner will risk criminal prosecution by passing on information without any expectation of financial reward or public praise, surely this is the exceptional case. Moreover, there is no basis for assuming that imposing sanctions upon respondents will deter the unidentified scanner from continuing to engage in surreptitious interceptions. Unusual cases fall far short of a showing that there is a "need ... of the highest order" for a rule supplementing the traditional means of deterring antisocial conduct. The justification for any such novel burden on expression must be "far stronger than mere speculation about serious harms." *United States v. Treasury Employees,* 513 U.S. 454, 475, 115 S.Ct. 1003, 130 L.Ed.2d 964 (1995). Accordingly, the Government's first suggested justification for applying § 2511(1)(c) to an otherwise innocent disclosure of public information is plainly insufficient.

The Government's second argument, however, is considerably stronger. Privacy of communication is an important interest, *Harper & Row, Publishers, Inc. v. Nation Enterprises,* 471 U.S. 539, 559, 105 S.Ct. 2218, 85 L.Ed.2d 588 (1985), and Title III's restrictions are intended to protect that interest, thereby "encouraging the uninhibited exchange of ideas and information among private parties...." Brief for United States 27. Moreover, the fear of public disclosure of private conversations might well have a chilling effect on private speech.

...Accordingly, it seems to us that there are important interests to be considered on *both* sides of the constitutional calculus. In considering that balance, we acknowledge that some intrusions on privacy are more offensive than others, and that the disclosure of the contents of a private conversation can be an even greater intrusion on privacy than the interception itself. As a result, there is a valid independent justification for prohibiting such disclosures by persons who lawfully obtained access to the contents of an illegally intercepted message, even if that prohibition does not play a significant role in preventing such interceptions from occurring in the first place.

We need not decide whether that interest is strong enough to justify the application of § 2511(c) to disclosures of trade secrets or domestic gossip or other information of purely private concern. Cf. *Time, Inc. v. Hill,* 385 U.S. 374, 387–388, 87 S.Ct. 534, 17 L.Ed.2d 456 (1967) (reserving the question whether truthful publication of private matters unrelated to public affairs can be constitutionally proscribed). In other words, the outcome of these cases does not turn on whether § 2511(1)(c) may be enforced with respect to most violations of the statute without offending the First Amendment. The enforcement of that provision in these cases, however, implicates the core purposes of the First Amendment because it imposes sanctions on the publication of truthful information of public concern.

In these cases, privacy concerns give way when balanced against the interest in publishing matters of public importance. As Warren and Brandeis stated in their classic law review article: "The right of privacy does not prohibit any publication of matter which is of public or general interest." The Right to Privacy, 4 Harv. L.Rev. 193, 214 (1890). One of the costs associated with participation in public affairs is an attendant loss of privacy.

> "Exposure of the self to others in varying degrees is a concomitant of life in a civilized community. The risk of this exposure is an essential incident of life in a society which places a primary value on freedom of speech and of press. 'Freedom of discussion, if it would fulfill its historic function in this nation, must embrace all issues about which information is needed or appropriate to enable the members of society to cope with the exigencies of their period.' " *Time, Inc. v. Hill,* 385 U.S., at 388, 87 S.Ct. 534 (quoting *Thornhill v. Alabama,* 310 U.S. 88, 102, 60 S.Ct. 736, 84 L.Ed. 1093 (1940)).

...

We think it clear that parallel reasoning requires the conclusion that a stranger's illegal conduct does not suffice to remove the First Amendment shield from speech about a matter of public concern. The months of negotiations over the proper level of compensation for teachers at the Wyoming Valley West High School were unquestionably a matter of public concern, and respondents were clearly engaged in debate about that concern. That debate may be more mundane than the Communist rhetoric that inspired Justice Brandeis' classic opinion in *Whitney v. California,* 274 U.S., at 372, 47 S.Ct. 641, but it is no less worthy of constitutional protection.

The judgment is affirmed.

It is so ordered.

Justice BREYER, with whom Justice O'CONNOR joins, concurring.

I join the Court's opinion. I agree with its narrow holding limited to the special circumstances present here...

As the Court recognizes, the question before us—a question of immunity from statutorily imposed civil liability—implicates competing constitutional concerns. *Ante,* at 1763–1764. The statutes directly interfere with free expression in that they prevent the media from publishing information. At the same time, they help to protect personal privacy—an interest here that includes not only the "right to be let alone," *Olmstead v. United States,* 277 U.S. 438 (1928) (Brandeis, J., dissenting), but also "the interest ... in fostering private speech"...

I would ask whether the statutes strike a reasonable balance between their speech-restricting and speech-enhancing consequences. Or do they instead impose restrictions on speech that are disproportionate when measured against their corresponding privacy and speech-related benefits, taking into account the kind, the importance, and the extent of these benefits, as well as the need for the restrictions in order to secure those benefits? ...

...[I]n finding a constitutional privilege to publish unlawfully intercepted conversations of the kind here at issue, the Court does not create a "public interest" exception that swallows up the statutes' privacy-protecting general rule. Rather, it finds constitutional protection for publication of intercepted information of a special kind. Here, the speakers' legitimate privacy expectations are unusually low, and the public interest in defeating those expectations is unusually high. Given these circumstances, along with the lawful nature of respondents' behavior, the statutes' enforcement would disproportionately harm media freedom.

I emphasize the particular circumstances before us because, in my view, the Constitution permits legislatures to respond flexibly to the challenges future technology may pose to the individual's interest in basic personal privacy. Clandestine and pervasive invasions of privacy, unlike the simple theft of documents from a bedroom, are genuine possibilities as a result of continuously advancing technologies. Eavesdropping on ordinary cellular phone conversations in the street (which many callers seem to tolerate) is a very different matter from eavesdropping on encrypted cellular phone conversations or those carried on in the bedroom. But the technologies that allow the former may come to permit the latter. And statutes that may seem less important in the former context may turn out to have greater importance in the latter. Legislatures also may decide to revisit statutes such as those before us, creating better tailored provisions designed to encourage, for example, more effective privacy-protecting technologies.

For these reasons, we should avoid adopting overly broad or rigid constitutional rules, which would unnecessarily restrict legislative flexibility. I consequently agree with the Court's holding that the statutes as applied here violate the Constitution, but I would not extend that holding beyond these present circumstances.

Chief Justice REHNQUIST, with whom Justice SCALIA and Justice THOMAS join, dissenting.

Technology now permits millions of important and confidential conversations to occur through a vast system of electronic networks. These advances, however, raise significant privacy concerns. We are placed in the uncomfortable position of not knowing who might have access to our personal and business e-mails, our medical and financial records, or our cordless and cellular telephone conversations. In an attempt to prevent some of the most egregious violations of privacy, the United States, the District of Columbia, and 40 States have enacted laws prohibiting the intentional interception and knowing disclosure of electronic communications. The Court holds that all of these statutes violate the First Amendment insofar as the illegally intercepted conversation touches upon a matter of "public concern," an amorphous concept that the Court does not even attempt to define. But the Court's decision diminishes, rather than enhances, the purposes of the First Amendment, thereby chilling the speech of the millions of Americans who rely upon electronic technology to communicate each day....

NOTES AND QUESTIONS

1. The common law does not shield journalists because they are not licensed and do not have a trust relationship with clients as lawyers and doctors do. But aren't some journalists highly trained professionals with graduate degrees from respected universities? And is not a reporter's promise of confidentiality made to a source predicated on a trust relationship? Do you think the common law should weigh these considerations and allow for a privilege in meritorious cases? Why or why not?
2. What is a journalist? In some countries, journalists are licensed by the state, but in the United States, anyone can claim to be a journalist. Should a never-published novelist be considered a journalist if the novelist uncovers relevant evidence in an actual case while conducting research? What about a blogger on a popular gossip website? Can there be a credential process for journalists that would be acceptable under the First Amendment? Should there be?
3. In his *Harper & Row* dissent, Justice Brennan argues that journalists are expressly covered by the "fair use" provisions contained in the Copyright Act of 1976. Why does the majority opinion not offer blanket protection to journalists acting in good faith? How does the First Amendment factor into the majority's analysis?
4. **The chilling effect of threatened litigation.** The absence of clear guidelines for "fair use" may chill the speech of individuals and companies lacking the resources to defend themselves from a threatened

copyright suit. Documentary producers and book authors may be less inclined to take advantage of "fair use" if they are threatened with a suit and the prospect of paying their own attorneys' fees even if they prevail. Should there be a "safe harbor" for "fair use"?

5. The Register of Copyrights at the Library of Congress affords special "fair use" status for educators, provided that the otherwise infringing use is limited to in-class instruction. In the digital age, in-class instruction is just one component of an educational environment that may include Web-based simulations and asynchronous online instruction. Should this special "fair use" status be extended to digital platforms outside the traditional classroom?
6. At the time of the *Sony* decision in 1984, home VCR use was not viewed as a significant threat to commercial television. Today, DVRs allow viewers to fast-forward through commercials at lightning speed, and some, like DirecTV's Hopper, can skip commercials entirely. Should the courts revisit the U.S. Supreme Court's decision in the so-called "Betamax case"?
7. Does the First Amendment require a president of the United States to support and protect a free press? In one of his first tweets after becoming president, Donald Trump referred to the American press as the "enemy of the people." In the Trump era, journalists have been screamed at, pepper-sprayed, physically restrained, and arrested for doing nothing more than trying to report a story. In May 2017, a reporter for the *Guardian* newspaper was body slammed by Greg Gianforte, a GOP candidate for Montana's seat in Congress. An audio recording, corroborated by witnesses, showed that the reporter was attacked after calmly posing a question about healthcare that the candidate did not want to answer. Gianforte was charged with misdemeanor assault, but won the election anyway.

CHAPTER 6

OBSCENITY & CHILD PORNOGRAPHY

The word "obscenity" has many meanings in the English language. People use the word frequently to describe something outrageous or offensive. Expensive dinner checks are sometimes referred to as obscene. Four-letter words are commonly called "obscenities" and the word is often used interchangeably with pornography. For the media lawyer, however, obscenity has a very specific legal meaning. As you can see in the first case infra, Miller v. California, for speech to be obscene it must fail a three-part test. If the speech passes the *Miller* test, then it is protected under the First Amendment—soft-core pornography and uses of four-letter words would fall into that category. If the speech does not pass the *Miller* test, it is unprotected speech, which means that the state can censor it with minimal scrutiny.

As you review *Miller*, you will see a long history of the courts trying to address obscenity. One of the problems with obscenity is that it can be subjective. Justice Potter Stewart famously summed up the subjective challenge of obscenity when he stated, in Jacobellis v. Ohio: "I know it when I see it." To address this subjectivity, the *Miller* court added some flexibility to the obscenity test, allowing juries to apply community standards in their analyses of the speech-at-issue's prurient impact.

The next cases in this chapter have to do with child pornography. No one would argue that someone who photographs children in sexual poses is a child abuser and criminal of the worst kind. But child pornography laws are not only about punishing the conduct of a sex offender. In Ferber v. New York infra, the Supreme Court ruled that the possession of pornographic images of identifiable children is not protected by the First Amendment. The government can—and does—prosecute and imprison individuals who possess this content, even if they had no knowledge of the minors depicted or the manner if its creation. In the wake of the digital revolution, the debate over child pornography has become more complicated as new technologies make it possible for pornographers to create computer-generated images of virtual children. To address this, Congress enacted a statute that, among other things, punished those who would create virtual child pornography. In Ashcroft v. Free Speech Coalition, the Supreme Court declared such provisions to be an unconstitutional departure from the logic of *Ferber*, which justified exceptional treatment for child pornography because real children suffered real harm.

MILLER V. CALIFORNIA
413 U.S. 15 (1973)

Mr. Chief Justice BURGER delivered the opinion of the Court.
This is one of a group of "obscenity-pornography" cases being reviewed by the Court in a re-examination of standards enunciated in earlier cases involving what Mr. Justice Harlan called "the intractable obscenity problem."

Appellant conducted a mass mailing campaign to advertise the sale of illustrated books, euphemistically called "adult" material. After a jury trial, he was convicted of violating California Penal Code § 311.2(a), a misdemeanor, by knowingly distributing obscene matter and the Appellate Department, Superior Court of California, County of Orange, summarily affirmed the judgment without opinion. Appellant's conviction was specifically based on his conduct in causing five unsolicited advertising brochures to be sent through the mail in an envelope addressed to a restaurant in Newport Beach, California. The envelope was opened by the manager of the restaurant and his mother. They had not requested the brochures; they complained to the police.

The brochures advertise four books entitled "Intercourse," "Man-Woman," "Sex Orgies Illustrated," and "An Illustrated History of Pornography," and a film entitled "Marital Intercourse." While the brochures contain some descriptive printed material, primarily they consist of pictures and drawings very explicitly depicting men and women in groups of two or more engaging in a variety of sexual activities, with genitals often prominently displayed.

I.
This case involves the application of a State's criminal obscenity statute to a situation in which sexually explicit materials have been thrust by aggressive sales action upon unwilling recipients who had in no way indicated any desire to receive such materials. This Court has recognized that the States have a legitimate interest in prohibiting dissemination or exhibition of obscene material when the mode of dissemination carries with it a significant danger of offending the sensibilities of unwilling recipients or of exposure to juveniles. . . . It is in this context that we are called on to define the standards which must be used to identify obscene material that a State may regulate without infringing on the First

Amendment as applicable to the States through the Fourteenth Amendment.

. . . While Roth presumed "obscenity" to be "utterly without redeeming social importance," Memoirs required that to prove obscenity it must be affirmatively established that the material is "utterly without redeeming social value." Thus, even as they repeated the words of Roth, the Memoirs plurality produced a drastically altered test that called on the prosecution to prove a negative, i.e., that the material was "utterly without redeeming social value"—a burden virtually impossible to discharge under our criminal standards of proof. Such considerations caused Mr. Justice Harlan to wonder if the "utterly without redeeming social value" test had any meaning at all. . . .

II.

This much has been categorically settled by the Court, that obscene material is unprotected by the First Amendment. . . . We acknowledge, however, the inherent dangers of undertaking to regulate any form of expression. State statutes designed to regulate obscene materials must be carefully limited. See Interstate Circuit, Inc. v. Dallas, supra, 390 U.S., at 682-685. As a result, we now confine the permissible scope of such regulation to works which depict or describe sexual conduct. That conduct must be specifically defined by the applicable state law, as written or authoritatively construed. A state offense must also be limited to works which, taken as a whole, appeal to the prurient interest in sex, which portray sexual conduct in a patently offensive way, and which, taken as a whole, do not have serious literary, artistic, political, or scientific value.

The basic guidelines for the trier of fact must be: (a) whether "the average person, applying contemporary community standards" would find that the work, taken as a whole, appeals to the prurient interest, Kois v. Wisconsin, supra, 408 U.S., at 230, quoting Roth v. United States, supra, 354 U.S., at 489; (b) whether the work depicts or describes, in a patently offensive way, sexual conduct specifically defined by the applicable state law; and (c) whether the work, taken as a whole, lacks serious literary, artistic, political, or scientific value. We do not adopt as a constituional standard the "utterly without redeeming social value" test of Memoirs v. Massachusetts, 383 U.S., at 419; that concept has never commanded the adherence of more than three Justices at one time. See supra, at 2613. If a state law that regulates obscene material is thus limited, as written or construed, the First Amendment values applicable to the States through the Fourteenth Amendment are adequately protected by the ultimate power of appellate courts to conduct an independent review of constitutional claims when necessary. . . .

We emphasize that it is not our function to propose regulatory schemes for the States. That must await their concrete legislative efforts. It is possible, however, to give a few plain examples of what a state statute could define for regulation under part (b) of the standard announced in this opinion, supra:

(a) Patently offensive representations or descriptions of ultimate sexual acts, normal or perverted, actual or simulated.

(b) Patently offensive representation or descriptions of masturbation, excretory functions, and lewd exhibition of the genitals.

Sex and nudity may not be exploited without limit by films or pictures exhibited or sold in places of public accommodation any more than live sex and nudity can be exhibited or sold without limit in such public places. At a minimum, prurient, patently offensive depiction or description of sexual conduct must have serious literary, artistic, political, or scientific value to merit First Amendment protection. See Kois v. Wisconsin, supra, 408 U.S., at 230-232; Roth v. United States, supra, 354 U.S., at 487; Thornhill v. Alabama, 310 U.S. 88 (1940). For example, medical books for the education of physicians and related personnel necessarily use graphic illustrations and descriptions of human anatomy. In resolving the inevitably sensitive questions of fact and law, we must continue to rely on the jury system, accompanied by the safeguards that judges, rules of evidence, presumption of innocence, and other protective features provide, as we do with rape, murder, and a host of other offenses against society and its individual members.

. . .

Under the holdings announced today, no one will be subject to prosecution for the sale or exposure of obscene materials unless these materials depict or describe patently offensive "hard core" sexual conduct specifically defined by the regulating state law, as written or construed. We are satisfied that these specific prerequisites will provide fair notice to a dealer in such materials that his public and commercial activities may bring prosecution. . . . If the inability to define regulated materials with ultimate, god-like precision altogether removes the power of the States or the Congress to regulate, then "hard core" pornography may be exposed without limit to the juvenile, the passerby, and the consenting adult alike, as, indeed, Mr. Justice Douglas contends. . . .

. . .

III.

We conclude that neither the State's alleged failure to offer evidence of "national standards," nor the trial court's charge that the jury consider state community standards, were constitutional errors. Nothing in the First Amendment requires that a jury must consider hypothetical and unascertainable "national standards" when attempting to determine whether certain materials are obscene as a matter of fact. Mr. Chief Justice Warren pointedly commented in his dissent in Jacobellis v. Ohio, supra, at 200:

> "It is my belief that when the Court said in Roth that obscenity is to be defined by reference to 'community standards,' it meant community standards—not a national standard, as is sometimes argued. I believe that there is no provable 'national standard' . . . . At all events, this Court has not been able to enunciate one, and it would be unreasonable to expect local courts to divine one."

It is neither realistic nor constitutionally sound to read the First Amendment as requiring that the people of Maine or Mississippi accept public depiction of conduct found tolerable in Las Vegas, or New York City. People in different States vary in their tastes and attitudes, and this diversity is not to be strangled by the absolutism of imposed uniformity. As the Court made clear in Mishkin v. New York, 383 U.S., at 508-509, the primary concern with requiring a jury to apply the standard of "the average person, applying contemporary community standards" is to be certain that, so far as material is not aimed at a deviant group, it will be judged by its impact on an average person, rather than a particularly susceptible or sensitive person—or indeed a totally insensitive one . . . We hold that the requirement that the jury evaluate the materials with reference to "contemporary standards of the State of California" serves this protective purpose and is constitutionally adequate.

IV.

. . .

In sum, we (a) reaffirm the Roth holding that obscene material is not protected by the First Amendment; (b) hold that such material can be regulated by the States, subject to the specific safeguards enunciated above, without a showing that the material is "utterly without redeeming social value"; and (c) hold that obscenity is to be determined by applying "contemporary community standards," not "national standards." The judgment of the Appellate Department of the Superior Court, Orange County, California, is vacated and the case remanded to that court for further proceedings not inconsistent with the First Amendment standards established by this opinion.

Vacated and remanded.
Mr. Justice DOUGLAS, dissenting.

I.

. . .

Today the Court retreats from the earlier formulations of the constitutional test and undertakes to make new definitions. This effort, like the earlier ones, is earnest and well intentioned. The difficulty is that we do not deal with constitutional terms, since "obscenity" is not mentioned in the Constitution or Bill of Rights. And the First Amendment makes no such exception from "the press" which it undertakes to protect nor, as I have said on other occasions, is an exception necessarily implied, for there was no recognized exception to the free press at the time the Bill of Rights was adopted which treated "obscene" publications differently from other types of papers, magazines, and books. So there are no constitutional guidelines for deciding what is and what is not "obscene." The Court is at large because we deal with tastes and standards of literature. What shocks me may be sustenance for my neighbor. What causes one person to boil up in rage over one pamphlet or movie may reflect only his neurosis, not shared by others. We deal here with a regime of censorship which, if adopted, should be done by constitutional amendment after full debate by the people.

Obscenity cases usually generate tremendous emotional outbursts. They have no business being in the courts. If a constitutional amendment authorized censorship, the censor would probably be an administrative agency. Then criminal prosecutions could follow as, if, and when publishers defied the censor and sold their literature. Under that regime a publisher would know when he was on dangerous ground. Under the present regime—whether the old standards or the new ones are used—

the criminal law becomes a trap. A brand new test would put a publisher behind bars under a new law improvised by the courts after the publication. That was done in Ginzburg and has all the evils of an ex post facto law.

. . .

II.

. . .

No such protective procedure has been designed by California in this case. Obscenity—which even we cannot define with precision—is a hodge-podge. To send men to jail for violating standards they cannot understand, construe, and apply is a monstrous thing to do in a Nation dedicated to fair trials and due process.

III.

While the right to know is the corollary of the right to speak or publish, no one can be forced by government to listen to disclosure that he finds offensive. That was the basis of my dissent in Public Utilities Comm'n v. Pollak, 343 U.S. 451, 467, where I protested against making streetcar passengers a "captive" audience. There is no "captive audience" problem in these obscenity cases. No one is being compelled to look or to listen. Those who enter newsstands or bookstalls may be offended by what they see. But they are not compelled by the State to frequent those places; and it is only state or governmental action against which the First Amendment, applicable to the States by virtue of the Fourteenth, raises a ban.

The idea that the First Amendment permits government to ban publications that are "offensive" to some people puts an ominous gloss on freedom of the press. That test would make it possible to ban any paper or any journal or magazine in some benighted place. The First Amendment was designed "to invite dispute," to induce "a condition of unrest," to "create dissatisfaction with conditions as they are," and even to stir "people to anger." Terminiello v. Chicago, 337 U.S. 1, 4. The idea that the First Amendment permits punishment for ideas that are "offensive" to the particular judge or jury sitting in judgment is astounding. No greater leveler of speech or literature has ever been designed. To give the power to the censor, as we do today, is to make a sharp and radical break with the traditions of a free society. The First Amendment was not fashioned as a vehicle for dispensing tranquilizers to the people. Its prime function was to keep debate open to "offensive" as well as to "staid" people. The tendency throughout history has been to subdue the individual and to exalt the power of government. The use of the standard "offensive" gives authority to government that cuts the very vitals out of the First Amendment. As is intimated by the Court's opinion, the materials before us may be garbage. But so is much of what is said in political campaigns, in the daily press, on TV, or over the radio. By reason of the First Amendment—and solely because of it—speakers and publishers have not been threatened or subdued because their thoughts and ideas may be "offensive" to some.

NEW YORK V. FERBER
458 U.S. 747 (1982)

Justice WHITE delivered the opinion of the Court.
At issue in this case is the constitutionality of a New York criminal statute which prohibits persons from knowingly promoting sexual performances by children under the age of 16 by distributing material which depicts such performances.

I.
In recent years, the exploitive use of children in the production of pornography has become a serious national problem. The Federal Government and 47 States have sought to combat the problem with statutes specifically directed at the production of child pornography. At least half of such statutes do not require that the materials produced be legally obscene. Thirty-five States and the United States Congress have also passed legislation prohibiting the distribution of such materials; 20 States prohibit the distribution of material depicting children engaged in sexual conduct without requiring that the material be legally obscene.

. . .

In 1977, the New York Legislature enacted Article 263 of its Penal Law. N.Y. Penal Law, Art. 263 (McKinney 1980). Section 263.05 criminalizes as a class C felony the use of a child in a sexual performance:

> "A person is guilty of the use of a child in a sexual performance if knowing the character and content thereof he employs, authorizes or induces a child less than sixteen years of age to engage in a sexual performance or being a parent, legal guardian or custodian of such child, he con-

> sents to the participation by such child in a sexual performance."

A "[s]exual performance" is defined as "any performance or part thereof which includes sexual conduct by a child less than sixteen years of age." § 263.00(1). "Sexual conduct" is in turn defined in § 263.00(3):

> "'Sexual conduct' means actual or simulated sexual intercourse, deviate sexual intercourse, sexual bestiality, masturbation, sado-masochistic abuse, or lewd exhibition of the genitals."

A performance is defined as "any play, motion picture, photograph or dance" or "any other visual representation exhibited before an audience." § 263.00(4).

At issue in this case is § 263.15, defining a class D felony:

> "A person is guilty of promoting a sexual performance by a child when, knowing the character and content thereof, he produces, directs or promotes any performance which includes sexual conduct by a child less than sixteen years of age."

To "promote" is also defined:

> "'Promote' means to procure, manufacture, issue, sell, give, provide, lend, mail, deliver, transfer, transmute, publish, distribute, circulate, disseminate, present, exhibit or advertise, or to offer or agree to do the same." § 263.00(5).

A companion provision bans only the knowing dissemination of obscene material. § 263.10.

This case arose when Paul Ferber, the proprietor of a Manhattan bookstore specializing in sexually oriented products, sold two films to an undercover police officer. The films are devoted almost exclusively to depicting young boys masturbating. Ferber was indicted on two counts of violating § 263.10 and two counts of violating § 263.15, the two New York laws controlling dissemination of child pornography. After a jury trial, Ferber was acquitted of the two counts of promoting an obscene sexual performance, but found guilty of the two counts under § 263.15, which did not require proof that the films were obscene. Ferber's convictions were affirmed without opinion by the Appellate Division of the New York State Supreme Court. 424 N.Y.S.2d 967 (1980).

. . .

The *Miller* standard, like its predecessors, was an accommodation between the State's interests in protecting the "sensibilities of unwilling recipients" from exposure to pornographic material and the dangers of censorship inherent in unabashedly content-based laws. Like obscenity statutes, laws directed at the dissemination of child pornography run the risk of suppressing protected expression by allowing the hand of the censor to become unduly heavy. For the following reasons, however, we are persuaded that the States are entitled to greater leeway in the regulation of pornographic depictions of children.

First. It is evident beyond the need for elaboration that a State's interest in "safeguarding the physical and psychological well-being of a minor" is "compelling." *Globe Newspaper Co. v. Superior Court*, 457 U.S. 596, 607 (1982). "A democratic society rests, for its continuance, upon the healthy, well-rounded growth of young people into full maturity as citizens." *Prince v. Massachusetts*, 321 U.S. 158, 168 (1944). Accordingly, we have sustained legislation aimed at protecting the physical and emotional well-being of youth even when the laws have operated in the sensitive area of constitutionally protected rights. In *Prince v. Massachusetts, supra*, the Court held that a statute prohibiting use of a child to distribute literature on the street was valid notwithstanding the statute's effect on a First Amendment activity. In *Ginsberg v. New York, supra*, we sustained a New York law protecting children from exposure to nonobscene literature. Most recently, we held that the Government's interest in the "well-being of its youth" justified special treatment of indecent broadcasting received by adults as well as children. *FCC v. Pacifica Foundation*, 438 U.S. 726 (1978).

The prevention of sexual exploitation and abuse of children constitutes a government objective of surpassing importance. The legislative findings accompanying passage of the New York laws reflect this concern:

> "[T]here has been a proliferation of exploitation of children as subjects in sexual performances. The care of children is a sacred trust and should not be abused by those who seek to profit through a commercial network based upon the exploitation of children. The public policy of the state demands the protection of children from exploitation

> through sexual performances." 1977 N.Y. Laws, ch. 910, § 1.

We shall not second-guess this legislative judgment. Respondent has not intimated that we do so. Suffice it to say that virtually all of the States and the United States have passed legislation proscribing the production of or otherwise combating "child pornography." The legislative judgment, as well as the judgment found in the relevant literature, is that the use of children as subjects of pornographic materials is harmful to the physiological, emotional, and mental health of the child. That judgment, we think, easily passes muster under the First Amendment.

Second. The distribution of photographs and films depicting sexual activity by juveniles is intrinsically related to the sexual abuse of children in at least two ways. First, the materials produced are a permanent record of the children's participation and the harm to the child is exacerbated by their circulation. Second, the distribution network for child pornography must be closed if the production of material which requires the sexual exploitation of children is to be effectively controlled. Indeed, there is no serious contention that the legislature was unjustified in believing that it is difficult, if not impossible, to halt the exploitation of children by pursuing only those who produce the photographs and movies. While the production of pornographic materials is a low-profile, clandestine industry, the need to market the resulting products requires a visible apparatus of distribution. The most expeditious if not the only practical method of law enforcement may be to dry up the market for this material by imposing severe criminal penalties on persons selling, advertising, or otherwise promoting the product. Thirty-five States and Congress have concluded that restraints on the distribution of pornographic materials are required in order to effectively combat the problem, and there is a body of literature and testimony to support these legislative conclusions. Cf. *United States v. Darby*, 312 U.S. 100 (1941) (upholding federal restrictions on sale of goods manufactured in violation of Fair Labor Standards Act).

Respondent does not contend that the State is unjustified in pursuing those who distribute child pornography. Rather, he argues that it is enough for the State to prohibit the distribution of materials that are legally obscene under the *Miller* test. While some States may find that this approach properly accommodates its interests, it does not follow that the First Amendment prohibits a State from going further. The *Miller* standard, like all general definitions of what may be banned as obscene, does not reflect the State's particular and more compelling interest in prosecuting those who promote the sexual exploitation of children. Thus, the question under the *Miller* test of whether a work, taken as a whole, appeals to the prurient interest of the average person bears no connection to the issue of whether a child has been physically or psychologically harmed in the production of the work. Similarly, a sexually explicit depiction need not be "patently offensive" in order to have required the sexual exploitation of a child for its production. In addition, a work which, taken on the whole, contains serious literary, artistic, political, or scientific value may nevertheless embody the hardest core of child pornography. "It is irrelevant to the child [who has been abused] whether or not the material . . . has a literary, artistic, political or social value." Memorandum of Assemblyman Lasher in Support of § 263.15. We therefore cannot conclude that the *Miller* standard is a satisfactory solution to the child pornography problem.

Third. The advertising and selling of child pornography provide an economic motive for and are thus an integral part of the production of such materials, an activity illegal throughout the Nation. "It rarely has been suggested that the constitutional freedom for speech and press extends its immunity to speech or writing used as an integral part of conduct in violation of a valid criminal statute." *Giboney v. Empire Storage & Ice Co.*, 336 U.S. 490, 498 (1949). We note that were the statutes outlawing the employment of children in these films and photographs fully effective, and the constitutionality of these laws has not been questioned, the First Amendment implications would be no greater than that presented by laws against distribution: enforceable production laws would leave no child pornography to be marketed.

Fourth. The value of permitting live performances and photographic reproductions of children engaged in lewd sexual conduct is exceedingly modest, if not *de minimis.* We consider it unlikely that visual depictions of children performing sexual acts or lewdly exhibiting their genitals would often constitute an important and necessary part of a literary performance or scientific or educational work. As a state judge in this case observed, if it were necessary for literary or artistic value, a person over the statutory age who perhaps looked younger could be utilized. Simulation outside of the prohibition of the statute could provide another alternative. Nor is there any question here of censoring a particular literary theme or portrayal of sexual activity. The First Amendment interest is limited to that of rendering the portrayal somewhat more "realistic" by utilizing or photographing children.

Fifth. Recognizing and classifying child pornography as a category of material outside the protection of the First Amendment is not, incompatible with our earlier decisions. "The question whether speech is, or is not protected by the First Amendment often depends on the content of the speech." . . . Thus, it is not rare that a content-based classification of speech has been accepted because it may be appropriately generalized that within the confines of the given classification, the evil to be restricted so overwhelmingly outweighs the expressive interests, if any, at stake, that no process of case-by-case adjudication is required. When a definable class of material, such as that covered by § 263.15, bears so heavily and pervasively on the welfare of children engaged in its production, we think the balance of competing interests is clearly struck and that it is permissible to consider these materials as without the protection of the First Amendment.

C.

There are, of course, limits on the category of child pornography which, like obscenity, is unprotected by the First Amendment. As with all legislation in this sensitive area, the conduct to be prohibited must be adequately defined by the applicable state law, as written or authoritatively construed. Here the nature of the harm to be combated requires that the state offense be limited to works that *visually* depict sexual conduct by children below a specified age. The category of "sexual conduct" proscribed must also be suitably limited and described.

The test for child pornography is separate from the obscenity standard enunciated in *Miller*, but may be compared to it for the purpose of clarity. The *Miller* formulation is adjusted in the following respects: A trier of fact need not find that the material appeals to the prurient interest of the average person; it is not required that sexual conduct portrayed be done so in a patently offensive manner; and the material at issue need not be considered as a whole. We note that the distribution of descriptions or other depictions of sexual conduct, not otherwise obscene, which do not involve live performance or photographic or other visual reproduction of live performances, retains First Amendment protection. As with obscenity laws, criminal responsibility may not be imposed without some element of scienter on the part of the defendant. . . .

D.

Section 263.15's prohibition incorporates a definition of sexual conduct that comports with the above-stated principles. The forbidden acts to be depicted are listed with sufficient precision and represent the kind of conduct that, if it were the theme of a work, could render it legally obscene: "actual or simulated sexual intercourse, deviate sexual intercourse, sexual bestiality, masturbation, sado-masochistic abuse, or lewd exhibition of the genitals." § 263.00(3). The term "lewd exhibition of the genitals" is not unknown in this area and, indeed, was given in *Miller* as an example of a permissible regulation. 413 U.S., at 25. A performance is defined only to include live or visual depictions: "any play, motion picture, photograph or dance . . . [or] other visual representation exhibited before an audience." § 263.00(4). Section 263.15 expressly includes a scienter requirement.

We hold that § 263.15 sufficiently describes a category of material the production and distribution of which is not entitled to First Amendment protection. It is therefore clear that there is nothing unconstitutionally "underinclusive" about a statute that singles out this category of material for proscription. It also follows that the State is not barred by the First Amendment from prohibiting the distribution of unprotected materials produced outside the State.

III.

It remains to address the claim that the New York statute is unconstitutionally overbroad because it would forbid the distribution of material with serious literary, scientific, or educational value or material which does not threaten the harms sought to be combated by the State. Respondent prevailed on that ground below, and it is to that issue that we now turn.

The New York Court of Appeals recognized that overbreadth scrutiny has been limited with respect to conduct-related regulation, *Broadrick v. Oklahoma*, 413 U.S. 601 (1973), but it did not apply the test enunciated in *Broadrick* because the challenged statute, in its view, was directed at "pure speech." The court went on to find that § 263.15 was fatally overbroad: "[T]he statute would prohibit the showing of any play or movie in which a child portrays a defined sexual act, real or simulated, in a nonobscene manner. It would also prohibit the sale, showing, or distributing of medical or educational materials containing photographs of such acts. Indeed, by its terms, the statute would prohibit those who oppose such portrayals from providing illustrations of what they oppose." 52 N.Y.2d, at 678.

While the construction that a state court gives a state statute is not a matter subject to our review, *Wainwright v. Stone*, 414 U.S. 21, 22-23 (1973); *Gooding v. Wilson*, 405 U.S. 518, 520 (1972), this Court is the final arbiter of whether the Federal Constitution necessitated the invalidation of a state law. It is only through this process of review that we may correct erroneous applications of the Constitution that err on the side of an overly broad reading of our doctrines and precedents, as well as state-court decisions giving the Constitution too little shrift. A state court is not free to avoid a proper facial attack on federal constitutional grounds. *Bigelow v. Virginia,* 421 U.S. 809, 817 (1975). By the same token, it should not be compelled to entertain an overbreadth attack when not required to do so by the Constitution.

A.

The traditional rule is that a person to whom a statute may constitutionally be applied may not challenge that statute on the ground that it may conceivably be applied unconstitutionally to others in situations not before the Court. . . . In *Broadrick,* we recognized that this rule reflects two cardinal principles of our constitutional order: the personal nature of constitutional rights, *McGowan v. Maryland,* 366 U.S. 420, 429 (1961), and prudential limitations on constitutional adjudication. In *United States v. Raines, supra,* 362 U.S., at 21, we noted the "incontrovertible proposition" that it "'would indeed be undesirable for this Court to consider every conceivable situation which might possibly arise in the application of complex and comprehensive legislation" . . . .

What has come to be known as the First Amendment overbreadth doctrine is one of the few exceptions to this principle and must be justified by "weighty countervailing policies." *United States v. Raines, supra,* 362 U.S., at 22-23. The doctrine is predicated on the sensitive nature of protected expression: "persons whose expression is constitutionally protected may well refrain from exercising their rights for fear of criminal sanctions by a statute susceptible of application to protected expression." *Village of Schaumburg v. Citizens for a Better Environment,* 444 U.S. 620, 634 (1980); *Gooding v. Wilson, supra,* at 521. It is for this reason that we have allowed persons to attack overly broad statutes even though the conduct of the person making the attack is clearly unprotected and could be proscribed by a law drawn with the requisite specificity. . . .

The scope of the First Amendment overbreadth doctrine, like most exceptions to established principles, must be carefully tied to the circumstances in which facial invalidation of a statute is truly warranted. Because of the wide-reaching effects of striking down a statute on its face at the request of one whose own conduct may be punished despite the First Amendment, we have recognized that the overbreadth doctrine is "strong medicine" and have employed it with hesitation, and then "only as a last resort." *Broadrick,* 413 U.S., at 613. We have, in consequence, insisted that the overbreadth involved be "substantial" before the statute involved will be invalidated on its face.

The requirement of substantial overbreadth is directly derived from the purpose and nature of the doctrine. While a sweeping statute, or one incapable of limitation, has the potential to repeatedly chill the exercise of expressive activity by many individuals, the extent of deterrence of protected speech can be expected to decrease with the declining reach of the regulation. This observation appears equally applicable to the publication of books and films as it is to activities, such as picketing or participation in election campaigns, which have previously been categorized as involving conduct plus speech. We see no appreciable difference between the position of a publisher or bookseller in doubt as to the reach of New York's child pornography law and the situation faced by the Oklahoma state employees with respect to that State's restriction on partisan political activity. Indeed, it could reasonably be argued that the bookseller, with an economic incentive to sell materials that may fall within the statute's scope, may be less likely to be deterred than the employee who wishes to engage in political campaign activity.

. . .

B.

Applying these principles, we hold that § 263.15 is not substantially overbroad. We consider this the paradigmatic case of a state statute whose legitimate reach dwarfs its arguably impermissible applications. New York, as we have held, may constitutionally prohibit dissemination of material specified in § 263.15. While the reach of the statute is directed at the hard core of child pornography, the Court of Appeals was understandably concerned that some protected expression, ranging from medical textbooks to pictorials in the National Geographic would fall prey to the statute. How often, if ever, it may be necessary to employ children to engage in conduct clearly within the reach of § 263.15 in order to produce educational, medical, or artistic works cannot be known with certainty. Yet we seriously doubt, and it has not been suggested, that these arguably impermissible applications of the statute amount to more than a tiny fraction of the materials within the statute's reach. Nor will we assume that the New York courts will widen the possibly invalid reach of the statute by giving an expansive construction to the proscription on "lewd exhibition[s] of the genitals." Under these circumstances, § 263.15 is "not substantially overbroad and . . . whatever overbreadth may exist should be cured through case-by-case analysis of the fact situations to which its sanctions, assertedly, may not be applied." *Broadrick v. Oklahoma*, 413 U.S., at 615- 616.

IV.

Because § 263.15 is not substantially overbroad, it is unnecessary to consider its application to material that does not depict sexual conduct of a type that New York may restrict consistent with the First Amendment. As applied to Paul Ferber and to others who distribute similar material, the statute does not violate the First Amendment as applied to the States through the Fourteenth. The judgment of the New York Court of Appeals is reversed, and the case is remanded to that court for further proceedings not inconsistent with this opinion.

So ordered.

Justice BRENNAN, with whom Justice MARSHALL joins, concurring in the judgment.

But in my view application of § 263.15 or any similar statute to depictions of children that in themselves do have serious literary, artistic, scientific, or medical value, would violate the First Amendment. As the Court recognizes, the limited classes of speech, the suppression of which does not raise serious First Amendment concerns, have two attributes. They are of exceedingly "slight social value," and the State has a compelling interest in their regulation. See *Chaplinsky v. New Hampshire*, 315 U.S. 568, 571-572 (1942). The First Amendment value of depictions of children that are in themselves serious contributions to art, literature, or science, is, by definition, simply not "*de minimis.*" See *ante*, at 3356-3357. At the same time, the State's interest in suppression of such materials is likely to be far less compelling. For the Court's assumption of harm to the child resulting from the "permanent record" and "circulation" of the child's "participation," *ante*, at 3355, lacks much of its force where the depiction is a serious contribution to art or science. The production of materials of serious value is not the "low-profile, clandestine industry" that according to the Court produces purely pornographic materials. See *ante*, at 3356. In short, it is inconceivable how a depiction of a child that is itself a serious contribution to the world of art or literature or science can be deemed "material outside the protection of the First Amendment." See *ante*, at 3358.

I, of course, adhere to my view that, in the absence of exposure, or particular harm, to juveniles or unconsenting adults, the State lacks power to suppress sexually oriented materials.... With this understanding, I concur in the Court's judgment in this case.

18 U.S.C.A. § 2251: SEXUAL EXPLOITATION OF CHILDREN

(a) Any person who employs, uses, persuades, induces, entices, or coerces any minor to engage in, or who has a minor assist any other person to engage in, or who transports any minor in interstate or foreign commerce, or in any Territory or Possession of the United States, with the intent that such minor engage in, any sexually explicit conduct for the purpose of producing any visual depiction of such conduct, shall be punished as provided under subsection (e), if such person knows or has reason to know that such visual depiction will be transported in interstate or foreign commerce or mailed, if that visual depiction was produced using materials that have been mailed, shipped, or transported in interstate or foreign commerce by any means, including by computer, or if such visual depiction has actually been transported in interstate or foreign commerce or mailed.

(b) Any parent, legal guardian, or person having custody or control of a minor who knowingly permits such minor to engage in, or to assist any other person to engage in, sexually explicit conduct for the purpose of producing any visual depiction of such conduct shall be punished as provided under subsection (e) of this section, if such parent, legal guardian, or person knows or has reason to know that such visual depiction will be transported in interstate or foreign commerce or mailed, if that visual depiction was produced using materials that have been mailed, shipped, or transported in interstate or foreign commerce by any means, including by computer, or if such visual depiction has actually been transported in interstate or foreign commerce or mailed.

(c)

(1) Any person who, in a circumstance described in paragraph (2), employs, uses, persuades, induces, entices, or coerces any minor to engage in, or who has a minor assist any other person to engage in, any sexually explicit conduct outside of the United States, its territories or possessions, for the purpose of producing any visual depiction of such conduct, shall be punished as provided under subsection (e).

(2) The circumstance referred to in paragraph (1) is that—

(A) the person intends such visual depiction to be transported to the United States, its territories or possessions, by any means, including by computer or mail; or

(B) the person transports such visual depiction to the United States, its territories or possessions, by any means, including by computer or mail.

(d)
(1) Any person who, in a circumstance described in paragraph (2), knowingly makes, prints, or publishes, or causes to be made, printed, or published, any notice or advertisement seeking or offering—

(A) to receive, exchange, buy, produce, display, distribute, or reproduce, any visual depiction, if the production of such visual depiction involves the use of a minor engaging in sexually explicit conduct and such visual depiction is of such conduct; or

(B) participation in any act of sexually explicit conduct by or with any minor for the purpose of producing a visual depiction of such conduct:

shall be punished as provided under subsection (e).

(2) The circumstance referred to in paragraph (1) is that—

(A) such person knows or has reason to know that such notice or advertisement will be transported in interstate or foreign commerce by any means including by computer or mailed; or

(B) such notice or advertisement is transported in interstate or foreign commerce by any means including by computer or mailed.

(e) Any individual who violates, or attempts or conspires to violate, this section shall be fined under this title and imprisoned not less than 15 years nor more than 30 years, but if such person has one prior conviction under this chapter, chapter 71, chapter 109A, or chapter 117, or under section 920 of title 10 (article 120 of the Uniform Code of Military Justice), or under the laws of any State relating to the sexual exploitation of children, such person shall be fined under this title and imprisoned for not less than 25 years nor more than 50 years, but if such person has 2 or more prior convictions under this chapter, chapter 71, chapter 109A, or chapter 117, or under section 920 of title 10 (article 120 of the Uniform Code of Military Justice), or under the laws of any State relating to the sexual exploitation of children, such person shall be fined under this title and imprisoned not less than 35 years nor more than life. Any organization that violates, or attempts or conspires to violate, this section shall be fined under this title. Whoever, in the course of an offense under this section, engages in conduct that results in the death of a person, shall be punished by death or imprisoned for any term of years or for life.

18 U.S.C.A. § 2256: Definitions for Chapter

For the purposes of this chapter, the term—

(1) "minor" means any person under the age of eighteen years;

(2)

(A) Except as provided in subparagraph (B), "sexually explicit conduct" means actual or simulated—

(i) sexual intercourse, including genital-genital, oral-genital, anal-genital, or oral-anal, whether between persons of the same or opposite sex;
(ii) bestiality;
(iii) masturbation;
(iv) sadistic or masochistic abuse; or
(v) lascivious exhibition of the genitals or pubic area of any person;

(B) For purposes of subsection 8(B) of this section, "sexually explicit conduct" means—

(i) graphic sexual intercourse, including genital-genital, oral- genital, anal-genital, or oral-anal, whether between persons of the same or opposite sex, or lascivious simulated sexual intercourse where the genitals, breast, or pubic area of any person is exhibited;
(ii) graphic or lascivious simulated;
(I) bestiality;
(II) masturbation; or
(III) sadistic or masochistic abuse; or
(iii) graphic or simulated lascivious exhibition of the genitals or pubic area of any person;

(3) "producing" means producing, directing, manufacturing, issuing, publishing, or advertising;

(4) "organization" means a person other than an individual;

(5) "visual depiction" includes undeveloped film and videotape, and data stored on computer disk or by electronic means which is capable of conversion into a visual image;

(6) "computer" has the meaning given that term in section 1030 of this title;

(7) "custody or control" includes temporary supervision over or responsibility for a minor whether legally or illegally obtained;

(8) "child pornography" means any visual depiction, including any photograph, film, video, picture, or computer or computer-generated image or picture, whether made or produced by electronic, mechanical, or other means, of sexually explicit conduct, where—

(A) the production of such visual depiction involves the use of a minor engaging in sexually explicit conduct;

(B) such visual depiction is a digital image, computer image, or computer-generated image that is, or is indistinguishable from, that of a minor engaging in sexually explicit conduct; or

(C) such visual depiction has been created, adapted, or modified to appear that an identifiable minor is engaging in sexually explicit conduct.

[**(D)** Repealed. Pub.L. 108-21, Title V, § 502(a)(3), Apr. 30, 2003, 117 Stat. 678]

(9) "identifiable minor"—
(A) means a person—

(i)
(I) who was a minor at the time the visual depiction was created, adapted, or modified; or
(II) whose image as a minor was used in creating, adapting, or modifying the visual depiction; and
(ii) who is recognizable as an actual person by the person's face, likeness, or other distinguishing characteristic, such as a unique birthmark or other recognizable feature; and
(B) shall not be construed to require proof of the actual identity of the identifiable minor.

(10) "graphic", when used with respect to a depiction of sexually explicit conduct, means that a viewer can observe any part of the genitals or pubic area of any depicted person or animal during any part of the time that the sexually explicit conduct is being depicted; and

(11) the term "indistinguishable" used with respect to a depiction, means virtually indistinguishable, in that the depiction is such that an ordinary person viewing the depiction would conclude that the depiction is of an actual minor engaged in sexually explicit conduct. This definition does not apply to depictions that are drawings, cartoons, sculptures, or paintings depicting minors or adults.

ASHCROFT V. FREE SPEECH COALITION
535 U.S. 234 (2002)

Justice KENNEDY delivered the opinion of the Court.
We consider in this case whether the Child Pornography Prevention Act of 1996 (CPPA), 18 U.S.C. § 2251 *et seq.,* abridges the freedom of speech. The CPPA extends the federal prohibition against child pornography to sexually explicit images that appear to depict minors but were produced without using any real children. The statute prohibits, in specific circumstances, possessing or distributing these images, which may be created by using adults who look like minors or by using computer imaging. The new technology, according to Congress, makes it possible to create realistic images of children who do not exist. . . .

By prohibiting child pornography that does not depict an actual child, the statute goes beyond *New York v. Ferber,* 458 U.S. 747 (1982), which distinguished child pornography from other sexually explicit speech because of the State's interest in protecting the children exploited by the production process. See *id.,* at 758. As a general rule, pornography can be banned only if obscene, but under *Ferber,* pornography showing minors can be proscribed whether or not the images are obscene under the definition set forth in *Miller v. California,* 413 U.S. 15 (1973). *Ferber* recognized that "[t]he *Miller* standard, like all general definitions of what may be banned as obscene, does not reflect the State's particular and more compelling interest in prosecuting those who promote the sexual exploitation of children." 458 U.S., at 761.

While we have not had occasion to consider the question, we may assume that the apparent age of persons engaged in sexual conduct is relevant to whether a depiction offends community standards. Pictures of young children engaged in certain acts might be obscene where similar depictions of adults, or perhaps even older adolescents, would not. The CPPA, however, is not directed at speech that is obscene; Congress has proscribed those materials through a separate statute. 18 U.S.C. §§ 1460-1466. Like the law in *Ferber,* the CPPA seeks to reach beyond obscenity, and it makes no attempt to conform to the *Miller* standard. For instance, the statute would reach visual depictions, such as movies, even if they have redeeming social value.

The principal question to be resolved, then, is whether the CPPA is constitutional where it proscribes a significant universe of speech that is neither obscene under *Miller* nor child pornography under *Ferber.*

I.

. . .

Section 2256(8)(B) prohibits "any visual depiction, including any photograph, film, video, picture, or computer or computer-generated image or picture," that "is, or appears to be, of a minor engaging in sexually explicit conduct." The prohibition on "any visual depiction" does not depend at all on how the image is produced. The section captures a range of depictions, sometimes called "virtual child pornography," which include computer-generated images, as well as images produced by more traditional means. For instance, the literal terms of the statute embrace a Renaissance painting depicting a scene from classical mythology, a "picture" that "appears to be, of a minor engaging in sexually explicit conduct." The statute also prohibits Hollywood movies, filmed without any child actors, if a jury believes an actor "appears to be" a minor engaging in "actual or simulated . . . sexual intercourse." § 2256(2).

These images do not involve, let alone harm, any children in the production process; but Congress decided the materials threaten children in other, less direct, ways. Pedophiles might use the materials to encourage children to participate in sexual activity. "[A] child who is reluctant to engage in sexual activity with an adult, or to pose for sexually explicit photographs, can sometimes be convinced by viewing depictions of other children 'having fun' participating in such activity." Congressional Finding (3), notes following § 2251. Furthermore, pedophiles might "whet their own sexual appetites" with the pornographic images, "thereby increasing the creation and distribution of child pornography and the sexual abuse and exploitation of actual children." *Id.,* Findings, (10)(B).

Under these rationales, harm flows from the content of the images, not from the means of their production. In addition, Congress identified another problem created by computer-generated images: Their existence can make it harder to prosecute pornographers who do use real minors. See *id.,* Finding (6)(A). As imaging technology improves, Congress found, it becomes more difficult to prove that a particular picture was produced using actual children. To ensure that defendants possessing child pornography using real minors cannot evade prosecution, Congress extended the ban to virtual child pornography.

Section 2256(8)(C) prohibits a more common and lower tech means of creating virtual images, known as computer morphing. Rather than creating original images, pornographers can alter innocent pictures of real children so that the children appear to be engaged in sexual activity. Although morphed images may fall within the definition of virtual child pornography, they implicate the interests of real children and are in that sense closer to the images in *Ferber.* Respondents do not challenge this provision, and we do not consider it.

Respondents do challenge § 2256(8)(D). Like the text of the "appears to be" provision, the sweep of this provision is quite broad. Section 2256(8)(D) defines child pornography to include any sexually explicit image that was "advertised, promoted, presented, described, or distributed in such a manner that conveys the impression" it depicts "a minor engaging in sexually explicit conduct." . . . The statute is not so limited in its reach, however, as it punishes even those possessors who took no part in pandering. Once a work has been described as child pornography, the taint remains on the speech in the hands of subsequent possessors, making possession unlawful even though the content otherwise would not be objectionable.

Fearing that the CPPA threatened the activities of its members, respondent Free Speech Coalition and others challenged the statute in the United States District Court for the Northern District of California. The Coalition, a California trade association for the adult-entertainment industry, alleged that its members did not use minors in their sexually explicit works, but they believed some of these materials might fall within the CPPA's expanded definition of child pornography. The other respondents are Bold Type, Inc., the publisher of a book advocating the nudist lifestyle; Jim Gingerich, a painter of nudes; and Ron Raffaelli, a photographer specializing in erotic images. Respondents alleged that the "appears to be" and "conveys the impression" provisions are overbroad and vague, chilling them from producing works protected by the First Amendment. . . .

II.

The First Amendment commands, "Congress shall make no law . . . abridging the freedom of speech." The government may violate this mandate in many ways, *e.g., Rosenberger v. Rector and Visitors of Univ. of Va.,* 515 U.S. 819 (1995); *Keller v. State Bar of Cal.,* 496 U.S. 1 (1990), but a law imposing criminal penalties on protected speech is a stark example of speech suppression. The CPPA's penalties are indeed severe. A first offender may be imprisoned for 15 years. § 2252A(b)(1). A repeat offender faces a prison sentence of not less than 5 years and not more than 30 years in prison. *Ibid.* While even minor punishments can chill protected speech, see *Wooley v. Maynard,* 430 U.S. 705 (1977), this case provides a textbook example of why we permit facial challenges to statutes that burden expression. With these severe penalties in force, few legitimate movie producers or book publishers, or few other speakers in any capacity, would risk distributing images in or near the uncertain reach of this law. The Constitution gives significant protection from overbroad laws that chill speech within the First Amendment's vast and privileged sphere. Under this principle, the CPPA is unconstitutional on its face if it prohibits a substantial amount of protected expression. . . .

Congress may pass valid laws to protect children from abuse, and it has. *E.g.,* 18 U.S.C. §§ 2241, 2251. The prospect of crime, however, by itself does not justify laws suppressing protected speech. See *Kingsley Int'l Pictures Corp. v. Regents of Univ. of N.Y.,* 360 U.S. 684, 689 (1959) ("Among free men, the deterrents ordinarily to be applied to prevent crime are education and punishment for violations of the law, not abridgment of the rights of free speech" (internal quotation marks and citation omitted)). It is also well established that speech may not be prohibited because it concerns subjects offending our sensibilities. See *FCC v. Pacifica Foundation,* 438 U.S. 726, 745 (1978) ("[T]he fact that society may find speech offensive is not a sufficient reason for suppressing it"); see also *Reno v. American Civil Liberties Union,* 521 U.S. 844, 874 (1997) ("In evaluating the free speech rights of adults, we have made it perfectly clear that '[s]exual expression which is indecent but not obscene is protected by the First Amendment'") (quoting *Sable Communications of Cal., Inc. v. FCC,* 492 U.S. 115, 126 (1989)); *Carey v. Population Services Int'l,* 431 U.S. 678, 701 (1977) ("[T]he fact that protected speech may be offensive to some does not justify its suppression").

As a general principle, the First Amendment bars the government from dictating what we see or read or speak or hear. The freedom of speech has its limits; it does not embrace certain categories of speech, including defamation, incitement, obscenity, and pornography produced with real children. See *Simon & Schuster, Inc. v. Members of N.Y. State Crime Victims Bd.,* 502 U.S. 105, 127 (1991) (KENNEDY, J., concurring). While these categories may be prohibited without violating the First Amendment, none of them includes the speech prohibited by the CPPA. In his dissent from the opinion of the Court of Appeals, Judge Ferguson recognized this to be the law and proposed that virtual child pornography should be regarded as an additional category of unprotected speech. See 198 F.3d, at 1101. It would be necessary for us to take this step to uphold the statute.

As we have noted, the CPPA is much more than a supplement to the existing federal prohibition on obscenity. Under *Miller v. California,* 413 U.S. 15 (1973), the Government must prove that the work, taken as a whole, appeals to the prurient interest, is patently offensive in light of community standards, and lacks serious literary, artistic, political, or scientific value. *Id.,* at 24. The CPPA, however, extends to images that appear to depict a minor engaging in sexually explicit activity without regard to the *Miller* requirements. The materials need not appeal to the prurient interest. Any depiction of sexually explicit activity, no matter how it is presented, is proscribed. The CPPA applies to a picture in a psychology manual, as well as a movie depicting the horrors of sexual abuse. It is not necessary, moreover, that the image be patently offensive. Pictures of what appear to be 17-year-olds engaging in sexually explicit activity do not in every case contravene community standards.

The CPPA prohibits speech despite its serious literary, artistic, political, or scientific value. The statute proscribes the visual depiction of an idea— that of teenagers engaging in sexual activity—that is a fact of modern society and has been a theme in art and literature throughout the ages. Under the CPPA, images are prohibited so long as the persons appear to be under 18 years of age. 18 U.S.C. § 2256(1). This is higher than the legal age for marriage in many States, as well as the age at which persons may consent to sexual relations... It is, of course, undeniable that some youths engage in sexual activity before the legal age, either on their own inclination or because they are victims of sexual abuse.

Both themes—teenage sexual activity and the sexual abuse of children—have inspired countless literary works. William Shakespeare created the most famous pair of teenage lovers, one of whom is just 13 years of age. . . . Shakespeare may not have written sexually explicit scenes for the Elizabethan audience, but were modern directors to adopt a less conventional approach, that fact alone would not compel the conclusion that the work was obscene.

Contemporary movies pursue similar themes. . . . If these films, or hundreds of others of lesser note that explore those subjects, contain a single graphic depiction of sexual activity within the statutory definition, the possessor of the film would be subject to severe punishment without inquiry into the work's redeeming value. This is inconsistent with an essential First Amendment rule: The artistic merit of a work does not depend on the presence of a single explicit scene. . . . Under *Miller,* the First Amendment requires that redeeming value be judged by considering the work as a whole. Where the scene is part of the narrative, the work itself does not for this reason become obscene, even though the scene in isolation might be offensive. See *Kois v. Wisconsin,* 408 U.S. 229, 231 (1972) *(per curiam).* For this reason, and the others we have noted, the CPPA cannot be read to prohibit obscenity, because it lacks the required link between its prohibitions and the affront to community standards prohibited by the definition of obscenity.

. . .

Ferber upheld a prohibition on the distribution and sale of child pornography, as well as its production, because these acts were "intrinsically related" to the sexual abuse of children in two ways. *Id.,* at 759. First, as a permanent record of a child's abuse, the continued circulation itself would harm the child who had participated. Like a defamatory statement, each new publication of the speech would cause new injury to the child's reputation and emotional well-being. See *id.,* at 759 and n. 10. Second, because the traffic in child pornography was an economic motive for its production, the State had an interest in closing the distribution network. "The most expeditious if not the only practical method of law enforcement may be to dry up the market for this material by imposing severe criminal penalties on persons selling, advertising, or otherwise promoting the product." *Id.,* at 760. Under either rationale, the speech had what the Court in effect held was a proximate link to the crime from which it came.

Later, in *Osborne v. Ohio,* 495 U.S. 103 (1990), the Court ruled that these same interests justified a ban on the possession of pornography produced by using children. "Given the importance of the State's interest in protecting the victims of child pornography," the State was justified in "attempting to stamp out this vice at all levels in the distribution chain." *Id.,* at 110. *Osborne* also noted the State's interest in preventing child pornography from being used as an aid in the solicitation of minors. *Id.,* at 111. The Court, however, anchored its holding in the concern for the participants, those whom it called the "victims of child pornography." *Id.,* at 110. It did not suggest that, absent this concern, other governmental interests would suffice. See *infra,* at 1402-1403.

In contrast to the speech in *Ferber,* speech that itself is the record of sexual abuse, the CPPA prohibits speech that records no crime and creates no victims by its production. Virtual child pornography is not "intrinsically related" to the sexual abuse of children, as were the materials in *Ferber.* 458 U.S., at 759. While the Government asserts that the images can lead to actual instances of child abuse, see *infra,* at 1402-1404, the causal link is contingent and indirect. The harm does not necessarily follow from the speech, but depends upon some unquantified potential for subsequent criminal acts.

The Government says these indirect harms are sufficient because, as *Ferber* acknowledged, child pornography rarely can be valuable speech. . . . This argument, however, suffers from two flaws. First, *Ferber's* judgment about child pornography was based upon how it was made, not on what it communicated. The case reaffirmed that where the speech is neither obscene nor the product of sexual abuse, it does not fall outside the protection of the First Amendment... The second flaw in the Government's position is that *Ferber* did not hold that child pornography is by definition without value. On the contrary, the Court recognized some works in this category might have significant value, see *id.,* at 761, but relied on virtual images—the very images prohibited by the CPPA—as an alternative and permissible means of expression: "[I]f it were necessary for literary or artistic value, a person over the statutory age who perhaps looked younger could be utilized. Simulation outside of the prohibition of the statute could provide another alternative." *Id.,* at 763. *Ferber,* then, not only referred to the distinction between actual and virtual child pornography, it relied on it as a reason supporting its holding. *Ferber* provides no support for a statute that eliminates the distinction and makes the alternative mode criminal as well.

III.

The CPPA, for reasons we have explored, is inconsistent with *Miller* and finds no support in *Ferber.* The Government seeks to justify its prohibitions in other ways. It argues that the CPPA is necessary because pedophiles may use virtual child pornography to seduce children. There are many things innocent in themselves, however, such as cartoons, video games, and candy, that might be used for immoral purposes, yet we would not expect those to be prohibited because they can be misused. The Government, of course, may punish adults who provide unsuitable materials to children, see *Ginsberg v. New York,* 390 U.S. 629 (1968), and it may enforce criminal penalties for unlawful solicitation. The precedents establish, however, that speech within the rights of adults to hear may not be silenced completely in an attempt to shield children from it. . . .

Here, the Government wants to keep speech from children not to protect them from its content but to protect them from those who would commit other crimes. The principle, however, remains the same: The Government cannot ban speech fit for adults simply because it may fall into the hands of children. The evil in question depends upon the actor's unlawful conduct, conduct defined as criminal quite apart from any link to the speech in question. This establishes that the speech ban is not narrowly drawn. The objective is to prohibit illegal conduct, but this restriction goes well beyond that interest by restricting the speech available to law-abiding adults.

The Government submits further that virtual child pornography whets the appetites of pedophiles and encourages them to engage in illegal conduct. This rationale cannot sustain the provision in question. The mere tendency of speech to encourage unlawful acts is not a sufficient reason for banning it. The government "cannot constitutionally premise legislation on the desirability of controlling a person's private thoughts." *Stanley v. Georgia,* 394 U.S. 557, 566 (1969). First Amendment freedoms are most in danger when the government seeks to control thought or to justify its laws for that impermissible end. The right to think is the beginning of freedom, and speech must be protected from the government because speech is the beginning of thought.

To preserve these freedoms, and to protect speech for its own sake, the Court's First Amendment cases draw vital distinctions between words and deeds, between ideas and conduct. . . . The government may not prohibit speech because it increases the chance an unlawful act will be committed "at some indefinite future time." *Hess v. Indiana,* 414 U.S. 105 (1973) *(per curiam).* The government may suppress speech for advocating the use of force or a violation of law only if "such advocacy is directed to inciting or producing imminent lawless action and is likely to incite or produce such action." *Brandenburg v. Ohio,* 395 U.S. 444, 447 (1969) *(per curiam).* There is here no attempt, incitement, solicitation, or conspiracy. The Government has shown no more than a remote connection between speech that might encourage thoughts or impulses and any resulting child abuse. Without a significantly stronger, more direct connection, the Government may not prohibit speech on the ground that it may encourage pedophiles to engage in illegal conduct.

The Government next argues that its objective of eliminating the market for pornography produced using real children necessitates a prohibition on virtual images as well. . . . In the case of the material covered by *Ferber,* the creation of the speech is itself the crime of child abuse; the prohibition deters the crime by removing the profit motive. See *Osborne,* 495 U.S., at 109-110. Even where there is an underlying crime, however, the Court has not allowed the suppression of speech in all cases. *E.g., Bartnicki, supra,* at 529 (market deterrence would not justify law prohibiting a radio commentator from distributing speech that had been unlawfully intercepted). We need not consider where to strike the balance in this case, because here, there is no underlying crime at all. Even if the Government's market deterrence theory were persuasive in some contexts, it would not justify this statute.

Finally, the Government says that the possibility of producing images by using computer imaging makes it very difficult for it to prosecute those who produce pornography by using real children. . . . The argument, in essence, is that protected speech may be banned as a means to ban unprotected speech. This analysis turns the First Amendment upside down.

The Government may not suppress lawful speech as the means to suppress unlawful speech. Protected speech does not become unprotected merely because it resembles the latter. The Constitution requires the reverse. "[T]he possible harm to society in permitting some unprotected speech to go unpunished is outweighed by the possibility that protected speech of others may be muted . . . ." *Broadrick v. Oklahoma,* 413 U.S., at 612. The overbreadth doctrine prohibits the Government from banning unprotected speech if a substantial amount of protected speech is prohibited or chilled in the process. . . .

In sum, § 2256(8)(B) covers materials beyond the categories recognized in *Ferber* and *Miller,* and the reasons the Government offers in support of limiting the freedom of speech have no justification in our precedents or in the law of the First Amendment. The provision abridges the freedom to engage in a substantial amount of lawful speech. For this reason, it is overbroad and unconstitutional.

IV.

Respondents challenge § 2256(8)(D) as well. This provision bans depictions of sexually explicit conduct that are "advertised, promoted, presented, described, or distributed in such a manner that conveys the impression that the material is or contains a visual depiction of a minor engaging in sexually explicit conduct." The parties treat the section as nearly identical to the provision prohibiting materials that appear to be child pornography. In the Government's view, the difference between the two is that "the 'conveys the impression' provision requires the jury to assess the material at issue in light of the manner in which it is promoted." Brief for Petitioners 18, n. 3. The Government's assumption, however, is that the determination would still depend principally upon the content of the prohibited work.

We disagree with this view. The CPPA prohibits sexually explicit materials that "conve[y] the impression" they depict minors. While that phrase may sound like the "appears to be" prohibition in § 2256(8)(B), it requires little judgment about the content of the image. Under § 2256(8)(D), the work must be sexually explicit, but otherwise the content is irrelevant. Even if a film contains no sexually explicit scenes involving minors, it could be treated as child pornography if the title and trailers convey the impression that the scenes would be found in the movie. The determination turns on how the speech is presented, not on what is depicted. While the legislative findings address at length the problems posed by materials that look like child pornography, they are silent on the evils posed by images simply pandered that way.

The Government does not offer a serious defense of this provision, and the other arguments it makes in support of the CPPA do not bear on § 2256(8)(D). The materials, for instance, are not likely to be confused for child pornography in a criminal trial. The Court has recognized that pandering may be relevant, as an evidentiary matter, to the question whether particular materials are obscene. See *Ginzburg v. United States,* 383 U.S. 463 (1966) ("[I]n close cases evidence of pandering may be probative with respect to the nature of the material in question and thus satisfy the [obscenity] test"). Where a defendant engages in the "commercial exploitation of erotica solely for the sake of their prurient appeal," *id.,* at 466, the context he or she creates may itself be relevant to the evaluation of the materials.

Section 2256(8)(D), however, prohibits a substantial amount of speech that falls outside *Ginzburg's* rationale. Materials falling within the proscription are tainted and unlawful in the hands of all who receive it, though they bear no responsibility for how it was marketed, sold, or described. The statute, furthermore, does not require that the context be part of an effort at "commercial exploitation." *Ibid.* As a consequence, the CPPA does more than prohibit pandering. It prohibits possession of material described, or pandered, as child pornography by someone earlier in the distribution chain. The provision prohibits a sexually explicit film containing no youthful actors, just because it is placed in a box suggesting a prohibited movie. Possession is a crime even when the possessor knows the movie was mislabeled. The First Amendment requires a more precise restriction. For this reason, § 2256(8)(D) is substantially overbroad and in violation of the First Amendment.

V.

For the reasons we have set forth, the prohibitions of §§ 2256(8)(B) and 2256(8)(D) are overbroad and unconstitutional. Having reached this conclusion, we need not address respondents' further contention that the provisions are unconstitutional because of vague statutory language.

The judgment of the Court of Appeals is affirmed.

It is so ordered.

Justice THOMAS, concurring in the judgment.

In my view, the Government's most persuasive asserted interest in support of the Child Pornography Prevention Act of 1996 (CPPA), 18 U.S.C. § 2251 *et seq.*, is the prosecution rationale—that persons who possess and disseminate pornographic images of real children may escape conviction by claiming that the images are computer generated, thereby raising a reasonable doubt as to their guilt. See Brief for Petitioners 37. At this time, however, the Government asserts only that defendants *raise* such defenses, not that they have done so successfully. In fact, the Government points to no case in which a defendant has been acquitted based on a "computer-generated images" defense. See *id.*, at 37-38, and n. 8. While this speculative interest cannot support the broad reach of the CPPA, technology may evolve to the point where it becomes impossible to enforce actual child pornography laws because the Government cannot prove that certain pornographic images are of real children. In the event this occurs, the Government should not be foreclosed from enacting a regulation of virtual child pornography that contains an appropriate affirmative defense or some other narrowly drawn restriction.

The Court suggests that the Government's interest in enforcing prohibitions against real child pornography cannot justify prohibitions on virtual child pornography, because "[t]his analysis turns the First Amendment upside down. The Government may not suppress lawful speech as the means to suppress unlawful speech." *Ante,* at 1404. But if technological advances thwart prosecution of "unlawful speech," the Government may well have a compelling interest in barring or otherwise regulating some narrow category of "lawful speech" in order to enforce effectively laws against pornography made through the abuse of real children. The Court does leave open the possibility that a more complete affirmative defense could save a statute's constitutionality, see *ante,* at 1405, implicitly accepting that some regulation of virtual child pornography might be constitutional. I would not prejudge, however, whether a more complete affirmative defense is the only way to narrowly tailor a criminal statute that prohibits the possession and dissemination of virtual child pornography. Thus, I concur in the judgment of the Court.

Justice O'CONNOR, with whom THE CHIEF JUSTICE and Justice SCALIA join as to Part II, concurring in the judgment in part and dissenting in part.

. . .

This litigation involves a facial challenge to the CPPA's prohibitions of pornographic images that "appea[r] to be . . . of a minor" and of material that "conveys the impression" that it contains pornographic images of minors. While I agree with the Court's judgment that the First Amendment requires that the latter prohibition be struck down, I disagree with its decision to strike down the former prohibition in its entirety. The "appears to be . . . of a minor" language in § 2256(8)(B) covers two categories of speech: pornographic images of adults that look like children ("youthful adult pornography") and pornographic images of children created wholly on a computer, without using any actual children ("virtual child pornography"). The Court concludes, correctly, that the CPPA's ban on youthful adult pornography is overbroad. In my view, however, respondents fail to present sufficient evidence to demonstrate that the ban on virtual child pornography is overbroad. Because invalidation due to overbreadth is such "strong medicine," *Broadrick v. Oklahoma,* 413 U.S. 601, 613 (1973), I would strike down the prohibition of pornography that "appears to be" of minors only insofar as it is applied to the class of youthful adult pornography.

. . .

II.
I disagree with the Court, however, that the CPPA's prohibition of virtual child pornography is overbroad. Before I reach that issue, there are two preliminary questions: whether the ban on virtual child pornography fails strict scrutiny and whether that ban is unconstitutionally vague. I would answer both in the negative.

The Court has long recognized that the Government has a compelling interest in protecting our Nation's children. See *Ferber, supra,* at 756-757 (citing cases). This interest is promoted by efforts directed against sexual offenders and actual child pornography. These efforts, in turn, are supported by the CPPA's ban on virtual child pornography. Such images whet the appetites of child molesters, § 121, 110 Stat. 3009-26, Congressional Findings (4), (10)(B), notes following 18 U.S.C. § 2251, who may use the images to seduce young children, *id.,* Finding (3). Of even more serious concern is the prospect that defendants indicted for the production, distribution, or possession of actual child pornography may evade liability by claiming that the images attributed to them are in fact computer-generated. *Id.,* Finding (6)(A). Respondents may be correct that no defendant has successfully employed this tactic. . . . But, given the rapid pace of advances in computer-graphics technology, the Government's concern is reasonable. . . .

Respondents argue that, even if the Government has a compelling interest to justify banning virtual child pornography, the "appears to be . . . of a minor" language is not narrowly tailored to serve that interest. See *Sable Communications of Cal., Inc. v. FCC,* 492 U.S. 115, 126 (1989). They assert that the CPPA would capture even cartoon sketches or statues of children that were sexually suggestive. Such images surely could not be used, for instance, to seduce children. I agree. A better interpretation of "appears to be . . . of" is "virtually indistinguishable from"—an interpretation that would not cover the examples respondents provide... Finally, to the extent that the phrase "appears to be . . . of" is ambiguous, the narrowing interpretation avoids constitutional problems such as overbreadth and lack of narrow tailoring.

Reading the statute only to bar images that are virtually indistinguishable from actual children would not only assure that the ban on virtual child pornography is narrowly tailored, but would also assuage any fears that the "appears to be . . . of a minor" language is vague. The narrow reading greatly limits any risks from "'discriminatory enforcement.'" *Reno v. American Civil Liberties Union,* 521 U.S. 844, 872 (1997). Respondents maintain that the "virtually indistinguishable from" language is also vague because it begs the question: from whose perspective? This problem is exaggerated. This Court has never required "mathematical certainty" or "'meticulous specificity'" from the language of a statute. *Grayned v. City of Rockford,* 408 U.S. 104, 110 (1972).

The Court concludes that the CPPA's ban on virtual child pornography is overbroad. The basis for this holding is unclear. Although a content-based regulation may serve a compelling state interest, and be as narrowly tailored as possible while substantially serving that interest, the regulation may unintentionally ensnare speech that has serious literary, artistic, political, or scientific value or that does not threaten the harms sought to be combated by the Government. If so, litigants may challenge the regulation on its face as overbroad, but in doing so they bear the heavy burden of demonstrating that the regulation forbids a substantial amount of valuable or harmless speech. See *Reno, supra,* at 896 (O'CONNOR, J., concurring in judgment in part and dissenting in part) (citing *Broadrick,* 413 U.S., at 615). Respondents have not made such a demonstration. Respondents provide no examples of films or other materials that are wholly computer generated and contain images that "appea[r] to be . . . of minors" engaging in indecent conduct, but that have serious value or do not facilitate child abuse. Their overbreadth challenge therefore fails. . . .

In sum, I would strike down the CPPA's ban on material that "conveys the impression" that it contains actual child pornography, but uphold the ban on pornographic depictions that "appea[r] to be" of minors so long as it is not applied to youthful adult pornography.

Chief Justice REHNQUIST, with whom Justice SCALIA joins in part, dissenting.

. . .

I also agree with Justice O'CONNOR that serious First Amendment concerns would arise were the Government ever to prosecute someone for simple distribution or possession of a film with literary or artistic value, such as Traffic or American Beauty. *Ante,* at 1408 (opinion concurring in judgment in part and dissenting in part). I write separately, however, because the Child Pornography Prevention Act of 1996 (CPPA), 18 U.S.C. § 2251 *et seq.,* need not be construed to reach such materials.

We normally do not strike down a statute on First Amendment grounds "when a limiting construction has been or could be placed on the challenged statute." . . . This case should be treated no differently.

Other than computer-generated images that are virtually indistinguishable from real children engaged in sexually explicit conduct, the CPPA can be limited so as not to reach any material that was not already unprotected before the CPPA. The CPPA's definition of "sexually explicit conduct" is quite explicit in this regard. It makes clear that the statute only reaches "visual depictions" of:

> "[A]ctual or simulated ... sexual intercourse, including genital-genital, oral-genital, anal-genital, or oral-anal, whether between persons of the same or opposite sex; ... bestiality; ... masturbation; ... sadistic or masochistic abuse; or ... lascivious exhibition of the genitals or pubic area of any person." 18 U.S.C. § 2256(2).

The Court and Justice O'CONNOR suggest that this very graphic definition reaches the depiction of youthful looking adult actors engaged in suggestive sexual activity, presumably because the definition extends to "simulated" intercourse. *Ante,* at 1400-1401 (majority opinion); *ante,* at 1408 (opinion concurring in judgment in part and dissenting in part). Read as a whole, however, I think the definition reaches only the sort of "hard core of child pornography" that we found without protection in *Ferber, supra,* at 773-774. So construed, the CPPA bans visual depictions of youthful looking adult actors engaged in *actual* sexual activity; mere *suggestions* of sexual activity, such as youthful looking adult actors squirming under a blanket, are more akin to written descriptions than visual depictions, and thus fall outside the purview of the statute.

. . .

This narrow reading of "sexually explicit conduct" not only accords with the text of the CPPA and the intentions of Congress; it is exactly how the phrase was understood prior to the broadening gloss the Court gives it today. Indeed, had "sexually explicit conduct" been thought to reach the sort of material the Court says it does, then films such as Traffic and American Beauty would not have been made the way they were . . . The chill felt by the Court, *ante,* at 1398 ("[F]ew legitimate movie producers . . . would risk distributing images in or near the uncertain reach of this law"), has apparently never been felt by those who actually make movies.

. . .

The First Amendment may protect the video shopowner or film distributor who promotes material as "entertaining" or "acclaimed" regardless of whether the material contains depictions of youthful looking adult actors engaged in nonobscene but sexually suggestive conduct. The First Amendment does not, however, protect the panderer. Thus, materials promoted as conveying the impression that they depict actual minors engaged in sexually explicit conduct do not escape regulation merely because they might warrant First Amendment protection if promoted in a different manner. . . .

The Court says that "conveys the impression" goes well beyond *Ginzburg* to "prohibi[t][the] possession of material described, or pandered, as child pornography by someone earlier in the distribution chain." *Ante,* at 1406. The Court's concern is that an individual who merely possesses protected materials (such as videocassettes of Traffic or American Beauty) might offend the CPPA regardless of whether the individual actually intended to possess materials containing unprotected images. . . .

This concern is a legitimate one, but there is, again, no need or reason to construe the statute this way. In *X-Citement Video, supra,* we faced a provision of the Protection of Children Against Sexual Exploitation Act of 1977, the precursor to the CPPA, which lent itself much less than the present statute to attributing a "knowingly" requirement to the contents of the possessed visual depictions. We held that such a requirement nonetheless applied, so that the Government would have to prove that a person charged with possessing child pornography actually knew that the materials contained depictions of real minors engaged in sexually explicit conduct. 513 U.S., at 77-78. In light of this holding, and consistent with the narrow class of images the CPPA is intended to prohibit, the CPPA can be construed to prohibit only the knowing possession of materials actually containing visual depictions of real minors engaged in sexually explicit conduct, or computer-generated images virtually indistinguishable from real minors engaged in sexually explicit conduct. The mere possession of materials containing only suggestive depictions of youthful looking adult actors need not be so included.

In sum, while potentially impermissible applications of the CPPA may exist, I doubt that they would be "substantial . . . in relation to the statute's plainly legitimate sweep." *Broadrick,* 413 U.S., at 615. The aim of ensuring the enforceability of our Nation's child pornography laws is a compelling one. The CPPA is targeted to this aim by extending the definition of child pornography to reach computer-generated images that are virtually indistinguishable from real children engaged in sexually explicit conduct. The statute need not be read to do any more than precisely this, which is not offensive to the First Amendment.

For these reasons, I would construe the CPPA in a manner consistent with the First Amendment, reverse the Court of Appeals' judgment, and uphold the statute in its entirety.

NOTES AND QUESTIONS

1. In Ginsberg v. New York, 390 U.S. 629 (1968), the Supreme Court ruled that a law protecting minors from exposure to pornographic displays at convenience stores and other public accommodations was constitutional. Shouldn't that be enough protection under the First Amendment? With respect to consensual displays of sexual conduct, what justifications exist apart from protecting minors?
2. If you are not convinced that there is a moral imperative to restrict obscenity, are there other compelling justifications? In Canada, pornography that humiliates women or depicts sexual violence may be regulated by the state. Feminist legal scholars Catherine McKinnon and Andrea Dworkin championed a similar approach in Indianapolis in the 1980s, which was subsequently declared unconstitutional. American Booksellers Ass'n, Inc. v. Hudnut, 771 F.2d 323 (7th Cir. 1985), summarily affirmed by the U.S. Supreme Court, 475 U.S. 1001 (1986).
3. **Secondary effects.** In City of Renton v. Playtime Theatres, Inc., 475 U.S. 41 (1986), the U.S. Supreme Court held that a city ordinance prohibiting adult theaters from operating near schools, churches, parks, and residential neighborhoods was a constitutional time, place, or manner regulation, even though the law targeted a specific type of content. A similar ordinance in New York City effectively prevented strip clubs from operating in Manhattan. Do you agree that law-abiding businesses that purvey in pornography may have a negative impact on a neighborhood or business district? Should the same rationale apply to liquor stores, housing for the mentally ill, or a community youth center, even if they obey all local laws?
4. **Child Pornography Possession.** Although the U.S. Supreme Court, in the cases supra, permits prosecution for the mere possession of child pornography, high fines and significant prison terms for possessors have generated considerable debate in the twenty-first century. Federal District Court Judge Jack B. Weinstein of the Eastern District of New York has argued that possession does not warrant the same

degree of punishment meted out to sex offenders and child porn distributors or creators. Do you agree?

5. **The challenge of bright lines.** In most U.S. jurisdictions, a pornographic image of a person under eighteen subjects its creator or possessor to prosecution for a sex crime. The same image taken after the person's eighteenth birthday is protected by the First Amendment, unless it is found to be obscene. Is this an arbitrary distinction? If children, on average, become sexually active at an earlier age, should the government lower the age at which child pornography laws apply? On the other hand, are not the actions of a sexual predator just as damaging to an eighteen-year-old as they are to a person one year younger?
6. **Sexting.** Sexting is when a person texts sexual comments or images to a friend or partner. While intimate phone-to-phone contact is legal for adults, minors who send and receive sexualized selfies run afoul of child pornography laws. While some prosecutors have taken a permissive approach to consensual exchanges of these images, teens and even middle school students have been arrested for texting nude photos of themselves or for posting intimate selfies online. These prosecutors argue that even good-natured distribution of photos among friends may humiliate these teens later in life, especially if the digital images get into the hands of pedophiles. Do you agree?
7. **Morphing.** Morphing is when an image is edited with a superimposed second image. A common form of morphing is taking an image of a celebrity's face and placing it on the image of someone else's body. In Ashcroft v. Free Speech Coalition supra, the Court takes no position on whether morphing is permitted under the First Amendment. Should it be permitted? What if a pedophile digitally copies the face of an identifiable minor from a family photo and realistically morphs it onto an adult model's naked body?

CHAPTER 7

FILM CENSORSHIP

While many today consider film to be an established, time-honored communication medium, it was, of course, not always viewed that way. A century ago, film was considered a novelty—more an article of commerce than a form of artistic expression. In the 1915 case of Mutual Film Corp. v. Industrial Commission of Ohio, the U.S. Supreme Court, sensing the power of motion pictures, declined to offer speech protections to the new medium, allowing states to impose prior restraint regimes on film, a technology that was then barely 20 years old. In *Mutual*, one gets the sense that none of the nine old men on the Court had seen a film; the first nationwide release of a full-length motion picture, D.W. Griffith's "The Birth of A Nation," was still months away when this case was decided. By 1952, film had emerged as a major art form; in Burstyn v. Wilson, all of the justices understood the expressive value of Charlie Chaplin's silent classics, the great movie musicals of the 1930s, and film noir. In the aftermath of World War II, they also understood that film has a persuasive power that is greater than that of a printed page or artist's canvas. Though the *Burstyn* court was willing to apply First Amendment protection to film, the justices did not fully reject the concerns about the medium that their predecessors expressed in *Mutual*. This medium-specific treatment of film allowed states to continue to require films to be submitted to and approved by government censors, provided that the censorship criteria did not violate the First Amendment. It was only in 1965, in the case of Freedman v. Maryland, that the U.S. Supreme Court decided that a state censorship board could not issue a prior restraint without first proving its case before a court of law. Film had finally matured enough as a medium to be treated the same as books and newspapers under the First Amendment. Following *Freedman*, the Motion Picture Association of America (MPAA) introduced its film rating system, which remains in place, with some changes, to this day.

MUTUAL FILM CORP. V. INDUSTRIAL COMMISSION OF OHIO

236 U.S. 230 (1915)

Mr. Justice McKenna . . . delivered the opinion of the court:
Complainant directs its argument to three propositions: (1) The statute in controversy imposes an unlawful burden on interstate commerce; (2) it

violates the freedom of speech and publication guaranteed by § 11, article 1, of the Constitution of the state of Ohio; and (3) it attempts to delegate legislative power to censors and to other boards to determine whether the statute offends in the particulars designated.

It is necessary to consider only §§ 3, 4, and 5. Section 3 makes it the duty of the board to examine and censor motion picture films to be publicly exhibited and displayed in the state of Ohio. The films are required to be exhibited to the board before they are delivered to the exhibitor for exhibition, for which a fee is charged.

Section 4. "Only such films as are, in the judgment and discretion of the board of censors, of a moral, educational, or amusing and harmless character shall be passed and approved by such board." The films are required to be stamped or designated in a proper manner.

Section 5. The board may work in conjunction with censor boards of other states as a censor congress, and the action of such congress in approving or rejecting films shall be considered as the action of the state board, and all films passed, approved, stamped, and numbered by such congress, when the fees therefor are paid, shall be considered approved by the board.

By § 7 a penalty is imposed for each exhibition of films without the approval of the board, and by § 8 any person dissatisfied with the order of the board is given the same rights and remedies for hearing and reviewing, amendment or vacation of the order "as is provided in the case of persons dissatisfied with the orders of the Industrial Commission."

The censorship, therefore, is only of films intended for exhibition in Ohio, and we can immediately put to one side the contention that it imposes a burden on interstate commerce. . . .

It is true that the statute requires them to be submitted to the board before they are delivered to the exhibitor, but we have seen that the films are shipped to "exchanges" and by them rented to exhibitors, and the "exchanges" are described as "nothing more or less than circulating libraries or clearing houses." And one film "serves in many theaters from day to day until it is worn out."

The next contention is that the statute violates the freedom of speech and publication guaranteed by the Ohio Constitution. In its discussion

Men enjoying films at a Kinetoscope parlor, San Francisco, 1894.

counsel have gone into a very elaborate description of moving picture exhibitions and their many useful purposes as graphic expressions of opinion and sentiments, as exponents of policies, as teachers of science and history, as useful, interesting, amusing, educational, and moral. And a list of the "campaigns," as counsel call them, which may be carried on, is given. We may concede the praise. It is not questioned by the Ohio statute, and under its comprehensive description, "campaigns" of an infinite variety may be conducted. Films of a "moral, educational, or amusing and harmless character shall be passed and approved," are the words of the statute. No exhibition, therefore, or "campaign" of complainant will be prevented if its pictures have those qualities. Therefore, however missionary of opinion films are or may become, however educational or entertaining, there is no impediment to their value or effect in the Ohio statute. But they may be used for evil, and against that possibility the statute was enacted. Their power of amusement, and, it may be, education, the audiences they assemble, not of women alone nor of men alone, but together, not of adults only, but of children, make them the more insidious in corruption by a pretense of worthy purpose or if they should degenerate from worthy purpose. Indeed, we may go beyond that possibility. They take their attraction from the general interest, eager and wholesome it may be, in their subjects, but a prurient interest may be excited and appealed to. Besides, there are some things which should not have pictorial representation in public places and to all audiences. And not only the state of Ohio, but other states, have considered it to be in the interest of the public morals and welfare to supervise moving picture exhibitions. We would have to shut our eyes to the facts of the world to regard the precaution unreasonable or the legislation to effect it a mere wanton interference with personal liberty.

We do not understand that a possibility of an evil employment of films is denied, but a freedom from the censorship of the law and a precedent right of exhibition are asserted, subsequent responsibility only, it is contended, being incurred for abuse. In other words, as we have seen, the Constitution of Ohio is invoked, and an exhibition of films is assimilated to the freedom of speech, writing, and publication assured by that instrument, and for the abuse of which only is there responsibility, and, it is insisted, that as no law may be passed "to restrain the liberty of speech or of the press," no law may be passed to subject moving pictures to censorship before their exhibition.

We need not pause to dilate upon the freedom of opinion and its expression, and whether by speech, writing, or printing. They are too certain to need discussion-of such conceded value as to need no supporting praise. Nor can there be any doubt of their breadth, nor that their underlying safeguard is, to use the words of another, "that opinion is free, and that conduct alone is amenable to the law."

Are moving pictures within the principle, as it is contended they are? They, indeed, may be mediums of thought, but so are many things. So is the theater, the circus, and all other shows and spectacles, and their performances may be thus brought by the like reasoning under the same immunity from repression or supervision as the public press,-made the same agencies of civil liberty.

Counsel have not shrunk from this extension of their contention, and cite a case in this court where the title of drama was accorded to pantomime; and such and other spectacles are said by counsel to be publications of ideas, satisfying the definition of the dictionaries,-that is, and we quote counsel, a means of making or announcing publicly something that otherwise might have remained private or unknown,-and this being peculiarly the purpose and effect of moving pictures, they come directly, it is contended, under the protection of the Ohio constitution.

The first impulse of the mind is to reject the contention. We immediately feel that the argument is wrong or strained which extends the guaranties of free opinion and speech to the multitudinous shows which are advertised on the billboards of our cities and towns, and which regards them as emblems of public safety, to use the words of Lord Camden, quoted by counsel, and which seeks to bring motion pictures and other spectacle into practical and legal similitude to a free press and liberty of opinion.

The judicial sense supporting the common sense of the country is against the contention. As pointed out by the district court, the police power is familiarly exercised in granting or withholding licenses for theatrical performances as a means of their regulation. . . .

It cannot be put out of view that the exhibition of moving pictures is a business, pure and simple, originated and conducted for profit, like other spectacles, not to be regarded, nor intended to be regarded by the Ohio Constitution, we think, as part of the press of the country, or as organs of public opinion. They are mere representations of events, of ideas and sentiments published and known; vivid, useful, and entertaining, no doubt, but, as we have said, capable of evil, having power for it, the greater because of their attractiveness and manner of exhibition. It was this capability and power, and it may be in experience of them, that induced the state of Ohio, in addition to prescribing penalties for immoral exhibitions, as it does in its Criminal Code, to require censorship before exhibition, as it does by the act under review. We cannot regard this as beyond the power of government.

It does not militate against the strength of these considerations that motion pictures may be used to amuse and instruct in other places than theaters,-in churches, for instance, and in Sunday schools and public schools. Nor are we called upon to say on this record whether such exceptions would be within the provisions of the statute, nor to anticipate that it will be so declared by the state courts, or so enforced by the state officers.

Decree affirmed.

JOSEPH BURSTYN, INC. V. WILSON

343 U.S. 495 (1952)

Mr. Justice CLARK delivered the opinion of the Court.

The issue here is the constitutionality, under the First and Fourteenth Amendments, of a New York statute which permits the banning of motion picture films on the ground that they are "sacrilegious." That statute makes it unlawful "to exhibit, or to sell, lease or lend for exhibition at any place of amusement for pay or in connection with any business in the state of New York, any motion picture film or reel (with specified exceptions not relevant here), unless there is at the time in full force and effect a valid license or permit therefor of the education department." The statute further provides:

> "The director of the (motion picture) division (of the education department) or, when authorized by the regents, the officers of a local office or bureau shall cause to be promptly examined every motion picture film submitted to them

> as herein required, and unless such film or a part thereof is obscene, indecent, immoral, inhuman, sacrilegious, or is of such a character that its exhibition would tend to corrupt morals or incite to crime, shall issue a license therefor. If such director or, when so authorized, such officer shall not license any film submitted, he shall furnish to the applicant therefor a written report of the reasons for his refusal and a description of each rejected part of a film not rejected in toto."

Appellant is a corporation engaged in the business of distributing motion pictures. It owns the exclusive rights to distribute throughout the United States a film produced in Italy entitled "The Miracle." On November 30, 1950, after having examined the picture, the motion picture division of the New York education department, acting under the statute quoted above, issued to appellant a license authorizing exhibition of "The Miracle," with English subtitles, as one part of a trilogy called "Ways of Love." Thereafter, for a period of approximately eight weeks, "Ways of Love" was exhibited publicly in a motion picture theater in New York City under an agreement between appellant and the owner of the theater whereby appellant received a stated percentage of the admission price.

During this period, the New York State Board of Regents, which by statute is made the head of the education department, received "hundreds of letters, telegrams, post cards, affidavits and other communications' both protesting against and defending the public exhibition of "The Miracle." The Chancellor of the Board or Regents requested three members of the Board to view the picture and to make a report to the entire Board. After viewing the film, this committee reported to the Board that in its opinion there was basis for the claim that the picture was "sacrilegious." Thereafter, on January 19, 1951, the Regents directed appellant to show cause, at a hearing to be held on January 30, why its license to show "The Miracle" should not be rescinded on that ground. Appellant appeared at this hearing, which was conducted by the same three-member committee of the Regents which had previously viewed the picture, and challenged the jurisdiction of the committee and of the Regents to proceed with the case. With the consent of the committee, various interested persons and organizations submitted to it briefs and exhibits bearing upon the merits of the picture and upon the constitutional and statutory questions involved. On February 16, 1951, the Regents, after viewing "The Miracle," determined that it was "sacrilegious" and for that reason ordered the Commissioner of Education to rescind appellant's license to exhibit the picture. The Commissioner did so.

Appellant brought the present action in the New York courts to review the determination of the Regents. Among the claims advanced by appellant were (1) that the statute violates the Fourteenth Amendment as a prior restraint upon freedom of speech and of the press; (2) that it is invalid under the same Amendment as a violation of the guaranty of separate church and state and as a prohibition of the free exercise of religion; and, (3) that the term "sacrilegious" is so vague and indefinite as to offend due process. The Appellate Division rejected all of appellant's contentions and upheld the Regents' determination. 104 N.Y.S.2d 740. On appeal the New York Court of Appeals, two judges dissenting, affirmed the order of the Appellate Division. 101 N.E.2d 665 [(N.Y.)]. The case is here on appeal. 28 U.S.C. § 1257(2), 28 U.S.C.A. § 1257(2).

As we view the case, we need consider only appellant's contention that the New York statute is an unconstitutional abridgment of free speech and a free press. In Mutual Film Corp. v. Industrial Comm. of Ohio, 1915, 236 U.S. 230, a distributor of motion pictures sought to enjoin the enforcement of an Ohio statute which required the prior approval of a board of censors before any motion picture could be publicly exhibited in the state, and which directed the board to approve only such films as it adjudged to be "of a moral, educational, or amusing and harmless character." The statute was assailed in part as an unconstitutional abridgment of the freedom of the press guaranteed by the First and Fourteenth Amendments. The District Court rejected this contention, stating that the first eight Amendments were not a restriction on state action. 215 F. 138, 141. On appeal to this Court, plaintiff in its brief abandoned this claim and contended merely that the statute in question violated the freedom of speech and publication guaranteed by the Constitution of Ohio. In affirming the decree of the District Court denying injunctive relief, this Court stated:

> "It cannot be put out of view that the exhibition of moving pictures is a business, pure and simple, originated and conducted for profit, like other spectacles, not to be regarded, nor intended to be regarded by the Ohio Constitution, we think, as part of the press of the country, or as organs of public opinion."

In a series of decisions beginning with Gitlow v. People of State of New York, 1925, 268 U.S. 652, this Court held that the liberty of speech and of the press which the First Amendment guarantees against abridgment by the federal government is within the liberty safeguarded by the Due

Process Clause of the Fourteenth Amendment from invasion by state action. That principle has been followed and reaffirmed to the present day. Since this series of decisions came after the Mutual decision, the present case is the first to present squarely to us the question whether motion pictures are within the ambit of protection which the First Amendment, through the Fourteenth, secures to any form of "speech" or "the press."

It cannot be doubted that motion pictures are a significant medium for the communication of ideas. They may affect public attitudes and behavior in a variety of ways, ranging from direct espousal of a political or social doctrine to the subtle shaping of thought which characterizes all artistic expression. The importance of motion pictures as an organ of public opinion is not lessened by the fact that they are designed to entertain as well as to inform. As was said in Winters v. People of State of New York, 1948, 333 U.S. 507, 510:

> "The line between the informing and the entertaining is too elusive for the protection of that basic right (a free press). Everyone is familiar with instances of propaganda through fiction. What is one man's amusement, teaches another's doctrine."

It is urged that motion pictures do not fall within the First Amendment's aegis because their production, distribution, and exhibition is a large-scale business conducted for private profit. We cannot agree. That books, newspapers, and magazines are published and sold for profit does not prevent them from being a form of expression whose liberty is safeguarded by the First Amendment. We fail to see why operation for profit should have any different effect in the case of motion pictures.

It is further urged that motion pictures possess a greater capacity for evil, particularly among the youth of a community, than other modes of expression. Even if one were to accept this hypothesis, it does not follow that motion pictures should be disqualified from First Amendment protection. If there be capacity for evil it may be relevant in determining the permissible scope of community control, but it does not authorize substantially unbridled censorship such as we have here.

For the foregoing reasons, we conclude that expression by means of motion pictures is included within the free speech and free press guaranty of the First and Fourteenth Amendments. To the extent that language in the opinion in Mutual Film Corp. v. Industrial Comm., supra, is out of harmony with the views here set forth, we no longer adhere to it.

To hold that liberty of expression by means of motion pictures is guaranteed by the First and Fourteenth Amendments, however, is not the end of our problem. It does not follow that the Constitution requires absolute freedom to exhibit every motion picture of every kind at all times and all places. That much is evident from the series of decisions of this Court with respect to other media of communication of ideas. Nor does it follow that motion pictures are necessarily subject to the precise rules governing any other particular method of expression. Each method tends to present its own peculiar problems. But the basic principles of freedom of speech and the press, like the First Amendment's command, do not vary. Those principles, as they have frequently been enunciated by this Court, make freedom of expression the rule. There is no justification in this case for making an exception to that rule.

The statute involved here does not seek to punish, as a past offense, speech or writing falling within the permissible scope of subsequent punishment. On the contrary, New York requires that permission to communicate ideas be obtained in advance from state officials who judge the content of the words and pictures sought to be communicated. This Court recognized many years ago that such a previous restraint is a form of infringement upon freedom of expression to be especially condemned. Near v. State of Minnesota ex rel. Olson, 1931, 283 U.S. 697. The Court there recounted the history which indicates that a major purpose of the First Amendment guaranty of a free press was to prevent prior restraints upon publication, although it was carefully pointed out that the liberty of the press is not limited to that protection. It was further stated that "the protection even as to previous restraint is not absolutely unlimited. But the limitation has been recognized only in exceptional cases." Id., 283 U.S. at page 716. In the light of the First Amendment's history and of the Near decision, the State has a heavy burden to demonstrate that the limitation challenged here presents such an exceptional case.

New York's highest court says there is "nothing mysterious" about the statutory provision applied in this case: "It is simply this: that no religion, as that word is understood by the ordinary, reasonable person, shall be treated with contempt, mockery, scorn and ridicule." This is far from the kind of narrow exception to freedom of expression which a state may carve out to satisfy the adverse demands of other interests of society. In seeking to apply the broad and all-inclusive definition of "sacrilegious" given by the New York courts, the censor is set adrift upon a boundless sea amid a myriad of conflicting currents of religious views, with no charts but those provided by the most vocal and powerful orthodoxies, New York cannot vest such unlimited restraining control over motion pictures in a censor. Cf. Kunz v. People of State of New York, 1951, 340 U.S. 290. Under such a standard the most careful and tolerant censor would find it virtually impossible to avoid favoring one religion over another, and he would be subject to an inevitable tendency to ban the expression of unpopular sentiments sacred to a religious minority. Application of the "sacrilegious" test, in these or other respects, might raise substantial questions under the First Amendment's guaranty of separate church and state with freedom of worship for all. However, from the standpoint of freedom of speech and the press, it is enough to point out that the state has no legitimate interest in protecting any or all religions from views distasteful to them which is sufficient to justify prior restraints upon the expression of those views. It is not the business of government in our nation to suppress real or imagined attacks upon a particular religious doctrine, whether they appear in publications, speeches, or motion pictures.

Since the term "sacrilegious" is the sole standard under attack here, it is not necessary for us to decide, for example, whether a state may censor motion pictures under a clearly drawn statute designed and applied to prevent the showing of obscene films. That is a very different question from the one now before us. We hold only that under the First and Fourteenth Amendments a state may not ban a film on the basis of a censor's conclusion that it is "sacrilegious."

Reversed.

FREEDMAN V. MARYLAND
380 U.S. 51 (1965)

Mr. Justice BRENNAN delivered the opinion of the Court.

Appellant sought to challenge the constitutionality of the Maryland motion picture censorship statute, Md.Ann.Code, 1957, Art. 66A, and exhibited the film "Revenge at Daybreak" at his Baltimore theatre without first submitting the picture to the State Board of Censors as required by § 2 thereof. The State concedes that the picture does not violate the statutory standards and would have received a license if properly submitted, but the appellant was convicted of a § 2 violation despite his contention that the statute in its entirety unconstitutionally impaired freedom of expression. The Court of Appeals of Maryland affirmed, 197 A.2d 232 [(Md.)], and we noted probable jurisdiction, 377 U.S. 987. We reverse.

I.

In Times Film Corp. v. City of Chicago, 365 U.S. 43, we considered and upheld a requirement of submission of motion pictures in advance of exhibition. The Court of Appeals held, on the authority of that decision, that "the Maryland censorship law must be held to be not void on its face as violative of the freedoms protected against State action by the First and Fourteenth Amendments." 197 A.2d, at 235. This reliance on Times Film was misplaced. The only question tendered for decision in that case was "whether a prior restraint was necessarily unconstitutional under all circumstances." Bantam Books, Inc. v. Sullivan, 372 U.S. 58, 70, n. 10 (emphasis in original). The exhibitor's argument that the requirement of submission without more amounted to a constitutionally prohibited prior restraint was interpreted by the Court in Times Film as a contention that the "constitutional protection includes complete and absolute freedom to exhibit, at least once, any and every kind of motion picture. . . . even if this film contains the basest type of pornography, or incitement to riot, or forceful overthrow of orderly government . . . ." 365 U.S., at 46, 47. The Court held that on this "narrow" question, id., at 46, the argument stated the principle against prior restraints too broadly; citing a number of our decisions, the Court quoted the statement from Near v. State of Minnesota, 283 U.S. 697, 716, that "(t)he protection even as to previous restraint is not absolutely unlimited." In rejecting the proffered proposition in Times Film the Court emphasized, however, that "(i)t is that question alone which we decide," 365 U.S., at 46, and it would therefore be inaccurate to say that Times Film upheld the specific features of the Chicago censorship ordinance.

Unlike the petitioner in Times Film, appellant does not argue that § 2 is unconstitutional simply because it may prevent even the first showing of a film whose exhibiting may legitimately be the subject of an obscenity prosecution. He presents a question quite distinct from that passed on in Times Film; accepting the rule in Times Film, he argues that § 2 constitutes an invalid prior restraint because, in the context of the remainder of the statute, it presents a danger of unduly suppressing protected expression. He focuses particularly on the procedure for an initial decision by the censorship board, which, without any judicial participation, effectively bars exhibition of any disapproved film, unless and until the exhibitor undertakes a time-consuming appeal to the Maryland courts and succeeds in having the Board's decision reversed. Under the statute, the exhibitor is required to submit the film to the Board for examination, but no time limit is imposed for completion of Board action, § 17. If the film is disapproved, or any elimination ordered, § 19 provides that

> "The person submitting such film or view for examination will receive immediate notice of such elimination or disapproval, and if appealed from, such film or view will be promptly reexamined, in the presence of such person, by two or more members of the Board, and the same finally approved or disapproved promptly after such re-examination, with the right of appeal from the decision of the Board to the Baltimore City Court of Baltimore City. There shall be a further right of appeal from the decision of the Baltimore City Court to the Court of Appeals of Maryland, subject generally to the time and manner provided for taking appeal to the Court of Appeals."

Thus there is no statutory provision for judicial participation in the procedure which bars a film, nor even assurance of prompt judicial review. Risk of delay is built into the Maryland procedure, as is borne out by experience; in the only reported case indicating the length of time required to complete an appeal, the initial judicial determination has taken four months and final vindication of the film on appellate review, six months. United Artists Corp. v. Maryland State Board of Censors, 124 A.2d 292.

In the light of the difference between the issues presented here and in Times Film, the Court of Appeals erred in saying that, since appellant's refusal to submit the film to the Board was a violation only of § 2, "he has restricted himself to an attack on that section alone, and lacks standing to challenge any of the other provisions (or alleged shortcomings) of the statute." 197 A.2d, at 236. Appellant has not challenged the submission requirement in a vacuum but in a concrete statutory context. His contention is that § 2 effects an invalid prior restraint because the structure of the other provisions of the statute contributes to the infirmity of § 2; he does not assert that the other provisions are independently invalid.

In the area of freedom of expression it is well established that one has standing to challenge a statute on the ground that it delegates overly broad licensing discretion to an administrative office, whether or not his conduct could be proscribed by a properly drawn statute, and whether or not he applied for a license. "One who might have had a license for the asking may . . . call into question the whole scheme of licensing when he is prosecuted for failure to procure it." . . . Standing is recognized in such cases because of the ". . . danger of tolerating, in the area of First Amendment freedoms, the existence of a penal statute susceptible of sweeping and improper application." ... Although we have no occasion to decide whether the vice of overbroadness infects the Maryland statute, we think that appellant's assertion of a similar danger in the Maryland apparatus of censorship—one always fraught with danger and viewed with suspicion—gives him standing to make that challenge. In substance his argument is that, because the apparatus operates in a statutory context in which judicial review may be too little and too late, the Maryland statute lacks sufficient safeguards for confining the censor's action to judicially determined constitutional limits, and therefore contains the same vice as a statute delegating excessive administrative discretion.

II.

Although the Court has said that motion pictures are not "necessarily subject to the precise rules governing any other particular method of expression," Joseph Burstyn, Inc. v. Wilson, 343 U.S. 495, 503, it is as true here as of other forms of expression that "(a)ny system of prior restraints of expression comes to this Court bearing a heavy presumption against its constitutional validity." Bantam Books, Inc. v. Sullivan, supra, 372 U.S. at 70. "... (U)nder the Fourteenth Amendment, a State is not free to adopt whatever procedures it pleases for dealing with obscenity ... without regard to the possible consequences for constitutionally protected speech." Marcus v. Search Warrant, 367 U.S. 717, 731. The administration of a censorship system for motion pictures presents peculiar dangers to constitutionally protected speech. Unlike a prosecution for obscenity, a censorship proceeding puts the initial burden on the exhibitor or distributor. Because the censor's business is to censor, there inheres the danger that he may well be less responsive than a court—part of an independent branch of government—to the constitutionally protected interests in free expression. And if it is made unduly onerous, by reason of delay or otherwise, to seek judicial review, the censor's determination may in practice be final.

Applying the settled rule of our cases, we hold that a noncriminal process which requires the prior submission of a film to a censor avoids constitutional infirmity only if it takes place under procedural safeguards designed to obviate the dangers of a censorship system. First, the burden of proving that the film is unprotected expression must rest on the censor ... Second, while the State may require advance submission of all films, in order to proceed effectively to bar all showings of unprotected films, the requirement cannot be administered in a manner which would lend an effect of finality to the censor's determination whether a film constitutes protected expression. The teaching of our cases is that, because only a judicial determination in an adversary proceeding ensures the necessary sensitivity to freedom of expression, only a procedure requiring a judicial determination suffices to impose a valid final restraint. . . . To this end, the exhibitor must be assured, by statute or authoritative judicial construction, that the censor will, within a specified brief period, either issue a license or go to court to restrain showing the film. Any restraint imposed in advance of a final judicial determination on the merits must similarly be limited to preservation of the status quo for the shortest fixed period compatible with sound judicial resolution. Moreover, we are well aware that, even after expiration of a temporary restraint, an administrative refusal to license, signifying the censor's view that the film is unprotected, may have a discouraging effect on the exhibitor. See Bantam Books, Inc. v. Sullivan, supra. Therefore, the procedure must also assure a prompt final judicial decision, to minimize the deterrent effect of an interim and possibly erroneous denial of a license.

Without these safeguards, it may prove too burdensome to seek review of the censor's determination. Particularly in the case of motion pictures, it may take very little to deter exhibition in a given locality. The exhibitor's stake in any one picture may be insufficient to warrant a protracted and onerous course of litigation. The distributor, on the other hand, may be equally unwilling to accept the burdens and delays of litigation in a particular area when, without such difficulties, he can freely exhibit his film in most of the rest of the country; for we are told that only four States and a handful of municipalities have active censorship laws.

It is readily apparent that the Maryland procedural scheme does not satisfy these criteria. First, once the censor disapproves the film, the exhibitor must assume the burden of instituting judicial proceedings and of persuading the courts that the film is protected expression. Second, once the Board has acted against a film, exhibition is prohibited pending judicial review, however protracted. Under the statute, appellant could have been convicted if he had shown the film after unsuccessfully seeking a license, even though no court had ever ruled on the obscenity of the film. Third, it is abundantly clear that the Maryland statute provides no assurance of prompt judicial determination. We hold, therefore, that appellant's conviction must be reversed. The Maryland scheme fails to provide adequate safeguards against undue inhibition of protected expression, and this renders the § 2 requirement of prior submission of films to the Board an invalid previous restraint.

III.

How or whether Maryland is to incorporate the required procedural safeguards in the statutory scheme is, of course, for the State to decide. But a model is not lacking: In Kingsley Books, Inc. v. Brown, 354 U.S. 436, we upheld a New York injunctive procedure designed to prevent the sale of obscene books. That procedure postpones any restraint against sale until a judicial determination of obscenity following notice and an adversary hearing. The statute provides for a hearing one day after joinder of issue; the judge must hand down his decision within two days after termination of the hearing. The New York procedure operates without prior submission to a censor, but the chilling effect of a censorship order, even one which requires judicial action for its enforcement, suggests all the more reason for expeditious determination of the question whether a particular film is constitutionally protected.

The requirement of prior submission to a censor sustained in Times Film is consistent with our recognition that films differ from other forms of expression. Similarly, we think that the nature of the motion picture industry may suggest different time limits for a judicial determination. It is common knowledge that films are scheduled well before actual exhibition, and the requirement of advance submission in § 2 recognizes this. One possible scheme would be to allow the exhibitor or distributor to submit his film early enough to ensure an orderly final disposition of the case before the scheduled exhibition date—far enough in advance so that the exhibitor could safely advertise the opening on a normal basis. Failing such a scheme or sufficiently early submission under such a scheme, the statute would have to require adjudication considerably more prompt than has been the case under the Maryland statute. Otherwise, litigation might be unduly expensive and protracted, or the victorious exhibitor might find the most propitious opportunity for exhibition past. We do not mean to lay down rigid time limits or procedures, but to suggest considerations in drafting legislation to accord with local exhibition practices, and in doing so to avoid the potentially chilling effect of the Maryland statute on protected expression.

Reversed.

Mr. Justice DOUGLAS, whom Mr. Justice BLACK joins, concurring.

On several occasions I have indicated my view that movies are entitled to the same degree and kind of protection under the First Amendment as other forms of expression. . . . I do not believe any form of censorship—no matter how speedy or prolonged it may be—is permissible. As I see it, a pictorial presentation occupies as preferred a position as any other form of expression. If censors are banned from the publishing business, from the pulpit, from the public platform—as they are—they should be banned from the theatre. I would not admit the censor even for the limited role accorded him in Kingsley Books, Inc. v. Brown, 354 U.S. 436, 77 S.Ct. 1325, 1 L.Ed.2d 1469. I adhere to my dissent in that case. Id., at 446-447. Any authority to obtain a temporary injunction gives the State "the paralyzing power of a censor." Id., at 446. The regime of Kingsley Books "substitutes punishment by contempt for punishment by jury trial." Id., at 477. I would put an end to all forms and types of censorship and give full literal meaning to the command of the First Amendment.

MPAA Ratings System

Rating symbol	Meaning
G	**G - General Audiences** All ages admitted. This movie contains little or no content that would offend parents for viewing by children.
PG	**PG - Parental Guidance Suggested** Some material may not be suitable for children. Parents are urged to give parental guidance as the motion picture contains some material that parents might not find suitable for their young children.
PG-13	**PG-13 - Parents Strongly Cautioned** Parents are urged to be cautious as the motion picture contains some material that parents might consider inappropriate for children under 13 years.
R	**R - Restricted** People under 17 years may only be admitted if accompanied by a parent or guardian.

NC-17

NC-17 – No One 17 and Under Admitted
This film is exclusively adult in content and people under 18 are not admitted.

Source: Wikipedia

The MPAA ratings system was developed in 1968 as a replacement for the Motion Picture Production Code, a Depression-era morals-based censorship regime, which had become outmoded by the 1950s. While the MPAA ratings system is voluntary, it carries considerable weight in the movie industry. The success of the system rests on the fact that all the major Hollywood studios and larger theater chains have agreed to abide by the ratings. The ratings themselves are determined by a Ratings Board and administered by the Classifications and Ratings Administration (CARA), which is independent of the MPAA. The categories "G," "PG," and "PG-13" are merely advisory; filmgoers of any age are permitted, even if a PG-13 film might otherwise be inappropriate for a young child. While the "R" rating denotes "restricted," it is only conditionally so, since children of any age may be permitted to see an R film in the presence of an adult.

Only an "NC-17" rating truly restricts a minor from being admitted to a film. NC-17 films are not necessarily pornographic; films that are excessively violent or focus on adult themes may receive the rating. As the heir to the MPAA's "X" rating, which, in the absence of a trademark, became co-opted by the porn industry, the NC-17 rating may denote a serious film with artistic ambition. That said, an NC-17 assignment can also be box-office poison for a film. Studios and directors will seek to recut a film in the hopes of avoiding an NC-17 rating since the potential audience for this restricted rating is much smaller, and many theaters will not show NC-17 films. Some newspapers and Web sites also may choose not to advertise NC-17 films.

While the MPAA has tried to enunciate clearer guidelines for each rating, there are many that criticize the system's fairness. Producers and directors have long complained that the ratings are too focused on sex and perhaps not enough on violence. Trey Parker and Matt Stone, the creators of the animated television show "South Park," were especially vocal in their criticism of the MPAA when the film "Orgasmo," Parker's satire about a Mormon missionary-turned-porn-star, fizzled at the box office after receiving an NC-17 rating. Their "South Park" film, laden with homoeroticism, sadistic violence, and subtitled with a sexual allusion unnoticed by the Ratings Board, received an R-rating and was regarded by many as a subversive critique of the MPAA.

Other critics say that the ratings system favors the major studios—and big-name directors—over those with less sway in Hollywood. Wes Craven had to recut his film, "Scream," and rescreen it for the MPAA in order to avoid an NC-17 rating for graphic violence; yet, Steven Spielberg's "Saving Private Ryan" received an R-rating without cuts, despite what the MPAA described as "intense prolonged realistically graphic sequences of war violence." Indeed, it was Steven Spielberg who persuaded the MPAA to add the PG-13 rating in 1984, in part to avoid a costly R-rating for "Gremlins," which he executive produced, and "Indiana Jones and the Temple of Doom," which he directed, because both featured gory fantasy violence. To educate consumers and filmmakers, the MPAA operates www.filmratings.com, which explains ratings criteria and lists ratings decisions for new releases.

NOTES AND QUESTIONS

1. **The Threat of the New.** In reflecting on the way American culture—and the courts—changed their view of cinema between the *Mutual Film* and *Burstyn* cases, do you see a pattern that could also apply to other media technologies? Has our culture's view of television, pop music, and video games similarly evolved as these technologies matured?
2. **Early attempts at industry censorship.** Beginning in the 1920s, Hollywood film studios like Metro-Goldwyn-Mayer, Paramount, and Fox collaborated with advocates of religion-inspired decency to develop a list of "don'ts" and "be carefuls." The "don'ts" included ridicule of the clergy, depictions of miscegenation, spoken or mouthed profanity, and suggestive nudity. Filmmakers were admonished to take "special care" in depicting use of the American flag, sympathy for criminals, the institution of marriage, unfavorable characterizations of other countries, and too much detail in the manner of which crimes are committed. Before 1934, there was no industry-based enforcement of these lists.
3. **The Hayes Code.** In 1934, the industry created the Production Code Administration under the direction of Will H. Hayes, to enforce a rigorous morals-based production code that now bears Hayes name. Watch a movie produced prior to 1934—a very popular example is "Gold Diggers of 1933"—and compare it to any number of "showgirl" movie musicals made later in the 1930s. Can you see the impact of strict code enforcement on the content of films made during this era?

4. After Freedman v. Maryland, the era of state censorship boards was effectively over. Why?
5. In 1972, the U.S. Supreme Court reversed an obscenity conviction in Georgia related to the release of "Carnal Knowledge," a Jack Nicholson film with frank sexual content. In reversing the Georgia Supreme Court, Justice Rehnquist makes it clear that films enjoy full First Amendment protection under the *Miller* obscenity test: "Nothing in the movie falls within . . . material which may constitutionally be found . . . 'patently offensive' . . . . There are occasional scenes of nudity, but nudity alone is not enough to make material legally obscene. . . ." Jenkins v. Georgia, 418 U.S. 153 (1974).
6. While voluntary, the MPAA ratings system has been the subject of occasional criticism for being too opaque and inconsistent in its application. Since the 1990s, the MPAA has included a brief explanation for a particular movie's rating. Even so, if you were asked to screen your favorite films blindly, would you correctly guess their ratings?
7. **Unintended consequences.** While an R or NC-17 rating can hurt a film's release in theaters, it may be a boon for DVD sales. Many violent thrillers and raunchy comedies often shoot an "uncut and unrated" version of the film for separate DVD release or as DVD bonus material. Since the MPAA does not control DVD marketing, the result is that children—and sensitive adults—may be exposed to objectionable content. Some kids may even seek this material without their parents' consent. Should the MPAA and studios voluntarily agree to restrict DVD content?

limited network programming on local stations to certain times of the day, and prevented companies from owning more than one network, among other things. By 1940, the National Broadcasting Company (NBC) owned two popular radio networks, NBC Red and NBC Blue. With the support of the Columbia Broadcasting System (CBS) and the Mutual Network, NBC challenged the federal government's authority to grant licenses under the Communications Act and the First Amendment. In the aftermath of its corporate parent's loss in the Supreme Court, NBC Blue was spun-off into a separate network, becoming the American Broadcasting Company (ABC) in 1951.

National Broadcasting Co. v. U.S.

319 U.S. 190 (1943)

Mr. Justice FRANKFURTER delivered the opinion of the Court.

In view of our dependence upon regulated private enterprise in discharging the far-reaching role which radio plays in our society, a somewhat detailed exposition of the history of the present controversy and the issues which it raises is appropriate.

. . .

On March 18, 1938, the Commission undertook a comprehensive investigation to determine whether special regulations applicable to radio stations engaged in chain broadcasting were required in the "public interest, convenience, or necessity." The Commission's order directed that inquiry be made, inter alia, in the following specific matters: the number of stations licensed to or affiliated with networks, and the amount of station time used or controlled by networks; the contractual rights and obligations of stations under their agreements with networks; the scope of network agreements containing exclusive affiliation provisions and restricting the network from affiliating with other stations in the same area; the rights and obligations of stations with respect to network advertisers; the nature of the program service rendered by stations licensed to networks; the policies of networks with respect to character of programs, diversification, and accommodation to the particular requirements of the areas served by the affiliated stations; the extent to which affiliated stations exercise control over programs, advertising contracts, and related matters; the nature and extent of network program duplication by stations serving the same area; the extent to which particular networks have exclusive coverage in some areas; the competitive [illegible]s of stations engaged in chain broadcasting; the effect of chain broadcasting upon stations not licensed to or affiliated with networks; practices or agreements in restraint of trade, or in furtherance of monopoly, in connection with chain broadcasting; and the scope of concentration of control over stations, locally, regionally, or nationally, through contracts, common ownership, or other means.

. . .

The Radio Act of 1927 created the Federal Radio Commission, composed of five members, and endowed the Commission with wide licensing and regulatory powers. We do not pause here to enumerate the scope of the Radio Act of 1927 and of the authority entrusted to the Radio Commission, for the basic provisions of that Act are incorporated in the Communications Act of 1934, 48 Stat. 1064, 47 U.S.C. § 151 et seq., 47 U.S.C.A. § 151 et seq., the legislation immediately before us. As we noted in Federal Communications Comm. v. Pottsville Broadcasting Co., 309 U.S. 134, 137, "In its essentials the Communications Act of 1934 (so far as its provisions relating to radio are concerned) derives from the Federal Radio Act of 1927 . . . . By this Act Congress, in order to protect the national interest involved in the new and far-reaching science of broadcasting, formulated a unified and comprehensive regulatory system for the industry. The common factors in the administration of the various statutes by which Congress had supervised the different modes of communication led to the creation, in the Act of 1934, of the Communications Commission. But the objectives of the legislation have remained substantially unaltered since 1927."

The FCC's commissioners, 1937.

Section 1 of the Communications Act states its "purpose of regulating interstate and foreign commerce in communication by wire and radio so as to make available, so far as possible, to all the people of the United States a rapid, efficient, Nationwide, and world-wide wire and radio communication service with adequate facilities at reasonable charges." Section 301 particularizes this general purpose with respect to radio: "It is the purpose of this Act, among other things, to maintain the control of the United States over all the channels of interstate and foreign radio transmission; and to provide for the use of such channels, but not the ownership thereof, by persons for limited periods of time, under licenses granted by Federal authority, and no such license shall be construed to create any right, beyond the terms, conditions, and periods of the license." To that end a Commission composed of seven members was created, with broad licensing and regulatory powers.

Section 303 provides:

"Except as otherwise provided in this Act, the Commission from time to time, as public convenience, interest, or necessity requires, shall-

"(a) Classify radio stations;

"b) Prescribe the nature of the service to be rendered by each class of licensed stations and each station within any class;

. . .

"(f) Make such regulations not inconsistent with law as it may deem necessary to prevent interference between stations and to carry out the provisions of this Act * * *;

"(g) Study new uses for radio, provide for experimental uses of frequencies, and generally encourage the larger and more effective use of radio in the public interest;

. . .

"(i) Have authority to make special regulations applicable to radio stations engaged in chain broadcasting;

. . .

"(r) Make such rules and regulations and prescribe such restrictions and conditions, not inconsistent with law, as may be necessary to carry out the provisions of this Act * * *."

The criterion governing the exercise of the Commission's licensing power is the "public interest, convenience, or necessity." §§ 307(a)(d), 309(a), 310, 312. In addition, § 307(b) directs the Commission that "In considering applications for licenses, and modifications and renewals thereof, when and insofar as there is demand for the same, the Commission shall make such distribution of licenses, frequencies, hours of operation, and of power among the several States and communities as to provide a fair, efficient, and equitable distribution of radio service to each of the same."

The Act itself establishes that the Commission's powers are not limited to the engineering and technical aspects of regulation of radio communication. Yet we are asked to regard the Commission as a kind of traffic officer, policing the wave lengths to prevent stations from interfering with each other. But the Act does not restrict the Commission merely to supervision of the traffic. It puts upon the Commission the burden of determining the composition of that traffic. The facilities of radio are not large enough to accommodate all who wish to use them. Methods must be devised for choosing from among the many who apply. And since Congress itself could not do this, it committed the task to the Commission.

. . .

We come, finally, to an appeal to the First Amendment. The Regulations, even if valid in all other respects, must fall because they abridge, say the appellants, their right of free speech. If that be so, it would follow that every person whose application for a license to operate a station is denied by the Commission is thereby denied his constitutional right of free speech. Freedom of utterance is abridged to many who wish to use the limited facilities of radio. Unlike other modes of expression, radio inherently is not available to all. That is its unique characteristic, and that is why, unlike other modes of expression, it is subject to governmental regulation. Because it cannot be used by all, some who wish to use it must be denied. But Congress did not authorize the Commission to choose among applicants upon the basis of their political, economic or social views, or upon any other capricious basis. If it did, or if the Commission by these Regulations proposed a choice among applicants upon some such basis, the issue before us would be wholly different. The question here is simply whether the Commission, by announcing that it will refuse licenses to persons who engage in specified network practices (a basis for choice which we hold is comprehended within the statutory criterion of "public interest"), is thereby denying such persons the constitutional right of free speech. The right of free speech does not include, however, the right to use the facilities of radio without a license. The licensing system established by Congress in the Communications Act of 1934 was a proper exercise of its power over commerce. The standard it provided for the licensing of stations was the "public interest, convenience, or necessity." Denial of a station license on that ground, if valid under the Act, is not a denial of free speech. . . .

RED LION BROADCASTING CO. V. FCC
395 U.S. 367 (1969)

Mr. Justice WHITE delivered the opinion of the Court.
The Federal Communications Commission has for many years imposed on radio and television broadcasters the requirement that discussion of public issues be presented on broadcast stations, and that each side of those issues must be given fair coverage. This is known as the fairness doctrine, which originated very early in the history of broadcasting and has maintained its present outlines for some time. It is an obligation whose content has been defined in a long series of FCC rulings in particular cases, and which is distinct from the statutory requirement of § 315 of the Communications Act that equal time be allotted all qualified candidates for public office. Two aspects of the fairness doctrine, relating to personal attacks in the context of controversial public issues and to political editorializing, were codified more precisely in the form of FCC regulations in 1967. The two cases before us now, which were decided separately below, challenge the constitutional and statutory bases of the doctrine and component rules. Red Lion involves the application of the fairness doctrine to a particular broadcast, and RTNDA arises as an action to review the FCC's 1967 promulgation of the personal attack and political editorializing regulations, which were laid down after the Red Lion litigation had begun.

I.
A.
The Red Lion Broadcasting Company is licensed to operate a Pennsylvania radio station, WGCB. On November 27, 1964, WGCB carried a 15-minute broadcast by the Reverend Billy James Hargis as part of a "Christian Crusade" series. A book by Fred J. Cook entitled "Goldwater—Extremist on the Right" was discussed by Hargis, who said that Cook had been fired by a newspaper for making false charges against city officials; that Cook had then worked for a Communist-affiliated publication; that he had defended Alger Hiss and attacked J. Edgar Hoover and the

Central Intelligence Agency; and that he had now written a "book to smear and destroy Barry Goldwater." When Cook heard of the broadcast he concluded that he had been personally attacked and demanded free reply time, which the station refused. After an exchange of letters among Cook, Red Lion, and the FCC, the FCC declared that the Hargis broadcast constituted a personal attack on Cook; that Red Lion had failed to meet its obligation under the fairness doctrine as expressed in Times-Mirror Broadcasting Co., 24 P & F Radio Reg. 404 (1962), to send a tape, transcript, or summary of the broadcast to Cook and offer him reply time; and that the station must provide reply time whether or not Cook would pay for it. On review in the Court of Appeals for the District of Columbia Circuit, the FCC's position was upheld as constitutional and otherwise proper. 381 F.2d 908 (1967).

B.

Not long after the Red Lion litigation was begun, the FCC issued a Notice of Proposed Rule Making, 31 Fed.Reg. 5710, with an eye to making the personal attack aspect of the fairness doctrine more precise and more readily enforceable, and to specifying its rules relating to political editorials. After considering written comments supporting and opposing the rules, the FCC adopted them substantially as proposed, 32 Fed.Reg. 10303. Twice amended, 32 Fed.Reg. 11531, 33 Fed.Reg. 5362, the rules were held unconstitutional in the RTNDA litigation by the Court of Appeals for the Seventh Circuit, on review of the rulemaking proceeding, as abridging the freedoms of speech and press. 400 F.2d 1002 (1968).

As they now stand amended, the regulations read as follows:

"Personal attacks; political editorials.

"(a) When, during the presentation of views on a controversial issue of public importance, an attack is made upon the honesty, character, integrity or like personal qualities of an identified person or group, the licensee shall, within a reasonable time and in no event later than 1 week after the attack, transmit to the person or group attacked (1) notification of the date, time and identification of the broadcast; (2) a script or tape (or an accurate summary if a script or tape is not available) of the attack, and (3) an offer of a reasonable opportunity to respond over the licensee's facilities.

"(b) The provisions of paragraph (a) of this section shall not be applicable (1) to attacks on foreign groups or foreign public figures; (2) to personal attacks which are made by legally qualified candidates, their authorized spokesmen, or those associated with them in the campaign, on other such candidates, their authorized spokesmen, or persons associated with the candidates in the campaign; and (3) to bona fide newscasts, bona fide news interviews, and on-the-spot coverage of a bona fide news event (including commentary or analysis contained in the foregoing programs, but the provisions of paragraph (a) of this section shall be applicable to editorials of the licensee).

"NOTE: The fairness doctrine is applicable to situations coming within ((3)), above, and, in a specific factual situation, may be applicable in the ((2)), above. See, section 315(a) of the Act, 47 U.S.C. § 315(a); Public Notice: Applicability of the Fairness Doctrine in the Handling of Controversial Issues of Public Importance. 29 F.R. 10415. The categories listed in ((3)) are the same as those specified in section 315(a) of the Act.

"(c) Where a licensee, in an editorial, (i) endorses or (ii) opposes a legally qualified candidate or candidates, the licensee shall, within 24 hours after the editorial, transmit to respectively (i) the other qualified candidate or candidates for the same office or (ii) the candidate opposed in the editorial (1) notification of the date and the time of the editorial; (2) a script or tape of the editorial; and (3) an offer of a reasonable opportunity for a candidate or a spokesman of the candidate to respond over the licensee's facilities: Provided, however, That where such editorials are broadcast within 72 hours prior to the day of the election, the licensee shall comply with the provisions of this paragraph sufficiently far in advance of the broadcast to enable the candidate or candidates to have a reasonable opportunity to prepare a response and to present it in a timely fashion." 47 CFR §§ 73.123, 73.300, 73.598, 73.679 (all identical).

C.

Believing that the specific application of the fairness doctrine in Red Lion, and the promulgation of the regulations in RTNDA, are both authorized by Congress and enhance rather than abridge the freedoms of speech and press protected by the First Amendment, we hold them valid and constitutional, reversing the judgment below in RTNDA and affirming the judgment below in Red Lion.

II.

The history of the emergence of the fairness doctrine and of the related legislation shows that the Commission's action in the Red Lion case did not exceed its authority, and that in adopting the new regulations the Commission was implementing congressional policy rather than embarking on a frolic of its own.

A.

Before 1927, the allocation of frequencies was left entirely to the private sector, and the result was chaos. It quickly became apparent that broadcast frequencies constituted a scarce resource whose use could be regulated and rationalized only by the Government. Without government control, the medium would be of little use because of the cacophony of competing voices, none of which could be clearly and predictably heard. Consequently, the Federal Radio Commission was established to allocate frequencies among competing applicants in a manner responsive to the public "convenience, interest, or necessity."

Very shortly thereafter the Commission expressed its view that the "public interest requires ample play for the free and fair competition of opposing views, and the commission believes that the principle applies * * * to all discussions of issues of importance to the public." . . . After an extended period during which the licensee was obliged not only to cover and to cover fairly the views of others, but also to refrain from expressing his own personal views, Mayflower Broadcasting Corp., 8 F.C.C. 333 (1940), the latter limitation on the licensee was abandoned and the doctrine developed into its present form.

There is a twofold duty laid down by the FCC's decisions and described by the 1949 Report on Editorializing by Broadcast Licensees, 13 F.C.C. 246 (1949). The broadcaster must give adequate coverage to public issues, United Broadcasting Co., 10 F.C.C. 515 (1945), and coverage must be fair in that it accurately reflects the opposing views. New Broadcasting Co., 6 P & F Radio Reg. 258 (1950). This must be done at the broadcaster's own expense if sponsorship is unavailable. Cullman Broadcasting Co., 25 P & F Radio Reg. 895 (1963). Moreover, the duty must be met by programming obtained at the licensee's own initiative if available from no other source. . . .

When a personal attack has been made on a figure involved in a public issue both the doctrine of cases such as Red Lion and Times-Mirror Broadcasting Co., 24 P & F Radio Reg. 404 (1962), and also the 1967 regulations at issue in RTNDA require that the individual attacked himself be offered an opportunity to respond. Likewise, where one candidate is endorsed in a political editorial, the other candidates must themselves be offered reply time to use personally or through a spokesman. These obligations differ from the general fairness requirement that issues be presented, and presented with coverage of competing views, in that the broadcaster does not have the option of presenting the attacked party's side himself or choosing a third party to represent that side. But insofar as there is an obligation of the broadcaster to see that both sides are presented, and insofar as that is an affirmative obligation, the personal attack doctrine and regulations do not differ from the preceding fairness doctrine. The simple fact that the attacked men or unendorsed candidates may respond themselves or through agents is not a critical distinction, and indeed, it is not unreasonable for the FCC to conclude that the objective of adequate presentation of all sides may best be served by allowing those most closely affected to make the response, rather than leaving the response in the hands of the station which has attacked their candidacies, endorsed their opponents, or carried a personal attack upon them.

B.

The statutory authority of the FCC to promulgate these regulations derives from the mandate to the "Commission from time to time, as public convenience, interest, or necessity requires" to promulgate "such rules and regulations and prescribe such restrictions and conditions * * * as may be necessary to carry out the provisions of this chapter * * *." 47 U.S.C. § 303 and § 303(r). The Commission is specifically directed to consider the demands of the public interest in the course of granting licenses. 47 U.S.C. §§ 307(a), 309(a); renewing them, 47 U.S.C. § 307; and modifying them. Ibid. Moreover, the FCC has included among the conditions of the Red Lion license itself the requirement that operation of the station be carried out in the public interest, 47 U.S.C. § 309(h). This mandate to the FCC to assure that broadcasters operate in the public interest is a broad one, a power "not niggardly but expansive," . . . It is broad enough to encompass these regulations.

The fairness doctrine finds specific recognition in statutory form, is in part modeled on explicit statutory provisions relating to political candidates, and is approvingly reflected in legislative history.

In 1959 the Congress amended the statutory requirement of § 315 that equal time be accorded each political candidate to except certain appearances on news programs, but added that this constituted no exception "from the obligation imposed upon them under this Act to operate in the public interest and to afford reasonable opportunity for the discussion of conflicting views on issues of public importance." Act of September 14, 1959, § 1, 73 Stat. 557, amending 47 U.S.C. § 315(a) (emphasis added). This language makes it very plain that Congress, in 1959, announced that the phrase "public interest," which had been in the Act since 1927, imposed a duty on broadcasters to discuss both sides of controversial public issues. In other words, the amendment vindicated the FCC's general view that the fairness doctrine inhered in the public interest standard. Subsequent legislation declaring the intent of an earlier statute is entitled to great weight in statutory construction. And here this principle is given special force by the equally venerable principle that the construction of a statute by those charged with its execution should be followed unless there are compelling indications that it is wrong, especially when Congress has refused to alter the administrative construction. Here, the Congress has not just kept its silence by refusing to overturn the administrative construction, but has ratified it with positive legislation. Thirty years of consistent administrative construction left undisturbed by Congress until 1959, when that construction was expressly accepted, reinforce the natural conclusion that the public interest language of the Act authorized the Commission to require licensees to use their stations for discussion of public issues, and that the FCC is free to implement this requirement by reasonable rules and regulations which fall short of abridgment of the freedom of speech and press, and of the censorship proscribed by § 326 of the Act.

The objectives of § 315 themselves could readily be circumvented but for the complementary fairness doctrine ratified by § 315. The section applies only to campaign appearances by candidates, and not by family, friends, campaign managers, or other supporters. Without the fairness doctrine, then, a licensee could ban all campaign appearances by candidates themselves from the air and proceed to deliver over his station entirely to the supporters of one slate of candidates, to the exclusion of all others. In this way the broadcaster could have a far greater impact on the favored candidacy than he could by simply allowing a spot appearance by the candidate himself. It is the fairness doctrine as an aspect of the obligation to operate in the public interest, rather than § 315, which prohibits the broadcaster from taking such a step.

The legislative history reinforces this view of the effect of the 1959 amendment. Even before the language relevant here was added, the Senate report on amending § 315 noted that "broadcast frequencies are limited and, therefore, they have been necessarily considered a public trust. Every licensee who is fortunate in obtaining a license is mandated to operate in the public interest and has assumed the obligation of presenting important public questions fairly and without bias." . . .

When the Congress ratified the FCC's implication of a fairness doctrine in 1959 it did not, of course, approve every past decision or pronouncement by the Commission on this subject, or give it a completely free hand for the future. The statutory authority does not go so far. But we cannot say that when a station publishes personal attacks or endorses political candidates, it is a misconstruction of the public interest standard to require the station to offer time for a response rather than to leave the response entirely within the control of the station which has attacked either the candidacies or the men who wish to reply in their own defense. When a broadcaster grants time to a political candidate, Congress itself requires that equal time be offered to his opponents. It would exceed our competence to hold that the Commission is unauthorized by the statute to employ a similar device where personal attacks or political editorials are broadcast by a radio or television station.

In light of the fact that the "public interest" in broadcasting clearly encompasses the presentation of vigorous debate of controversial issues of importance and concern to the public; the fact that the FCC has rested upon that language from its very inception a doctrine that these issues must be discussed, and fairly; and the fact that Congress has acknowledged that the analogous provisions of § 315 are not preclusive in this area, and knowingly preserved the FCC's complementary efforts, we think the fairness doctrine and its component personal attack and political editorializing regulations are a legitimate exercise of congressionally delegated authority. The Communications Act is not notable for the precision of its substantive standards and in this respect the explicit provisions of § 315, and the doctrine and rules at issue here which are closely modeled upon that section, are far more explicit than the generalized "public interest" standard in which the Commission ordinarily finds its sole guidance, and which we have held a broad but adequate standard before... We cannot say that the FCC's declaratory ruling in Red Lion, or the regulations at issue in RTNDA, are beyond the scope of the congressionally conferred power to assure that stations are operated by those whose possession of a license serves "the public interest."

III.

The broadcasters challenge the fairness doctrine and its specific manifestations in the personal attack and political editorial rules on conventional First Amendment grounds, alleging that the rules abridge their freedom of speech and press. Their contention is that the First Amendment protects their desire to use their allotted frequencies continuously to broadcast whatever they choose, and to exclude whomever they choose from ever using that frequency. No man may be prevented from saying or publishing what he thinks, or from refusing in his speech or other utterances to give equal weight to the views of his opponents. This right, they say, applies equally to broadcasters.

A.
Although broadcasting is clearly a medium affected by a First Amendment interest, United States v. Paramount Pictures, Inc., 334 U.S. 131, 166 (1948), differences in the characteristics of new media justify differences in the First Amendment standards applied to them. Joseph Burstyn, Inc. v. Wilson, 343 U.S. 495, 503 (1952). For example, the ability of new technology to produce sounds more raucous than those of the human voice justifies restrictions on the sound level, and on the hours and places of use, of sound trucks so long as the restrictions are reasonable and applied without discrimination. . . .

Just as the Government may limit the use of sound-amplifying equipment potentially so noisy that it drowns out civilized private speech, so may the Government limit the use of broadcast equipment. The right of free speech of a broadcaster, the user of a sound truck, or any other individual does not embrace a right to snuff out the free speech of others. Associated Press v. United States, 326 U.S. 1, 20 (1945) . . . .

It was . . . the chaos which ensued from permitting anyone to use any frequency at whatever power level he wished, which made necessary the enactment of the Radio Act of 1927 and the Communications Act of 1934, as the Court has noted at length before. National Broadcasting Co. v. United States, 319 U.S. 190, 210-214 (1943). It was this reality which at the very least necessitated first the division of the radio spectrum into portions reserved respectively for public broadcasting and for other important radio uses such as amateur operation, aircraft, police, defense, and navigation; and then the subdivision of each portion, and assignment of specific frequencies to individual users or groups of users. Beyond this, however, because the frequencies reserved for public broadcasting were limited in number, it was essential for the Government to tell some applicants that they could not broadcast at all because there was room for only a few.

Where there are substantially more individuals who want to broadcast than there are frequencies to allocate, it is idle to posit an unabridgeable First Amendment right to broadcast comparable to the right of every individual to speak, write, or publish. If 100 persons want broadcast licenses but there are only 10 frequencies to allocate, all of them may have the same "right" to a license; but if there is to be any effective communication by radio, only a few can be licensed and the rest must be barred from the airwaves. It would be strange if the First Amendment, aimed at protecting and furthering communications, prevented the Government from making radio communication possible by requiring licenses to broadcast and by limiting the number of licenses so as not to overcrowd the spectrum.

This has been the consistent view of the Court. Congress unquestionably has the power to grant and deny licenses and to eliminate existing stations. FRC v. Nelson Bros. Bond & Mortgage Co., 289 U.S. 266 (1933). No one has a First Amendment right to a license or to monopolize a radio frequency; to deny a station license because "the public interest" requires it "is not a denial of free speech." . . .

By the same token, as far as the First Amendment is concerned those who are licensed stand no better than those to whom licenses are refused. A license permits broadcasting, but the licensee has no constitutional right to be the one who holds the license or to monopolize a radio frequency to the exclusion of his fellow citizens. There is nothing in the First Amendment which prevents the Government from requiring a licensee to share his frequency with others and to conduct himself as a proxy or fiduciary with obligations to present those views and voices which are representative of his community and which would otherwise, by necessity, be barred from the airwaves.

This is not to say that the First Amendment is irrelevant to public broadcasting. On the contrary, it has a major role to play as the Congress itself recognized in § 326, which forbids FCC interference with "the right of free speech by means of radio communication." Because of the scarcity of radio frequencies, the Government is permitted to put restraints on licensees in favor of others whose views should be expressed on this unique medium. But the people as a whole retain their interest in free speech by radio and their collective right to have the medium function consistently with the ends and purposes of the First Amendment. It is the right of the viewers and listeners, not the right of the broadcasters, which is paramount. . . . It is the purpose of the First Amendment to preserve an uninhibited marketplace of ideas in which truth will ultimately prevail, rather than to countenance monopolization of that market, whether it be by the Government itself or a private licensee. . . . It is the right of the public to receive suitable access to social, political, esthetic, moral, and other ideas and experiences which is crucial here. That right may not constitutionally be abridged either by Congress or by the FCC.

B.

Rather than confer frequency monopolies on a relatively small number of licensees, in a Nation of 200,000,000, the Government could surely have decreed that each frequency should be shared among all or some of those who wish to use it, each being assigned a portion of the broadcast day or the broadcast week. The ruling and regulations at issue here do not go quite so far. They assert that under specified circumstances, a licensee must offer to make available a reasonable amount of broadcast time to those who have a view different from that which has already been expressed on his station. The expression of a political endorsement, or of a personal attack while dealing with a controversial public issue, simply triggers this time sharing. As we have said, the First Amendment confers no right on licensees to prevent others from broadcasting on "their" frequencies and no right to an unconditional monopoly of a scarce resource which the Government has denied others the right to use.

In terms of constitutional principle, and as enforced sharing of a scarce resource, the personal attack and political editorial rules are indistinguishable from the equal-time provision of § 315, a specific enactment of Congress requiring stations to set aside reply time under specified circumstances and to which the fairness doctrine and these constituent regulations are important complements. That provision, which has been part of the law since 1927, Radio Act of 1927, § 18, 44 Stat. 1170, has been held valid by this Court as an obligation of the licensee relieving him of any power in any way to prevent or censor the broadcast, and thus insulating him from liability for defamation. The constitutionality of the statute under the First Amendment was unquestioned.

Nor can we say that it is inconsistent with the First Amendment goal of producing an informed public capable of conducting its own affairs to require a broadcaster to permit answers to personal attacks occurring in the course of discussing controversial issues, or to require that the political opponents of those endorsed by the station be given a chance to communicate with the public. Otherwise, station owners and a few networks would have unfettered power to make time available only to the highest bidders, to communicate only their own views on public issues, people and candidates, and to permit on the air only those with whom they agreed. There is no sanctuary in the First Amendment for unlimited private censorship operating in a medium not open to all. "Freedom of the press from governmental interference under the First Amendment does not sanction repression of that freedom by private interests." Associated Press v. United States, 326 U.S. 1, 20 (1945).

C.

It is strenuously argued, however, that if political editorials or personal attacks will trigger an obligation in broadcasters to afford the opportunity for expression to speakers who need not pay for time and whose views are unpalatable to the licensees, then broadcasters will be irresistibly forced to self-censorship and their coverage of controversial public issues will be eliminated or at least rendered wholly ineffective. Such a result would indeed be a serious matter, for should licensees actually eliminate their coverage of controversial issues, the purposes of the doctrine would be stifled.

At this point, however, as the Federal Communications Commission has indicated, that possibility is at best speculative. The communications industry, and in particular the networks, have taken pains to present controversial issues in the past, and even now they do not assert that they intend to abandon their efforts in this regard. It would be better if the FCC's encouragement were never necessary to induce the broadcasters to meet their responsibility. And if experience with the administration of those doctrines indicates that they have the net effect of reducing rather than enhancing the volume and quality of coverage, there will be time enough to reconsider the constitutional implications. The fairness doctrine in the past has had no such overall effect.

That this will occur now seems unlikely, however, since if present licensees should suddenly prove timorous, the Commission is not powerless to insist that they give adequate and fair attention to public issues. It does not violate the First Amendment to treat licensees given the privilege of using scarce radio frequencies as proxies for the entire community, obligated to give suitable time and attention to matters of great public concern. To condition the granting or renewal of licenses on a willingness to present representative community views on controversial issues is consistent with the ends and purposes of those constitutional provisions forbidding the abridgment of freedom of speech and freedom of the press. Congress need not stand idly by and permit those with licenses to ignore the problems which beset the people or to exclude from the airways anything but their own views of fundamental questions. The statute, long administrative practice, and cases are to this effect.

Licenses to broadcast do not confer ownership of designated frequencies, but only the temporary privilege of using them. 47 U.S.C. § 301. . . . The statute mandates the issuance of licenses if the "public convenience, interest, or necessity will be served thereby." 47 U.S.C. § 307(a). In applying this standard the Commission for 40 years has been choosing licensees based in part on their program proposals. In FRC v. Nelson Bros. Bond & Mortgage Co., 289 U.S. 266, 279 (1933), the Court noted that in "view of the limited number of available broadcasting frequencies, the Congress has authorized allocation and licenses." In determining how best to allocate frequencies, the Federal Radio Commission considered the needs of competing communities and the programs offered by competing stations to meet those needs; moreover, if needs or programs shifted, the Commission could alter its allocations to reflect those shifts. Id., at 285. In the same vein, in FCC v. Pottsville Broadcasting Co., 309 U.S. 134, 137-138 (1940), the Court noted that the statutory standard was a supple instrument to effect congressional desires "to maintain * * * a grip on the dynamic aspects of radio transmission" and to allay fears that "in the absence of governmental control the public interest might be subordinated to monopolistic domination in the broadcasting field." Three years later the Court considered the validity of the Commission's chain broadcasting regulations, which among other things forbade stations from devoting too much time to network programs in order that there be suitable opportunity for local programs serving local needs. The Court upheld the regulations, unequivocally recognizing that the Commission was more than a traffic policeman concerned with the technical aspects of broadcasting and that it neither exceeded its powers under the statute nor transgressed the First Amendment in interesting itself in general program format and the kinds of programs broadcast by licensees. National Broadcasting Co. v. United States, 319 U.S. 190 (1943).

D.

. . . We need not and do not now ratify every past and future decision by the FCC with regard to programming. There is no question here of the Commission's refusal to permit the broadcaster to carry a particular program or to publish his own views; of a discriminatory refusal to require the licensee to broadcast certain views which have been denied access to the airwaves; of government censorship of a particular program contrary to § 326; or of the official government view dominating public broadcasting. Such questions would raise more serious First Amendment issues. But we do hold that the Congress and the Commission do not violate the First Amendment when they require a radio or television station to give reply time to answer personal attacks and political editorials.

Scarcity and Media Access after *Red Lion*

By the time *Red Lion* was decided, in 1969, broadcast scarcity had become a more complex issue than Justice Frankfurter would have imagined in the *National Broadcasting Co.* case. There are those today who argue that broadcasting is just a small slice of a media universe that now includes cable, satellite, video playback, and the Internet. Because there are a large number of content distribution options in this universe, the scarcity that justifies special regulations for broadcasting is no longer present. For people who look to this type of scarcity, also called "numerical" scarcity, use of public airwaves should not be subject to exceptional regulation since it is merely one of many distribution platforms available to content providers. Those who favor continued regulation of broadcasting argue that the public airwaves are still scarce. Though there is an abundance of other media available today, electromagnetic frequencies are still a finite, natural resource, and there are not enough frequencies available to all who want them. This type of scarcity, also known as "allocational" scarcity, continues to provide a justification for many of the special rules and obligations that apply only to radio and television licensees.

In 1986, the Supreme Court determined that, as a result of a legislative oversight in 1959, Congress had never incorporated the Fairness Doctrine into the Communications Act as a law. No longer required to enforce the doctrine as law, a deregulatory-minded FCC slowly repealed the doctrine as policy, citing a lack of numerical scarcity. While the Fairness Doctrine is no longer operative, *Red Lion* is still cited as good law by the Supreme Court. Congress or the FCC could revive the doctrine, or a new iteration of it, without violating the first amendment.

The centrality of the scarcity concept, along with the public's ownership of the airwaves, is what allowed the Supreme Court to uphold the Fairness Doctrine as constitutional in *Red Lion*. Consider, however, whether a law granting similar access to another, increasingly scarce media platform—a newspaper—would be upheld under the first amendment. The answer, evident in Miami Herald v. Tornillo infra, is a resounding no. Yet, isn't scarcity a big issue here as well? Some would argue that newspapers are more scarce than broadcast stations. Many major cities have one newspaper (and some have none), though there may be dozens of radio and television stations broadcasting locally. Pat Tornillo, a candidate who was attacked by the Miami Herald, does not have the resources to start a competing newspaper, nor would he want to; he simply desires access to the newspaper's editorial page so he can respond in a forum that reaches those who read the attack. The case, decided only four years after *Red Lion*, makes no mention of the earlier precedent. Why? What's different about the scarcity of a newspaper that would lead the Supreme Court to strike down Florida's access law as unconstitutional?

MIAMI HERALD PUBLISHING CO. V. TORNILLO
418 U.S. 241 (1974)

Mr. Chief Justice BURGER delivered the opinion of the Court.
The issue in this case is whether a state statute granting a political candidate a right to equal space to reply to criticism and attacks on his record by a newspaper violates the guarantees of a free press.

I.
In the fall of 1972, appellee, Executive Director of the Classroom Teachers Association, apparently a teachers' collective-bargaining agent, was a candidate for the Florida House of Representatives. On September 20, 1972, and again on September 29, 1972, appellant printed editorials critical of appellee's candidacy. In response to these editorials appellee demanded that appellant print verbatim his replies, defending the role of the Classroom Teachers Association and the organization's accomplishments for the citizens of Dade County. Appellant declined to print the appellee's replies and appellee brought suit in Circuit Court, Dade County, seeking declaratory and injunctive relief and actual and punitive damages in excess of $5,000. The action was premised on Florida Statute § 104.38 (1973), F.S.A., a "right of reply" statute which provides that if a candidate for nomination or election is assailed regarding his personal character or official record by any newspaper, the candidate has the right to demand that the newspaper print, free of cost to the candidate, any reply the candidate may make to the newspaper's charges. The reply must appear in as conspicuous a place and in the same kind of type as the charges which prompted the reply, provided it does not take up more space than the charges. Failure to comply with the statute constitutes a first-degree misdemeanor.

Appellant sought a declaration that § 104.38 was unconstitutional. After an emergency hearing requested by appellee, the Circuit Court denied injunctive relief because, absent special circumstances, no injunction could properly issue against the commission of a crime, and held that § 104.38 was unconstitutional as an infringement on the freedom of the press under the First and Fourteenth Amendments to the Constitution. 38 Fla.Supp. 80 (1972). The Circuit Court concluded that dictating what a newspaper must print was no different from dictating what it must not print. The Circuit Judge viewed the statute's vagueness as serving "to restrict and stifle protected expression." Id., at 83. Appellee's cause was dismissed with prejudice.

On direct appeal, the Florida Supreme Court reversed, holding that § 104.38 did not violate constitutional guarantees. 287 So.2d 78 (1973). It held that free speech was enhanced and not abridged by the Florida right-of-reply statute, which in that court's view, furthered the "broad societal interest in the free flow of information to the public." Id., at 82. . . .

. . .

III.

A.

The challenged statute creates a right to reply to press criticism of a candidate for nomination or election. The statute was enacted in 1913, and this is only the second recorded case decided under its provisions.

Appellant contends the statute is void on its face because it purports to regulate the content of a newspaper in violation of the First Amendment. Alternatively it is urged that the statute is void for vagueness since no editor could know exactly what words would call the statute into operation. It is also contended that the statute fails to distinguish between critical comment which is and which is not defamatory.

B.

The appellee and supporting advocates of an enforceable right of access to the press vigorously argue that government has an obligation to ensure that a wide variety of views reach the public. The contentions of access proponents will be set out in some detail. It is urged that at the time the First Amendment to the Constitution was ratified in 1791 as part of our Bill of Rights the press was broadly representative of the people it was serving. While many of the newspapers were intensely partisan and narrow in their views, the press collectively presented a broad range of opinions to readers. Entry into publishing was inexpensive; pamphlets and books provided meaningful alternatives to the organized press for the expression of unpopular ideas and often treated events and expressed views not covered by conventional newspapers. A true marketplace of ideas existed in which there was relatively easy access to the channels of communication.

Access advocates submit that although newspapers of the present are superficially similar to those of 1791 the press of today is in reality very different from that known in the early years of our national existence. In the past half century a communications revolution has seen the introduction of radio and television into our lives, the promise of a global community through the use of communications satellites, and the spectre of a "wired" nation by means of an expanding cable television network with two-way capabilities. The printed press, it is said, has not escaped the effects of this revolution. Newspapers have become big business and there are far fewer of them to serve a larger literate population. Chains of newspapers, national newspapers, national wire and news services, and one-newspaper towns, are the dominant features of a press that has become noncompetitive and enormously powerful and influential in its capacity to manipulate popular opinion and change the course of events. Major metropolitan newspapers have collaborated to establish news services national in scope. Such national news organizations provide syndicated "interpretive reporting" as well as syndicated features and commentary, all of which can serve as part of the new school of "advocacy journalism."

The elimination of competing newspapers in most of our large cities, and the concentration of control of media that results from the only newspaper's being owned by the same interests which own a television station and a radio station, are important components of this trend toward concentration of control of outlets to inform the public.

The result of these vast changes has been to place in a few hands the power to inform the American people and shape public opinion. Much of the editorial opinion and commentary that is printed is that of syndicated columnists distributed nationwide and, as a result, we are told, on national and world issues there tends to be a homogeneity of editorial opinion, commentary, and interpretive analysis. The abuses of bias and manipulative reportage are, likewise, said to be the result of the vast accumulations of unreviewable power in the modern media empires. In effect, it is claimed, the public has lost any ability to respond or to contribute in a meaningful way to the debate on issues. The monopoly of the means of communication allows for little or no critical analysis of the media except in professional journals of very limited readership. . . .

The obvious solution, which was available to dissidents at an earlier time when entry into publishing was relatively inexpensive, today would be to have additional newspapers. But the same economic factors which have caused the disappearance of vast numbers of metropolitan newspapers, have made entry into the marketplace of ideas served by the print media almost impossible. It is urged that the claim of newspapers to be "surrogates for the public" carries with it a concomitant fiduciary obligation to account for that stewardship. From this premise it is reasoned that the only effective way to insure fairness and accuracy and to provide for some accountability is for government to take affirmative action. The

First Amendment interest of the public in being informed is said to be in peril because the "marketplace of ideas" is today a monopoly controlled by the owners of the market.

Proponents of enforced access to the press take comfort from language in several of this Court's decisions which suggests that the First Amendment acts as a sword as well as a shield, that it imposes obligations on the owners of the press in addition to protecting the press from government regulation. In Associated Press v. United States, 326 U.S. 1, 20 (1945), the Court, in rejecting the argument that the press is immune from the antitrust laws by virtue of the First Amendment, stated:

> "The First Amendment, far from providing an argument against application of the Sherman Act, here provides powerful reasons to the contrary. That Amendment rests on the assumption that the widest possible dissemination of information from diverse and antagonistic sources is essential to the welfare of the public, that a free press is a condition of a free society. Surely a command that the government itself shall not impede the free flow of ideas does not afford non-governmental combinations a refuge if they impose restraints upon that constitutionally guaranteed freedom. Freedom to publish means freedom for all and not for some. Freedom to publish is guaranteed by the Constitution, but freedom to combine to keep others from publishing is not. Freedom of the press from governmental interference under the First Amendment does not sanction repression of that freedom by private interests." (Footnote omitted.)

In New York Times Co. v. Sullivan, 376 U.S. 254, 270 (1964), the Court spoke of "a profound national commitment to the principle that debate on public issues should be uninhibited, robust, and wide-open." It is argued that the "uninhibited, robust" debate is not "wide-open" but open only to a monopoly in control of the press. Appellee cites the plurality opinion in Rosenbloom v. Metromedia, Inc., 403 U.S. 29, 47, and n. 15 (1971), which he suggests seemed to invite experimentation by the State in right-to-access regulation of the press. . . .

IV.

However much validity may be found in these arguments, at each point the implementation of a remedy such as an enforceable right of access necessarily calls for some mechanism, either governmental or consensual. If it is governmental coercion, this at once brings about a confrontation with the express provisions of the First Amendment and the judicial gloss on that Amendment developed over the years. . . .

We see the beginning with Associated Press, supra, the Court has expressed sensitivity as to whether a restriction or requirement constituted the compulsion exerted by government on a newspaper to print that which it would not otherwise print. The clear implication has been that any such compulsion to publish that which "'reason' tells them should not be published" is unconstitutional. A responsible press is an undoubtedly desirable goal, but press responsibility is not mandated by the Constitution and like many other virtues it cannot be legislated.

Appellee's argument that the Florida statute does not amount to a restriction of appellant's right to speak because "the statute in question here has not prevented the Miami Herald from saying anything it wished" begs the core question. Compelling editors or publishers to publish that which "'reason' tells them should not be published" is what is at issue in this case. The Florida statute operates as a command in the same sense as a statue or regulation forbidding appellant to publish specified matter. Governmental restraint on publishing need not fall into familiar or traditional patterns to be subject to constitutional limitations on governmental powers. Grosjean v. American Press Co., 297 U.S. 233, 244-245 (1936). The Florida statute exacts a penalty on the basis of the content of a newspaper. The first phase of the penalty resulting from the compelled printing of a reply is exacted in terms of the cost in printing and composing time and materials and in taking up space that could be devoted to other material the newspaper may have preferred to print. It is correct, as appellee contends, that a newspaper is not subject to the finite technological limitations of time that confront a broadcaster but it is not correct to say that, as an economic reality, a newspaper can proceed to infinite expansion of its column space to accommodate the replies that a government agency determines or a statute commands the readers should have available.

Faced with the penalties that would accrue to any newspaper that published news or commentary arguably within the reach of the right-of-access statute, editors might well conclude that the safe course is to avoid controversy. Therefore, under the operation of the Florida statute, political and electrol coverage would be blunted or reduced. Government-enforced right of access inescapably "dampens the vigor and limits the variety of public debate," New York Times Co. v. Sullivan, supra, 376

U.S., at 279. The Court, in Mills v. Alabama, 384 U.S. 214, 218 (1966), stated:

> "[T]here is practically universal agreement that a major purpose of [the First] Amendment was to protect the free discussion of governmental affairs. This of course includes discussions of candidates . . ."

Even if a newspaper would face no additional costs to comply with a compulsory access law and would not be forced to forgo publication of news or opinion by the inclusion of a reply, the Florida statute fails to clear the barriers of the First Amendment because of its intrusion into the function of editors. A newspaper is more than a passive receptacle or conduit for news, comment, and advertising. The choice of material to go into a newspaper, and the decisions made as to limitations on the size and content of the paper, and treatment of public issues and public officials—whether fair or unfair—constitute the exercise of editorial control and judgment. It has yet to be demonstrated how governmental regulation of this crucial process can be exercised consistent with First Amendment guarantees of a free press as they have evolved to this time. Accordingly, the judgment of the Supreme Court of Florida is reversed.

It is so ordered. Reversed.

Mr. Justice BRENNAN, with whom Mr. Justice REHNQUIST joins, concurring.
I join the Court's opinion which, as I understand it, addresses only "right of reply" statutes and implies no view upon the constitutionality of "retraction" statutes affording plaintiffs able to prove defamatory falsehoods a statutory action to require publication of a retraction. . . .

Mr. Justice WHITE, concurring.
The Court today holds that the First Amendment bars a State from requiring a newspaper to print the reply of a candidate for public office whose personal character has been criticized by that newspaper's editorials. According to our accepted jurisprudence, the First Amendment erects a virtually insurmountable barrier between government and the print media so far as government tampering, in advance of publication, with news and editorial content is concerned. New York Times Co. v. United States, 403 U.S. 713 (1971). A newspaper or magazine is not a public utility subject to "reasonable" governmental regulation in matters affecting the exercise of journalistic judgment as to what shall be printed. Cf. Mills v. Alabama, 384 U.S. 214, 220 (1966). We have learned, and

continue to learn, from what we view as the unhappy experiences of other nations where government has been allowed to meddle in the internal editorial affairs of newspapers. Regardless of how beneficent-sounding the purposes of controlling the press might be, we prefer "the power of reason as applied through public discussion" and remain intensely skeptical about those measures that would allow government to insinuate itself into the editorial rooms of this Nation's press.

"Whatever differences may exist about interpretations of the First Amendment, there is practically universal agreement that a major purpose of that Amendment was to protect the free discussion of governmental affairs. This of course includes discussions of candidates, structures and forms of government, the manner in which government is operated or should be operated, and all such matters relating to political processes. The Constitution specifically selected the press . . . to play an important role in the discussion of public affairs. Thus the press serves and was designed to serve as a powerful antidote to any abuses of power by governmental officials and as a constitutionally chosen means for keeping officials elected by the people responsible to all the people whom they were selected to serve. Suppression of the right of the press to praise or criticize governmental agents and to clamor and contend for or against change . . . muzzles one of the very agencies the Framers of our Constitution thoughtfully and deliberately selected to improve our society and keep it free." Mills v. Alabama, supra, at 218-219.

. . .

The press would be unlicensed because, in Jefferson's words, "(w)here the press is free, and every man able to read, all is safe." Any other accommodation—any other system that would supplant private control of the press with the heavy hand of government intrusion—would make the government the censor of what the people may read and know.

. . .

[T]his law runs afoul of the elementary First Amendment proposition that government may not force a newspaper to print copy which, in its journalistic discretion, it chooses to leave on the newsroom floor. Whatever power may reside in government to influence the publishing of certain narrowly circumscribed categories of material, see, e.g., Pittsburgh Press Co. v. Pittsburgh Commission on Human Relations, 413 U.S. 376 (1973); New York Times Co. v. United States, 403 U.S., at 730 (White, J., concurring), we have never thought that the First Amendment permitted public officials to dictate to the press the contents of its news columns or the slant of its editorials.

But though a newspaper may publish without government censorship, it has never been entirely free from liability for what it chooses to print. See ibid. Among other things, the press has not been wholly at liberty to publish falsehoods damaging to individual reputation. At least until today, we have cherished the average citizen's reputation interest enough to afford him a fair chance to vindicate himself in an action for libel characteristically provided by state law. He has been unable to force the press to tell his side of the story or to print a retraction, but he has had at least the opportunity to win a judgment if he has been able to prove the falsity of the damaging publication, as well as a fair chance to recover reasonable damages for his injury. . . .

Of course, these two decisions do not mean that because government may not dictate what the press is to print, neither can it afford a remedy for libel in any form. Gertz itself leaves a putative remedy for libel intact, albeit in severely emaciated form; and the press certainly remains liable for knowing or reckless falsehoods under New York Times Co. v. Sullivan, 376 U.S. 254 (1964), and its progeny, however improper an injunction against publication might be.

One need not think less of the First Amendment to sustain reasonable methods for allowing the average citizen to redeem a falsely tarnished reputation. Nor does one have to doubt the genuine decency, integrity, and good sense of the vast majority of professional journalists to support the right of any individual to have his day in court when he has been falsely maligned in the public press. The press is the servant, not the master, of the citizenry, and its freedom does not carry with it an unrestricted hunting license to prey on the ordinary citizen. . . . To me it is a near absurdity to so deprecate individual dignity, as the Court does in Gertz, and to leave the people at the complete mercy of the press, at least in this stage of our history when the press, as the majority in this case so well documents, is steadily becoming more powerful and much less likely to be deterred by threats of libel suits.

NOTES AND QUESTIONS

1. Section 326 of the Communications Act says nothing "shall be understood or construed to give the Commission the power of cen-

sorship over radio communications or signals transmitted." In Trinity Methodist Church, South v. Fed. Radio Comm'n, 62 F.2d 850 (D.C. Cir. 1932), the precursor to the FCC, operating under the same censorship constraint, denied renewal of a station license controlled by a minister who used the airwaves to derogate the government and attack minorities and labor groups. The court concluded that denying a license renewal to a station which broadcasts "without facts" is "neither censorship nor previous restraint." Do you agree?

2. **Qualifications.** Under section 308 of the Communications Act, license applicants must be U.S. citizens and meet financial, technical, and character qualifications. In 1994, Rupert Murdoch's News Corporation, an Australian corporation, was ultimately permitted to renew Fox Television Stations' (FTS) licenses, despite a cap on 25 percent foreign ownership of a broadcast licensee. The FCC determined that News Corporation created its corporate structure "in good faith reliance on our published rulings" and that there was no evidence of foreign influence on FTS. In re Fox Television Stations, Inc., 11 FCC Rcd. 5714 (1995). Do you think the FCC would waive section 310(b)(4)'s foreign ownership restriction for a corporation controlled by entities based in countries, for example, like China or Saudi Arabia?
3. **Format Changes.** For many years, the FCC required licensees to "ascertain" the programming needs of the communities in which they operated. Today, much of the "regulatory underbrush" relating to renewals, including ascertainment, is no longer in place. A community's only classical music station can, overnight, and without notice, switch its format to become the area's fifth country station. See FCC v. WNCN Listeners Guild, 450 U.S. 582 (1981). What if format changes lead to a loss of all news stations in a particular city or stations that program in a language used by a sizeable population in that city?
4. If broadcasters in good standing want to transfer their licenses, they are free to sell them to qualified third-party buyers at market rates, even if their licenses were acquired for free decades ago. Should incumbent broadcasters be required to share some of their windfalls with the U.S. government? Why should broadcasters be allowed to sell their licenses?
5. **The Repeal of the Fairness Doctrine.** In 1986, the FCC determined that, contrary to the Supreme Court's assumption in *Red Lion*, the Fairness Doctrine had never been ratified by Congress in 1959. Without a statutory mandate, a deregulatory FCC an-

nounced that they would no longer enforce it. See Syracuse Peace Council v. FCC, 867 F.2d 654 (D.C. Cir. 1989).

6. In the rulemaking that led to the *Syracuse Peace Council* case supra, the FCC determined that the Fairness Doctrine "restricts the journalistic freedom of broadcasters . . . [and] actually inhibits the presentation of controversial issues of public importance to the detriment of the public and the degradation of the editorial prerogative of broadcast journalists." Citing the numerical abundance of electronic media, the FCC questioned the continued constitutionality of *Red Lion*. Do you agree? Does the Supreme Court agree?
7. Which is scarcer in a community? Daily newspapers or television stations? In Los Angeles, for example, there are 27 full-power stations on the broadcast dial, but only two daily newspapers. Some major cities no longer have a daily newspaper. Should we reexamine the *Miami Herald* decision in light of this economic scarcity?

CHAPTER 9

POLITICAL PROGRAMMING

The statutory provision infra, section 315 of the 1934 Communications Act, underscores the delicate balance that Congress has tried to maintain between free speech rights of a political candidate and fair access to the public's airwaves by all candidates. Section 315 is actually two distantly related provisions. Section 315(a), the "equal opportunities" or "equal time" statute, permits a candidate free access to a broadcast station if an opposing candidate makes a "positive appearance," as long as that appearance is not subject to a news-related exemption. Section 315(b) is the "Lowest Unit Rate" provision. Section 315(b) requires broadcast stations to charge political candidates the lowest rate for commercial time—the rate stations give their best customers—within forty-five days of a primary and sixty days of a general election; at other times, stations must charge candidates no differently than their other customers.

47 U.S.C.A. § 315: CANDIDATES FOR PUBLIC OFFICE

(a) Equal opportunities requirement; censorship prohibition; allowance of station use; news appearances exception; public interest; public issues discussion opportunities

If any licensee shall permit any person who is a legally qualified candidate for any public office to use a broadcasting station, he shall afford equal opportunities to all other such candidates for that office in the use of such broadcasting station: *Provided,* That such licensee shall have no power of censorship over the material broadcast under the provisions of this section. No obligation is imposed under this subsection upon any licensee to allow the use of its station by any such candidate. Appearance by a legally qualified candidate on any—

(1) bona fide newscast,
(2) bona fide news interview,
(3) bona fide news documentary (if the appearance of the candidate is incidental to the presentation of the subject or subjects covered by the news documentary), or

(4) on-the-spot coverage of bona fide news events (including but not limited to political conventions and activities incidental thereto),

shall not be deemed to be use of a broadcasting station within the meaning of this subsection. Nothing in the foregoing sentence shall be construed as relieving broadcasters, in connection with the presentation of newscasts, news interviews, news documentaries, and on-the-spot coverage of news events, from the obligation imposed upon them under this chapter to operate in the public interest and to afford reasonable opportunity for the discussion of conflicting views on issues of public importance.

(b) Charges

(1) In general

The charges made for the use of any broadcasting station by any person who is a legally qualified candidate for any public office in connection with his campaign for nomination for election, or election, to such office shall not exceed—

(A) subject to paragraph (2), during the forty-five days preceding the date of a primary or primary runoff election and during the sixty days preceding the date of a general or special election in which such person is a candidate, the lowest unit charge of the station for the same class and amount of time for the same period; and

(B) at any other time, the charges made for comparable use of such station by other users thereof.

(2) Content of broadcasts

(A) In general

In the case of a candidate for Federal office, such candidate shall not be entitled to receive the rate under paragraph (1)(A) for the use of any broadcasting station unless the candidate provides written certification to the broadcast station that the candidate (and any authorized committee of the candidate) shall not make any direct reference to another candidate for the same office, in any broadcast using the rights and conditions of access under this chapter, unless such reference meets the requirements of subparagraph (C) or (D).

(B) Limitation on charges

If a candidate for Federal office (or any authorized committee of such candidate) makes a reference described in subparagraph (A) in any broadcast that does not meet the requirements of subparagraph (C) or (D), such candidate shall not be entitled to receive the rate under paragraph (1)(A) for such broadcast or any other broadcast during any portion of the 45-day and 60-day periods described in paragraph (1)(A), that occur on or after the date of such broadcast, for election to such office.

. . .

Section 315(a). Equal Opportunities.

Section 315(a) is triggered when a licensee airs a non-exempt positive appearance of a legally qualified candidate for public office. If that happens for any reason, the station must give every opposing candidate for the same office an equal amount of time on the station. The station does not have the discretion to deny or condition the opposing candidate's access to the station; nor does it have the right to edit or censor the opposing candidate's triggered appearance. The burden is wholly on the licensee—that is, the local broadcast station. If a network program triggers the statute, neither the producers of the show nor the network, for that matter, have any obligation to offer free time on the show or on the network. In such a case, every station that aired the program would potentially be required to furnish the triggered time—even if the station had no foreknowledge of the triggering appearance.

To stay in compliance with this statute, station management must diligently scrutinize the content that gets aired on the station. The station, for one, needs to determine if an individual schedule to appear on air is a legally qualified candidate. In most cases, that is easy to figure out; to be legally qualified, the candidate must have either announced or taken concrete steps to announcing a candidacy, and be legally qualified to hold the office if elected. Under section 315(a), it does not matter if it is election season or not. If a candidate announces years in advance of an election, his or her appearance will still trigger the statute. Once the candidate is known to the station, program management will need to review scripts or pre-screen content to make sure that the candidate is not making a non-exempt positive appearance. Although it is not entirely clear what makes an appearance "positive," the FCC applies the statute to voice "appearances" by candidates on radio and television. Only a candidate's appearance triggers, however. Surrogates on behalf of a candidate, or impersonators of a candidate, do not count as positive appearances. But if a candidate appears as herself on an episode of *The Big Bang Theory* or as a character in an old movie like *Conan the Barbarian*, that would be a triggering event, even though the appearance was unrelated to the announced candidacy, or created before the candidate entered politics.

While section 315(a), at first blush, appears to impose a Draconian burden upon local stations, the section is rarely invoked today. For one thing, licensees, in cooperation with networks, producers and lawyers, are careful to scrutinize for triggering appearances. After former senator Fred Dalton Thompson, who played a district attorney on *Law & Order*, announced his candidacy for president in 2011, the show's producers edited him out of episodes being prepared for broadcast syndication. For the same reason, NBC would almost certainly have prohibited candidate Donald Trump from continuing as the star of *The Apprentice*, had the broadcast network not parted way with him because of provocative anti-immigrant comments made when he announced his presidential campaign.

Another way stations avoid a trigger event is to argue that the candidate's appearance is exempt under the statute. In 1959, Congress enacted four exemptions to section 315(a) for newscasts, incidental appearances in a documentary, bona fide news interview programs, and on-the-spot political coverage. Candidates appearing in these types of programs do not trigger. The reason for these exemptions, made at the behest of the broadcast industry, was that a broad application of section 315(a) would act as a chilling effect on broadcast news coverage, since stations would be less likely to cover candidates if it meant yielding free time to opposing candidates. This concern is still present today, which is one reason that the FCC broadly applies the newsworthy exemption to shows that are topical, even if they would not qualify under most viewers' definitions of broadcast journalism. The FCC's 2003 Infinity Broadcasting Declaratory Ruling is perhaps the best example of how far the FCC is willing to go to thaw section 315(a)'s potential chilling effect on news coverage by licensees. However, in the *Branch* case infra, the DC Circuit upheld the FCC's denial of an exemption to a news anchor running for office. The FCC will also strictly apply section 315(a)'s trigger to appearances on scripted entertainment shows, as the comedian Pat Paulsen discovered in the FCC's 1972 Walt Disney Productions Declaratory Ruling.

IN RE INFINITY BROADCASTING OPERATIONS INC.

18 FCC Rcd. 18603 (2003)

By the Chief, Media Bureau:

1. This refers to the request for declaratory ruling filed by Infinity Broadcasting Operations Inc. ("Infinity"), licensee of Station WXRK(FM), New York City, New York, asking the Commission to declare that the program "The Howard Stern Show," which airs on Station WXRK(FM) and forty-four other stations nationwide, is a *bona fide* news interview program and therefore exempt from the equal opportunities requirements of Section 315(a) of the Communications Act of 1934, as amended (the "Act"), 47 U.S.C. § 315(a). . . .

2. Section 315(a) of the Act provides that, if a licensee allows a legally qualified candidate for public office to use a broadcast station, it must afford equal opportunities to other such candidates for that office. Section 315(a) also states, however, that appearances by legally qualified candidates on certain categories of *bona fide* news programming, including *bona fide* news interviews, are exempt from equal opportunities. When adopting these exemptions in 1959, Congress indicated that, to qualify as a *bona fide* news interview program, the program must be regularly scheduled; the content, format, and participants must be determined by the licensee; and the determination must have been made by the station "in the exercise of its bona fide news judgment and not for the political advantage of the candidate for political office." Although Congress did not specifically define the term "news" when adopting these exemptions, the Commission has stated that "it is clear that in enacting the exemptions Congress envisioned increased news coverage of the political process. It would seem elemental that Congress contemplated interviews with elected officials and candidates for elected office as newsworthy subject matter." . . .

3. Initially, the Commission found only programs with traditional question and answer formats such as "Meet the Press" and "Face the Nation," which were noted by Congress as examples of the kind of news interview programs in existence at the time the news exemptions were adopted, qualified as news interview programs. In 1984, in determining

that *bona fide* news interview segments on the "Donahue" show were exempt from Section 315(a), the Commission recognized less conventional interview formats as being consistent with Congress' intent in adopting the exemptions to increase news coverage of the political campaign process. The Commission stated that "it would be unsound to rule that a program involving a unique or innovative approach to interviewing its guests somehow lacks sufficient licensee control evident in traditional news interview programs like 'Meet the Press' or 'Face the Nation"' and that "[t]o do so would discourage programming innovation by sending a signal to broadcasters that to be exempt an interview program should adhere only to the format of certain programs mentioned by Congress over 25 years ago." The Commission also stated that "the fact that other 'Donahue' segments may not include discussions pertaining directly to the political arena, or even to current news events, would appear immaterial." . . . Since the *Donahue* decision, other news interview programs or segments thereof with unique and innovative format elements, such as the "Sally Jessy Raphael Show", "Jerry Springer," and "Politically Incorrect," . . . have qualified for the news interview exemption under Section 315(a).

Howard Stern, bona fide journalist. © Bill Norton. Used under license: http://creativecommons.org/licenses/by/2.0/legalcode.

4. Infinity states that the news interview segments of "The Howard Stern Show" satisfy the Commission's requirements for exempt *bona fide* news interview programming because the program is regularly scheduled; Infinity, which broadcasts the program, has control over all aspects of the show; Infinity's decisions on format, content, and participants are based on newsworthiness; and guests that happen to be political candidates are not selected to advance their candidacies.

5. Based on the record before us, we conclude that the news interview segments of "The Howard Stern Show" qualify for the *bona fide* news interview exemption under Section 315(a)(2), and that news interviews conducted on that program are exempt from the equal opportunities requirements of Section 315(a) of the Act. Although we take this action in

response to Infinity's request, we emphasize that licensees airing programs that meet the statutory news exemption, as clarified in our case law, need not seek formal declaration from the Commission that that such programs qualify as news exempt programming under Section 315(a).

6. Accordingly, Infinity's request for declaratory ruling IS GRANTED to the extent indicated herein.

FEDERAL COMMUNICATIONS COMMISSION

W. Kenneth Ferree
Chief
Media Bureau

BRANCH V. FCC
824 F.2d 37 (D.C. Cir. 1987)

BORK, Circuit Judge.
A television news reporter who wishes to run for public office challenges the Federal Communications Commission's decision that the station which employs him would be required to provide "equal time" to his political opponents. This decision would require the station to offer his opponents opportunities to appear on the station that are equivalent to the newscaster's regular daily appearances. The Commission's determination rested on a federal statute. The reporter challenges both the interpretation of the statute and its constitutionality. We deny the petition for review.

I.
The petitioner, William Branch, is a television reporter who covers general assignments for station KOVR in Sacramento, California. He appears on the air in newscasts, on average, about three minutes per day, reporting stories assigned to him by the station. Branch lives in nearby Loomis, California, a small community of about 4,000 people. Beginning late in 1982, he participated in a successful effort to incorporate Loomis as a town. In 1984 Branch decided to seek election to the new Loomis town council.

Branch was aware that a federal statute—47 U.S.C. § 315(a) (1982)—imposes certain "equal time" burdens on broadcasters. He therefore consulted with station management for advice before commencing his campaign. The KOVR news editors calculated that the station would be required to provide thirty-three hours—or about one and a half broadcast days—of response time to Branch's opponents if he continued to work there during his campaign. They told Branch that KOVR was unwilling to provide that amount of time to his opponents, and that if he wished to maintain his candidacy he must take an unpaid leave of absence during the campaign, with no guarantee that he would be able to resume his duties after the election.

Branch immediately sought judicial and administrative determination of his rights, but was unable to get a ruling before the 1984 election. Put to a choice, he continued his work at KOVR and dropped out of the town council race. Upon terminating his candidacy, however, he filed a petition for a declaratory ruling from the Commission on the effect of the "equal opportunities" requirement in 47 U.S.C. § 315(a) on newscaster candidates. Branch sought a ruling that would enable him to run for the Loomis town council in a future election without requiring his employer to offer equal time to his opponents. He specifically asked the Commission to rule on two issues: whether the statute required broadcast stations to provide equal time to the opponents of newscaster candidates; and whether the statute was constitutional as so applied.

The Commission denied the petition. After reviewing the language and purposes of the statute, as well as its legislative history, the Commission concluded that newscaster candidates do not come within any special exemption from a station's statutory obligation to provide equal time to other candidates. *In re William H. Branch,* 101 F.C.C.2d 901, 902-04, 906 (1985). The Commission initially refused to review its previous determinations that section 315 is constitutional, mindful "that such constitutional decisions have 'generally been thought beyond the jurisdiction of administrative agencies.'" *Id.* at 904 n. 4 (quoting *Oestereich v. Selective Serv. Bd.,* 393 U.S. 233, 242 (1968) (Harlan, J., concurring)). The Commission went on, however, to state that it would defer to Congress' determination "in enacting section 315 that there is a governmental interest in assuring that licensees afford equitable treatment to all candidates running for a particular office, and that this interest justifies imposing certain limitations on broadcast speech. . . . [that treat] all candidates for public office . . . in the same manner." *Id.* at 904-05. The Commission also ruled that the statute is not unconstitutionally overbroad. *Id.* at 905. Branch's petition for reconsideration was denied by the Commission, and he now seeks review in this court.

. . .

III.

Branch initially contends that the statute's "equal time" provisions do not apply to him because the statute exempts the television appearances of a newscaster candidate from their coverage. In matters of statutory construction, we "employ[ ] traditional tools of statutory construction," and "[i]f the intent of Congress is clear, that is the end of the matter." *Chevron U.S.A. Inc. v. Natural Resources Defense Council, Inc.*, 467 U.S. 837, 843-44 & n. 9, 104 S.Ct. 2778, 2781 & n. 9, 81 L.Ed.2d 694 (1984). The statutory language at issue reads in full:

> If any licensee shall permit any person who is a legally qualified candidate for any public office to use a broadcasting station, he shall afford equal opportunities to all other candidates for the office in the use of such broadcasting station: *Provided,* That such licensee shall have no power of censorship over the material broadcast under the provision of this section. No obligation is hereby imposed under this subsection upon any licensee to allow the use of its station by any such candidate. Appearance by a legally qualified candidate on any—
>
> (1) bona fide newscast,
>
> (2) bona fide news interview,
>
> (3) bona fide news documentary (if the appearance of the candidate is incidental to the presentation of the subject or subjects covered by the news documentary), or
>
> (4) on-the-spot coverage of bona fide news events (including but not limited to political conventions and activities incidental thereto),
>
> shall not be deemed to be use of a broadcasting station within the meaning of this subsection. Nothing in the foregoing sentence shall be construed as relieving broadcasters, in connection with the presentation of newscasts, news interviews, news documentaries, and on-the-spot coverage of news events, from the obligation imposed upon them under this chapter to operate in the public interest and to afford reasonable opportunity for the discussion of

conflicting views on issues of public importance.

47 U.S.C. § 315(a) (1982). Branch reads the statutory language to mean: the "equal opportunities" requirement applies only when there is a "use" of a broadcasting station; a candidate's appearance on a bona fide newscast does not constitute such a "use"; thus Branch's appearances on KOVR's bona fide news broadcasts are not subject to the "equal opportunities" requirement. The apparent simplicity of this argument, however, is misleading.

The statutory language just quoted comprises four sentences. The first two, which contain Congress' statement of the equal opportunities rule, have been in effect since 1927, about as long as the broadcasting industry has existed in this country. *See* Radio Act of 1927, § 18, 44 Stat. 1162, 1170. For thirty-two years, these sentences stood alone as Congress' entire treatment of the issue. During that period, the Commission interpreted the statute to require "equal opportunities" whenever any candidate appeared on the air, unless the candidate was the subject of "a routine news broadcast."... The news broadcast exception that the Commission formulated was understood as preserving for the station "the exercise of its judgment as to newsworthy events." 23 Fed.Reg. at 7818.

Branch does not deny that his on-the-air work as a news reporter would be classified as a "use" if we looked solely at the first two sentences of section 315. His statutory argument rests instead on the third sentence.

. . .

Thus Congress' intent in enacting the amended section 315 is readily discernible. "Appearance by a legally qualified candidate," which is not "deemed to be use of a broadcasting station," is coverage of the candidate that is presented to the public as news. The "appearance" of the candidate is itself expected to be the newsworthy item that activates the exemption. "By modifying all four categories [not deemed to be 'use' with the phrase 'bona fide,' Congress plainly emphasized its reliance on newsworthiness as the basis for an exemption." *Office of Communication of the United Church of Christ v. FCC,* 590 F.2d 1062, 1065 (D.C. Cir. 1978).

The thrust of the language is brought out further in the third and fourth specific exemptions. The "news documentary" exemption applies only "if the appearance of the candidate is incidental to *the presentation of the subject or subjects covered by the news documentary.*" 47 U.S.C. § 315(a)(3) (1982) (emphasis added). This passage relates the candidate's appearance to the subjects covered in the program. If the candidate's appearance has nothing to do with the subjects that are being covered as news—whether because the candidate is a regular employee on all such programs or, to take another example, because the candidate is being offered a gratuitous appearance that realistically is unrelated to the news content of the program—then the exemption does not apply. Similarly, the fourth exemption for "on-the-spot coverage" of news applies only to "coverage of bona fide news events." *Id.* § 315(a)(4). Here again the focus is on a news *event* that is being covered, with the candidate's appearance expected to occur as part of the event *being covered.*

When a broadcaster's employees are sent out to cover a news story involving other persons, therefore, the "bona fide news event" is the activity engaged in by those other persons, not the work done by the employees covering the event. The work done by the broadcaster's employees is not a part of the event, for the event would occur without them and they serve only to communicate it to the public. For example, when a broadcaster's employees are sent out to cover a fire, the fire is the "bona fide news" event and the reporter does not become a part of that event merely by reporting it. There is nothing at all "newsworthy" about the work being done by the broadcaster's own employees, regardless of whether any of those employees happens also to be a candidate for public office. . . .

Moreover, Congress' objection to *Lar Daly* was that it discouraged wide broadcast coverage of political news events by restricting a station's ability to determine which news *events* to present to the public. Congress solved this problem by exempting any on-air appearance by a candidate who is the *subject* of news coverage. It is irrelevant to that problem whether a station has broad discretion to determine which of its employees will actually present the news on the air. That issue may raise very different problems, which we will consider later, but it did not arise at all in Congress' debates on the 1959 amendments. On the contrary, considerable concern was voted about the possibility that "sham" news events—events that are not bona fide news but are staged by the candidate—might be seen as exempt from the "equal opportunities" rule. *See, e.g.,* H.R.Rep. No. 802, *supra,* at 6; 105 Cong.Rec. 14,462 (1959) (Sen. Long) (the amendments apply to a candidate "when he was making news"); *id.* at 16,236 (Rep. MacDonald) ("staged events . . . should not be viewed as news"). This possibility was eventually foreclosed, however, by the wording of the fourth exemption. In denying any exemption for candidate appearances through "sham" news events, Congress once again expressed its view that exemption should be made only for on-air appearances that are intrinsically newsworthy. At all times, the focus was not on preserving anyone's "right" to appear on the air, but on preserving broadcasters' ability to present to the public certain kinds of news programs and news events.

In opposition to that consistent approach, Branch asks this court to read the phrase "[a]ppearance by a legally qualified candidate on any [news program]" as exempting from the "equal opportunities" rule all on-air work done by newscaster candidates. We cannot do so. As we have already noted, such a reading would be at odds with the law before *Lar Daly,* which Congress explicitly sought to restore through the 1959 amendments. In addition, this reading would raise a station's news employees to an elevated status not shared by any of its other employees: although the work done on the air by any other employee on any other program would not be exempt, *see, e.g., Paulsen v. FCC,* 491 F.2d 887 (9th Cir. 1974), the work done on the air by news employees would be. Yet this novel division was never endorsed, or even discussed, by Congress.

. . .

IV.

We have determined that section 315 does not exempt newscaster candidates from the strictures of the "equal opportunities" rule. Branch challenges the statute, as so interpreted, on several constitutional grounds. Common to all of the challenges is Branch's assertion that the Commission acted arbitrarily and capriciously by initially refusing "to undertake a review here of previous determinations as to the constitutionality of section 315." *Branch,* 101 F.C.C.2d at 904 n. 4. The Commission did not err in taking this position, for although an administrative agency may be influenced by constitutional considerations in the way it interprets or applies statutes, it does not have jurisdiction to declare statutes unconstitutional. *See e.g., Weinberger v. Salfi,* 422 U.S. 749, 765 (1975); *Johnson v. Robison,* 415 U.S. 361, 368 (1974); *Public Utils. Comm'n v. United States,* 355 U.S. 534, 539 (1958). In addition, the Commission did consider Branch's constitutional arguments insofar as they had a bearing on its own interpretation and application of section 315. *See Branch,* 101 F.C.C.2d at 904-05. We think this approach was entirely proper, and we turn now to Branch's substantive challenges to the constitutionality of section 315.

A.

Branch's first objection is that the statute extinguishes his right to seek political office. That he has such a right is undeniable, though the Constitution and the Supreme Court's cases in the area do not pinpoint the precise grounds on which it rests. . . . But whatever its source, the right is not implicated in this case. "In approaching candidate restrictions, it is essential to examine in a realistic light the extent and nature of their impact on voters." *Bullock,* 405 U.S. at 143. Here that impact is slight. The "equal opportunities" rule does not extinguish anyone's right to run for office. It simply provides that certain uses of a broadcast station by a candidate entitle other candidates for the same office to equal time. That the rule will affect some candidates favorably and others unfavorably is obvious. It may cause certain candidates to receive less time on the air than if the statute did not exist. But the Supreme Court has held that no individual has any right of access to the broadcast media. *Columbia Broadcasting System, Inc. v. Democratic Nat'l Comm.,* 412 U.S. 94 (1973). "It is the right of the viewers and listeners, not the right of the broadcasters, which is paramount." *Red Lion Broadcasting Co. v. FCC,* 395 U.S. 367, 390.

The core of Branch's challenge on this point is that the statute imposes an undue burden on his ability to run for office because he cannot, during the time he is a candidate, do his normal work of reporting news on the air for station KOVR. But nobody has ever thought that a candidate has a right to run for office and at the same time to avoid all personal sacrifice. *See United States Civil Serv. Comm'n v. National Ass'n of Letter Carriers,* 413 U.S. 548, 567 (1973) ("Neither the right to associate nor the right to participate in political activities is absolute in any event."). Even if the practicalities of campaigning for office are put to one side, many people find it necessary to choose between their jobs and their candidacies. The Hatch Act requires government employees to resign from work if they wish to run for certain political offices, *see* 5 U.S.C. §§ 7324-7327 (1982), and involves many more intrusive restrictions as well, yet the Supreme Court has upheld it against constitutional challenge. *See Letter Carriers,* 413 U.S. 548; *United Public Workers v. Mitchell,* 330 U.S. 75 (1947). More recently, the Court upheld a Texas law that required certain public officials to resign from office if they wished to become candidates for certain other offices. *Clements v. Fashing,* 457 U.S. 957 (1982).

Indeed, the burdens Branch complains of are borne by all other radio and television personalities under section 315, though the exception he seeks would apply only to newscasters. In *Paulsen v. FCC,* 491 F.2d 887 (9th Cir. 1974), those burdens were upheld against essentially the same objection made here. The petitioner, a television performer who had announced his candidacy for President, contended that section 315 "forces him to give up his means of livelihood as a television performer in order to run for office." *Id.* at 891-92. In *Paulsen* the challenge was clothed in an equal protection guise, and perhaps at bottom Branch's challenge is also one of equal protection. However that may be, the argument is the same, and so is the result. Under established law, *Paulsen* was correct in finding the burdens imposed by section 315 justifiable as "both reasonable and necessary to achieve the important and legitimate objectives of encouraging political discussion and preventing unfair and unequal use of the broadcast media." *Id.* at 892.

B.

Branch's second constitutional objection to section 315 is that the "equal opportunities" rule violates the First Amendment. He cites *Miami Herald Publishing Co. v. Tornillo,* 418 U.S. 241 (1974), where the Supreme Court unanimously struck down a Florida law that gave political candidates a right to reply to criticisms and attacks published in newspapers. The Court held that the law compelled editors or publishers to publish material against their will, thus exacting an unconstitutional "penalty on the basis of the content of a newspaper." *Id.* at 256. The Court broadly declared that a "[g]overnment-enforced right of access inescapably 'dampens the vigor and limits the variety of public debate.'" *Id.* at 257 (quoting *New York Times Co. v. Sullivan,* 376 U.S. 254, 279 (1964)). The "equal opportunities" rule, in Branch's view, is identical to a right-of-reply statute in its impact.

The Supreme Court has expressly held, however, that the First Amendment's protections for the press do not apply as powerfully to the broadcast media. In *Red Lion Broadcasting Co. v. FCC,* 395 U.S. 367 (1969), the Court upheld the government's authority "to put restraints on licensees in favor of others whose views should be expressed on this unique medium." *Id.* at 390. What makes the broadcast medium unique, in the Court's view, is the scarcity of broadcast frequencies. *Id.* at 389-90.

While doubts have been expressed that the scarcity rationale is adequate to support differing degrees of First Amendment protection for the print and electronic media, *see, e.g., Telecommunications Research & Action Center v. FCC,* 801 F.2d 501, 506-09 (D.C. Cir.), *reh'g denied,* 806 F.2d 1115 (1986); *Meredith Corp. v. FCC,* 809 F.2d 863, 866-67 (D.C. Cir. 1987), it remains true, nonetheless, that Branch's First Amendment challenge is squarely foreclosed by *Red Lion.* In *Red Lion,* the Supreme Court upheld as constitutional the Commission's authority to enforce the fairness doctrine, which requires broadcast stations to give fair coverage to each side of a public issue, and in particular upheld "its specific manifestations in the personal attack and political editorial rules." 395 U.S. at 386. In the course of its opinion, the Court held that the statutory "equal opportunities" rule in section 315 and the Commission's own fairness doctrine rested on the same constitutional basis of the government's power to regulate "a scarce resource which the Government has denied others the right to use" . . . *Red Lion* thus compels us to reject Branch's First Amendment claim.

Nor can we adopt Branch's suggestion that this court would be justified in stepping away from *Red Lion.* The Supreme Court recently reaffirmed *Red Lion* and disavowed any intention "to reconsider our longstanding approach without some signal from Congress or the FCC that technological developments have advanced so far that some revision of the system of broadcast regulation may be required." *FCC v. League of Women Voters of Cal.,* 468 U.S. 364, 376 n. 11 (1984). The Commission may now have sent just such a signal by issuing a report which concludes that section 315 is unconstitutional and should be abandoned. *See General Fairness Doctrine Obligations of Broadcast Licensees,* 102 F.C.C.2d 143 (1985). But unless the Court itself were to overrule *Red Lion,* we remain bound by it.

C.

Branch's final constitutional challenge to section 315 is that it impermissibly limits the discretion of broadcast stations to select the particular people who will present news on the air to the public. Branch thus attempts to press the third-party rights of broadcasters who are not themselves parties to this case. Although the general rule is that a party "must assert his own legal rights and interests, and cannot rest his claim to relief on the legal rights or interests of third parties," *Warth v. Seldin,* 422 U.S. 490, 499 (1975), the Supreme Court has also stated that "[w]ithin the context of the First Amendment, the Court has enunciated . . . concerns that justify a lessening of prudential limitations on standing." . . .

Here, as in *Munson,* the "activity sought to be protected is at the heart of the business relationship between" Branch and KOVR, and Branch's "interests in challenging the statute are completely consistent with the First Amendment interests of the [broadcasters he] represents." 467 U.S. at 958. It makes no difference that a broadcaster could bring this challenge in a separate suit. *Id.* at 957-58.

Nonetheless, the third-party challenge Branch advances is rebutted by *Red Lion.* A burden on the ability to present a particular broadcaster on the air, which applies to all broadcasters irrespective of the content of the news they present, is a much less significant burden than rules requiring the transmission of replies to personal attacks and political editorials, which were upheld in *Red Lion.* The latter provisions apply directly to political speech, and weigh more heavily on some messages than on others, depending on the precise content of the message conveyed. In contrast, the burdens on broadcasters that Branch asserts here do not "impair the discretion of broadcasters to present their views on any issue or to carry any particular type of programming." *Columbia Broadcasting System, Inc. v. FCC*, 453 U.S. 367, 396-97 (1981). Moreover, we note again that there is no right of any particular individual to appear on television. . . .

The petition for review is, therefore, *Denied.*

IN RE REQUEST BY WALT DISNEY PRODUCTIONS, INC.

For Declaratory Ruling With Respect to Political Broadcast Equal Opportunities [Pat Paulsen] (JANUARY 25, 1972)

DEAR MR. BADER: This is in reference to your request for declaratory ruling filed January 18, 1972 "with respect to the 'equal opportunities" implications of the scheduled appearance of Pat Paulsen on episode 4 of the new Disney television series, "The Mouse Factory."

You state that you seek to terminate a controversy and remove uncertainty as to the obligations to other candidates under Section 315 of the Communications Act of 1934, as amended, of broadcast stations not operating in or serving New Hampshire which carry the Paulsen episode; that Mr. Paulsen is a candidate for the Republican presidential nomination in New Hampshire to be held March 7, 1972; that Mr. Paulsen's appearance on "Mouse Factory" will be telecast throughout the United States; and that one station licensee "refused to schedule the Paulsen program episode on its five stations because of its concern that such broadcasts would create a nation-wide, rather than a New Hampshire, equal time obligation in favor of all other Republican candidates for the Presidency."

You further state that Mr. Paulsen became a candidate "at the last minute for acquiring status on the New Hampshire primary ballot," and that the circumstances surrounding his decision to enter the New Hampshire primary are described in the Hollywood Reporter of Wednesday, January 12, 1972. That paper quotes Mr. Paulsen:

"As far as going beyond New Hampshire," Paulsen said, "I haven't thought much about it. We'll see how it goes. There's a possibility I might enter another primary in Oregon, but it depends on how things go in New Hampshire."

You contend that Mr. Paulsen's appearance does not give rise to "equal opportunities" obligations to any candidate except candidates for the New Hampshire Republican presidential nomination, and that any such obligation is limited to television stations located in or serving New Hampshire. You state that, as indicated by the above quotation in the newspaper, Mr. Paulsen has stated his intention to campaign only in New Hampshire and that he hasn't 'thought much' about going beyond that state. You state that you do not think it was the intention of Congress to cause stations which do not serve the area of the primary election to provide "equal opportunities" to all primary candidates; that if this were the case a candidate eligible for a write-in in Alaska could demand time because Mr. Paulsen is campaigning in New Hampshire. You question whether Mr. Paulsen's opposing candidates in the Republican New Hampshire primary have "equal opportunities" rights on stations in other states. You submit that 'the answer to this question is no' since "the local or regional character of a state nominating primary is not changed by reason of the national prominence of some of the participants" and the "essential fact is that the electorate to be informed is only the state's population."

Comedian Pat Paulsen on the campaign trail

You refer to proposed legislation before Congress (passed and sent to the President on January 19, 1972) to promote fair practices in federal elections and state that in this legislation Congress provided for state-by-state limitations on media expenditures by candidates for Presidential nomination, and that, therefore, it is the intention of Congress that primaries be treated as state-wide, not nation-wide, factors in the electoral process. You distinguish the Commission's ruling in Letter to CBS, 40 FCC 244 (1952), by asserting that in that case William R. Schneider was an announced Presidential candidate and had stated his intention of seeking the Republican nomination at the Republican convention, had entered the primaries in Oregon and New Hampshire, and otherwise actively solicited support for his candidacy. You contend that although Schneider was engaged in nation-wide campaigning and had made it clear that he would go all the way for the Presidency, Mr. Paulsen states only that "as far as going beyond New Hampshire he hasn't thought much about it," and that his future course "depends on how things go in New Hampshire."

Section 73.657 (a) of the Commission's rules states:

Legally qualified candidate. A "legally qualified candidate" means any person who has publicly announced that he is a candidate for nomination by a convention of a political party or for nomination or election in a primary, special, or general election, municipal, county, state or national, and who meets the qualifications prescribed by the applicable laws to hold the office for which he is a candidate, so that he may be voted for by the electorate directly or by means of delegates or electors, and who:

(1) Has qualified for a place on the ballot, or

(2) Is eligible under the applicable law to be voted for by sticker, by writing in his name on the ballot, or other method, and (i) has been duly nominated by a political party which is commonly known and regarded as such, or (ii) makes a substantial showing that he is a bona fide candidate for nomination or office.

Section IV, Question and Answer 5, of the Primer on Section 315 of the Communications Act, Use of Broadcast Facilities by Candidates for Public Office, 35 F.R. 13048, 13057 (1970) states:

Q. When is a person a legally qualified candidate for nomination as the candidate of a party for President or Vice President of the United States?

A. In view of the fact that a person may be nominated for these offices by the conventions of his party without having appeared on the ballot of any State having presidential primary elections, or having any pledged votes prior to the convention, or even announcing his willingness to be a candidate, no fixed rule can be promulgated in answer to this question. Whether a person so claiming is in fact a bona fide candidate will depend on the particular facts of each situation, including consideration of what efforts, if any, he has taken to secure delegates or preferential votes in State primaries. It cannot, however, turn on the licensee's evaluation of the claimant's chances for success. (Letter to Columbia Broadcasting

System, Inc., 40 FCC 244 (1952); and see also par.(f) of §§ 73.120, 73.290, 73.657, and par. (e) of § 74.1113 of the Commission rules.)

The question before us is whether Mr. Paulsen meets the criteria for being a legally qualified candidate for nomination for the office of President of the United States and, if so, whether he may be treated as a candidate only in the State in which he has entered a primary. We think that in the absence of further indication to the contrary Mr. Paulsen should be considered a bona fide candidate, and that under established principles he should be considered a candidate on a national basis. While we do not wish to make a definitive ruling on the first question upon the basis of the record before us and without the benefit of the views of an affected licensee, we note that Mr. Paulsen has qualified to be on the ballot for the Republican Presidential nomination in the New Hampshire primary and is apparently actively campaigning. The Hollywood Reporter article which you cite also attributes the following statements to Mr. Paulsen:

I'm serious about it and I think I have a chance to make it now.

and, . . .
I think I have the right to run. But now that I'm on the ballot I have to get people to vote for me.

Under the foregoing circumstances, and particularly in the absence of a clear-cut statement from Mr. Paulsen to the contrary, it appears that Mr. Paulsen is a legally qualified candidate for the Republican nomination for President, who has taken steps to secure delegates to the Republican National Convention.

On the second issue, your contention that Mr. Paulsen is legally qualified only in New Hampshire would require us to reach an unworkable conclusion. As Question and Answer 5, quoted above states, a person may be a legally qualified candidate for President "without having appeared on the ballot of any State having primary elections." Thus your contention is contrary to Commission precedent which does not make appearance in a primary ballot the touchstone. In this connection, we note that many States do not have presidential primaries; to adopt your concept would seem to lead to the result that unless a State has a primary election, there is no such thing as a candidate for a party nomination in that State, or at least that an announced candidate for President would be treated as such only in the States where he chose to appear in a primary. The practicalities are of course not so limited, and such a result is not mandated by the Communications Act or the Federal Election Campaign

Act of 1971. The purpose of that bill is "to promote fair practices in the conduct of election campaigns for Federal political offices." Federal Election Campaign Act of 1971, Conference Report, 92d Congress, 1st Session, Dec. 14, 1971, p. 21. That Congress limited campaign expenditures on a State-by-State basis does not indicate that Congress intended to affect the working of Section 315 (a) of the Communications Act. Moreover, Section 73.657 of the Rules, quoted above, specifically refers to elections in "municipal, county, state, or national" geographical areas and the office of President clearly is a national office.

Staff action is taken here under delegated authority. Application for review by the full Commission may be requested within thirty (30) days by writing the Secretary, Federal Communications Commission, Washington, D.C. 20554, stating the factors warranting consideration. Copies must be sent to the parties to the complaint. See Code of Federal Regulations, Volume 47, Section 1.115.

Sincerely yours,
WILLIAM B. RAY, Chief, Complaints and Compliance Division, (For Chief, Broadcast Bureau).

Section 312(a)(7). Reasonable Access

In 1972, Congress amended the Communications Act by adding Section 312(a)(7), a provision that requires licensees to provide access to candidates for federal office. This is a much smaller group of candidates than under Section 315(a), which applies to any legally qualified candidate. As the statute gives the broadcaster the option to charge a fee for this access, 312(a)(7) is primarily used by candidates seeking to get paid commercial access to a station. In the *CBS* case infra, the U.S. Supreme Court sets forth specific guidelines that broadcasters can use to determine if a candidate's access request is reasonable. Broadcasters are not required to accede to a candidate's request, but they must offer a reasonable justification for a denial. If they respond to a request in good faith, the FCC will give them deference, meaning that a well-advised broadcaster will usually prevail if challenged by a candidate. If a broadcaster has reason to deny a request, it can almost always fulfill its 312(a)(7) obligation by offering a good faith counterproposal to the candidate.

47 C.F.R. § 73.1944: Reasonable Access

(a) Section 312(a)(7) of the Communications Act provides that the Commission may revoke any station license or construction permit for willful or repeated failure to allow reasonable access to, or to permit purchase of, reasonable amounts of time for the use of a broadcasting station by a legally qualified candidate for Federal elective office on behalf of his candidacy.

(b) Weekend access. For purposes of providing reasonable access, a licensee shall make its facilities available for use by federal candidates on the weekend before the election if the licensee has provided similar access to commercial advertisers during the year preceding the relevant election period. Licensees shall not discriminate between candidates with regard to weekend access.

CBS, Inc. v. FCC

453 U.S. 367 (1981)

Chief Justice BURGER delivered the opinion of the Court.

We granted certiorari to consider whether the Federal Communications Commission properly construed 47 U.S.C. § 312(a)(7) and determined that petitioners failed to provide "reasonable access to . . . the use of a broadcasting station" as required by the statute. 449 U.S. 950 (1980).

I.

A.

On October 11, 1979, Gerald M. Rafshoon, President of the Carter-Mondale Presidential Committee, requested each of the three major television networks to provide time for a 30-minute program between 8 p. m. and 10:30 p. m. on either the 4th, 5th, 6th, or 7th of December 1979. The Committee intended to present, in conjunction with president carter's formal announcement of his candidacy, a documentary outlining the record of his administration.

The networks declined to make the requested time available. Petitioner CBS emphasized the large number of candidates for the Republican and Democratic Presidential nominations and the potential disruption of regular programming to accommodate requests for equal treatment, but it offered to sell two 5-minute segments to the Committee, one at 10:55 p.m. on December 8 and one in the daytime. Petitioner American Broadcasting Cos. replied that it had not yet decided when it would begin selling political time for the 1980 Presidential campaign, but subsequently indicated that it would allow such sales in January 1980. App. 58. Petitioner National Broadcasting Co., noting the number of potential requests for time from Presidential candidates, stated that it was not prepared to sell time for political programs as early as December 1979.

On October 29, 1979, the Carter-Mondale Presidential Committee filed a complaint with the Federal Communications Commission, charging that the networks had violated their obligation to provide "reasonable access" under § 312(a)(7) of the Communications Act of 1934, as amended. Title 47 U.S.C. § 312(a)(7), as added to the Act, 86 Stat. 4, states:

> "The Commission may revoke any station license or construction permit—
>
> . . .
>
> "(7) for willful or repeated failure to allow reasonable access to or to permit purchase of reasonable amounts of time for the use of a broadcasting station by a legally qualified candidate for Federal elective office on behalf of his candidacy."

At an open meeting on November 20, 1979, the Commission, by a 4-to-3 vote, ruled that the networks had violated § 312(a)(7). In its memorandum opinion and order, the Commission concluded that the networks' reasons for refusing to sell the time requested were "deficient" under its standards of reasonableness, and directed the networks to indicate by November 26, 1979, how they intended to fulfill their statutory obligations. 74 F.C.C.2d 631.

. . .

III.

A.

Although Congress provided in § 312(a)(7) for greater use of broadcasting stations by federal candidates, it did not give guidance on how the Commission should implement the statute's access requirement. Essentially, Congress adopted a "rule of reason" and charged the Commission with its enforcement. Pursuant to 47 U.S.C. § 303(r), which empowers the Commission to "[m]ake such rules and regulations and prescribe such restrictions and conditions, not inconsistent with law, as may be necessary to carry out the provisions of [the Communications Act]," the agency has developed standards to effectuate the guarantees of § 312(a)(7). See also 47 U.S.C. § 154(i). The Commission has issued some general interpretative statements, but its standards implementing § 312(a)(7) have evolved principally on a case-by-case basis and are not embodied in formalized rules. The relevant criteria broadcasters must employ in evaluating access requests under the statute can be summarized from the Commission's 1978 Report and Order and the memorandum opinions and orders in these cases.

Broadcasters are free to deny the sale of air time prior to the commencement of a campaign, but once a campaign has begun, they must give reasonable and good-faith attention to access requests from "legally qualified" candidates for federal elective office. Such requests must be considered on an individualized basis, and broadcasters are required to tailor their responses to accommodate, as much as reasonably possible, a candidate's stated purposes in seeking air time. In responding to access requests, however, broadcasters may also give weight to such factors as the amount of time previously sold to the candidate, the disruptive impact on regular programming, and the likelihood of requests for time by rival candidates under the equal opportunities provision of § 315(a). These considerations may not be invoked as pretexts for denying access; to justify a negative response, broadcasters must cite a realistic danger of substantial program disruption—perhaps caused by insufficient notice to allow adjustments in the schedule—or of an excessive number of equal time requests. Further, in order to facilitate review by the Commission, broadcasters must explain their reasons for refusing time or making a more limited counteroffer. If broadcasters take the appropriate factors into account and act reasonably and in good faith, their decisions will be entitled to deference even if the Commission's analysis would have differed in the first instance. But if broadcasters adopt "across-the-board policies" and do not attempt to respond to the individualized situation of a particular candidate, the Commission is not compelled to sustain their denial of access. See 74 F.C.C.2d at 665-674; 74 F.C.C.2d, at 642-651; 1978 Report and Order, 68 F.C.C.2d, at 1089-1092, 1094. Petitioners argue that certain of these standards are contrary to the statutory objectives of § 312(a)(7).

(1)

The Commission has concluded that, as a threshold matter, it will independently determine whether a campaign has begun and the obligations imposed by § 312(a)(7) have attached. 74 F.C.C.2d, at 665-666. Petitioners assert that, in undertaking such a task, the Commission becomes improperly involved in the electoral process and seriously impairs broadcaster discretion.

However, petitioners fail to recognize that the Commission does not set the starting date for a campaign. Rather, on review of a complaint alleging denial of "reasonable access," it examines objective evidence to find whether the campaign has already commenced, "taking into account the position of the candidate *and the networks* as well as other factors." *Id.*, at 665 (emphasis added). As the Court of Appeals noted, the "determination of when the statutory obligations attach does not control the electoral process, . . . the determination is controlled by the process." 629 F.2d, at 16. Such a decision is not, and cannot be, purely one of editorial judgment.

Moreover, the Commission's approach serves to narrow § 312(a)(7), which might be read as vesting access rights in an individual candidate as soon as he becomes "legally qualified" without regard to the status of the campaign. See n. 11, *supra*. By confining the applicability of the statute to the period after a campaign commences, the Commission has limited its impact on broadcasters and given substance to its command of *reasonable* access.

(2)
Petitioners also challenge the Commission's requirement that broadcasters evaluate and respond to access requests on an individualized basis. In petitioners' view, the agency has attached inordinate significance to candidates' needs, thereby precluding fair assessment of broadcasters' concerns and prohibiting the adoption of uniform policies regarding requests for access.

While admonishing broadcasters not to "'second guess' the 'political' wisdom or . . . effectiveness" of the particular format sought by a candidate, the Commission has clearly acknowledged that "the candidate's . . . request is by no means conclusive of the question of how much time, if any, is appropriate. Other . . . factors, such as the disruption or displacement of regular programming (particularly as affected by a reasonable probability of requests by other candidates), must be considered in the balance." 74 F.C.C.2d, at 667-668. Thus, the Commission mandates careful consideration of, not blind assent to, candidates' desires for air time.

Petitioners are correct that the Commission's standards proscribe blanket rules concerning access; each request must be examined on its own merits. While the adoption of uniform policies might well prove more convenient for broadcasters, such an approach would allow personal campaign strategies and the exigencies of the political process to be ignored. A broadcaster's "evenhanded" response of granting only time spots of a fixed duration to candidates may be "unreasonable" where a particular candidate desires less time for an advertisement or a longer format to discuss substantive issues. In essence, petitioners seek the unilateral right to determine in advance how much time to afford *all* candidates. Yet § 312(a)(7) assures a right of reasonable access to *individual* candidates for federal elective office, and the Commission's requirement that their requests be considered on an *individualized* basis is consistent with that guarantee.

(3)
The Federal Communications Commission is the experienced administrative agency long entrusted by Congress with the regulation of broadcasting, and the Commission is responsible for implementing and enforcing § 312(a)(7) of the Communications Act. Accordingly, its construction of the statute is entitled to judicial deference "unless there are compelling indications that it is wrong." . . . Like the Court of Appeals, we cannot say that the Commission's standards are arbitrary and capricious or at odds with the language and purposes of § 312(a)(7). See 5 U.S.C. § 706(2)(A). Indeed, we are satisfied that the Commission's action represents a reasoned attempt to effectuate the statute's access requirement, giving broadcasters room to exercise their discretion but demanding that they act in good faith.

B.
There can be no doubt that the Commission's standards have achieved greater clarity as a result of the orders in these cases. However laudable that may be, it raises the question whether § 312(a)(7) was properly applied to petitioners. Based upon the Commission's prior decisions and 1978 Report and Order, however, we must conclude that petitioners had adequate notice that their conduct in responding to the Carter-Mondale Presidential Committee's request for access would contravene the statute.

. . . "[A]n arbitrary 'blanket' ban on the use by a candidate of a particular class or length of time in a particular period cannot be considered reasonable. A Federal candidate's decisions as to the best method of pursuing his or her media campaign should be honored as much as possible under the 'reasonable' limits imposed by the licensee." *Id.*, at 1090.

Here, the Carter-Mondale Presidential Committee sought broadcast time approximately 11 months before the 1980 Presidential election and 8 months before the Democratic National Convention. In determining that a national campaign was underway at that point, the Commission stressed: (a) that 10 candidates formally had announced their intention to seek the Republican nomination, and 2 candidates had done so for the Democratic nomination; (b) that various states had started the delegate selection process; (c) that candidates were traveling across the country making speeches and attempting to raise funds; (d) that national campaign organizations were established and operating; (e) that the Iowa caucus would be held the following month; (f) that public officials and private groups were making endorsements; and (g) that the national print media had given campaign activities prominent coverage for almost two months. 74 F.C.C.2d, at 645-647. The Commission's conclusion about the status of the campaign accorded with its announced position on the vesting of § 312(a)(7) rights and was adequately supported by the objective factors on which it relied.

Nevertheless, petitioners ABC and NBC refused to sell the Carter-Mondale Presidential Committee any time in December 1979 on the ground that it was "too early in the political season." App. 41-43, 52-74; nn. 3 and 4, *supra*. These petitioners made no counteroffers, but adopted "blanket" policies refusing access despite the admonition against such an approach in the 1978 Report and Order. Cf. *Donald W. Riegle*, 59 F.C.C.2d 1314 (1976); *WALB- TV, Inc.*, 59 F.C.C.2d 1246 (1976). Likewise, petitioner CBS, while not barring access completely, had an across-the-board policy of selling only 5- minute spots to all candidates, notwithstanding the Commission's directive in the 1978 Report and Order that broadcasters consider "a candidate's desires as to the method of conducting his or her media campaign." 68 F.C.C.2d, at 1089, n. 14. See App. 44-45, 75-93; n. 2, *supra*. Petitioner CBS responded with its standard offer of separate 5-minute segments, even though the Carter-Mondale Presidential Committee sought 30 minutes of air time to present a comprehensive statement launching President Carter's re-election campaign. Moreover, the Committee's request was made almost two months before the intended date of broadcast, was flexible in that it could be satisfied with any prime time slot during a 4-day period, was accompanied by an offer to pay the normal commercial rate, and was not preceded by other requests from President Carter for access. See App. 27-40; n. 1, *supra*. Although petitioners adverted to the disruption of regular programming and the potential equal time requests from rival candidates in their responses to the Carter-Mondale Presidential Committee's complaint, the Commission rejected these claims as "speculative and unsubstantiated at best." 74 F.C.C.2d, at 674.

Under these circumstances, we cannot conclude that the Commission abused its discretion in finding that petitioners failed to grant the "reasonable access" required by § 312(a)(7). See 5 U.S.C. § 706(2)(A). "[T]he fact that we might not have made the same determination on the same facts does not warrant a substitution of judicial for administrative discretion since Congress has confided the problem to the latter." *FCC v. WOKO, Inc.*, 329 U.S. 223, 229 (1946). "[C]ourts should not overrule an administrative decision merely because they disagree with its wisdom." *Radio Corp. of America v. United States*, 341 U.S. 412, 420 (1951).

IV.

Finally, petitioners assert that § 312(a)(7) as implemented by the Commission violates the First Amendment rights of broadcasters by unduly circumscribing their editorial discretion. . . . We disagree.

A licensed broadcaster is "granted the free and exclusive use of a limited and valuable part of the public domain; when he accepts that franchise it is burdened by enforceable public obligations." This Court has noted the limits on a broadcast license:

> "A license permits broadcasting, but the licensee has no constitutional right to be the one who holds the license or to monopolize a . . . frequency to the exclusion of his fellow citizens. There is nothing in the First Amendment which prevents the Government from requiring a licensee to share his frequency with others . . . ." *Red Lion Broadcasting Co. v. FCC*, 395 U.S., at 389.

Although the broadcasting industry is entitled under the First Amendment to exercise "the widest journalistic freedom consistent with its public [duties]," *Columbia Broadcasting System, Inc. v. Democratic National Committee, supra*, 412 U.S., at 110, 93 S.Ct., at 2090, the Court has made clear that:

> "*It is the right of the viewers and listeners, not the right of the broadcasters which is paramount.* It is the purpose of the First Amendment to preserve an uninhibited marketplace of ideas in which truth will ultimately prevail, rather than to countenance monopolization of that market . . . . It is the right of the public to receive suitable access to social, polit-

> ical, esthetic, moral, and other ideas and experience which is crucial here." *Red Lion Broadcasting Co. v. FCC, supra*, 395 U.S., at 390 (citations omitted) (emphasis added).

The First Amendment interests of candidates and voters, as well as broadcasters, are implicated by § 312(a)(7). We have recognized that "it is of particular importance that candidates have the . . . opportunity to make their views known so that the electorate may intelligently evaluate the candidates' personal qualities and their positions on vital public issues before choosing among them on election day." *Buckley v. Valeo*, 424 U.S. 1, 52-53 (1976). Indeed, "speech concerning public affairs is . . . the essence of self-government," *Garrison v. Louisiana*, 379 U.S. 64, 74-75 (1964). The First Amendment "has its fullest and most urgent application precisely to the conduct of campaigns for political office." *Monitor Patriot Co. v. Roy*, 401 U.S. 265, 272 (1971). Section 312(a)(7) thus makes a significant contribution to freedom of expression by enhancing the ability of candidates to present, and the public to receive, information necessary for the effective operation of the democratic process.

. . . Section 312(a)(7) creates a *limited* right to "reasonable" access that pertains only to legally qualified federal candidates and may be invoked by them only for the purpose of advancing their candidacies once a campaign has commenced. The Commission has stated that, in enforcing the statute, it will "provide leeway to broadcasters and not merely attempt *de novo* to determine the reasonableness of their judgments . . . ." 74 F.C.C.2d, at 672. If broadcasters have considered the relevant factors in good faith, the Commission will uphold their decisions. See 629 F.2d, at 25. Further, § 312(a)(7) impair the discretion of broadcasters to present their views on any issue or to carry any particular type of programming.

Section 312(a)(7) represents an effort by Congress to assure that an important resource—the airwaves—will be used in the public interest. We hold that the statutory right of access, as defined by the Commission and applied in these cases, properly balances the First Amendment rights of federal candidates, the public, and broadcasters.

The judgment of the Court of Appeals is *Affirmed.*

Justice WHITE, with whom Justice REHNQUIST and Justice STEVENS join, dissenting.

The Court's opinion is disarmingly simple and seemingly straightforward: in 1972, Congress created a right of reasonable access for candidates for federal office; the Federal Communications Commission, charged with enforcing the statute, has defined that right; as long as the agency's action is within the zone of reasonableness, it should be accepted even though a court would have preferred a different course. This approach, however, conceals the fundamental issue in these cases, which is whether Congress intended not only to create a right of reasonable access but also to negate the longstanding statutory policy of deferring to editorial judgments that are not destructive of the goals of the Act. In these cases, such a policy would require acceptance of network or station decisions on access as long as they are within the range of reasonableness, even if the Commission would have preferred different responses by the networks. It is demonstrable that Congress did not intend to set aside this traditional policy, and the Commission seriously misconstrued the statute when it assumed that it had been given authority to insist on its own views as to reasonable access even though this entailed rejection of media judgments representing different but nevertheless reasonable reactions to access requests. As this litigation demonstrates, the result is an administratively created right of access which, in light of the preexisting statutory policies concerning access, is far broader than Congress could have intended to allow. The Court unfortunately accepts this major departure from the underlying themes of the Communications Act and from the cases that have construed that statute. With all due respect, I dissent.

. . .

None of these justifications is patently unreasonable. They become so only because of the Commission's conclusion, adopted by the majority, that the reasonableness of access is to be considered from the individual candidate's perspective, including that candidate's particular "needs." While both the Court and the Commission describe other factors considered relevant such as the number of candidates and disruption in programming, the overarching focus is directed to the perceived needs of the individual candidate. This highly skewed approach is required because, as the Court sees it, the networks "seek the unilateral right to determine in advance how much time to afford *all* candidates." *Ante*, at 2826. But such a right, reasonably applied, would seem to fall squarely within the traditionally recognized discretion of the broadcaster. Instead of adhering to this traditional approach, the Court has laid the foundation for the unilateral right of candidates to demand and receive any "reasonable" amount of time a candidate determines to be necessary to execute a particular campaign strategy. The concomitant Commission involvement is obvious. There is no basis in the statute for this very broad and unworkable scheme of access.

Justice STEVENS, dissenting.
In my judgment, the question whether a broadcast licensee has violated 47 U.S.C. § 312(a)(7) by denying a political candidate reasonable access to broadcast time must be answered in the context of an entire political campaign, rather than by focusing upon the licensee's rejection of a single request for access. The licensee has a duty to act impartially and to make an adequate quantity of desirable time available. The performance of that duty cannot be evaluated adequately by focusing solely on particular requests or the particular needs of individual candidates. The approach the Federal Communications Commission has taken in this litigation, now adopted by the Court, creates an impermissible risk that the Commission's evaluation of a given refusal by a licensee will be biased—or will appear to be biased—by the character of the office held by the candidate making the request. Indeed, anyone who listened to the campaign rhetoric that was broadcast during 1980 must wonder how an impartial administrator could conclude that any Presidential candidate was denied "reasonable access" to the electronic media. That wonderment is not dispelled by anything said in the opinions for the majority of the Commission in this litigation.

In sum, I find Justice WHITE'S analysis of the issue compelling. I accordingly join his opinion.

BECKER v. FCC
95 F.3d 75 (D.C. Cir. 1996)

BUCKLEY, Senior Circuit Judge.
These consolidated cases arise from the efforts of a candidate for federal office to air political advertisements portraying images of aborted fetuses during time periods of his selection. Petitioners Washington Area Citizens Coalition Interested in Viewers' Constitutional Rights ("WACCI") and the candidate, Daniel Becker, seek review of a Federal Communications Commission order permitting a broadcast licensee to restrict the broadcast of campaign advertisements that may be "harmful to children" to times of the day when children are less likely to be in the viewing audience. Petitioners claim that the ruling violates sections 312(a)(7) and 315(a) of the Communications Act of 1934 ("Act"). We agree.

I. BACKGROUND
A. Legal Framework

Petitioners' challenge involves two sections of the Communications Act. The first requires broadcasters to provide candidates for federal office with "reasonable access" to the broadcast media. 47 U.S.C. § 312(a)(7) (1994). The second guarantees all candidates for elective office equal opportunities in the use of the broadcast media, and it deprives licensees of the power of censorship over the material a candidate may wish to broadcast. *Id.* § 315(a). Of peripheral relevance here is a federal criminal statute prohibiting the broadcast of obscene, indecent, or profane language. . . .

B. The Facts

The 1992 election season witnessed the advent of political advertisements depicting the aftermath of abortions... In that year, Daniel Becker was a qualified candidate for election to the United States House of Representatives from Georgia's Ninth Congressional District. At 7:58 p.m. on July 19, Station WAGA-TV, which was then licensed to Gillett Communications of Atlanta, Inc. ("Gillett"), aired, at Mr. Becker's request, a campaign advertisement that included photographs of aborted fetuses. WAGA-TV received numerous complaints from viewers who saw the advertisement.

Anticipating that Mr. Becker would wish to broadcast similar materials later in the campaign, Gillett filed a petition with the Commission requesting a declaratory ruling on the following question: Whether a licensee may channel a use by a legally-qualified federal candidate to a safe harbor when children are not generally present in the audience if the licensee determines in good faith that the proposed use is indecent or otherwise unsuitable for children . . . This was followed by a petition . . . requesting a declaratory ruling that broadcast licensees may decline to air political advertisements that "present[ ] graphic depictions or descriptions of aborted fetuses or any other similar graphic depictions of excised or bloody fetal tissue, where there is, in the good-faith judgment of the licensee, a reasonable risk that children may be in the audience. . . ." The firm also asked for a ruling that any determination by a broadcast licensee that such advertisements are "indecent" within the meaning of 18 U.S.C. § 1464 will be upheld by the Commission. *Id.* at 2.

After viewing a tape of Mr. Becker's July 1992 advertisement, and in response to the two petitions, the FCC's Mass Media Bureau ("Bureau") found, in a letter released on August 21, 1992, that the advertisement was not indecent. *Letter Ruling*, 7 F.C.C.R. 5599, 5560 (Aug. 21, 1992). It also concluded that "the broad prospective relief that petitioners seek [was] inconsistent with the 'reasonable access' provision of the Act. . . ." *Id.* Specifically, the Bureau stated that "[s]uch channeling would violate . . .

Section 312(a)(7) of the Act," because "channeling material that is not indecent . . . would deprive federal candidates of their rights to determine how best to conduct their campaigns." . . .

In October 1992, Mr. Becker again sought to purchase air time from WAGA-TV. He wished to broadcast a 30-minute political program entitled "Abortion in America: The Real Story" on November 1 between 4:00 p.m. and 5:00 p.m., following a televised professional football game. WAGA-TV refused to air the program at the time requested, claiming that the advertisement would violate the indecency provision of 18 U.S.C. § 1464. It stated that it would carry the program only within the safe harbor hours of midnight to 6:00 a.m. Mr. Becker filed a complaint with the FCC on October 27, 1992.

Faced with Mr. Becker's complaint and Kaye Scholer's application for review, the FCC issued a Request for Comments: [W]e seek comment on all issues concerning what, if any, right or obligation a broadcast licensee has to channel political advertisements that it reasonably and in good faith believes are indecent. We also seek comment as to whether broadcasters have any right to channel material that, while not indecent, may be otherwise harmful to children. That same day, the Bureau responded to Mr. Becker's complaint. *Letter Ruling*, 7 F.C.C.R. 7282 (Oct. 30, 1992). Noting that the FCC had solicited comments on the interplay of sections 312(a)(7) and 315(a) and the indecency provision of the criminal code, the letter stated that until the Commission provides definitive guidance, . . . it would not be unreasonable for the licensee to . . . conclude that Section 312(a)(7) does not require it to air, outside the "safe harbor", material that it reasonably and in good faith believes is indecent. *Id.* Mr. Becker subsequently filed an Application for Review with the Commission.

On November 22, 1994, the FCC issued the Memorandum Opinion and Order that is the subject of this appeal, denying Mr. Becker's Application for Review and granting Kaye Scholer's in part. *In re Petition for Declaratory Ruling Concerning Section 312(a)(7) of the Communications Act*, 9 F.C.C.R. 7638, 7649 (1994) ("*Declaratory Ruling*"). In it, the FCC concluded (1) that Mr. Becker's initial advertisement was not indecent, *id.* at 7643; (2) that there was evidence in the record "indicating that the graphic political advertisements at issue can be psychologically damaging to children," *id.* at 7646; (3) that "nothing in 312(a)(7) precludes a broadcaster's exercise of some discretion with respect to placement of political advertisements so as to protect children," *id.*; and (4) that channeling would not violate the no-censorship provision of section 315(a). *Id.* at 7649.

WACCI and Mr. Becker petition the court for review of this FCC order. WAGA License, Inc., has intervened on behalf of the FCC.

II. ANALYSIS

At the outset, we must dispose of a preliminary issue. The Commission asks us to treat the petitions for review as facial challenges to a legislative act, thus requiring petitioners to demonstrate that there is no set of circumstances under which channeling would be permissible. *See, e.g., Rust v. Sullivan,* 500 U.S. 173, 183 (1991). This argument is creative but hardly persuasive. Petitioners do not challenge the validity of sections 312(a)(7) and 315(a); they question the FCC's interpretation that those sections allow channeling. Therefore, because the administration of the Communications Act is entrusted to the FCC, the appropriate standard for review of the *Declaratory Ruling* is that set forth in *Chevron U.S.A. Inc. v. Natural Resources Defense Council, Inc.,* 467 U.S. 837, 842-43 (1984).

In that case, the Supreme Court stated that unless Congress has "directly spoken to the precise question at issue" (in which case "that is the end of the matter"), a court must defer to the agency's construction of the statute, so long as it is "permissible." *Id.* The Court has defined "permissible" as "rational and consistent with the statute." *NLRB v. United Food & Commercial Workers Union,* 484 U.S. 112, 123 (1987). Because it is conceded here that Congress did not directly address the propriety of channeling, our task is to determine whether the Commission's construction of sections 312(a)(7) and 315(a) meets those criteria.

A. Section 312(a)(7)

Section 312(a)(7) was added to the Communications Act by the Federal Election Campaign Act of 1971, Pub.L. No. 92-225. It provides that a station's license may be revoked for willful or repeated failure to allow *reasonable access* to or to permit purchase of reasonable amounts of time for the use of a broadcasting station by a legally qualified candidate for Federal elective office on behalf of his candidacy. 47 U.S.C. § 312(a)(7) (emphasis added). The Act does not define "reasonable access." The FCC's policy guidelines, however, have indicated the nature of the access that the section guarantees a qualified candidate.

In the first of those guidelines, the Commission stated that the provisions of Section 312(a)(7) impose upon licensees . . . the specific responsibility to afford . . . the opportunity to purchase reasonable amounts of time to legally qualified candidates for Federal elective office. . . . [T]he test of whether a licensee has fulfilled its obligations under Section 312(a)(7) is one of reasonableness. . . .

While the statute does not establish a precise or definite standard, . . . we believe it is unreasonable and not in compliance with the statute for a licensee to adopt a rigid policy of refusing to sell or give prime-time programming to legally qualified candidates. . . .

> *Such a refusal would deny the candidates access to the time periods with the greatest audience potential and would be inconsistent with the Congressional intent to give ". . . candidates for public office greater access to the media so that they may better explain their stand on the issues, and thereby more fully and completely inform the voters."*

. . .

The Supreme Court found the Commission's approach to section 312(a)(7) to be "a reasoned attempt to effectuate the statute's access requirement," while at the same time accommodating broadcasters' discretion to the extent necessary. *CBS, Inc. v. FCC,* 453 U.S. 367, 390 (1981). In so holding, the Court recognized that "Federal candidates are the intended beneficiary of § 312(a)(7)," *id.* at 392, and that the section "did more than simply codify the pre-existing public interest standard" governing broadcasters by "singl[ing] out" qualified candidates and "grant[ing] them a special right of access on an individual basis." *Id.* at 379.

More recently, the Commission issued "[f]ormal guidelines for reasonable access for federal candidates" in which it states that commercial broadcasters "must make program time available . . . during prime time and other time periods unless unusual circumstances exist that render it reasonable to deny access." *Codification of the Commission's Political Programming Policies,* 7 F.C.C.R. 678, 681 (1991) ("*1991 Policy Statement*"). "Prime time" constitutes that part of the day in which the audience is likely to be the largest; the FCC has identified the hours of 7-11 p.m. as comprising prime time in the Eastern and Pacific time zones, and the hours of 6-10 p.m. in the Central and Mountain time zones...

The FCC has also advised that [a] station may not use a denial of reasonable access as means to censor or otherwise exercise control over the content of political material . . . [and that] . . . Licensees may not adopt a policy that flatly bans federal candidates from access to the types, lengths, and classes of time which they sell to commercial advertisers.

Petitioners argue that the *Declaratory Ruling* deviates from its policy guidelines because there is nothing in them that would allow broadcasters to take the content of a political advertisement into account in determining what constitutes "reasonable access"; nor do they permit a licensee to deny a candidate access to adult audiences of his choice merely because significant numbers of children may also be watching television. Mr. Becker also objects to the ruling on the basis that it gives broadcasters a standardless discretion to determine whether an advertisement "may be harmful to children." For its part, the FCC contends that the ruling is consistent with both its past policies and the language and purpose of section 312(a)(7). Emphasizing its past practice of deferring to a broadcaster's reasonable and good faith discretion in making reasonable access decisions, the FCC argues that there is no basis for the position that it may never be appropriate for a broadcaster to take the graphic nature of abortion images into consideration when deciding at what hour to broadcast a particular advertisement.

We believe that petitioners have the better part of the argument. As we explain below, by permitting a licensee to channel political advertisements that it believes may harm children, the *Declaratory Ruling* frustrates what the Commission itself has identified as Congress's primary purpose in enacting section 312(a)(7); namely, to ensure "candidates access to the time periods with the greatest audience potential. . . ." *Licensee Responsibility,* 47 F.C.C.2d at 517; *see also Section 312(a)(7) Policy,* 68 F.C.C.2d at 1090. The FCC claims, nevertheless, that its order is consistent with this policy, citing the following passage from *Declaratory Ruling*:

> If licensees do channel, . . . they are expected to provide access to times with as broad an audience potential as is consistent with the federal candidate's right to reasonable access. This is consistent with our general policy under Section 312(a)(7) that licensees should afford access to federal candidates in prime time, when access to voters is greatest.
> 9 F.C.C.R. at 7647. We are unpersuaded.

The problem with this statement is that it is not possible, on the one hand, to channel a political advertisement to a time when there is little risk "that large numbers of children may be in the audience," *id.,* and, on the other, to assure the candidate of "as broad an audience potential as is consistent with [his] right of reasonable access." *Id.* We recently concluded, on the basis of an FCC study issued in 1993, that "there is a reasonable risk that large numbers of children would be exposed to any . . . material broadcast between 6:00 a.m. and midnight." *Action for Children's Television v.*

FCC, 58 F.3d 654, 665 (D.C. Cir. 1995) (en banc) ("*ACT*"), *cert. denied*, 116 S.Ct. 701 (1996). It is apparent, then, that a licensee will not be able to channel the advertisement to a time "when access to voters is greatest" without exposing it to substantial numbers of children.

We are faced, then, with competing interests—the licensee's desire to spare children the sight of images that are not indecent but may nevertheless prove harmful, and the interest of a political candidate in exercising his statutory right of "access to the time periods with the greatest audience potential." *Licensee Responsibility*, 47 F.C.C.2d at 517. The Commission has made it clear that when these two interests are in conflict, the licensee is free to decide in favor of the children. *See Declaratory Ruling*, 9 F.C.C.R. at 7646 ("we are unwilling to infer that Congress . . . intended to strip licensees of all discretion to consider the impact of political advertisements featuring graphic depictions of abortions on children in their audience.").

Finally, while it is possible to visualize accommodations at the margin in which a political message is broadcast during school hours or the late, late evening when significantly fewer children are watching television, any such accommodation is apt to deprive a candidate of particular *categories* of adult viewers whom he may be especially anxious to reach. It is common knowledge that campaign strategists rely on survey research to target specific voting groups with television advertisements. *See generally* Dan Koeppel, *The High-Tech Election (of 1992)*, Brandweek 18, Mar. 2, 1992. We can surmise, for example, that early shift factory workers whom a candidate wishes to reach are not apt to stay up beyond their normal bedtimes just to see his political advertisements. Thus, the ruling creates a situation where a candidate's ability to reach his target audience may be limited and his "personal campaign strategies . . . ignored." *See CBS, Inc.*, 453 U.S. at 389.

The FCC points out that it has previously acknowledged that "'there may be circumstances when a licensee might reasonably refuse broadcast time to political candidates during certain parts of the broadcast day.'" Brief for Respondents at 25 (quoting *Section 312(a)(7) Policy*, 68 F.C.C.2d at 1091). The FCC has never defined those circumstances; but in describing the circumstances that a licensee is entitled to take into consideration in refusing candidates' access to particular time frames, the Commission's concerns have focused on making sure that the exercise by candidates of their rights under the section would not "disrupt a station's broadcast schedule." *Section 312(a)(7) Policy*, 68 F.C.C.2d at 1090; *cf. CBS, Inc.*, 453 U.S. at 387, 101 S.Ct. at 2825 (to justify a denial of access, "broadcasters must cite a realistic danger of substantial program disruption . . . or of an excessive number of equal time requests"). Thus, the FCC has advised that a licensee may take into account its "broader programming and business commitments, including the multiplicity of candidates in a particular race, the program disruption that will be caused by political advertising, and the amount of time already sold to a candidate in a particular race." *1991 Policy Statement,* 7 F.C.C.R. at 681-82; *see also Section 312(a)(7) Policy,* 68 F.C.C.2d at 1090. None of these circumstances is remotely concerned with the content of a campaign advertisement, and we can see no connection between a licensee's right to protect his programming from disruption and a licensee's asserted right to shield children from the sight of disturbing images.

The Commission states, quite correctly, that in applying section 312(a)(7), it has always "rel[ied] upon the reasonable good faith judgments of licensees to determine what constitutes reasonable access." *1991 Policy Statement,* 7 F.C.C.R. at 679; *see also Section 312(a)(7) Policy,* 68 F.C.C.2d at 1089. The Supreme Court has cautioned, however, that "endowing licensees with a 'blank check' to determine what constitutes 'reasonable access' would eviscerate § 312(a)(7)." *CBS, Inc.,* 453 U.S. at 390 n. 12, 101 S.Ct. at 2827 n. 12. We believe that the standardless discretion that the FCC has granted broadcasters to channel political messages will do just that. While the *Declaratory Ruling* emphasizes that broadcasters may not channel an advertisement "out of disagreement with the candidate's political position," and that "[t]he licensee's discretion should relate to the nature of the graphic imagery in question and not to any political position the candidate espouses," 9 F.C.C.R. at 7647-48, the Commission now allows licensees to channel images based entirely on a subjective judgment that a particular advertisement *might* prove harmful to children. All that it asks is that that judgment be "reasonable" and made in good faith.

These are slippery standards, and it is of small solace to a losing candidate that an appellate court might eventually find that the Commission's approval of a licensee's channeling decision was an abuse of discretion or contrary to law. Moreover, the acceptance of a subjective standard renders it impossible to determine whether it was the advertisement's message rather than its images that the licensee found too shocking for tender minds.

In many instances, of course, it will be impossible to separate the message from the image, when the point of the political advertisement is to call attention to the perceived horrors of a particular issue. Indeed, this was the apparent purpose of many of the candidates who ran abortion advertisements similar to Mr. Becker's. *See Anti-Abortion Political Advertising,* III Vill. Sports & Ent. L.J. at 89 n.11 (discussing candidates who felt the advertisements were "a necessary offense," in order to "show that it's a life or death issue"). And the political uses of television for shock effect is not limited to abortion. *See id.* at 95 ("Other subjects that could easily lead to shocking and graphic visual treatment include the death penalty, gun control, rape, euthanasia and animal rights.")

Finally, in arguing that a licensee has the authority under the Act to channel material that might harm the young, the Commission points to Congress's "concern with protecting children from the adverse effects of televised material," Brief for Respondents at 19, and contends that "the public interest standard of the [Communications] Act clearly contemplates that appropriate measures may be taken to protect the well-being of children, as reflected in" other provisions of the Act. . . .

We have a couple of problems with this argument. First of all, the first of the cited provisions deals with the quantity and duration of advertisements during children's programs, not their content; and the second places no restraints on the broadcasting of materials that are not indecent. Secondly, the Commission offers no evidence that Congress intended to subordinate a candidate's right of reasonable access to a licensee's assessment of the public interest. To the contrary, it seems to us that the right of access accorded candidates by sections 312(a)(7) and 315(a) overrides the programming discretion that is otherwise allowed licensees by the Act, except in those circumstances already specified in the Commission's policy guidelines.

B. Section 315(a)

> Section 315(a) contains the Act's "equal opportunity" and "no censorship" provisions:
>
> If any licensee shall permit any person who is a legally qualified candidate for any public office to use a broadcasting station, he shall afford equal opportunities to all other such candidates for that office in the use of such broadcasting station: *Provided,* That such licensee shall have no power of censorship over the material broadcast under the provisions of this section. . . .

47 U.S.C. § 315(a).

The FCC has recognized that the "[c]ase law interpreting [section 315(a)] has uniformly barred licensees from exercising any power of censorship over the content of political broadcasts whether they are 'first' uses or responses to first uses." *Hammond for Governor Committee,* 69 F.C.C.2d 946, 947 (Broadcast Bur.1978). In its *Declaratory Ruling,* the FCC stated:

> We are not granting licensees the ability to delete political statements. We are simply recognizing that a licensee may, consistent with its public interest obligations, channel political advertisements containing graphic abortion imagery to times when, although consistent with its obligation to provide reasonable access, the likelihood that children will be in the audience is diminished. This added measure of licensee discretion does not constitute "censorship" as that term is used in the Communications Act.

9 F.C.C.R. at 7649.

According to the FCC, that ruling is consistent with section 315(a)'s no censorship provision because the Commission was careful to emphasize broadcasters' continuing obligation to air, in full, political advertisements with graphic abortion images should they choose to channel them to times when there were not large numbers of children in the viewing audience. The Commission also insists that the ruling does not allow licensees to dictate what issues a candidate may address in its advertisement or to "exercise their discretion in a manner that has the practical effect of censorship" by, for example, airing the advertisement during a period of "minimal viewership," such as 2:00 a.m. to 6:00 a.m. Brief for Respondent at 27. The FCC further argues that, in any event, the competing public interest in protecting the welfare of children outweighs "the minimal intrusion on a candidate's unfettered ability to present his message at the particular time preferred by the candidate." *Id.* at 30.

For their part, petitioners assert that the ruling compromises section 315(a)'s no censorship provision in two ways: First, by granting licensees the content-based discretion to refuse to broadcast particular advertisements during a particular period, it enables them not only to discriminate against a candidate on the basis of speech, but to inhibit the manner in which he is able to discuss public issues. Second, by enabling the licensee to determine when an advertisement that "may be harmful to children" will air, the ruling deprives the candidate of the ability to convey his message when and how he sees fit by presenting him with the choice of either changing its content or accepting a time slot that deprives him of his preferred audience.

The FCC has never defined censorship in the context of section 315(a), although it has provided guidance in the form of lists of acts that constitute censorship and of those that do not—neither of which refers to channeling. *See Political Primer 1984,* 100 F.C.C.2d at 1510-13. The Supreme Court, however, has stated that

> [t]he term censorship, . . . as commonly understood, connotes *any* examination of thought or expression in order to prevent publication of "objectionable" material. We find no clear expression of legislative intent, nor any other convincing reason to indicate Congress meant to give "censorship" a narrower meaning in § 315.

Farmers Educ. & Coop. Union of Am. v. WDAY, Inc., 360 U.S. 525, 527 (1959). In *WDAY, Inc.,* the Court held that section 315(a) prohibited a broadcaster from removing defamatory statements from the advertisements of a legally qualified candidate. From the Court's discussion, we may discern two guiding principles: First, the basic purpose of section 315(a) is to permit the "full and unrestricted discussion of political issues by legally qualified candidates." *Id.* at 529. Second, the section reflects Congress's "deep hostility to censorship either by the Commission or by a licensee." *Id.* at 528.

Although the Court was discussing a case in which a licensee sought to excise certain references in a political advertisement, we believe that these principles apply with equal force to this case because of the leverage that the threat of channeling provides a licensee in the heat of a political election. As the Court observed in *WDAY, Inc.,* [b]ecause of the time limitation inherent in a political campaign, erroneous decisions by a station could not be corrected by the courts promptly enough to permit the candidate to bring improperly excluded material before the public. It follows from all this that allowing censorship . . . would almost inevitably force a candidate to avoid controversial issues during political debates . . . and hence restrict the coverage of consideration relevant to intelligent political decision. We . . . are unwilling to assume[ ] that Congress intended any such result.

. . .

Not only does the power to channel confer on a licensee the power to discriminate between candidates, it can force one of them to back away from what he considers to be the most effective way of presenting his position on a controversial issue lest he be deprived of the audience he is most anxious to reach. This self-censorship must surely frustrate the "full and unrestricted discussion of political issues" envisioned by Congress.

. . . "[C]ensorship" encompasses more than the refusal to run a candidate's advertisement or the deletion of material contained in it. The FCC itself has indicated that it understands the Supreme Court's definition of censorship to be broader than it will now acknowledge. In *Radio Station WPAM,* 81 F.C.C.2d 492 (1980), after initially refusing to run a candidate's potentially defamatory advertisement, Station WPAM informed the political committee that was paying for it that "the spot would be broadcast 'as is', but stated that [the committee] would thereby risk the consequences of a later lawsuit" for defamation. *Id.* at 493. As a result, the candidate revised the text of his advertisement. *Id.* The Commission observed that

> were it not for WPAM's intimidating actions in the present case, i.e., [its] initial refusal to accept the announcement as submitted, followed by grudging acceptance coupled with a threat of subsequent legal action, the candidate would not have been required by the sponsoring Committee to revise the spot. We believe that this result was reasonably foreseeable. We further believe that the actions here constituted censorship, within the Supreme Court's definition in *WDAY, Inc.* . . . in violation of Section 315(a) of the Act.

Id. at 495. It concluded by "serving notice . . . that in the future any attempts by a licensee to coerce a candidate to revise his political announcement, albeit by threat of litigation or otherwise, will be considered censorship. . . ." *Id.*

In *D.J. Leary,* 37 F.C.C.2d 576 (1972), the FCC affirmed that a licensee may not require a candidate to execute an agreement to indemnify the licensee against liability resulting from the candidate's political advertisement because such an agreement "is likely to inhibit a candidate's use of a broadcast facility and possibly to affect his decision on whether to utilize a station to address the public." *Id.* at 577. The FCC explained that

> it was the intent of Congress to insure complete freedom of expression by political candidates, and therefore the no-censorship provision of Section 315 prohibits any interference, *direct or indirect,* with such expression.

Id. at 578 (emphasis added). We believe that a licensee's right to channel political advertisements will inevitably interfere with a candidate's freedom of expression by requiring him to choose between what he wishes to say and the audience he wishes to address. *See Gray Communications Systems, Inc.,* 19 F.C.C.2d 532, 535 (1969) ("the basic objective of section 315 [is] to permit a candidate to present himself to the electorate in a manner wholly unfettered by licensee judgment as to the propriety or content of that presentation"); *id.* (section 315(a) applies to "all program material presented as part of a candidate's use of a broadcast facility, with no right of prior approval of format or content on the part of the licensee"); *In re Inquiry Concerning "Equal Time" Requirements under Section 315,* 40 F.C.C. 357, 359 (1962) ("the Act bestows upon the candidate the right to choose the format and other similar aspects of the material broadcast") (internal quotations omitted).

Finally, section 315(a) not only prohibits censorship, it also requires that candidates be given "equal opportunities" to use a broadcaster's facilities. To satisfy this requirement, a broadcaster must "make available periods of approximately equal audience potential to competing candidates to the extent that this is possible." *Political Primer 1984,* 100 F.C.C.2d at 1505. The FCC claims that the *Declaratory Ruling* does not involve the equal opportunity provision because there was no equal opportunity request before it. Because the equal opportunity requirements "forbid any kind of discrimination by a station between competing candidates," however, channeling clearly implicates the equal opportunity provision of section 315(a).

This is so because if a station channels one candidate's message but allows his opponent to broadcast his messages in prime time, the first candidate will have been denied the equal opportunity guaranteed by this section. On the other hand, if the station relegates the opponent's advertisements to the broadcasting Siberia to which the first candidate was assigned, it would be violating the opponent's right of reasonable access under section 312(a)(7). We agree with petitioners that these provisions may not be read to create such a tension.

We conclude from the above that permitting the content-based channeling of political advertisements thwarts the objectives of both section 312(a)(7) and section 315(a) by restricting candidates' ability to "fully and completely inform the voters," *CBS, Inc.,* 453 U.S. at 379 (internal quotation marks and citation omitted), and by inhibiting the "full and unrestricted discussion of political issues by legally qualified candidates," *WDAY, Inc.,* 360 U.S. at 529. Because the *Declaratory Ruling* is based on impermissible constructions of the Act to which we owe no deference, *see Chevron,* 467 U.S. at 843, we hold that it is without legal effect.

In light of the above, we decline to address Mr. Becker's argument that channeling a candidate's campaign advertisements violates that candidate's First Amendment rights. . . .

III. CONCLUSION

The Commission's *Declaratory Ruling* violates the "reasonable access" requirement of section 312(a)(7) by permitting content-based channeling of non-indecent political advertisements, thus denying qualified candidates the access to the broadcast media envisioned by Congress. The ruling also permits licensees to review political advertisements and to discriminate against candidates on the basis of their content, in violation of both the "no censorship" and "equal opportunities" provisions of section 315(a). Therefore, we grant the petitions for review and vacate the ruling.

So ordered.

NOTES AND QUESTIONS

1. **Positive appearance.** Only the visual (or audio) appearance of the candidate himself or herself will trigger section 315(a). A candidate's surrogates do not trigger section 315(a), nor do impersonators. So, if a candidate voices a character on an animated program, that will trigger section 315(a)—even if the candidate is playing someone else. On the other hand, if a show portrays a cartoon image of a candidate, but the candidate is voiced by someone else, it will not trigger section 315(a). Do these distinctions make sense?
2. **Donald Trump and positive appearances.** Did Trump gain name-recognition and a reputation as a take-charge business titan because of the role he played on *The Apprentice*, NBC's long-running "reality" television series? Should a candidate be able to take advantage of positive appearances that predate a formal decision to run for office? Note that Trump had flirted with the prospect of a presidential run for years before he announced his successful candidacy in 2015.
3. **Section 315(a) and incumbents.** In the late 1960s, President Lyndon Johnson delayed announcing his candidacy for reelection, which allowed him to use his presidential bully pulpit without triggering

equal access for opposing candidates. Within weeks of becoming president in 2017, Donald Trump announced his candidacy for reelection in 2020. What do these two opposite approaches say about the application of Section 315(a)?

4. In 1980, broadcasters covered a live White House press conference during which President Jimmy Carter verbally attacked Senator Edward Kennedy, an opposing primary candidate for president. Senator Kennedy sued for equal time under section 315(a). However, as long as broadcasters do not know that the news conference is being used for reelection purposes, section 315(a) will not be triggered by live coverage of a press conference. Kennedy for President Committee v. FCC, 636 F2d 432 (D.C. Cir. 1980) (*Kennedy I*).
5. Can section 315(a) be triggered if a candidate airs a commercial under section 312(a)(7)? The answer is no, since it would undermine the purpose of 312(a)(7) if a paid commercial triggered free time for opposing candidates. Kennedy for President Committee v. FCC, 636 F2d 417 (D.C. Cir. 1980). (*Kennedy II*).
6. On November 7, 2015, candidate Donald Trump hosted NBC's *Saturday Night Live*, triggering Section 315(a). Three lesser-known opponents in the GOP primary, John Kasich, Lindsay Graham and Geroge Pataki, sought 12 minutes and 5 seconds of airtime from NBC stations—the amount of time that Trump had appeared on camera during the program. Trump's hosting gig gave *SNL* its highest ratings since 2012.
7. **Appearances that predate a candidacy.** In 1976, the FCC decided that airing old Ronald Reagan films would trigger equal time for opposing Republican primary candidates. Adrien Weiss, 58 F.C.C.2d 342 (1976). After some wavering, the FCC reconfirmed that old images of a candidate constitute a triggering use under the statute. Political Programming Policies, 9 FCC Rcd. 651 (1994).

CHAPTER 10

PROTECTING & ENRICHING CHILDREN

Indecency

Indecency is defined as patently offensive depictions of sexual or excretory organs or functions. Unlike obscenity, indecency is speech that is protected by the First Amendment. The FCC, however, regulates this protected speech on broadcast television and radio. Because of the pervasiveness and intrusiveness of broadcasting, the FCC requires that this content air between 10 p.m. and 6 a.m., when children are less likely to watch. The FCC knows that we live in an age when kids can easily access DVRs and have headphone radios, but the real purpose of these regulations is to help those parents who do wish to keep their children away from content that they feel is inappropriate. By channeling indecent content into the overnight hours, concerned parents can be confident that when their kids turn on the radio or television before 10 p.m., the content transmitted will be free of indecency. Put differently, indecency regulations are really designed to help parents control what their kids consume. For some, including many broadcasters, the problem with indecency is not the regulations themselves, but the way in which the FCC enforces them. After a few high-profile incidents on television and radio during the last decade, the FCC announced that it would enforce indecency more strictly, and Congress increased the fines for indecency against licensees exponentially. Among broadcasters, there is also a good deal of concern that the FCC enforces indecency selectively and subjectively. Though the FCC has, for example, focused aggressively on Nicole Ritchie's "potty mouth" or Janet Jackson's "wardrobe malfunction," it has refrained from pursuing complaints against similar content in the movie "Saving Private Ryan" and on "The Oprah Winfrey Show." Depending on one's perspective, broadcast indecency regulations can be a valuable parenting tool or a politically biased form of censorship.

In 2012, the U.S. Supreme Court, in Fox Television Stations v. FCC, had the opportunity to revisit the constitutionality of indecency regulations and the continued validity of its 1978 landmark *Pacifica* case. The Court, however, ruled on narrower grounds, unanimously invalidating FCC fines levied against Fox as unconstitutionally vague. Only Justice Ginsburg, in a brief concurrence, opined that the time was ripe for a wholesale reassessment of indecency regulations under the First Amendment.

FCC v. Pacifica Foundation
438 U.S. 726 (1978)

Mr. Justice STEVENS delivered the opinion of the Court (Parts I, II, III and IV-C) and an opinion in which THE CHIEF JUSTICE and Mr. Justice REHNQUIST joined (Parts IV-A and IV-B).
This case requires that we decide whether the Federal Communications Commission has any power to regulate a radio broadcast that is indecent but not obscene.

A satiric humorist named George Carlin recorded a 12-minute monologue entitled "Filthy Words" before a live audience in a California theater. He began by referring to his thoughts about "the words you couldn't say on the public, ah, airwaves, um, the ones you definitely wouldn't say, ever." He proceeded to list those words and repeat them over and over again in a variety of colloquialisms. . . .

Comedian George Carlin performing in the 1970s.

At about 2 o'clock in the afternoon on Tuesday, October 30, 1973, a New York radio station, owned by respondent Pacifica Foundation, broadcast the "Filthy Words" monologue. A few weeks later a man, who stated that he had heard the broadcast while driving with his young son, wrote a letter complaining to the Commission. He stated that, although he could perhaps understand the "record's being sold for private use, I certainly cannot understand the broadcast of same over the air that, supposedly, you control."

The complaint was forwarded to the station for comment. In its response, Pacifica explained that the monologue had been played during a program about contemporary society's attitude toward language and that, immediately before its broadcast, listeners had been advised that it included "sensitive language which might be regarded as offensive to some." Pacifica characterized George Carlin as "a significant social satirist" who "like Twain and Sahl before him, examines the language of ordinary people. . . . Carlin is not mouthing obscenities, he is merely using words to satirize as harmless and essentially silly our attitudes towards those words." Pacifica stated that it was not aware of any other complaints about the broadcast.

On February 21, 1975, the Commission issued a declaratory order granting the complaint and holding that Pacifica "could have been the subject of administrative sanctions." 56 F.C.C.2d 94, 99. The Commission did not impose formal sanctions, but it did state that the order would be "associated with the station's license file, and in the event that subsequent complaints are received, the Commission will then decide whether it should utilize any of the available sanctions it has been granted by Congress."

In its memorandum opinion the commission stated that it intended to "clarify the standards which will be utilized in considering" the growing number of complaints about indecent speech on the airwaves. *Id.*, at 94. Advancing several reasons for treating broadcast speech differently from other forms of expression, the Commission found a power to regulate indecent broadcasting in two statutes: 18 U.S.C. § 1464 (1976 ed.), which forbids the use of "any obscene, indecent, or profane language by means of radio communications," and 47 U.S.C. § 303(g), which requires the Commission to "encourage the larger and more effective use of radio in the public interest."

The Commission characterized the language used in the Carlin monologue as "patently offensive," though not necessarily obscene, and expressed the opinion that it should be regulated by principles analogous to those found in the law of nuisance where the "law generally speaks to *channeling* behavior more than actually prohibiting it. . . . [T]he concept of 'indecent' is intimately connected with the exposure of children to language that describes, in terms patently offensive as measured by contemporary community standards for the broadcast medium, sexual or excretory activities and organs at times of the day when there is a reasonable risk that children may be in the audience." 56 F.C.C.2d, at 98.

Applying these considerations to the language used in the monologue as broadcast by respondent, the Commission concluded that certain words depicted sexual and excretory activities in a patently offensive manner, noted that they "were broadcast at a time when children were undoubtedly in the audience (i. e., in the early afternoon)," and that the prerecorded language, with these offensive words "repeated over and over," was "deliberately broadcast." *Id.*, at 99. In summary, the Commission stated: "We therefore hold that the language as broadcast was indecent and prohibited by 18 U.S.C. [§] 1464." *Ibid.*

After the order issued, the Commission was asked to clarify its opinion by ruling that the broadcast of indecent words as part of a live newscast would not be prohibited. The Commission issued another opinion in which it pointed out that it "never intended to place an absolute prohibition on the broadcast of this type of language, but rather sought to channel it to times of day when children most likely would not be exposed to it." 59 F.C.C.2d 892 (1976). The Commission noted that its "declaratory order was issued in a specific factual context," and declined to comment on various hypothetical situations presented by the petition. *Id.*, at 893. It relied on its "long standing policy of refusing to issue interpretive rulings or advisory opinions when the critical facts are not explicitly stated or there is a possibility that subsequent events will alter them." *Ibid.*

. . .

Having granted the Commission's petition for certiorari, 434 U.S. 1008, we must decide: (1) whether the scope of judicial review encompasses more than the Commission's determination that the monologue was indecent "as broadcast"; (2) whether the Commission's order was a form of censorship forbidden by § 326; (3) whether the broadcast was indecent within the meaning of § 1464; and (4) whether the order violates the First Amendment of the United States Constitution.

. . .

II.

The relevant statutory questions are whether the Commission's action is forbidden "censorship" within the meaning of 47 U.S.C. § 326 and wheth er speech that concededly is not obscene may be restricted as "indecent" under the authority of 18 U.S.C. § 1464 (1976 ed.). The questions are not unrelated, for the two statutory provisions have a common origin. Nevertheless, we analyze them separately.

Section 29 of the Radio Act of 1927 provided:

> "Nothing in this Act shall be understood or construed to give the licensing authority the power of censorship over the radio communications or signals transmitted by any radio station, and no regulation or condition shall be promulgated or fixed by the licensing authority which shall interfere with the right of free speech by means of radio communications. No person within the jurisdiction of the United States shall utter any obscene, indecent, or profane language by means of radio communication." 44 Stat. 1172-1173.

The prohibition against censorship unequivocally denies the Commission any power to edit proposed broadcasts in advance and to excise material considered inappropriate for the airwaves. The prohibition, however, has never been construed to deny the Commission the power to review the content of completed broadcasts in the performance of its regulatory duties.

During the period between the original enactment of the provision in 1927 and its re-enactment in the Communications Act of 1934, the courts and the Federal Radio Commission held that the section deprived the Commission of the power to subject "broadcasting matter to scrutiny prior to its release," but they concluded that the Commission's "undoubted right" to take note of past program content when considering a licensee's renewal application "is not censorship."

. . .

We conclude, therefore, that § 326 does not limit the Commission's authority to impose sanctions on licensees who engage in obscene, indecent, or profane broadcasting.

III.

The only other statutory question presented by this case is whether the afternoon broadcast of the "Filthy Words" monologue was indecent within the meaning of § 1464. Even that question is narrowly confined by the arguments of the parties.

The Commission identified several words that referred to excretory or sexual activities or organs, stated that the repetitive, deliberate use of those words in an afternoon broadcast when children are in the audience was patently offensive, and held that the broadcast was indecent. Pacifica takes issue with the Commission's definition of indecency, but does not dispute the Commission's preliminary determination that each of the components of its definition was present. Specifically, Pacifica does not quarrel with the conclusion that this afternoon broadcast was patently offensive. Pacifica's claim that the broadcast was not indecent within the meaning of the statute rests entirely on the absence of prurient appeal.

The plain language of the statute does not support Pacifica's argument. The words "obscene, indecent, or profane" are written in the disjunctive, implying that each has a separate meaning. Prurient appeal is an element of the obscene, but the normal definition of "indecent" merely refers to nonconformance with accepted standards of morality.

Pacifica argues, however, that this Court has construed the term "indecent" in related statutes to mean "obscene," as that term was defined in *Miller v. California*, 413 U.S. 15. Pacifica relies most heavily on the construction this Court gave to 18 U.S.C. § 1461 in *Hamling v. United States*, 418 U.S. 87. See also *United States v. 12 200-ft. Reels of Film*, 413 U.S. 123, 130 n. 7 (18 U.S.C. § 1462) (dicta). *Hamling* rejected a vagueness attack on § 1461, which forbids the mailing of "obscene, lewd, lascivious, indecent, filthy or vile" material. In holding that the statute's coverage is limited to obscenity, the Court followed the lead of Mr. Justice Harlan in *Manual Enterprises, Inc. v. Day*, 370 U.S. 478. In that case, Mr. Justice Harlan recognized that § 1461 contained a variety of words with many shades of meaning. Nonetheless, he thought that the phrase "obscene, lewd, lascivious, indecent, filthy or vile," taken as a whole, was clearly limited to the obscene, a reading well grounded in prior judicial constructions: "[T]he statute since its inception has always been taken as aimed at obnoxiously debasing portrayals of sex." 370 U.S., at 483. In *Hamling* the Court agreed with Mr. Justice Harlan that § 1461 was meant only to regulate obscenity in the mails; by reading into it the limits set by *Miller v. California, supra*, the Court adopted a construction which assured the statute's constitutionality.

. . .

Because neither our prior decisions nor the language or history of § 1461 supports the conclusion that prurient appeal is an essential component of indecent language, we reject Pacifica's construction of the statute. When that construction is put to one side, there is no basis for disagreeing with the Commission's conclusion that indecent language was used in this broadcast.

IV.

Pacifica makes two constitutional attacks on the Commission's order. First, it argues that the Commission's construction of the statutory language broadly encompasses so much constitutionally protected speech that reversal is required even if Pacifica's broadcast of the "Filthy Words" monologue is not itself protected by the First Amendment. Second, Pacifica argues that inasmuch as the recording is not obscene, the Constitution forbids any abridgment of the right to broadcast it on the radio.

A.
The first argument fails because our review is limited to the question whether the Commission has the authority to proscribe this particular broadcast. As the Commission itself emphasized, its order was "issued in a specific factual context." 59 F.C.C.2d, at 893. That approach is appropriate for courts as well as the Commission when regulation of indecency is at stake, for indecency is largely a function of context—it cannot be adequately judged in the abstract.

. . .

It is true that the Commission's order may lead some broadcasters to censor themselves. At most, however, the Commission's definition of indecency will deter only the broadcasting of patently offensive references to excretory and sexual organs and activities. While some of these references may be protected, they surely lie at the periphery of First Amendment concern. . . . The danger dismissed so summarily in *Red Lion,* in contrast, was that broadcasters would respond to the vagueness of the regulations by refusing to present programs dealing with important social and political controversies. Invalidating any rule on the basis of its hypothetical application to situations not before the Court is "strong medicine" to be applied "sparingly and only as a last resort." *Broadrick v. Oklahoma,* 413 U.S. 601, 613. We decline to administer that medicine to preserve the vigor of patently offensive sexual and excretory speech.

B.
When the issue is narrowed to the facts of this case, the question is whether the First Amendment denies government any power to restrict the public broadcast of indecent language in any circumstances. For if the government has any such power, this was an appropriate occasion for its exercise.

The words of the Carlin monologue are unquestionably "speech" within the meaning of the First Amendment. It is equally clear that the Commission's objections to the broadcast were based in part on its content. The order must therefore fall if, as Pacifica argues, the First Amendment prohibits all governmental regulation that depends on the content of speech. Our past cases demonstrate, however, that no such absolute rule is mandated by the Constitution.

. . .

The government may forbid speech calculated to provoke a fight. See *Chaplinsky v. New Hampshire,* 315 U.S. 568. It may pay heed to the "'commonsense differences' between commercial speech and other varieties." *Bates v. State Bar of Arizona, supra,* 433 U.S., at 381. It may treat libels against private citizens more severely than libels against public officials. See *Gertz v. Robert Welch, Inc.,* 418 U.S. 323. Obscenity may be wholly prohibited. *Miller v. California,* 413 U.S. 15. And only two Terms ago we refused to hold that a "statutory classification is unconstitutional because it is based on the content of communication protected by the First Amendment." *Young v. American Mini Theatres, Inc., supra,* 427 U.S., at 52.

The question in this case is whether a broadcast of patently offensive words dealing with sex and excretion may be regulated because of its content. Obscene materials have been denied the protection of the First Amendment because their content is so offensive to contemporary moral standards. *Roth v. United States,* 354 U.S. 476. But the fact that society may find speech offensive is not a sufficient reason for suppressing it. Indeed, if it is the speaker's opinion that gives offense, that consequence is a reason for according it constitutional protection. For it is a central tenet of the First Amendment that the government must remain neutral in the marketplace of ideas. If there were any reason to believe that the Commission's characterization of the Carlin monologue as offensive could be traced to its political content—or even to the fact that it satirized contemporary attitudes about four-letter words—First Amendment protection might be required. But that is simply not this case. These words offend for the same reasons that obscenity offends. Their place in the hierarchy of First Amendment values was aptly sketched by Mr. Justice Murphy when he said: "Such utterances are no essential part of any exposition of ideas, and are of such slight social value as a step to truth that any benefit that may be derived from them is clearly outweighed by the social interest in order and morality." *Chaplinsky v. New Hampshire,* 315 U.S., at 572.

Although these words ordinarily lack literary, political, or scientific value, they are not entirely outside the protection of the First Amendment. Some uses of even the most offensive words are unquestionably protected. See, *e. g., Hess v. Indiana*, 414 U.S. 105. Indeed, we may assume, *arguendo*, that this monologue would be protected in other contexts. Nonetheless, the constitutional protection accorded to a communication containing such patently offensive sexual and excretory language need not be the same in every context. It is a characteristic of speech such as this that both its capacity to offend and its "social value," to use Mr. Justice Murphy's term, vary with the circumstances. Words that are commonplace in one setting are shocking in another. To paraphrase Mr. Justice Harlan, one occasion's lyric is another's vulgarity. Cf. *Cohen v. California*, 403 U.S. 15, 25.

In this case it is undisputed that the content of Pacifica's broadcast was "vulgar," "offensive," and "shocking." Because content of that character is not entitled to absolute constitutional protection under all circumstances, we must consider its context in order to determine whether the Commission's action was constitutionally permissible.

C.

We have long recognized that each medium of expression presents special First Amendment problems. *Joseph Burstyn, Inc. v. Wilson*, 343 U.S. 495, 502-503. And of all forms of communication, it is broadcasting that has received the most limited First Amendment protection. Thus, although other speakers cannot be licensed except under laws that carefully define and narrow official discretion, a broadcaster may be deprived of his license and his forum if the Commission decides that such an action would serve "the public interest, convenience, and necessity." Similarly, although the First Amendment protects newspaper publishers from being required to print the replies of those whom they criticize, *Miami Herald Publishing Co. v. Tornillo*, 418 U.S. 241, it affords no such protection to broadcasters; on the contrary, they must give free time to the victims of their criticism. *Red Lion Broadcasting Co. v. FCC*, 395 U.S. 367, 89.

The reasons for these distinctions are complex, but two have relevance to the present case. First, the broadcast media have established a uniquely pervasive presence in the lives of all Americans. Patently offensive, indecent material presented over the airwaves confronts the citizen, not only in public, but also in the privacy of the home, where the individual's right to be left alone plainly outweighs the First Amendment rights of an intruder. *Rowan v. Post Office Dept.*, 397 U.S. 728. Because the broadcast audience is constantly tuning in and out, prior warnings cannot completely protect the listener or viewer from unexpected program content. To say that one may avoid further offense by turning off the radio when he hears indecent language is like saying that the remedy for an assault is to run away after the first blow. One may hang up on an indecent phone call, but that option does not give the caller a constitutional immunity or avoid a harm that has already taken place.

Second, broadcasting is uniquely accessible to children, even those too young to read. Although Cohen's written message might have been incomprehensible to a first grader, Pacifica's broadcast could have enlarged a child's vocabulary in an instant. Other forms of offensive expression may be withheld from the young without restricting the expression at its source. Bookstores and motion picture theaters, for example, may be prohibited from making indecent material available to children. We held in *Ginsberg v. New York*, 390 U.S. 629, that the government's interest in the "well-being of its youth" and in supporting "parents' claim to authority in their own household" justified the regulation of otherwise protected expression. *Id.*, at 640 and 639. The ease with which children may obtain access to broadcast material, coupled with the concerns recognized in *Ginsberg*, amply justify special treatment of indecent broadcasting.

It is appropriate, in conclusion, to emphasize the narrowness of our holding. This case does not involve a two-way radio conversation between a cab driver and a dispatcher, or a telecast of an Elizabethan comedy. We have not decided that an occasional expletive in either setting would justify any sanction or, indeed, that this broadcast would justify a criminal prosecution. The Commission's decision rested entirely on a nuisance rationale under which context is all-important. The concept requires consideration of a host of variables. The time of day was emphasized by the Commission. The content of the program in which the language is used will also affect the composition of the audience, and differences between radio, television, and perhaps closed-circuit transmissions, may also be relevant. As Mr. Justice Sutherland wrote a "nuisance may be merely a right thing in the wrong place,—like a pig in the parlor instead of the barnyard." *Euclid v. Ambler Realty Co.*, 272 U.S. 365, 388. We simply hold that when the Commission finds that a pig has entered the parlor, the exercise of its regulatory power does not depend on proof that the pig is obscene.

The judgment of the Court of Appeals is reversed. *It is so ordered.*

FCC Memorandum Opinion and Order

IN THE MATTER OF COMPLAINTS AGAINST VARIOUS BROADCAST LICENSEES REGARDING THEIR AIRING OF THE "GOLDEN GLOBE AWARDS" PROGRAM

Adopted: March 3, 2004

I. INTRODUCTION

In this Memorandum Opinion and Order, issued pursuant to section 1.115 of the Commission's rules, we grant an Application for Review filed by the Parents Television Council ("PTC") on November 3, 2003. PTC seeks reversal of an October 3, 2003, Memorandum Opinion and Order ("Bureau Order") issued by the Chief, Enforcement Bureau ("Bureau") that denied complaints alleging various licensees violated restrictions regarding the broadcast of obscene and indecent material by airing the "Golden Globe Awards" on January 19, 2003.

We conclude that, based on the specific facts before us, the live broadcast of the "Golden Globe Awards" included material in violation of the applicable indecency and profanity prohibitions.

II. BACKGROUND

The Commission received numerous complaints from individuals associated with PTC alleging that the licensees named on the complaints broadcast the "Golden Globe Awards" program, during which the performer Bono uttered a phrase allegedly in violation of the FCC's rules restricting the broadcast of indecent material. The Golden Globe Awards are sponsored by the Hollywood Foreign Press Association. Bono made the statement in response to winning the award for "Best Original Song." The complainants maintained that such language was obscene and/or indecent, and requested that the Commission levy sanctions against the licensees for broadcasting the subject material. The Bureau, however, concluded that the material was not obscene or indecent, finding in particular with respect to indecency that the language used by Bono did not describe, in context, sexual or excretory organs or activities and that the utterance was fleeting and isolated. . . .

With respect to the first step of the indecency analysis, we disagree with the Bureau and conclude that use of the phrase at issue is within the scope of our indecency definition because it does depict or describe sexual activities. We recognize NBC's argument that the "F-Word" here was used "as an intensifier." Nevertheless, we believe that, given the core meaning of the "F-Word," any use of that word or a variation, in any context, inherently has a sexual connotation, and therefore falls within the first prong of our indecency definition. This conclusion is consistent with the Commission's original Pacifica decision, affirmed by the Supreme Court, in which the Commission held that the "F-Word" does depict or describe sexual activities.

We now turn to the second step of the analysis—whether the broadcast of the phrase at issue here is patently offensive under contemporary community standards for the broadcast medium and therefore indecent. We conclude that the answer to this question is yes. The "F-Word" is one of the most vulgar, graphic and explicit descriptions of sexual activity in the English language. Its use invariably invokes a coarse sexual image. The use of the "F-Word" here, on a nationally telecast awards ceremony, was shocking and gratuitous. In this regard, NBC does not claim that there was any political, scientific or other independent value of use of the word here, or any other factors to mitigate its offensiveness. If the Commission were routinely not to take action against isolated and gratuitous uses of such language on broadcasts when children were expected to be in the audience, this would likely lead to more widespread use of the offensive language. Neither Congress nor the courts have ever indicated that broadcasters should be given free rein to air any vulgar language, including isolated and gratuitous instances of vulgar language. The fact that the use of this word may have been unintentional is irrelevant; it still has the same effect of exposing children to indecent language. Our action today furthers our responsibility to safeguard the well-being of the nation's children from the most objectionable, most offensive language.

. . .

While prior Commission and staff action have indicated that isolated or fleeting broadcasts of the "F-Word" such as that here are not indecent or would not be acted upon, consistent with our decision today we conclude that any such interpretation is no longer good law. In Pacifica Foundation, Inc., 2 FCC Rcd 2698, 2699 (1987) (subsequent history omitted), for example, the Commission stated as follows: "If a complaint focuses solely on the use of expletives, we believe that . . . deliberate and repetitive use in a patently offensive manner is a requisite to a finding of indecency." The staff has since found that the isolated or fleeting use of the "F-Word" is not indecent in situations arguably similar to that here. We now depart from this portion of the Commission's 1987 Pacifica decision as well as all of the ... cases holding that isolated or fleeting use of the "F-Word" or a variant thereof in situations such as this is not indecent and conclude that such cases are not good law to that extent. . . .

We also find, as an independent ground, that the use of the phrase at issue here in the context and at the time of day here constitutes "profane" language under 18 U.S.C. § 1464. The term "profanity" is commonly defined as "vulgar, irreverent, or coarse language." . . .

We recognize that the Commission's limited case law on profane speech has focused on what is profane in the context of blasphemy, but nothing in those cases suggests either that the statutory definition of profane is limited to blasphemy . . . Broadcasters are on notice that the Commission in the future will not limit its definition of profane speech to only those words and phrases that contain an element of blasphemy or divine imprecation, but, depending on the context, will also consider under the definition of "profanity" the "F-Word" and those words (or variants thereof) that are as highly offensive as the "F-Word," to the extent such language is broadcast between 6 a.m. and 10 p.m. We will analyze other potentially profane words or phrases on a case-by-case basis.

Finally, our decision is not inconsistent with the Supreme Court ruling in Pacifica. The Court explicitly left open the issue of whether an occasional expletive could be considered indecent. Just as the Court held that Pacifica's broadcast of the George Carlin routine "could have enlarged a child's vocabulary in an instant," we believe that even isolated broadcasts of the "F-Word" in situations such as that here could do so as well, in a manner that many, if not most, parents would find highly detrimental and objectionable.

FCC v. Fox Television Stations, Inc. (*Fox I*)
556 U.S. 502 (2009)

Justice SCALIA delivered the opinion of the Court, except as to Part III-E.

Federal law prohibits the broadcasting of "any . . . indecent . . . language," 18 U.S.C. § 1464, which includes expletives referring to sexual or excretory activity or organs, see *FCC v. Pacifica Foundation,* 438 U.S. 726 (1978). This case concerns the adequacy of the Federal Communications Commission's explanation of its decision that this sometimes forbids the broadcasting of indecent expletives even when the offensive words are not repeated.

I. Statutory and Regulatory Background

The Communications Act of 1934, 48 Stat. 1064, 47 U.S.C. § 151 *et seq.* (2000 ed. and Supp. V), established a system of limited-term broadcast licenses subject to various "conditions" designed "to maintain the control of the United States over all the channels of radio transmission," § 301 (2000 ed.). Twenty-seven years ago we said that "[a] licensed broadcaster is granted the free and exclusive use of a limited and valuable part of the public domain; when he accepts that franchise it is burdened by enforceable public obligations." *CBS, Inc. v. FCC,* 453 U.S. 367, 395 (1981) (internal quotation marks omitted).

One of the burdens that licensees shoulder is the indecency ban—the statutory proscription against "utter[ing] any obscene, indecent, or profane language by means of radio communication,"18 U.S.C. § 1464—which Congress has instructed the Commission to enforce between the hours of 6 a.m. and 10 p.m. Public Telecommunications Act of 1992, § 16(a), 106 Stat. 954, note following 47 U.S.C. § 303. Congress has given the Commission various means of enforcing the indecency ban, including civil fines, see § 503(b)(1), and license revocations or the denial of license renewals, see §§ 309(k), 312(a)(6).

The Commission first invoked the statutory ban on indecent broadcasts in 1975, declaring a daytime broadcast of George Carlin's "Filthy Words" monologue actionably indecent. *Pacifica Foundation,* 56 F.C.C.2d 94, 1975 WL 29897. At that time, the Commission announced the definition of indecent speech that it uses to this day, prohibiting "language that describes, in terms patently offensive as measured by contemporary community standards for the broadcast medium, sexual or excretory activities or organs, at times of the day when there is a reasonable risk that children may be in the audience." *Id.,* at 98.

In *FCC v. Pacifica Foundation, supra,* we upheld the Commission's order against statutory and constitutional challenge. We rejected the broadcasters' argument that the statutory proscription applied only to speech appealing to the prurient interest, noting that "the normal definition of 'indecent' merely refers to nonconformance with accepted standards of morality." *Id.,* at 740, 98 S.Ct. 3026. And we held that the First Amendment allowed Carlin's monologue to be banned in light of the "uniquely pervasive presence" of the medium and the fact that broadcast programming is "uniquely accessible to children." *Id.,* at 748-749, 98 S.Ct. 3026.

In the ensuing years, the Commission took a cautious, but gradually expanding, approach to enforcing the statutory prohibition against indecent broadcasts. Shortly after *Pacifica,* 438 U.S. 726, the Commission expressed its "inten[tion] strictly to observe the narrowness of the *Pacifica* holding," which "relied in part on the repetitive occurrence of the 'indecent' words" contained in Carlin's monologue. *In re Application of WGBH Educ. Foundation,* 69 F.C.C.2d 1250, 1254, ¶ 10, 1978 WL 36042 (1978). When the full Commission next considered its indecency standard, however, it repudiated the view that its enforcement power was limited to "deliberate, repetitive use of the seven words actually contained in the George Carlin monologue." *In re Pacifica Foundation, Inc.,* 2 FCC Rcd. 2698, 2699, ¶ 12, 1987 WL 345577 (1987). The Commission determined that such a "highly restricted enforcement standard ... was unduly narrow as a matter of law and inconsistent with [the Commission's] enforcement responsibilities under Section 1464." *In re Infinity Broadcasting Corp. of Pa.,* 3 F.C.C. Rcd. 930, ¶ 5, 1987 WL 345514 (1987). The Court of Appeals for the District of Columbia Circuit upheld this expanded enforcement standard against constitutional and Administrative Procedure Act challenge. See *Action for Children's Television v. FCC,* 852 F.2d 1332 (1988) (R. Ginsburg, J.), superseded in part by *Action for Children's Television v. FCC,* 58 F.3d 654 (1995) (en banc).

Although the Commission had expanded its enforcement beyond the "repetitive use of specific words or phrases," it preserved a distinction between literal and nonliteral (or "expletive") uses of evocative language. *In re Pacifica Foundation, Inc.,* 2 FCC Rcd., at 2699, ¶ 13. The Commission explained that each literal "description or depiction of sexual or excretory functions must be examined in context to determine whether it is patently offensive," but that "deliberate and repetitive use ... is a requisite to a finding of indecency" when a complaint focuses solely on the use of nonliteral expletives. *Ibid.*

Over a decade later, the Commission emphasized that the "full context" in which particular materials appear is "critically important," but that a few "principal" factors guide the inquiry, such as the "explicitness or graphic nature" of the material, the extent to which the material "dwells on or repeats" the offensive material, and the extent to which the material was presented to "pander," to "titillate," or to "shock." *In re Industry Guidance On the Commission's Case Law Interpreting 18 U.S.C. § 1464 and Enforcement Policies Regarding Broadcast Indecency,* 16 FCC Rcd. 7999, 8002, ¶ 9, 8003, ¶ 10, 2001 WL 332787 (2001) (emphasis deleted). "No single factor," the Commission said, "generally provides the basis for an indecency finding," but "where sexual or excretory references have been made once or have been passing or fleeting in nature, this characteristic has tended to weigh against a finding of indecency." *Id.,* at 8003, ¶ 10, 8008, ¶ 17.

In 2004, the Commission took one step further by declaring for the first time that a nonliteral (expletive) use of the F- and S-Words could be actionably indecent, even when the word is used only once. The first order to this effect dealt with an NBC broadcast of the Golden Globe Awards, in which the performer Bono commented, "'This is really, really, f***ing brilliant.'" *In re Complaints Against Various Broadcast Licensees Regarding Their Airing of the "Golden Globe Awards" Program,* 19 FCC Rcd. 4975, 4976, n. 4, 2004 WL 540339 (2004) *(Golden Globes Order).* Although the Commission had received numerous complaints directed at the broadcast, its enforcement bureau had concluded that the material was not indecent because "Bono did not describe, in context, sexual or excretory organs or activities and . . . the utterance was fleeting and isolated." *Id.,* at 4975-4976, ¶ 3. The full Commission reviewed and reversed the staff ruling.

The Commission first declared that Bono's use of the F-Word fell within its indecency definition, even though the word was used as an intensifier rather than a literal descriptor. "[G]iven the core meaning of the 'F-Word,'" it said, "any use of that word . . . inherently has a sexual connotation." *Id.,* at 4978, ¶ 8. The Commission determined, moreover, that the broadcast was "patently offensive" because the F-Word "is one of the most vulgar, graphic and explicit descriptions of sexual activity in the English language," because "[i]ts use invariably invokes a coarse sexual image," and because Bono's use of the word was entirely "shocking and gratuitous." *Id.,* at 4979, ¶ 9.

The Commission observed that categorically exempting such language from enforcement actions would "likely lead to more widespread use." *Ibid.* Commission action was necessary to "safeguard the well-being of the nation's children from the most objectionable, most offensive language." *Ibid.* The order noted that technological advances have made it far easier to delete ("bleep out") a "single and gratuitous use of a vulgar expletive," without adulterating the content of a broadcast. *Id.,* at 4980, ¶ 11.

The order acknowledged that "prior Commission and staff action have indicated that isolated or fleeting broadcasts of the 'F-Word' . . . are not indecent or would not be acted upon." It explicitly ruled that "any such interpretation is no longer good law." *Ibid.,* ¶ 12. It "clarif[ied] . . . that the mere fact that specific words or phrases are not sustained or repeated does not mandate a finding that material that is otherwise patently offensive to the broadcast medium is not indecent." *Ibid.* Because, however, "existing precedent would have permitted this broadcast," the Commission determined that "NBC and its affiliates necessarily did not have the requisite notice to justify a penalty." *Id.*, at 4981-4982, ¶ 15.

II. The Present Case

This case concerns utterances in two live broadcasts aired by Fox Television Stations, Inc., and its affiliates prior to the Commission's *Golden Globes Order*. The first occurred during the 2002 Billboard Music Awards, when the singer Cher exclaimed, "I've also had critics for the last 40 years saying that I was on my way out every year. Right. So f*** 'em." Brief for Petitioners 9. The second involved a segment of the 2003 Billboard Music Awards, during the presentation of an award by Nicole Richie and Paris Hilton, principals in a Fox television series called "The Simple Life." Ms. Hilton began their interchange by reminding Ms. Richie to "watch the bad language," but Ms. Richie proceeded to ask the audience, "Why do they even call it 'The Simple Life?' Have you ever tried to get cow s*** out of a Prada purse? It's not so f***ing simple." *Id.*, at 9-10. Following each of these broadcasts, the Commission received numerous complaints from parents whose children were exposed to the language.

On March 15, 2006, the Commission released Notices of Apparent Liability for a number of broadcasts that the Commission deemed actionably indecent, including the two described above. *In re Complaints Regarding Various Television Broadcasts Between February 2, 2002 and March 8, 2005,* 21 FCC Rcd. 2664, 2006 WL 656783 (2006). Multiple parties petitioned the Court of Appeals for the Second Circuit for judicial review of the order, asserting a variety of constitutional and statutory challenges. Since the order had declined to impose sanctions, the Commission had not previously given the broadcasters an opportunity to respond to the indecency charges. It therefore requested and obtained from the Court of Appeals a voluntary remand so that the parties could air their objections. 489 F.3d 444, 453 (2007). The Commission's order on remand upheld the indecency findings for the broadcasts described above. See *In re Complaints Regarding Various Television Broadcasts Between February 2, 2002, and March 8, 2005,* 21 FCC Rcd. 13299, 2006 WL 3207085 (2006)*(Remand Order).*

The order first explained that both broadcasts fell comfortably within the subject-matter scope of the Commission's indecency test because the 2003 broadcast involved a literal description of excrement and both broadcasts invoked the "F-Word," which inherently has a sexual connotation. *Id.*, at 13304, ¶ 16, 13323, ¶ 58. The order next determined that the broadcasts were patently offensive under community standards for the medium. Both broadcasts, it noted, involved entirely gratuitous uses of "one of the most vulgar, graphic, and explicit words for sexual activity in the English language." *Id.*, at 13305, ¶ 17, 13324, ¶ 59. It found Ms. Richie's use of the "F-Word" and her "explicit description of the handling of excrement" to be "vulgar and shocking," as well as to constitute "pandering," after Ms. Hilton had playfully warned her to "'watch the bad language.'" *Id.*, at 13305, ¶ 17. And it found Cher's statement patently offensive in part because she metaphorically suggested a sexual act as a means of expressing hostility to her critics. *Id.*, at 13324, ¶ 60. The order relied upon the "critically important" context of the utterances, *id.*, at 13304, ¶ 15, noting that they were aired during prime-time awards shows "designed to draw a large nationwide audience that could be expected to include many children interested in seeing their favorite music stars," *id.*, at 13305, ¶ 18, 13324, ¶ 59. Indeed, approximately 2.5 million minors witnessed each of the broadcasts. *Id.*, at 13306, ¶ 18, 13326, ¶ 65.

The order asserted that both broadcasts under review would have been actionably indecent under the staff rulings and Commission dicta in effect prior to the *Golden Globes Order*-the 2003 broadcast because it involved a literal description of excrement, rather than a mere expletive, because it used more than one offensive word, and because it was planned, 21 FCC Rcd., at 13307, ¶ 22; and the 2002 broadcast because Cher used the F-Word not as a mere intensifier, but as a description of the sexual act to express hostility to her critics, *id.*, at 13324, ¶ 60. The order stated, however, that the pre-*Golden Globes* regime of immunity for isolated indecent expletives rested only upon staff rulings and Commission dicta, and that the Commission itself had never held "that the isolated use of an expletive . . . was not indecent or could not be indecent,"21 FCC Rcd., at 13307, ¶ 21. In any event, the order made clear, the *Golden Globes Order* eliminated any doubt that fleeting expletives could be actionably indecent, 21 FCC Rcd., at 13308, ¶ 23, 13325, ¶ 61, and the Commission disavowed the bureau-level decisions and its own dicta that had said otherwise, *id.*, at 13306-13307, ¶¶ 20, 21. Under the new policy, a lack of repetition "weigh[s] against a finding of indecency," *id.*, at 13325, ¶ 61, but is not a safe harbor.

The order explained that the Commission's prior "strict dichotomy between 'expletives' and 'descriptions or depictions of sexual or excretory functions' is artificial and does not make sense in light of the fact that an 'expletive's' power to offend derives from its sexual or excretory meaning." *Id.*, at 13308, ¶ 23. In the Commission's view, "granting an automatic exemption for 'isolated or fleeting' expletives unfairly forces viewers (including children)" to take "'the first blow'" and would allow broadcasters "to air expletives at all hours of a day so long as they did so one at a time." *Id.,* at 13309, ¶ 25. Although the Commission determined that Fox encouraged the offensive language by using suggestive scripting in the 2003 broadcast, and unreasonably failed to take adequate precautions in both broadcasts, *id.,* at 13311-13314, ¶¶ 31-37, the order again declined to impose any forfeiture or other sanction for either of the broadcasts, *id.,* at 13321, ¶ 53, 13326, ¶ 66.

Fox returned to the Second Circuit for review of the *Remand Order,* and various intervenors including CBS, NBC, and ABC joined the action. The Court of Appeals reversed the agency's orders, finding the Commission's reasoning inadequate under the Administrative Procedure Act. 489 F.3d 444. The majority was "skeptical that the Commission [could] provide a reasoned explanation for its 'fleeting expletive' regime that would pass constitutional muster," but it declined to reach the constitutional question. *Id.,* at 462. Judge Leval dissented, *id.,* at 467. We granted certiorari, 128 S.Ct. 1647 (2008).

III. Analysis

A. Governing Principles

The Administrative Procedure Act, 5 U.S.C. § 551 *et seq.,* which sets forth the full extent of judicial authority to review executive agency action for procedural correctness. . . .

In overturning the Commission's judgment, the Court of Appeals here relied in part on Circuit precedent requiring a more substantial explanation for agency action that changes prior policy. . . .

To be sure, the requirement that an agency provide reasoned explanation for its action would ordinarily demand that it display awareness that it *is* changing position. An agency may not, for example, depart from a prior policy *sub silentio* or simply disregard rules that are still on the books. See *United States v. Nixon,* 418 U.S. 683, 696 (1974). And of course the agency must show that there are good reasons for the new policy. But it need not demonstrate to a court's satisfaction that the reasons for the new policy are *better* than the reasons for the old one; it suffices that the new policy is permissible under the statute, that there are good reasons for it, and that the agency *believes* it to be better, which the conscious change of course adequately indicates. This means that the agency need not always provide a more detailed justification than what would suffice for a new policy created on a blank slate. Sometimes it must when, for example, its new policy rests upon factual findings that contradict those which underlay its prior policy; or when its prior policy has engendered serious reliance interests that must be taken into account. *Smiley v. Citibank*

(South Dakota), N. A., 517 U.S. 735, 742 (1996). It would be arbitrary or capricious to ignore such matters. In such cases it is not that further justification is demanded by the mere fact of policy change; but that a reasoned explanation is needed for disregarding facts and circumstances that underlay or were engendered by the prior policy.

In this appeal from the Second Circuit's setting aside of Commission action for failure to comply with a procedural requirement of the Administrative Procedure Act, the broadcasters' arguments have repeatedly referred to the First Amendment. If they mean to invite us to apply a more stringent arbitrary-and-capricious review to agency actions that implicate constitutional liberties, we reject the invitation. The so-called canon of constitutional avoidance is an interpretive tool, counseling that ambiguous statutory language be construed to avoid serious constitutional doubts. . . . We know of no precedent for applying it to limit the scope of authorized executive action. In the same section authorizing courts to set aside "arbitrary [or] capricious" agency action, the Administrative Procedure Act separately provides for setting aside agency action that is "unlawful," 5 U.S.C. § 706(2)(A), which of course includes unconstitutional action. We think that is the only context in which constitutionality bears upon judicial review of authorized agency action. If the Commission's action here was not arbitrary or capricious in the ordinary sense, it satisfies the Administrative Procedure Act's "arbitrary [or] capricious" standard; its lawfulness under the Constitution is a separate question to be addressed in a constitutional challenge.

B. Application to This Case

Judged under the above described standards, the Commission's new enforcement policy and its order finding the broadcasts actionably indecent were neither arbitrary nor capricious. First, the Commission forthrightly acknowledged that its recent actions have broken new ground, taking account of inconsistent "prior Commission and staff action" and explicitly disavowing them as "no longer good law." *Golden Globes Order,* 19 FCC Rcd., at 4980, ¶ 12. To be sure, the (superfluous) explanation in its *Remand Order* of why the Cher broadcast would even have violated its earlier policy may not be entirely convincing. But that unnecessary detour is irrelevant. There is no doubt that the Commission knew it was making a change. That is why it declined to assess penalties; and it relied on the *Golden Globes Order* as removing any lingering doubt. *Remand Order,* 21 FCC Rcd., at 13308, ¶ 23, 13325, ¶ 61.

Moreover, the agency's reasons for expanding the scope of its enforcement activity were entirely rational. It was certainly reasonable to determine that it made no sense to distinguish between literal and nonliteral uses of offensive words, requiring repetitive use to render only the latter indecent. As the Commission said with regard to expletive use of the F-Word, "the word's power to insult and offend derives from its sexual meaning." *Id.*, at 13323, ¶ 58. And the Commission's decision to look at the patent offensiveness of even isolated uses of sexual and excretory words fits with the context-based approach we sanctioned in *Pacifica*, 438 U.S., at 750. Even isolated utterances can be made in "pander[ing,] . . . vulgar and shocking" manners, *Remand Order*, 21 FCC Rcd., at 13305, ¶ 17, and can constitute harmful "'first blow[s]'" to children, *id.*, at 13309, ¶ 25. It is surely rational (if not inescapable) to believe that a safe harbor for single words would "likely lead to more widespread use of the offensive language," *Golden Globes Order, supra*, at 4979, ¶ 9.

When confronting other requests for *per se* rules governing its enforcement of the indecency prohibition, the Commission has declined to create safe harbors for particular types of broadcasts. See *In re Pacifica Foundation, Inc.*, 2 FCC Rcd., at 2699, ¶ 12 (repudiating the view that the Commission's enforcement power was limited to "deliberate, repetitive use of the seven words actually contained in the George Carlin monologue"); *In re Infinity Broadcasting Corp. of Pa.*, 3 FCC Rcd., at 932, ¶ 17 ("reject[ing] an approach that would hold that if a work has merit, it is *per se* not indecent"). The Commission could rationally decide it needed to step away from its old regime where nonrepetitive use of an expletive was *per se* nonactionable because that was "at odds with the Commission's overall enforcement policy." *Remand Order, supra*, at 13308, ¶ 23.

The fact that technological advances have made it easier for broadcasters to bleep out offending words further supports the Commission's stepped-up enforcement policy. *Golden Globes Order, supra*, at 4980, ¶ 11. And the agency's decision not to impose any forfeiture or other sanction precludes any argument that it is arbitrarily punishing parties without notice of the potential consequences of their action.

C. The Court of Appeals' Reasoning

The Court of Appeals found the Commission's action arbitrary and capricious on three grounds. First, the court criticized the Commission for failing to explain why it had not previously banned fleeting expletives as "harmful 'first blow[s].'" 489 F.3d, at 458. In the majority's view, without "evidence that suggests a fleeting expletive is harmful [and] . . . serious enough to warrant government regulation," the agency could not regulate more broadly. *Id.*, at 461. As explained above, the fact that an agency had a prior stance does not alone prevent it from changing its view or create a higher hurdle for doing so. And it is not the Commission, but Congress that has proscribed "any . . . indecent . . . language." 18 U.S.C. § 1464.

There are some propositions for which scant empirical evidence can be marshaled, and the harmful effect of broadcast profanity on children is one of them. One cannot demand a multiyear controlled study, in which some children are intentionally exposed to indecent broadcasts (and insulated from all other indecency), and others are shielded from all indecency. . . . Here it suffices to know that children mimic the behavior they observe-or at least the behavior that is presented to them as normal and appropriate. Programming replete with one-word indecent expletives will tend to produce children who use (at least) one-word indecent expletives. Congress has made the determination that indecent material is harmful to children, and has left enforcement of the ban to the Commission. If enforcement had to be supported by empirical data, the ban would effectively be a nullity.

The Commission had adduced no quantifiable measure of the harm caused by the language in *Pacifica,* and we nonetheless held that the "government's interest in the 'well-being of its youth' . . . justified the regulation of otherwise protected expression." 438 U.S., at 749 (quoting *Ginsberg v. New York,* 390 U.S. 629, 640, 639 (1968)). If the Constitution itself demands of agencies no more scientifically certain criteria to comply with the First Amendment, neither does the Administrative Procedure Act to comply with the requirement of reasoned decisionmaking.

The court's second objection is that fidelity to the agency's "first blow" theory of harm would require a categorical ban on *all* broadcasts of expletives; the Commission's failure to go to this extreme thus undermined the coherence of its rationale. 489 F.3d, at 458-459. This objection, however, is not responsive to the Commission's actual policy under review-the decision to include patently offensive fleeting expletives within the definition of indecency. The Commission's prior enforcement practice, unchallenged here, already drew distinctions between the offensiveness of particular words based upon the context in which they appeared. Any complaint about the Commission's failure to ban only some fleeting expletives is better directed at the agency's context-based system generally rather than its inclusion of isolated expletives.

More fundamentally, however, the agency's decision to consider the patent offensiveness of isolated expletives on a case-by-case basis is not arbitrary or capricious. "Even a prime-time recitation of Geoffrey Chaucer's Miller's Tale," we have explained, "would not be likely to command the attention of many children who are both old enough to understand and young enough to be adversely affected." *Pacifica, supra,* at 750, n. 29. The same rationale could support the Commission's finding that a broadcast of the film Saving Private Ryan was not indecent-a finding to which the broadcasters point as supposed evidence of the Commission's inconsistency. The frightening suspense and the graphic violence in the movie could well dissuade the most vulnerable from watching and would put parents on notice of potentially objectionable material. See *In re Complaints Against Various Television Licensees Regarding Their Broadcast on Nov. 11, 2004 of the ABC Television Network's Presentation of the Film "Saving Private Ryan,"* 20 FCC Rcd. 4507, 4513, ¶ 15, 2005 WL 474210 (2005) (noting that the broadcast was not "intended as family entertainment"). The agency's decision to retain some discretion does not render arbitrary or capricious its regulation of the deliberate and shocking uses of offensive language at the award shows under review-shows that were expected to (and did) draw the attention of millions of children.

Finally, the Court of Appeals found unconvincing the agency's prediction (without any evidence) that a *per se* exemption for fleeting expletives would lead to increased use of expletives one at a time. 489 F.3d, at 460. But even in the absence of evidence, the agency's predictive judgment (which merits deference) makes entire sense. To predict that complete immunity for fleeting expletives, ardently desired by broadcasters, will lead to a substantial increase in fleeting expletives seems to us an exercise in logic rather than clairvoyance. The Court of Appeals was perhaps correct that the Commission's prior policy had not yet caused broadcasters to "barrag[e] the airwaves with expletives," *ibid.* That may have been because its prior permissive policy had been confirmed (save in dicta) only at the staff level. In any event, as the *Golden Globes* order demonstrated, it did produce more expletives than the Commission (which has the first call in this matter) deemed in conformity with the statute.

D. Respondents' Arguments

Respondents press some arguments that the court did not adopt. They claim that the Commission failed to acknowledge its change in enforcement policy. That contention is not tenable in light of the *Golden Globes Order* 's specific declaration that its prior rulings were no longer good law, 19 FCC Rcd., at 4980, ¶ 12, and the *Remand Order* 's disavowal of those staff rulings and Commission dicta as "seriously flawed," 21 FCC Rcd., at 13308, ¶ 23. The broadcasters also try to recharacterize the nature of the Commission's shift, contending that the old policy was not actually a *per se* rule against liability for isolated expletives and that the new policy is a presumption of indecency for certain words. This description of the prior agency policy conflicts with the broadcasters' own prior position in this case. See, *e.g.*, Brief in Opposition for Respondent Fox Television Stations, Inc., et al. ("For almost 30 years following Pacifica, the FCC did not consider fleeting, isolated or inadvertent expletives to be indecent"). And we find no basis for the contention that the Commission has now adopted a presumption of indecency; its repeated reliance on context refutes this claim.

The broadcasters also make much of the fact that the Commission has gone beyond the scope of authority approved in *Pacifica,* which it once regarded as the farthest extent of its power. But we have never held that *Pacifica* represented the outer limits of permissible regulation, so that fleeting expletives *may not* be forbidden. To the contrary, we explicitly left for another day whether "an occasional expletive" in "a telecast of an Elizabethan comedy" could be prohibited. 438 U.S., at 748. By using the narrowness of *Pacifica* 's holding to require empirical evidence of harm before the Commission regulates more broadly, the broadcasters attempt to turn the sword of *Pacifica,* which allowed *some* regulation of broadcast indecency, into an administrative-law shield preventing any regulation beyond what *Pacifica* sanctioned. Nothing prohibits federal agencies from moving in an incremental manner. Cf. *National Cable & Telecommunications Assn. v. Brand X Internet Services,* 545 U.S. 967, 1002 (2005).

Finally, the broadcasters claim that the Commission's repeated appeal to "context" is simply a smokescreen for a standardless regime of unbridled discretion. But we have previously approved Commission regulation based "on a nuisance rationale under which context is all-important," *Pacifica, supra,* at 750, 98 S.Ct. 3026, and we find no basis in the Administrative Procedure Act for mandating anything different.

E. The Dissents' Arguments

Justice BREYER purports to "begin with applicable law," *post,* at 1829, but in fact begins by stacking the deck. He claims that the FCC's status as an "independent" agency sheltered from political oversight requires courts to be "all the more" vigilant in ensuring "that major policy decisions be based upon articulable reasons." *Post,* at 1829, 1829-1830. Not so. The independent agencies are sheltered not from politics but from the President, and it has often been observed that their freedom from presidential oversight (and protection) has simply been replaced by increased subservience to congressional direction. See, *e.g., In re Sealed Case,* 838 F.2d 476, 507-508 (C.A.D.C.) (Silberman, J.), rev'd *sub nom. Morrison v. Olson,* 487 U.S. 654 (1988); Kagan, Presidential Administration,

114 Harv. L.Rev. 2245, 2271, n. 93 (2001); Calabresi & Prakash, The President's Power to Execute the Laws, 104 Yale L.J. 541, 583 (1994); Easterbrook, The State of Madison's Vision of the State: A Public Choice Perspective, 107 Harv. L.Rev. 1328, 1341 (1994). Indeed, the precise policy change at issue here was spurred by significant political pressure from Congress.

Justice STEVENS apparently recognizes this political control by Congress, and indeed sees it as the manifestation of a principal-agency relationship. In his judgment, the FCC is "better viewed as an agent of Congress" than as part of the Executive. *Post,* at 1825-1826 (dissenting opinion). He nonetheless argues that this is a good reason for requiring the FCC to explain "why its prior policy is no longer sound before allowing it to change course." *Post,* at 1826. Leaving aside the unconstitutionality of a scheme giving the power to enforce laws to agents of Congress, see *Bowsher v. Synar,* 478 U.S. 714, 726 (1986), it seems to us that Justice STEVENS' conclusion does not follow from his premise. If the FCC is indeed an agent of Congress, it would seem an adequate explanation of its change of position that Congress made clear its wishes for stricter enforcement, see n. 4, *supra.* The Administrative Procedure Act, after all, does not apply to Congress and its agencies.

Regardless, it is assuredly not "applicable law" that rulemaking by independent regulatory agencies is subject to heightened scrutiny. The Administrative Procedure Act, which provides judicial review, makes no distinction between independent and other agencies, neither in its definition of agency, 5 U.S.C. § 701(b)(1), nor in the standards for reviewing agency action, § 706. Nor does any case of ours express or reflect the "heightened scrutiny" Justice BREYER and Justice STEVENS would impose. Indeed, it is hard to imagine any closer scrutiny than that we have given to the Environmental Protection Agency, which is not an independent agency. . . . There is no reason to magnify the separation-of-powers dilemma posed by the Headless Fourth Branch . . . by letting Article III judges-like jackals stealing the lion's kill-expropriate some of the power that Congress has wrested from the unitary Executive.

Justice BREYER and Justice STEVENS rely upon two supposed omissions in the FCC's analysis that they believe preclude a finding that the agency did not act arbitrarily. Neither of these omissions could undermine the coherence of the rationale the agency gave, but the dissenters' evaluation of each is flawed in its own right.

First, both claim that the Commission failed adequately to explain its consideration of the constitutional issues inherent in its regulation, *post,* at 1832-1835 (opinion of BREYER, J.); *post,* at 1826-1828 (opinion of STEVENS, J.). We are unaware that we have ever before reversed an executive agency, not for violating our cases, but for failure to discuss them adequately. But leave that aside. According to Justice BREYER, the agency said "next to nothing about the relation between the change it made in its prior 'fleeting expletive' policy and the First-Amendment-related need to avoid 'censorship,'" *post,* at 1832-1833. The *Remand Order* does, however, devote four full pages of small-type, single-spaced text (over 1,300 words not counting the footnotes) to explaining why the Commission believes that its indecency-enforcement regime (which includes its change in policy) is consistent with the First Amendment-and therefore not censorship as the term is understood. More specifically, Justice BREYER faults the FCC for "not explain[ing] why the agency changed its mind about the line that *Pacifica* draws or its policy's relation to that line," *post,* at 1834. But in fact (and as the Commission explained) this Court's holding in *Pacifica,* 438 U.S. 726, drew no constitutional line; to the contrary, it expressly declined to express any view on the constitutionality of prohibiting isolated indecency. Justice BREYER and Justice STEVENS evidently believe that when an agency has obtained this Court's determination that a less restrictive rule is constitutional, its successors acquire some special burden to explain why a more restrictive rule is not *un*constitutional. We know of no such principle.

Second, Justice BREYER looks over the vast field of particular factual scenarios unaddressed by the FCC's 35-page *Remand Order* and finds one that is fatal: the plight of the small local broadcaster who cannot afford the new technology that enables the screening of live broadcasts for indecent utterances. Cf. *post,* at 1834-1838. The Commission has failed to address the fate of this unfortunate, who will, he believes, be subject to sanction.

We doubt, to begin with, that small-town broadcasters run a heightened risk of liability for indecent utterances. In programming that they originate, their down-home local guests probably employ vulgarity less than big-city folks; and small-town stations generally cannot afford or cannot attract foul-mouthed glitteratae from Hollywood. Their main exposure with regard to self-originated programming is live coverage of news and public affairs. But the *Remand Order* went out of its way to note that the case at hand did not involve "breaking news coverage," and that "it may be inequitable to hold a licensee responsible for airing offensive speech during live coverage of a public event,"21 FCC Rcd., at 13311, ¶ 33. As for the programming that small stations receive on a network "feed": This *will* be cleansed by the expensive technology small stations (by Justice BREYER's hypothesis) cannot afford.

But never mind the detail of whether small broadcasters are uniquely subject to a great risk of punishment for fleeting expletives. The fundamental fallacy of Justice BREYER's small-broadcaster gloomy scenario is its demonstrably false assumption that the *Remand Order* makes no provision for the avoidance of unfairness-that the single-utterance prohibition will be invoked uniformly, in all situations. The *Remand Order* made very clear that this is not the case. It said that in determining "what, if any, remedy is appropriate" the Commission would consider the facts of each individual case, such as the "possibility of human error in using delay equipment," *id.,* at 13313, ¶ 35. Thus, the fact that the agency believed that Fox (a large broadcaster that used suggestive scripting and a deficient delay system to air a prime-time awards show aimed at millions of children) "fail[ed] to exercise 'reasonable judgment, responsibility and sensitivity,'" *id.,* at 13311, ¶ 33, and n. 91 (quoting *Pacifica Foundation, Inc.,* 2 FCC Rcd., at 2700, ¶ 18), says little about how the Commission would treat smaller broadcasters who cannot afford screening equipment. Indeed, that they would not be punished for failing to purchase equipment they cannot afford is positively suggested by the *Remand Order's* statement that "[h]olding Fox responsible for airing indecent material in this case does not ... impose undue burdens on broadcasters." 21 FCC Rcd., at 13313, ¶ 36.

There was, in sum, no need for the Commission to compose a special treatise on local broadcasters. And Justice BREYER can safely defer his concern for those yeomen of the airwaves until we have before us a case that involves one.

IV. Constitutionality

The Second Circuit did not definitively rule on the constitutionality of the Commission's orders, but respondents nonetheless ask us to decide their validity under the First Amendment. This Court, however, is one of final review, "not of first view." *Cutter v. Wilkinson,* 544 U.S. 709, 718, n. 7 (2005). It is conceivable that the Commission's orders may cause some broadcasters to avoid certain language that is beyond the Commission's reach under the Constitution. Whether that is so, and, if so, whether it is unconstitutional, will be determined soon enough, perhaps in this very case. Meanwhile, any chilled references to excretory and sexual material "surely lie at the periphery of First Amendment concern," *Pacifica,* 438 U.S., at 743 (plurality opinion of STEVENS, J.). We see no reason to abandon our usual procedures in a rush to judgment without a lower court opinion. We decline to address the constitutional questions at this time.

. . .

The Second Circuit believed that children today "likely hear this language far more often from other sources than they did in the 1970's when the Commission first began sanctioning indecent speech," and that this cuts against more stringent regulation of broadcasts. 489 F.3d, at 461. Assuming the premise is true (for this point the Second Circuit did not demand empirical evidence) the conclusion does not necessarily follow. The Commission could reasonably conclude that the pervasiveness of foul language, and the coarsening of public entertainment in other media such as cable, justify more stringent regulation of broadcast programs so as to give conscientious parents a relatively safe haven for their children. In the end, the Second Circuit and the broadcasters quibble with the Commission's policy choices and not with the explanation it has given. We decline to "substitute [our] judgment for that of the agency," *State Farm,* 463 U.S., at 43, and we find the Commission's orders neither arbitrary nor capricious.

The judgment of the United States Court of Appeals for the Second Circuit is reversed, and the case is remanded for further proceedings consistent with this opinion.

It is so ordered.

Justice THOMAS, concurring.
I join the Court's opinion, which, as a matter of administrative law, correctly upholds the Federal Communications Commission's (FCC) policy with respect to indecent broadcast speech under the Administrative Procedure Act. I write separately, however, to note the questionable viability of the two precedents that support the FCC's assertion of constitutional authority to regulate the programming at issue in this case. See *Red Lion Broadcasting Co. v. FCC,* 395 U.S. 367 (1969); *FCC v. Pacifica Foundation,* 438 U.S. 726 (1978). *Red Lion* and *Pacifica* were unconvincing when they were issued, and the passage of time has only increased doubt regarding their continued validity. "The text of the First Amendment makes no distinctions among print, broadcast, and cable media, but we have done so" in these cases. *Denver Area Ed. Telecommunications Consortium, Inc. v. FCC,* 518 U.S. 727, 812 (1996) (THOMAS, J., concurring in judgment in part and dissenting in part). . . .

These dramatic changes in factual circumstances [*e.g., scarcity, pervasiveness – ed.*] might well support a departure from precedent under the prevailing approach to *stare decisis*. See *Planned Parenthood of Southeastern Pa. v. Casey*, 505 U.S. 833, 855 (1992) (asking "whether facts have so changed, or come to be seen so differently, as to have robbed the old rule of significant application or justification"); see also *American Trucking Assns., Inc. v. Scheiner*, 483 U.S. 266, 302 (1987) (O'Connor, J., dissenting) ("Significantly changed circumstances can make an older rule, defensible when formulated, inappropriate . . ."). "In cases involving constitutional issues" that turn on a particular set of factual assumptions, "this Court must, in order to reach sound conclusions, feel free to bring its opinions into agreement with experience and with facts newly ascertained." *Burnet v. Coronado Oil & Gas Co.*, 285 U.S. 393, 412 (1932) (Brandeis, J., dissenting). For all these reasons, I am open to reconsideration of *Red Lion* and *Pacifica* in the proper case.

Justice KENNEDY, concurring in part and concurring in the judgment. I join Parts I, II, III-A through III-D, and IV of the opinion of the Court and agree that the judgment must be reversed. This separate writing is to underscore certain background principles for the conclusion that an agency's decision to change course may be arbitrary and capricious if the agency sets a new course that reverses an earlier determination but does not provide a reasoned explanation for doing so. In those circumstances I agree with the dissenting opinion of Justice BREYER that the agency must explain why "it now reject[s] the considerations that led it to adopt that initial policy." *Post*, at 1831.

The question whether a change in policy requires an agency to provide a more-reasoned explanation than when the original policy was first announced is not susceptible, in my view, to an answer that applies in all cases. There may be instances when it becomes apparent to an agency that the reasons for a longstanding policy have been altered by discoveries in science, advances in technology, or by any of the other forces at work in a dynamic society. If an agency seeks to respond to new circumstances by modifying its earlier policy, the agency may have a substantial body of data and experience that can shape and inform the new rule. In other cases the altered circumstances may be so new that the agency must make predictive judgments that are as difficult now as when the agency's earlier policy was first announced. Reliance interests in the prior policy may also have weight in the analysis.

The question in each case is whether the agency's reasons for the change, when viewed in light of the data available to it, and when informed by the experience and expertise of the agency, suffice to demonstrate that the new policy rests upon principles that are rational, neutral, and in accord with the agency's proper understanding of its authority. That showing may be required if the agency is to demonstrate that its action is not "arbitrary, capricious, an abuse of discretion, or otherwise not in accordance with law." 5 U.S.C. § 706(2)(A). And, of course, the agency action must not be "in excess of statutory jurisdiction, authority, or limitations, or short of statutory right." § 706(2)(C).

These requirements stem from the administrative agency's unique constitutional position. The dynamics of the three branches of Government are well understood as a general matter. But the role and position of the agency, and the exact locus of its powers, present questions that are delicate, subtle, and complex. The Federal Government could not perform its duties in a responsible and effective way without administrative agencies. Yet the amorphous character of the administrative agency in the constitutional system escapes simple explanation.

If agencies were permitted unbridled discretion, their actions might violate important constitutional principles of separation of powers and checks and balances. To that end the Constitution requires that Congress' delegation of lawmaking power to an agency must be "specific and detailed." *Mistretta v. United States,* 488 U.S. 361, 374 (1989). Congress must "clearly delineat[e] the general policy" an agency is to achieve and must specify the "boundaries of [the] delegated authority." *Id.,* at 372-373. Congress must "'lay down by legislative act an intelligible principle,'" and the agency must follow it. *Id.,* at 372 (quoting *J.W. Hampton, Jr., & Co. v. United States,* 276 U.S. 394, 409 (1928)).

Congress passed the Administrative Procedure Act (APA) to ensure that agencies follow constraints even as they exercise their powers. One of these constraints is the duty of agencies to find and formulate policies that can be justified by neutral principles and a reasoned explanation. To achieve that end, Congress confined agencies' discretion and subjected their decisions to judicial review. See R. Stewart & C. Sunstein, Public Programs and Private Rights, 95 Harv. L.Rev. 1193, 1248 (1982) (the APA was a "working compromise, in which broad delegations of discretion were tolerated as long as they were checked by extensive procedural safeguards"). If an agency takes action not based on neutral and rational principles, the APA grants federal courts power to set aside the agency's action as "arbitrary" or "capricious." 5 U.S.C. § 706(2)(A); *Citizens to*

Preserve Overton Park, Inc. v. Volpe, 401 U.S. 402, 416 (1971). For these reasons, agencies under the APA are subject to a "searching and careful" review by the courts. *Ibid.*

Where there is a policy change the record may be much more developed because the agency based its prior policy on factual findings. In that instance, an agency's decision to change course may be arbitrary and capricious if the agency ignores or countermands its earlier factual findings without reasoned explanation for doing so. An agency cannot simply disregard contrary or inconvenient factual determinations that it made in the past, any more than it can ignore inconvenient facts when it writes on a blank slate.

. . .

Rather than base its prior policy on its knowledge of the broadcast industry and its audience, the FCC instead based its policy on what it considered to be our holding in *FCC v. Pacifica Foundation,* 438 U.S. 726 (1978). See *In re Application of WGBH Educ. Foundation,* 69 F.C.C.2d 1250, 1254, ¶ 10, 1978 WL 36042 (1978) ("We intend strictly to observe the narrowness of the *Pacifica* holding"). The FCC did not base its prior policy on factual findings.

The FCC's *Remand Order* explains that the agency has changed its reading of *Pacifica.* The reasons the agency announces for this change are not so precise, detailed, or elaborate as to be a model for agency explanation. But, as the opinion for the Court well explains, the FCC's reasons for its action were the sort of reasons an agency may consider and act upon. The Court's careful and complete analysis-both with respect to the procedural history of the FCC's indecency policies, and the reasons the agency has given to support them-is quite sufficient to sustain the FCC's change of course against respondents' claim that the agency acted in an arbitrary or capricious fashion.

The holding of the Court of Appeals turned on its conclusion that the agency's explanation for its change of policy was insufficient, and that is the only question presented here. I agree with the Court that as this case comes to us from the Court of Appeals we must reserve judgment on the question whether the agency's action is consistent with the guarantees of the Constitution.

Justice STEVENS, dissenting.

While I join Justice BREYER's cogent dissent, I think it important to emphasize two flaws in the Court's reasoning. Apparently assuming that the Federal Communications Commission's (FCC or Commission) rulemaking authority is a species of executive power, the Court espouses the novel proposition that the Commission need not explain its decision to discard a longstanding rule in favor of a dramatically different approach to regulation. See *ante,* at 1810-1811. Moreover, the Court incorrectly assumes that our decision in *FCC v. Pacifica Foundation,* 438 U.S. 726 (1978), decided that the word "indecent," as used in 18 U.S.C. § 1464, permits the FCC to punish the broadcast of *any* expletive that has a sexual or excretory origin. *Pacifica* was not so sweeping, and the Commission's changed view of its statutory mandate certainly would have been rejected if presented to the Court at the time.

I.

"The structure of our Government as conceived by the Framers of our Constitution disperses the federal power among the three branches-the Legislative, the Executive, and the Judicial-placing both substantive and procedural limitations on each." ... Strict lines of authority are particularly elusive when Congress and the President both exert a measure of control over an agency. As a landmark decision involving the Federal Trade Commission (FTC) made clear, however, when Congress grants rulemaking and adjudicative authority to an expert agency composed of commissioners selected through a bipartisan procedure and appointed for fixed terms, it substantially insulates the agency from executive control. See *Humphrey's Executor v. United States,* 295 U.S. 602, 623-628 (1935).

With the view that broadcast regulation "should be as free from political influence or arbitrary control as possible," S.Rep. No. 772, 69th Cong., 1st Sess., 2 (1926), Congress established the FCC with the same measure of independence from the Executive that it had provided the FTC. Just as the FCC's commissioners do not serve at the will of the President, see 47 U.S.C. § 154(c) (2000 ed.), its regulations are not subject to change at the President's will. And when the Commission fashions rules that govern the airwaves, it exercises legislative power delegated to it by Congress. See *Whitman v. American Trucking Assns., Inc.*, 531 U.S. 457, 489-490 (2001) (STEVENS, J., concurring in part and concurring in judgment); *Bowsher,* 478 U.S., at 752 (opinion of STEVENS, J.). Consequently, the FCC "cannot in any proper sense be characterized as an arm or an eye of the executive" and is better viewed as an agent of Congress established "to carry into effect legislative policies embodied in the statute in accordance with the legislative standard therein prescribed, and to perform other specified duties as a legislative . . . aid." *Humphrey's Executor,* 295 U.S., at 628.

The FCC, like all agencies, may revise its regulations from time to time, just as Congress amends its statutes as circumstances warrant. But the FCC is constrained by its congressional mandate. There should be a strong presumption that the FCC's initial views, reflecting the informed judgment of independent commissioners with expertise in the regulated area, also reflect the views of the Congress that delegated the Commission authority to flesh out details not fully defined in the enacting statute. The rules adopted after *Pacifica,* 438 U.S. 726, have been in effect for decades and have not proved unworkable in the intervening years. As Justice BREYER's opinion explains, broadcasters have a substantial interest in regulatory stability; the threat of crippling financial penalties looms large over these entities. See *post,* at 1834-1836. The FCC's shifting and impermissibly vague indecency policy only imperils these broadcasters and muddles the regulatory landscape. It therefore makes eminent sense to require the Commission to justify why its prior policy is no longer sound before allowing it to change course. The FCC's congressional charter, 47 U.S.C. § 151 *et seq.,* the Administrative Procedure Act, 5 U.S.C. § 706(2)(A) (2006 ed.) (instructing courts to "hold unlawful and set aside . . . arbitrary [or] capricious" agency action), and the rule of law all favor stability over administrative whim.

II.

The Court commits a second critical error by assuming that *Pacifica* endorsed a construction of the term "indecent," as used in 18 U.S.C. § 1464, that would include any expletive that has a sexual or excretory origin. Neither the opinion of the Court, nor Justice Powell's concurring opinion, adopted such a far-reaching interpretation. Our holding was narrow in two critical respects. First, we concluded, over the dissent of four Justices, that the statutory term "indecent" was not limited to material that had prurient appeal and instead included material that was in "nonconformance with accepted standards of morality." *Pacifica,* 438 U.S., at 740. Second, we upheld the FCC's adjudication that a 12-minute, expletive-filled monologue by satiric humorist George Carlin was indecent "as broadcast." *Id.,* at 735. We did not decide whether an *isolated* expletive could qualify as indecent. *Id.,* at 750; *id.,* at 760-761 (Powell, J., concurring in part and concurring in judgment). And we certainly did not hold that any word with a sexual or scatological origin, however used, was indecent.

The narrow treatment of the term "indecent" in *Pacifica* defined the outer boundaries of the enforcement policies adopted by the FCC in the ensuing years. The Commission originally explained that "under the legal standards set forth in *Pacifica,* deliberate and repetitive use [of expletives] in a patently offensive manner is a requisite to a finding of indecency." *In re Pacifica Foundation,* 2 FCC Rcd. 2698, 2699, ¶ 13, 1987 WL 345577 (1987). While the "repetitive use" issue has received the most attention in this case, it should not be forgotten that *Pacifica* permitted the Commission to regulate only those words that describe sex or excrement. See 438 U.S., at 743, 98 S.Ct. 3026 (plurality opinion) ("[T]he Commission's definition of indecency will deter only the broadcasting of patently offensive *references* to excretory and sexual organs and activities" (emphasis added)). The FCC minimizes the strength of this limitation by now claiming that any use of the words at issue in this case, in any context and in any form, *necessarily* describes sex or excrement. See *In re Complaints Regarding Various Television Broadcasts Between February 2, 2002 and March 8, 2005,* 21 FCC Rcd. 13299, 13308, ¶ 23, 2006 WL 3207085 (2006) *(Remand Order)* ("[A]ny strict dichotomy between expletives and descriptions or depictions of sexual or excretory functions is artificial and does not make sense in light of the fact that an expletive's power to offend derives from its sexual or excretory meaning" (internal quotation marks omitted)). The customs of speech refute this claim: There is a critical distinction between the use of an expletive to describe a sexual or excretory function and the use of such a word for an entirely different purpose, such as to express an emotion. One rests at the core of indecency; the other stands miles apart. As any golfer who has watched his partner shank a short approach knows, it would be absurd to accept the suggestion that the resultant four-letter word uttered on the golf course describes sex or excrement and is therefore indecent. But that is the absurdity the FCC has embraced in its new approach to indecency. See *In re Complaints Against Various Broadcast Licensees Regarding Their Airing of the "Golden Globe Awards" Program,* 19 FCC Rcd. 4975, 4978-4979, ¶¶ 8-9, 2004 WL 540339 (2004) (declaring that even the use of an expletive to emphasize happiness "invariably invokes a coarse sexual image").

Even if the words that concern the Court in this case *sometimes* retain their sexual or excretory meaning, there are surely countless instances in which they are used in a manner unrelated to their origin. These words may not be polite, but that does not mean they are necessarily "indecent" under § 1464. By improperly equating the two, the Commission has adopted an interpretation of " indecency" that bears no resemblance to what *Pacifica* contemplated. . . .

III.

For these reasons and those stated in Justice BREYER's dissenting opinion, I would affirm the judgment of the Court of Appeals.

Justice GINSBURG, dissenting.

The mainspring of this case is a Government restriction on spoken words. This appeal, I recognize, arises under the Administrative Procedure Act. Justice BREYER's dissenting opinion, which I join, cogently describes the infirmities of the Federal Communications Commission's (FCC or Commission) policy switch under that Act. The Commission's bold stride beyond the bounds of *FCC v. Pacifica Foundation,* 438 U.S. 726 (1978), I agree, exemplified "arbitrary" and "capricious" decisionmaking. I write separately only to note that there is no way to hide the long shadow the First Amendment casts over what the Commission has done. Today's decision does nothing to diminish that shadow.

More than 30 years ago, a sharply divided Court allowed the FCC to sanction a midafternoon radio broadcast of comedian George Carlin's 12-minute "Filthy Words" monologue. *Ibid.* Carlin satirized the "original" seven dirty words and repeated them relentlessly in a variety of colloquialisms. The monologue was aired as part of a program on contemporary attitudes toward the use of language. *In re Citizen's Complaint Against Pacifica Foundation Station WBAI (FM),* 56 F.C.C.2d 94, 95, 1975 WL 29897 (1975). In rejecting the First Amendment challenge, the Court "emphasize[d] the narrowness of [its] holding." *Pacifica,* 438 U.S., at 750. See also *ante,* at 1824-1825 (STEVENS, J., dissenting). In this regard, the majority stressed that the Carlin monologue deliberately repeated the dirty words "over and over again." 438 U.S., at 729, 751-755, 98 S.Ct. 3026 (Appendix). Justice Powell, concurring, described Carlin's speech as "verbal shock treatment." *Id.,* at 757 (concurring in part and concurring in judgment).

In contrast, the unscripted fleeting expletives at issue here are neither deliberate nor relentlessly repetitive. Nor does the Commission's policy home in on expressions used to describe sexual or excretory activities or organs. Spontaneous utterances used simply to convey an emotion or intensify a statement fall within the order's compass. Cf. *Cohen v. California,* 403 U.S. 15, 26 (1971) ("[W]ords are often chosen as much for their emotive as their cognitive force. We cannot sanction the view that the Constitution, while solicitous of the cognitive content of individual speech, has little or no regard for that emotive function which, practically speaking, may often be the more important element of the overall message sought to be communicated."); *Denver Area Ed. Telecommunications Consortium, Inc. v. FCC,* 518 U.S. 727, 805 (1996) (KENNEDY, J., concurring in part, concurring in judgment in part, and dissenting in part) (a word categorized as indecent "often is inseparable from the ideas and viewpoints conveyed, or separable only with loss of truth or expressive power").

The *Pacifica* decision, however it might fare on reassessment, see *ante,* at 1822 (THOMAS, J., concurring), was tightly cabined, and for good reason. In dissent, Justice Brennan observed that the Government should take care before enjoining the broadcast of words or expressions spoken by many "in our land of cultural pluralism." 438 U.S., at 775. That comment, fitting in the 1970's, is even more potent today. If the reserved constitutional question reaches this Court, see *ante,* at 1819 (majority opinion), we should be mindful that words unpalatable to some may be "commonplace" for others, "the stuff of everyday conversations." 438 U.S., at 776 (Brennan, J., dissenting).

Justice BREYER, with whom Justice STEVENS, Justice SOUTER, and Justice GINSBURG join, dissenting.

In my view, the Federal Communications Commission failed adequately to explain *why* it *changed* its indecency policy from a policy permitting a single "fleeting use" of an expletive, to a policy that made no such exception. Its explanation fails to discuss two critical factors, at least one of which directly underlay its original policy decision. Its explanation instead discussed several factors well known to it the first time around, which by themselves provide no significant justification for a *change* of policy. Consequently, the FCC decision is "arbitrary, capricious, an abuse of discretion." 5 U.S.C. § 706(2)(A); *Motor Vehicle Mfrs. Assn. of United States, Inc. v. State Farm Mut. Automobile Ins. Co.,* 463 U.S. 29, 41-43 (1983); *Citizens to Preserve Overton Park, Inc. v. Volpe,* 401 U.S. 402, 420-421 (1971). And I would affirm the Second Circuit's similar determination.

I.

I begin with applicable law. That law grants those in charge of independent administrative agencies broad authority to determine relevant policy. But it does not permit them to make policy choices for purely political reasons nor to rest them primarily upon unexplained policy preferences. Federal Communications Commissioners have fixed terms of office; they are not directly responsible to the voters; and they enjoy an independence expressly designed to insulate them, to a degree, from "'the exercise of political oversight.'" *Freytag v. Commissioner,* 501 U.S. 868, 916 (1991) (SCALIA, J., concurring in part and concurring in judgment); see also *Morrison v. Olson,* 487 U.S. 654, 691, n. 30 (1988). That insulation helps to secure important governmental objectives, such as the constitutionally related objective of maintaining broadcast regulation that does not bend too readily before the political winds. But that agency's comparative freedom from ballot-box control makes it all the more important that courts review its decisionmaking to assure compliance with applicable provisions of the law-including law requiring that major policy decisions be based upon articulable reasons.

The statutory provision applicable here is the Administrative Procedure Act's (APA) prohibition of agency action that is "arbitrary, capricious, [or] an abuse of discretion,"5 U.S.C. § 706(2)(A). This legal requirement helps assure agency decisionmaking based upon more than the personal preferences of the decisionmakers. Courts have applied the provision sparingly, granting agencies broad policymaking leeway. But they have also made clear that agency discretion is not "'unbounded.'" *Burlington Truck Lines, Inc. v. United States,* 371 U.S. 156, 167-168 (1962). In so holding, American courts have followed a venerable legal tradition, stretching back at least to the days of Sir Edward Coke and the draining of the English fens. See *Rooke's Case,* 77 Eng. Rep. 209, 210, 5 Coke Rep. 99b, 100a (C.P. 1598) (Coke, J.) (members of sewer commission with authority to act according "to their discretio[n]" are nonetheless "limited and bound with the rule of reason and law . . . and [cannot act] according to their wills and private affections" (quoted in Jaffe, Judicial Review: Constitutional and Jurisdictional Fact, 70 Harv. L.Rev. 953, 954 (1957)).

The law has also recognized that it is not so much a particular set of substantive commands but rather it is a *process,* a process of learning through reasoned argument, that is the antithesis of the "arbitrary." This means agencies must follow a "logical and rational" decisionmaking "process." . . .

Moreover, an agency must act consistently. The agency must follow its own rules. *Arizona Grocery Co. v. Atchison, T. & S.F.R. Co.,* 284 U.S. 370, 389-390 (1932). And when an agency seeks to change those rules, it must focus on the fact of change and explain the basis for that change. See, *e.g.,National Cable & Telecommunications Assn. v. Brand X Internet Services,* 545 U.S. 967, 981 (2005) ("*Unexplained* inconsistency is" a "reason for holding an interpretation to be an arbitrary and capricious change from agency practice" (emphasis added)).

To explain a change requires more than setting forth reasons why the new policy is a good one. It also requires the agency to answer the question, "Why did you change?" And a rational answer to this question typically requires a more complete explanation than would prove satisfactory were change itself not at issue. An (imaginary) administrator explaining why he chose a policy that requires driving on the right-side, rather than the left-side, of the road might say, "Well, one side seemed as good as the other, so I flipped a coin." But even assuming the rationality of that explanation for an *initial* choice, that explanation is not at all rational if offered to explain why the administrator *changed* driving practice, from right-side to left-side, 25 years later.

. . .

Contrary to the majority's characterization of this dissent, it would not (and *[admin law precedent]* does not) require a *"heightened standard"* of review. *Ante,* at 1810-1811 (emphasis added). Rather, the law requires application of the *same standard* of review to different circumstances, namely circumstances characterized by the fact that *change* is at issue. It requires the agency to focus upon the fact of change where change is relevant, just as it must focus upon any other relevant circumstance. It requires the agency here to focus upon the reasons that led the agency to adopt the initial policy, and to explain why it now comes to a new judgment.

I recognize that *sometimes* the ultimate explanation for a change may have to be, "We now weigh the relevant considerations differently." But at other times, an agency can and should say more. Where, for example, the agency rested its previous policy on particular factual findings, see *ante,* at 1823-1824 (KENNEDY, J., concurring in part and concurring in judgment); or where an agency rested its prior policy on its view of the governing law, see *infra,* at 1832-1835 or where an agency rested its previous policy on, say, a special need to coordinate with another agency, one would normally expect the agency to focus upon those earlier views of fact, of law, or of policy and explain why they are no longer controlling. Regardless, to say that the agency here must answer the question "why change" is not to require the agency to provide a justification that is "*better* than the reasons for the old [policy]." *Ante,* at 1834-1835. It is only to recognize the obvious fact that *change* is sometimes (not always) a relevant background feature that sometimes (not always) requires focus (upon prior justifications) and explanation lest the adoption of the new policy (in that circumstance) be "arbitrary, capricious, an abuse of discretion."

That is certainly how courts of appeals, the courts that review agency decisions, have always treated the matter in practice. . . . After all, if it is *always* legally sufficient for the agency to reply to the question "why change?" with the answer "we prefer the new policy" (even when the agency *has not considered* the major factors that led it to adopt its old policy), then why bother asking the agency to focus on the fact of change? More to the point, *why* would the law exempt this and no other aspect of an agency decision from "arbitrary, capricious" review? Where does, and why would, the APA grant agencies the freedom to change major policies on the basis of nothing more than political considerations or even personal whim?

Avoiding the application of any *heightened* standard of review, the Court in *State Farm* recognized that the APA's "nonarbitrary" requirement affords agencies generous leeway when they set policy. 463 U.S., at 42, 103 S.Ct. 2856. But it also recognized that this leeway is not absolute. The Court described its boundaries by then listing considerations that help determine whether an explanation is adequate. Mirroring and elaborating upon its statement in *Overton Park,* 401 U.S. 402, the Court said that a reviewing court should take into account whether the agency had "relied on factors which Congress has not intended it to consider, entirely failed to consider an important aspect of the problem, offered an explanation for its decision that runs counter to the evidence before the agency, or is so implausible that it could not be ascribed to a difference in view or the product of agency expertise." *State Farm, supra,* at 43; see also *Overton Park, supra,* at 416.

II.

We here must apply the general standards set forth in *State Farm* and *Overton Park* to an agency decision that changes a 25-year-old "fleeting expletive" policy from (1) the old policy that would normally permit broadcasters to transmit a single, fleeting use of an expletive to (2) a new policy that would threaten broadcasters with large fines for transmitting even a single use (including its use by a member of the public) of such an expletive, alone with nothing more. The question is whether that decision satisfies the minimal standards necessary to assure a reviewing court that such a change of policy is not "arbitrary, capricious, [or] an abuse of discretion,"5 U.S.C. § 706(2)(A), particularly as set forth in, *e.g., State Farm* and *Overton Park, supra,* at 1829-1832. The decision, in my view, does not satisfy those standards.

Consider the requirement that an agency at least minimally "consider . . . important aspect[s] of the problem." *State Farm, supra,* at 43. The FCC failed to satisfy this requirement, for it failed to consider two critically important aspects of the problem that underlay its initial policy judgment (one of which directly, the other of which indirectly). First, the FCC said next to nothing about the relation between the change it made in its prior "fleeting expletive" policy and the First-Amendment-related need to avoid "censorship," a matter as closely related to broadcasting regulation as is health to that of the environment. The reason that discussion of the matter is particularly important here is that the FCC had *explicitly* rested its prior policy in large part upon the need to avoid treading too close to the constitutional line.

Thirty years ago, the Court considered the location of that constitutional line. In *FCC v. Pacifica Foundation,* 438 U.S. 726 (1978), the Court reviewed an FCC decision forbidding the broadcast of a monologue that deliberately and repeatedly uttered the expletives here at issue more than 100 times in one hour at a time of day when children were likely to hear the broadcast. *Id.,* at 739. The Court held that the FCC's prohibition did not violate the First Amendment. But the Court divided 5 to 4. And two Members of the majority, Justices Powell and Blackmun, explicitly noted that the Court "does not speak to cases involving *the isolated use* of a potentially offensive word ... as distinguished from the verbal shock treatment administered by respondent here." *Id.,* at 760-761 (Powell, J., concurring in part and concurring in judgment) (emphasis added). This statement by two Members of the majority suggested that they could reach a different result, finding an FCC prohibition unconstitutional, were that prohibition aimed at the fleeting or single use of an expletive.

The FCC subsequently made clear that it thought that Justice Powell's concurrence set forth a constitutional line that its indecency policy should embody. In 1978, the Commission wrote that the First Amendment "severely limit [s]" the Commission's role in regulating indecency. It added that the Court, in *Pacifica,* had "relied ... on the repetitive occurrence of the 'indecent' words in question." And it said that, in setting policy, it "intend [ed] strictly to observe the narrowness of the *Pacifica* holding." *In re Application of WGBH Educ. Foundation,* 69 F.C.C.2d 1250, 1254, ¶ 10, 1978 WL 36042.

In 1983, the Commission again wrote that it understood the Court's decision in *Pacifica* to rest on the "repetitive occurrence of the 'indecent' words in question." And, again, the Commission explained that its regulation of fleeting or isolated offensive words would reflect Justice Powell's understanding of the First Amendment's scope. *In re Application of Pacifica Foundation,* 95 F.C.C.2d 750, 760, ¶¶ 17-18, 1983 WL 182971. In 1987, the Commission once more explained that its "fleeting expletives" policy reflected the Court's decision in *Pacifica.* It said that, under its policy, "speech that is indecent *must* involve more than an isolated use of an offensive word," adding that "we believe that under the legal standards set forth in *Pacifica,* deliberate and repetitive use in a patently offensive manner is a requisite to a finding of indecency." *In re Pacifica Foundation,* 2 FCC Rcd. 2698, 2699, ¶ 13, 1987 WL 345577 (emphasis added). In another order that same year, the Commission stated that "the First Amendment dictate[s] a careful and restrained approach with regard to review of matters involving broadcast programming"; it then explained, citing *Pacifica,* that "[s]peech that is indecent *must* involve more than the isolated use of an offensive word." *In re Infinity Broadcasting,* 2 FCC Rcd. 2705, 2705, ¶¶ 6-7, 1987 WL 344896 (1987) (emphasis added). And in 2001, in giving the industry guidance, the FCC once again said in respect to its regulation of indecent speech that it "must both identify a compelling interest for any regulation . . . and choose the least restrictive means to further that interest." *In re Industry Guidance On Commission's Case Law Interpreting 18 U.S.C. § 1464 and Enforcement Policies Regarding Broadcast Indecency,* 16 FCC Rcd. 7999, 8000-8001, ¶ 3-5, 2001 WL 332787.

The FCC thus repeatedly made clear that it based its "fleeting expletive" policy upon the need to avoid treading too close to the constitutional line as set forth in Justice Powell's *Pacifica* concurrence. What then did it say, when it changed its policy, about *why* it abandoned this Constitution-based reasoning? The FCC devoted "four full pages of small-type, single-spaced text," *ante,* at 1817-1818, responding to industry arguments that, *e.g.,* changes in the nature of the broadcast industry made *all* indecency regulation, *i.e.,*18 U.S.C. § 1464, unconstitutional. In doing so it repeatedly *reaffirmed* its view that *Pacifica* remains good law. . . . All the more surprising then that, in respect to *why* it abandoned its prior view about the critical relation between its prior fleeting expletive policy and Justice Powell's *Pacifica* concurrence, it says no more than the following:

"[O]ur decision is not inconsistent with the Supreme Court ruling in *Pacifica.* The Court explicitly left open the issue of whether an occasional expletive could be considered indecent." . . . And, (repeating what it already had said), "*[Pacifica]* specifically reserved the question of 'an occasional expletive' and noted that it addressed only the 'particular broadcast' at issue in that case." *Remand Order, supra,* at 13308-13309, ¶ 24.

These two sentences are not a summary of the FCC's discussion about why it abandoned its prior understanding of *Pacifica.* They *are* the discussion. These 28 words (repeated in two opinions) do not acknowledge that an entirely different understanding of *Pacifica* underlay the FCC's earlier policy; they do not explain why the agency changed its mind about the line that *Pacifica* draws or its policy's relation to that line; and they tell us nothing at all about what happened to the FCC's earlier determination to search for "compelling interests" and "less restrictive alternatives." They do not explain the transformation of what the FCC had long thought an insurmountable obstacle into an open door. The result is not simply *Hamlet* without the prince, but *Hamlet* with a prince who, in mid-play and without explanation, just disappears.

I have found one other related reference to *Pacifica,* but that reference occurs in an opinion written by a *dissenting* Commissioner. That dissenter said that the FCC had "'fail[ed] to address the many serious [constitutional] concerns raised'" by the new policy, while adding that the new policy was "not the restrained enforcement policy encouraged by the Supreme Court in *Pacifica.*" *Remand Order, supra,* at 13331, 13334. Neither that Commissioner in his dissent, nor I in this dissent, claim that agencies must always take account of possible constitutional issues when they formulate policy. Cf. *ante,* at 1835. But the FCC works in the shadow of the First Amendment and its view of the application of that Amendment to "fleeting expletives" directly informed its initial policy choice. Under these circumstances, the FCC's failure to address this "aspect" of the problem calls for a remand to the agency. *Overton Park,* 401 U.S., at 420-421.

Second, the FCC failed to consider the potential impact of its new policy upon local broadcasting coverage. This "aspect of the problem" is particularly important because the FCC explicitly took account of potential broadcasting impact. *Golden Globe Order, supra,* at 4980, ¶ 11 ("The ease with which broadcasters today can block even fleeting words in a live broadcast is an element in our decision"). Indeed, in setting forth "bleeping" technology changes (presumably lowering bleeping costs) as justifying the policy change, it implicitly reasoned that lower costs, making it easier for broadcasters to install bleeping equipment, made it less likely that the new policy would lead broadcasters to reduce coverage, say by canceling coverage of public events. *Ibid.* ("[T]echnological advances have made it possible . . . to prevent the broadcast of a single offending word or action without blocking or disproportionately disrupting the message of the speaker or performer").

What then did the FCC say about the likelihood that smaller independent broadcasters, including many public service broadcasters, still would not be able to afford "bleeping" technology and, as a consequence, would reduce local coverage, indeed cancel coverage, of many public events? It said nothing at all.

The FCC cannot claim that local coverage lacks special importance. To the contrary, "the concept of localism has been a cornerstone of broadcast regulation for decades." *In re Broadcast Localism,* 23 FCC Rcd. 1324, 1326, 1327, ¶¶ 3, 5, 2008 WL 216994 (2008). That policy seeks to provide "viewers and listeners ... access to locally responsive programming including, but not limited to, local news and public affairs matter" and to ensure "diversity in what is seen and heard over the airwaves." That policy has long favored local broadcasting, both as a means to increase coverage of local events and, insofar as it increases the number of broadcast voices, as an end in itself. See, *e.g., In re Reexamination of Comparative Standards for Noncommercial Educ. Applicants,* 15 FCC Rcd. 7386, 7399, ¶ 29, 2000 WL 756503 (2000) (adopting a system for selecting applicants for broadcast channels that "would foster our goal of broadcast diversity by enabling the local public to be served by differing . . . licensees") . . . .

Neither can the FCC now claim that the impact of its new policy on local broadcasting is insignificant and obviously so. Broadcasters tell us, as they told the FCC, the contrary. . . . They told the FCC, for example, that the costs of bleeping/delay systems, up to $100,000 for installation and annual operation, place that technology beyond the financial reach of many smaller independent local stations. . . . And they ask what the FCC thinks will happen when a small local station without bleeping equipment wants to cover, say a local city council meeting, a high school football game, a dance contest at community center, or a Fourth of July parade.

Relevant literature supports the broadcasters' financial claims. See, *e.g.,* Ho, Taking No Chances, Austin American-Statesman, June 18, 2006, p. J1; Dotinga, Dirty-Word Filters Prove Costly, Wired.com, July 9, 2004, http:// www. wired.com/entertainment/music/news/2004/07/64127; Stations, Cable Networks Finding Indecency Rules Expensive, Public Broadcasting Report, Aug. 4, 2006. It also indicates that the networks with which some small stations are affiliated are not liable for the stations' local transmissions (unless the networks own them). Ho, *supra,* at J1; Public Stations Fear Indecency Fine Jump Means Premium Hikes, Public Broadcasting Report, July 7, 2006. The result is that smaller stations, fearing "fleeting expletive" fines of up to $325,000, may simply cut back on their coverage. See Romano, Reporting Live. Very Carefully, Broadcasting & Cable, July 4, 2005, p. 8; see also *ibid.* ("Afraid to take chances" of getting fined under the FCC's new policy, "local broadcasters are responding by altering-or halting altogether-the one asset that makes local stations so valuable to their communities: live TV"); Daneman, WRUR Drops Its Live Radio Programs, Rochester Democrat and Chronicle, May 27, 2004, p. 1B (reporting that a local broadcast station ceased broadcasting all local live programming altogether in response to the Commission's policy change). And there are many such smaller stations. See, *e.g.*, Corporation for Public Broadcasting, Frequently Asked Questions, available at http://www.cpb.org/aboutpb/faq/stations.html (noting there are over 350 local public television stations and nearly 700 local public radio stations that receive support from the Corporation for Public Broadcasting).

As one local station manager told the FCC,

> "To lessen the risk posed by the new legal framework . . . I have directed [the station's] news staff that [our station] may no longer provide live, direct-to-air coverage" of "live events where crowds are present . . . unless they affect matters of public safety or convenience. Thus, news coverage by [my station] of live events where crowds are present essentially will be limited to civil emergencies." App. 236-237 (declaration of Dennis Fisher).

What did the FCC say in response to this claim? What did it say about the likely impact of the new policy on the coverage that its new policy is most likely to affect, coverage of *local* live events-city council meetings, local sports events, community arts productions, and the like? It said nothing at all.

The plurality acknowledges that the Commission entirely failed to discuss this aspect of the regulatory problem. But it sees "no need" for discussion in light of its, *i.e.*, the plurality's, own "doubt[s]" that "small-town broadcasters run a heightened risk of liability for indecent utterances" as a result of the change of policy. *Ante*, at 1818-1819. The plurality's "doubt[s]" rest upon its views (1) that vulgar expression is less prevalent (at least among broadcast guests) in smaller towns, *ante*, at 1818; (2) that the greatest risk the new policy poses for "small-town broadcasters" arises when they broadcast local "news and public affairs," *ibid.*, and (3) that the *Remand Order* says "little about how the Commission would treat smaller broadcasters who cannot afford screening equipment," while also pointing out that the new policy "'does not . . . impose undue burdens on broadcasters'" and emphasizing that the case before it did not involve "'breaking news.'" *Ante*, at 1818-1819.

As to the first point, about the prevalence of vulgarity in small towns, I confess ignorance. But I do know that there are independent stations in many large and medium sized cities. See Television & Cable Factbook, Directory of Television Stations in Operation 2008. As to the second point, I too believe that coverage of local public events, if not news, lies at the heart of the problem.

I cannot agree with the plurality, however, about the critical third point, namely that the new policy obviously provides smaller independent broadcasters with adequate assurance that they will not be fined. The new policy removes the "fleeting expletive" exception, an exception that assured smaller independent stations that they would not be fined should someone swear at a public event. In its place, it puts a policy that places all broadcasters at risk when they broadcast fleeting expletives, including expletives uttered at public events. The *Remand Order* says that there "is *no outright news exemption from our indecency rules.*" 21 FCC Rcd., at 13327, ¶ 71 (emphasis added). The best it can provide by way of assurance is to say that "it *may* be inequitable to hold a licensee responsible for airing offensive speech during live coverage of a public event *under some circumstances.*" *Id.*, at 13311, ¶ 33 (emphasis added). It does list those circumstances as including the "possibility of human error in using delay equipment." *Id.*, at 13313, ¶ 35. But it says *nothing* about a station's *inability to afford* delay equipment (a matter that in individual cases could itself prove debatable). All the FCC had to do was to *consider* this matter and either grant an exemption or explain why it did not grant an exemption. But it did not. And the result is a rule that may well chill coverage-the kind of consequence that the law has considered important for decades, to which the broadcasters pointed in their arguments before the FCC, and which the FCC nowhere discusses. . . .

Had the FCC used traditional administrative notice-and-comment procedures, 5 U.S.C. § 553, the two failures I have just discussed would clearly require a court to vacate the resulting agency decision. See *ACLU v. FCC,* 823 F.2d 1554, 1581 (C.A.D.C.1987) ("Notice and comment rulemaking procedures obligate the FCC to respond to *all* significant comments, for the opportunity to comment is meaningless unless the agency responds to significant points raised by the public" (emphasis added; internal quotation marks omitted)). Here the agency did not make new policy through the medium of notice and comment proceedings. But the same failures here-where the policy is important, the significance of the issues clear, the failures near complete-should lead us to the same conclusion. The agency's failure to discuss these two "important aspect[s] of the problem" means that the resulting decision is "'arbitrary, capricious, an abuse of discretion'" requiring us to remand the matter to the agency. *State Farm,* 463 U.S., at 43; *Overton Park,* 401 U.S., at 416.

III.

The three reasons the FCC did set forth in support of its change of policy cannot make up for the failures I have discussed. Consider each of them. First, as I have pointed out, the FCC based its decision in part upon the fact that "bleeping/delay systems" technology has advanced. I have already set forth my reasons for believing that that fact, without more, cannot provide a sufficient justification for its policy change. *Supra,* at 1834-1838.

Second, the FCC says that the expletives here in question always invoke a coarse excretory or sexual image; hence it makes no sense to distinguish between whether one uses the relevant terms as an expletive or as a literal description. The problem with this answer is that it does not help to justify the *change* in policy. The FCC was aware of the coarseness of the "image" the first time around. See, *e.g., Remand Order,* 21 FCC Rcd., at 13308, ¶ 23 (asserting that FCC has always understood the words as coarse and indecent). And it explained the first time around why it nonetheless distinguished between their literal use and their use as fleeting expletives. See, *e.g., In re Application of WGBH Educ. Foundation,* 69 F.C.C.2d, at 1254-1255, ¶¶ 10-11 (discussing First Amendment considerations and related need to avoid reduced broadcast coverage). Simply to announce that the words, whether used descriptively or as expletives, call forth similar "images" is not to address those reasons.

Third, the FCC said that "perhaps" its "most importan[t]" justification for the new policy lay in the fact that its new "contextual" approach to fleeting expletives is better and more "[c]onsistent with" the agency's "general approach to indecency" than was its previous "categorica[l]" approach, which offered broadcasters virtual immunity for the broadcast of fleeting expletives. *Remand Order, supra,* at 13308, ¶ 23. This justification, however, offers no support for the change without an understanding of *why, i.e., in what way,* the FCC considered the new approach better or more consistent with the agency's general approach.

The Solicitor General sets forth one way in which the new policy might be more consistent with statutory policy. The indecency statute prohibits the broadcast of "any . . . indecent . . . language." 18 U.S.C. § 1464. The very point of the statute, he says, is to eliminate nuisance; and the use of expletives, even once, can constitute such a nuisance. The Solicitor

General adds that the statutory word "any" indicates that Congress did not intend a safe-harbor for a fleeting use of that language. Brief for Petitioners 24-25. The fatal flaw in this argument, however, lies in the fact that the Solicitor General and not the agency has made it. We must consider the lawfulness of an agency's decision on the basis of the reasons the agency gave, not on the basis of those it *might have* given. . . . And the FCC did not make this claim. Hence, we cannot take it into account and need not evaluate its merits.

In fact, the FCC found that the new policy was better in part because, in its view, the new policy better protects children against what it described as "'the first blow'" of broadcast indecency that results from the "'pervasive'" nature of broadcast media. It wrote that its former policy of "granting an automatic exemption for 'isolated or fleeting' expletives unfairly forces viewers (including children) to take 'the first blow.'" *Remand Order, supra,* at 13309, ¶ 25.

The difficulty with this argument, however, is that it does not explain the *change*. The FCC has long used the theory of the "first blow" to justify its regulation of broadcast indecency. . . . Yet the FCC has also long followed its original "fleeting expletives" policy. Nor was the FCC ever aware of the fact to which the majority points, namely that children's surroundings influence their behavior. . . . So, to repeat the question: What, in respect to the "first blow," has changed?

The FCC points to no empirical (or other) evidence to demonstrate that it previously understated the importance of avoiding the "first blow." Like the majority, I do not believe that an agency must always conduct full empirical studies of such matters. *Ante,* at 1813-1814. But the FCC could have referred to, and explained, relevant empirical studies that suggest the contrary. One review of the empirical evidence, for example, reports that "[i]t is doubtful that children under the age of 12 understand sexual language and innuendo; therefore it is unlikely that vulgarities have any negative effect." Kaye & Sapolsky, Watch Your Mouth! An Analysis of Profanity Uttered by Children on Prime-Time Television, 2004 Mass Communication & Soc'y 429, 433 (Vol.7) (citing two studies). The Commission need not have accepted this conclusion. But its failure to discuss this or any other such evidence, while providing no empirical evidence at all that favors its position, must weaken the logical force of its conclusion. See *State Farm,* 463 U.S., at 43 (explaining that an agency's failure to "examine the relevant data" is a factor in determining whether the decision is "arbitrary").

The FCC also found the new policy better because it believed that its prior policy "would as a matter of logic permit broadcasters to air expletives at all hours of a day so long as they did so one at a time." *Remand Order,* 21 FCC Rcd., at 13309, ¶ 25. This statement, however, raises an obvious question: Did that happen? The FCC's initial "fleeting expletives" policy was in effect for 25 years. Had broadcasters during those 25 years aired a series of expletives "one at a time?" If so, it should not be difficult to find evidence of that fact. But the FCC refers to none. Indeed, the FCC did not even claim that a change had taken place in this respect. It spoke only of the pure "logic" of the initial policy "permitting" such a practice. That logic would have been apparent to anyone, including the FCC, in 1978 when the FCC set forth its initial policy.

Finally, the FCC made certain statements that suggest it did not believe it was changing prior policy in any major way. It referred to that prior policy as based on "staff letters and dicta" and it said that at least one of the instances before it (namely, the Cher broadcast) would have been actionably indecent under that prior policy. Id., at 13306-13307, 13324, ¶¶ 20-21, 60. As we all agree, however, in fact the FCC did change its policy in a major way. See *ante,* at 1812. To the extent that the FCC minimized that fact when considering the change, it did not fully focus on the fact of change. And any such failure would make its decision still less supportable. See *National Cable,* 545 U.S., at 981.

IV.

Were the question a closer one, the doctrine of constitutional avoidance would nonetheless lead me to remand the case. See *United States v. Jin Fuey Moy,* 241 U.S. 394, 401 (1916) ("A statute must be construed, if fairly possible, so as to avoid not only the conclusion that it is unconstitutional but also *grave doubts* upon that score" (emphasis added)). That doctrine seeks to avoid unnecessary judicial consideration of constitutional questions, assumes that Congress, no less than the Judicial Branch, seeks to act within constitutional bounds, and thereby diminishes the friction between the branches that judicial holdings of unconstitutionality might otherwise generate. . . . The doctrine assumes that Congress would prefer a less-than-optimal interpretation of its statute to the grave risk of a constitutional holding that would set the statute entirely aside. . . .

Unlike the majority, I can find no convincing reason for refusing to apply a similar doctrine here. The Court has often applied that doctrine where an agency's regulation relies on a plausible but constitutionally suspect interpretation of a statute. See, *e.g., Solid Waste Agency, supra,* at 172-174; *NLRB v. Catholic Bishop of Chicago,* 440 U.S. 490, 506-507 (1979). The values the doctrine serves apply whether the agency's decision does, or does not, rest upon a constitutionally suspect interpretation of a statute. And a remand here would do no more than ask the agency to reconsider its policy decision in light of the concerns raised in a judicial opinion. . . . I would not now foreclose, as the majority forecloses, our further consideration of this matter. (Of course, nothing in the Court's decision today prevents the Commission from reconsidering its current policy in light of potential constitutional considerations or for other reasons.)

V

In sum, the FCC's explanation of its change leaves out two critically important matters underlying its earlier policy, namely *Pacifica* and local broadcasting coverage. Its explanation rests upon three considerations previously known to the agency ("coarseness," the "first blow," and running single expletives all day, one at a time). With one exception, it provides no empirical or other information explaining why those considerations, which did not justify its new policy before, justify it now. Its discussion of the one exception (technological advances in bleeping/delay systems), failing to take account of local broadcast coverage, is seriously incomplete.

I need not decide whether one or two of these features, standing alone, would require us to remand the case. Here all come together. And taken together they suggest that the FCC's answer to the question, "Why change?" is, "We like the new policy better." This kind of answer, might be perfectly satisfactory were it given by an elected official. But when given by an agency, in respect to a major change of an important policy where much more might be said, it is not sufficient. *State Farm,* 463 U.S., at 41-42.

For these reasons I would find the FCC's decision "arbitrary, capricious, an abuse of discretion,"5 U.S.C. § 706(2)(A), requiring remand of this case to the FCC. And I would affirm the Second Circuit's similar determination.

With respect, I dissent.

FCC v. Fox Television Stations, Inc. (*Fox II*)

132 S. Ct. 2307 (2012)

Justice KENNEDY delivered the opinion of the Court.

In *FCC v. Fox Television Stations, Inc.*, 556 U.S. 502, 529 (2009) *(Fox I)*, the Court held that the Federal Communication Commission's decision to modify its indecency enforcement regime to regulate so-called fleeting expletives was neither arbitrary nor capricious. The Court then declined to address the constitutionality of the policy, however, because the United States Court of Appeals for the Second Circuit had yet to do so. On remand, the Court of Appeals found the policy was vague and, as a result, unconstitutional. 613 F.3d 317 (2010). The case now returns to this Court for decision upon the constitutional question.

I.

In *Fox I*, the Court described both the regulatory framework through which the Commission regulates broadcast indecency and the long procedural history of this case. The Court need not repeat all that history, but some preliminary discussion is necessary to understand the constitutional issue the case now presents.

A.

Title 18 U.S.C. § 1464 provides that "[w]hoever utters any obscene, indecent, or profane language by means of radio communication shall be fined . . . or imprisoned not more than two years, or both." The Federal Communications Commission (Commission) has been instructed by Congress to enforce § 1464 between the hours of 6 a.m. and 10 p.m., see Public Telecommunications Act of 1992, § 15(a), 106 Stat. 954, note following 47 U.S.C. § 303, p. 113 (Broadcasting of Indecent Programming). And the Commission has applied its regulations to radio and television broadcasters alike, see *Fox I, supra*, at 505–506, 129 S.Ct. 1800; see also 47 CFR § 73.3999 (2010) (Commission regulation prohibiting the broadcast of any obscene material or any indecent material between 6 a.m. and 10 p.m.). Although the Commission has had the authority to regulate indecent broadcasts under § 1464 since 1948 (and its predecessor commission, the Federal Radio Commission, since 1927), it did not begin to enforce § 1464 until the 1970's. See Campbell, *Pacifica* Reconsidered: Implications for the Current Controversy over Broadcast Indecency, 63 Fed. Com. L.J. 195, 198 (2010).

This Court first reviewed the Commission's indecency policy in *FCC v. Pacifica Foundation*, 438 U.S. 726 (1978). In *Pacifica*, the Commission determined that George Carlin's "Filthy Words" monologue was indecent. It contained "'language that describes, in terms patently offensive as measured by contemporary community standards for the broadcast medium, sexual or excretory activities and organs, at times of the day when there is a reasonable risk that children may be in the audience.'"

Id., at 732 (quoting 56 F.C.C.2d 94, 98 (1975)). This Court upheld the Commission's ruling. The broadcaster's statutory challenge was rejected. The Court held the Commission was not engaged in impermissible censorship within the meaning of 47 U.S.C. § 326 (1976 ed.), see 438 U.S., at 735–739, and that § 1464's definition of indecency was not confined to speech with an appeal to the prurient interest, see *id.,* at 738–741. Finding no First Amendment violation, the decision explained the constitutional standard under which regulations of broadcasters are assessed. It observed that "broadcast media have established a uniquely pervasive presence in the lives of all Americans," *id.,* at 748, and that "broadcasting is uniquely accessible to children, even those too young to read," *id.,* at 749. In light of these considerations, "broadcasting . . . has received the most limited First Amendment protection." *Id.,* at 748. Under this standard the Commission's order passed constitutional scrutiny. The Court did note the narrowness of its holding, explaining that it was not deciding whether "an occasional expletive . . . would justify any sanction." *Id.,* at 750; see also *id.,* at 760–761 (Powell, J., concurring in part and concurring in judgment) ("[C]ertainly the Court's holding . . . does not speak to cases involving the isolated use of a potentially offensive word in the course of a radio broadcast, as distinguished from the verbal shock treatment administered by respondent here").

From 1978 to 1987, the Commission did not go beyond the narrow circumstances of *Pacifica* and brought no indecency enforcement actions. See *In re Infinity Broadcasting Corp.,* 3 FCC Rcd. 930 (1987); see also *In re Application of WGBH Educ. Foundation,* 69 F.C.C.2d 1250, 1254 (1978) (Commission declaring it "intend[s] strictly to observe the narrowness of the *Pacifica* holding"). Recognizing that *Pacifica* provided "no general prerogative to intervene in any case where words similar or identical to those in *Pacifica* are broadcast over a licensed radio or television station," the Commission distinguished between the "repetitive occurrence of the 'indecent' words" (such as in the Carlin monologue) and an "isolated" or "occasional" expletive, that would not necessarily be actionable. 69 F.C.C.2d, at 1254.

In 1987, the Commission determined it was applying the *Pacifica* standard in too narrow a way. It stated that in later cases its definition of indecent language would "appropriately includ[e] a broader range of material than the seven specific words at issue in [the Carlin monologue]." *In re Pacifica Foundation Inc.,* 2 FCC Rcd. 2698, 2699. Thus, the Commission indicated it would use the "generic definition of indecency" articulated in its 1975 *Pacifica* order, *Infinity* Order, 3 FCC Rcd., at 930, and assess the full context of allegedly indecent broadcasts rather than limiting its regulation to a "comprehensive index . . . of indecent words or pictorial depictions," *id.*, at 932.

Even under this context based approach, the Commission continued to note the important difference between isolated and repeated broadcasts of indecent material. See *ibid.* (considering variables in determining whether material is patently offensive including "whether allegedly offensive material is isolated or fleeting"). In the context of expletives, the Commission determined "deliberate and repetitive use in a patently offensive manner is a requisite to a finding of indecency." *Pacifica* Order, 2 FCC Rcd., at 2699. For speech "involving the description or depiction of sexual or excretory functions . . . [t]he mere fact that specific words or phrases are not repeated does not mandate a finding that material that is otherwise patently offensive . . . is not indecent." *Ibid.*

In 2001, the Commission issued a policy statement intended "to provide guidance to the broadcast industry regarding [its] caselaw interpreting 18 U.S.C. § 1464 and [its] enforcement policies with respect to broadcast indecency." *In re Industry Guidance on Commission's Case Law Interpreting 18 U.S.C. § 1464 and Enforcement Policies Regarding Broadcast Indecency,* 16 FCC Rcd. 7999. In that document the Commission restated that for material to be indecent it must depict sexual or excretory organs or activities and be patently offensive as measured by contemporary community standards for the broadcast medium. *Id.*, at 8002. Describing the framework of what it considered patently offensive, the Commission explained that three factors had proved significant:

> "(1) [T]he explicitness or graphic nature of the description or depiction of sexual or excretory organs or activities; (2) whether the material dwells on or repeats at length descriptions of sexual or excretory organs or activities; (3) whether the material appears to pander or is used to titillate, or whether the material appears to have been presented for its shock value." *Id.*, at 8003 (emphasis deleted).

As regards the second of these factors, the Commission explained that "[r]epetition of and persistent focus on sexual or excretory material have been cited consistently as factors that exacerbate the potential offensiveness of broadcasts. In contrast, where sexual or excretory references have been made once or have been passing or fleeting in nature, this characteristic has tended to weigh against a finding of indecency." *Id.*, at 8008. The Commission then gave examples of material that was not found indecent because it was fleeting and isolated, *id.*, at 8008–8009 (citing, *e.g.*,

L.M. Communications of South Carolina, Inc. (*WYBB(FM)*), 7 FCC Rcd. 1595 (MMB 1992) (finding "a fleeting and isolated utterance" in the context of live and spontaneous programming not actionable)), and contrasted it with fleeting references that were found patently offensive in light of other factors, 16 FCC Rcd., at 8009 (citing, *e.g.*, *Temple Radio, Inc. (KUPD-FM),* 12 FCC Rcd. 21828 (MMB 1997) (finding fleeting language that clearly refers to sexual activity with a child to be patently offensive)).

B.

It was against this regulatory background that the three incidents of alleged indecency at issue here took place. First, in the 2002 Billboard Music Awards, broadcast by respondent Fox Television Stations, Inc., the singer Cher exclaimed during an unscripted acceptance speech: "I've also had my critics for the last 40 years saying that I was on my way out every year. Right. So f*** 'em." 613 F.3d, at 323. Second, Fox broadcast the Billboard Music Awards again in 2003. There, a person named Nicole Richie made the following unscripted remark while presenting an award: "Have you ever tried to get cow s*** out of a Prada purse? It's not so f***ing simple." *Ibid.* The third incident involved an episode of NYPD Blue, a regular television show broadcast by respondent ABC Television Network. The episode broadcast on February 25, 2003, showed the nude buttocks of an adult female character for approximately seven seconds and for a moment the side of her breast. During the scene, in which the character was preparing to take a shower, a child portraying her boy-friend's son entered the bathroom. A moment of awkwardness followed. 404 Fed. Appx. 530, 533–534 (C.A.2 2011). The Commission received indecency complaints about all three broadcasts. See *Fox I,* 556 U.S., at 510.

After these incidents, but before the Commission issued Notices of Apparent Liability to Fox and ABC, the Commission issued a decision sanctioning NBC for a comment made by the singer Bono during the 2003 Golden Globe Awards. Upon winning the award for Best Original Song, Bono exclaimed: "'This is really, really, f***ing brilliant. Really, really great.'" *In re Complaints Against Various Broadcast Licensees Regarding Their Airing of the "Golden Globe Awards" Program,* 19 FCC Rcd. 4975, 4976, n. 4 (2004) (*Golden Globes* Order). Reversing a decision by its enforcement bureau, the Commission found the use of the F-word actionably indecent. *Id.,* at 4975–4976. The Commission held that the word was "one of the most vulgar, graphic and explicit descriptions of sexual activity in the English language," and thus found "any use of that word or a variation, in any context, inherently has a sexual connotation." *Id.,* at 4978–4979. Turning to the isolated nature of the expletive, the Commission reversed prior rulings that had found fleeting expletives not indecent. The Commission held "the mere fact that specific words or phrases are not sustained or repeated does not mandate a finding that material that is otherwise patently offensive to the broadcast medium is not indecent." *Id.*, at 4980; see also *id.*, at 4982 ("Just as the Court [in *Pacifica*] held that . . . the George Carlin routine 'could have enlarged a child's vocabulary in an instant,' we believe that even isolated broadcasts of the 'F-Word' in situations such as that here could do so as well").

C.

Even though the incidents at issue in these cases took place before the *Golden Globes* Order, the Commission applied its new policy regarding fleeting expletives and fleeting nudity. It found the broadcasts by respondents Fox and ABC to be in violation of this standard.

1.

As to Fox, the Commission found the two Billboard Awards broadcasts indecent in *In re Complaints Regarding Various Television Broadcasts Between February 2, 2002, and March 8, 2005,* 21 FCC Rcd. 2664 (2006). Numerous parties petitioned for a review of the order in the United States Court of Appeals for the Second Circuit. The Court of Appeals granted the Commission's request for a voluntary remand so that it could respond to the parties' objections. *Fox Television Stations, Inc. v. FCC,* 489 F.3d 444, 453 (2007). In its remand order, the Commission applied its tripartite definition of patently offensive material from its 2001 Order and found that both broadcasts fell well within its scope. See *In re Complaints Regarding Various Television Broadcasts Between February 2, 2002, and March 8, 2005,* 21 FCC Rcd. 13299 (2006) (*Remand* Order); see also *Fox I, supra,* at 511-513 (discussing in detail the Commission's findings). As pertains to the constitutional issue in these cases, the Commission noted that under the policy clarified in the *Golden Globes* Order, "categorically requiring repeated use of expletives in order to find material indecent is inconsistent with our general approach to indecency enforcement." *Remand* Order, 21 FCC Rcd., at 13308; see also *id.,* at 13325 ("[U]nder our *Golden Globe* precedent, the fact that Cher used the 'F-word' once does not remove her comment from the realm of actionable indecency"). Though the Commission deemed Fox should have known Nicole Richie's comments were actionably indecent even prior to the *Golden Globes* Order, 21 FCC Rcd., at 13307, it declined to propose a forfeiture in light of the limited nature of the Second Circuit's remand. *Id.,* at 13321. The Commission acknowledged that "it was not apparent that Fox could be penalized for Cher's comment at the time it was broadcast." And so, as in the Golden Globes case it imposed no penalty for that broadcast. *Id.,* at 13324, 13326.

Fox and various intervenors returned to the United States Court of Appeals for the Second Circuit, raising administrative, statutory, and constitutional challenges to the Commission's indecency regulations. See *Fox Television Stations, Inc. v. FCC,* 489 F.3d 444. In a 2–to–1 decision, with Judge Leval dissenting, the Court of Appeals found the *Remand* Order arbitrary and capricious because "the FCC has made a 180–degree turn regarding its treatment of 'fleeting expletives' without providing a reasoned explanation justifying the about-face." 489 F.3d, at 455. While noting its skepticism as to whether the Commission's fleeting expletive regime "would pass constitutional muster," the Court of Appeals found it unnecessary to address the issue. *Id.,* at 462.

The case came here on certiorari. Citing the Administrative Procedure Act, 5 U.S.C. § 551 *et seq.,* this Court noted that the Judiciary may set aside agency action that is arbitrary or capricious. In the context of a change in policy (such as the Commission's determination that fleeting expletives could be indecent), the decision held an agency, in the ordinary course, should acknowledge that it is in fact changing its position and "show that there are good reasons for the new policy." *Fox I,* 556 U.S., at 515. There is no need, however, for an agency to provide detailed justifications for every change or to show that the reasons for the new policy are better than the reasons for the old one. *Ibid.*

Judged under this standard, the Court in *Fox I* found the Commission's new indecency enforcement policy neither arbitrary nor capricious. *Id.,* at 517. The Court noted the Commission had acknowledged breaking new ground in ruling that fleeting and nonliteral expletives could be indecent under the controlling standards; the Court concluded the agency's reasons for expanding the scope of its enforcement activity were rational. *Ibid.* Not only was it "certainly reasonable to determine that it made no sense to distinguish between literal and nonliteral uses of offensive words," *ibid.,* but the Court agreed that the Commission's decision to "look at the patent offensiveness of even isolated uses of sexual and excretory words fits with the context-based approach [approved] . . . in *Pacifica.*" *Ibid.* Given that "[e]ven isolated utterances can . . . constitute harmful 'first blow[s]' to children," the Court held that the Commission could "decide it needed to step away from its old regime where nonrepetitive use of an expletive was *per se* nonactionable." *Id.,* at 518, 129 S.Ct. 1800. Having found the agency's action to be neither arbitrary nor capricious, the Court remanded for the Court of Appeals to address respondents' First Amendment challenges. *Id.*, at 529–530.

On remand from *Fox I*, the Court of Appeals held the Commission's indecency policy unconstitutionally vague and invalidated it in its entirety. 613 F.3d, at 327. The Court of Appeals found the policy, as expressed in the 2001 Guidance and subsequent Commission decisions, failed to give broadcasters sufficient notice of what would be considered indecent. Surveying a number of Commission adjudications, the court found the Commission was inconsistent as to which words it deemed patently offensive. See *id.*, at 330. It also determined that the Commission's presumptive prohibition on the F-word and the S-word was plagued by vagueness because the Commission had on occasion found the fleeting use of those words not indecent provided they occurred during a bona fide news interview or were "demonstrably essential to the nature of an artistic or educational work." *Id.*, at 331 (internal quotation marks omitted). The Commission's application of these exceptions, according to the Court of Appeals, left broadcasters guessing whether an expletive would be deemed artistically integral to a program or whether a particular broadcast would be considered a bona fide news interview. The Court of Appeals found the vagueness inherent in the policy had forced broadcasters to "choose between not airing . . . controversial programs [or] risking massive fines or possibly even loss of their licenses." *Id.*, at 334. And the court found that there was "ample evidence in the record" that this harsh choice had led to a chill of protected speech. *Ibid.*

2.

The procedural history regarding ABC is more brief. On February 19, 2008, the Commission issued a forfeiture order finding the display of the woman's nude buttocks in NYPD Blue was actionably indecent. See *In re Complaints Against Various Television Licensees Concerning Their February 24, 2003 Broadcast of the Program "NYPD Blue"*, 23 FCC Rcd. 3147 (2008). The Commission determined that, regardless of medical definitions, displays of buttocks fell within the category of displays of sexual or excretory organs because the depiction was "widely associated with sexual arousal and closely associated by most people with excretory activities." *Id.*, at 3150. The scene was deemed patently offensive as measured by contemporary community standards, *ibid.*; and the Commission determined that "[t]he female actor's nudity is presented in a manner that clearly panders to and titillates the audience," *id.*, at 3153. Unlike in the Fox case, the Commission imposed a forfeiture of $27,500 on each of the 45 ABC-affiliated stations that aired the indecent episode. In a summary order the United States Court of Appeals for the Second Circuit vacated the forfeiture order, determining that it was bound by its *Fox* decision striking down the entirety of the Commission's indecency policy. See 404 Fed. Appx., at 533.

The Government sought review of both judgments, see Brief for Petitioners 1, and this Court granted certiorari, 564 U.S. ---- (2011). These are the cases before us.

II.

A fundamental principle in our legal system is that laws which regulate persons or entities must give fair notice of conduct that is forbidden or required. See *Connally v. General Constr. Co.*, 269 U.S. 385, 391 (1926) ("[A] statute which either forbids or requires the doing of an act in terms so vague that men of common intelligence must necessarily guess at its meaning and differ as to its application, violates the first essential of due process of law"); *Papachristou v. Jacksonville,* 405 U.S. 156, 162 (1972) ("Living under a rule of law entails various suppositions, one of which is that '[all persons] are entitled to be informed as to what the State commands or forbids'" (quoting *Lanzetta v. New Jersey,* 306 U.S. 451, 453 (1939) (alteration in original)). This requirement of clarity in regulation is essential to the protections provided by the Due Process Clause of the Fifth Amendment. See *United States v. Williams,* 553 U.S. 285, 304 (2008). It requires the invalidation of laws that are impermissibly vague. A conviction or punishment fails to comply with due process if the statute or regulation under which it is obtained "fails to provide a person of ordinary intelligence fair notice of what is prohibited, or is so standardless that it authorizes or encourages seriously discriminatory enforcement." *Ibid.* As this Court has explained, a regulation is not vague because it may at times be difficult to prove an incriminating fact but rather because it is unclear as to what fact must be proved. See *id.,* at 306.

Even when speech is not at issue, the void for vagueness doctrine addresses at least two connected but discrete due process concerns: first, that regulated parties should know what is required of them so they may act accordingly; second, precision and guidance are necessary so that those enforcing the law do not act in an arbitrary or discriminatory way. See *Grayned v. City of Rockford,* 408 U.S. 104, 108-109 (1972). When speech is involved, rigorous adherence to those requirements is necessary to ensure that ambiguity does not chill protected speech.

These concerns are implicated here because, at the outset, the broadcasters claim they did not have, and do not have, sufficient notice of what is proscribed. And leaving aside any concerns about facial invalidity, they contend that the lengthy procedural history set forth above shows that the broadcasters did not have fair notice of what was forbidden. Under the 2001 Guidelines in force when the broadcasts occurred, a key consideration was "'whether the material dwell[ed] on or repeat[ed] at length'" the offending description or depiction. 613 F.3d, at 322. In the 2004 *Golden Globes* Order, issued after the broadcasts, the Commission changed course and held that fleeting expletives could be a statutory violation. *Fox I,* 556 U.S., at 512. In the challenged orders now under review the Commission applied the new principle promulgated in the *Golden Globes* Order and determined fleeting expletives and a brief moment of indecency were actionably indecent. This regulatory history, however, makes it apparent that the Commission policy in place at the time of the broadcasts gave no notice to Fox or ABC that a fleeting expletive or a brief shot of nudity could be actionably indecent; yet Fox and ABC were found to be in violation. The Commission's lack of notice to Fox and ABC that its interpretation had changed so the fleeting moments of indecency contained in their broadcasts were a violation of § 1464 as interpreted and enforced by the agency "fail[ed] to provide a person of ordinary intelligence fair notice of what is prohibited." *Williams, supra,* at 304. This would be true with respect to a regulatory change this abrupt on any subject, but it is surely the case when applied to the regulations in question, regulations that touch upon "sensitive areas of basic First Amendment freedoms," *Baggett v. Bullitt,* 377 U.S. 360, 372 (1964); see also *Reno v. American Civil Liberties Union,* 521 U.S. 844, 870-871 (1997) ("The vagueness of [a content-based regulation of speech] raises special First Amendment concerns because of its obvious chilling effect").

The Government raises two arguments in response, but neither is persuasive. As for the two fleeting expletives, the Government concedes that "Fox did not have reasonable notice at the time of the broadcasts that the Commission would consider non-repeated expletives indecent." Brief for Petitioners 28, n. 3. The Government argues, nonetheless, that Fox "cannot establish unconstitutional vagueness on that basis . . . because the Commission did not impose a sanction where Fox lacked such notice." *Ibid.* As the Court observed when the case was here three Terms ago, it is true that the Commission declined to impose any forfeiture on Fox, see 556 U.S., at 513, and in its order the Commission claimed that it would not consider the indecent broadcasts either when considering whether to renew stations' licenses or "in any other context," 21 FCC Rcd., at 13321, 13326. This "policy of forbearance," as the Government calls it, does not suffice to make the issue moot. Brief for Petitioners 31. Though the Commission claims it will not consider the prior indecent broadcasts "in any context," it has the statutory power to take into account "any history of prior offenses" when setting the level of a forfeiture penalty. See 47 U.S.C. § 503(b)(2)(E). Just as in the First Amendment context, the due process protection against vague regulations "does not leave [regulated parties] . . . at the mercy of *noblesse oblige*." *United States v. Stevens,* 130 S.Ct. 1577 (2010). Given that the Commission found it was "not inequitable to hold Fox responsible for [the 2003 broadcast]," 21 FCC Rcd., at 13314, and that it has the statutory authority to use its finding to increase any future penalties, the Government's assurance it will elect not to do so is insufficient to remedy the constitutional violation.

In addition, when combined with the legal consequence described above, reputational injury provides further reason for granting relief to Fox. Cf. *Paul v. Davis,* 424 U.S. 693, 708–709 (1976) (explaining that an "alteration of legal status . . . combined with the injury resulting from the defamation" justifies the invocation of procedural safeguards). As respondent CBS points out, findings of wrongdoing can result in harm to a broadcaster's "reputation with viewers and advertisers." Brief for Respondent CBS Television Network Affiliates Assn. et al. 17. This observation is hardly surprising given that the challenged orders, which are contained in the permanent Commission record, describe in strongly disapproving terms the indecent material broadcast by Fox, see, *e.g.,* 21 FCC Rcd., at 13310-13311, ¶ 30 (noting the "explicit, graphic, vulgar, and shocking nature of Ms. Richie's comments"), and Fox's efforts to protect children from being exposed to it, see *id.,* at 13311, ¶ 33 (finding Fox had failed to exercise "'reasonable judgment, responsibility, and sensitivity to the public's needs and tastes to avoid [a] patently offensive broadcas[t]'"). Commission sanctions on broadcasters for indecent material are widely publicized. See, *e.g.,* F.C.C. Fines Fox, N.Y. Times, Feb. 26, 2008, p. E2; F.C.C. Plans Record Fine for CBS, Washington Post, Sept. 24, 2004, p. E1. The challenged orders could have an adverse impact on Fox's reputation that audiences and advertisers alike are entitled to take into account.

With respect to ABC, the Government with good reason does not argue no sanction was imposed. The fine against ABC and its network affiliates for the seven seconds of nudity was nearly $1.24 million. See Brief for Respondent ABC, Inc., et al. 7 (hereinafter ABC Brief). The Government argues instead that ABC had notice that the scene in NYPD Blue would be considered indecent in light of a 1960 decision where the Commission declared that the "televising of nudes might well raise a serious question of programming contrary to 18 U.S.C. § 1464." Brief for Petitioners 32 (quoting *Enbanc Programming Inquiry,* 44 FCC 2303, 2307 (internal quotation marks omitted)). This argument does not prevail. An isolated and ambiguous statement from a 1960 Commission decision does not suffice for the fair notice required when the Government intends to impose over a $1 million fine for allegedly impermissible speech. The Commission, furthermore, had released decisions before sanctioning ABC that declined to find isolated and brief moments of nudity actionably indecent. See, *e.g., In re Application of WGBH,* 69 F.C.C.2d, at 1251, 1255 (declining to find broadcasts containing nudity to be indecent and emphasizing the difference between repeated and isolated expletives); *In re WPBN/WTOM License Subsidiary, Inc.,* 15 FCC Rcd. 1838, 1840 (2000) (finding full frontal nudity in Schindler's List not indecent). This is not to say, of course, that a graphic scene from Schindler's List involving nude concentration camp prisoners is the same as the shower scene from NYPD Blue. It does show, however, that the Government can point to nothing that would have given ABC affirmative notice that its broadcast would be considered actionably indecent. It is likewise not sufficient for the Commission to assert, as it did in its order, that though "the depiction [of nudity] here is not as lengthy or repeated" as in some cases, the shower scene nonetheless "does contain more shots or lengthier depictions of nudity" than in other broadcasts found not indecent. 23 FCC Rcd., at 3153. This broad language fails to demonstrate that ABC had fair notice that its broadcast could be found indecent. In fact, a Commission ruling prior to the airing of the NYPD Blue episode had deemed 30 seconds of nude buttocks "very brief" and not actionably indecent in the context of the broadcast. See Letter from Norman Goldstein to David Molina, FCC File No. 97110028 (May 26, 1999), in App. to Brief for Respondent ABC Television Affiliates Assn. et al.; see also Letter from Edythe Wise to Susan Cavin, FCC File No. 91100738 (Aug. 13, 1992), *id.,* at 18a, 19a. In light of this record of agency decisions, and the absence of any notice in the 2001 Guidance that seven seconds of nude buttocks would be found indecent, ABC lacked constitutionally sufficient notice prior to being sanctioned.

The Commission failed to give Fox or ABC fair notice prior to the broadcasts in question that fleeting expletives and momentary nudity could be found actionably indecent. Therefore, the Commission's standards as applied to these broadcasts were vague, and the Commission's orders must be set aside.

III.

It is necessary to make three observations about the scope of this decision. First, because the Court resolves these cases on fair notice grounds under the Due Process Clause, it need not address the First Amendment implications of the Commission's indecency policy. It is argued that this Court's ruling in *Pacifica* (and the less rigorous standard of scrutiny it provided for the regulation of broadcasters, see 438 U.S. 726) should be overruled because the rationale of that case has been overtaken by technological change and the wide availability of multiple other choices for listeners and viewers. See, *e.g.*, ABC Brief 48–57; Brief for Respondent Fox Television Stations, Inc., et al. 15–26. The Government for its part maintains that when it licenses a conventional broadcast spectrum, the public may assume that the Government has its own interest in setting certain standards. See Brief for Petitioners 40–53. These arguments need not be addressed here. In light of the Court's holding that the Commission's policy failed to provide fair notice it is unnecessary to reconsider *Pacifica* at this time.

This leads to a second observation. Here, the Court rules that Fox and ABC lacked notice at the time of their broadcasts that the material they were broadcasting could be found actionably indecent under then-existing policies. Given this disposition, it is unnecessary for the Court to address the constitutionality of the current indecency policy as expressed in the *Golden Globes* Order and subsequent adjudications. The Court adheres to its normal practice of declining to decide cases not before it. See, *e.g.*, *Sweatt v. Painter*, 339 U.S. 629, 631, 70 S.Ct. 848, 94 L.Ed. 1114 (1950) ("Broader issues have been urged for our consideration, but we adhere to the principle of deciding constitutional questions only in the context of the particular case before the Court").

Third, this opinion leaves the Commission free to modify its current indecency policy in light of its determination of the public interest and applicable legal requirements. And it leaves the courts free to review the current policy or any modified policy in light of its content and application.

. . .

The judgments of the United States Court of Appeals for the Second Circuit are vacated, and the cases are remanded for further proceedings consistent with the principles set forth in this opinion.

It is so ordered.

Justice SOTOMAYOR took no part in the consideration or decision of these cases.

Justice GINSBURG, concurring in the judgment.

In my view, the Court's decision in *FCC v. Pacifica Foundation*, 438 U.S. 726 (1978), was wrong when it issued. Time, technological advances, and the Commission's untenable rulings in the cases now before the Court show why *Pacifica* bears reconsideration. Cf. *FCC v. Fox Television Stations, Inc.*, 556 U.S. 502, 532-535 (2009) (THOMAS, J., concurring).

Children's Programming

In 1990, Congress enacted the Children's Television Act (CTA). The CTA introduced a number of broadcast programming requirements designed to enrich children, and to protect them from undue consumerism. Sec. 317, for example, prevents a station from airing commercials featuring the same characters appearing in the program that the commercial supports. This means that *The Smurfs'* toy commercials cannot air during *The Smurfs* television show, although the toys could still be advertised during other programs. The CTA also requires broadcasters to announce when they are going to commercial during a children's program. As you can see from the Report and Order infra, the FCC is concerned that children may be easy prey for the type of consumerism that adults take for granted. In 1984, the commission removed limits on the number of commercials that can air on adult programs, ushering in the era of the infomercial. Left intact, however, were strict limitations in the number of commercial minutes that can be aired during children's programming. Infomercials for children, as a result, are an impossibility on broadcast television.

The main concern of the Report and Order is enforcement of the CTA's requirement that each broadcaster air three hours of educational children's programming each week. After stations attempted compliance with shows such as *The Flintstones* and *The Jetsons*, the FCC stiffened the requirements for the three hours. Children's programs must now be specifically designed to be educational and informative—designated by an " e/i" onscreen. As you complete your review of the policy statement infra, ask on what basis these content regulations are regarded as consistent with the First Amendment.

FCC REPORT AND ORDER

IN THE MATTER OF POLICIES AND RULES CONCERNING CHILDREN'S TELEVISION PROGRAMMING
11 FCC RCD. 10660 (1996)

1. In this Order, we take action to strengthen our enforcement of the Children's Television Act of 1990 ("CTA"), which requires the Commission, in its review of each television broadcast license renewal application, to "consider the extent to which the licensee . . . has served the educational and informational needs of children through the licensee's overall programming, including programming specifically designed to serve such needs." In enacting the CTA, Congress found that television has the power to teach children—that "television can assist children to learn important information, skills, values, and behavior, while entertaining them and exciting their curiosity to learn about the world around them." Congress also found, however, that there are significant market disincentives for commercial broadcasters to air children's educational and informational programming. The rules we adopt today are intended to counteract these market disincentives and to ensure that broadcasters fulfill the promise of the Children's Television Act to our nation's children. We alter our regulations to provide greater clarity about broadcasters' obligation under the CTA to air programming "specifically designed" to serve the educational and informational needs of children and to improve public access to information about the availability of these programs.

Big Bird meets First Lady Michelle Obama in the White House kitchen, 2013. Begun in 1969, "Sesame Street" is a venerable model for educational and instructional kid's programming.

2. As explained in greater detail below, we conclude that our initial regulations implementing the CTA have not been fully effective in

prompting broadcasters "to increase the amount of educational and informational broadcast television programming available to children." Our review of the record in this proceeding reveals several problems. First, because of their imprecision in defining the scope of a broadcaster's obligation under the Children's Television Act, our rules have led to a variation in the level and nature of broadcasters' compliance efforts that is incompatible with the intent of the CTA. . . . Second, some broadcasters are claiming to have satisfied their statutory obligations with shows that, by any reasonable benchmark, cannot be said to be "specifically designed" to educate and inform children within the meaning of the CTA. Third, parents and others frequently lack timely access to information about the availability of programming in their communities specifically designed to educate and inform children, exacerbating market disincentives. Therefore, as proposed in the Notice of Proposed Rule Making ("NPRM") we released in April 1995, we refine our policies and rules implementing the CTA to remedy these problems.

. . .

14. For over 30 years, the Commission has recognized that, as part of their obligation as trustees of the public's airwaves, broadcasters must provide programming that serves the special needs of children. The Commission's efforts to promote programming for children began in 1960 with the statement that children were one of the several groups whose programming needs television licensees must meet to fulfill their community public interest responsibilities. In 1974, the Commission specifically recognized that broadcasters have an obligation to provide children's educational programming. . . . The Commission concluded at that time, however, that it was not necessary to prescribe the number of hours of such programming that broadcasters should show per week. Instead, the Commission stated that it expected the industry to take steps voluntarily to increase the amount of educational and informational programming for children.

. . .

29. . . . (I)n enacting the CTA, Congress found that market forces were not sufficient to ensure that commercial stations would provide children's educational and information programming. Congress concluded that the same problems that the Commission found in 1976 still existed and that market forces had not worked to increase the educational and information programming available to children on commercial television.

. . .

84. . . . We believe that, to qualify as core programming, a show must have serving the educational and informational needs of children ages 16 and under as a significant purpose. The "significant purpose" standard appropriately acknowledges the point advanced by broadcasters and others that to be successful, and thus to serve children's needs as mandated by the CTA, educational and informational programming must also be entertaining and attractive to children. Accordingly, as proposed in the NPRM, we will require that core programming be specifically designed to meet the educational and informational needs of children ages 16 and under and have educating and informing children as a significant purpose.

. . .

93. . . . We are persuaded that we should adopt our proposal to require that the educational and informational objective of core programming be specified in writing. Requiring a statement of educational and informational purpose will ensure that broadcasters devote attention to the educational and informational goals of core programming and how those goals may be achieved. A written statement of educational and information purpose should also assist licensees to distinguish programs specifically designed to serve children's educational and informational needs from programs whose primary purpose is to entertain children. . . .

95. We will also require licensees to indicate a specific target age group for core programs. . . . Requiring licensees to specify the age group [for] a core program is intended to encourage them to consider whether the content of the program is suited to the interests, knowledge, vocabulary, and other abilities of that group. In addition, this requirement will provide information to parents regarding the appropriate age for core programs, thereby facilitating increased program audience and ratings. We decline, however, to identify particular age ranges of children to which core programs may be directed. We prefer to leave broadcasters the discretion to develop programs suited to children with similar educational and informational needs and to counterprogram to distinct portions of the child audience as they believe appropriate.

96. In addition, we decline to require broadcasters to serve particular segments of the child audience. . . . (W)e tentatively concluded that it would be undesirable to require broadcasters to serve particular segments of the child audience, in part because we did not have adequate

data showing that in fact younger age groups are underserved relative to other children. . . . Accordingly, we adhere to our view that we should not at this time require broadcasters to serve particular segments of the child audience, particularly in light of the significant new steps we have adopted to promote the overall availability of children's educational and informational programming.

. . .

99. . . . After considering the evidence, we will limit the hours within which programming may qualify as core to a narrower time frame than that proposed in the NPRM. To qualify as core, a program must air between the hours of 7:00 a.m. and 10:00 p.m. In specifying this time period, our intention is to encourage broadcasters to air educational programming at times the maximum number of child viewers will be watching. . . .

. . .

110. . . . We believe that core programming should be at least 30 minutes in length. In enacting the CTA, Congress identified a number of examples of worthwhile educational and informational programs, all of which are at least one half-hour in length. . . . There was no evidence presented in response to the NPRM to support claims by some parties that children have short attention spans and thus will not benefit from substantial length programming.

. . .

147. . . . The First Amendment arguments raised by opponents of our proposed CTA regulations essentially fall into two categories—arguments that attack the CTA obligation and arguments that attack the quantification of the CTA obligation. To the extent that some commenters argue that the CTA is unconstitutional, Congress itself addressed that issue. It specifically concluded that "it is well within the First Amendment strictures to require the FCC to consider, during the license renewal process, whether a television licensee has provided information specifically designed to serve the educational and informational needs of children in the context of its overall programming." As the Senate Report noted, broadcasters, in exchange for "the free and exclusive use of a valuable part of the public domain," can be expected to serve as a public fiduciary, obliged to serve the needs and interests of their viewers. That obligation includes the obligation to serve the needs of children. Even

more specifically, as the FCC, the courts, and Congress have concluded, a broadcaster's public interest obligation properly includes an obligation to serve the educational and informational needs of children. The question in this proceeding is not whether the Commission should give effect to the CTA, but how it should do so.

. . .

149. The course we adopt today—defining what qualifies as programming "specifically designed" to serve the educational needs of children and giving broadcasters clear but nonmandatory guidance on how to guarantee compliance—is a constitutional means of giving effect to the CTA's programming requirement. "It does not violate the First Amendment to treat licensees given the privilege of using scarce radio frequencies as proxies for the entire community, obligated to give suitable time and attention to matters of great public concern." Red Lion Broadcasting Co. v. FCC, 395 U.S. 367, 394 (1969). Congress's authority to order "suitable time and attention to matters of great public concern" includes the authority to require broadcasters to air programming specifically designed to further the educational needs of children. The airwaves belong to the public, not to any individual broadcaster. As the Supreme Court observed in CBS, Inc. v. FCC, "a licensed broadcaster is 'granted the free and exclusive use of a limited and valuable part of the public domain; when he accepts that franchise it is burdened by enforceable public obligations.'" The fact that Congress elected to retain public ownership of the broadcast spectrum and to lease it for free to private licensees for limited periods carries significant First Amendment consequences.

. . .

152. Our new regulations, like the CTA itself, impose reasonable, viewpoint-neutral conditions on a broadcaster's free use of the public airwaves. They do not censor or foreclose speech of any kind. They do not tell licensees what topics they must address. They provide only that broadcasters report the educational objective of the program and the expected educational effects. Moreover, they expressly provide that broadcasters need not describe the viewpoint of the program or the opinions expressed on the program.

153. The CTA and our regulations directly advance the government's substantial, and indeed compelling, interest in the education of America's children. As Congress recognized, "[i]t is difficult to think of an interest more substantial than the promotion of the welfare of children who

watch so much television and rely upon it for so much of the information they receive." In other contexts, the courts and commentators have recognized the government's "compelling" interest in "safeguarding the physical and psychological well being" of minors.

. . .

157. . . . But even if evaluated under a heightened standard, our rules would pass muster because the interest advanced is compelling and our regulations are narrowly tailored. As detailed above, our regulations are no more burdensome than necessary to ensure that children will be able to watch educational and informational programming. Like the CTA, our regulations require broadcasters to air children's educational and informational programming, but do not "exclude any programming that does in fact serve the educational and informational needs of children; rather the broadcaster has discretion to meet its public service obligation in the way it deems best suited." Specifically, the processing guideline that we adopt today does not limit this discretion. . . . In addition, a broadcaster can rely on other more general programming and related non-programming efforts to satisfy its CTA obligation—albeit after full Commission review.

NOTES AND QUESTIONS

1. Note that scarcity is not a justification for indecency regulation. But should it be? Otherwise, how is indecency different from the public display of "Fuck the Draft" outside a courtroom as in *Cohen* in Chapter 1?
2. At the time of *Pacifica*, broadcast television and radio stations were relatively few and content distribution was subject to control by licensees. Today, children can access all sorts of indecent content online—from intimate live chats to pornography—often without their parents knowing. Has broadcast indecency become a relic in an age of digital production and user-controlled distribution?
3. The V-chip, discussed in the next chapter, now makes it possible for parents to filter programming based on ratings that denote age-appropriateness and categories relating to sex and violence. Is this filtering technology, required by law on every modern television, a less-restrictive means of accomplishing the government's goals than channeling? If so, what impact would it have on the constitutionality of indecency regulation?

4. **After-hours indecency.** As a general matter, broadcast stations do not air indecency during the safe harbor, even though they may do so. Hip late-night talk shows still avoid expletives or nudity, and even "Saturday Night Live" has occasionally operated on a seven-second delay. Why?
5. In 2004, after several run-ins with the FCC over indecency, "shock jock" Howard Stern left his syndicated broadcast-radio perch for satellite radio, a subscription service that is exempt from indecency regulation. In the last decade, satellite radio has grown from a little-known novelty to a ubiquitous radio service that is preloaded into cars and aired in public places. Should the government apply indecency regulations to this service? Are the government's interests somehow different because satellite radio offers subscriptions?
6. **Newsworthy indecency.** Vice President Nelson Rockefeller flipped his middle finger at a heckler during a rally's live broadcast. In the *Becker* case supra, the FCC argued that broadcasters had the right to channel indecent political ads. Does a political or news context change your analysis of the constitutionality of indecency regulation? Should it matter that the news or political coverage was live-to-air or pre-taped? See *Pacifica Foundation*, 59 F.C.C. 2d 892 (1976).
7. In its 1996 Report and Order, the FCC concluded that its children's television program regulations are constitutional as part of a broadcaster's public-interest obligation, citing the scarcity rationale of *Red Lion*. In the final paragraphs, the FCC suggested that the interest is compelling enough, and the burden sufficiently tailored, to withstand strict scrutiny. Do you agree with either or both of these justifications?
8. **The politics of indecency**. During the May 1, 2017 broadcast of *The Late Show* on CBS, Stephen Colbert used a crude sexual term in a political joke about Donald Trump and Russian president Vladimir Putin. The FCC received thousands of complaints, mainly from Trump supporters and from some gay rights advocates. After initially announcing an investigation, the FCC determined that Colbert's joke did not warrant any action by the agency. Note that *The Late Show* airs at 11:35 pm in most markets, well within the overnight safe harbor for broadcasters.

CHAPTER 11

VIOLENCE & PUBLIC SAFETY

For decades, psychologists and communications scholars have explored the relationship between violent representations in media and aggressive behavior among those who consume those representations. Whether it's a crime drama on television, a gory video game, or a "crush video" on YouTube, depictions of violence—real and fabricated—saturate today's media landscape. What to do about media violence remains an intractable issue in our culture.

As the *Stevens* and *Brown* cases infra make clear, there is little support in the courts for treating violence as a form of unprotected speech, in the same manner that the courts regulate obscene speech. Obscenity, to paraphrase Justice Potter Stewart, is easy to recognize. Violence, on the other hand, is a pervasive part of culture. We see it exhibited on the nightly news, choreographed in Quentin Tarantino films, and spoofed in "Road Runner" cartoons. The taboo that exists in our culture for even explicit images of loving, consensual sex does not exist for even the most extreme images of gore and mayhem. The National Association of Broadcasters (NAB), until the 1980s, enforced restrictions on violent content among its constituent television stations. After the NAB abandoned its code, restrictions against violence on television became a matter of individual station policy, which often meant little or no curbs.

With the First Amendment as a bar to state action and market forces as an effective deterrent against industry efforts, Congress devised a system in which the government mandated a filtering system, but left it to broadcasters to decide how to rate the content subject to the filter. This hybrid filter-ratings system, created by section 551 of the Telecommunications Act of 1996, requires all televisions to have a device known as a V-chip, and directed broadcasters to develop ratings that would allow parents and others to block violent or sexually suggestive content they may find objectionable. Although some networks and program producers were initially opposed to any form of government intervention on violence, few are critical of the V-chip today, especially since studies have shown that few households actually use it to filter programs.

In addition to depictions of violence, there is also an issue as to whether media outlets should be liable for the impact that a violent representation allegedly had on third parties. In the *Olivia N.* case infra, the plaintiff tried unsuccessfully to sue NBC in tort for "indirect harm" that a young girl suffered at the hands of boys who were allegedly inspired by a violent network program. Victims who injure themselves after watching a violent show have also tried to sue for the "direct harm" allegedly caused by the media company, again without success. In the absence of inducement, courts are unwilling to impose a duty on mass media to avoid causing injury to the public; they are also unwilling to find proximate causation for the subjective reaction of third parties outside of their control. The FCC, however, does have rules in place to assure that broadcasters do not fabricate hoaxes or create panic to the public-at-large. With the exception of some radio "shock jocks" who used hoaxes for self-promotion, most broadcasters avoid running afoul of the regulation by using disclaimers. Even Orson Welles' famous 1938 "War of the Worlds" radio broadcast, a performance of a fictional real-time alien invasion account that caused panic among his audience, would have been in compliance with the current regulation because it was punctuated with disclaimers.

The final two cases in this chapter deal with the complicated issue of true threats, a relatively narrow category of intimidating speech directed toward individuals that is unprotected by the First Amendment. In Planned Parenthood of Columbia/Willamette, Inc. v. ACLA, a bitterly divided Ninth Circuit addresses media liability under a federal statute designed to protect abortion providers from true threats. Sitting en banc, a narrow majority ultimately held an anti-abortion Web site liable for posting photos of doctors who performed abortions. Those doctors felt threatened because a third party unrelated and unknown to the website was killing the pictured doctors. The majority found for the doctors, even though ACLA did not subjectively intend to threaten bodily harm. Judge Kozinski's dissent, reprinted here in part, excoriates the majority for trampling over the anti-abortion activists' First Amendment right to engage in political speech.

In June 2015, the U.S. Supreme Court decided Elonis v. United States, a case involving a self-styled rapper who posted graphically violent lyrics about his estranged wife and others on Facebook. Elonis, writing as "Tone Dougie,"used disclaimers to emphasize that his lyrics were imaginative expressions of artistry protected by the First Amendment. Confining the Court's analysis to the concept of mens rea under criminal law, Chief Justice Roberts's majority opinion determined that the Federal true threat statute at issue requires a subjective intent to threaten, not an objective intent. Only Justices Alito and Thomas, in two separate opinions, considered the First Amendment issue timely, though neither would have deemed Elonis's posts to be protected speech.

Violence in Media

BROWN V. ENTERTAINMENT MERCHANTS ASS'N
131 S. Ct. 2729 (2011)

Justice SCALIA delivered the opinion of the Court.
We consider whether a California law imposing restrictions on violent video games comports with the First Amendment.

I.
California Assembly Bill 1179 (2005), Cal. Civ. Code Ann. §§ 1746-1746.5 (West 2009) (Act), prohibits the sale or rental of "violent video games" to minors, and requires their packaging to be labeled "18." The Act covers games "in which the range of options available to a player includes killing, maiming, dismembering, or sexually assaulting an image of a human being, if those acts are depicted" in a manner that "[a] reasonable person, considering the game as a whole, would find appeals to a deviant or morbid interest of minors," that is "patently offensive to prevailing standards in the community as to what is suitable for minors," and that "causes the game, as a whole, to lack serious literary, artistic, political, or scientific value for minors." § 1746(d)(1)(A). Violation of the Act is punishable by a civil fine of up to $1,000. § 1746.3.

Respondents, representing the video-game and software industries, brought a preenforcement challenge to the Act in the United States District Court for the Northern District of California. . . .

II.
California correctly acknowledges that video games qualify for First Amendment protection. The Free Speech Clause exists principally to protect discourse on public matters, but we have long recognized that it is difficult to distinguish politics from entertainment, and dangerous to try. "Everyone is familiar with instances of propaganda through fiction. What is one man's amusement, teaches another's doctrine." *Winters v. New York,* 333 U.S. 507, 510 (1948). Like the protected books, plays, and movies that preceded them, video games communicate ideas—and even social messages—through many familiar literary devices (such as characters, dialogue, plot, and music) and through features distinctive to the medium (such as the player's interaction with the virtual world). That

suffices to confer First Amendment protection. Under our Constitution, "esthetic and moral judgments about art and literature . . . are for the individual to make, not for the Government to decree, even with the mandate or approval of a majority." *United States v. Playboy Entertainment Group, Inc.,* 529 U.S. 803, 818 (2000). And whatever the challenges of applying the Constitution to ever-advancing technology, "the basic principles of freedom of speech and the press, like the First Amendment's command, do not vary" when a new and different medium for communication appears. *Joseph Burstyn, Inc. v. Wilson,* 343 U.S. 495, 503 (1952).

The most basic of those principles is this: "[A]s a general matter, . . . government has no power to restrict expression because of its message, its ideas, its subject matter, or its content." *Ashcroft v. American Civil Liberties Union,* 535 U.S. 564, 573 (2002) (internal quotation marks omitted). There are of course exceptions. "'From 1791 to the present,' . . . the First Amendment has 'permitted restrictions upon the content of speech in a few limited areas,' and has never 'include[d] a freedom to disregard these traditional limitations.'" *United States v. Stevens*, 130 S.Ct. 1577, 1584 (2010) (quoting *R.A.V. v. St. Paul,* 505 U.S. 377, 382-383 (1992)). These limited areas—such as obscenity, *Roth v. United States,* 354 U.S. 476, 483 (1957), incitement, *Brandenburg v. Ohio,* 395 U.S. 444, 447-449 (1969) *(per curiam),* and fighting words, *Chaplinsky v. New Hampshire,* 315 U.S. 568, 572 (1942)—represent "well-defined and narrowly limited classes of speech, the prevention and punishment of which have never been thought to raise any Constitutional problem," *id.,* at 571-572.

Last Term, in *Stevens,* we held that new categories of unprotected speech may not be added to the list by a legislature that concludes certain speech is too harmful to be tolerated. *Stevens* concerned a federal statute purporting to criminalize the creation, sale, or possession of certain depictions of animal cruelty. See 18 U.S.C. § 48 (amended 2010). The statute covered depictions "in which a living animal is intentionally maimed, mutilated, tortured, wounded, or killed" if that harm to the animal was illegal where the "the creation, sale, or possession t[ook] place," § 48(c)(1). A saving clause largely borrowed from our obscenity jurisprudence, see *Miller v. California,* 413 U.S. 15, 24 (1973), exempted depictions with "serious religious, political, scientific, educational, journalistic, historical, or artistic value," § 48(b). We held that statute to be an impermissible content-based restriction on speech. There was no American tradition of forbidding the *depiction of* animal cruelty—though States have long had laws against *committing* it.

The Government argued in *Stevens* that lack of a historical warrant did not matter; that it could create new categories of unprotected speech by applying a "simple balancing test" that weighs the value of a particular category of speech against its social costs and then punishes that category of speech if it fails the test. *Stevens*, 130 S.Ct., at 1585. We emphatically rejected that "startling and dangerous" proposition. *Ibid.* "Maybe there are some categories of speech that have been historically unprotected, but have not yet been specifically identified or discussed as such in our case law." *Id.*, at 1586. But without persuasive evidence that a novel restriction on content is part of a long (if heretofore unrecognized) tradition of proscription, a legislature may not revise the "judgment [of] the American people," embodied in the First Amendment, "that the benefits of its restrictions on the Government outweigh the costs." *Id.*, at 1585.

That holding controls this case. As in *Stevens*, California has tried to make violent-speech regulation look like obscenity regulation by appending a saving clause required for the latter. That does not suffice. Our cases have been clear that the obscenity exception to the First Amendment does not cover whatever a legislature finds shocking, but only depictions of "sexual conduct," *Miller, supra*, at 24. See also *Cohen v. California*, 403 U.S. 15, 20 (1971); *Roth, supra*, at 487, and n. 20.

Stevens was not the first time we have encountered and rejected a State's attempt to shoehorn speech about violence into obscenity. In *Winters*, we considered a New York criminal statute "forbid[ding] the massing of stories of bloodshed and lust in such a way as to incite to crime against the person," 333 U.S., at 514. The New York Court of Appeals upheld the provision as a law against obscenity. "[T]here can be no more precise test of written indecency or obscenity," it said, "than the continuing and changeable experience of the community as to what types of books are likely to bring about the corruption of public morals or other analogous injury to the public order." *Id.*, at 514 (internal quotation marks omitted). That is of course the same expansive view of governmental power to abridge the freedom of speech based on interest-balancing that we rejected in *Stevens*. Our opinion in *Winters*, which concluded that the New York statute failed a heightened vagueness standard applicable to restrictions upon speech entitled to First Amendment protection, 333 U.S., at 517–519, made clear that violence is not part of the obscenity that the Constitution permits to be regulated. The speech reached by the statute contained "no indecency or obscenity in any sense heretofore known to the law." *Id.*, at 519.

Because speech about violence is not obscene, it is of no consequence that California's statute mimics the New York statute regulating obscenity-for-minors that we upheld in *Ginsberg v. New York,* 390 U.S. 629 (1968). That case approved a prohibition on the sale to minors of *sexual* material that would be obscene from the perspective of a child. We held that the legislature could "adjus[t] the definition of obscenity 'to social realities by permitting the appeal of this type of material to be assessed in terms of the sexual interests . . .' of . . . minors." *Id.,* at 638 (quoting *Mishkin v. New York,* 383 U.S. 502, 509 (1966)). And because "obscenity is not protected expression," the New York statute could be sustained so long as the legislature's judgment that the proscribed materials were harmful to children "was not irrational." 390 U.S., at 641.

The California Act is something else entirely. It does not adjust the boundaries of an existing category of unprotected speech to ensure that a definition designed for adults is not uncritically applied to children. California does not argue that it is empowered to prohibit selling offensively violent works *to adults*—and it is wise not to, since that is but a hair's breadth from the argument rejected in *Stevens.* Instead, it wishes to create a wholly new category of content-based regulation that is permissible only for speech directed at children.

That is unprecedented and mistaken. "[M]inors are entitled to a significant measure of First Amendment protection, and only in relatively narrow and well-defined circumstances may government bar public dissemination of protected materials to them." *Erznoznik v. Jacksonville,* 422 U.S. 205, 212–213 (1975) (citation omitted). No doubt a State possesses legitimate power to protect children from harm, *Ginsberg, supra,* at 640–641; *Prince v. Massachusetts,* 321 U.S. 158, 165 (1944), but that does not include a free-floating power to restrict the ideas to which children may be exposed. "Speech that is neither obscene as to youths nor subject to some other legitimate proscription cannot be suppressed solely to protect the young from ideas or images that a legislative body thinks unsuitable for them." *Erznoznik, supra,* at 213–214.

California's argument would fare better if there were a longstanding tradition in this country of specially restricting children's access to depictions of violence, but there is none. Certainly the *books* we give children to read—or read to them when they are younger—contain no shortage of gore. Grimm's Fairy Tales, for example, are grim indeed. As her just deserts for trying to poison Snow White, the wicked queen is made to dance in red hot slippers "till she fell dead on the floor, a sad example of envy and jealousy." The Complete Brothers Grimm Fairy

Tales 198 (2006 ed.). Cinderella's evil stepsisters have their eyes pecked out by doves. *Id.,* at 95. And Hansel and Gretel (children!) kill their captor by baking her in an oven. *Id.,* at 54.

High-school reading lists are full of similar fare. Homer's Odysseus blinds Polyphemus the Cyclops by grinding out his eye with a heated stake. The Odyssey of Homer, Book IX, p. 125 (S. Butcher & A. Lang transls. 1909) ("Even so did we seize the fiery-pointed brand and whirled it round in his eye, and the blood flowed about the heated bar. And the breath of the flame singed his eyelids and brows all about, as the ball of the eye burnt away, and the roots thereof crackled in the flame"). In the Inferno, Dante and Virgil watch corrupt politicians struggle to stay submerged beneath a lake of boiling pitch, lest they be skewered by devils above the surface. Canto XXI, pp. 187-189 (A. Mandelbaum transl. Bantam Classic ed.1982). And Golding's Lord of the Flies recounts how a schoolboy called Piggy is savagely murdered *by other children* while marooned on an island. W. Golding, Lord of the Flies 208-209 (1997 ed.).

This is not to say that minors' consumption of violent entertainment has never encountered resistance. In the 1800's, dime novels depicting crime and "penny dreadfuls" (named for their price and content) were blamed in some quarters for juvenile delinquency. See Brief for Cato Institute as *Amicus Curiae* 6-7. When motion pictures came along, they became the villains instead. "The days when the police looked upon dime novels as the most dangerous of textbooks in the school for crime are drawing to a close .... They say that the moving picture machine ... tends even more than did the dime novel to turn the thoughts of the easily influenced to paths which sometimes lead to prison." Moving Pictures as Helps to Crime, N.Y. Times, Feb. 21, 1909, quoted in Brief for Cato Institute, at 8. For a time, our Court did permit broad censorship of movies because of their capacity to be "used for evil," see *Mutual Film Corp. v. Industrial Comm'n of Ohio,* 236 U.S. 230, 242 (1915), but we eventually reversed course, *Joseph Burstyn, Inc.,* 343 U.S., at 502; see also *Erznoznik, supra,* at 212-214 (invalidating a drive-in movies restriction designed to protect children). Radio dramas were next, and then came comic books. Brief for Cato Institute, at 10-11. Many in the late 1940's and early 1950's blamed comic books for fostering a "preoccupation with violence and horror" among the young, leading to a rising juvenile crime rate. See Note, Regulation of Comic Books, 68 Harv. L. Rev. 489, 490 (1955). But efforts to convince Congress to restrict comic books failed. Brief for Comic Book Legal Defense Fund as *Amicus Curiae* 11-15. And, of course, after comic books came television and music lyrics.

California claims that video games present special problems because they are "interactive," in that the player participates in the violent action on screen and determines its outcome. The latter feature is nothing new: Since at least the publication of The Adventures of You: Sugarcane Island in 1969, young readers of choose-your-own-adventure stories have been able to make decisions that determine the plot by following instructions about which page to turn to. Cf. *Interactive Digital Software Assn. v. St. Louis County,* 329 F.3d 954, 957–958 ([8th Cir.] 2003). As for the argument that video games enable participation in the violent action, that seems to us more a matter of degree than of kind. As Judge Posner has observed, all literature is interactive. "[T]he better it is, the more interactive. Literature when it is successful draws the reader into the story, makes him identify with the characters, invites him to judge them and quarrel with them, to experience their joys and sufferings as the reader's own." *American Amusement Machine Assn. v. Kendrick,* 244 F.3d 572, 577 ([7th Cir.] 2001) (striking down a similar restriction on violent video games).

Justice ALITO has done considerable independent research to identify, see *post,* at ---- - ----, nn. 13–18, video games in which "the violence is astounding," *post,* at ----. "Victims are dismembered, decapitated, disemboweled, set on fire, and chopped into little pieces.... Blood gushes, splatters, and pools." *Ibid.* Justice ALITO recounts all these disgusting video games in order to disgust us—but disgust is not a valid basis for restricting expression. And the same is true of Justice ALITO's description, *post,* at ---- - ----, of those video games he has discovered that have a racial or ethnic motive for their violence—"'ethnic cleansing' [of] . . . African Americans, Latinos, or Jews." To what end does he relate this? Does it somehow increase the "aggressiveness" that California wishes to suppress? Who knows? But it does arouse the reader's ire, and the reader's desire to put an end to this horrible message. Thus, ironically, Justice ALITO's argument highlights the precise danger posed by the California Act: that the *ideas* expressed by speech—whether it be violence, or gore, or racism—and not its objective effects, may be the real reason for governmental proscription.

III.

Because the Act imposes a restriction on the content of protected speech, it is invalid unless California can demonstrate that it passes strict scrutiny—that is, unless it is justified by a compelling government interest and is narrowly drawn to serve that interest. *R.A.V.,* 505 U.S., at 395. The State must specifically identify an "actual problem" in need of solving, *Playboy,* 529 U.S., at 822–823, and the curtailment of free speech must be actually necessary to the solution, see *R.A.V., supra,* at 395. That is a demanding standard. "It is rare that a regulation restricting speech because of its content will ever be permissible." *Playboy, supra,* at 818.

California cannot meet that standard. At the outset, it acknowledges that it cannot show a direct causal link between violent video games and harm to minors. Rather, relying upon our decision in *Turner Broadcasting System, Inc. v. FCC,* 512 U.S. 622 (1994), the State claims that it need not produce such proof because the legislature can make a predictive judgment that such a link exists, based on competing psychological studies. But reliance on *Turner Broadcasting* is misplaced. That decision applied *intermediate scrutiny* to a content-neutral regulation. *Id.,* at 661–662. California's burden is much higher, and because it bears the risk of uncertainty, see *Playboy, supra,* at 816–817, ambiguous proof will not suffice.

The State's evidence is not compelling. California relies primarily on the research of Dr. Craig Anderson and a few other research psychologists whose studies purport to show a connection between exposure to violent video games and harmful effects on children. These studies have been rejected by every court to consider them, and with good reason: They do not prove that violent video games *cause* minors to *act* aggressively (which would at least be a beginning). Instead, "[n]early all of the research is based on correlation, not evidence of causation, and most of the studies suffer from significant, admitted flaws in methodology." . . .

Of course, California has (wisely) declined to restrict Saturday morning cartoons, the sale of games rated for young children, or the distribution of pictures of guns. The consequence is that its regulation is wildly underinclusive when judged against its asserted justification, which in our view is alone enough to defeat it. Underinclusiveness raises serious doubts about whether the government is in fact pursuing the interest it invokes, rather than disfavoring a particular speaker or viewpoint. . . . Here, California has singled out the purveyors of video games for disfavored treatment—at least when compared to booksellers, cartoonists, and movie producers—and has given no persuasive reason why.

The Act is also seriously underinclusive in another respect—and a respect that renders irrelevant the contentions of the concurrence and the dissents that video games are qualitatively different from other portrayals of violence. The California Legislature is perfectly willing to leave this dangerous, mind-altering material in the hands of children so long as one parent (or even an aunt or uncle) says it's OK. And there are not even any requirements as to how this parental or avuncular relationship is to be verified; apparently the child's or putative parent's, aunt's, or uncle's say-so suffices. That is not how one addresses a serious social problem.

California claims that the Act is justified in aid of parental authority: By requiring that the purchase of violent video games can be made only by adults, the Act ensures that parents can decide what games are appropriate. At the outset, we note our doubts that punishing third parties for conveying protected speech to children *just in case* their parents disapprove of that speech is a proper governmental means of aiding parental authority. Accepting that position would largely vitiate the rule that "only in relatively narrow and well-defined circumstances may government bar public dissemination of protected materials to [minors]." *Erznoznik*, 422 U.S., at 212–213.

But leaving that aside, California cannot show that the Act's restrictions meet a substantial need of parents who wish to restrict their children's access to violent video games but cannot do so. The video-game industry has in place a voluntary rating system designed to inform consumers about the content of games. The system, implemented by the Entertainment Software Rating Board (ESRB), assigns age-specific ratings to each video game submitted: EC (Early Childhood); E (Everyone); E10+ (Everyone 10 and older); T (Teens); M (17 and older); and AO (Adults Only—18 and older). App. 86. The Video Software Dealers Association encourages retailers to prominently display information about the ESRB system in their stores; to refrain from renting or selling adults-only games to minors; and to rent or sell "M" rated games to minors only with parental consent. *Id.*, at 47. In 2009, the Federal Trade Commission (FTC) found that, as a result of this system, "the video game industry outpaces the movie and music industries" in "(1) restricting target-marketing of mature-rated products to children; (2) clearly and prominently disclosing rating information; and (3) restricting children's access to mature-rated products at retail." FTC, Report to Congress, Marketing Violent Entertainment to Children 30 (Dec.2009), online at http://www.ftc.gov/os/2009/12/P994511violententertainment.pdf (as visited June 24, 2011, and available in Clerk of Court's case file) (FTC Report). This system does much to ensure that minors cannot purchase seriously violent games on their own, and that parents who care about the matter can readily evaluate the games their children bring home. Filling the remaining modest gap in concerned-parents' control can hardly be a compelling state interest.

And finally, the Act's purported aid to parental authority is vastly overinclusive. Not all of the children who are forbidden to purchase violent video games on their own have parents who *care* whether they purchase violent video games. While some of the legislation's effect may indeed be in support of what some parents of the restricted children actually want, its entire effect is only in support of what the State thinks parents *ought* to want. This is not the narrow tailoring to "assisting parents" that restriction of First Amendment rights requires.

. . .

California's effort to regulate violent video games is the latest episode in a long series of failed attempts to censor violent entertainment for minors. While we have pointed out above that some of the evidence brought forward to support the harmfulness of video games is unpersuasive, we do not mean to demean or disparage the concerns that underlie the attempt to regulate them—concerns that may and doubtless do prompt a good deal of parental oversight. We have no business passing judgment on the view of the California Legislature that violent video games (or, for that matter, any other forms of speech) corrupt the young or harm their moral development. Our task is only to say whether or not such works constitute a "well-defined and narrowly limited clas[s] of speech, the prevention and punishment of which have never been thought to raise any Constitutional problem," *Chaplinsky*, 315 U.S., at 571–572 (the answer plainly is no); and if not, whether the regulation of such works is justified by that high degree of necessity we have described as a compelling state interest (it is not). Even where the protection of children is the object, the constitutional limits on governmental action apply.

California's legislation straddles the fence between (1) addressing a serious social problem and (2) helping concerned parents control their children. Both ends are legitimate, but when they affect First Amendment rights they must be pursued by means that are neither seriously underinclusive nor seriously overinclusive. See *Church of Lukumi Babalu Aye, Inc. v. Hialeah*, 508 U.S. 520, 546 (1993). As a means of protecting children from portrayals of violence, the legislation is seriously underinclusive, not only because it excludes portrayals other than video games, but also because it permits a parental or avuncular veto. And as a means of assisting concerned parents it is seriously overinclusive because it abridges the First Amendment rights of young people whose parents (and aunts and uncles) think violent video games are a harmless pastime. And the overbreadth in achieving one goal is not cured by the underbreadth in achieving the other. Legislation such as this, which is neither fish nor fowl, cannot survive strict scrutiny.

We affirm the judgment below.

It is so ordered.

Justice ALITO, with whom THE CHIEF JUSTICE joins, concurring in the judgment.

The California statute that is before us in this case represents a pioneering effort to address what the state legislature and others regard as a potentially serious social problem: the effect of exceptionally violent video games on impressionable minors, who often spend countless hours immersed in the alternative worlds that these games create. Although the California statute is well intentioned, its terms are not framed with the precision that the Constitution demands, and I therefore agree with the Court that this particular law cannot be sustained.

. . .

In the view of the Court, all those concerned about the effects of violent video games—federal and state legislators, educators, social scientists, and parents—are unduly fearful, for violent video games really present no serious problem. See *ante,* at 2737–2739, 2740–2741. Spending hour upon hour controlling the actions of a character who guns down scores of innocent victims is not different in "kind" from reading a description of violence in a work of literature. See *ante,* at 2737–2738.

The Court is sure of this; I am not. There are reasons to suspect that the experience of playing violent video games just might be very different from reading a book, listening to the radio, or watching a movie or a television show.

I.

Respondents in this case, representing the video-game industry, ask us to strike down the California law on two grounds: The broad ground adopted by the Court and the narrower ground that the law's definition of "violent video game," see Cal. Civ. Code Ann. § 1746(d)(1)(A) (West 2009), is impermissibly vague. See Brief for Respondents 23-61. Because I agree with the latter argument, I see no need to reach the broader First Amendment issues addressed by the Court.

. . .

For better or worse, our society has long regarded many depictions of killing and maiming as suitable features of popular entertainment, including entertainment that is widely available to minors. The California law's threshold requirement would more closely resemble the limitation in *Miller* if it targeted a narrower class of graphic depictions.

Because of this feature of the California law's threshold test, the work of providing fair notice is left in large part to the three requirements that follow, but those elements are also not up to the task. In drafting the violent video game law, the California Legislature could have made its own judgment regarding the kind and degree of violence that is acceptable in games played by minors (or by minors in particular age groups). Instead, the legislature relied on undefined societal or community standards.

One of the three elements at issue here refers expressly to "prevailing standards in the community as to what is suitable for minors." § 1746(d)(1)(A)(ii). Another element points in the same direction, asking whether "[a] reasonable person, considering [a] game as a whole," would find that it "appeals to a *deviant* or *morbid* interest of minors." § 1746(d)(1)(A)(i) (emphasis added).

The terms "deviant" and "morbid" are not defined in the statute, and California offers no reason to think that its courts would give the terms anything other than their ordinary meaning. . . .

There is a critical difference, however, between obscenity laws and laws regulating violence in entertainment. By the time of this Court's landmark obscenity cases in the 1960's, obscenity had long been prohibited, see *Roth,* 354 U.S., at 484-485, and this experience had helped to shape certain generally accepted norms concerning expression related to sex.

There is no similar history regarding expression related to violence. As the Court notes, classic literature contains descriptions of great violence, and even children's stories sometimes depict very violent scenes. See *ante,* at 2736–2737.

Although our society does not generally regard all depictions of violence as suitable for children or adolescents, the prevalence of violent depictions in children's literature and entertainment creates numerous opportunities for reasonable people to disagree about which depictions may excite "deviant" or "morbid" impulses. See Edwards & Berman, Regulating Violence on Television, 89 Nw. U.L.Rev. 1487, 1523 (1995) (observing that the *Miller* test would be difficult to apply to violent expression because "there is nothing even approaching a consensus on low-value violence").

Finally, the difficulty of ascertaining the community standards incorporated into the California law is compounded by the legislature's decision to lump all minors together. The California law draws no distinction between young children and adolescents who are nearing the age of majority.

For these reasons, I conclude that the California violent video game law fails to provide the fair notice that the Constitution requires. And I would go no further. I would not express any view on whether a properly drawn statute would or would not survive First Amendment scrutiny. We should address that question only if and when it is necessary to do so.

. . .

Justice THOMAS, dissenting.
The Court's decision today does not comport with the original public understanding of the First Amendment. The majority strikes down, as facially unconstitutional, a state law that prohibits the direct sale or rental of certain video games to minors because the law "abridg[es] the freedom of speech." U.S. Const., Amdt. 1. But I do not think the First Amendment stretches that far. The practices and beliefs of the founding generation establish that "the freedom of speech," as originally understood, does not include a right to speak to minors (or a right of minors to access speech) without going through the minors' parents or guardians. I would hold that the law at issue is not facially unconstitutional under the First Amendment, and reverse and remand for further proceedings. . . .

I respectfully dissent.

Justice BREYER, dissenting.
California imposes a civil fine of up to $1,000 upon any person who distributes a violent video game in California without labeling it "18," or who sells or rents a labeled violent video game to a person under the age of 18. Representatives of the video game and software industries, claiming that the statute violates the First Amendment on its face, seek an injunction against its enforcement. Applying traditional First Amendment analysis, I would uphold the statute as constitutional on its face and would consequently reject the industries' facial challenge.

. . .

In determining whether the statute is unconstitutional, I would apply both this Court's "vagueness" precedents and a strict form of First Amendment scrutiny. In doing so, the special First Amendment category I find relevant is not (as the Court claims) the category of "depictions of violence," *ante,* at ----, but rather the category of "protection of children." This Court has held that the "power of the state to control the conduct of children reaches beyond the scope of its authority over adults." *Prince v. Massachusetts,* 321 U.S. 158, 170 (1944). And the "'regulatio[n] of communication addressed to [children] need not conform to the requirements of the [F]irst [A]mendment in the same way as those applicable to adults.'" *Ginsberg v. New York,* 390 U.S. 629, 638, n. 6, (1968) (quoting Emerson, Toward a General Theory of the First Amendment, 72 Yale L.J. 877, 939 (1963)).

The majority's claim that the California statute, if upheld, would create a "new categor[y] of unprotected speech," *ante,* at ----, ----, is overstated. No one here argues that depictions of violence, even extreme violence, *automatically* fall outside the First Amendment's protective scope as, for example, do obscenity and depictions of child pornography. We properly speak of *categories* of expression that lack protection when, like "child pornography," the category is broad, when it applies automatically, and when the State can prohibit everyone, including adults, from obtaining access to the material within it. But where, as here, careful analysis must precede a narrower judicial conclusion (say, denying protection to a shout of "fire" in a crowded theater, or to an effort to teach a terrorist group how to peacefully petition the United Nations), we do not normally describe the result as creating a "new category of unprotected speech." See *Schenck v. United States,* 249 U.S. 47, 52 (1919); *Holder v. Humanitarian Law Project,* 130 S.Ct. 2705 (2010).

Thus, in *Stevens,* after rejecting the claim that *all* depictions of animal cruelty (a category) fall outside the First Amendment's protective scope, we went on to decide whether the particular statute at issue violates the First Amendment under traditional standards; and we held that, because the statute was overly broad, it was invalid. Similarly, here the issue is whether, applying traditional First Amendment standards, this statute does, or does not, pass muster.

This Court upheld the New York statute in *Ginsberg* (which is sometimes unfortunately confused with a very different, earlier case, *Ginzburg v. United States,* 383 U.S. 463 (1966)). The five-Justice majority, in an opinion written by Justice Brennan, wrote that the statute was sufficiently clear.

390 U.S., at 643–645. No Member of the Court voiced any vagueness objection. See *id.*, at 648–650 (Stewart, J., concurring in result); *id.*, at 650–671 (Douglas, J., joined by Black, J., dissenting); *id.*, at 671–675 (Fortas, J., dissenting).

Comparing the language of California's statute (set forth *supra*, at ----- ----) with the language of New York's statute (set forth immediately above), it is difficult to find any vagueness-related difference. Why are the words "kill," "maim," and "dismember" any more difficult to understand than the word "nudity?" ... California only departed from the *Miller* formulation in two significant respects: It substituted the word "deviant" for the words "prurient" and "shameful," and it three times added the words "for minors." The word "deviant" differs from "prurient" and "shameful," but it would seem no less suited to defining and narrowing the reach of the statute. And the addition of "for minors" to a version of the *Miller* standard was approved in *Ginsberg*, 390 U.S., at 643, even though the New York law "dr[ew] no distinction between young children and adolescents who are nearing the age of majority," *ante*, at ---- (opinion of ALITO, J.).

Both the *Miller* standard and the law upheld in *Ginsberg* lack perfect clarity. But that fact reflects the difficulty of the Court's long search for words capable of protecting expression without depriving the State of a legitimate constitutional power to regulate. As is well known, at one point Justice Stewart thought he could do no better in defining obscenity than, "I know it when I see it." *Jacobellis v. Ohio*, 378 U.S. 184, 197 (1964) (concurring opinion). And Justice Douglas dissented from *Miller*'s standard, which he thought was still too vague. 413 U.S., at 39-40. Ultimately, however, this Court accepted the "community standards" tests used in *Miller* and *Ginsberg*.

. . .

U. S. v. STEVENS
559 U.S. 460 (2010)

Chief Justice ROBERTS delivered the opinion of the Court.
Congress enacted 18 U.S.C. § 48 to criminalize the commercial creation, sale, or possession of certain depictions of animal cruelty. The statute does not address underlying acts harmful to animals, but only portrayals of such conduct. The question presented is whether the prohibition in the

statute is consistent with the freedom of speech guaranteed by the First Amendment.

I.

Section 48 establishes a criminal penalty of up to five years in prison for anyone who knowingly "creates, sells, or possesses a depiction of animal cruelty," if done "for commercial gain" in interstate or foreign commerce. § 48(a). A depiction of "animal cruelty" is defined as one "in which a living animal is intentionally maimed, mutilated, tortured, wounded, or killed," if that conduct violates federal or state law where "the creation, sale, or possession takes place." § 48(c)(1). In what is referred to as the "exceptions clause," the law exempts from prohibition any depiction "that has serious religious, political, scientific, educational, journalistic, historical, or artistic value." § 48(b).

The legislative background of § 48 focused primarily on the interstate market for "crush videos." According to the House Committee Report on the bill, such videos feature the intentional torture and killing of helpless animals, including cats, dogs, monkeys, mice, and hamsters. H.R.Rep. No. 106-397, p. 2 (1999) (hereinafter H.R. Rep.). Crush videos often depict women slowly crushing animals to death "with their bare feet or while wearing high heeled shoes," sometimes while "talking to the animals in a kind of dominatrix patter" over "[t]he cries and squeals of the animals, obviously in great pain." *Ibid.* Apparently these depictions "appeal to persons with a very specific sexual fetish who find them sexually arousing or otherwise exciting." *Id.*, at 2-3. The acts depicted in crush videos are typically prohibited by the animal cruelty laws enacted by all 50 States and the District of Columbia. See Brief for United States 25, n. 7 (listing statutes). But crush videos rarely disclose the participants' identities, inhibiting prosecution of the underlying conduct. See H.R. Rep., at 3; accord, Brief for State of Florida et al. as *Amici Curiae* 11.

This case, however, involves an application of § 48 to depictions of animal fighting. Dogfighting, for example, is unlawful in all 50 States and the District of Columbia, see Brief for United States 26, n. 8 (listing statutes), and has been restricted by federal law since 1976. Animal Welfare Act Amendments of 1976, § 17, 90 Stat. 421, 7 U.S.C. § 2156. Respondent Robert J. Stevens ran a business, "Dogs of Velvet and Steel," and an associated Web site, through which he sold videos of pit bulls engaging in dogfights and attacking other animals. Among these videos were Japan Pit Fights and Pick-A-Winna: A Pit Bull Documentary, which include contemporary footage of dogfights in Japan (where such conduct is allegedly legal) as well as footage of American dogfights from the

1960's and 1970's. A third video, Catch Dogs and Country Living, depicts the use of pit bulls to hunt wild boar, as well as a "gruesome" scene of a pit bull attacking a domestic farm pig. 533 F.3d 218, 221 (C.A.3 2008) (en banc). On the basis of these videos, Stevens was indicted on three counts of violating § 48. . . .

II.

The Government's primary submission is that § 48 necessarily complies with the Constitution because the banned depictions of animal cruelty, as a class, are categorically unprotected by the First Amendment. We disagree.

. . .

"From 1791 to the present," however, the First Amendment has "permitted restrictions upon the content of speech in a few limited areas," and has never "include[d] a freedom to disregard these traditional limitations." . . . These "historic and traditional categories long familiar to the bar," . . . including obscenity, . . . defamation, . . . fraud, . . . incitement, . . . and speech integral to criminal conduct, . . . [and] are "well-defined and narrowly limited classes of speech, the prevention and punishment of which have never been thought to raise any Constitutional problem." . . .

The Government argues that "depictions of animal cruelty" should be added to the list. It contends that depictions of "illegal acts of animal cruelty" that are "made, sold, or possessed for commercial gain" necessarily "lack expressive value," and may accordingly "be regulated as *unprotected* speech." Brief for United States 10 (emphasis added). The claim is not just that Congress may regulate depictions of animal cruelty subject to the First Amendment, but that these depictions are outside the reach of that Amendment altogether-that they fall into a "'First Amendment Free Zone.'" *Board of Airport Comm'rs of Los Angeles v. Jews for Jesus, Inc.*, 482 U.S. 569, 574 (1987).

As the Government notes, the prohibition of animal cruelty itself has a long history in American law, starting with the early settlement of the Colonies. Reply Brief 12, n. 8; see, *e.g.*, The Body of Liberties § 92 (Mass. Bay Colony 1641), reprinted in American Historical Documents 1000-1904, 43 Harvard Classics 66, 79 (C. Eliot ed. 1910) ("No man shall exercise any Tirranny or Crueltie towards any bruite Creature which are usuallie kept for man's use"). But we are unaware of any similar tradition excluding *depictions* of animal cruelty from "the freedom of speech" codified in the First Amendment, and the Government points us to none.

The Government contends that "historical evidence" about the reach of the First Amendment is not "a necessary prerequisite for regulation today," Reply Brief 12, n. 8, and that categories of speech may be exempted from the First Amendment's protection without any long-settled tradition of subjecting that speech to regulation. Instead, the Government points to Congress's "'legislative judgment that . . . depictions of animals being intentionally tortured and killed [are] of such minimal redeeming value as to render [them] unworthy of First Amendment protection,'" Brief for United States 23 (quoting 533 F.3d, at 243 (Cowen, J., dissenting)), and asks the Court to uphold the ban on the same basis. The Government thus proposes that a claim of categorical exclusion should be considered under a simple balancing test: "Whether a given category of speech enjoys First Amendment protection depends upon a categorical balancing of the value of the speech against its societal costs." Brief for United States 8; see also *id.*, at 12.

As a free-floating test for First Amendment coverage, that sentence is startling and dangerous. The First Amendment's guarantee of free speech does not extend only to categories of speech that survive an ad hoc balancing of relative social costs and benefits. The First Amendment itself reflects a judgment by the American people that the benefits of its restrictions on the Government outweigh the costs. Our Constitution forecloses any attempt to revise that judgment simply on the basis that some speech is not worth it. The Constitution is not a document "prescribing limits, and declaring that those limits may be passed at pleasure." *Marbury v. Madison,* 2 L.Ed. 60 ([U.S.] 1803).

To be fair to the Government, its view did not emerge from a vacuum. As the Government correctly notes, this Court has often *described* historically unprotected categories of speech as being "'of such slight social value as a step to truth that any benefit that may be derived from them is clearly outweighed by the social interest in order and morality.'" *R.A.V., supra,* at 383 (quoting *Chaplinsky, supra,* at 572). In *New York v. Ferber,* 458 U.S. 747 (1982), we noted that within these categories of unprotected speech, "the evil to be restricted so overwhelmingly outweighs the expressive interests, if any, at stake, that no process of case-by-case adjudication is required," because "the balance of competing interests is clearly struck," *id.,* at 763-764. The Government derives its proposed test from these descriptions in our precedents. See Brief for United States 12-13.

But such descriptions are just that-descriptive. They do not set forth a test that may be applied as a general matter to permit the Government to imprison any speaker so long as his speech is deemed valueless or unnecessary, or so long as an ad hoc calculus of costs and benefits tilts in a statute's favor.

When we have identified categories of speech as fully outside the protection of the First Amendment, it has not been on the basis of a simple cost-benefit analysis. In *Ferber*, for example, we classified child pornography as such a category, 458 U.S., at 763. We noted that the State of New York had a compelling interest in protecting children from abuse, and that the value of using children in these works (as opposed to simulated conduct or adult actors) was *de minimis*. *Id.*, at 756-757, 762. But our decision did not rest on this "balance of competing interests" alone. *Id.*, at 764. We made clear that *Ferber* presented a special case: The market for child pornography was "intrinsically related" to the underlying abuse, and was therefore "an integral part of the production of such materials, an activity illegal throughout the Nation." *Id.*, at 759, 761. As we noted, "'[i]t rarely has been suggested that the constitutional freedom for speech and press extends its immunity to speech or writing used as an integral part of conduct in violation of a valid criminal statute.'" *Id.*, at 761-762 (quoting *Giboney*, *supra*, at 498). *Ferber* thus grounded its analysis in a previously recognized, long-established category of unprotected speech, and our subsequent decisions have shared this understanding. See *Osborne v. Ohio*, 495 U.S. 103, 110 (1990) (describing *Ferber* as finding "persuasive" the argument that the advertising and sale of child pornography was "an integral part" of its unlawful production (internal quotation marks omitted)); *Ashcroft v. Free Speech Coalition*, 535 U.S. 234, 249-250 (2002) (noting that distribution and sale "were intrinsically related to the sexual abuse of children," giving the speech at issue "a proximate link to the crime from which it came" (internal quotation marks omitted)).

Our decisions in *Ferber* and other cases cannot be taken as establishing a freewheeling authority to declare new categories of speech outside the scope of the First Amendment. Maybe there are some categories of speech that have been historically unprotected, but have not yet been specifically identified or discussed as such in our case law. But if so, there is no evidence that "depictions of animal cruelty" is among them. We need not foreclose the future recognition of such additional categories to reject the Government's highly manipulable balancing test as a means of identifying them.

III.

Because we decline to carve out from the First Amendment any novel exception for § 48, we review Stevens's First Amendment challenge under our existing doctrine.

A.

Stevens challenged § 48 on its face, arguing that any conviction secured under the statute would be unconstitutional. The court below decided the case on that basis, 533 F.3d, at 231, n. 13, and we granted the Solicitor General's petition for certiorari to determine "whether 18 U.S.C. 48 is facially invalid under the Free Speech Clause of the First Amendment," Pet. for Cert. i.

To succeed in a typical facial attack, Stevens would have to establish "that no set of circumstances exists under which [§ 48] would be valid," *United States v. Salerno,* 481 U.S. 739, 745 (1987), or that the statute lacks any "plainly legitimate sweep," *Washington v. Glucksberg,* 521 U.S. 702, 740, n. 7 (1997) (STEVENS, J., concurring in judgments) (internal quotation marks omitted). Which standard applies in a typical case is a matter of dispute that we need not and do not address, and neither *Salerno* nor *Glucksberg* is a speech case. Here the Government asserts that Stevens cannot prevail because § 48 is plainly legitimate as applied to crush videos and animal fighting depictions. Deciding this case through a traditional facial analysis would require us to resolve whether these applications of § 48 are in fact consistent with the Constitution.

In the First Amendment context, however, this Court recognizes "a second type of facial challenge," whereby a law may be invalidated as overbroad if "a substantial number of its applications are unconstitutional, judged in relation to the statute's plainly legitimate sweep." *Washington State Grange v. Washington State Republican Party,* 552 U.S. 442, 449, n. 6 (2008) (internal quotation marks omitted). Stevens argues that § 48 applies to common depictions of ordinary and lawful activities, and that these depictions constitute the vast majority of materials subject to the statute. Brief for Respondent 22-25. The Government makes no effort to defend such a broad ban as constitutional. Instead, the Government's entire defense of § 48 rests on interpreting the statute as narrowly limited to specific types of "extreme" material. Brief for United States 8. As the parties have presented the issue, therefore, the constitutionality of § 48 hinges on how broadly it is construed. It is to that question that we now turn.

. . .

We read § 48 to create a criminal prohibition of alarming breadth. To begin with, the text of the statute's ban on a "depiction of animal cruelty" nowhere requires that the depicted conduct be cruel. That text applies to "any . . . depiction" in which "a living animal is intentionally maimed, mutilated, tortured, wounded, or killed." § 48(c)(1). "[M]aimed, mutilated, [and] tortured" convey cruelty, but "wounded" or "killed" do not suggest any such limitation.

. . .

What is more, the application of § 48 to depictions of illegal conduct extends to conduct that is illegal in only a single jurisdiction. Under subsection (c)(1), the depicted conduct need only be illegal in "the State in which the creation, sale, or possession takes place, regardless of whether the . . . wounding . . . or killing took place in [that] State." A depiction of entirely lawful conduct runs afoul of the ban if that depiction later finds its way into another State where the same conduct is unlawful. This provision greatly expands the scope of § 48, because although there may be "a broad societal consensus" against cruelty to animals, Brief for United States 2, there is substantial disagreement on what types of conduct are properly regarded as cruel. Both views about cruelty to animals and regulations having no connection to cruelty vary widely from place to place.

In the District of Columbia, for example, all hunting is unlawful. D.C. Munic. Regs., tit. 19, § 1560 (2009). Other jurisdictions permit or encourage hunting, and there is an enormous national market for hunting-related depictions in which a living animal is intentionally killed. Hunting periodicals have circulations in the hundreds of thousands or millions, see Mediaweek, Sept. 29, 2008, p. 28, and hunting television programs, videos, and Web sites are equally popular, see Brief for Professional Outdoor Media Association et al. as *Amici Curiae* 9-10. . . .

Those seeking to comply with the law thus face a bewildering maze of regulations from at least 56 separate jurisdictions. Some States permit hunting with crossbows, Ga. Code Ann. § 27-3-4(1) (2007); Va.Code Ann. § 29.1-519(A)(6) (Lexis 2008 Cum.Supp.), while others forbid it, Ore. Admin. Reg. 635-065-0725 (2009), or restrict it only to the disabled, N.Y. Envir. Conserv. Law Ann. § 11-0901(16) (West 2005). Missouri allows the "canned" hunting of ungulates held in captivity, Mo. Code Regs. Ann., tit. 3, 10-9.560(1), but Montana restricts such hunting to certain bird species, Mont. Admin. Rule 12.6.1202(1) (2007). The sharp-tailed grouse may be hunted in Idaho, but not in Washington. Compare Idaho Admin. Code § 13.01.09.606 (2009) with Wash. Admin. Code § 232-28-342 (2009).

. . .

C.

The only thing standing between defendants who sell such depictions and five years in federal prison-other than the mercy of a prosecutor-is the statute's exceptions clause. Subsection (b) exempts from prohibition "any depiction that has serious religious, political, scientific, educational, journalistic, historical, or artistic value." The Government argues that this clause substantially narrows the statute's reach: News reports about animal cruelty have "journalistic" value; pictures of bullfights in Spain have "historical" value; and instructional hunting videos have "educational" value. Reply Brief 6. Thus, the Government argues, § 48 reaches only crush videos, depictions of animal fighting (other than Spanish bullfighting, see Brief for United States 47-48), and perhaps other depictions of "extreme acts of animal cruelty." *Id.*, at 41.

The Government's attempt to narrow the statutory ban, however, requires an unrealistically broad reading of the exceptions clause. As the Government reads the clause, any material with "redeeming societal value," *id.*, at 9, 16, 23, "'at least some minimal value,'" Reply Brief 6 (quoting H.R. Rep., at 4), or anything more than "scant social value," Reply Brief 11, is excluded under § 48(b). But the text says "serious" value, and "serious" should be taken seriously. We decline the Government's invitation-advanced for the first time in this Court-to regard as "serious" anything that is not "scant." (Or, as the dissent puts it, "'trifling.'" *Post*, at ----.) As the Government recognized below, "serious" ordinarily means a good bit more. The District Court's jury instructions required value that is "significant and of great import," App. 132, and the Government defended these instructions as properly relying on "a commonly accepted meaning of the word 'serious,'" Brief for United States in No. 05-2497(CA3), p. 50.

Quite apart from the requirement of "serious" value in § 48(b), the excepted speech must also fall within one of the enumerated categories. Much speech does not. Most hunting videos, for example, are not obviously instructional in nature, except in the sense that all life is a lesson.

. . .

In *Miller* we held that "serious" value shields depictions of sex from regulation as obscenity. 413 U.S., at 24-25. Limiting *Miller* 's exception to "serious" value ensured that "'[a] quotation from Voltaire in the flyleaf of a book [would] not constitutionally redeem an otherwise obscene publication.'" *Id.*, at 25, n. 7 (quoting *Kois v. Wisconsin*, 408 U.S. 229, 231 (1972) (*per curiam*)). We did not, however, determine that serious value could be used as a general precondition to protecting *other* types of speech in the first place. *Most* of what we say to one another lacks "religious, political, scientific, educational, journalistic, historical, or artistic value" (let alone serious value), but it is still sheltered from government regulation. Even "'[w]holly neutral futilities . . . come under the protection of free speech as fully as do Keats' poems or Donne's sermons.'" *Cohen v. California*, 403 U.S. 15 . . . Thus, the protection of the First Amendment presumptively extends to many forms of speech that do not qualify for the serious-value exception of § 48(b), but nonetheless fall within the broad reach of § 48(c).

. . .

The judgment of the United States Court of Appeals for the Third Circuit is affirmed.

It is so ordered.

Justice ALITO, dissenting.
The Court strikes down in its entirety a valuable statute, 18 U.S.C. § 48, that was enacted not to suppress speech, but to prevent horrific acts of animal cruelty-in particular, the creation and commercial exploitation of "crush videos," a form of depraved entertainment that has no social value.

. . .

In light of the practical problems thwarting the prosecution of the creators of crush videos under state animal cruelty laws, Congress concluded that the only effective way of stopping the underlying criminal conduct was to prohibit the commercial exploitation of the videos of that conduct. And Congress' strategy appears to have been vindicated. We are told that "[b]y 2007, sponsors of § 48 declared the crush video industry dead. Even overseas Websites shut down in the wake of § 48. Now, after the Third Circuit's decision [facially invalidating the statute], crush videos are already back online."

. . .

The First Amendment protects freedom of speech, but it most certainly does not protect violent criminal conduct, even if engaged in for expressive purposes. Crush videos present a highly unusual free speech issue because they are so closely linked with violent criminal conduct. The videos record the commission of violent criminal acts, and it appears that these crimes are committed for the sole purpose of creating the videos. . . .

The most relevant of our prior decisions is *Ferber*, 458 U.S. 747, which concerned child pornography. The Court there held that child pornography is not protected speech, and I believe that *Ferber* 's reasoning dictates a similar conclusion here.

In *Ferber,* an important factor-I would say the most important factor-was that child pornography involves the commission of a crime that inflicts severe personal injury to the "children who are made to engage in sexual conduct for commercial purposes.'" *Id.*, at 753 (internal quotation marks omitted). The *Ferber* Court repeatedly described the production of child pornography as child "abuse," "molestation," or "exploitation." . . . As later noted in *Ashcroft v. Free Speech Coalition*, . . . , in *Ferber* "[t]he production of the work, not its content, was the target of the statute."

. . .

Second, *Ferber* emphasized the fact that these underlying crimes could not be effectively combated without targeting the distribution of child pornography. As the Court put it, "the distribution network for child pornography must be closed if the production of material which requires the sexual exploitation of children is to be effectively controlled." 458 U.S., at 759. The Court added:

> "[T]here is no serious contention that the legislature was unjustified in believing that it is difficult, if not impossible, to halt the exploitation of children by pursuing only those who produce the photographs and movies . . . . The most expeditious if not the only practical method of law enforcement may be to dry up the market for this material by imposing severe criminal penalties on persons selling, advertising, or otherwise promoting the product." *Id.*, at 759-760.

See also *id.*, at 761 ("The advertising and selling of child pornography provide an economic motive for and are thus an integral part of the production of such materials").

Third, the *Ferber* Court noted that the value of child pornography "is exceedingly modest, if not *de minimis*" and that any such value was "overwhelmingly outweigh[ed]" by "the evil to be restricted." *Id.*, at 762-763.

All three of these characteristics are shared by § 48, as applied to crush videos.

. . .

It must be acknowledged that § 48 differs from a child pornography law in an important respect: preventing the abuse of children is certainly much more important than preventing the torture of the animals used in crush videos. It was largely for this reason that the Court of Appeals concluded that *Ferber* did not support the constitutionality of § 48. 533 F.3d, at 228 ("Preventing cruelty to animals, although an exceedingly worthy goal, simply does not implicate interests of the same magnitude as protecting children from physical and psychological harm"). But while protecting children is unquestionably *more* important than protecting animals, the Government also has a compelling interest in preventing the torture depicted in crush videos.

. . .

OLIVIA N. V. NATIONAL BROADCASTING CO., INC.
178 Cal. Rptr. 888 (Ct. App. 1981)

CHRISTIAN, J.
Olivia N. appeals from a judgment of nonsuit terminating her action against the National Broadcasting Company and the Chronicle Broadcasting Company. Appellant sought damages for physical and emotional injury inflicted by assailants who had seen a television broadcast of a film drama. . . .

On appeal from the judgment this court recognized that certain narrowly limited classes of speech may be prevented or punished by the state consistent with the principles of the First Amendment and held that "the trial court's action in viewing the film, and thereupon making fact findings and rendering judgment for respondents, was a violation of appellant's constitutional right to trial by jury." (*Olivia N. v. National Broadcasting Co.* (1977) 74 Cal. App.3d 383, 389.) Therefore, the judgment was reversed with directions to impanel a jury and proceed to trial of the action.

. . .

At 8 p.m. on September 10, 1974, NBC telecast nationwide, and Chronicle Broadcasting Company broadcast locally, a film entitled "Born Innocent." "The subject matter of the television film was the harmful effect of a state-run home upon an adolescent girl who had become a ward of the state. In one scene of the film, the young girl enters the community bathroom of the facility to take a shower. She is then shown taking off her clothes and stepping into the shower, where she bathes for a few moments. Suddenly, the water stops and a look of fear comes across her face. Four adolescent girls are standing across from her in the shower room. One of the girls is carrying a 'plumber's helper,' waving it suggestively by her side. The four girls violently attack the younger girl, wrestling her to the floor. The young girl is shown naked from the waist up, struggling as the older girls force her legs apart. Then, the television film shows the girl with the plumber's helper making intense thrusting motions with the handle of the plunger until one of the four says, 'That's enough.' The young girl is left sobbing and naked on the floor." (*Olivia N. v. National Broadcasting Co., supra,* 74 Cal. App.3d 383, 386.) It is alleged that on September 14, 1974, appellant, aged 9, was attacked and forcibly "artifically raped" with a bottle by minors at a San Francisco beach. (*Id.,* at pp. 386-387.) The assailants had viewed and discussed the "artificial rape" scene in "Born Innocent," and the film allegedly caused the assailants to decide to commit a similar act on appellant. Appellant offered to show that NBC had knowledge of studies on child violence and should have known that susceptible persons might imitate the crime enacted in the film. Appellant alleged that "Born Innocent" was particularly likely to cause imitation and that NBC televised the film without proper warning in an effort to obtain the largest possible viewing audience. Appellant alleged that as a proximate result of respondents' telecast, she suffered physical and psychological damage.

Appellant contends that where there is negligence liability could constitutionally be imposed despite the absence of proof of incitement as defined in *Brandenburg v. Ohio, supra,* 395 U.S. 444, 447. Appellant argues in the alternative that a different definition of "incitement" should be applied to the present circumstances.

Analysis of this appeal commences with recognition of the overriding constitutional principle that material communicated by the public media, including fictional material such as the television drama here at issue, is generally to be accorded protection under the First Amendment to the Constitution of the United States. . . . First Amendment rights are accorded a preferred place in our democratic society. (*Thomas v. Collins* (1945) 323 U.S. 516, 530.) First Amendment protection extends to a communication, to its source and to its recipients. . . . Applied to the electronic media, the First Amendment means that it is the broadcaster that has authority to make programming decisions. (*Writers Guild of America, West, Inc. v. F.C.C.* (C.D.Cal. 1976) 423 F.Supp. 1064, 1154.)

Motion pictures are accorded First Amendment protections. (*Joseph Burstyn, Inc. v. Wilson, supra,* 343 U.S. 495, 501.) "[T]he central concern of the First Amendment in this area is that there be a free flow from creator to audience of whatever message a film or a book might convey. . . . [T]he central First Amendment concern remains the need to maintain free access of the public to the expression." (*Young v. American Mini Theatres* (1976) 427 U.S. 50, 77 [conc. opn. of Powell, J.]) Freedom of speech is not limited to political expression or comment on public affairs. (*Time, Inc. v. Hill* (1967) 385 U.S. 374, 388.) Free speech must "embrace all issues about which information is needed or appropriate to enable the members of society to cope with the exigencies of their period." (*Thornhill v. Alabama* (1940) 310 U.S. 88, 102.) The commercial nature of an enterprise does not introduce a nonspeech element or relax the scrutiny required by the First Amendment.

. . .

The electronic media are also entitled to First Amendment protection.... Television broadcasting poses "unique and special problems not present in the traditional free speech case." . . . Nonetheless, the First Amendment precludes censorship of programming content even where the restraint is designed to protect children. (See Note, *Regulation of Program Content to Protect Children After Pacifica* (1979) 32 Vand.L.Rev. 1377, 1410-1411.) "Congress intended to permit private broadcasting to develop with the widest journalistic freedom consistent with its public obligations."

. . .

Appellant does not seek to impose a prior restraint on speech; rather, she asserts civil liability premised on traditional negligence concepts. But the chilling effect of permitting negligence actions for a television broadcast is obvious. "The fear of damage awards . . . may be markedly more inhibiting than the fear of prosecution under a criminal statute." (*New*

York Times Co. v. Sullivan, supra, 376 U.S. 254, 277.) Realistically, television networks would become significantly more inhibited in the selection of controversial materials if liability were to be imposed on a simple negligence theory. "[T]he pall of fear and timidity imposed upon those who would give voice to public criticism is an atmosphere in which the First Amendment freedoms cannot survive." (*New York Times Co. v. Sullivan, supra,* 376 U.S. 254, 278.) The deterrent effect of subjecting the television networks to negligence liability because of their programming choices would lead to self-censorship which would dampen the vigor and limit the variety of public debate. (*Id.,* at p. 279.)

Although the First Amendment is not absolute, the television broadcast of "Born Innocent" does not, on the basis of the opening statement of appellant's attorney, fall within the scope of unprotected speech. Appellant concedes that the film did not advocate or encourage violent acts and did not constitute an "incitement" within the meaning of *Brandenburg v. Ohio, supra,* 395 U.S. 444, 447-448. Notwithstanding the pervasive effect of the broadcasting media (see *FCC v. Pacifica Foundation* (1978) 438 U.S. 726, 748; Note, *The Future of Content Regulation in Broadcasting* (1981) 69 Cal.L.Rev. 555, 580-581) and the unique access afforded children (*F.C.C. v. Pacifica Foundation, supra,* 438 U.S. 726, 749), the effect of the imposition of liability could reduce the U.S. adult population to viewing only what is fit for children. (See *Butler v. Michigan* (1957) 352 U.S. 380, 383.) Incitement is the proper test here. (See *Kingsley Pictures Corp. v. Regents* (1959) 360 U.S. 684, 688.) In areas outside of obscenity the United States Supreme Court has "consistently held that the fact that protected speech may be offensive to some does not justify its suppression. See, *e.g., Cohen v. California,* 403 U.S. 15 (1971)." (*Carey v. Population Services International* (1977) 431 U.S. 678, 701.) Just as the advertising in *Carey, supra,* was not "directed to inciting or producing imminent lawless action and . . . likely to incite or produce such action" (*Brandenburg v. Ohio, supra,* 395 U.S. 444, 447, quoted in *Carey v. Population Services International, supra,* 431 U.S. 678, 701), the television broadcast which is the subject of this action concededly did not fulfill the incitement requirements of *Brandenburg.* Thus it is constitutionally protected.

Appellant would distinguish between the fictional presentation of "Born Innocent" and news programs and documentaries. But that distinction is too blurred to protect adequately First Amendment values. "Everyone is familiar with instances of propaganda through fiction. What is one man's amusement, teaches another's doctrine." (*Winters v. New York, supra,* 333 U.S. 507, 510.) If a negligence theory is recognized, a television network or local station could be liable when a child imitates activities portrayed in a news program or documentary. Thus, the distinction urged by appellant cannot be accepted. (See Krattenmaker & Powe, Jr., *Televised Violence: First Amendment Principles and Social Science Theory* (1978) 64 Va.L.Rev. 1123, 1169 fn. 253. For a similar conclusion regarding content regulation, see Note, *Regulation of Programming Content to Protect Children After Pacifica* (1979) 32 Vand.L.Rev. 1377, 1410-1411.) "Among free men, the deterrents ordinarily to be applied to prevent crime are education and punishment for violations of the law, not abridgement of the rights of free speech . . . ." (*Whitney v. California* (1927) 274 U.S. 357, 378 [conc. opn. of Brandeis, J.], overruled by *Brandenburg v. Ohio, supra*, 395 U.S. 444; see *Kingsley Pictures Corp. v. Regents, supra*, 360 U.S. 684, 689; *Zamora v. Columbia Broadcasting System* (S.D.Fla. 1979) 480 F.Supp. 199, 206.) The trial court's determination that the First Amendment bars appellant's claim where no incitement is alleged must be upheld.

Appellant argues from *Weirum v. RKO General, Inc.* (1975) 539 P.2d 36, that the First Amendment should not bar a negligence action. In *Weirum*, the California Supreme Court upheld a jury finding that a Los Angeles rock radio station was liable for the wrongful death of a motorist killed by two teenagers participating in a contest sponsored by the station. The court emphasized that the youthful contestants' reckless conduct was stimulated by the radio station's broadcast. (*Id.*, at p. 47.) Limiting its ruling, the court indicated that "[t]he giveaway contest was no commonplace invitation to an attraction available on a limited basis. It was a competitive scramble in which the thrill of the chase to be the one and only victor was intensified by the live broadcasts which accompanied the pursuit. . . . In [other] situations there [was] no attempt, as here, to generate a competitive pursuit on public streets, accelerated by *repeated importuning* by radio to be the very first to arrive at a particular destination." (*Id.*, at p. 48; italics added.) Disposing of the radio station's First Amendment claim, the court said: "Defendant's contention that the giveaway contest must be afforded the deference due society's interest in the First Amendment is clearly without merit. The issue here is civil accountability for the foreseeable results of a broadcast which created an undue risk of harm to decedent. The First Amendment does not sanction the infliction of physical injury merely because achieved by word, rather than act." (*Id.*) Although the language utilized by the Supreme Court was broad, it must be understood in light of the particular facts of that case. The radio station's broadcast was designed to encourage its youthful listeners to be the first to arrive at a particular location in order to win a prize and gain momentary glory. The *Weirum* broadcasts actively and repeatedly encouraged listeners to speed to announced locations. Liability was imposed on the broadcaster for urging listeners to act in an inherently dangerous manner. No such urging can be imputed to respondents here. Appellant only alleges that the teenage viewers of "Born Innocent" acted on the stimulus of the broadcast rather than in response to encouragement of such conduct. *Weirum* does not control the present case.

Appellant also relies on *FCC v. Pacifica Foundation, supra,* 438 U.S. 726. But the narrowness of the *Pacifica* decision precludes its application here. "We simply hold that when the Commission finds that a pig has entered the parlor, the exercise of its *regulatory* power does not depend on proof that the pig is obscene." (*Id.,* at pp. 750-751; italics added.) Furthermore, Justice Powell in his concurrence emphasized that the court is not free "to decide on the basis of its content which speech protected by the First Amendment is most 'valuable' and hence deserving of the most protection, and which is less 'valuable' and hence deserving of less protection." (*Id.,* at p. 761 [conc. opn. of Powell, J.].) As the United States District Court indicated in *Zamora v. Columbia Broadcasting System, supra,* 480 F.Supp. 199, 206, reliance on *FCC v. Pacifica Foundation* "is misplaced because of both the factual and legal bases for that decision." Other methods of controlling violence on television must be found. *Pacifica* deals with regulation of indecency, not the imposition of general tort liability. Imposing liability on a simple negligence theory here would frustrate vital freedom of speech guarantees. *Gertz v. Robert Welch, Inc.* (1974) 418 U.S. 323, is also to be distinguished: There the United States Supreme Court recognized the power of the states to impose civil liability for defamation "so long as the States [do] not impose liability without fault." (418 U.S. at p. 339.) The holding does not extend more broadly to tort liability for speech in areas outside the law of defamation.

The judgment is affirmed.

FCC Report and Order

IN RE AMENDMENT OF PART 73 REGARDING BROADCAST HOAXES

MM Docket No. 91-314
Adopted: May 14, 1992

Part 73 of Title 47 of the Code of Federal Regulations is amended as follows:

. . .

Section 73.1217, Broadcast hoaxes, is added to Part 73 to read as follows:

§ 73.1217 Broadcast hoaxes.

No licensee or permittee of any broadcast station shall broadcast false information concerning a crime or a catastrophe if (a) the licensee knows this information is false, (b) it is foreseeable that broadcast of the information will cause substantial public harm, and (c) broadcast of the information does in fact directly cause substantial public harm. Any programming accompanied by a disclaimer will be presumed not to pose foreseeable harm if the disclaimer clearly characterizes the program as a fiction and is presented in a way that is reasonable under the circumstances.

FCC Report and Order

IN THE MATTER OF IMPLEMENTATION OF SECTION 551 OF THE TELECOMMUNICATIONS ACT OF 1996

Video Programming Ratings

CS Docket No. 97-55
Adopted: March 12, 1998

I. INTRODUCTION

In the Telecommunications Act of 1996 (the "1996 Act"), Congress determined that parents should be provided with timely information about the nature of upcoming video programming and with the technological tools that would allow them to easily block violent, sexual, or other programming they believe is harmful to their children. . . . Following enactment of the 1996 Act, and over the course of the next year, the broadcasting, cable and program production industries worked together to develop a rating system, which they implemented in early January 1997 . . . The revised *TV Parental Guidelines* were implemented on October 1, 1997.

. . .

III. THE TV PARENTAL GUIDELINES

. . .

The Industry states that the *TV Parental Guidelines* will apply to all television programming except for news, sports, and unedited MPAA rated movies on premium cable channels. The *TV Parental Guidelines* (labels and content indicators, and respective meanings) are:

For programs designed solely for children:
TV-Y (All Children—*This program is designed to be appropriate for all children*). Whether animated or live-action, the themes and elements in this program are specifically designed for a very young audience, including children from ages 2-6. This program is not expected to frighten younger children.

TV-Y7 (Directed to Older Children—*This program is designed for children age 7 and above*). It may be more appropriate for children who have acquired the developmental skills needed to distinguish between make-believe and reality. Themes and elements in this program may include mild fantasy or comedic violence, or may frighten children under the age of 7. Therefore, parents may wish to consider the suitability of this program for their very young children. Note: For those programs where fantasy violence may be more intense or more combative than other programs in this category, such programs will be designated **TV-Y7-FV.**
For programs designed for the entire audience, the general categories are:

TV-G (General Audience—*Most parents would find this program suitable for all ages*). Although this rating does not signify a program designed specifically for children, most parents may let younger children watch this program unattended. It contains little or no violence, no strong language and little or no sexual dialogue or situations.

TV-PG (Parental Guidance Suggested—*This program contains material that parents may find unsuitable for younger children*). Many parents may want to watch it with their younger children. The theme itself may call for parental guidance and/or the program contains one or more of the following: moderate violence (V), some sexual situations (S), infrequent coarse language (L), or some suggestive dialogue (D).

TV-14 (Parents Strongly Cautioned—*This program contains some material that many parents would find unsuitable for children under 14 years of age*). Parents are strongly urged to exercise greater care in monitoring this program and are cautioned against letting children under the age of 14 watch unattended. This program contains one or more of the following: intense violence (V), intense sexual situations (S), strong coarse language (L), or intensely suggestive dialogue (D).

TV-MA (Mature Audience Only—*This program is specifically designed to be viewed by adults and therefore may be unsuitable for children under 17*). This program contains one or more of the following: graphic violence (V), explicit sexual activity (S), or crude indecent language (L).

As proposed by the Industry, rating icons and associated content symbols appear for 15 seconds at the beginning of all rated programming and through the use of a display button on a remote control device thereafter. Under the *TV Parental Guidelines,* the rating guidelines will typically be applied to television programs by broadcast and cable networks and producers, while television stations retain the right to substitute the rating they deem appropriate for their audience. The v-chip, which will be installed in television sets, or available through set-top boxes, will read information encoded in the program and block based on the overall age category or by the S, L, V, or D rating assigned to the program, or by a combination of the two.

True Threats

PLANNED PARENTHOOD OF COLUMBIA/WILLAMETTE, INC. V. AMERICAN COALITION OF LIFE ACTIVISTS

290 F.3d 1058 (9th Cir. 2002)

Opinion by Judge RYMER.

For the first time we construe what the Freedom of Access to Clinics Entrances Act (FACE), 18 U.S.C. § 248, means by "threat of force." FACE gives aggrieved persons a right of action against whoever by "threat of force . . . intentionally . . . intimidates . . . any person because that person is or has been . . . providing reproductive health services." 18 U.S.C. § 248(a)(1) and (c)(1)(A). This requires that we define "threat of force" in a way that comports with the First Amendment, and it raises the question whether the conduct that occurred here falls within the category of unprotected speech.

Four physicians, Dr. Robert Crist, Dr. Warren M. Hern, Dr. Elizabeth Newhall, and Dr. James Newhall, and two health clinics that provide medical services to women including abortions, Planned Parenthood of the Columbia/Willamette, Inc. (PPCW) and the Portland Feminist Women's Health Center (PFWHC), brought suit under FACE claiming that they were targeted with threats by the American Coalition of Life

Activists (ACLA), Advocates for Life Ministries (ALM), and numerous individuals. Three threats remain at issue: the Deadly Dozen "GUILTY" poster which identifies Hern and the Newhalls among ten others; the Crist "GUILTY" poster with Crist's name, addresses and photograph; and the "Nuremberg Files," which is a compilation about those whom the ACLA anticipated one day might be put on trial for crimes against humanity. The "GUILTY" posters identifying specific physicians were circulated in the wake of a series of "WANTED" and "unWANTED" posters that had identified other doctors who performed abortions before they were murdered.

Although the posters do not contain a threat on their face, the district court held that context could be considered. It defined a threat under FACE in accordance with our "true threat" jurisprudence, as a statement made when "a reasonable person would foresee that the statement would be interpreted by those to whom the maker communicates the statement as a serious expression of intent to harm." Applying this definition, the court denied ACLA's motion for summary judgment in a published opinion. *Planned Parenthood of the Columbia/Willamette, Inc. v. ACLA (PPCW II)*, 23 F.Supp.2d 1182 (D. Or. 1998). The jury returned a verdict in physicians' favor, and the court enjoined ACLA from publishing the posters or providing other materials with the specific intent to threaten Crist, Hern, Elizabeth Newhall, James Newhall, PPCW, or the Health Center. *Planned Parenthood of the Columbia/Willamette, Inc. v. ACLA (PPCW III)*, 41 F.Supp.2d 1130 (D.Or.1999). ACLA timely appealed.

A panel of this court reversed. In its view, the standard adopted by the district court allowed the jury to find ACLA liable for putting the doctors in harm's way by singling them out for the attention of unrelated but violent third parties, conduct which is protected by the First Amendment, rather than for authorizing or directly threatening harm itself, which is not. *Planned Parenthood of the Columbia/Willamette, Inc. v. ACLA (PPCW IV)*, 244 F.3d 1007 (9th Cir.), *reh'g en banc granted*, 268 F.3d 908 (9th Cir. 2001). The panel decided that it should evaluate the record independently to determine whether ACLA's statements could reasonably be construed as saying that ACLA, or its agents, would physically harm doctors who did not stop performing abortions. Having done so, the panel found that the jury's verdict could not stand.

We reheard the case en banc because these issues are obviously important. We now conclude that it was proper for the district court to adopt our long-standing law on "true threats" to define a "threat" for purposes of FACE. FACE itself requires that the threat of force be made with the intent to intimidate. Thus, the jury must have found that ACLA made statements to intimidate the physicians, reasonably foreseeing that physicians would interpret the statements as a serious expression of ACLA's intent to harm them because they provided reproductive health services. Construing the facts in the light most favorable to physicians, the verdict is supported by substantial evidence. ACLA was aware that a "wanted"-type poster would likely be interpreted as a serious threat of death or bodily harm by a doctor in the reproductive health services community who was identified on one, given the previous pattern of "WANTED" posters identifying a specific physician followed by that physician's murder. The same is true of the posting about these physicians on that part of the "Nuremberg Files" where lines were drawn through the names of doctors who provided abortion services and who had been killed or wounded. We are independently satisfied that to this limited extent, ACLA's conduct amounted to a true threat and is not protected speech.

As we see no reversible error on liability or in the equitable relief that was granted, we affirm. However, we remand for consideration of whether the punitive damages award comports with due process.

I.

The facts are fully set out in the district court's order granting injunctive relief, *PPWC III*, 41 F.Supp.2d at 1131-1155, and we shall not belabor them. In sum:

On March 10, 1993, Michael Griffin shot and killed Dr. David Gunn as he entered an abortion clinic in Pensacola, Florida. Before this, a "WANTED" and an "unWANTED" poster with Gunn's name, photograph, address and other personal information were published. The "WANTED" poster describes Gunn as an abortionist and invites participation by prayer and fasting, by writing and calling him and sharing a willingness to help him leave his profession, and by asking him to stop doing abortions; the "unWANTED" poster states that he kills children at designated locations and "[t]o defenseless unborn babies Gunn in [sic] heavily armed and very dangerous." After Gunn's murder, Bray and Paul Hill (a non-party who was later convicted of murdering a different doctor) prepared a statement supporting Griffin's acquittal on a justifiable homicide theory, which ALM, Burnett, Crane, Dodds, Foreman, McMillan, Ramey and Stover joined.

On August 21, 1993, Dr. George Patterson, who operated the clinic where Gunn worked, was shot to death. A "WANTED" poster had been circulated prior to his murder, indicating where he performed abortions and that he had Gunn perform abortions for his Pensacola clinic.

In July 1994, Dr. John Bayard Britton was murdered by Paul Hill after being named on an "unWANTED" poster that Hill helped to prepare. One gives Britton's physical description together with his home and office addresses and phone numbers, and charges "crimes against humanity"; another also displays his picture and states that "he is considered armed and extremely dangerous to women and children. Pray that he is soon apprehended by the love of Jesus!!!" In addition to these items, a third version of the Britton "unWANTED" poster lists personal achievements and Britton's "crimes against humanity," also warning that "John Bayard Britton is considered armed and extremely dangerous, especialy [sic] to women and children." ALM, Bray, Burnett, Crane, McMillan, Ramey and Stover signed a petition supporting Hill.

Many pro-life activists in Operation Rescue condemned these acts of violence. As a result, ALM, Bray, Burnett, Crane, Foreman, McMillan, Ramey and Stover, who espoused a "pro-force" point of view, split off to form ACLA. Burnett observed, "if someone was to condemn any violence against abortion, they probably wouldn't have felt comfortable working with us." Organizational meetings were held in the spring of 1994, and ACLA's first event was held in August 1994. ACLA is based in Portland, Oregon, as is ALM. ALM publishes *Life Advocate,* a magazine that is distributed nationally and advocates the use of force to oppose the delivery of abortion services. Except for Bray, who authored *A Time to Kill* and served time in federal prison for conspiring to bomb ten clinics, the individual defendants were directors of ACLA and actively involved in its affairs. ALM commissioned and published Bray's book, noting that it "shows the connection between the [justifiable homicide] position and clinic destruction and the shootings of abortionists." Wysong and ACLA also drafted and circulated a "Contract on the Abortion Industry," having deliberately chosen that language to allude to mafia hit contracts.

ACLA presented the Deadly Dozen poster during a January 25, 1995 press conference at the March for Life event in Washington, D.C. Bray, Burnett, Crane, Dodds, Foreman, McMillan, Murch, Ramey, Stover, Treshman and Wysong were there; Dreste later ratified the poster's release. This poster is captioned "GUILTY" at the top (which meant the same thing to Crane, who drafted it, as "wanted"), beneath which in slightly smaller print the poster indicates "OF CRIMES AGAINST HUMANITY." The poster continues: "Abortion was provided as a choice for East European and Jewish women by the (Nazi) National Socialist

Regime, and was prosecuted during the Nuremberg Trials (1945-46) under Allied Control Order No. 10 as a 'war crime.'" Under the heading "THE DEADLY DOZEN," the poster identifies thirteen doctors of whom James Newhall, Elizabeth Newhall, and Warren Hern are three. The poster provides Hern's residence and the home address of James Newhall and Elizabeth Newhall; it also lists the name and home address of Dr. George Kabacy, a doctor who provided abortions at PPCW. It offers a "$5,000 REWARD" "for information leading to arrest, conviction and revocation of license to practice medicine." At the bottom the poster bears the legend "ABORTIONIST" in large, bold typeface. The day after the Deadly Dozen poster was released, the FBI offered protection to doctors identified on it and advised them to wear bulletproof vests and take other security precautions, which they did. Knowing this, ALM reprinted the poster in the March 1995 edition of its magazine *Life Advocate* under a cover with the "grim reaper" holding a scythe; Murch printed it in his newsletter *Salt & Light;* and ACLA republished the Deadly Dozen poster at events in August 1995 and January 1996.

ACLA released the Crist poster along with five others in August 1995 at the old federal courthouse in St. Louis where the *Dred Scott* decision had been handed down. Burnett, Crane, Dreste, McMillan, Ramey, Stover and Wysong attended the event. Three of the posters identify doctors; the others identify reproductive health care clinics, one of which was a Planned Parenthood affiliate where Crist worked. The Crist poster has "GUILTY" in large bold letters at the top followed by "OF CRIMES AGAINST HUMANITY" in smaller font. It also gives his home and work addresses; states "Please write, leaflet or picket his neighborhood to expose his blood guilt"; offers a "$500 REWARD" "to any ACLA organization that successfully persuades Crist to turn from his child killing through activities within ACLA guidelines"; and has "ABORTIONIST" in large bold type at the bottom.

At its January 1996 conference, ACLA displayed the Deadly Dozen poster, held a "White Rose Banquet" to honor prisoners convicted of anti-abortion violence, and introduced ALM's Paul deParrie to unveil the "Nuremberg Files." ACLA sent a hard copy of some of the Files to Neal Horsley (a non-party) to post on the internet, and ACLA's name appeared on the Nuremberg Files website opened in January 1997. Approximately 200 people are listed under the label "ABORTIONISTS: the shooters," and 200 more are listed under Files for judges, politicians, law enforcement, spouses, and abortion rights supporters. Crist, Hern and the Newhalls are listed in the "abortionists" section, which bears the legend: "Black font (working); Greyed-out Name (wounded);

Strikethrough (fatality)." The names of Gunn, Patterson and Britton are struck through.

By January 1995 ACLA knew the effect that "WANTED," "unWANTED," or "GUILTY" posters had on doctors named in them. For example, in a September 1993 issue of *Life Advocate* which reported that an "unwanted" poster was being prepared for Britton, ALM remarked of the Gunn murder that it "sent shock waves of fear through the ranks of abortion providers across the country. As a result, many more doctors quit out of fear for their lives, and the ones who are left are scared stiff." Of another doctor who decided to quit performing abortions after circulation of a "Not Wanted" poster, Bray wrote that "it is clear to all who possess faculties capable of inductive analysis: he was bothered and afraid." Wysong also stated: "Listening to what abortionists said, abortionists who have quit the practice who are no longer killing babies but are now pro-life. They said the two things they feared the most were being sued for malpractice and having their picture put on a poster." And Burnett testified with respect to the danger that "wanted" or "guilty" posters pose to the lives of those who provide abortions: "I mean, if I was an abortionist, I would be afraid."

By January 1995 the physicians knew about the Gunn, Patterson and Britton murders and the posters that preceded each. Hern was terrified when his name appeared on the Deadly Dozen poster; as he put it: "The fact that wanted posters about these doctors had been circulated, prior to their assassination, and that the-that the posters, then, were followed by the doctor's assassination, emphasized for me the danger posed by this document, the Deadly Dozen List, which meant to me that-that, as night follows day, that my name was on this wanted poster . . . and that I would be assassinated, as had the other doctors been assassinated." Hern interpreted the poster as meaning "Do what we tell you to do, or we will kill you. And they do." Crist was "truly frightened," and stopped practicing medicine for a while out of fear for his life. Dr. Elizabeth Newhall interpreted the Deadly Dozen poster as saying that if she didn't stop doing abortions, her life was at risk. Dr. James Newhall was "severely frightened" in light of the "clear pattern" of a wanted poster and a murder when there was "another wanted poster with my name on it."

The jury found for plaintiffs on all claims except for Bray and Treshman on the RICO claims. . . . .

Given that the verdict for physicians and the injunctive relief granted in their favor restrict speech, we review the record independently in order to satisfy ourselves that the posters and the Files constitute a "true threat" such that they lack First Amendment protection...

III.

ACLA argues that the First Amendment requires reversal because liability was based on political speech that constituted neither an incitement to imminent lawless action nor a true threat. It suggests that the key question for us to consider is whether these posters can be considered "true threats" when, in fact, the posters on their face contain no explicitly threatening language. Further, ACLA submits that classic political speech cannot be converted into non-protected speech by a context of violence that includes the independent action of others.

Physicians counter that this threats case must be analyzed under the settled threats law of this circuit. Following precedent, it was proper for the jury to take context into account. They point out that the district court limited evidence of anti-abortion violence to evidence tending to show knowledge of a particular defendant, and maintain that the objective standard on which the jury was instructed comports both with Ninth Circuit law and congressional intent. As the First Amendment does not protect true threats of force, physicians conclude, ACLA's speech was not protected.

A.

We start with the statute under which this action arises. Section 248(c)(1)(A) gives a private right of action to any person aggrieved by reason of the conduct prohibited by subsection (a). Subsection (a)(1) provides:

> (a) . . . Whoever—
> (1) by force or threat of force or by physical obstruction, intentionally injures, intimidates or interferes with or attempts to injure, intimidate or interfere with any person because that person is or has been, or in order to intimidate such person or any other person or any class of persons from, obtaining or providing reproductive health services . . . shall be subject to the . . . civil remedies provided in subsection (c) . . . .

18 U.S.C. § 248(a)(1). The statute also provides that "[n]othing in this section shall be construed . . . to prohibit any expressive conduct (including peaceful picketing or other peaceful demonstration) protected from

legal prohibition by the First Amendment to the Constitution." 18 U.S.C. § 248(d)(1).

FACE does not define "threat," although it does provide that "[t]he term 'intimidate' means to place a person in reasonable apprehension of bodily harm to him-or herself or to another." 18 U.S.C. § 248(e)(3). Thus, the first task is to define "threat" for purposes of the Act. This requires a definition that comports with the First Amendment, that is, a "true threat."

The Supreme Court has provided benchmarks, but no definition.

Brandenburg v. Ohio, 395 U.S. 444, 447 (1969), makes it clear that the First Amendment protects speech that advocates violence, so long as the speech is not directed to inciting or producing imminent lawless action and is not likely to incite or produce such action. So do *Hess v. Indiana,* 414 U.S. 105 (1973) (overturning disorderly conduct conviction of antiwar protestor who yelled "We'll take the fucking street later (or again)"), and *NAACP v. Claiborne Hardware Co.,* 458 U.S. 886 (1982). If ACLA had merely endorsed or encouraged the violent actions of others, its speech would be protected.

However, while advocating violence is protected, threatening a person with violence is not. In *Watts v. United States,* 394 U.S. 705 (1969), the Court explicitly distinguished between political hyperbole, which is protected, and true threats, which are not. Considering how to construe a statute which prohibited "knowingly and willfully . . . (making) any threat to take the life of or to inflict bodily harm upon the President," the Court admonished that any statute which criminalizes a form of pure speech "must be interpreted with the commands of the First Amendment clearly in mind. What is a threat must be distinguished from what is constitutionally protected speech." *Id.* at 705, 707. In that case, an 18-year old war protester told a discussion group of other young people at a public rally on the Washington Monument grounds: "They always holler at us to get an education. And now I have already received my draft classification as 1-A and I have got to report for my physical this Monday coming. I am not going. If they ever make me carry a rifle the first man I want to get in my sights is L.B.J." *Id.* at 706. His audience laughed. Taken in context, and given the conditional nature of the statement and the reaction of the listeners, the Court concluded that the speech could not be interpreted other than as "a kind of very crude offensive method of stating a political opposition to the President." *Id.* at 708. Accordingly, it ordered judgment entered for Watts.

ACLA's position is that the posters, including the Nuremberg Files, are protected political speech under *Watts,* and cannot lose this character by context. But this is not correct. The Court itself considered context and determined that Watts's statement was political hyperbole instead of a true threat because of context. *Id.* at 708. Beyond this, ACLA points out that the posters contain no language that is a threat. We agree that this is literally true. Therefore, ACLA submits, this case is really an incitement case in disguise. So viewed, the posters are protected speech under *Brandenburg* and *Claiborne,* which ACLA suggests is the closest analogue. We disagree that *Claiborne* is closely analogous.

In March 1966 black citizens in Claiborne County made a list of demands for racial equality and integration. Unsatisfied by the response, several hundred black persons at a meeting of the local National Association for the Advancement of Colored People (NAACP) voted to place a boycott on white merchants in the area. The boycott continued until October 1969. During this period, stores were watched and the names of persons who violated the boycott were read at meetings of the NAACP at the First Baptist Church, and published in a local paper called "Black Times." These persons were branded as traitors to the black cause, were called demeaning names, and were socially ostracized. A few incidents of violence occurred. Birdshot was fired at the houses of two boycott violators; a brick was thrown through a windshield; and a flower garden was damaged. None of the victims ceased trading with white merchants. Six other incidents of arguably unlawful conduct occurred. White business owners brought suit against the NAACP and Charles Evers, its field secretary, along with other individuals who had participated in the boycott, for violating Mississippi state laws on malicious interference with a business, antitrust, and illegal boycott. Plaintiffs pursued several theories of liability: participating in management of the boycott; serving as an "enforcer" or monitor; committing or threatening acts of violence, which showed that the perpetrator wanted the boycott to succeed by coercion when it could not succeed by persuasion; and as to Evers, threatening violence against boycott breakers, and as to the NAACP because he was its field secretary when he committed tortious and constitutionally unprotected acts. Damages for business losses during the boycott and injunctive relief were awarded.

The Court held that there could be no recovery based on intimidation by threats of social ostracism, because offensive and coercive speech is protected by the First Amendment. "The use of speeches, marches, and threats of social ostracism cannot provide the basis for a damages award.

But violent conduct is beyond the pale of constitutional protection." 458 U.S. at 933. There was some evidence of violence, but the violence was not pervasive as it had been in *Milk Wagon Drivers Union Local 753 v. Meadowmoor Dairies, Inc.,* 312 U.S. 287 (1941). Accordingly, the Court made clear that only losses proximately caused by unlawful conduct could be recovered. Further, civil liability could not be imposed consistent with the First Amendment solely on account of an individual's association with others who have committed acts of violence; he must have incited or authorized them himself.

For the same reasons the Court held that liability could not be imposed on Evers for his participation in the boycott itself, or for his threats of vilification or ostracism. However, the merchants also sought damages from Evers for his speeches. He gave one in April 1966, and two others in April 1969. In the first, he told his audience that they would be watched and that blacks who traded with white merchants would be answerable to him; he also said that any "uncle toms" who broke the boycott would "have their necks broken" by their own people. In his April 19, 1969 speech, Evers stated that boycott violators would be "disciplined" by their own people and warned that the Sheriff could not sleep with boycott violators at night. And on April 21, Evers gave another speech to several hundred people calling for a total boycott of white-owned businesses and saying: "If we catch any of you going in any of them racist stores, we're gonna break your damn neck." The Court concluded that the "emotionally charged rhetoric" of Evers's speeches was within the bounds of *Brandenburg.* It was not followed by violence, and there was no evidence-apart from the speeches themselves-that Evers authorized, ratified, or directly threatened violence. "If there were other evidence of his authorization of wrongful conduct, the references to discipline in the speeches could be used to corroborate that evidence." *Claiborne,* 458 U.S. at 929. As there was not, the findings were constitutionally inadequate to support the damages judgment against him and, in turn, the NAACP.

Claiborne, of course, did not arise under a threats statute. The Court had no need to consider whether Evers's statements were true threats of force within the meaning of a threats statute; it held only that his speeches did not incite illegal activity, thus could not have caused business losses and could not be the basis for liability to white merchants. As the opinion points out, there was no context to give the speeches (including the expression "break your neck") the implication of authorizing or directly threatening unlawful conduct. To the extent there was any intimidating overtone, Evers's rhetoric was extemporaneous, surrounded by statements supporting non-violent action, and primarily of the social ostracism sort. No specific individuals were targeted. For all that appears, "the break your neck" comments were hyperbolic vernacular. Certainly there was no history that Evers or anyone else associated with the NAACP had broken anyone's neck who did not participate in, or opposed, this boycott or any others. Nor is there any indication that Evers's listeners took his statement that boycott breakers' "necks would be broken" as a serious threat that *their* necks would be broken; they kept on shopping at boycotted stores.

Thus, *Watts* was the only Supreme Court case that discussed the First Amendment in relation to true threats before we first confronted the issue. Apart from holding that Watts's crack about L.B.J. was not a true threat, the Court set out no standard for determining when a statement is a true threat that is unprotected speech under the First Amendment. Shortly after *Watts* was rendered, we had to decide in *Roy v. United States,* 416 F.2d 874 (9th Cir. 1969), whether a Marine Corps private made a true threat for purposes of 18 U.S.C. § 871 against the President, who was coming to his base the next day, by saying: "I am going to get him." We adopted a "reasonable speaker" test. As it has come to be articulated, the test is:

Whether a particular statement may properly be considered to be a threat is governed by an objective standard-whether a reasonable person would foresee that the statement would be interpreted by those to whom the maker communicates the statement as a serious expression of intent to harm or assault. *United States v. Orozco-Santillan,* 903 F.2d 1262, 1265 (9th Cir. 1990)....

Under our cases, a threat is "an expression of an intention to inflict evil, injury, or damage on another." *Gilbert II,* 884 F.2d at 457; *Orozco-Santillan,* 903 F.2d at 1265. "Alleged threats should be considered in light of their entire factual context, including the surrounding events and reaction of the listeners." *Orozco-Santillan,* 903 F.2d at 1265; *see also Mitchell,* 812 F.2d at 1255 (citing *Watts,* 394 U.S. at 708; *Merrill,* 746 F.2d at 462; *Roy,* 416 F.2d at 876). "'The fact that a threat is subtle does not make it less of a threat.'" *Orozco-Santillan,* 903 F.2d at 1265 (quoting *Gilbert II,* 884 F.2d at 457). A true threat, that is one "where a reasonable person would foresee that the listener will believe he will be subjected to physical violence upon his person, is unprotected by the First Amendment." *Id.* (citing *Merrill,* 746 F.2d at 462).

It is not necessary that the defendant intend to, or be able to carry out his threat; the only intent requirement for a true threat is that the defendant intentionally or knowingly communicate the threat. *Orozco-Santillan,* 903 F.2d at 1265 n. 3; *Gilbert II,* 884 F.2d at 456-57; *Mitchell,* 812 F.2d at 1256 (upholding § 871 conviction of defendant with no capacity to carry out threat); *Roy,* 416 F.2d at 877. Other circuits are in accord. Nevertheless, we are urged to adopt a subjective intent requirement for FACE. In particular, amicus ACLU Foundation of Oregon, Inc., advocates a subjective intent component to "require evidence, albeit circumstantial or inferential in many cases, that the speaker actually *intended* to induce fear, intimidation, or terror; namely, that the speaker intended to threaten. If a person did not intend to threaten or intimidate (*i.e.,* did not intend that his or her statement be understood as a threat), then the speech should not be considered to be a 'true threat,' unprotected by the First Amendment." However, this much is subsumed within the statutory standard of FACE itself, which requires that the threat of force be made with the intent to intimidate. The "requirement of intent to intimidate serves to insulate the statute from unconstitutional application to protected speech." *Gilbert I,* 813 F.2d at 1529 (construing the Fair Housing Act's threat provision, 42 U.S.C. § 3631, which is essentially the same as FACE's). No reason appears to engraft another intent requirement onto the statute, because whether or not the maker of the threat has an actual intention to carry it out, "an apparently serious threat may cause the mischief or evil toward which the statute was in part directed." *Gilbert II,* 884 F.2d at 458 (quoting *Roy,* 416 F.2d at 877).

The dissents would change the test, either to require that the speaker actually intend to carry out the threat or be in control of those who will, or to make it inapplicable when the speech is public rather than private. However, for years our test has focused on what *a reasonable speaker* would foresee the *listener's* reaction to be under the circumstances, and that is where we believe it should remain. *See Madsen,* 512 U.S. at 773 (noting that "threats . . . however communicated, are proscribable under the First Amendment, and indicating that display of signs "that could be interpreted as threats or veiled threats" could be prohibited"). Threats are outside the First Amendment to "protect[ ] individuals from the fear of violence, from the disruption that fear engenders, and from the possibility that the threatened violence will occur." *R.A.V. v. City of St. Paul, Minn.,* 505 U.S. 377, 388 (1992). This purpose is not served by hinging constitutionality on the speaker's subjective intent or capacity to do (or not to do) harm. Rather, these factors go to how reasonably foreseeable it is to a speaker that the listener will seriously take his communication as an intent to inflict bodily harm. This suffices to distinguish a "true threat" from speech that is merely frightening. Thus, no reasonable speaker would foresee that a patient would take the statement "You have cancer and will die within six months," or that a pedestrian would take a warning "Get out of the way of that bus," as a serious expression of intent *to inflict* bodily harm; the harm is going to happen anyway.

Neither do we agree that threatening speech made in public is entitled to heightened constitutional protection just because it is communicated publicly rather than privately. As *Madsen* indicates, threats are unprotected by the First Amendment "however communicated." *Madsen,* 512 U.S. at 753.

Therefore, we hold that "threat of force" in FACE means what our settled threats law says a true threat is: a statement which, in the entire context and under all the circumstances, a reasonable person would foresee would be interpreted by those to whom the statement is communicated as a serious expression of intent to inflict bodily harm upon that person. So defined, a threatening statement that violates FACE is unprotected under the First Amendment.

B.

Although ACLA does not believe we should reach this point, if we do it submits that no claim was made out even under "true threats" cases. First, it argues that other threats cases were criminal actions against someone who made a real threat directly to others, not political speech as is the case here. It contrasts what it calls "a threat plus context" present in *United States v. Dinwiddie,* 76 F.3d 913 (8th Cir. 1996), and in other out-of-circuit cases, with the absence of a direct threat in this case. However, our cases do not require that the maker of the threat personally cause physical harm to the listener. ...

ACLA also maintains that "context" means the direct circumstances surrounding delivery of the threat, or evidence sufficient to resolve ambiguity in the words of the statement-not two weeks of testimony as occurred here in the district court. Otherwise, ACLA submits, FACE is facially invalid. However, none of our cases has limited "context" to explaining ambiguous words, or to delivery. We, and so far as we can tell, other circuits as well, consider the whole factual context and "all of the circumstances," *Merrill,* 746 F.2d at 462, in order to determine whether a statement is a true threat. ...

Indeed, context is critical in a true threats case and history can give meaning to the medium. ... Of the courts to consider the constitutionality of threats statutes, including the United States Supreme Court in *Watts,* all have upheld constitutionality and ACLA points to none that has disallowed consideration of context. This makes sense, because without context, a burning cross or dead rat mean nothing. In any event, the requirement of intent to intimidate cures whatever risk there might be of overbreadth.

Nor does consideration of context amount to viewpoint discrimination, as ACLA contends. ACLA's theory appears to be that because the posters did not contain any threat on their face, the views of abortion foes are chilled more than the views of abortion-right proponents because of the random acts of violence committed by some people against abortion providers. However, FACE itself is viewpoint neutral. *See, e.g., United States v. Weslin,* 156 F.3d 292, 296-97 (2d Cir. 1998); *United States v. Wilson,* 154 F.3d 658, 663 (7th Cir. 1998) ("The Act punishes anyone who engages in the prohibited conduct, irrespective of the person's viewpoint and does not target any message based on content. 'The Access Act thus does not play favorites: it protects from violent or obstructive activity not only abortion clinics, but facilities providing pre-pregnancy and pregnancy counseling services, as well as facilities counseling alternatives to abortion.'") (quoting *Terry v. Reno,* 101 F.3d 1412, 1419 (D.C. Cir. 1996)). Moreover, ACLA could not be liable under FACE unless *it* made a true threat *with the intent to intimidate* physicians. Thus it is making a threat to intimidate that makes ACLA's conduct unlawful, not its viewpoint.

Because of context, we conclude that the Crist and Deadly Dozen posters are not just a political statement. Even if the Gunn poster, which was the first "WANTED" poster, was a purely political message when originally issued, and even if the Britton poster were too, by the time of the Crist poster, the poster format itself had acquired currency as a death threat for abortion providers. Gunn was killed after his poster was released; Britton was killed after his poster was released; and Patterson was killed after his poster was released. Knowing this, and knowing the fear generated among those in the reproductive health services community who were singled out for identification on a "wanted"-type poster, ACLA deliberately identified Crist on a "GUILTY" poster and intentionally put the names of Hern and the Newhalls on the Deadly Dozen "GUILTY" poster to intimidate them. This goes well beyond the political message (regardless of what one thinks of it) that abortionists are killers who deserve death too.

The Nuremberg Files are somewhat different. Although they name individuals, they name hundreds of them. The avowed intent is "collecting dossiers on abortionists in anticipation that one day we may be able to hold them on trial for crimes against humanity." The web page states:

"One of the great tragedies of the Nuremberg trials of Nazis after WWII was that complete information and documented evidence had not been collected so many war criminals went free or were only found guilty of minor crimes. We do not want the same thing to happen when the day comes to charge abortionists with their crimes. We anticipate the day when these people will be charged in PERFECTLY LEGAL COURTS once the tide of this nation's opinion turns against child-killing (as it surely will)." However offensive or disturbing this might be to those listed in the Files, being offensive and provocative is protected under the First Amendment. But, in two critical respects, the Files go further. In addition to listing judges, politicians and law enforcement personnel, the Files separately categorize "Abortionists" and list the names of individuals who provide abortion services, including, specifically, Crist, Hern, and both Newhalls. Also, names of abortion providers who have been murdered because of their activities are lined through in black, while names of those who have been wounded are highlighted in grey. As a result, we cannot say that it is clear as a matter of law that listing Crist, Hern, and the Newhalls on *both* the Nuremberg Files *and* the GUILTY posters is purely protected, political expression.

Accordingly, whether the Crist Poster, the Deadly Dozen poster, and the identification of Crist, Hern, Dr. Elizabeth Newhall and Dr. James Newhall in the Nuremberg Files as well as on "wanted"-type posters, constituted true threats was properly for the jury to decide.

C.

ACLA next argues that the true threat instructions require reversal because they permitted consideration of motive, history of violence including the violent actions of others, and the defendants' subjective motives as part of context. We have already explained why it is proper for the whole factual context and all the circumstances bearing on a threat to be considered. The court also instructed the jury to consider evidence presented by the defense of non-violence and permissive exercise of free speech. That the contextual facts may have included the violent actions of others does not infect the instruction, because the issue is whether a reasonable person should have foreseen that the Crist Guilty Poster, the Deadly Dozen Poster, and the Nuremberg Files, would be interpreted as a serious threat of harm by doctors who provide abortions and were identified on them.

ACLA also contends that the district court employed the wrong standard of intent, allowing the jury to find in physicians' favor regardless of ACLA's subjective intent. The court instructed: "A statement is a 'true threat' when a reasonable person making the statement would foresee that the statement would be interpreted by those to whom it is communicated as a serious expression of an intent to bodily harm or assault." This language is taken from *Orozco-Santillan,* 903 F.2d at 1265, is an accurate statement of our law, and is faithful to the objective standard we use for determining whether a statement is a true threat. For reasons we have already explained, we decline to read into FACE (or the Hobbs Act) a specific intent to threaten violence or to commit unlawful acts in addition to the intent to intimidate which the statute itself requires.. . .

F.

Having concluded that "threat of force" was properly defined and that no trial error requires reversal, we consider whether the core constitutional fact-a true threat-exists such that the Crist and Deadly Dozen Posters, and the Nuremberg Files as to Crist, Hern, and the Newhalls, are without First Amendment protection. The task in this case does not seem dramatically different from determining that the issue should have gone to the jury and that the jury was properly instructed under FACE. Nevertheless, we review the evidence on true threats independently.

The true threats analysis turns on the poster pattern. Neither the Crist poster nor the Deadly Dozen poster contains any language that is overtly threatening. Both differ from prior posters in that the prior posters were captioned "WANTED" while these are captioned "GUILTY." The text also differs somewhat, but differences in caption or words are immaterial because the language itself is not what is threatening. Rather, it is use of the "wanted"-type format in the context of the poster pattern-poster followed by murder-that constitutes the threat. Because of the pattern, a "wanted"-type poster naming a specific doctor who provides abortions was perceived by physicians, who are providers of reproductive health services, as a serious threat of death or bodily harm. After a "WANTED" poster on Dr. David Gunn appeared, he was shot and killed. After a "WANTED" poster on Dr. George Patterson appeared, he was shot and killed. After a "WANTED" poster on Dr. John Britton appeared, he was shot and killed. None of these "WANTED" posters contained threatening language, either. Neither did they identify who would pull the trigger. But knowing this pattern, knowing that unlawful action had followed "WANTED" posters on Gunn, Patterson and Britton, and knowing that "wanted"-type posters were intimidating and caused fear of serious harm to those named on them, ACLA published a "GUILTY" poster in essentially the same format on Dr. Crist and a Deadly Dozen "GUILTY" poster in similar format naming Dr. Hern, Dr. Elizabeth Newhall and Dr. James Newhall because they perform abortions. Physicians could well believe that ACLA would make good on the threat. One of the other doctors on the Deadly Dozen poster had in fact been shot before the poster was published. This is not political hyperbole. Nor is it merely "vituperative, abusive, and inexact." *Watts,* 394 U.S. at 708 (comparing language used in political arena to language used in labor disputes). In the context of the poster pattern, the posters were precise in their meaning to those in the relevant community of reproductive health service providers. They were a true threat.

The posters are a true threat because... they connote something they do not literally say, yet both the actor and the recipient get the message. To the doctor who performs abortions, these posters meant "You're Wanted or You're Guilty; You'll be shot or killed." This was reinforced by the scorecard in the Nuremberg Files. The communication was not conditional or casual. It was specifically targeted. Crist, Hern, and the Newhalls, who performed abortions, were not amused...

The "GUILTY" posters were publicly distributed, but personally targeted. While a privately communicated threat is generally more likely to be taken seriously than a diffuse public one, this cannot be said of a threat that is made publicly but is about a specifically identified doctor and is in the same format that had previously resulted in the death of three doctors who had also been publicly, yet specifically, targeted. There were no individualized threats in *Brandenburg, Watts* or *Claiborne.* However, no one putting Crist, Hern, and the Newhalls on a "wanted"-type poster, or participating in selecting these particular abortion providers for such a poster or publishing it, could possibly believe anything other than that each would be seriously worried about being next in line to be shot and killed. And they were seriously worried.

As a direct result of having a "GUILTY" poster out on them, physicians wore bullet-proof vests and took other extraordinary security measures to protect themselves and their families. ACLA had every reason to foresee that its expression of intent to harm (the "GUILTY" poster identifying Crist, Hern, Elizabeth Newhall and James Newhall by name and putting them in the File that tracks hits and misses) would elicit this reaction. Physicians' fear did not simply happen; ACLA intended to intimidate them from doing what they do.

This is the point of the statute and is conduct that we are satisfied lacks any protection under the First Amendment.

Violence is not a protected value. Nor is a *true threat* of violence *with intent to intimidate.* ACLA may have been staking out a position for debate when it merely advocated violence as in Bray's *A Time to Kill,* or applauded it, as in the Defense Action petitions. Likewise, when it created the Nuremberg Files in the abstract, because the First Amendment does not preclude calling people demeaning or inflammatory names, or threatening social ostracism or vilification to advocate a political position. *Claiborne,* 458 U.S. at 903, 909-12. But, after being on "wanted"-type posters, Dr. Gunn, Dr. Patterson, and Dr. Britton can no longer participate in the debate. By replicating the poster pattern that preceded the elimination of Gunn, Patterson and Britton, and by putting Crist, Hern, and the Newhalls in an abortionists' File that scores fatalities, ACLA was not staking out a position of debate but of threatened demise. This turns the First Amendment on its head....Holding ACLA accountable for this conduct does not impinge on legitimate protest or advocacy. Restraining it from continuing to threaten these physicians burdens speech no more than necessary.

Therefore, we affirm the judgment in all respects but for punitive damages, as to which we remand.

AFFIRMED IN PART; VACATED AND REMANDED IN PART.

KOZINSKI, Circuit Judge, with whom Circuit Judges REINHARDT, O'SCANNLAIN, KLEINFELD and BERZON join, dissenting.

The majority writes a lengthy opinion in a vain effort to justify a crushing monetary judgment and a strict injunction against speech protected by the First Amendment. The apparent thoroughness of the opinion, addressing a variety of issues that are not in serious dispute, masks the fact that the majority utterly fails to apply its own definition of a threat, and affirms the verdict and injunction when the evidence in the record does not support a finding that defendants threatened plaintiffs.

After meticulously canvassing the caselaw, the majority correctly distills the following definition of a true threat: "a statement which, in the entire context and under all the circumstances, a reasonable person would foresee would be interpreted by those to whom the statement is communicated as *a serious expression of intent to inflict bodily harm* upon that person." Maj. op. at 1076-77 (emphasis added). The emphasized language is crucial, because it is not illegal-and cannot be made so-merely to say things that would frighten or intimidate the listener. For example, when a doctor says, "You have cancer and will die within six months," it is not a threat, even though you almost certainly will be frightened.

Similarly, "Get out of the way of that bus" is not a threat, even though it is said in order to scare you into changing your behavior. By contrast, "If you don't stop performing abortions, I'll kill you" is a true threat and surely illegal.

The difference between a true threat and protected expression is this: A true threat warns of violence or other harm that the speaker controls. Thus, when a doctor tells a patient, "Stop smoking or you'll die of lung cancer," that is not a threat because the doctor obviously can't cause the harm to come about. Similarly, "If you walk in that neighborhood late at night, you're going to get mugged" is not a threat, unless it is clear that the speaker himself (or one of his associates) will be doing the mugging.

In this case, none of the statements on which liability was premised were overtly threatening. On the contrary, the two posters and the web page, by their explicit terms, foreswore the use of violence and advocated lawful means of persuading plaintiffs to stop performing abortions or punishing them for continuing to do so. Nevertheless, because context matters, the statements could reasonably be interpreted as an effort to intimidate plaintiffs into ceasing their abortion-related activities. If that were enough to strip the speech of First Amendment protection, there would be nothing left to decide. But the Supreme Court has told us that "[s]peech does not lose its protected character . . . simply because it may embarrass others *or coerce them into action.*" *NAACP v. Claiborne Hardware Co.,* 458 U.S. 886, 910 (1982) (emphasis added). In other words, some forms of intimidation enjoy constitutional protection.

Only a year after *Claiborne Hardware,* we incorporated this principle into our circuit's true threat jurisprudence. Striking down as overbroad a Montana statute that made it a crime to communicate to another "a threat to . . . commit a criminal offense," we stated: "The mere fact that communication induces or 'coerces' action in others does not remove it from First Amendment protection." *Wurtz v. Risley,* 719 F.2d 1438, 1441 (9th Cir. 1983) (quoting *Claiborne Hardware,* 458 U.S. at 911). We noted—referring to *Claiborne Hardware* again—that the statute criminalized pure speech designed to alter someone else's conduct, so that a "civil rights activist who states to a restaurant owner, 'if you don't desegregate this restaurant I am going to organize a boycott' could be punished for the mere statement, even if no action followed." *Id.* at 1442. *Claiborne Hardware* and *Wurtz* hold that statements that are intimidating, even coercive, are protected by the First Amendment, so long as the speaker does not threaten that he, or someone acting in concert with him, will resort to violence if the warning is not heeded.

The majority recognizes that this is the standard it must apply, yet when it undertakes the critical task of canvassing the record for evidence that defendants made a true threat-a task the majority acknowledges we must perform de novo, Maj. op at 1070-its opinion fails to come up with any proof that defendants communicated an intent to inflict bodily harm upon plaintiffs.

Buried deep within the long opinion is a single paragraph that cites evidence supporting the finding that the two wanted posters prepared by defendants constituted a true threat. Maj. op at 1079-80; *see also id.* at 1085-86 (same analysis). The majority does not point to any statement by defendants that they intended to inflict bodily harm on plaintiffs, nor is there any evidence that defendants took any steps whatsoever to plan or carry out physical violence against anyone. Rather, the majority relies on the fact that "the poster format itself had acquired currency as a death threat for abortion providers. Gunn was killed after his poster was released; Britton was killed after his poster was released; and Patterson was killed after his poster was released." *Id.* at 1079; *see also id.* at 1085-86. But neither Dr. Gunn nor Dr. Patterson was killed by anyone connected with the posters bearing their names. *Planned Parenthood of the Columbia/Willamette, Inc. v. Am. Coalition of Life Activists,* 41 F.Supp.2d 1130, 1134-35 (D.Or. 1999). In fact, Dr. Patterson's murder may have been unrelated to abortion: He was killed in what may have been a robbery attempt five months after his poster was issued; the crime is unsolved and plaintiffs' counsel conceded that no evidence ties his murderer to any anti-abortion group. R.T. at 131, 1197.

The record reveals one instance where an individual—Paul Hill, who is not a defendant in this case—participated in the preparation of the poster depicting a physician, Dr. Britton, and then murdered him some seven months later. All others who helped to make that poster, as well as those who prepared the other posters, did not resort to violence. And for years, hundreds of other posters circulated, condemning particular doctors with no violence ensuing. *See* R.T. at 1775-76, 1783-84, 2487, 2828. There is therefore no pattern showing that people who prepare wanted-type posters then engage in physical violence. To the extent the posters indicate a pattern, it is that almost all people engaged in poster-making were non-violent.

The majority tries to fill this gaping hole in the record by noting that defendants "kn[ew] the fear generated among those in the reproductive health services community who were singled out for identification on a 'wanted'-type poster." Maj. op at 1079. But a statement does not become a true threat because it instills fear in the listener; as noted above, many statements generate fear in the listener, yet are not true threats and therefore may not be punished or enjoined consistent with the First Amendment. *See* pp. 1089-90 *supra.* In order for the statement to be a threat, it must send the message that the speakers themselves-or individuals acting in concert with them-will engage in physical violence. The majority's own definition of true threat makes this clear. Yet the opinion points to no evidence that defendants who prepared the posters would have been understood by a reasonable listener as saying that *they* will cause the harm.

Plaintiffs themselves explained that the fear they felt came, not from defendants, but from being singled out for attention by abortion protesters across the country. For example, plaintiff Dr. Elizabeth Newhall testified, "I feel like my risk comes from being identified as a target. And . . . all the John Salvis in the world know who I am, and that's my concern." *Planned Parenthood of the Columbia/Willamette, Inc. v. Am. Coalition of Life Activists,* No. CV-95-01671-JO, at 302 (D.Or. Jan. 8, 1999); *see also id.* at 290 ("[U]p until January of '95, I felt relatively diluted by the-you know, in the pool of providers of abortion services. I didn't feel particularly visible to the people who were-you know, to the John Salvis of the world, you know. I sort of felt one of a big, big group."). Likewise, Dr. Warren Martin Hern, another plaintiff, testified that when he heard he was on the list, "I was terrified. [I]t's hard to describe the feeling that-that you are on a list of people to-who have been brought to public attention in this way. I felt that this was a-a list of doctors to be killed." *Planned Parenthood,* No. CV-95-01671 JO, at 625 (Jan. 11, 1999).

From the point of view of the victims, it makes little difference whether the violence against them will come from the makers of the posters or from unrelated third parties; bullets kill their victims regardless of who pulls the trigger. But it makes a difference for the purpose of the First Amendment. Speech-especially political speech, as this clearly was-may not be punished or enjoined unless it falls into one of the narrow categories of unprotected speech recognized by the Supreme Court: true threat, *Watts v. United States,* 394 U.S. 705, 707 (1969), incitement, *Brandenburg v. Ohio,* 395 U.S. 444, 447 (1969), conspiracy to commit criminal acts, *Scales v. United States,* 367 U.S. 203, 229 (1961), fighting words, *Chaplinsky v. New Hampshire,* 315 U.S. 568, 572-73 (1942), etc.

Even assuming that one could somehow distill a true threat from the posters themselves, the majority opinion is still fatally defective because it contradicts the central holding of *Claiborne Hardware:* Where the speaker is engaged in public political speech, the public statements themselves cannot be the sole proof that they were true threats, unless the speech directly threatens actual injury to identifiable individuals. Absent such an unmistakable, specific threat, there must be evidence *aside from the political statements themselves* showing that the public speaker would himself or in conspiracy with others inflict unlawful harm. 458 U.S. at 932-34. The majority cites not a scintilla of evidence-other than the posters themselves-that plaintiffs or someone associated with them would carry out the threatened harm.

Given this lack of evidence, the posters can be viewed, at most, as a call to arms for *other* abortion protesters to harm plaintiffs. However, the Supreme Court made it clear that under *Brandenburg,* encouragement or even advocacy of violence is protected by the First Amendment: "[M]ere *advocacy* of the use of force or violence does not remove speech from the protection of the First Amendment." *Claiborne Hardware,* 458 U.S. at 927 (citing *Brandenburg,* 395 U.S. at 447) (emphasis in the original). *Claiborne Hardware* in fact goes much farther; it cautions that where liability is premised on "politically motivated" activities, we must "examine critically the basis on which liability was imposed." *Id.* at 915. As the Court explained, "Since respondents would impose liability on the basis of a public address-which predominantly contained highly charged political rhetoric lying at the core of the First Amendment-we approach this suggested basis for liability with extreme care." *Id.* at 926-27. This is precisely what the majority does *not* do; were it to do so, it would have no choice but to reverse.

The activities for which the district court held defendants liable were unquestionably of a political nature....This political agenda may not be to the liking of many people-political dissidents are often unpopular-but the speech, including the intimidating message, does not constitute a direct threat because there is no evidence other than the speech itself that the speakers intend to resort to physical violence if their threat is not heeded....

We have recognized that statements communicated directly to the target are much more likely to be true threats than those, as here, communicated as part of a public protest. Our caselaw also instructs that, in deciding whether the coercive speech is protected, it makes a big difference whether it is contained in a private communication-a face-to-face confrontation, a telephone call, a dead fish wrapped in newspaper or is made during the course of public discourse. The reason for this distinction is obvious:

Private speech is aimed only at its target. Public speech, by contrast, seeks to move public opinion and to encourage those of like mind. Coercive speech that is part of public discourse enjoys far greater protection than identical speech made in a purely private context. . . .

ELONIS v. UNITED STATES

575 U.S. ___, 135 S.Ct 2001 (2015)

CHIEF JUSTICE ROBERTS delivered the opinion of the Court.

Federal law makes it a crime to transmit in interstate commerce "any communication containing any threat . . . to injure the person of another." 18 U. S. C. §875(c). Petitioner was convicted of violating this provision under instructions that required the jury to find that he communicated what a reasonable person would regard as a threat. The question is whether the statute also requires that the defendant be aware of the threatening nature of the communication, and—if not—whether the First Amendment requires such a showing.

. . . Anthony Douglas Elonis was an active user of the social networking Web site Facebook. Users of that Web site may post items on their Facebook page that are accessible to other users, including Facebook "friends" who are notified when new content is posted. In May 2010, Elonis's wife of nearly seven years left him, taking with her their two young children. Elonis began "listening to more violent music" and posting self-styled "rap" lyrics inspired by the music. App. 204, 226. Eventually, Elonis changed the user name on his Facebook page from his actual name to a rap-style nom de plume, "Tone Dougie," to distinguish himself from his "on-line persona." *Id.*, at 249, 265. The lyrics Elonis posted as "Tone Dougie" included graphically violent language and imagery. This material was often interspersed with disclaimers that the lyrics were "fictitious," with no intentional "resemblance to real persons." *Id.*, at 331, 329. Elonis posted an explanation to another Facebook user that "I'm doing this for me. My writing is therapeutic." *Id.*, at 329; see also *id.*, at 205 (testifying that it "helps me to deal with the pain").

Elonis's co-workers and friends viewed the posts in a different light. Around Halloween of 2010, Elonis posted a photograph of himself and a co-worker at a "Halloween Haunt" event at the amusement park where they worked. In the photograph, Elonis was holding a toy knife against his co-worker's neck, and in the caption Elonis wrote, "I wish." *Id.*, at 340. Elonis was not Facebook friends with the co-worker and did not "tag" her, a Facebook feature that would have alerted her to the posting. *Id.,* at 175; Brief for Petitioner 6, 9. But the chief of park security was a Facebook "friend" of Elonis, saw the photograph, and fired him. App. 114–116; Brief for Petitioner 9.

In response, Elonis posted a new entry on his Facebook page:

"Moles! Didn't I tell y'all I had several? Y'all sayin' I had access to keys for all the f***in' gates. That I have sinister plans for all my friends and must have taken home a couple. Y'all think it's too dark and foggy to secure your facility from a man as mad as me? You see, even without a paycheck, I'm still the main attraction. Whoever thought the Halloween Haunt could be so f***in' scary?" App. 332. This post became the basis for Count One of Elonis's subsequent indictment, threatening park patrons and employees.

Elonis's posts frequently included crude, degrading, and violent material about his soon-to-be ex-wife. Shortly after he was fired, Elonis posted an adaptation of a satirical sketch that he and his wife had watched together. *Id.,* at 164–165, 207. In the actual sketch, called "It's Illegal to Say . . . ," a comedian explains that it is illegal for a person to say he wishes to kill the President, but not illegal to explain that it is illegal for him to say that. When Elonis posted the script of the sketch, however, he substituted his wife for the President. The posting was part of the basis for Count Two of the indictment, threatening his wife:

"Hi, I'm Tone Elonis. Did you know that it's illegal for me to say I want to kill my wife? . . . It's one of the only sentences that I'm not allowed to say. . . . Now it was okay for me to say it right then because I was just telling you that it's illegal for me to say I want to kill my wife. . . . Um, but what's interesting is that it's very illegal to say I really, really think someone out there should kill my wife. . . . But not illegal to say with a mortar launcher. Because that's its own sentence. . . . I also found out that it's incredibly illegal, extremely illegal to go on Facebook and say something like the best place to fire a mortar launcher at her house would be from the cornfield behind it because of easy access to a getaway road and you'd have a clear line of sight through the sun room. . . . Yet even more illegal to show an illustrated diagram. [diagram of the house]. . . ." *Id.,* at 333.

The details about the home were accurate. *Id.,* at 154. At the bottom of the post, Elonis included a link to the video of the original skit, and wrote,

"Art is about pushing limits. I'm willing to go to jail for my Constitutional rights. Are you?" *Id.,* at 333.

After viewing some of Elonis's posts, his wife felt "extremely afraid for [her] life." *Id.,* at 156. A state court granted her a three-year protection-from-abuse order against Elonis (essentially, a restraining order). *Id.,* at 148–150. Elonis referred to the order in another post on his "Tone Dougie" page, also included in Count Two of the indictment:

"Fold up your [protection-from-abuse order] and put it in your pocket / Is it thick enough to stop a bullet? / Try to enforce an Order that was improperly granted in the first place / Me thinks the Judge needs an education on true threat jurisprudence / And prison time'll add zeros to my settlement . . . / And if worse comes to worse I've got enough explosives to take care of the State Police and the Sheriff 's Department." *Id.,* at 334.

At the bottom of this post was a link to the Wikipedia article on "Freedom of speech." *Ibid.* Elonis's reference to the police was the basis for Count Three of his indictment, threatening law enforcement officers.

That same month, interspersed with posts about a movie Elonis liked and observations on a comedian's social commentary, *id.,* at 356–358, Elonis posted an entry that gave rise to Count Four of his indictment:

"That's it, I've had about enough I'm checking out and making a name for myself / Enough elementary schools in a ten mile radius to initiate the most heinous school shooting ever imagined / And hell hath no fury like a crazy man in a Kindergarten class / The only question is . . . which one?" *Id.,* at 335.

Meanwhile, park security had informed both local police and the Federal Bureau of Investigation about Elonis's posts, and FBI Agent Denise Stevens had created a Facebook account to monitor his online activity. *Id.,* at 49–51, 125. After the post about a school shooting, Agent Stevens and her partner visited Elonis at his house. *Id.,* at 65–66. Following their visit, during which Elonis was polite but uncooperative, Elonis posted another entry on his Facebook page, called "Little Agent Lady," which led to Count Five:

"You know your s***'s ridiculous when you have the FBI knockin' at yo' door / Little Agent lady stood so close / Took all the strength I had not to turn the b**** ghost / Pull my knife, flick my wrist, and slit her throat

/Leave her bleedin' from her jugular in the arms of her partner [laughter] /So the next time you knock, you best be serving a warrant /And bring yo' SWAT and an explosives expert while you're at it /Cause little did y'all know, I was strapped wit' a bomb /Why do you think it took me so long to get dressed with no shoes on? /I was jus' waitin' for y'all to handcuff me and pat me down /Touch the detonator in my pocket and we're all goin' [BOOM!] /Are all the pieces comin' together? /S***, I'm just a crazy sociopath that gets off playin' you stupid f***s like a fiddle /And if y'all didn't hear, I'm gonna be famous /Cause I'm just an aspiring rapper who likes the attention who happens to be under investigation for terrorism cause y'all think I'm ready to turn the Valley into Fallujah /But I ain't gonna tell you which bridge is gonna fall into which river or road /And if you really believe this s*** I'll have some bridge rubble to sell you tomorrow [BOOM!][BOOM!][BOOM!]" *Id.*, at 336.

...A grand jury indicted Elonis for making threats to injure patrons and employees of the park, his estranged wife, police officers, a kindergarten class, and an FBI agent, all in violation of 18 U. S. C. §875(c). App. 14–17. In the District Court, Elonis moved to dismiss the indictment for failing to allege that he had intended to threaten anyone. The District Court denied the motion, holding that Third Circuit precedent required only that Elonis "intentionally made the communication, not that he intended to make a threat." App. to Pet. for Cert. 51a. At trial, Elonis testified that his posts emulated the rap lyrics of the well-known performer Eminem, some of which involve fantasies about killing his ex-wife. App. 225. In Elonis's view, he had posted "nothing . . . that hasn't been said already." *Id.*, at 205. The Government presented as witnesses Elonis's wife and co-workers, all of whom said they felt afraid and viewed Elonis's posts as serious threats. See, *e.g.*, *id.*, at 153, 158.

Elonis requested a jury instruction that "the government must prove that he intended to communicate a true threat." *Id.*, at 21. See also *id.*, at 267–269, 303. The District Court denied that request. The jury instructions instead informed the jury that

"A statement is a true threat when a defendant intentionally makes a statement in a context or under such circumstances wherein a reasonable person would foresee that the statement would be interpreted by those to whom the maker communicates the statement as a serious expression of an intention to inflict bodily injury or take the life of an individual." *Id.*, at 301.

The Government's closing argument emphasized that it was irrelevant whether Elonis intended the postings to be threats—"it doesn't matter what he thinks." *Id.,* at 286. A jury convicted Elonis on four of the five counts against him, acquitting only on the charge of threatening park patrons and employees. *Id.,* at 309. Elonis was sentenced to three years, eight months' imprisonment and three years' supervised release.

Elonis renewed his challenge to the jury instructions in the Court of Appeals, contending that the jury should have been required to find that he intended his posts to be threats. The Court of Appeals disagreed, holding that the intent required by Section 875(c) is only the intent to communicate words that the defendant understands, and that a reasonable person would view as a threat. 730 F. 3d 321, 332 (CA3 2013).

We granted certiorari. 573 U. S. ___ (2014). …

An individual who "transmits in interstate or foreign commerce any communication containing any threat to kidnap any person or any threat to injure the person of another" is guilty of a felony and faces up to five years' imprisonment. 18 U. S. C. §875(c). This statute requires that a communication be transmitted and that the communication contain a threat. It does not specify that the defendant must have any mental state with respect to these elements. In particular, it does not indicate whether the defendant must intend that his communication contain a threat.

Elonis argues that the word "threat" itself in Section 875(c) imposes such a requirement. According to Elonis, every definition of "threat" or "threaten" conveys the notion of an intent to inflict harm. Brief for Petitioner 23. See *United States* v. *Jeffries,* 692 F. 3d 473, 483 (CA6 2012) (Sutton, J., *dubitante*). *E.g.,* 11 Oxford English Dictionary 353 (1933) ("to declare (usually conditionally) one's intention of inflicting injury upon"); Webster's New International Dictionary 2633 (2d ed. 1954) ("*Law,* specif., an expression of an intention to inflict loss or harm on another by illegal means"); Black's Law Dictionary 1519 (8th ed. 2004) ("A communicated intent to inflict harm or loss on another").

These definitions, however, speak to what the statement conveys—not to the mental state of the author. For example, an anonymous letter that says "I'm going to kill you" is "an expression of an intention to inflict loss or harm" regardless of the author's intent. A victim who receives that letter in the mail has received a threat, even if the author believes (wrongly) that his message will be taken as a joke.

. . . . The "central thought" is that a defendant must be "blameworthy in mind" before he can be found guilty, a concept courts have expressed over time through various terms such as *mens rea*, scienter, malice aforethought, guilty knowledge, and the like. *Id.*, at 252; 1 W. LaFave, Substantive Criminal Law §5.1, pp. 332–333 (2d ed. 2003). Although there are exceptions, the "general rule" is that a guilty mind is "a necessary element in the indictment and proof of every crime." *United States* v. *Balint*, 258 U. S. 250, 251 (1922). We therefore generally "interpret[] criminal statutes to include broadly applicable scienter requirements, even where the statute by its terms does not contain them." *United States* v. *X-Citement Video, Inc.*, 513 U. S. 64, 70 (1994).

This is not to say that a defendant must know that his conduct is illegal before he may be found guilty. The familiar maxim "ignorance of the law is no excuse" typically holds true. Instead, our cases have explained that a defendant generally must "know the facts that make his conduct fit the definition of the offense," *Staples* v. *United States*, 511 U. S. 600, 608, n. 3 (1994), even if he does not know that those facts give rise to a crime.

. . . *[I]*n *X-Citement Video,* we considered a statute criminalizing the distribution of visual depictions of minors engaged in sexually explicit conduct. 513 U. S., at 68. We rejected a reading of the statute which would have required only that a defendant knowingly send the prohibited materials, regardless of whether he knew the age of the performers. *Id.*, at 68–69. We held instead that a defendant must also know that those depicted were minors, because that was "the crucial element separating legal innocence from wrongful conduct." *Id.*, at 73. See also *Staples,* 511 U. S., at 619 (defendant must know that his weapon had automatic firing capability to be convicted of possession of such a weapon). . . .

Section 875(c), as noted, requires proof that a communication was transmitted and that it contained a threat. The "presumption in favor of a scienter requirement should apply to *each* of the statutory elements that criminalize otherwise innocent conduct." *X-Citement Video,* 513 U. S., at 72 (emphasis added). The parties agree that a defendant under Section 875(c) must know that he is transmitting a communication. But communicating *something* is not what makes the conduct "wrongful." Here "the crucial element separating legal innocence from wrongful conduct" is the threatening nature of the communication. *Id.*, at 73. The mental state requirement must therefore apply to the fact that the communication contains a threat.

Elonis's conviction, however, was premised solely on how his posts would be understood by a reasonable person. Such a "reasonable person" standard is a familiar feature of civil liability in tort law, but is inconsistent with "the conventional requirement for criminal conduct—*awareness* of some wrongdoing." *Staples*, 511 U. S., at 606–607 (quoting *United States* v. *Dotterweich*, 320 U. S. 277, 281 (1943); emphasis added). Having liability turn on whether a "reasonable person" regards the communication as a threat—regardless of what the defendant thinks—"reduces culpability on the all-important element of the crime to negligence," *Jeffries*, 692 F. 3d, at 484 (Sutton, J., *dubitante*), and we "have long been reluctant to infer that a negligence standard was intended in criminal statutes," *Rogers* v. *United States*, 422 U. S. 35, 47 (1975) (Marshall, J., concurring) (citing *Morissette*, 342 U. S. 246). See 1 C. Torcia, Wharton's Criminal Law §27, pp. 171–172 (15th ed. 1993); *Cochran* v. *United States*, 157 U. S. 286, 294 (1895) (defendant could face "liability in a civil action for negligence, but he could only be held criminally for an evil intent actually existing in his mind"). Under these principles, "what [Elonis] thinks" does matter. App. 286. . . .

In light of the foregoing, Elonis's conviction cannot stand. The jury was instructed that the Government need prove only that a reasonable person would regard Elonis's communications as threats, and that was error. Federal criminal liability generally does not turn solely on the results of an act without considering the defendant's mental state. That understanding "took deep and early root in American soil" and Congress left it intact here: Under Section 875(c), "wrongdoing must be conscious to be criminal." *Morissette*, 342 U. S., at 252.

There is no dispute that the mental state requirement in Section 875(c) is satisfied if the defendant transmits a communication for the purpose of issuing a threat, or with knowledge that the communication will be viewed as a threat. See Tr. of Oral Arg. 25, 56. In response to a question at oral argument, Elonis stated that a finding of recklessness would not be sufficient. See *id.*, at 8–9. Neither Elonis nor the Government has briefed or argued that point, and we accordingly decline to address it. See *Department of Treasury, IRS* v. *FLRA*, 494 U. S. 922, 933 (1990) (this Court is "poorly situated" to address an argument the Court of Appeals did not consider, the parties did not brief, and counsel addressed in "only the most cursory fashion at oral argument"). Given our disposition, it is not necessary to consider any First Amendment issues.

Both JUSTICE ALITO and JUSTICE THOMAS complain about our not deciding whether recklessness suffices for liability under Section 875(c).

Post, at 1–2 (ALITO, J., concurring in part and dissenting in part); *post*, at 1–2 (opinion of THOMAS, J.). JUSTICE ALITO contends that each party "argued" this issue, *post*, at 2, but they did not address it at all until oral argument, and even then only briefly. See Tr. of Oral Arg. at 8, 38–39.

JUSTICE ALITO also suggests that we have not clarified confusion in the lower courts. That is wrong. Our holding makes clear that negligence is not sufficient to support a conviction under Section 875(c), contrary to the view of nine Courts of Appeals. Pet. for Cert. 17. There was and is no circuit conflict over the question JUSTICE ALITO and JUSTICE THOMAS would have us decide—whether recklessness suffices for liability under Section 875(c). No Court of Appeals has even addressed that question. We think that is more than sufficient "justification," *post*, at 2 (opinion of ALITO, J.), for us to decline to be the first appellate tribunal to do so. . . .

We may be "capable of deciding the recklessness issue," *post*, at 2 (opinion of ALITO, J.), but following our usual practice of awaiting a decision below and hearing from the parties would help ensure that we decide it correctly.

The judgment of the United States Court of Appeals for the Third Circuit is reversed, and the case is remanded for further proceedings consistent with this opinion.

It is so ordered.

JUSTICE ALITO, concurring in part and dissenting in part.

I

. . . The Court's disposition of this case is certain to cause confusion and serious problems. Attorneys and judges need to know which mental state is required for conviction under 18 U. S. C. §875(c), an important criminal statute. This case squarely presents that issue, but the Court provides only a partial answer. The Court holds that the jury instructions in this case were defective because they required only negligence in conveying a threat. But the Court refuses to explain what type of intent was necessary. Did the jury need to find that Elonis had the *purpose* of conveying a true threat? Was it enough if he *knew* that his words conveyed such a threat? Would *recklessness* suffice? The Court declines to say. Attorneys and judges are left to guess.

I agree with the Court that we should presume that criminal statutes require some sort of *mens rea* for conviction. . . .

Once we have passed negligence, however, no further presumptions are defensible. . . . There can be no real dispute that recklessness regarding a risk of serious harm is wrongful conduct. In a wide variety of contexts, we have described reckless conduct as morally culpable. See, *e.g., Farmer, supra,* at 835–836 (deliberate indifference to an inmate's harm); *Garrison* v. *Louisiana,* 379 U. S. 64, 75 (1964) (criminal libel); *New York Times Co.* v. *Sullivan,* 376 U. S. 254, 279–280 (1964) (civil libel). Indeed, this Court has held that "reckless disregard for human life" may justify the death penalty. *Tison* v. *Arizona,* 481 U. S. 137, 157 (1987). Someone who acts recklessly with respect to conveying a threat necessarily grasps that he is not engaged in innocent conduct. He is not merely careless. He is aware that others could regard his statements as a threat, but he delivers them anyway.

Accordingly, I would hold that a defendant may be convicted under §875(c) if he or she consciously disregards the risk that the communication transmitted will be interpreted as a true threat. Nothing in the Court's noncommittal opinion prevents lower courts from adopting that standard.

II

There remains the question whether interpreting §875(c) to require no more than recklessness with respect to the element at issue here would violate the First Amendment. Elonis contends that it would. I would reject that argument.

It is settled that the Constitution does not protect true threats. See *Virginia* v. *Black,* 538 U. S. 343, 359–360 (2003); *R. A. V.* v. *St. Paul,* 505 U. S. 377, 388 (1992); *Watts,* 394 U. S., at 707–708. And there are good reasons for that rule: True threats inflict great harm and have little if any social value. A threat may cause serious emotional stress for the person threatened and those who care about that person, and a threat may lead to a violent confrontation. It is true that a communication containing a threat may include other statements that have value and are entitled to protection. But that does not justify constitutional protection for the threat itself.

Elonis argues that the First Amendment protects a threat if the person making the statement does not actually intend to cause harm. In his view, if a threat is made for a " 'therapeutic' " purpose, "to 'deal with the pain' . . . of a wrenching event," or for "cathartic" reasons, the threat is protected. Brief for Petitioner 52–53. But whether or not the person making a threat intends to cause harm, the damage is the same. And the fact that making a threat may have a therapeutic or cathartic effect for the speaker is not sufficient to justify constitutional protection. Some people may experience a therapeutic or cathartic benefit only if they know that their words will cause harm or only if they actually plan to carry out the threat, but surely the First Amendment does not protect them.

Elonis also claims his threats were constitutionally protected works of art. Words like his, he contends, are shielded by the First Amendment because they are similar to words uttered by rappers and singers in public performances and recordings. To make this point, his brief includes a lengthy excerpt from the lyrics of a rap song in which a very well-compensated rapper imagines killing his ex-wife and dumping her body in a lake. If this celebrity can utter such words, Elonis pleads, amateurs like him should be able to post similar things on social media. But context matters. "Taken in context," lyrics in songs that are performed for an audience or sold in recorded form are unlikely to be interpreted as a real threat to a real person. *Watts, supra,* at 708. Statements on social media that are pointedly directed at their victims, by contrast, are much more likely to be taken seriously. To hold otherwise would grant a license to anyone who is clever enough to dress up a real threat in the guise of rap lyrics, a parody, or something similar.

The facts of this case illustrate the point. Imagine the effect on Elonis's estranged wife when she read this: "'If I only knew then what I know now . . . I would have smothered your ass with a pillow, dumped your body in the back seat, dropped you off in Toad Creek and made it look like a rape and murder.' " 730 F. 3d 321, 324 (CA3 2013). Or this: "There's one way to love you but a thousand ways to kill you. I'm not going to rest until your body is a mess, soaked in blood and dying from all the little cuts." *Ibid.* Or this: "Fold up your [protection from abuse order] and put it in your pocket[.] Is it thick enough to stop a bullet?" *Id.,* at 325.

There was evidence that Elonis made sure his wife saw his posts. And she testified that they made her feel "'extremely afraid'" and "'like [she] was being stalked.'" *Ibid.* Considering the context, who could blame her? Threats of violence and intimidation are among the most favored weapons of domestic abusers, and the rise of social media has only made those tactics more commonplace. See Brief for The National Network to End Domestic Violence et al. as *Amici Curiae* 4–16. A fig leaf of artistic expression cannot convert such hurtful, valueless threats into protected speech.

It can be argued that §875(c), if not limited to threats made with the intent to harm, will chill statements that do not qualify as true threats, *e.g.*, statements that may be literally threatening but are plainly not meant to be taken seriously. We have sometimes cautioned that it is necessary to "exten[d] a measure of strategic protection" to otherwise unprotected false statements of fact in order to ensure enough "'breathing space'" for protected speech. *Gertz* v. *Robert Welch, Inc.*, 418 U. S. 323, 342 (1974) (quoting *NAACP* v. *Button*, 371 U. S. 415, 433 (1963)). A similar argument might be made with respect to threats. But we have also held that the law provides adequate breathing space when it requires proof that false statements were made with reckless disregard of their falsity. . . .

JUSTICE THOMAS, dissenting.

We granted certiorari to resolve a conflict in the lower courts over the appropriate mental state for threat prosecutions under 18 U. S. C. §875(c).

. . .

Elonis nonetheless suggests that an intent-to-threaten element is necessary in order to avoid the risk of punishing innocent conduct. But there is nothing absurd about punishing an individual who, with knowledge of the words he uses and their ordinary meaning in context, makes a threat. For instance, a high-school student who sends a letter to his principal stating that he will massacre his classmates with a machine gun, even if he intended the letter as a joke, cannot fairly be described as engaging in innocent conduct. But see *ante*, at 4–5, 16 (concluding that Elonis' conviction under §875(c) for discussing a plan to "'initiate the most heinous school shooting ever imagined'" against "'a Kindergarten class'" cannot stand with out proof of some unspecified heightened mental state).

Elonis also insists that we read an intent-to-threaten element into §875(c) in light of the First Amendment. But our practice of construing statutes "to avoid constitutional questions . . . is not a license for the judiciary to rewrite language enacted by the legislature," *Salinas* v. *United States*, 522 U. S. 52, 59–60 (1997) (internal quotation marks omitted), and ordinary background principles of criminal law do not support rewriting §875(c) to include an intent-to-threaten requirement. We have not altered our traditional approach to *mens rea* for other constitutional provisions. See, *e.g., Dean* v. *United States*, 556 U. S. 568, 572–574 (2009) (refusing to read an intent-to-discharge the-firearm element into a mandatory minimum provision concerning the discharge of a firearm during a particular crime). The First Amendment should be treated no differently. . . .

There is always a risk that a criminal threat statute may be deployed by the Government to suppress legitimate speech. But the proper response to that risk is to adhere to our traditional rule that only a narrow class of true threats, historically unprotected, may be constitutionally proscribed.

. . .

I respectfully dissent.

NOTES AND QUESTIONS

1. Why not devise a flexible test for violence, as the U.S. Supreme Court did in the *Miller* case *supra*, Chapter 6? Could jurors, for example, be asked to determine if an average person in their community would find a violent depiction to be horrifying? Why not let judges use the equivalent of the *Miller* test's third prong to protect speech deemed horrifying if it has redeeming social value?
2. Justice Alito, in the *Stevens* case *supra*, dissents on the basis that those who possess images of animal abuse should be treated like those who possess images of child pornography. Does Justice Alito do enough to justify this analogy? Does the victim's incapacity to consent make it a tenable comparison?
3. Should there be any distinctions between depictions of actual violence and imagined violence? Is it less gratuitous if it appears on a newscast? What if a reality show aired the violence?
4. If a broadcaster aired content that it had been advised might inspire copycats or cause many viewers emotional distress, do you think the court should allow recovery for any ensuing injury?
5. According to a yearlong study published by the Annenberg Public Policy Center, only eight percent of households with children aged seven-to-ten regularly filtered programs with the V-chip, even after some were instructed on how to use it; seventy percent never used it. Should Congress and the FCC reevaluate the effectiveness of the V-chip if usage remains low?
6. V-chip ratings are not used for news or sports. While parental filtering of news programs may spark concern that broadcasters may limit or modify their news coverage to reduce filtering, why exempt sports?
7. In reviewing the *Planned Parenthood* case *supra*, consider, instead of the abortion context, a human rights group posting images of known racists who are then being murdered by third-party vigilantes without any hint of collusion. Would that change your view of the case?

8. Judge Rymer's majority opinion in *Planned Parenthood* applies an objective standard of intent to threats under the FACES statute. In the *Elonis* case supra, the U.S. Supreme Court requires a subjective standard to threats under a different statute. Is the legal conclusion in *Planned Parenthood* still viable in light of Chief Justice Roberts' mens rea analysis in *Elonis*?

CHAPTER 12

CABLE & SATELLITE

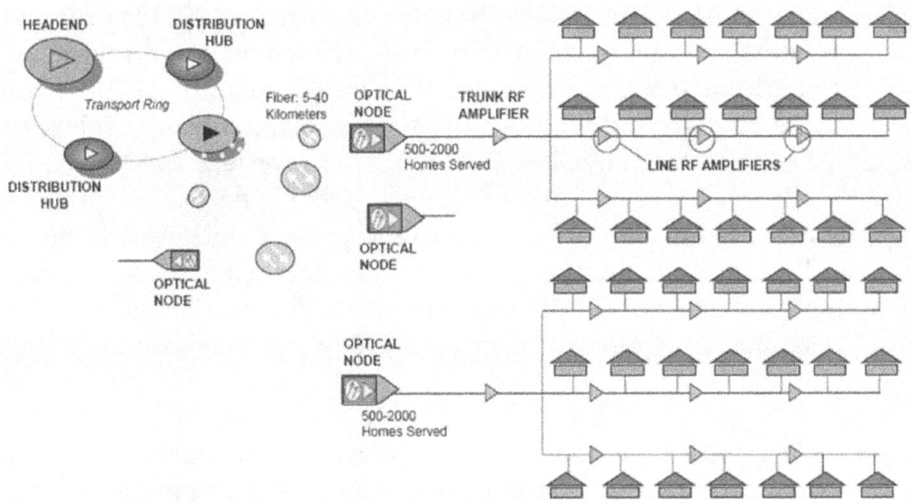

Cable television "pipeline," from head-end to household.

As its name suggests, cable television is about the transmission of a signal through wire—a coaxial cable or fiber-optic (glass tubing)—from a source to an end user. For a local cable provider, the signal pathway begins with the "head-end," a satellite or terrestrial connection from which the provider receives a signal from a content provider—in most cases, a cable channel like CNN, ESPN, or Comedy Central. In digital cable systems today, fiber-optic tubes transmit the signal along trunk lines to various distribution hubs in a community, which in turn branch out to optical nodes located in neighborhoods. At that point, the fiber-optic signal, which is encoded in a beam of light, is converted into a radio frequency that is amplified and then transmitted by insulated wire cable to subscribing households in that neighborhood.

Conceptually, it is a simple process of transmission and reception. Legally, however, it is anything but simple. Back in the late 1940s, when cable—then known as Community Antenna Television—was first introduced, it largely escaped the scrutiny of federal and state regulators. These early CATV systems were designed merely to extend the reach of broadcast signals into areas where the signal could not travel—in Oregon's Willamette Valley and Pennsylvania's Poconos, the nation's first cable systems, local providers ran wires from antennas placed atop mountains to homes in signal-blocked valleys below. For broadcasters, CATV was a technology that facilitated reception of their own signals—and increased their audience.

In 1961, a cable provider in San Diego successfully introduced distant signals from independent stations based in Los Angeles. Cable providers and regulators soon understood that audiences would be willing to pay more for additional television channels in local markets. At this point, the FCC asserted general jurisdiction over cable systems to regulate the importation of distant signals. In U.S. v. Southwestern Cable Co., 392 U.S. 157 (1968), the U.S. Supreme Court upheld the FCC's power to regulate cable as ancillary to its mandate to protect and promote broadcasting. Though the Communications Act did not then expressly address cable, the Court ruled that the importation of distant signals may "destroy or seriously degrade the service offered by a television broadcaster."

In the 1970s, the FCC tested the limits of its ancillary jurisdiction over cable, successfully requiring larger cable providers to originate a portion of their programming—U.S. v. Midwest Video Corp. (*Midwest Video I*), 406 U.S. 649 (1972)—and overstepping its authority to require cable systems to set aside public access channels—U.S. v. Midwest Video Corp. (*Midwest Video II*), 440 U.S. 689 (1979). These regulations were considered to be "structural," since they sought to regulate the infrastructure or economics of the cable industry. Because cable systems need public rights-of-way in order to lay their lines, states also have the authority to issue structural regulation, subject to federal preemption, relating to technical specifications and municipal franchising. Today, municipalities still franchise cable systems, although federal law requires franchises to be non-exclusive.

In 1984, Congress passed the Cable Communications Policy Act as an amendment to the Communications Act, granting the FCC specific authority to regulate cable for the first time. The 1984 Cable Act authorized the FCC to regulate basic cable "tier" rates in markets where effective competition was lacking. The 1992 Cable Act gave the FCC more power to regulate rates, requiring subscribers, for example, to pay for basic cable before accessing premium tiers and removing rate regulation from municipal franchise authorities. The 1992 Act also required municipalities to adopt customer service standards for their cable-provider franchisees, ensured equipment compatibility for cable systems and video recorders, and set forth the must-carry rules, which allow local broadcasters to elect compulsory carriage on a local cable system.

While the U.S. Supreme Court, in the *Turner* case infra, determined that the must-carry rules were a content-neutral structural regulation, many—including cable companies—argued that it was, in fact, a content regulation. With the advent of alternative programming on basic cable channels and premium channels like Home Box Office (HBO) in the 1970s, cable's increased audience share led the government to adopt a more permissive attitude toward cable content regulation. In the Copyright Act of 1976, Congress effectively overruled Supreme Court precedent by redefining cable retransmission of broadcast signals as copyright infringement. These precedents, Fortnightly Corp. v. United Artists Television, Inc., 392 U.S. 390 (1968), and Teleprompter Corp. v. Columbia Broadcasting System, Inc., 415 U.S. 294 (1974), play a significant role in the Supreme Court's analysis in the *Aereo* case infra.

Congress also enacted a compulsory copyright license for a cable system's use of distant signals—the so-called "may-carry" rules, which required broadcasters to make their stations available in other markets, leading to the growth of "superstations." The "may-carry" compulsory license was especially controversial for content stakeholders like sports leagues, studios, syndicators, and the broadcasters themselves, and the government has tried a number of methods to pool royalties among various claimants. Under the 1992 Cable Act, broadcasters may choose to negotiate for retransmission of their local signals at market rates as an alternative to royalty-free compulsory carriage. Today, most network-affiliated stations attempt to negotiate for high royalty payments from cable providers, leading to brinksmanship that occasionally results in a blackout of a broadcaster's channel on a local cable system.

Cable Indecency

In addition to copyright-related content regulations, Congress has set out to regulate indecent programming on cable systems. To shield children from adult content, Congress passed section 505 of the Telecommunications Act of 1996, which required cable providers to "fully block or otherwise scramble" cable channels "primarily dedicated to sexually-oriented programming." Because scrambling technology in the 1990s resulted in "signal bleed," which allowed viewers to hear or see fleeting portions of blocked content, cable systems complied with the statute by limiting adult channels to overnight hours. Since the statute adversely affected the Playboy Channel, the Playboy Entertainment Group sued, arguing that the statute fails strict scrutiny and, thus, violates the First Amendment.

U.S. v. Playboy Entertainment Group, Inc.

529 U.S. 803 (2000)

Justice KENNEDY delivered the opinion of the Court.

This case presents a challenge to § 505 of the Telecommunications Act of 1996, Pub.L. 104-104, 110 Stat. 136, 47 U.S.C. § 561 (1994 ed., Supp. III). Section 505 requires cable television operators who provide channels "primarily dedicated to sexually-oriented programming" either to "fully scramble or otherwise fully block" those channels or to limit their transmission to hours when children are unlikely to be viewing, set by administrative regulation as the time between 10 p.m. and 6 a.m. 47 U.S.C. § 561(a) (1994 ed., Supp. III); 47 CFR § 76.227 (1999). Even before enactment of the statute, signal scrambling was already in use. Cable operators used scrambling in the regular course of business, so that only paying customers had access to certain programs. Scrambling could be imprecise, however; and either or both audio and visual portions of the scrambled programs might be heard or seen, a phenomenon known as "signal bleed." The purpose of § 505 is to shield children from hearing or seeing images resulting from signal bleed.

To comply with the statute, the majority of cable operators adopted the second, or "time channeling," approach. The effect of the widespread adoption of time channeling was to eliminate altogether the transmission of the targeted programming outside the safe harbor period in affected cable service areas. In other words, for two-thirds of the day no household in those service areas could receive the programming, whether or not the household or the viewer wanted to do so.

Appellee Playboy Entertainment Group, Inc., challenged the statute as unnecessarily restrictive content-based legislation violative of the First Amendment. After a trial, a three-judge District Court concluded that a regime in which viewers could order signal blocking on a household-by-household basis presented an effective, less restrictive alternative to § 505. 30 F.Supp.2d 702, 719 (D.Del. 1998). Finding no error in this conclusion, we affirm.

I.

Playboy Entertainment Group owns and prepares programs for adult television networks, including Playboy Television and Spice. Playboy transmits its programming to cable television operators, who retransmit it to their subscribers, either through monthly subscriptions to premium channels or on a so-called "pay-per-view" basis. Cable operators transmit Playboy's signal, like other premium channel signals, in scrambled form. The operators then provide paying subscribers with an "addressable converter," a box placed on the home television set. The converter permits the viewer to see and hear the descrambled signal. It is conceded that almost all of Playboy's programming consists of sexually explicit material as defined by the statute.

The statute was enacted because not all scrambling technology is perfect. Analog cable television systems may use either "RF" or "baseband" scrambling systems, which may not prevent signal bleed, so discernible pictures may appear from time to time on the scrambled screen. Furthermore, the listener might hear the audio portion of the program.

These imperfections are not inevitable. The problem is that at present it appears not to be economical to convert simpler RF or baseband scrambling systems to alternative scrambling technologies on a systemwide scale. Digital technology may one day provide another solution, as it presents no bleed problem at all. Indeed, digital systems are projected to become the technology of choice, which would eliminate the signal bleed problem. Digital technology is not yet in widespread use, however. With imperfect scrambling, viewers who have not paid to receive Playboy's channels may happen across discernible images of a sexually explicit nature. How many viewers, how discernible the scene or sound, and how often this may occur are at issue in this case.

Section 505 was enacted to address the signal bleed phenomenon. As noted, the statute and its implementing regulations require cable operators either to scramble a sexually explicit channel in full or to limit the channel's programming to the hours between 10 p.m. and 6 a.m. 47 U.S.C. § 561 (1994 ed., Supp. III); 47 CFR § 76.227 (1999) . . .

The District Court denied Playboy a preliminary injunction, . . . and we summarily affirmed, . . . The TRO was lifted, and the Federal Communications Commission announced it would begin enforcing § 505 on May 18, 1997.

. . .

When the statute became operative, most cable operators had "no practical choice but to curtail [the targeted] programming during the [regulated] sixteen hours or risk the penalties imposed . . . if any audio or video signal bleed occur[red] during [those] times." 30 F.Supp.2d, at 711. The majority of operators—"in one survey, 69%"—complied with § 505 by time channeling the targeted programmers. *Ibid.* Since "30 to 50% of all adult programming is viewed by households prior to 10 p.m.," the result was a significant restriction of communication, with a corresponding reduction in Playboy's revenues. *Ibid.*

In March 1998, the District Court held a full trial and concluded that § 505 violates the First Amendment. . . . The United States filed a direct appeal in this Court pursuant to § 561. The District Court thereafter dismissed for lack of jurisdiction two post-trial motions filed by the Government. . . . We noted probable jurisdiction, and now affirm.

II.

Two essential points should be understood concerning the speech at issue here. First, we shall assume that many adults themselves would find the material highly offensive; and when we consider the further circumstance that the material comes unwanted into homes where children might see or hear it against parental wishes or consent, there are legitimate reasons for regulating it. Second, all parties bring the case to us on the premise that Playboy's programming has First Amendment protection. As this case has been litigated, it is not alleged to be obscene; adults have a constitutional right to view it; the Government disclaims any interest in preventing children from seeing or hearing it with the consent of their parents; and Playboy has concomitant rights under the First Amendment to transmit it. These points are undisputed.

The speech in question is defined by its content; and the statute which seeks to restrict it is content based. Section 505 applies only to channels primarily dedicated to "sexually explicit adult programming or other programming that is indecent." The statute is unconcerned with signal bleed from any other channels. . . . The overriding justification for the regulation is concern for the effect of the subject matter on young viewers. Section 505 is not "'justified without reference to the content of the regulated speech.'" . . . This is the essence of content-based regulation.

Not only does § 505 single out particular programming content for regulation, it also singles out particular programmers. The speech in question was not thought by Congress to be so harmful that all channels were subject to restriction. Instead, the statutory disability applies only to channels "primarily dedicated to sexually-oriented programming." 47 U.S.C. § 561(a) (1994 ed., Supp. III). One sponsor of the measure even identified appellee by name. See 141 Cong. Rec. 15587 (1995) (statement of Sen. Feinstein) (noting the statute would apply to channels "such as the Playboy and Spice channels"). Laws designed or intended to suppress or restrict the expression of specific speakers contradict basic First Amendment principles. Section 505 limited Playboy's market as a penalty for its programming choice, though other channels capable of transmitting like material are altogether exempt.

The effect of the federal statute on the protected speech is now apparent. It is evident that the only reasonable way for a substantial number of cable operators to comply with the letter of § 505 is to time channel, which silences the protected speech for two-thirds of the day in every home in a cable service area, regardless of the presence or likely presence of children or of the wishes of the viewers. According to the District Court, "30 to 50% of all adult programming is viewed by households prior to 10 p.m.," when the safe-harbor period begins. 30 F.Supp.2d, at 711. To prohibit this much speech is a significant restriction of communication between speakers and willing adult listeners, communication which enjoys First Amendment protection. It is of no moment that the statute does not impose a complete prohibition. The distinction between laws burdening and laws banning speech is but a matter of degree. The Government's content-based burdens must satisfy the same rigorous scrutiny as its content-based bans.

Since § 505 is a content-based speech restriction, it can stand only if it satisfies strict scrutiny. *Sable Communications of Cal., Inc. v. FCC*, 492 U.S. 115 (1989). If a statute regulates speech based on its content, it must be narrowly tailored to promote a compelling Government interest. *Ibid.* If a less restrictive alternative would serve the Government's purpose, the legislature must use that alternative.

. . .

Our precedents teach these principles. Where the designed benefit of a content-based speech restriction is to shield the sensibilities of listeners, the general rule is that the right of expression prevails, even where no less restrictive alternative exists. We are expected to protect our own sensibilities "simply by averting [our] eyes." . . . Here, of course, we consider images transmitted to some homes where they are not wanted and where parents often are not present to give immediate guidance. Cable television, like broadcast media, presents unique problems, which inform our assessment of the interests at stake, and which may justify restrictions that would be unacceptable in other contexts. . . . No one suggests the Government must be indifferent to unwanted, indecent speech that comes into the home without parental consent. The speech here, all agree, is protected speech; and the question is what standard the Government must meet in order to restrict it. As we consider a content-based regulation, the answer should be clear: The standard is strict scrutiny. This case involves speech alone; and even where speech is indecent and enters the home, the objective of shielding children does not suffice to support a blanket ban if the protection can be accomplished by a less restrictive alternative.

In *Sable Communications,* for instance, the feasibility of a technological approach to controlling minors' access to "dial-a-porn" messages required invalidation of a complete statutory ban on the medium. 492 U.S., at 130-131. And, while mentioned only in passing, the mere possibility that user-based Internet screening software would "'soon be widely available'" was relevant to our rejection of an overbroad restriction of indecent cyberspeech. *Reno, supra,* at 876-877 . . . .

Our zoning cases, on the other hand, are irrelevant to the question here. *Post,* at 1899 (BREYER, J., dissenting) (citing *Renton v. Playtime Theatres, Inc.,* 475 U.S. 41 (1986), and *Young v. American Mini Theatres, Inc.,* 427 U.S. 50 (1976)). We have made clear that the lesser scrutiny afforded regulations targeting the secondary effects of crime or declining property values has no application to content-based regulations targeting the primary effects of protected speech. . . . The statute now before us burdens speech because of its content; it must receive strict scrutiny.

There is, moreover, a key difference between cable television and the broadcasting media, which is the point on which this case turns: Cable systems have the capacity to block unwanted channels on a household-by-household basis. The option to block reduces the likelihood, so concerning to the Court in *Pacifica, supra,* at 744, that traditional First Amendment scrutiny would deprive the Government of all authority to address this sort of problem. The corollary, of course, is that targeted blocking enables the Government to support parental authority without affecting the First Amendment interests of speakers and willing listeners-listeners for whom, if the speech is unpopular or indecent, the privacy of their own homes may be the optimal place of receipt. Simply put, targeted blocking is less restrictive than banning, and the Government cannot ban speech if targeted blocking is a feasible and effective means of furthering its compelling interests. This is not to say that the absence of an effective blocking mechanism will in all cases suffice to support a law restricting the speech in question; but if a less restrictive means is available for the Government to achieve its goals, the Government must use it.

III.

The District Court concluded that a less restrictive alternative is available: § 504, with adequate publicity. . . . No one disputes that § 504, which requires cable operators to block undesired channels at individual households upon request, is narrowly tailored to the Government's goal of supporting parents who want those channels blocked. The question is whether § 504 can be effective.

When a plausible, less restrictive alternative is offered to a content-based speech restriction, it is the Government's obligation to prove that the alternative will be ineffective to achieve its goals. The Government has not met that burden here. In support of its position, the Government cites empirical evidence showing that § 504, as promulgated and implemented before trial, generated few requests for household-by-household blocking. Between March 1996 and May 1997, while the Government was enjoined from enforcing § 505, § 504 remained in operation. A survey of cable operators determined that fewer than 0.5% of cable subscribers requested full blocking during that time. *Id.,* at 712. The uncomfortable fact is that § 504 was the sole blocking regulation in effect for over a year; and the public greeted it with a collective yawn.

The District Court was correct to direct its attention to the import of this tepid response. Placing the burden of proof upon the Government, the District Court examined whether § 504 was capable of serving as an effective, less restrictive means of reaching the Government's goals. *Id.,* at 715, 718-719. It concluded that § 504, if publicized in an adequate manner, could be. *Id.,* at 719-720.

The District Court employed the proper approach. When the Government restricts speech, the Government bears the burden of proving the constitutionality of its actions. . . . When the Government seeks to restrict speech based on its content, the usual presumption of constitutionality afforded congressional enactments is reversed. "Content-based regulations are presumptively invalid," . . . and the Government bears the burden to rebut that presumption.

. . .

With this burden in mind, the District Court explored three explanations for the lack of individual blocking requests. 30 F.Supp.2d, at 719. First, individual blocking might not be an effective alternative, due to technological or other limitations. Second, although an adequately advertised blocking provision might have been effective, § 504 as written did not require sufficient notice to make it so. Third, the actual signal bleed problem might be far less of a concern than the Government at first had supposed. *Ibid.*

To sustain its statute, the Government was required to show that the first was the right answer. According to the District Court, however, the first and third possibilities were "equally consistent" with the record before it. *Ibid.* As for the second, the record was "not clear" as to whether enough notice had been issued to give § 504 a fighting chance. *Ibid.* The case, then, was at best a draw. Unless the District Court's findings are clearly erroneous, the tie goes to free expression.

The District Court began with the problem of signal bleed itself, concluding "the Government has not convinced us that [signal bleed] is a pervasive problem." *Id.*, at 708-709, 718. The District Court's thorough discussion exposes a central weakness in the Government's proof: There is little hard evidence of how widespread or how serious the problem of signal bleed is. Indeed, there is no proof as to how likely any child is to view a discernible explicit image, and no proof of the duration of the bleed or the quality of the pictures or sound. To say that millions of children are subject to a risk of viewing signal bleed is one thing; to avoid articulating the true nature and extent of the risk is quite another. Under § 505, sanctionable signal bleed can include instances as fleeting as an image appearing on a screen for just a few seconds. The First Amendment requires a more careful assessment and characterization of an evil in order to justify a regulation as sweeping as this. . . .

Spurred by the District Court's express request for more specific evidence of the problem, see 945 F.Supp., at 779, n. 16, the Government also presented an expert's spreadsheet estimate that 39 million homes with 29.5 million children had the potential to be exposed to signal bleed, 30 F.Supp.2d, at 708-709. The Government made no attempt to confirm the accuracy of its estimate through surveys or other field tests, however. Accordingly, the District Court discounted the figures and made this finding: "[T]he Government presented no evidence on the number of households actually exposed to signal bleed and thus has not quantified the actual extent of the problem of signal bleed." . . . The finding is not clearly erroneous; indeed it is all but required.

Once § 505 went into effect, of course, a significant percentage of cable operators felt it necessary to time channel their sexually explicit programmers. *Id.*, at 711, and n. 14. This is an indication that scrambling technology is not yet perfected. That is not to say, however, that scrambling is completely ineffective. Different cable systems use different scrambling systems, which vary in their dependability. "The severity of the problem varies from time to time and place to place, depending on the weather, the quality of the equipment, its installation, and maintenance." *Id.*, at 708. At even the good end of the spectrum a system might bleed to an extent sufficient to trigger the time-channeling requirement for a cautious cable operator. (The statute requires the signal to be "*fully* block[ed]." 47 U.S.C. § 561(a) (1994 ed., Supp. III) (emphasis added).) A rational cable operator, faced with the possibility of sanctions for intermittent bleeding, could well choose to time channel even if the bleeding is too momentary to pose any concern to most households. To affirm that the Government failed to prove the existence of a problem, while at the same time observing that the statute imposes a severe burden on speech, is consistent with the analysis our cases require. Here, there is no probative evidence in the record which differentiates among the extent of bleed at individual households and no evidence which otherwise quantifies the signal bleed problem.

In addition, market-based solutions such as programmable televisions, VCR's, and mapping systems (which display a blue screen when tuned to a scrambled signal) may eliminate signal bleed at the consumer end of the cable. 30 F.Supp.2d, at 708. Playboy made the point at trial that the Government's estimate failed to account for these factors. *Id.*, at 708-709. Without some sort of field survey, it is impossible to know how widespread the problem in fact is, and the only indicator in the record is a handful of complaints. . . . If the number of children transfixed by even flickering pornographic television images in fact reached into the millions we, like the District Court, would have expected to be directed to more than a handful of complaints.

. . .

Nor did the District Court err in its second conclusion. The Government also failed to prove § 504 with adequate notice would be an ineffective alternative to § 505. Once again, the District Court invited the Government to produce its proof . . . Once again, the Government fell short. . . . It is not clear, however, from the record that notices of the provisions of § 504 have been adequate"). There is no evidence that a well-promoted voluntary blocking provision would not be capable at least of informing parents about signal bleed (if they are not yet aware of it) and about their rights to have the bleed blocked (if they consider it a problem and have not yet controlled it themselves).

. . .

The Government also contends a publicized § 504 will be just as restrictive as § 505, on the theory that the cost of installing blocking devices will outstrip the revenues from distributing Playboy's programming and lead to its cancellation. See 30 F.Supp.2d, at 713. This conclusion rests on the assumption that a sufficient percentage of households, informed of the potential for signal bleed, would consider it enough of a problem to order blocking devices-an assumption for which there is no support in the record. *Id.*, at 719. It should be noted, furthermore, that Playboy is willing to incur the costs of an effective § 504. One might infer that Playboy believes an advertised § 504 will be ineffective for its object, or one might infer the company believes the signal bleed problem is not widespread. In the absence of proof, it is not for the Court to assume the former.

It is no response that voluntary blocking requires a consumer to take action, or may be inconvenient, or may not go perfectly every time. A court should not assume a plausible, less restrictive alternative would be ineffective; and a court should not presume parents, given full information, will fail to act. If unresponsive operators are a concern, moreover, a notice statute could give cable operators ample incentive, through fines or other penalties for noncompliance, to respond to blocking requests in prompt and efficient fashion.

Having adduced no evidence in the District Court showing that an adequately advertised § 504 would not be effective to aid desirous parents in keeping signal bleed out of their own households, the Government can now cite nothing in the record to support the point. The Government instead takes quite a different approach. After only an offhand suggestion that the success of a well-communicated § 504 is "highly unlikely," the Government sets the point aside, arguing instead that society's independent interests will be unserved if parents fail to act on that information.

. . .

The whole point of a publicized § 504 would be to advise parents that indecent material may be shown and to afford them an opportunity to block it at all times, even when they are not at home and even after 10 p.m. Time channeling does not offer this assistance. The regulatory alternative of a publicized § 504, which has the real possibility of promoting more open disclosure and the choice of an effective blocking system, would provide parents the information needed to engage in active supervision.

It must be remembered, however, that children will be exposed to signal bleed under time channeling as well. Time channeling, unlike blocking, does not eliminate signal bleed around the clock. Just as adolescents may be unsupervised outside of their own households, it is hardly unknown for them to be unsupervised in front of the television set after 10 p.m. The record is silent as to the comparative effectiveness of the two alternatives.

. . .

Basic speech principles are at stake in this case. When the purpose and design of a statute is to regulate speech by reason of its content, special consideration or latitude is not accorded to the Government merely because the law can somehow be described as a burden rather than outright suppression. We cannot be influenced, moreover, by the perception that the regulation in question is not a major one because the speech is not very important. The history of the law of free expression is one of vindication in cases involving speech that many citizens may find shabby, offensive, or even ugly. It follows that all content-based restrictions on speech must give us more than a moment's pause. If television broadcasts can expose children to the real risk of harmful exposure to indecent materials, even in their own home and without parental consent, there is a problem the Government can address. It must do so, however, in a way consistent with First Amendment principles. Here the Government has not met the burden the First Amendment imposes.

The Government has failed to show that § 505 is the least restrictive means for addressing a real problem; and the District Court did not err in holding the statute violative of the First Amendment. In light of our ruling, it is unnecessary to address the second question presented: whether the District Court was divested of jurisdiction to consider the Government's postjudgment motions after the Government filed a notice of appeal in this Court. The judgment of the District Court is affirmed.

It is so ordered.

APPENDIX TO OPINION OF THE COURT.

Section 505 of the Telecommunications Act of 1996, Pub.L. 104-104, 110 Stat. 136, 47 U.S.C. § 561 (1994 ed., Supp. III), provides in relevant part:

> "(a) Requirement
>
> "In providing sexually explicit adult programming or other programming that is indecent on any channel of its service primarily dedicated to sexually-oriented programming, a multichannel video programming distributor shall fully scramble or otherwise fully block the video and audio portion of such channel so that one not a subscriber to such channel or programming does not receive it.
>
> "(b) Implementation
>
> "Until a multichannel video programming distributor complies with the requirement set forth in subsection (a) of this section, the distributor shall limit the access of children to the programming referred to in that subsection by not providing such programming during the hours of the day (as determined by the Commission) when a significant number of children are likely to view it.
>
> "(c) 'Scramble' defined
>
> "As used in this section, the term 'scramble' means to rearrange the content of the signal of the programming so that the programming cannot be viewed or heard in an understandable manner."

Section 504 of the Telecommunications Act of 1996, Pub.L. 104-104, 110 Stat. 136, 47 U.S.C. § 560 (1994 ed., Supp. III), provides in relevant part:

> "(a) Subscriber request
>
> "Upon request by a cable service subscriber, a cable operator shall, without charge, fully scramble or otherwise fully block the audio and video programming of each channel carrying such programming so that one not a subscriber does not receive it.
>
> "(b) 'Scramble' defined

> "As used in this section, the term 'scramble' means to rearrange the content of the signal of the programming so that the programming cannot be viewed or heard in an understandable manner."

Justice STEVENS, concurring.
Because Justice SCALIA has advanced an argument that the parties have not addressed, a brief response is in order. Relying on *Ginzburg v. United States,* 383 U.S. 463 (1966), Justice SCALIA would treat programs whose content is, he assumes, protected by the First Amendment as though they were obscene because of the way they are advertised. . . .

Justice THOMAS, concurring.
It would seem to me that, with respect to at least some of the cable programming affected by § 505 of the Telecommunications Act of 1996, the Government has ample constitutional and statutory authority to prohibit its broadcast entirely. . . . Applying the First Amendment's exacting standards, the Court has correctly determined that § 505 cannot be upheld on the theory argued by the Government. Accordingly, I join the opinion of the Court.

Justice SCALIA, dissenting.
I agree with the principal dissent in this case that § 505 of the Telecommunications Act of 1996, Pub.L. 104-104, 110 Stat. 136, 47 U.S.C. § 561 (1994 ed., Supp. III), is supported by a compelling state interest and is narrowly tailored. I write separately to express my view that § 505 can be upheld in simpler fashion: by finding that it regulates the business of obscenity.

. . .

Justice BREYER, with whom THE CHIEF JUSTICE, Justice O'CONNOR, and Justice SCALIA join, dissenting.
This case involves the application, not the elucidation, of First Amendment principles. We apply established First Amendment law to a statute that focuses upon the broadcast of "sexually explicit adult programming" on AdulTVision, Adam & Eve, Spice, and Playboy cable channels. These channels are, as the statute requires, "primarily dedicated to sexually-oriented programming." Telecommunications Act of 1996, Pub.L. 104-104, § 505(a), 110 Stat. 136, 47 U.S.C. § 561(a) (1994 ed., Supp. III). Section 505 prohibits cable operators from sending these adult channels into the homes of viewers who do not request them. In practice, it requires a significant number of cable operators either to upgrade their scrambling

technology or to avoid broadcasting these channels during daylight and evening hours (6 a.m. to 10 p.m.). . . .

I.

At the outset, I would describe the statutory scheme somewhat differently than does the majority. I would emphasize three background points. First, the statutory scheme reflects more than a congressional effort to control incomplete scrambling. Previously, federal law had left cable operators free to decide whether, when, and how to transmit adult channels.

. . .

The statute is carefully tailored to respect viewer preferences. It regulates transmissions by creating two "default rules" applicable unless the subscriber decides otherwise. Section 504 requires a cable operator to "fully scramble" any channel (whether or not it broadcasts adult programming) *if* a subscriber asks *not* to receive it. Section 505 requires a cable operator to "fully scramble" every adult channel *unless* a subscriber asks to receive it. Taken together, the two provisions create a scheme that permits subscribers to choose to see what they want. But each law creates a different "default" assumption about silent subscribers. Section 504 assumes a silent subscriber wants to see the ordinary (non-adult) channels that the cable operator includes in the paid-for bundle sent into the home. Section 505 assumes that a silent subscriber does not want to receive adult channels. Consequently, a subscriber wishing to view an adult channel must "opt in," and specifically request that channel. See § 505. A subscriber wishing not to view any other channel (sent into the home) must "opt out." See § 504.

The scheme addresses signal bleed but only indirectly. From the statute's perspective signal "bleeding"--*i.e.*, a failure to fully "rearrange the content of the signal . . . so that the programming cannot be viewed or heard in an understandable manner," § 504(c)—amounts to transmission into a home. Hence "bleeding" violates the statute whenever a clear transmission of an unrequested adult channel would violate the statute.

Second, the majority's characterization of this statutory scheme as "prohibit[ing] . . . speech" is an exaggeration. *Ante*, at 1885-1886. Rather, the statute places a *burden* on adult channel speech by requiring the relevant cable operator either to use better scrambling technology, or, if that technology is too expensive, to broadcast only between 10 p.m. and 6 a.m. Laws that burden speech, say, by making speech less profitable, may create serious First Amendment issues, but they are not the equivalent of an absolute ban on speech itself. . . . The difference-between imposing a burden and enacting a ban-can matter even when strict First Amendment rules are at issue.

Third, this case concerns only the regulation of commercial actors who broadcast "virtually 100% sexually explicit" material. 30 F.Supp.2d 702, 707 (D.Del.1998). The channels do not broadcast more than trivial amounts of more serious material such as birth control information, artistic images, or the visual equivalents of classical or serious literature. This case therefore does not present the kind of narrow tailoring concerns seen in other cases. See, *e.g., Reno,* 521 U.S., at 877-879 ("The breadth of the [statute's] coverage is wholly unprecedented . . . . [It] cover[s] large amounts of nonpornographic material with serious educational or other value"); *Butler, supra,* at 381-384 (invalidating ban on books "'tending to the corruption of the morals of youth'").

With this background in mind, the reader will better understand my basic disagreement with each of the Court's two conclusions.

II.

The majority first concludes that the Government failed to prove the seriousness of the problem-receipt of adult channels by children whose parents did not request their broadcast. *Ante,* at 1889-1891. This claim is flat-out wrong. For one thing, the parties concede that basic RF scrambling does not scramble the audio portion of the program. 30 F.Supp.2d, at 707. For another, Playboy itself conducted a survey of cable operators who were asked: "Is your system in full compliance with Section 505 (no discernible audio or video bleed)?" To this question, 75% of cable operators answered "no." See Def. Exh. 254, 2 Record 2. Further, the Government's expert took the number of homes subscribing to Playboy or Spice, multiplied by the fraction of cable households with children and the average number of children per household, and found 29 million children are potentially exposed to audio and video bleed from adult programming. Def. Exh. 82, 10 Record 11-12. Even discounting by 25% for systems that might be considered in full compliance, this left 22 million children in homes with faulty scrambling systems. See *id.,* at 12. And, of course, the record contains additional anecdotal evidence and the concerns expressed by elected officials, probative of a larger problem. See 30 F.Supp.2d, at 709, and n. 10; see also 141 Cong. Rec. 15586 (1995).

. . .

If, as the majority suggests, the signal bleed problem is not significant, then there is also no significant burden on speech created by § 505. The majority cannot have this evidence both ways. And if, given this logical difficulty and the quantity of empirical evidence, the majority still believes that the Government has not proved its case, then it imposes a burden upon the Government beyond that suggested in any other First Amendment case of which I am aware.

III.

The majority's second claim-that the Government failed to demonstrate the absence of a "less restrictive alternative"-presents a closer question. The specific question is whether § 504's "opt-out" amounts to a "less restrictive," but *similarly* practical and *effective,* way to accomplish § 505's child-protecting objective. As *Reno* tells us, a "less restrictive alternativ[e]" must be "at least as effective in achieving the legitimate purpose that the statute was enacted to serve." 521 U.S., at 874.

The words I have just emphasized, "similarly" and "effective," are critical. In an appropriate case they ask a judge not to apply First Amendment rules mechanically, but to decide whether, in light of the benefits and potential alternatives, the statute works speech-related harm (here to adult speech) out of proportion to the benefits that the statute seeks to provide (here, child protection). . . . Section 504 gives parents the power to tell cable operators to keep any channel out of their home. Section 505 does more. Unless parents explicitly consent, it inhibits the transmission of adult cable channels to children whose parents may be unaware of what they are watching, whose parents cannot easily supervise television viewing habits, whose parents do not know of their § 504 "opt-out" rights, or whose parents are simply unavailable at critical times. In this respect, § 505 serves the same interests as the laws that deny children access to adult cabarets or X-rated movies. . . . These laws, and § 505, all act in the absence of direct parental supervision.

This legislative objective is perfectly legitimate. Where over 28 million school age children have both parents or their only parent in the work force, where at least 5 million children are left alone at home without supervision each week, and where children may spend afternoons and evenings watching television outside of the home with friends, § 505 offers independent protection for a large number of families. . . . Government has a compelling interest in helping parents by preventing minors from accessing sexually explicit materials in the absence of parental supervision. . . .

By definition, § 504 does *nothing at all* to further the compelling interest I have just described. How then is it a similarly effective § 505 alternative?

. . .

Even if better notice did adequately inform viewers of their § 504 rights, exercise of those rights by more than 6% of the subscriber base would itself raise Playboy's costs to the point that Playboy would be forced off the air entirely, 30 F.Supp.2d, at 713-a consequence that would not seem to further anyone's interest in free speech. The majority, resting on its own earlier conclusion that signal bleed is not widespread, denies any likelihood that more than 6% of viewers would need § 504. But that earlier conclusion is unsound. See *supra,* at 1900-1901. The majority also relies on the fact that Playboy, presumably aware of its own economic interests, "is willing to incur the costs of an effective § 504." *Ante,* at 1892. Yet that denial, as the majority admits, may simply reflect Playboy's knowledge that § 504, even with better notice, will not work. Section 504 is not a similarly effective alternative to § 505 (in respect to the Government's interest in protecting children), unless more than a minimal number of viewers actually use it; yet the economic evidence shows that if more than 6% do so, Playboy's programming would be totally eliminated. The majority provides no answer to this argument in its opinion-and this evidence is sufficient in and of itself to dispose of this case.

Of course, it is logically *possible* that "better notice" will bring about near perfect parental knowledge (of what children watch and § 504 opt-out rights), that cable operators will respond rapidly to blocking requests, and that still 94% of all informed parents will decided not to have adult channels blocked for free. But the *probability* that this remote *possibility* will occur is neither a "draw" nor a "tie." *Ante,* at 1889. And that fact is sufficient for the Government to have met its burden of proof.

. . .

IV.

Section 505 raises the cost of adult channel broadcasting. In doing so, it restricts, but does not ban, adult speech. Adults may continue to watch adult channels, though less conveniently, by watching at night, recording programs with a VCR, or by subscribing to digital cable with better blocking systems.... The Government's justification for imposing this restriction—limiting the access of children to channels that broadcast virtually 100% "sexually explicit" material—is "compelling." The record shows no similarly effective, less restrictive alternative. Consequently § 505's restriction, viewed in light of the proposed alternative, is proportionate to need. That is to say, it restricts speech no more than necessary to further that compelling need. Taken together, these considerations lead to the conclusion that § 505 is lawful.

. . .

Congress has taken seriously the importance of maintaining adult access to the sexually explicit channels here at issue. It has tailored the restrictions to minimize their impact upon adults while offering parents help in keeping unwanted transmissions from their children. By finding "adequate alternatives" where there are none, the Court reduces Congress' protective power to the vanishing point. That is not what the First Amendment demands.

I respectfully dissent.

The Must-Carry Rules

As Justice Kennedy points out in the *Turner* case infra, the must-carry provisions were intended to benefit weak broadcasters who would otherwise not get access to a cable system through negotiation—even without a royalty payment. To view a broadcast station not on a cable system, a subscriber would have to disconnect her television from cable and reconnect it to an antenna, and then reverse the process to return to the cable dial. In Quincy Cable TV, Inc. v. FCC, 768 F.2d 1434 (D.C. Cir. 1985), the FCC's first attempt to issue must-carry rules was struck down as unduly burdensome on cable systems' speech interests. In the late 1980s, the FCC even conducted an experiment with a so-called A/B switch, which would have facilitated the transition between broadcast and cable tuners. Viewers, however, were simply unwilling to interrupt their channel surfing with even minimal extra effort. Without a means to require cable systems to carry them, certain broadcast stations, the FCC concluded, would lose access to the cable audience, now well over 90 percent of all American viewers.

After the FCC tried and failed again to promulgate less burdensome must-carry rules, Congress enacted its own must-carry legislation, sections 614 and 615 of the 1992 Cable Act. To address speech-burden concerns, Congress scaled the carriage requirements. Section 614, which covers commercial stations, exempts systems with fewer than 300 subscribers from the rules and reduces the number of stations that must be carried to three if the system has fewer than twelve channels. Systems with more than twelve channels (most systems today) may be required to carry stations equal to one-third of their total channels.

Under section 615, cable systems with twelve or fewer channels may be required to carry one local noncommercial educational station, systems with twelve-to-thirty-six channels must carry all noncommercial educational stations up to three, and systems with more than thirty-six channels (most systems today) must carry all local noncommercial educational stations. In focusing on reducing speech burdens, Congress presupposed that the must-carry rules were a content-neutral structural regulation designed primarily to protect the economic interests of broadcasters. Cable companies, including Turner Broadcasting System and Time Warner Entertainment, challenged the rationale behind Congress' legislation, arguing that, since the rules compel a cable system to carry speech, they should be subject to strict scrutiny as a content regulation.

TURNER BROADCASTING SYSTEM, INC., V. FCC (*TURNER II*)
520 U.S. 180 (1997)

Justice KENNEDY delivered the opinion of the Court, except as to a portion of Part II-A-1.

Sections 4 and 5 of the Cable Television Consumer Protection and Competition Act of 1992 require cable television systems to dedicate some of their channels to local broadcast television stations. Earlier in this case, we held the so-called "must-carry" provisions to be content-neutral restrictions on speech, subject to intermediate First Amendment scrutiny under *United States v. O'Brien,* 391 U.S. 367, 377 (1968). A plurality of the Court considered the record as then developed insufficient to determine whether the provisions were narrowly tailored to further important governmental interests, and we remanded the case to the District Court for the District of Columbia for additional factfinding.

On appeal from the District Court's grant of summary judgment for appellees, the case now presents the two questions left open during the first appeal: First, whether the record as it now stands supports Congress' predictive judgment that the must-carry provisions further important governmental interests; and second, whether the provisions do not burden substantially more speech than necessary to further those interests. We answer both questions in the affirmative, and conclude the must-carry provisions are consistent with the First Amendment.

I.

Soon after Congress enacted the Cable Television Consumer Protection and Competition Act of 1992 (Cable Act), Pub.L. 102-385, 106 Stat. 1460, appellants brought suit against the United States and the Federal Communications Commission (FCC) (both referred to here as the Government) in the United States District Court for the District of Columbia, challenging the constitutionality of the must-carry provisions under the First Amendment. The three-judge District Court, in a divided opinion, granted summary judgment for the Government and intervenor-defendants. A majority of the court sustained the must-carry provisions under the intermediate standard of scrutiny set forth in *United States v. O'Brien, supra,* concluding the must-carry provisions were content-neutral "industry-specific antitrust and fair trade" legislation narrowly tailored to preserve local broadcasting beset by monopoly power in most cable systems, growing concentration in the cable industry, and concomitant risks of programming decisions driven by anticompetitive policies. 819 F.Supp. 32, 40, 45-47 (1993).

Ted Turner, cable television pioneer and philanthropist.

On appeal, we agreed with the District Court that must-carry does not "distinguish favored speech from disfavored speech on the basis of the ideas or views expressed," 512 U.S., at 643, but is a content-neutral regulation designed "to prevent cable operators from exploiting their economic power to the detriment of broadcasters," and "to ensure that all Americans, especially those unable to subscribe to cable, have access to free television programming-whatever its content." *Id.,* at 649. We held that, under the intermediate level of scrutiny applicable to content-neutral regulations, must-carry would be sustained if it were shown to further an important or substantial governmental interest unrelated to the suppression of free speech, provided the incidental restrictions did not "'burden substantially more speech than is necessary to further'" those interests... Although we "ha[d] no difficulty concluding" the interests must-carry was designed to serve were important in the abstract, 512 U.S., at 663, a four-Justice plurality concluded genuine issues of material fact remained regarding whether "the economic health of local broadcasting is in genuine jeopardy and in need of the protections afforded by must-carry," and whether must-carry "'burden[s] substantially more speech than is necessary to further the government's legitimate interests.'" *Id.*, at 665, 114 S.Ct., at 2470 (quoting *Ward, supra,* at 799). Justice STEVENS would have found the statute valid on the record then before us; he agreed to remand the case to ensure a judgment of the Court, and the case was returned to the District Court for further proceedings. 512 U.S., at 673-674 (opinion concurring in part and concurring in judgment); *id.*, at 667-668.

The District Court oversaw another 18 months of factual development on remand "yielding a record of tens of thousands of pages" of evidence, *Turner Broadcasting v. FCC,* 910 F.Supp. 734, 755 (1995), comprised of materials acquired during Congress' three years of preenactment hearings, see *Turner, supra,* at 632-634, as well as additional expert submissions, sworn declarations and testimony, and industry documents obtained on remand. Upon consideration of the expanded record, a divided panel of the District Court again granted summary judgment to appellees. 910 F.Supp., at 751. The majority determined "Congress drew reasonable inferences" from substantial evidence before it to conclude that " in the absence of must-carry rules, 'significant' numbers of broadcast stations would be refused carriage." *Id.*, at 742. The court found Congress drew on studies and anecdotal evidence indicating "cable operators had already dropped, refused to carry, or adversely repositioned significant numbers of local broadcasters," and suggesting that in the vast majority of cases the broadcasters were not restored to carriage in their prior position. *Ibid.* Noting evidence in the record before Congress and the testimony of experts on remand, *id.*, at 743, the court decided the noncarriage problem would grow worse without must-carry because cable operators had refrained from dropping broadcast stations during Congress' investigation and the pendency of this litigation, *id.*, at 742-743, and possessed increasing incentives to use their growing economic power to capture broadcasters' advertising revenues and promote affiliated cable programmers, *ibid.*

. . .

II.

We begin where the plurality ended in *Turner,* applying the standards for intermediate scrutiny enunciated in *O'Brien.* A content-neutral regulation will be sustained under the First Amendment if it advances important governmental interests unrelated to the suppression of free speech and does not burden substantially more speech than necessary to further those interests. *O'Brien,* 391 U.S., at 377. As noted in *Turner,* must-carry was designed to serve " three interrelated interests: (1) preserving the benefits of free, over-the-air local broadcast television, (2) promoting the widespread dissemination of information from a multiplicity of sources, and (3) promoting fair competition in the market for television programming." 512 U.S., at 662. We decided then, and now reaffirm, that each of those is an important governmental interest. We have been most explicit in holding that "'protecting noncable households from loss of regular television broadcasting service due to competition from cable systems' is an important federal interest." *Id.,* at 663 (quoting *Capital Cities Cable, Inc. v. Crisp,* 467 U.S. 691, 714 (1984)). Forty percent of American households continue to rely on over-the-air signals for television programming. Despite the growing importance of cable television and alternative technologies, "'broadcasting is demonstrably a principal source of information and entertainment for a great part of the Nation's population.'" *Turner, supra,* at 663 (quoting *United States v. Southwestern Cable Co.,* 392 U.S. 157, 177 (1968)). We have identified a corresponding "governmental purpose of the highest order" in ensuring public access to "a multiplicity of information sources," 512 U.S., at 663. And it is undisputed the Government has an interest in "eliminating restraints on fair competition . . . , even when the individuals or entities subject to particular regulations are engaged in expressive activity protected by the First Amendment." *Id.,* at 664.

. . .

In explicit factual findings, Congress expressed clear concern that the "marked shift in market share from broadcast television to cable television services," Cable Act § 2(a)(13), note following 47 U.S.C. § 521, resulting from increasing market penetration by cable services, as well as the expanding horizontal concentration and vertical integration of cable operators, combined to give cable systems the incentive and ability to delete, reposition, or decline carriage to local broadcasters in an attempt to favor affiliated cable programmers. §§ 2a(2)-(5), (15). Congress predicted that "absent the reimposition of [must-carry], additional local broadcast signals will be deleted, repositioned, or not carried," § 2(a)(15); see also § 2(a)(8)(D), with the end result that "the economic viability of free local broadcast television and its ability to originate quality local programming will be seriously jeopardized," § 2(a)(16).

At the same time, Congress was under no illusion that there would be a complete disappearance of broadcast television nationwide in the absence of must-carry. Congress recognized broadcast programming (and network programming in particular) "remains the most popular programming on cable systems," § 2(a)(19). Indeed, reflecting the popularity and strength of some broadcasters, Congress included in the Cable Act a provision permitting broadcasters to charge cable systems for carriage of the broadcasters' signals. See § 6, codified at 47 U.S.C. § 325. Congress was concerned not that broadcast television would disappear in its entirety without must-carry, but that without it, "significant numbers of broadcast stations will be refused carriage on cable systems," and those "broadcast stations denied carriage will either deteriorate to a substantial degree or fail altogether." 512 U.S., at 666. See, *e.g.*, H.R.Rep. No. 102-628, p. 51 (1992) (House Report) (the absence of must-carry "will result in a weakening of the over-the-air television industry and a reduction in competition"); *id.*, at 64 ("The Committee wishes to make clear that its concerns are not limited to a situation where stations are dropped wholesale by large numbers of cable systems"); S.Rep. No. 102-92, p. 62 (1991) (Senate Report) ("Without congressional action, . . . the role of local television broadcasting in our system of communications will steadily decline . . ."); see also Brief for Federal Appellees in *Turner Broadcasting System, Inc. v. FCC*, No. 93-44 p. 32, n. 22 (the question is not whether " the evidence shows that broadcast television is likely to be totally eliminated" but "whether the broadcast services available to viewers [without cable] are likely to be reduced to a significant extent, because of either loss of some stations altogether or curtailment of services by others").

Nor do the congressional findings support appellants' suggestion that legitimate legislative goals would be satisfied by the preservation of a rump broadcasting industry providing a minimum of broadcast service to Americans without cable. We have noted that "'it has long been a basic tenet of national communications policy that "the widest possible dissemination of information from diverse and antagonistic sources is essential to the welfare of the public."'" *Turner*, 512 U.S., at 663-664 . . . Congress identified a specific interest in "ensuring [the] continuation" of "the local origination of [broadcast] programming," § 2(a)(10), an interest consistent with its larger purpose of promoting multiple types of media, § 2(a)(6), and found must-carry necessary "to serve the goals" of the original Communications Act of 1934 of "providing a fair, efficient, and equitable distribution of broadcast services," § 2(a)(9). In short, Congress enacted must-carry to "preserve the existing structure of the Nation's broadcast television medium while permitting the concomitant expansion and development of cable television." 512 U.S., at 652.

Although Congress set no definite number of broadcast stations sufficient for these purposes, the Cable Act's requirement that all cable operators with more than 12 channels set aside one-third of their channel capacity for local broadcasters, § 4, 47 U.S.C. § 534(b)(1)(B), refutes the notion that Congress contemplated preserving only a bare minimum of stations. Congress' evident interest in "preserve[ing] the existing structure," 512 U.S., at 652, of the broadcast industry discloses a purpose to prevent any significant reduction in the multiplicity of broadcast programming sources available to noncable households. To the extent the appellants question the substantiality of the Government's interest in preserving something more than a minimum number of stations in each community, their position is meritless. It is for Congress to decide how much local broadcast television should be preserved for noncable households, and the validity of its determination "'does not turn on a judge's agreement with the responsible decisionmaker concerning' . . . the degree to which [the Government's] interests should be promoted."

. . .

The dissent proceeds on the assumption that must-carry is designed solely to be (and can only be justified as) a measure to protect broadcasters from cable operators' anticompetitive behavior. See *post,* at 1216, 1217, 1219. Federal policy, however, has long favored preserving a multiplicity of broadcast outlets regardless of whether the conduct that threatens it is motivated by anticompetitive animus or rises to the level of an antitrust violation. See *Capital Cities Cable, Inc. v. Crisp,* 467 U.S., at 714 . . . . While many of the network practices raise serious questions under the antitrust laws, . . . [i]t is not [the FCC's] function to apply the antitrust laws as such'" (quoting FCC Report on Chain Broadcasting Regulations (1941)). Broadcast television is an important source of information to many Americans. Though it is but one of many means for communication, by tradition and use for decades now it has been an essential part of the national discourse on subjects across the whole broad spectrum of speech, thought, and expression. . . . Congress has an independent interest in preserving a multiplicity of broadcasters to ensure that all households have access to information and entertainment on an equal footing with those who subscribe to cable.

A.

On our earlier review, we were constrained by the state of the record to assessing the importance of the Government's asserted interests when " viewed in the abstract," *Turner,* 512 U.S., at 663. The expanded record now permits us to consider whether the must-carry provisions were designed to address a real harm, and whether those provisions will alleviate it in a material way. *Id.*, at 663-664. We turn first to the harm or risk which prompted Congress to act. The Government's assertion that " the economic health of local broadcasting is in genuine jeopardy and in need of the protections afforded by must-carry," *id.*, at 664-665, rests on two component propositions: First, "significant numbers of broadcast stations will be refused carriage on cable systems" absent must-carry, *id.*, at 666. Second, "the broadcast stations denied carriage will either deteriorate to a substantial degree or fail altogether." *Ibid.*

In reviewing the constitutionality of a statute, "courts must accord substantial deference to the predictive judgments of Congress." . . . Our sole obligation is " to assure that, in formulating its judgments, Congress has drawn reasonable inferences based on substantial evidence." . . . We owe Congress' findings deference in part because the institution "is far better equipped than the judiciary to 'amass and evaluate the vast amounts of data' bearing upon" legislative questions. . . . This principle has special significance in cases, like this one, involving congressional judgments concerning regulatory schemes of inherent complexity and assessments about the likely interaction of industries undergoing rapid economic and technological change. Though different in degree, the deference to Congress is in one respect akin to deference owed to administrative agencies because of their expertise. . . . Even in the realm of First Amendment questions where Congress must base its conclusions upon substantial evidence, deference must be accorded to its findings as to the harm to be avoided and to the remedial measures adopted for that end, lest we infringe on traditional legislative authority to make predictive judgments when enacting nationwide regulatory policy.

1.

We have no difficulty in finding a substantial basis to support Congress' conclusion that a real threat justified enactment of the must-carry provisions. We examine first the evidence before Congress and then the further evidence presented to the District Court on remand to supplement the congressional determination.

As to the evidence before Congress, there was specific support for its conclusion that cable operators had considerable and growing market power over local video programming markets. Cable served at least 60 percent of American households in 1992, see Cable Act § 2(a)(3), and evidence indicated cable market penetration was projected to grow beyond 70 percent. See Cable TV Consumer Protection Act of 1991:

Hearing on S. 12 before the Subcommittee on Communications of the Senate Committee on Commerce, Science, and Transportation, 102d Cong., 1st Sess., 259 (1991) (statement of Edward O. Fritts) (App.1253); see also Defendants' Joint Statement of Evidence Before Congress ¶¶ 9, 10 (JSCR) (App.1252-1253). As Congress noted, § 2(a)(2), cable operators possess a local monopoly over cable households. Only one percent of communities are served by more than one cable system, JSCR ¶¶ 31-40 (App. 1262-1266). Even in communities with two or more cable systems, in the typical case each system has a local monopoly over its subscribers. See Comments of NAB before the FCC on MM Docket No. 85-349, ¶ 47 (Apr. 25, 1986) (App.26). Cable operators thus exercise " control over most (if not all) of the television programming that is channeled into the subscriber's home [and] can thus silence the voice of competing speakers with a mere flick of the switch." *Turner,* 512 U.S., at 656.

Evidence indicated the structure of the cable industry would give cable operators increasing ability and incentive to drop local broadcast stations from their systems, or reposition them to a less-viewed channel. Horizontal concentration was increasing as a small number of multiple system operators (MSO's) acquired large numbers of cable systems nationwide. § 2(a)(4). The trend was accelerating, giving the MSO's increasing market power.

. . .

Vertical integration in the industry also was increasing. As Congress was aware, many MSO's owned or had affiliation agreements with cable programmers. § 2(a)(5); Senate Report, at 24-29. Evidence indicated that before 1984 cable operators had equity interests in 38 percent of cable programming networks. In the late 1980's, 64 percent of new cable programmers were held in vertical ownership. . . .

After hearing years of testimony, and reviewing volumes of documentary evidence and studies offered by both sides, Congress concluded that the cable industry posed a threat to broadcast television. The Constitution gives to Congress the role of weighing conflicting evidence in the legislative process. Even when the resulting regulation touches on First Amendment concerns, we must give considerable deference, in examining the evidence, to Congress' findings and conclusions, including its findings and conclusions with respect to conflicting economic predictions. See *supra,* at 1189-1190. Furthermore, much of the testimony, though offered by interested parties, was supported by verifiable information and citation to independent sources. . . .

. . .

In addition, evidence before Congress, supplemented on remand, indicated that cable systems would have incentives to drop local broadcasters in favor of other programmers less likely to compete with them for audience and advertisers. Independent local broadcasters tend to be the closest substitutes for cable programs, because their programming tends to be similar, . . . and because both primarily target the same type of advertiser: those interested in cheaper (and more frequent) ad spots than are typically available on network affiliates...The ability of broadcast stations to compete for advertising is greatly increased by cable carriage, which increases viewership substantially. See Second Meek Declaration ¶ 34 (App.1866-1867). With expanded viewership, broadcast presents a more competitive medium for television advertising. Empirical studies indicate that cable-carried broadcasters so enhance competition for advertising that even modest increases in the numbers of broadcast stations carried on cable are correlated with significant decreases in advertising revenue to cable systems. . . .

Cable systems also have more systemic reasons for seeking to disadvantage broadcast stations: Simply stated, cable has little interest in assisting, through carriage, a competing medium of communication. As one cable-industry executive put it, "' our job is to promote cable television, not broadcast television.'" . . . The incentive to subscribe to cable is lower in markets with many over-the-air viewing options. . . . Evidence adduced on remand indicated cable systems have little incentive to carry, and a significant incentive to drop, broadcast stations that will only be strengthened by access to the 60 percent of the television market that cable typically controls. . . . Congress could therefore reasonably conclude that cable systems would drop broadcasters in favor of programmers-even unaffiliated ones-less likely to compete with them for audience and advertisers. . . .

The dissent contends Congress could not reasonably conclude cable systems would engage in such predation because cable operators, whose primary source of revenue is subscriptions, would not risk dropping a widely viewed broadcast station in order to capture advertising revenues. *Post,* at 1210. However, if viewers are faced with the choice of sacrificing a handful of broadcast stations to gain access to dozens of cable channels (plus network affiliates), it is likely they would still subscribe to cable even if they would prefer the dropped television stations to the cable programming that replaced them. Substantial evidence introduced on remand bears this out: With the exception of a handful of very popular broadcast stations (typically network affiliates), a cable system's choice between carrying a cable programmer or broadcast station has little or no effect on cable subscriptions, and subscribership thus typically does not bear on carriage decisions.

. . .

The record before Congress contained extensive anecdotal evidence about scores of adverse carriage decisions against broadcast stations. . . . Congress considered an FCC-sponsored study detailing cable system carriage practices in the wake of decisions by the United States Court of Appeals for the District of Columbia Circuit striking down prior must-carry regulations. . . . It indicated that in 1988, 280 out of 912 responding broadcast stations had been dropped or denied carriage in 1,533 instances. App. 47. Even assuming that every station dropped or denied coverage responded to the survey, it would indicate that nearly a quarter (21 percent) of the approximately 1,356 broadcast stations then in existence, *id.*, at 40, had been denied carriage. The same study reported 869 of 4,303 reporting cable systems had denied carriage to 704 broadcast stations in 1,820 instances, *id.*, at 48, and 279 of those stations had qualified for carriage under the prior must-carry rules, *id.*, at 49. A contemporaneous study of public television stations indicated that in the vast majority of cases, dropped stations were not restored to the cable service. Record, CR Vol. I.Z, Exh. 140, pp. CR 15297-15298, 15306-15307.

Substantial evidence demonstrated that absent must-carry the already "serious," Senate Report, at 43, problem of noncarriage would grow worse because "additional local broadcast signals will be deleted, repositioned, or not carried," § 2(a)(15). The record included anecdotal evidence showing the cable industry was acting with restraint in dropping broadcast stations in an effort to discourage reregulation. . . . A contemporaneous FCC report noted that "[c]able operators' incentive to deny carriage . . . appears to be particularly great as against local broadcasters . . . . As [cable] systems mature and penetration levels off, systems will turn increasingly to advertising for revenues. The incentive to deny carriage to local stations is a logical, rational and, without must carry, a legal business strategy."

. . .

Additional evidence developed on remand supports the reasonableness of Congress' predictive judgment. Approximately 11 percent of local broadcasters were not carried on the typical cable system in 1989.... According to one of appellants' own experts, between 19 and 31 percent of all local broadcast stations, including network affiliates, were not carried by the typical cable system. See Declaration of Stanley Besen, Exhs. C-2, C-3 (App.907-908). Based on the same data, another expert concluded that 47 percent of local independent commercial stations, and 36 percent of noncommercial stations, were not carried by the typical cable system. The rate of noncarriage was even higher for new stations. Third Meek Declaration ¶ 4 (App.2054). Appellees introduced evidence drawn from an empirical study concluding the 1988 FCC survey substantially underestimated the actual number of drops (Declaration of Tom Meek ¶¶ 5, 25, 36 (Meek Declaration) (App.619, 625, 626)), and the noncarriage problem grew steadily worse during the period without must-carry. By the time the Cable Act was passed, 1,261 broadcast stations had been dropped for at least one year, in a total of 7,945 incidents. *Id.*, ¶¶ 12, 15 (App.621, 622).

The dissent cites evidence indicating that many dropped broadcasters were stations few viewers watch, *post*, at 1211-1212, and it suggests that must-carry thwarts noncable viewers' preferences, *ibid.* Undoubtedly, viewers without cable—the immediate, though not sole, beneficiaries of efforts to preserve broadcast television—would have a strong preference for carriage of any broadcast program over any cable program, for the simple reason that it helps to preserve a medium to which they have access. The methodological flaws in the cited evidence are of concern. See *post*, at 1212.... On average, even the lowest rated station added pursuant to must-carry had ratings better than or equal to at least nine basic cable program services carried on the system. Third Meek Declaration ¶ 20, and n. 5 (App.2061). If cable systems refused to carry certain local broadcast stations because of their subscribers' preferences for the cable services carried in their place, one would expect that all cable programming services would have ratings exceeding those of broadcasters not carried. That is simply not the case.

The evidence on remand also indicated that the growth of cable systems' market power proceeded apace. The trend toward greater horizontal concentration continued, driven by "[e]nhanced growth prospects for advertising sales." . . . MSO's began to gain control of as many cable systems in a given market as they could, in a trend known as " clustering." . . . The vertical integration of the cable industry also continued, so by 1994, MSO's serving about 70 percent of the Nation's cable subscribers held equity interests in cable programmers. . . .

This is not a case in which we are called upon to give our best judgment as to the likely economic consequences of certain financial arrangements or business structures, or to assess competing economic theories and predictive judgments, as we would in a case arising, say, under the antitrust laws. "Statutes frequently require courts to make policy judgments. The Sherman Act, for example, requires courts to delve deeply into the theory of economic organization." See *Holder v. Hall*, 512 U.S. 874, 966, (1994) (separate opinion of STEVENS, J.). The issue before us is whether, given conflicting views of the probable development of the television industry, Congress had substantial evidence for making the judgment that it did. We need not put our imprimatur on Congress' economic theory in order to validate the reasonableness of its judgment.

2.

The harm Congress feared was that stations dropped or denied carriage would be at a " serious risk of financial difficulty," 512 U.S., at 667, and would " deteriorate to a substantial degree or fail altogether," *id.*, at 666. Congress had before it substantial evidence to support its conclusion. Congress was advised the viability of a broadcast station depends to a material extent on its ability to secure cable carriage. . . .

"Simply put, a television station's audience size directly translates into revenue-large audiences attract larger revenues, through the sale of advertising time. If a station is not carried on cable, and thereby loses a substantial portion of its audience, it will lose revenue. With less revenue, the station can not serve its community as well. The station will have less money to invest in equipment and programming. The attractiveness of its programming will lessen, as will its audience. Revenues will continue to decline, and the cycle will repeat."

. . .

Considerable evidence, consisting of statements compiled from dozens of broadcasters who testified before Congress and the FCC, confirmed that broadcast stations had fallen into bankruptcy, . . . The record also reflected substantial evidence that stations without cable carriage encountered severe difficulties obtaining financing for operations, reflecting the financial markets' judgment that the prospects are poor for broadcasters unable to secure carriage. . . . Evidence before Congress suggested the potential adverse impact of losing carriage was increasing as the growth of clustering gave MSO's centralized control over more local markets.

See JSCR ¶¶ 150-153 (App.1311-1313). Congress thus had ample basis to conclude that attaining cable carriage would be of increasing importance to ensuring a station's viability. We hold Congress could conclude from the substantial body of evidence before it that " absent legislative action, the free local off-air broadcast system is endangered." . . .

The evidence assembled on remand confirms the reasonableness of the congressional judgment. . . .

To be sure, the record also contains evidence to support a contrary conclusion. Appellants (and the dissent in the District Court) make much of the fact that the number of broadcast stations and their advertising revenue continued to grow during the period without must-carry, albeit at a diminished rate. Evidence introduced on remand indicated that only 31 broadcast stations actually went dark during the period without must-carry (one of which failed after a tornado destroyed its transmitter), and during the same period some 263 new stations signed on the air. Meek Declaration ¶¶ 76-77 (App.627-628). New evidence appellants produced on remand indicates the average cable system voluntarily carried local broadcast stations accounting for about 97 percent of television ratings in noncable households. Declaration of Stanley Besen, Part III-D (App.808). Appellants, as well as the dissent in the District Court, contend that in light of such evidence, it is clear " the must-carry law is not necessary to assure the economic viability of the broadcast system as a whole." NCTA Brief 18.

This assertion misapprehends the relevant inquiry. The question is not whether Congress, as an objective matter, was correct to determine must-carry is necessary to prevent a substantial number of broadcast stations from losing cable carriage and suffering significant financial hardship. Rather, the question is whether the legislative conclusion was reasonable and supported by substantial evidence in the record before Congress. . . . In making that determination, we are not to "reweigh the evidence *de novo*, or to replace Congress' factual predictions with our own." . . .

Although evidence of continuing growth in broadcast could have supported the opposite conclusion, a reasonable interpretation is that expansion in the cable industry was causing harm to broadcasting. . . . Broadcast advertising revenues declined in real terms by 11 percent between 1986 and 1991, during a period in which cable's real advertising revenues nearly doubled. See 910 F.Supp., at 790, App. 1. While these phenomena could be thought to stem from factors quite separate from the increasing market power of cable (for example, a recession in 1990-1992), it was for

Congress to determine the better explanation. We are not at liberty to substitute our judgment for the reasonable conclusion of a legislative body.

. . .

We think it apparent must-carry serves the Government's interests " in a direct and effective way." *Ward,* 491 U.S., at 800, 109 S.Ct., at 2759. Must-carry ensures that a number of local broadcasters retain cable carriage, with the concomitant audience access and advertising revenues needed to support a multiplicity of stations. Appellants contend that even were this so, must-carry is broader than necessary to accomplish its goals. We turn to this question.

B.

The second portion of the *O'Brien* inquiry concerns the fit between the asserted interests and the means chosen to advance them. Content-neutral regulations do not pose the same "inherent dangers to free expression," *Turner, supra,* at 661, that content-based regulations do, and thus are subject to a less rigorous analysis, which affords the Government latitude in designing a regulatory solution.... Under intermediate scrutiny, the Government may employ the means of its choosing "'so long as the ... regulation promotes a substantial governmental interest that would be achieved less effectively absent the regulation,'" and does not "'burden substantially more speech than is necessary to further'" that interest. *Turner,* 512 U.S., at 662 (quoting *Ward, supra,* at 799).

The must-carry provisions have the potential to interfere with protected speech in two ways. First, the provisions restrain cable operators' editorial discretion in creating programming packages by "reduc[ing] the number of channels over which [they] exercise unfettered control." *Turner,* 512 U.S., at 637. Second, the rules "render it more difficult for cable programmers to compete for carriage on the limited channels remaining." *Ibid.*

Appellants say the burden of must-carry is great, but the evidence adduced on remand indicates the actual effects are modest. Significant evidence indicates the vast majority of cable operators have not been affected in a significant manner by must-carry. Cable operators have been able to satisfy their must-carry obligations 87 percent of the time using previously unused channel capacity, . . . 94.5 percent of the 11,628 cable systems nationwide have not had to drop any programming in order to fulfill their must-carry obligations; the remaining 5.5 percent have had to drop an average of only 1.22 services from their programming, . . . and cable operators nationwide carry 99.8 percent of the programming they carried before enactment of must-carry. *Id.*, ¶ 21 (App.694-695). Appellees note that only 1.18 percent of the approximately 500,000 cable channels nationwide is devoted to channels added because of must-carry, see *id.*, ¶ 11(b) (App.688-689); weighted for subscribership, the figure is 2.4 percent . . . .

We do not understand appellants to dispute in any fundamental way the accuracy of those figures, only their significance. . . . Appellants argue that the rate of growth in cable programming outstrips cable operators' creation of new channel space, that the rate of cable growth is lower than claimed, Turner Brief 39, and that must-carry infringes First Amendment rights now irrespective of future growth, Turner Brief 40; Reply Brief for Appellants Turner Broadcasting System, Inc., et al. 12-13. Finally, they say that regardless of the percentage of channels occupied, must-carry still represents "thousands of real and individual infringements of speech."

. . .

While the parties' evidence is susceptible of varying interpretations, a few definite conclusions can be drawn about the burdens of must-carry. It is undisputed that broadcast stations gained carriage on 5,880 channels as a result of must-carry. While broadcast stations occupy another 30,006 cable channels nationwide, this carriage does not represent a significant First Amendment harm to either system operators or cable programmers because those stations were carried voluntarily before 1992, and even appellants represent, Tr. of Oral Arg. 6, that the vast majority of those channels would continue to be carried in the absence of any legal obligation to do. . . .

Because the burden imposed by must-carry is congruent to the benefits it affords, we conclude must-carry is narrowly tailored to preserve a multiplicity of broadcast stations for the 40 percent of American households without cable. . . . Congress took steps to confine the breadth and burden of the regulatory scheme. For example, the more popular stations (which appellants concede would be carried anyway) will likely opt to be paid for cable carriage under the "retransmission consent" provision of the Cable Act; those stations will nonetheless be counted toward systems' must-carry obligations. Congress exempted systems of 12 or fewer channels, and limited the must-carry obligation of larger systems to one-third of capacity, 47 U.S.C. § 534(b)(1); see also §§ 535(b)(2)-(3); allowed cable operators discretion in choosing which competing and qualified signals would be carried, § 534(b)(2); and permitted operators to carry public stations on unused public, educational, and governmental channels in some circumstances, § 535(d).

Appellants say the must-carry provisions are overbroad because they require carriage in some instances when the Government's interests are not implicated: The must-carry rules prohibit a cable system operator from dropping a broadcaster "even if the operator has no anticompetitive motives, and even if the broadcaster that would have to be dropped . . . would survive without cable access." . . . We are not persuaded that either possibility is so prevalent that must-carry is substantially overbroad. As discussed *supra,* at 1192, cable systems serving 70 percent of subscribers are vertically integrated with cable programmers, so anti competitive motives may be implicated in a majority of systems' decisions not to carry broadcasters. Some broadcasters will opt for must-carry although they would not suffer serious financial harm in its absence. . . . Broadcasters with stronger finances tend, however, to be popular ones that ordinarily seek payment from cable systems for transmission, so their reliance on must-carry should be minimal. . . .

Appellants posit a number of alternatives in an effort to demonstrate a less restrictive means to achieve the Government's aims. . . . Our precedents establish that when evaluating a content-neutral regulation which incidentally burdens speech, we will not invalidate the preferred remedial scheme because some alternative solution is marginally less intrusive on a speaker's First Amendment interests. "So long as the means chosen are not substantially broader than necessary to achieve the government's interest, . . . the regulation will not be invalid simply because a court concludes that the government's interest could be adequately served by some less-speech-restrictive alternative" . . . In any event, after careful examination of each of the alternatives suggested by appellants, we cannot conclude that any of them is an adequate alternative to must-carry for promoting the Government's legitimate interests. First among appellants' suggested alternatives is a proposal to revive a more limited set of must-carry rules, known as the "*Century* rules" after the 1987 court decision striking them down, see *Century Communications Corp. v. FCC,* 835 F.2d 292 (C.A.D.C.). Those rules included a minimum viewership standard for eligibility and limited the must-carry obligation to 25 percent of channel capacity. The parties agree only 14 percent of broadcasters added to cable systems under the Cable Act would be eligible for carriage under the *Century* rules. . . . While we acknowledge appellants' criticism of any rationale that more is better, . . . [t]he record reflects a deliberate congressional choice to adopt the present levels of protection, to which this Court must defer.

The second alternative appellants urge is the use of input selector or "A/B" switches, which, in combination with antennas, would permit viewers to switch between cable and broadcast input, allowing cable subscribers to watch broadcast programs not carried on cable. Congress examined the use of A/B switches as an alternative to must-carry and concluded it was "not an enduring or feasible method of distribution and . . . not in the public interest." § 2(a)(18). The data showed that: many households lacked adequate antennas to receive broadcast signals . . . ; viewers might be required to reset channel settings repeatedly in order to view both UHF and cable channels, House Report, at 54; and installation and use of the switch with other common video equipment (such as videocassette recorders) could be "cumbersome or impossible" . . . Even the cable industry trade association (one of appellants here) determined that "the A/B switch is not a workable solution to the carriage problem. . . ."

Congress also had before it "considerable evidence," including two empirical studies, that "it is rare for [cable subscribers] ever to switch to receive an over-the-air signal. . . . Of the small number of households possessing the switch, an even smaller number (only 38 percent) had ever used it.

. . .

Appellants also suggest a leased-access regime, under which both broadcasters and cable programmers would have equal access to cable channels at regulated rates. Turner Brief 46-47. Appellants do not specify what kind of regime they would propose, or how it would operate, making this alternative difficult to compare to the must-carry rules. Whatever virtues the proposal might otherwise have, it would reduce the number of cable channels under cable systems' control in the same manner as must-carry. Because this alternative is aimed solely at addressing the bottleneck control of cable operators, it would not be as effective in achieving Congress' further goal of ensuring that significant programming remains available for the 40 percent of American households without cable. . . .

Appellants next suggest a system of subsidies for financially weak stations. Appellants have not proposed any particular subsidy scheme, so it is difficult to determine whether this option presents a feasible means of achieving the Government's interests, let alone one preferable to must-carry under the First Amendment. To begin with, a system of subsidies would serve a very different purpose than must-carry. Must-carry is intended not to guarantee the financial health of all broadcasters, but to ensure a base number of broadcasters survive to provide service to noncable households. . . .

Appellants also suggest a system of antitrust enforcement or an administrative complaint procedure to protect broadcasters from cable operators' anticompetitive conduct. See Turner Brief 47-48. Congress could conclude, however, that the considerable expense and delay inherent in antitrust litigation, and the great disparities in wealth and sophistication between the average independent broadcast station and average cable system operator, would make these remedies inadequate substitutes for guaranteed carriage. The record suggests independent broadcasters simply are not in a position to engage in complex antitrust litigation. . . .

There is a final argument made by appellants that we do not reach. Appellant Time Warner Entertainment raises in its brief a separate First Amendment challenge to a subsection of the Cable Act, 47 U.S.C. § 534(c), that requires carriage on unfilled must-carry channels of low power broadcast stations if the FCC determines that the station's programming " would address local news and informational needs which are not being adequately served by full power television broadcast stations because of the geographic distance of such full power stations from the low power station's community of license." § 534(h)(2)(B). We earlier reserved this question and invited the District Court to address it on remand. See *Turner,* 512 U.S., at 643-644, n. 6, 114 S.Ct., at 2460, n. 6. Because this question has received " only the most glancing" attention, . . . we have insufficient basis to make an informed judgment on this discrete issue. Even if the issue is "fairly included" in the broadly worded question presented, it is tangential to the main issue, and prudence dictates that we not decide this question based on such scant argumentation. . . .

III.

Judgments about how competing economic interests are to be reconciled in the complex and fast-changing field of television are for Congress to make. Those judgments "cannot be ignored or undervalued simply because [appellants] cas[t] [their] claims under the umbrella of the First Amendment." *Columbia Broadcasting v. Democratic National Committee,* 412 U.S., at 103. Appellants' challenges to must-carry reflect little more than disagreement over the level of protection broadcast stations are to be afforded and how protection is to be attained. We cannot displace Congress' judgment respecting content-neutral regulations with our own, so long as its policy is grounded on reasonable factual findings supported by evidence that is substantial for a legislative determination. Those requirements were met in this case, and in these circumstances the First Amendment requires nothing more. The judgment of the District Court is affirmed.

It is so ordered.

Justice STEVENS, concurring.
As Justice KENNEDY clearly explains, the policy judgments made by Congress in the enactment of legislation that is intended to forestall the abuse of monopoly power are entitled to substantial deference. *Ante,* at 1189, 1203. That is true even when the attempt to protect an economic market imposes burdens on communication. . . . If this statute regulated the content of speech rather than the structure of the market, our task would be quite different. . . . Though I write to emphasize this important point, I fully concur in the Court's thorough opinion.

Justice BREYER, concurring in part.
I join the opinion of the Court except insofar as Part II-A-1 relies on an anticompetitive rationale. I agree with the majority that the statute must be "sustained under the First Amendment if it advances important governmental interests unrelated to the suppression of free speech and does not burden substantially more speech than necessary to further those interests." *Ante,* at 1186 (citing *United States v. O'Brien,* 391 U.S. 367, 377 (1968)). I also agree that the statute satisfies this standard. My conclusion rests, however, not upon the principal opinion's analysis of the statute's efforts to "promot[e] fair competition," see *post,* at 1206-1207, 1209-1210, but rather upon its discussion of the statute's other objectives, namely, "'(1) preserving the benefits of free, over-the-air local broadcast television,'" and "'(2) promoting the widespread dissemination of information from a multiplicity of sources,'" *ante,* at 1186 (quoting *Turner Broadcasting System, Inc. v. FCC,* 512 U.S. 622, 662 (1994) (*Turner*)). Whether or not the statute does or does not sensibly compensate for some significant market defect, it undoubtedly seeks to provide over-the-air viewers who *lack* cable with a rich mix of over-the-air programming by guaranteeing the over-the-air stations that provide such programming with the extra dollars that an additional cable audience will generate. I believe that this purpose-to assure the over-the-air public "access to a multiplicity of information sources," *id.,* at 663, 114 S.Ct., at 2469—provides sufficient basis for rejecting appellants' First Amendment claim.

I do not deny that the compulsory carriage that creates the "guarantee" extracts a serious First Amendment price. It interferes with the protected interests of the cable operators to choose their own programming; it prevents displaced cable program providers from obtaining an audience; and it will sometimes prevent some cable viewers from watching what, in its absence, would have been their preferred set of programs. *Ante,* at 1198; *post,* at 1215. This "price" amounts to a "suppression of speech."

But there are important First Amendment interests on the other side as well. The statute's basic noneconomic purpose is to prevent too precipitous a decline in the quality and quantity of programming choice for an ever-shrinking non-cable-subscribing segment of the public. *Ante,* at 1186, 1187-1189. This purpose reflects what " has long been a basic tenet of national communications policy," namely, that "the widest possible dissemination of information from diverse and antagonistic sources is essential to the welfare of the public." . . . That policy, in turn, seeks to facilitate the public discussion and informed deliberation, which, as Justice Brandeis pointed out many years ago, democratic government presupposes and the First Amendment seeks to achieve . . . *United States, supra,* at 20. Indeed, *Turner* rested in part upon the proposition that "assuring that the public has access to a multiplicity of information sources is a governmental purpose of the highest order, for it promotes values central to the First Amendment."

. . .

With important First Amendment interests on both sides of the equation, the key question becomes one of proper fit. That question, in my view, requires a reviewing court to determine both whether there are significantly less restrictive ways to achieve Congress' over-the-air programming objectives, and also to decide whether the statute, in its effort to achieve those objectives, strikes a reasonable balance between potentially speech-restricting and speech-enhancing consequences. *Ward v. Rock Against Racism,* 491 U.S. 781, 799-800 (1989); *ante,* at 1200. The majority's opinion analyzes and evaluates those consequences, and I agree with its conclusions in respect to both of these matters. *Ante,* at 1197-1203.

In particular, I note (and agree) that a cable system, physically dependent upon the availability of space along city streets, at present (perhaps less in the future) typically faces little competition, that it therefore constitutes a kind of bottleneck that controls the range of viewer choice (whether or not it uses any consequent economic power for economically predatory purposes), and that *some* degree-at least a limited degree-of governmental intervention and control through regulation can prove appropriate when justified under *O'Brien* (at least when not "content based"). . . . I also agree that, without the statute, cable systems would likely carry significantly fewer over-the-air stations, *ante,* at 1187, 1192-1193, that station revenues would therefore decline, *ante,* at 1195-1197, and that the quality of over-the-air programming on such stations would almost inevitably suffer. . . . I agree further that the burden the statute imposes upon the cable system, potential cable programmers, and cable viewers is limited and will diminish as typical cable system capacity grows over time.

Finally, I believe that Congress could reasonably conclude that the statute will help the typical over-the-air viewer (by maintaining an expanded range of choice) more than it will hurt the typical cable subscriber (by restricting cable slots otherwise available for preferred programming). The latter's cable choices are many and varied, and the range of choice is rapidly increasing. The former's over-the-air choice is more restricted; and, as cable becomes more popular, it may well become still more restricted insofar as the over-the-air market shrinks and thereby, by itself, becomes less profitable. In these circumstances, I do not believe the First Amendment dictates a result that favors the cable viewers' interests.

These and other similar factors discussed by the majority lead me to agree that the statute survives "intermediate scrutiny," whether or not the statute is properly tailored to Congress' purely economic objectives.

Justice O'CONNOR, with whom Justice SCALIA, Justice THOMAS, and Justice GINSBURG join, dissenting.

In sustaining the must-carry provisions of the Cable Television Protection and Competition Act of 1992 (Cable Act), Pub.L. 102-385, §§ 4-5, 106 Stat. 1460, against a First Amendment challenge by cable system operators and cable programmers, the Court errs in two crucial respects. First, the Court disregards one of the principal defenses of the statute urged by appellees on remand: that it serves a substantial interest in preserving "diverse," "quality" programming that is "responsive" to the needs of the local community. The course of this litigation on remand and the proffered defense strongly reinforce my view that the Court adopted the wrong analytic framework in the prior phase of this case. . . . Second, the Court misapplies the "intermediate scrutiny" framework it adopts. Although we owe deference to Congress' predictive judgments and its evaluation of complex economic questions, we have an independent duty to identify with care the Government interests supporting the scheme, to inquire into the reasonableness of congressional findings regarding its necessity, and to examine the fit between its goals and its consequences. . . . The Court fails to discharge its duty here.

I.

I did not join those portions of the principal opinion in *Turner* holding that the must-carry provisions of the Cable Act are content-neutral and therefore subject to intermediate First Amendment scrutiny. . . . The Court there referred to the "unusually detailed statutory findings" accompanying the Cable Act, in which Congress recognized the importance of preserving sources of local news, public affairs, and educational programming. . . . Nevertheless, the Court minimized the significance of these findings, suggesting that they merely reflected Congress' view of the " intrinsic value" of broadcast programming generally, rather than a congressional preference for programming with local, educational, or informational content.

. . .

In (*Turner I*), the Court drew upon Senate and House Reports to identify three " interests" that the must-carry provisions were designed to serve: "(1) preserving the benefits of free, over-the-air local broadcast television, (2) promoting the widespread dissemination of information from a multiplicity of sources, and (3) promoting fair competition in the market for television programming." . . . The Court reiterates these interests here, *ante,* at 1186, but neither the principal opinion nor the partial concurrence ever explains the relationship between them with any clarity.

Much of the principal opinion treats the must-carry provisions as a species of antitrust regulation enacted by Congress in response to a perceived threat that cable system operators would otherwise engage in various forms of anticompetitive conduct resulting in harm to broadcasters. . . . The Court recognizes that appellees cannot show an anticompetitive threat to broadcast television simply by demonstrating that " a few" broadcast stations would be forced off the air in the absence of must-carry.

. . .

I fully agree that promoting fair competition is a legitimate and substantial Government goal. But the Court nowhere examines whether the breadth of the must-carry provisions comports with a goal of preventing anticompetitive harms. Instead, in the course of its inquiry into whether the must-carry provisions are " narrowly tailored," the principal opinion simply assumes that most adverse carriage decisions are anticompetitively motivated, and that must-carry is therefore a measured response to a problem of anticompetitive behavior. . . .

Perhaps because of the difficulty of defending the must-carry provisions as a measured response to anticompetitive behavior, the Court asserts an "independent" interest in preserving a "multiplicity" of broadcast programming sources. . . . In doing so, the Court posits existence of "conduct that threatens" the availability of broadcast television outlets, quite apart from anticompetitive conduct. *Ante,* at 1188. We are left to wonder what precisely that conduct might be. Moreover, when separated from anticompetitive conduct, this interest in preserving a "multiplicity of broadcast programming sources" becomes poorly defined. Neither the principal opinion nor the partial concurrence offers any guidance on what might constitute a "significant reduction" in the availability of broadcast programming. The proper analysis, in my view, necessarily turns on the present *distribution* of broadcast stations among the local broadcast markets that make up the national broadcast "system." Whether cable poses a "significant" threat to a local broadcast market depends first on how many broadcast stations in that market will, in the absence of must-carry, remain available to viewers in noncable households. It also depends on whether viewers actually watch the stations that are dropped or denied carriage. The Court provides some raw data on adverse carriage decisions, but it never connects those data to markets and viewership. Instead, the Court proceeds from the assumptions that adverse carriage decisions nationwide will affect broadcast markets in proportion to their size; and that all broadcast programming is watched by viewers. Neither assumption is logical or has any factual basis in the record.

Appellees bear the burden of demonstrating that the provisions of the Cable Act restricting expressive activity survive constitutional scrutiny. See *Turner, supra,* at 664. As discussed below, the must-carry provisions cannot be justified as a narrowly tailored means of addressing anticompetitive behavior. See *infra,* at 1208-1218; *ante,* at 1203, 1204 (BREYER, J., concurring in part). As a result, the Court's inquiry into whether must-carry would prevent a "significant reduction in the multiplicity of broadcast programming sources" collapses into an analysis of an ill-defined and generalized interest in maintaining broadcast stations, wherever they might be threatened and whatever their viewership. Neither the principal opinion nor the partial concurrence ever explains what kind of conduct, apart from anticompetitive conduct, threatens the "multiplicity" of broadcast programming sources. Indeed, the only justification advanced by the parties for furthering this interest is heavily content based. It is undisputed that the broadcast stations protected by must-carry are the "marginal" stations within a given market, see *infra,* at 1212; the record on remand reveals that any broader threat to the broadcast system was entirely mythical. Pressed to explain the importance of preserving noncable viewers' access to "vulnerable" broadcast stations, appellees emphasize that the must-carry rules are necessary to ensure that broadcast stations maintain "diverse," "quality" programming that is "responsive" to the needs of the local community. Brief for Federal Appellees 13, 30; see Brief for Appellees National Association of Broadcasters et al. 36-37 (NAB Brief); Tr. of Oral Arg. 29, 42; see also *ante,* at 1204 (BREYER, J., concurring in part) (justifying must-carry as a means of preventing a decline in "quality and quantity of programming choice"). Must-carry is thus justified as a way of preserving viewers' access to a Spanish or Chinese language station or of preventing an independent station from adopting a home-shopping format. NAB Brief 28, 33; Brief for Federal Appellees 31; Tr. of Oral Arg. 32-33. Undoubtedly, such goals are reasonable and important, and the stations in question may well be worthwhile targets of Government subsidies. But appellees' characterization of must-carry as a means of protecting these stations, like the Court's explicit concern for promoting "'community self-expression'" and the "'local origination of broadcast programming,'" *ante,* at 1188 (brackets omitted), reveals a content-based preference for broadcast programming. This justification of the regulatory scheme is, in my view, wholly at odds with the *Turner* Court's premise that must-carry is a means of preserving "access to free television programming—*whatever its content,*" 512 U.S., at 649 (emphasis added).

I do not read Justice BREYER's opinion-which analyzes the must-carry rules in part as a "speech-enhancing" measure designed to ensure a "rich mix" of over-the-air programming, see *ante,* at 1204, 1205-to treat the content of over-the-air programming as irrelevant to whether the Government's interest in promoting it is an important one. The net result appears to be that five Justices of this Court *do not* view must-carry as a narrowly tailored means of serving a substantial governmental interest in preventing anticompetitive behavior; and that five Justices of this Court *do* see the significance of the content of over-the-air programming to the Government's and appellees' efforts to defend the law. Under these circumstances, the must-carry provisions should be subject to strict scrutiny, which they surely fail.

II.

The principal opinion goes to great lengths to avoid acknowledging that preferences for "quality," "diverse," and "responsive" local programming underlie the must-carry scheme, although the partial concurrence's reliance on such preferences is explicit. See *ante,* at 1204 (opinion of BREYER, J.). I take the principal opinion at its word and evaluate the claim that the threat of anticompetitive behavior by cable operators supplies a content-neutral basis for sustaining the statute. It does not.

The *Turner(I)* Court remanded the case for a determination whether the must-carry provisions satisfy intermediate scrutiny under *United States v. O'Brien* .... On whether must-carry furthers a substantial governmental interest, the *Turner* Court remanded the case to test two essential and unproven propositions: "(1) that unless cable operators are compelled to carry broadcast stations, *significant numbers* of broadcast stations will be refused carriage on cable systems; and (2) that the broadcast stations denied carriage will either *deteriorate to a substantial degree or fail altogether.*" ... As for whether must-carry restricts no more speech than essential to further Congress' asserted purpose, the *Turner* plurality found evidence lacking on the extent of the burden that the must-carry provisions would place on cable operators and cable programmers. *Id.,* at 667-668.

The District Court resolved this case on cross-motions for summary judgment. As the Court recognizes, *ante,* at 1196-1197, the fact that the evidence before Congress might have been in conflict will not necessarily preclude summary judgment upholding the must-carry scheme. The question, rather, is what the undisputed facts show about the reasonableness of Congress' conclusions. We are not, however, at liberty to substitute speculation for evidence or to ignore factual disputes that call the reasonableness of Congress' findings into question. The evidence on remand demonstrates that appellants, not appellees, are entitled to summary judgment.

A.

As of 1992, cable already served 60 percent of American households. I agree with the observation that Congress could reasonably predict an increase in cable penetration of the local video programming market....

What was not resolved in *Turner* was whether "reasonable inferences based on substantial evidence" ... supported Congress' judgment that the must-carry provisions were necessary "to prevent cable operators from exploiting their economic power to the detriment of broadcasters" .... Because I remain convinced that the statute is not a measured response to congressional concerns about monopoly power, ... in my view the principal opinion's discussion on this point is irrelevant. But even if it were relevant, it is incorrect.

1.

The *Turner* plurality recognized that Congress' interest in curtailing anticompetitive behavior is substantial " in the abstract." 512 U.S., at 664. The principal opinion now concludes that substantial evidence supports the congressional judgment that cable operators have incentives to engage in significant anticompetitive behavior. It appears to accept two related arguments on this point: first, that vertically integrated cable operators prefer programming produced by their affiliated cable programming networks to broadcast programming, *ante,* at 1190-1191, 1191; and second, that potential advertising revenues supply cable system operators, whether affiliated with programmers or not, with incentives to prefer cable programming to broadcast programming. . . .

To support the first proposition, the principal opinion states that "[e]xtensive testimony" before Congress showed that in fact operators do have incentives to favor vertically integrated programmers. *Ante,* at 1190. This testimony, noteworthy as it may be, is primarily that of persons appearing before Congress on behalf of the private appellees in this case. . . . Moreover, even accepting as reasonable Congress' conclusion that cable operators have incentives to favor affiliated programmers, Congress has already limited the number of channels on a cable system that can be occupied by affiliated programmers. . . . Once a cable system operator reaches that cap, it can no longer bump a broadcaster in favor of an affiliated programmer. If Congress were concerned that broadcasters favored too many affiliated programmers, it could simply adjust the cap. Must-carry simply cannot be justified as a response to the allegedly "substantial" problem of vertical integration.

The second argument, that the quest for advertising revenue will supply cable operators with incentives to drop local broadcasters, takes two forms. First, some cable programmers offer blank slots within a program into which a cable operator can insert advertisements; appellees argue that "[t]he opportunity to sell such advertising gives cable programmers an additional value to operators above broadcast stations. . . ." Second, appellees claim that since cable operators compete directly with broadcasters for some advertising revenue, operators will profit if they can drive broadcasters out of the market and capture their advertising revenue. Even if the record before Congress included substantial evidence that "advertising revenue would be of increasing importance to cable operators as subscribership growth began to flatten," *ante,* at 1193, it does not necessarily follow that Congress could reasonably find that the quest for advertising revenues supplies cable operators with incentives to engage in predatory behavior, or that must-carry is a reasonable response to such incentives. There is no dispute that a cable system depends primarily upon its subscriber base for revenue. A cable operator is therefore unlikely to drop a widely viewed station in order to capture advertising revenues-which, according to the figures of appellees' expert, account for between one and five percent of the total revenues of most large cable systems.... In doing so, it would risk losing subscribers. Nevertheless, appellees contend that cable operators will drop some broadcast stations in spite of, and not because of, viewer preferences. The principal opinion suggests that viewers are likely to subscribe to cable even though they prefer certain over-the-air programming to cable programming, because they would be willing to trade access to their preferred channel for access to dozens of cable channels.... Even assuming that, at the margin, advertising revenues would drive cable systems to drop some stations-invariably described as " vulnerable" or " smaller" independents....

2.

Under the standard articulated by the *Turner* plurality, the conclusion that must-carry serves a substantial governmental interest depends upon the "essential propositio[n]" that, without must-carry, "significant numbers of broadcast stations will be refused carriage on cable systems." ... In analyzing whether this undefined standard is satisfied, the Court focuses almost exclusively on raw numbers of stations denied carriage or "repositioned"—that is, shifted out of their traditional channel positions.

The Court begins its discussion of evidence of adverse carriage decisions with the 1988 study sponsored by the Federal Communications Commission (FCC).... But in *Turner,* the plurality criticized this very study, noting that it did not indicate the timeframe within which carriage denials occurred or whether the stations were later restored to their positions....

In canvassing the additional evidence offered on remand, the Court focuses on the suggestion of one of appellees' experts that the 1988 FCC survey underestimated the number of drops of broadcast stations in the non-must-carry era. The data do not indicate which of these stations would now qualify for mandatory carriage.... Two-thirds of the "subscriber instances" of drops existing as of mid-1992 remained uncured as of mid-1994, fully 19 months after the present must-carry rules went into effect.... It seems obvious, however, that if the must-carry rules will not reverse those adverse carriage decisions on which appellees rely to illustrate the Government " interest" supporting the rules, then a significant question remains as to whether the rules in fact serve the articulated interest. Without some further analysis, I do not see how the Court can, in the course of its independent scrutiny on a question of constitutional law, deem Congress' judgment "reasonable."

In any event, the larger problem with the Court's approach is that neither the FCC study nor the additional evidence on remand canvassed by the Court, *ante*, at 1193-1195, says anything about the broadcast markets in which adverse carriage decisions take place. The Court accepts Congress' stated concern about preserving the availability of a "multiplicity" of broadcast stations, but apparently thinks it sufficient to evaluate that concern in the abstract, without considering how much local service is already available in a given broadcast market.

. . .

Nor can we evaluate whether must-carry is necessary to serve an interest in preserving broadcast stations without examining the value of the stations protected by the must-carry scheme to viewers in noncable households. By disregarding the distribution and viewership of stations not carried on cable, the Court upholds the must-carry provisions without addressing the interests of the over-the-air television viewers that Congress purportedly seeks to protect.

. . .

Appellees claim there are various methodological flaws in each study, including appellants' expert's reliance on Nielsen data to measure viewership shares. A protective order entered by the District Court in this case prevents the parties from contesting the accuracy of such data. App. 321. But appellees-who bear the burden of proof in this case-offer no alternative measure of the viewership in noncable households of stations dropped or denied carriage. Instead, appellees and their experts repeatedly emphasize the importance of preserving "vulnerable" or "marginal" independent stations serving "relatively small" audiences. . . . The Court suggests that it is appropriate to disregard the low noncable viewership of stations denied carriage, because in some instances *cable* viewers preferred the dropped broadcast channels to the cable channels that replaced them. *Ante*, at 1193. The viewership statistics in question, as well as their significance, are sharply disputed, but they are also irrelevant. The issue is whether the Government can demonstrate a substantial interest in forced carriage of certain *broadcast* stations, for the benefit of viewers who lack access to cable. That inquiry is not advanced by an analysis of relative *cable* household viewership of broadcast and cable programming. When appellees are pressed to explain the Government's "substantial interest" in preserving noncable viewers' access to "vulnerable" or "marginal" stations with "relatively small" audiences, it becomes evident that the interest has nothing to do with anticompetitive behavior, but has everything to do with content-preserving "quality" local programming that is "responsive" to community needs. . . . Indeed, Justice BREYER expressly declines to accept the anticompetitive rationale for the must-carry rules embraced by the principal opinion, and instead explicitly relies on a need to preserve a " rich mix" of " quality" programming. *Ante,* at 1204 (opinion concurring in part).

3.

I turn now to the evidence of harm to broadcasters denied carriage or repositioned. The Court remanded for a determination whether broadcast stations denied carriage would be at "'serious risk of financial difficulty'" and would "'deteriorate to a substantial degree or fail altogether.'" *Ante,* at 1195 (quoting *Turner,* 512 U.S., at 667). The *Turner* plurality noted that there was no evidence that "local broadcast stations have fallen into bankruptcy, turned in their broadcast licenses, curtailed their broadcast operations, or suffered a serious reduction in operating revenues" because of adverse carriage decisions. *Id.,* at 667. The record on remand does not permit the conclusion, at the summary judgment stage, that Congress could reasonably have predicted serious harm to a significant number of stations in the absence of must-carry.

The purported link between an adverse carriage decision and severe harm to a station depends on yet another untested premise. Even accepting the conclusion that a cable system operator has a monopoly over *cable* services to the home, *supra,* at 1209, it does not necessarily follow that the operator also has a monopoly over all *video* services to cabled households. Cable subscribers using an input selector switch and an antenna can receive broadcast signals. Widespread use of such switches would completely eliminate any cable system "monopoly" over sources of video input. . . . Growing use of direct-broadcast satellite television also tends to undercut the notion that cable operators have an inevitable monopoly over video services entering cable households. . . .

In the Cable Act, Congress rejected the wisdom of any "substantial societal investment" in developing input selector switch technology. § 2(a)(18). In defending this choice, the Court purports to identify "substantial evidence of technological shortcomings" that prevent widespread, efficient use of such devices. But nearly all of the " data" in question are drawn from sources predating the enactment of must-carry by roughly six years. . . . The Court notes the importance of deferring to congressional judgments about the "interaction of industries undergoing rapid economic and technological change." *Ante,* at 1189. But this principle does not require wholesale deference to judgments about rapidly changing technologies that are based on unquestionably outdated information.

The Court concludes that the evidence on remand meets the threshold of harm established in *Turner.* The Court begins with the "[c]onsiderable evidence" that broadcast stations denied carriage have fallen into bankruptcy. . . . The analysis, however, does not focus on features of the market in which these stations were located or on the size of the audience they commanded. The "considerable evidence" relied on by the Court consists of repeated references to the bankruptcies of the same 23 commercial independent stations-apparently, new stations. . . . Because the must-carry provisions have never been justified as a means of *enhancing* broadcast television, I do not understand the relevance of this evidence, or of the evidence concerning the difficulties encountered by *new* stations seeking financing.

. . .

The Court also claims that the record on remand reflects "considerable evidence" of stations curtailing their broadcast operations or suffering reductions in operating revenues. *Ante,* at 1195. Most of the anecdotal accounts of harm on which the Court relies are sharply disputed. . . . Congress' reasonable conclusions are entitled to deference, and for that reason the fact that the evidence is in conflict will not necessarily preclude summary judgment in appellees' favor. Nevertheless, in the course of our independent review, we cannot ignore sharp conflicts in the record that call into question the reasonableness of Congress' findings.

Moreover, unlike other aspects of the record on remand, the station-specific accounts cited by the Court do permit an evaluation of trends in the various broadcast markets, or "areas of dominant influence," in which carriage denials allegedly caused harm. The Court does not conduct this sort of analysis. Were it to do so, the Court would have to recognize that all but *one* of the commercial broadcast stations cited as claiming a curtailment in operations or a decline in revenue was broadcasting within an area of dominant influence that experienced net growth, or at least no net reduction, in the number of commercial broadcast stations operating during the non-must-carry era. . . . Indeed, in 499 of 504 areas of dominant influence nationwide, the number of commercial broadcast stations operating in 1992 equaled or exceeded the number operating in 1987. . . . Only two areas of dominant influence experienced a reduction in the number of noncommercial broadcast stations operating between 1987 and 1992.

. . .

In sum, appellees are not entitled to summary judgment on whether Congress could conclude, based on reasonable inferences drawn from substantial evidence, that "'absent legislative action, the free local off-air broadcast system is endangered.'" *Ante,* at 1196 (quoting S.Rep. No. 102-92, at 42). The Court acknowledges that the record contains much evidence of the health of the broadcast industry, including evidence that 263 new broadcast stations signed on the air in the period without must-carry rules, evidence of growth in stations' advertising revenue, and evidence of voluntary carriage of broadcast stations accounting for virtually all measurable viewership in noncable households. *Ante,* at 1196. But the Court dismisses such evidence, emphasizing that the question is not whether Congress correctly determined that must-carry is necessary to prevent significant financial hardship to a substantial number of stations, but whether "the legislative conclusion was reasonable and supported by substantial evidence in the record before Congress." *Ante,* at 1196. Even accepting the Court's articulation of the relevant standard, it is not properly applied here. The principal opinion disavows a need to closely scrutinize the logic of the regulatory scheme at issue on the ground that it "need not put [its] imprimatur on Congress' economic theory in order to validate the reasonableness of its judgment." *Ante,* at 1195. That approach trivializes the First Amendment issue at stake in this case. A highly dubious economic theory has been advanced as the "substantial interest" supporting a First Amendment burden on cable operators and cable programmers. In finding that must-carry serves a substantial interest, the principal opinion necessarily accepts that theory. The partial concurrence does not, but neither does it articulate what threat to the availability of a "multiplicity" of broadcast stations would exist in a perfectly competitive market.

B.

I turn now to the second portion of the *O'Brien* inquiry, which concerns the fit between the Government's asserted interests and the means chosen to advance them. The Court observes that "broadcast stations gained carriage on 5,880 channels as a result of must-carry," and recognizes that this forced carriage imposes a burden on cable system operators and cable programmers. *Ante,* at 1198. But the Court also concludes that the other 30,006 cable channels occupied by broadcast stations are irrelevant to measuring the burden of the must-carry scheme. The must-carry rules prevent operators from dropping these broadcast stations should other more desirable cable programming become available, even though operators have carried these stations voluntarily in the past. The must-carry requirements thus burden an operator's First Amendment freedom to exercise unfettered control over a number of channels in its system, whether or not the operator's present choice is aligned with that of the Government.

Even assuming that the Court is correct that the 5,880 channels occupied by added broadcasters "represent the actual burden of the regulatory scheme," . . . the Court's leap to the conclusion that must-carry "is narrowly tailored to preserve a multiplicity of broadcast stations," *ante,* at 1199, is nothing short of astounding. The Court's logic is circular. Surmising that most of the 5,880 channels added by the regulatory scheme would be dropped in its absence, the Court concludes that the figure also approximates the "benefit" of must-carry. Finding the scheme's burden "congruent" to the benefit it affords, the Court declares the statute narrowly tailored. The Court achieves this result, however, only by equating the *effect* of the statute-requiring cable operators to add 5,880 stations-with the governmental *interest* sought to be served. . . . Positing the effect of a statute as the governmental interest " can sidestep judicial review of almost any statute, because it makes all statutes look narrowly tailored." . . . Without a sense whether *most* adverse carriage decisions are anticompetitively motivated, it is improper to conclude that the statute is narrowly tailored simply because it prevents *some* adverse carriage decisions.

. . .

In my view, the statute is not narrowly tailored to serve a substantial interest in preventing anticompetitive conduct. I do not understand Justice BREYER to disagree with this conclusion. *Ante,* at 1204 (examining fit between "speech-restricting and speech-enhancing consequences" of must-carry). Congress has commandeered up to one-third of each cable system's channel capacity for the benefit of local broadcasters, without any regard for whether doing so advances the statute's alleged goals. To the extent that Congress was concerned that anticompetitive impulses would lead vertically integrated operators to prefer those programmers in which the operators have an ownership stake, the Cable Act is overbroad, since it does not impose its requirements solely on such operators. . . . The principal opinion reasons that "cable systems serving

70 percent of subscribers are vertically integrated with cable programmers, *so anticompetitive motives may be implicated in a majority of systems' decisions not to carry broadcasters." Ante,* at 1199 (emphasis added). It is unclear whether the principal opinion means that anticompetitive motives may be implicated in a majority of *decisions,* or in decisions by a majority of *systems.* In either case, the principal opinion's conclusion is wholly speculative. We do not know which of these vertically integrated systems are affiliated with one cable programmer and which are affiliated with five cable programmers. Moreover, Congress has placed limits upon the number of channels that can be used for affiliated programming. 47 U.S.C. § 533(f)(1)(B). The principal opinion does not suggest why these limits are inadequate or explain why, once a system reaches the limit, its remaining carriage decisions would also be anticompetitively motivated. Even if the channel limits are insufficient, the principal opinion does not explain why requiring carriage of *broadcast* stations on *one-third* of the system's channels is a measured response to the problem.

Finally, I note my disagreement with the Court's suggestion that the availability of less-speech-restrictive alternatives is never relevant to *O'Brien's* narrow tailoring inquiry. . . .

Our cases suggest only that we have not interpreted the narrow tailoring inquiry to "require elimination of *all* less restrictive alternatives." *Fox, supra,* at 478. Put another way, we have refrained from imposing a *least*-restrictive-means requirement in cases involving intermediate First Amendment scrutiny. . . . It is one thing to say that a regulation need not be the *least*-speech-restrictive means of serving an important governmental objective. It is quite another to suggest, as I read the majority to do here, that the availability of less-speech-restrictive alternatives cannot establish or confirm that a regulation is substantially broader than necessary to achieve the Government's goals. While the validity of a Government regulation subject to intermediate First Amendment scrutiny does not turn on our "agreement with the responsible decisionmaker concerning the most appropriate method for promoting significant government interests," . . . the availability of less intrusive approaches to a problem serves as a benchmark for assessing the reasonableness of the fit between Congress' articulated goals and the means chosen to pursue them . . . .

If Congress truly sought to address anticompetitive behavior by cable system operators, it passed the wrong law. . . . Nevertheless, the availability of less restrictive alternatives-a leased access regime and subsidies-reinforces my conclusion that the must-carry provisions are overbroad.

Consider first appellants' proposed leased access scheme, under which a cable system operator would be required to make a specified proportion of the system's channels available to broadcasters and independent cable programmers alike at regulated rates. Leased access would directly address both vertical integration and predatory behavior, by placing broadcasters and cable programmers on a level playing field for access to cable. The principal opinion never explicitly identifies any threat to the availability of broadcast television to noncable households *other than* anticompetitive conduct, nor does Justice BREYER's partial concurrence. Accordingly, to the extent that leased access would address problems of anticompetitive behavior, I fail to understand why it would not achieve the goal of "ensuring that significant programming remains available" for noncable households. *Ante,* at 1201. The Court observes that a leased access regime would, like must-carry, "reduce the number of cable channels under cable systems' control in the same manner as must-carry." *Ibid.* No leased access scheme is currently before the Court, and I intimate no view on whether leased access, like must-carry, imposes unacceptable burdens on cable operators' free speech interests. It is important to note, however, that the Court's observation that a leased access scheme may, like must-carry, impose First Amendment burdens does not dispose of the narrow tailoring inquiry in this case. As noted, a leased access regime would respond directly to problems of vertical integration and problems of predatory behavior. Must-carry quite clearly does not respond to the problem of vertical integration. *Supra,* at 1215-1216. In addition, the must-carry scheme burdens the rights of cable programmers *and* cable operators; there is no suggestion here that leased access would burden cable *programmers* in the same way as must-carry does. In both of these respects, leased access is a more narrowly tailored guard against anticompetitive behavior. Finally, if, as the Court suggests, Congress were concerned that a leased access scheme would impose a burden on "small broadcasters" forced to pay for access, subsidies would eliminate the problem.

Subsidies would not, of course, eliminate anticompetitive behavior by cable system operators-a problem that Congress could address directly or through a leased-access scheme. . . . If the Government is indeed worried that imprecision in allocation of subsidies would prop up stations that would not survive even with cable carriage, then it could tie subsidies to a percentage of stations' advertising revenues (or, for public stations, member contributions), determined by stations' access to viewers. For example, in a broadcast market where 50 percent of television-viewing households subscribe to cable, a broadcaster has access to all households without cable as well as to those households served by cable systems on which the broadcaster has secured carriage. If a broadcaster is carried on cable systems serving only 20 percent of cable households (*i.e.*, 10 percent of all television-viewing households in the broadcast market), the broadcaster has access to 60 percent of the television-viewing households. If the Government provided a subsidy to compensate for the loss in advertising revenue or member contributions that a station would sustain by virtue of its failure to reach 40 percent of its potential audience, it could ensure that its allocation would do no more than protect those broadcasters that would survive with full access to television-viewing households. In sum, the alleged barrier to a precise allocation of subsidies is not insurmountable. The Court also suggests that a subsidy scheme would "involve the Government in making content-based determinations about programming." *Ante,* at 1202. Even if that is so, it does not distinguish subsidies from the must-carry provisions. In light of the principal opinion's steadfast adherence to the position that a preference for "diverse" or local-content broadcasting is not a content-based preference, the argument is ironic indeed.

IV.

In sustaining the must-carry provisions of the Cable Act, the Court ignores the main justification of the statute urged by appellees and subjects restrictions on expressive activity to an inappropriately lenient level of scrutiny. The principal opinion then misapplies the analytic framework it chooses, exhibiting an extraordinary and unwarranted deference for congressional judgments, a profound fear of delving into complex economic matters, and a willingness to substitute untested assumptions for evidence. In light of gaps in logic and evidence, it is improper to conclude, at the summary judgment stage, that the must-carry scheme serves a significant governmental interest " in a direct and effective way." . . . Moreover, because the undisputed facts demonstrate that the must-carry scheme is plainly not narrowly tailored to serving the only governmental interest the principal opinion fully explains and embraces-preventing anticompetitive behavior-appellants are entitled to summary judgment in their favor.

Justice BREYER disavows the principal opinion's position on anticompetitive behavior, and instead treats the must-carry rules as a "speech-enhancing" measure designed to ensure access to "quality" programming for noncable households. Neither the principal opinion nor the partial concurrence explains the nature of the alleged threat to the availability of a "multiplicity of broadcast programming sources," if that threat does not arise from cable operators' anticompetitive conduct. Such an approach makes it impossible to discern whether Congress was addressing a problem that is "real, not merely conjectural," and whether must-carry addresses the problem in a "direct and material way." *Turner, supra,* at 664, 114 S.Ct., at 2470 (plurality opinion).

I therefore respectfully dissent, and would reverse the judgment below.

Retransmission Consent

In the nearly twenty years since the *Turner* case, the must-carry rules have become almost an afterthought. While some weak-signal independent stations rely on compulsory carriage to maintain an audience, most network-owned or -affiliated stations have opted out of the rules. Recall that, under the 1992 Act, broadcasters can choose to negotiate (and periodically renegotiate) retransmission consent with cable systems at market rates. Broadcasters have discovered that they can exact a high price for their programming, including primetime shows, and especially, sports coverage. When cable systems and broadcasters find themselves unable to agree on these fees, nasty public relations battles can lead to prolonged station blackouts, causing concern and frustration for regulators and consumers. Today, cable systems generally accept these high fees as a cost of doing business and pass most of that cost on to subscribers. Broadcasters—and the studios and sports teams that license to them—have grown to rely on retransmission fees as a second revenue stream. When an upstart company named Aereo marketed a technology that allowed monthly subscribers to access antenna television signals on digital devices, broadcasters saw this as an imminent threat to their retransmission consent revenue. Attempts to stop Aereo's technology led to a split in the circuit courts, and, in 2014, to an expedited appeal before the U.S. Supreme Court.

AMERICAN BROADCASTING COS. V. AEREO, INC.

573 U.S. ___, 134 S. Ct. 2498 (2014)

Justice BREYER delivered the opinion of the Court.

The Copyright Act of 1976 gives a copyright owner the "exclusive righ[t]" to "perform the copyrighted work publicly." 17 U.S.C. § 106(4). The Act's Transmit Clause defines that exclusive right as including the right to

> *"transmit or otherwise communicate a performance . . . of the [copyrighted] work . . . to the public, by means of any device or process, whether the members of the public capable of receiving the performance . . . receive it in the same place or in separate places and at the same time or at different times." § 101* (italics added).

We must decide whether respondent Aereo, Inc., infringes this exclusive right by selling its subscribers a technologically complex service that allows them to watch television programs over the Internet at about the same time as the programs are broadcast over the air. We conclude that it does.

I.

A

For a monthly fee, Aereo offers subscribers broadcast television programming over the Internet, virtually as the programming is being broadcast. Much of this programming is made up of copyrighted works. Aereo neither owns the copyright in those works nor holds a license from the copyright owners to perform those works publicly.

Aereo's system is made up of servers, transcoders, and thousands of dime-sized antennas housed in a central warehouse. It works roughly as follows: First, when a subscriber wants to watch a show that is currently being broadcast, he visits Aereo's Web site and selects, from a list of the local programming, the show he wishes to see.

Second, one of Aereo's servers selects an antenna, which it dedicates to the use of that subscriber (and that subscriber alone) for the duration of the selected show. A server then tunes the antenna to the over-the-air broadcast carrying the show. The antenna begins to receive the broadcast, and an Aereo transcoder translates the signals received into data that can be transmitted over the Internet.

Third, rather than directly send the data to the subscriber, a server saves the data in a subscriber-specific folder on Aereo's hard drive. In other words, Aereo's system creates a subscriber-specific copy—that is, a "personal" copy—of the subscriber's program of choice.

Fourth, once several seconds of programming have been saved, Aereo's server begins to stream the saved copy of the show to the subscriber over the Internet. (The subscriber may instead direct Aereo to stream the program at a later time, but that aspect of Aereo's service is not before us.) The subscriber can watch the streamed program on the screen of his personal computer, tablet, smart phone, Internet-connected television, or other Internet-connected device. The streaming continues, a mere few seconds behind the over-the-air broadcast, until the subscriber has received the entire show. . . .

Aereo emphasizes that the data that its system streams to each subscriber are the data from his own personal copy, made from the broadcast signals received by the particular antenna allotted to him. Its system does not transmit data saved in one subscriber's folder to any other subscriber. When two subscribers wish to watch the same program, Aereo's system activates two separate antennas and saves two separate copies of the program in two separate folders. It then streams the show to the subscribers through two separate transmissions—each from the subscriber's personal copy.

B

Petitioners are television producers, marketers, distributors, and broadcasters who own the copyrights in many of the programs that Aereo's system streams to its subscribers. They brought suit against Aereo for copyright infringement in Federal District Court. They sought a preliminary injunction, arguing that Aereo was infringing their right to "perform" their works "publicly," as the Transmit Clause defines those terms.

The District Court denied the preliminary injunction. Relying on prior Circuit precedent, a divided panel of the Second Circuit affirmed. *WNET, Thirteen v. Aereo, Inc.*, 712 F.3d 676 (2d Cir. 2013) (citing *Cartoon Network LP v. CSC Holdings, Inc.*, 536 F.3d 121 (2008)). In the Second Circuit's view, Aereo does not perform publicly within the meaning of the Transmit Clause because it does not transmit "to the public." Rather, each time Aereo streams a program to a subscriber, it sends a *private* transmission that is available only to that subscriber. . . .

II

This case requires us to answer two questions: First, in operating in the manner described above, does Aereo "perform" at all? And second, if so, does Aereo do so "publicly"? . . .

Does Aereo "perform"? *See* . . . § 101 ("To *perform* . . . a work 'publicly' means [among other things] to transmit . . . a performance . . . of the work . . . to the public . . ." (emphasis added)). Phrased another way, does Aereo "transmit . . . a performance" when a subscriber watches a show using Aereo's system, or is it only the subscriber who transmits? In Aereo's view, it does not perform. It does no more than supply equipment that "emulate[s] the operation of a home antenna and [digital video recorder (DVR)]." . . . Like a home antenna and DVR, Aereo's equipment simply responds to its subscribers' directives. So it is only the subscribers who "perform" when they use Aereo's equipment to stream television programs to themselves.

Considered alone, the language of the Act does not clearly indicate when an entity "perform[s]" (or "transmit[s]") and when it merely supplies equipment that allows others to do so. But when read in light of its purpose, the Act is unmistakable: An entity that engages in activities like Aereo's performs.

A

History makes plain that one of Congress' primary purposes in amending the Copyright Act in 1976 was to overturn this Court's determination that community antenna television (CATV) systems (the precursors of modern cable systems) fell outside the Act's scope. In *Fortnightly Corp. v. United Artists Television, Inc.*, 392 U.S. 390 (1968), the Court considered a CATV system that carried local television broadcasting, much of which was copyrighted, to its subscribers in two cities. The CATV provider placed antennas on hills above the cities and used coaxial cables to carry the signals received by the antennas to the home television sets of its subscribers. The system amplified and modulated the signals in order to improve their strength and efficiently transmit them to subscribers. A subscriber "could choose any of the . . . programs he wished to view by simply turning the knob on his own television set." *Id.*, at 392. The CATV provider "neither edited the programs received nor originated any programs of its own." *Ibid.*

Asked to decide whether the CATV provider infringed copyright holders' exclusive right to perform their works publicly, the Court held that the provider did not "perform" at all. See 17 U.S.C. § 1(c) (1964 ed.) (granting copyright holder the exclusive right to "perform . . . in public for profit" a nondramatic literary work), § 1(d) (granting copyright holder the exclusive right to "perform . . . publicly" a dramatic work). The Court drew a line: "Broadcasters perform. Viewers do not perform." 392 U.S., at 398 (footnote omitted). And a CATV provider "falls on the viewer's side of the line." *Id.*, at 399.

The Court reasoned that CATV providers were unlike broadcasters:

> "Broadcasters select the programs to be viewed; CATV systems simply carry, without editing, whatever programs they receive. Broadcasters procure programs and propagate them to the public; CATV systems receive programs that have been released to the public and carry them by private channels to additional viewers." *Id.,* at 400.

Instead, CATV providers were more like viewers, for "the basic function [their] equipment serves is little different from that served by the equipment generally furnished by" viewers. *Id.,* at 399. "Essentially," the Court said, "a CATV system no more than enhances the viewer's capacity to receive the broadcaster's signals [by] provid[ing] a well-located antenna with an efficient connection to the viewer's television set." *Ibid.* Viewers do not become performers by using "amplifying equipment," and a CATV provider should not be treated differently for providing viewers the same equipment. *Id.,* at 398–400.

In *Teleprompter Corp. v. Columbia Broadcasting System, Inc.,* 415 U.S. 394 (1974), the Court considered the copyright liability of a CATV provider that carried broadcast television programming into subscribers' homes from hundreds of miles away. Although the Court recognized that a viewer might not be able to afford amplifying equipment that would provide access to those distant signals, it nonetheless found that the CATV provider was more like a viewer than a broadcaster. *Id.,* at 408–409. It explained: "The reception and rechanneling of [broadcast television signals] for simultaneous viewing is essentially a viewer function, irrespective of the distance between the broadcasting station and the ultimate viewer." *Id.,* at 408.

The Court also recognized that the CATV system exercised some measure of choice over what to transmit. But that fact did not transform the CATV system into a broadcaster. A broadcaster exercises significant creativity in choosing what to air, the Court reasoned. *Id.,* at 410. In contrast, the CATV provider makes an initial choice about which broadcast stations to retransmit, but then "'simply carr[ies], without editing, whatever programs [it] receive[s].'" *Ibid.* (quoting *Fortnightly, supra,* at 400 (alterations in original)).

B

In 1976 Congress amended the Copyright Act in large part to reject the Court's holdings in *Fortnightly* and *Teleprompter*. See H.R.Rep. No. 94–1476, pp. 86–87 (1976) (hereinafter H.R. Rep.) (The 1976 amendments "completely overturned" this Court's narrow construction of the Act in

Fortnightly and *Teleprompter*). Congress enacted new language that erased the Court's line between broadcaster and viewer, in respect to "perform[ing]" a work. The amended statute clarifies that to "perform" an audiovisual work means "to show its images in any sequence or to make the sounds accompanying it audible." § 101; see *ibid.* (defining "[a]udiovisual works" as "works that consist of a series of related images which are intrinsically intended to be shown by the use of machines . . . , together with accompanying sounds"). Under this new language, *both* the broadcaster *and* the viewer of a television program "perform," because they both show the program's images and make audible the program's sounds. See H.R. Rep., at 63 ("[A] broadcasting network is performing when it transmits [a singer's performance of a song] . . . and any individual is performing whenever he or she . . . communicates the performance by turning on a receiving set").

Congress also enacted the Transmit Clause, which specifies that an entity performs publicly when it "transmit[s] . . . a performance . . . to the public." § 101; see *ibid.* (defining "[t]o 'transmit' a performance" as "to communicate it by any device or process whereby images or sounds are received beyond the place from which they are sent"). Cable system activities, like those of the CATV systems in *Fortnightly* and *Teleprompter,* lie at the heart of the activities that Congress intended this language to cover. See H.R. Rep., at 63 ("[A] cable television system is performing when it retransmits [a network] broadcast to its subscribers"); see also *ibid.* ("[T]he concep[t] of public performance . . . cover[s] not only the initial rendition or showing, but also any further act by which that rendition or showing is transmitted or communicated to the public"). The Clause thus makes clear that an entity that acts like a CATV system itself performs, even if when doing so, it simply enhances viewers' ability to receive broadcast television signals.

Congress further created a new section of the Act to regulate cable companies' public performances of copyrighted works. See § 111. Section 111 creates a complex, highly detailed compulsory licensing scheme that sets out the conditions, including the payment of compulsory fees, under which cable systems may retransmit broadcasts. H.R. Rep., at 88 (Section 111 is primarily "directed at the operation of cable television systems and the terms and conditions of their liability for the retransmission of copyrighted works").

Congress made these three changes to achieve a similar end: to bring the activities of cable systems within the scope of the Copyright Act.

C

This history makes clear that Aereo is not simply an equipment provider. Rather, Aereo, and not just its subscribers, "perform[s]" (or "transmit[s]"). Aereo's activities are substantially similar to those of the CATV companies that Congress amended the Act to reach. See *id.*, at 89 ("[C]able systems are commercial enterprises whose basic retransmission operations are based on the carriage of copyrighted program material"). Aereo sells a service that allows subscribers to watch television programs, many of which are copyrighted, almost as they are being broadcast. In providing this service, Aereo uses its own equipment, housed in a centralized warehouse, outside of its users' homes. By means of its technology (antennas, transcoders, and servers), Aereo's system "receive[s] programs that have been released to the public and carr[ies] them by private channels to additional viewers." *Fortnightly,* 392 U.S., at 400. It "carr[ies] . . . whatever programs [it] receive[s]," and it offers "all the programming" of each over-the-air station it carries. *Id.,* at 392, 400.

Aereo's equipment may serve a "viewer function"; it may enhance the viewer's ability to receive a broadcaster's programs. It may even emulate equipment a viewer could use at home. But the same was true of the equipment that was before the Court, and ultimately before Congress, in *Fortnightly* and *Teleprompter.*

We recognize, and Aereo and the dissent emphasize, one particular difference between Aereo's system and the cable systems at issue in *Fortnightly* and *Teleprompter*. The systems in those cases transmitted constantly; they sent continuous programming to each subscriber's television set. In contrast, Aereo's system remains inert until a subscriber indicates that she wants to watch a program. Only at that moment, in automatic response to the subscriber's request, does Aereo's system activate an antenna and begin to transmit the requested program.

This is a critical difference, says the dissent. It means that Aereo's subscribers, not Aereo, "selec[t] the copyrighted content" that is "perform [ed]," *post,* at 2513 (opinion of SCALIA, J.), and for that reason they, not Aereo, "transmit" the performance. Aereo is thus like "a copy shop that provides its patrons with a library card." *Post,* at 2514. A copy shop is not directly liable whenever a patron uses the shop's machines to "reproduce" copyrighted materials found in that library. See § 106(1) ("exclusive righ[t] . . . to reproduce the copyrighted work"). And by the same token, Aereo should not be directly liable whenever its patrons use its equipment to "transmit" copyrighted television programs to their screens.

In our view, however, the dissent's copy shop argument, in whatever form, makes too much out of too little. Given Aereo's overwhelming likeness to the cable companies targeted by the 1976 amendments, this sole technological difference between Aereo and traditional cable companies does not make a critical difference here. The subscribers of the *Fortnightly* and *Teleprompter* cable systems also selected what programs to display on their receiving sets. Indeed, as we explained in *Fortnightly,* such a subscriber "could choose any of the . . . programs he wished to view by simply turning the knob on his own television set." 392 U.S., at 392. The same is true of an Aereo subscriber. Of course, in *Fortnightly* the television signals, in a sense, lurked behind the screen, ready to emerge when the subscriber turned the knob. Here the signals pursue their ordinary course of travel through the universe until today's "turn of the knob"—a click on a Web site—activates machinery that intercepts and reroutes them to Aereo's subscribers over the Internet. But this difference means nothing to the subscriber. It means nothing to the broadcaster. We do not see how this single difference, invisible to subscriber and broadcaster alike, could transform a system that is for all practical purposes a traditional cable system into "a copy shop that provides its patrons with a library card."

In other cases involving different kinds of service or technology providers, a user's involvement in the operation of the provider's equipment and selection of the content transmitted may well bear on whether the provider performs within the meaning of the Act. But the many similarities between Aereo and cable companies, considered in light of Congress' basic purposes in amending the Copyright Act, convince us that this difference is not critical here. We conclude that Aereo is not just an equipment supplier and that Aereo "perform[s].

III

Next, we must consider whether Aereo performs petitioners' works "publicly," within the meaning of the Transmit Clause. Under the Clause, an entity performs a work publicly when it "transmit[s] . . . a performance . . . of the work . . . to the public." § 101. Aereo denies that it satisfies this definition. It reasons as follows: First, the "performance" it "transmit[s]" is the performance created by its act of transmitting. And second, because each of these performances is capable of being received by one and only one subscriber, Aereo transmits privately, not publicly. Even assuming Aereo's first argument is correct, its second does not follow.

We begin with Aereo's first argument. . . . When an Aereo subscriber selects a program to watch, Aereo streams the program over the Internet to that subscriber. Aereo thereby "communicate[s]" to the subscriber, by means of a "device or process," the work's images and sounds. § 101. And those images and sounds are contemporaneously visible and audible on the subscriber's computer (or other Internet-connected device). So under our assumed definition, Aereo transmits a performance whenever its subscribers watch a program.

But what about the Clause's further requirement that Aereo transmit a performance "to the public"? As we have said, an Aereo subscriber receives broadcast television signals with an antenna dedicated to him alone. Aereo's system makes from those signals a personal copy of the selected program. It streams the content of the copy to the same subscriber and to no one else. One and only one subscriber has the ability to see and hear each Aereo transmission. The fact that each transmission is to only one subscriber, in Aereo's view, means that it does not transmit a performance "to the public."

In terms of the Act's purposes, these differences do not distinguish Aereo's system from cable systems, which do perform "publicly." Viewed in terms of Congress' regulatory objectives, why should any of these technological differences matter? They concern the behind-the-scenes way in which Aereo delivers television programming to its viewers' screens. They do not render Aereo's commercial objective any different from that of cable companies. Nor do they significantly alter the viewing experience of Aereo's subscribers. Why would a subscriber who wishes to watch a television show care much whether images and sounds are delivered to his screen via a large multisubscriber antenna or one small dedicated antenna, whether they arrive instantaneously or after a few seconds' delay, or whether they are transmitted directly or after a personal copy is made? And why, if Aereo is right, could not modern CATV systems simply continue the same commercial and consumer-oriented activities, free of copyright restrictions, provided they substitute such new technologies for old? . . .

. . .

The Transmit Clause . . . provides that one may transmit a performance to the public "whether the members of the public capable of receiving the performance . . . receive it . . . at the same time or at different times." § 101. Were the words "to transmit . . . a performance" limited to a single act of communication, members of the public could not receive the performance communicated "at different times." Therefore, in light of the purpose and text of the Clause, we conclude that when an entity communicates the same contemporaneously perceptible images and sounds to multiple people, it transmits a performance to them regardless of the number of discrete communications it makes.

We do not see how the fact that Aereo transmits via personal copies of programs could make a difference. The Act applies to transmissions "by means of any device or process." *Ibid.* . . . [W]hether Aereo transmits from the same or separate copies, it performs the same work; it shows the same images and makes audible the same sounds. Therefore, when Aereo streams the same television program to multiple subscribers, it "transmit[s] . . . a performance" to all of them.

. . .

Finally, we note that Aereo's subscribers may receive the same programs at different times and locations. This fact does not help Aereo, however, for the Transmit Clause expressly provides that an entity may perform publicly "whether the members of the public capable of receiving the performance . . . receive it in the same place or in separate places and at the same time or at different times." *Ibid.* In other words, "the public" need not be situated together, spatially or temporally. For these reasons, we conclude that Aereo transmits a performance of petitioners' copyrighted works to the public, within the meaning of the Transmit Clause.

IV

Aereo and many of its supporting *amici* argue that to apply the Transmit Clause to Aereo's conduct will impose copyright liability on other technologies, including new technologies, that Congress could not possibly have wanted to reach. We agree that Congress, while intending the Transmit Clause to apply broadly to cable companies and their equivalents, did not intend to discourage or to control the emergence or use of different kinds of technologies. But we do not believe that our limited holding today will have that effect.

For one thing, the history of cable broadcast transmissions that led to the enactment of the Transmit Clause informs our conclusion that Aereo "perform[s]," but it does not determine whether different kinds of providers in different contexts also "perform." For another, an entity only transmits a performance when it communicates contemporaneously perceptible images and sounds of a work. See Brief for Respondent at 31 ("[I]f a distributor . . . sells [multiple copies of a digital video disc] by mail to consumers, . . . [its] distribution of the DVDs merely makes it possible for the recipients to perform the work themselves—it is not a 'device or process' by which the *distributor* publicly performs the work" (emphasis in original)).

. . .

Finally, the doctrine of "fair use" can help to prevent inappropriate or inequitable applications of the Clause. *See Sony Corp. of America v. Universal City Studios, Inc.*, 464 U.S. 417 (1984).

We cannot now answer more precisely how the Transmit Clause or other provisions of the Copyright Act will apply to technologies not before us. We agree with the Solicitor General that "[q]uestions involving cloud computing, [remote storage] DVRs, and other novel issues not before the Court, as to which 'Congress has not plainly marked [the] course,' should await a case in which they are squarely presented." Brief for United States as *Amicus Curiae* at 34 (quoting *Sony, supra,* at 431 (alteration in original)). And we note that, to the extent commercial actors or other interested entities may be concerned with the relationship between the development and use of such technologies and the Copyright Act, they are of course free to seek action from Congress. . . .

In sum, having considered the details of Aereo's practices, we find them highly similar to those of the CATV systems in *Fortnightly* and *Teleprompter*. And those are activities that the 1976 amendments sought to bring within the scope of the Copyright Act. Insofar as there are differences, those differences concern not the nature of the service that Aereo provides so much as the technological manner in which it provides the service. We conclude that those differences are not adequate to place Aereo's activities outside the scope of the Act.

For these reasons, we conclude that Aereo "perform[s]" petitioners' copyrighted works "publicly," as those terms are defined by the Transmit Clause. We therefore reverse the contrary judgment of the Court of Appeals, and we remand the case for further proceedings consistent with this opinion.

It is so ordered.

Justice SCALIA, with whom Justice THOMAS and Justice ALITO join, dissenting.

. . .

[W]e are here concerned with a single claim: that Aereo violates the Networks' "exclusive righ[t]" to "perform" their programs "publicly." 17 U.S.C. § 106(4). That claim fails at the very outset because Aereo does not "perform" at all. The Court manages to reach the opposite conclusion only by disregarding widely accepted rules for service-provider liability and adopting in their place an improvised standard ("looks-like-cable-TV") that will sow confusion for years to come.

. . .

Unlike video-on-demand services, Aereo does not provide a prearranged assortment of movies and television shows. Rather, it assigns each subscriber an antenna that—like a library card—can be used to obtain whatever broadcasts are freely available. . . . The key point is that subscribers call all the shots: Aereo's automated system does not relay any program, copyrighted or not, until a subscriber selects the program and tells Aereo to relay it. Aereo's operation of that system is a volitional act and a but-for cause of the resulting performances, but, as in the case of the copy shop, that degree of involvement is not enough for direct liability. . . .

In sum, Aereo does not "perform" for the sole and simple reason that it does not make the choice of content. And because Aereo does not perform, it cannot be held directly liable for infringing the Networks' public-performance right. That conclusion does not necessarily mean that Aereo's service complies with the Copyright Act. Quite the contrary. The Networks' complaint alleges that Aereo is directly *and* secondarily liable for infringing their public-performance rights (§ 106(4)) *and also* their reproduction rights (§ 106(1)). Their request for a preliminary injunction—the only issue before this Court—is based exclusively on the direct-liability portion of the public-performance claim . . . . Affirming the judgment below would merely return this case to the lower courts for consideration of the Networks' remaining claims.

. . .

[T]he Court's reasoning fails on its own terms because there are material differences between the cable systems at issue in [*Teleprompter* and *Fortnightly*], on the one hand and Aereo on the other. The former . . . captured the full range of broadcast signals and forwarded them to all subscribers at all times, whereas Aereo transmits only specific programs selected by the user, at specific times selected by the user. The Court acknowledges this distinction but blithely concludes that it "does not make a critical difference." Even if that were true, the Court fails to account for other salient differences between the two technologies. . . . At the time of our *Teleprompter* decision, cable companies "perform[ed] the same functions as 'broadcasters' by deliberately selecting and importing distant signals, originating programs, [and] selling commercials," thus making them curators of content—more akin to video-on-demand services than copy shops. . . .

[M]ost importantly, even accepting that the 1976 amendments had as their purpose the overruling of our cable-TV cases, what they were meant to do and how they did it are two different questions—and it is the latter that governs the case before us here. The injury claimed is not violation of a law that says operations similar to cable TV are subject to copyright liability, but violation of § 106(4) of the Copyright Act. And whatever soothing reasoning the Court uses to reach its result ("this looks like cable TV"), the consequence of its holding is that someone who implements this technology *"perform[s]" under that provision*. That greatly disrupts settled jurisprudence which, before today, applied the straightforward, bright-line test of volitional conduct directed at the copyrighted work. If that test is not outcome determinative in this case, presumably it is not outcome determinative elsewhere as well. And it is not clear what the Court proposes to replace it. . . .

Satellite Television

To DirecTV and Dish Network subscribers, direct-broadcast satellite (DBS) may seem a lot like cable television. Home satellite systems offer the same channels that cable offers, plus programming from stations originating in different time zones. The technology, however, is quite different. Instead of transmitting a television signal by wire, DBS beams an encoded signal from a geo-synchronous satellite to a small "dish" installed on a rooftop. Unlike traditional broadcast television, the signal is not diffused widely to the public. Only subscribers who purchase proprietary equipment can decode the signal. Even so, satellite transmissions use the scarce frequencies of the radio spectrum. In 1984, the DC Circuit recognized that DBS systems used for two-way communications may be treated as common carriers, like a telephone. At the same time, the court ruled that DBS systems that offer subscription programming to the public should be subject to broadcast regulations, including candidate access rules such as Communications Act sections 315(a) and 312(a)(7).

Nat'l Ass'n of Broadcasters v. FCC, 740 F.2d 1190 (D.C. Cir. 1984). With the passage of the 1992 Cable Act, Congress expressly directed the FCC to apply the candidate access statutes to DBS, and required DBS systems to set aside as much as seven percent of their channel capacity to noncommercial educational program channels. These broadcast-style public interest regulations, codified into section 335 of the Communications Act, were challenged by Time Warner on constitutional grounds in 1996.

TIME WARNER ENTERTAINMENT CO. V. FCC
93 F.3d 957 (D.C. Cir. 1996)

Opinion for the Court filed PER CURIAM.

Opinion dissenting in part filed by Circuit Judge TATEL.

PER CURIAM:

. . .

THE DBS PROVISIONS

A direct broadcast satellite ("DBS") service utilizes satellites to retransmit signals from the Earth to small, inexpensive terminals. It operates on a specified band of the radio frequency spectrum. The FCC prescribes the manner in which parts of that spectrum are made available for DBS systems. *See* 47 C.F.R. pt. 100. With the emergence of DBS technology, nations of the Western Hemisphere entered into an agreement to assign orbital satellite positions and channels. *See Processing Procedures Regarding the Direct Broadcast Satellite Serv.,* 95 F.C.C.2d 250, 251 (1983). The United States was assigned 32 channels at each of eight orbital positions. *Id.* at 252 n. 4. Through the use of compression technology, one satellite channel can deliver up to four channels of video service. DBS providers are allotted a number of channels of a specified spectrum width.
Section 25 of the 1992 Act provides:

> The Commission shall require, as a condition of any provision, initial authorization, or authorization renewal for a provider of direct broadcast satellite service providing video programming, that the provider of such service reserve a portion of its channel capacity, equal to not less than 4 percent nor more than 7 percent, exclusively for noncommercial programming of an educational or infor-

mational nature.

47 U.S.C. § 335(b)(1). DBS providers have no editorial control over the educational or informational programming they are required to carry under this provision. *Id.* § 335(b)(3). The district court held that section 25 is invalid because the government provided no evidence that regulation of DBS providers is necessary to serve any significant interest. *Daniels Cablevision,* 835 F.Supp. at 8–9.

A

RIPENESS

We must first address a threshold question of ripeness. PBS argues that the challenge is not ripe because the nature of the regulations will be determined only through further FCC rulemaking. "We test ripeness of this facial, pre-enforcement challenge . . . by balancing two factors: the 'fitness of the issue for judicial decision' and the 'hardship to the parties of withholding court consideration.'" *Beach Communications,* 959 F.2d at 984 (quoting *Abbott Labs.,* 387 U.S. at 149). . . . Here, we are faced with the purely legal question of whether section 25 presents an unconstitutional infringement on DBS providers' First Amendment rights, which we are able to resolve without further agency action or factual development. Contrary to PBS's contention, *Beach Communications* does not dictate a finding that Time Warner's challenge is unripe. . . . (B)ecause the potential impact on speech is known and a resolution of the claim does not depend on undeveloped facts, the challenge to section 25 is suitable for judicial review; and because the issue is "clearly fit to be heard," we need not consider whether petitioners would "suffer any hardship from our postponing its resolution." *Consolidated Rail Corp. v. United States,* 896 F.2d 574, 577–78 (D.C. Cir. 1990).

B

MERITS

Time Warner insists, for a variety of reasons, that the DBS set-aside provisions must be subjected to strict scrutiny; it also maintains that we may not consider the government's argument that DBS systems are analogous to broadcast television and therefore subject to no more than heightened scrutiny, because that argument had not been raised before the district court. While it is true that we will not ordinarily entertain an argument that the trial court had no opportunity to consider, the Supreme Court has recognized that "there are circumstances in which a federal appellate court is justified in resolving an issue not passed on below. . . ." *Singleton v. Wulff*, 428 U.S. 106, 121 (1976).

We have noted that the discretion to consider issues not raised earlier will be exercised

> only in [such] exceptional circumstances . . . [as] uncertainty in the state of the law; a novel, important and recurring question of federal law; an intervening change in the law; and extraordinary situations in which review is necessary to prevent a miscarriage of justice or to preserve the integrity of the judicial process.

Roosevelt v. E.I. Du Pont de Nemours & Co., 958 F.2d 416, 419 & n. 5 (D.C. Cir. 1992) (citations omitted). In *Roosevelt,* we considered an issue raised for the first time on appeal because it was "purely one of law important in the administration of federal justice, and resolution of the issue [did] not depend on any additional facts not considered by the district court." *Id.* The instant case is concerned with the validity of a federal statute governing the application of a new technology of enormous significance. Our resolution of the legal issue presented here does not require the consideration of facts not already in the record, and for us to ignore the obvious similarity between DBS and broadcasting would do nothing to preserve the integrity of the judicial process.

The Supreme Court recognized, in 1969, that because of the limited availability of the radio spectrum for broadcast purposes, "only a tiny fraction of those with resources and intelligence can hope to communicate by radio at the same time. . . ." *Red Lion Broadcasting Co., Inc. v. FCC,* 395 U.S. 367, 388, (1969). The same is true for DBS today. Because the United States has only a finite number of satellite positions available for DBS use, the opportunity to provide such services will necessarily be limited. Even before the first DBS communications satellite was launched in 1994, the FCC found that "the demand for channel/orbit allocations far exceeds the available supply." *Continental Satellite Corp.,* 4 F.C.C.R. 6292, 6293 (1989). Recently, the last DBS license was auctioned off for $682.5 million, the largest sum ever received by the FCC for any single license to use the airwaves. Mike Mills, *MCI Becomes a Broadcaster,* WASH. POST, Jan. 26, 1996, at A1, A24. As the Supreme Court observed,

> [w]here there are substantially more individuals who want to broadcast than there are frequencies to allocate, it is idle to posit an unabridgeable First Amendment right to

> broadcast comparable to the right of every individual to speak, write, or publish.

Red Lion, 395 U.S. at 388.

In such cases, the Court applies a "less rigorous standard of First Amendment scrutiny," based on a recognition that

> the inherent physical limitation on the number of speakers who may use the . . . medium has been thought to require some adjustment in traditional First Amendment analysis to permit the Government to place limited content restraints, and impose certain affirmative obligations, on broadcast licensees.

Turner, 114 S.Ct. at 2456, 2457. Because the new DBS technology is subject to similar limitations, we conclude that section 25 should be analyzed under the same relaxed standard of scrutiny that the court has applied to the traditional broadcast media.

Both broadcasters and the public have First Amendment rights that must be balanced when the government seeks to regulate access to the radio spectrum. *Columbia Broadcasting Sys., Inc. v. Democratic Nat'l Comm.,* 412 U.S. 94, 102–03, 110 (1973) ("*DNC*"). Nonetheless, the Supreme Court has held that "[i]t is the right of the viewers and listeners, not the right of the broadcasters, which is paramount. . . . It is the right of the public to receive suitable access to social, political, esthetic, moral and other ideas and experiences which is crucial here." *Red Lion,* 395 U.S. at 390; *accord DNC,* 412 U.S. at 102. An essential goal of the First Amendment is to achieve "the widest possible dissemination of information from diverse and antagonistic sources." *FCC v. National Citizens Comm. for Broadcasting,* 436 U.S. 775, 799 (1978) ("*NCCB* ") (quoting *Associated Press,* 326 U.S. at 20,). Broadcasting regulations that affect speech have been upheld when they further this First Amendment goal. For example, in *NCCB,* the Supreme Court recognized that "efforts to enhance the volume and quality of coverage of public issues through regulation of broadcasting may be permissible where similar efforts to regulate the print media would not be." *Id.* at 800 (internal quotation marks, citations, and brackets omitted); *see also CBS, Inc. v. FCC,* 453 U.S. 367, 395 (1981) ("preserv[ation] [of] an uninhibited marketplace of ideas" is proper consideration in imposing public interest obligations on broadcasters); *FCC v. League of Women Voters,* 468 U.S. 364, 377 (1984) (Congress may "seek to assure that the public receives through this medium a balanced presentation of information on issues of public importance. . . .").

The government asserts an interest in assuring public access to diverse sources of information by requiring DBS operators to reserve four to seven percent of their channel capacity for noncommercial educational and informational programming. Indeed, a stated policy of the 1992 Act is to "promote the availability to the public of a diversity of views and information through cable television and other video distribution media." 1992 Act, § 2(b)(1), 106 Stat. at 1463. This interest lies at the core of the First Amendment: "Assuring that the public has access to a multiplicity of informational sources is a governmental purpose of the highest order, for it promotes values central to the First Amendment." *Turner,* 512 U.S. at– . . . .

So ordered.

TATEL, Circuit Judge, dissenting in part(omitted) . . . .

NOTES AND QUESTIONS

1. Although a cable franchise can no longer be exclusive, this does not mean that your local cable provider does not have a de facto monopoly in a community. This is because the barriers of entry into the market are too high for many competitors. In some large markets, upstart companies, known as overbuilders, have enjoyed a measure of success. But the costs are high, since an overbuilder must build its own cable infrastructure, advertise to become known, and compete on price with a dominant incumbent provider. Look at your local market. Does an overbuilder offer service in your neighborhood?
2. In the *Turner* case supra, Justice Kennedy's plurality opinion defers to Congress' economic concerns to conclude that the must-carry rules are constitutional content-neutral legislation. Justice O'Connor, writing for four dissenting justices, argues that must-carry is a content regulation that requires—and fails—strict scrutiny. How should one interpret Justice Breyer's concurrence?
3. In his *Aereo* dissent, Justice Scalia posits that the Court has improvised a "looks-like-cable-TV" standard in support of broadcasters. What does he mean by that? Is *Aereo* a case about structural regulation or content regulation?
4. **À la carte pricing.** In the United States, pay-television subscribers pay for a bundle of basic tier program channels with optional bundled

premium offerings. This means that you are required to pay for some channels, like ESPN, which can be quite costly, even if you never watch them. In 2006, FCC Chairman Kevin Martin advised Congress that subscribers with à la carte pricing would save an average of thirteen percent on their monthly bills. Cable channels with small audiences argue that à la carte pricing will put them out of business. Would you save money if you switched to à la carte pricing? How many channels do you watch?

5. In the *Time Warner* case supra, the DC Circuit, per curium, cited *Red Lion* to justify the constitutionality of public interest set-asides and candidate access obligations. Although a motion to rehear en banc was denied, Judge Stephen Williams, writing for five dissenting judges, rejected *Red Lion* as a justification, citing the lack of channel scarcity in DBS systems. 105 F.3d 723 (D.C. Cir. 1997). Should it be enough that satellite communications use scarce airwaves, or should the scarcity of channels be the dispositive factor?
6. **Cable set-asides.** Communications Act § 611, added by the 1984 Cable Act, authorized local franchise authorities to require cable operators to set aside channel capacity for public, educational, and governmental access when negotiating new franchises or renewing old ones. 47 U.S.C. § 531(b). Local authorities can bargain for conditions not inconsistent with federal law, in exchange for the grant of rights to lay cable on public land. *Red Lion* is not a factor because cable wires are not scarce.

CHAPTER 13

ONLINE MEDIA CHALLENGES

The Internet

If you asked most people what the Internet was prior to the early 1990s, odds are you would be greeted with an indifferent shrug. Today, of course, the Internet—and its graphical interface known as the World Wide Web—has become a constant presence in our everyday lives. Whether we are using email, shopping, posting to Facebook, filing taxes, streaming Netflix, or banking, an interconnectivity of computer networks—the "Internet"—is what powers most of our social and commercial interactions.

The freedoms that the Internet provides for all of us, however, is not without consequences. Issues such as pornography, privacy, defamation and copyright piracy have taken on greater urgency as our reliance on the Internet has increased. Despite repeated attempts. Congress has found the First Amendment to be a potent foil in its efforts to regulate content on the Internet. In ACLU v. Reno infra, the U.S. Supreme Court strikes down an early attempt to criminalize indecent online content, the Communications Decency Act. In Ashcroft v. American Civil Liberties Union infra, the Court, in a narrow ruling on the Child Online Protection Act, leaves open the possibility that it may be possible for Congress to assert "community standards"—an essential facet of the *Miller* obscenity test—for the Internet, even though the Internet is not tied to a particular geographic space.

Congress has had more success protecting websites from defamation claims, although the landmark Fourth Circuit case, Zeran v. America Online, Inc. infra, makes it clear that what is good for an Internet content provider may not be so good for the victim of an anonymous online attack. The final section of this chapter examines the issue of network neutrality and whether the Federal Communications Commission has the legal authority—and political will—to prevent Internet service providers from blocking or slowing access to websites and web-based applications for commercial reasons.

Internet Indecency

Reno v. American Civil Liberties Union
521 U.S. 844 (1997)

JUSTICE STEVENS delivered the opinion of the Court.
At issue is the constitutionality of two statutory provisions enacted to protect minors from "indecent" and "patently offensive" communications on the Internet. Notwithstanding the legitimacy and importance of the congressional goal of protecting children from harmful materials, we agree with the three-judge District Court that the statute abridges "the freedom of speech" protected by the First Amendment.

I.
The District Court made extensive findings of fact, most of which were based on a detailed stipulation prepared by the parties. See 929 F. Supp. 824, 830-849 (ED Pa. 1996). The findings describe the character and the dimensions of the Internet, the availability of sexually explicit material in that medium, and the problems confronting age verification for recipients of Internet communications. Because those findings provide the underpinnings for the legal issues, we begin with a summary of the undisputed facts.

The Internet
The Internet is an international network of interconnected computers . . . Individuals can obtain access to the Internet from many different sources, generally hosts themselves or entities with a host affiliation. . . .

Anyone with access to the Internet may take advantage of a wide variety of communication and information retrieval methods. These methods are constantly evolving and difficult to categorize precisely. But, as presently constituted, those most relevant to this case are electronic mail ("e-mail"), automatic mailing list services ("mail exploders," sometimes referred to as "listservs"), "newsgroups," "chat rooms," and the "World Wide Web." All of these methods can be used to transmit text; most can transmit sound, pictures, and moving video images. Taken together, these tools constitute a unique medium—known to its users as "cyberspace"—located in no particular geographical location but available to anyone, anywhere in the world, with access to the Internet.

. . .

The best known category of communication over the Internet is the World Wide Web, which allows users to search for and retrieve information stored in remote computers, as well as, in some cases, to communicate back to designated sites. In concrete terms, the Web consists of a vast number of documents stored in different computers all over the world. Some of these documents are simply files containing information. However, more elaborate documents, commonly known as Web "pages," are also prevalent. Each has its own address—"rather like a telephone number." Web pages frequently contain information and sometimes allow the viewer to communicate with the page's (or "site's") author. They generally also contain "links" to other documents created by that site's author or to other (generally) related sites. Typically, the links are either blue or underlined text—sometimes images.

. . .

The Web is thus comparable, from the readers' viewpoint, to both a vast library including millions of readily available and indexed publications and a sprawling mall offering goods and services.

From the publishers' point of view, it constitutes a vast platform from which to address and hear from a world-wide audience of millions of readers, viewers, researchers, and buyers. Any person or organization with a computer connected to the Internet can "publish" information. Publishers include government agencies, educational institutions, commercial entities, advocacy groups, and individuals. Publishers may either make their material available to the entire pool of Internet users, or confine access to a selected group, such as those willing to pay for the privilege. "No single organization controls any membership in the Web, nor is there any centralized point from which individual Web sites or services can be blocked from the Web."

Sexually Explicit Material

Sexually explicit material on the Internet includes text, pictures, and chat and "extends from the modestly titillating to the hardest-core." These files are created, named, and posted in the same manner as material that is not sexually explicit, and may be accessed either deliberately or unintentionally during the course of an imprecise search. "Once a provider posts its content on the Internet, it cannot prevent that content from entering any community." ... Some of the communications over the Internet that originate in foreign countries are also sexually explicit.

Though such material is widely available, users seldom encounter such content accidentally. "A document's title or a description of the document will usually appear before the document itself . . . and in many cases the user will receive detailed information about a site's content before he or she need take the step to access the document. Almost all sexually explicit images are preceded by warnings as to the content." For that reason, the "odds are slim" that a user would enter a sexually explicit site by accident. Unlike communications received by radio or television, "the receipt of information on the Internet requires a series of affirmative steps more deliberate and directed than merely turning a dial. A child requires some sophistication and some ability to read to retrieve material and thereby to use the Internet unattended."

Systems have been developed to help parents control the material that may be available on a home computer with Internet access. A system may either limit a computer's access to an approved list of sources that have been identified as containing no adult material, it may block designated inappropriate sites, or it may attempt to block messages containing identifiable objectionable features. "Although parental control software currently can screen for certain suggestive words or for known sexually explicit sites, it cannot now screen for sexually explicit images." Nevertheless, the evidence indicates that "a reasonably effective method by which parents can prevent their children from accessing sexually explicit and other material which parents may believe is inappropriate for their children will soon be available."

Age Verification

The problem of age verification differs for different uses of the Internet. The District Court categorically determined that there "is no effective way to determine the identity or the age of a user who is accessing material through e-mail, mail exploders, newsgroups or chat rooms." The Government offered no evidence that there was a reliable way to screen recipients and participants in such fora for age. Moreover, even if it were technologically feasible to block minors' access to newsgroups and chat rooms containing discussions of art, politics or other subjects that potentially elicit "indecent" or "patently offensive" contributions, it would not be possible to block their access to that material and "still allow them access to the remaining content, even if the overwhelming majority of that content was not indecent."

Technology exists by which an operator of a Web site may condition access on the verification of requested information such as a credit card number or an adult password. Credit card verification is only feasible, however, either in connection with a commercial transaction in which the card is used, or by payment to a verification agency. Using credit card possession as a surrogate for proof of age would impose costs on non-commercial Web sites that would require many of them to shut down. For that reason, at the time of the trial, credit card verification was "effectively unavailable to a substantial number of Internet content providers." 929 F. Supp. at 846 (finding 102). Moreover, the imposition of such a requirement "would completely bar adults who do not have a credit card and lack the resources to obtain one from accessing any blocked material."

Commercial pornographic sites that charge their users for access have assigned them passwords as a method of age verification. The record does not contain any evidence concerning the reliability of these technologies. Even if passwords are effective for commercial purveyors of indecent material, the District Court found that an adult password requirement would impose significant burdens on noncommercial sites, both because they would discourage users from accessing their sites and because the cost of creating and maintaining such screening systems would be "beyond their reach."

. . .

In sum, the District Court found:

"Even if credit card verification or adult password verification were implemented, the Government presented no testimony as to how such systems could ensure that the user of the password or credit card is in fact over 18. The burdens imposed by credit card verification and adult password verification systems make them effectively unavailable to a substantial number of Internet content providers." *Ibid.* (finding 107).

II.

The Telecommunications Act of 1996, Pub. L. 104-104, 110 Stat. 56, was an unusually important legislative enactment. As stated on the first of its 103 pages, its primary purpose was to reduce regulation and encourage "the rapid deployment of new telecommunications technologies." . . .

The first, 47 U.S.C. § 223(a) (Supp. 1997), prohibits the knowing transmission of obscene or indecent messages to any recipient under 18 years of age. . . .

The second provision, § 223(d), prohibits the knowing sending or displaying of patently offensive messages in a manner that is available to a person under 18 years of age. . . .

The breadth of these prohibitions is qualified by two affirmative defenses. See § 223(e)(5). One covers those who take "good faith, reasonable, effective, and appropriate actions" to restrict access by minors to the prohibited communications. § 223(e)(5)(A). The other covers those who restrict access to covered material by requiring certain designated forms of age proof, such as a verified credit card or an adult identification number or code. § 223(e)(5)(B).

IV.

In arguing for reversal, the Government contends that the CDA is plainly constitutional under three of our prior decisions: (1) *Ginsberg v. New York,* 390 U.S. 629 (1968); (2) *FCC v. Pacifica Foundation*, 438 U.S. 726 (1978); and (3) *Renton v. Playtime Theatres, Inc.*, 475 U.S. 41 (1986). . . .

These precedents, then, surely do not require us to uphold the CDA and are fully consistent with the application of the most stringent review of its provisions.

V.

In *Southeastern Promotions, Ltd. v. Conrad,* 420 U.S. 546, 557 (1975), we observed that "each medium of expression . . . may present its own problems." Thus, some of our cases have recognized special justifications for regulation of the broadcast media that are not applicable to other speakers, see *Red Lion Broadcasting Co. v. FCC,* 395 U.S. 367 (1969); *FCC v. Pacifica Foundation,* 438 U.S. 726 (1978). In these cases, the Court relied on the history of extensive government regulation of the broadcast medium, see, *e.g., Red Lion,* 395 U.S. at 399-400; the scarcity of available frequencies at its inception, see, *e.g., Turner Broadcasting System, Inc. v. FCC,* 512 U.S. 622, 637-638 (1994); and its "invasive" nature, see *Sable Communications of Cal., Inc. v. FCC,* 492 U.S. 115, 128 (1989).

Those factors are not present in cyberspace. Neither before nor after the enactment of the CDA have the vast democratic forums of the Internet been subject to the type of government supervision and regulation that has attended the broadcast industry. Moreover, the Internet is not as "invasive" as radio or television. The District Court specifically found that "communications over the Internet do not 'invade' an individual's home or appear on one's computer screen unbidden. Users seldom encounter content 'by accident.'" 929 F. Supp. at 844 (finding 88). It also found that "almost all sexually explicit images are preceded by warnings as to the content," and cited testimony that "'odds are slim' that a user would come across a sexually explicit sight by accident." *Ibid.* . . .

Finally, unlike the conditions that prevailed when Congress first authorized regulation of the broadcast spectrum, the Internet can hardly be considered a "scarce" expressive commodity. It provides relatively unlimited, low-cost capacity for communication of all kinds. The Government estimates that "as many as 40 million people use the Internet today, and that figure is expected to grow to 200 million by 1999." This dynamic, multifaceted category of communication includes not only traditional print and news services, but also audio, video, and still images, as well as interactive, real-time dialogue. Through the use of chat rooms, any person with a phone line can become a town crier with a voice that resonates farther than it could from any soapbox. Through the use of Web pages, mail exploders, and newsgroups, the same individual can become a pamphleteer. As the District Court found, "the content on the Internet is as diverse as human thought." 929 F. Supp. at 842 (finding 74). We agree with its conclusion that our cases provide no basis for qualifying the level of First Amendment scrutiny that should be applied to this medium.

VI.

Regardless of whether the CDA is so vague that it violates the Fifth Amendment, the many ambiguities concerning the scope of its coverage render it problematic for purposes of the First Amendment. For instance, each of the two parts of the CDA uses a different linguistic form. The first uses the word "indecent," 47 U.S.C. § 223(a) (Supp. 1997), while the second speaks of material that "in context, depicts or describes, in terms patently offensive as measured by contemporary community standards, sexual or excretory activities or organs," § 223(d). Given the absence of a definition of either term, this difference in language will provoke uncertainty among speakers about how the two standards relate to each other and just what they mean. Could a speaker confidently assume that a serious discussion about birth control practices, homosexuality, the First Amendment issues raised by the Appendix to our *Pacifica* opinion, or the consequences of prison rape would not violate the CDA? This uncertainty undermines the likelihood that the CDA has been carefully tailored to the congressional goal of protecting minors from potentially harmful materials.

"Indecent" does not benefit from any textual embellishment at all. "Patently offensive" is qualified only to the extent that it involves "sexual or excretory activities or organs" taken "in context" and "measured by contemporary community standards."

The vagueness of the CDA is a matter of special concern for two reasons. First, the CDA is a content-based regulation of speech. The vagueness of such a regulation raises special First Amendment concerns because of its obvious chilling effect on free speech. See, *e.g.*, *Gentile v. State Bar of Nev.*, 501 U.S. 1030, 1048-1051 (1991). Second, the CDA is a criminal statute. In addition to the opprobrium and stigma of a criminal conviction, the CDA threatens violators with penalties including up to two years in prison for each act of violation. The severity of criminal sanctions may well cause speakers to remain silent rather than communicate even arguably unlawful words, ideas, and images. See, *e.g.*, *Dombrowski v. Pfister*, 380 U.S. 479, 494 (1965). As a practical matter, this increased deterrent effect, coupled with the "risk of discriminatory enforcement" of vague regulations, poses greater First Amendment concerns than those implicated by the civil regulation reviewed in *Denver Area Ed. Telecommunications Consortium, Inc.* v. *FCC*, 518 U.S. 727 (1996).

The Government argues that the statute is no more vague than the obscenity standard this Court established in *Miller v. California*, 413 U.S. 15 (1973). But that is not so. In *Miller*, this Court reviewed a criminal conviction against a commercial vendor who mailed brochures containing pictures of sexually explicit activities to individuals who had not requested such materials. *Id.*, at 18. Having struggled for some time to establish a definition of obscenity, we set forth in *Miller* the test for obscenity that controls to this day:

> "(a) whether the average person, applying contemporary community standards would find that the work, taken as a whole, appeals to the prurient interest; (b) whether the work depicts or describes, in a patently offensive way, sexual conduct specifically defined by the applicable state law; and (c) whether the work, taken as a whole, lacks serious literary, artistic, political, or scientific value." *Id., at* 24 (internal quotation marks and citations omitted).

Because the CDA's "patently offensive" standard (and, we assume *arguendo*, its synonymous "indecent" standard) is one part of the three-prong *Miller* test, the Government reasons, it cannot be unconstitutionally vague.

The Government's assertion is incorrect as a matter of fact. The second prong of the *Miller* test—the purportedly analogous standard—contains a critical requirement that is omitted from the CDA: that the proscribed material be "specifically defined by the applicable state law." This requirement reduces the vagueness inherent in the open-ended term "patently offensive" as used in the CDA. Moreover, the *Miller* definition is limited to "sexual conduct," whereas the CDA extends also to include (1) "excretory activities" as well as (2) "organs" of both a sexual and excretory nature.

The Government's reasoning is also flawed. Just because a definition including three limitations is not vague, it does not follow that one of those limitations, standing by itself, is not vague. Each of *Miller*'s additional two prongs—(1) that, taken as a whole, the material appeal to the "prurient" interest, and (2) that it "lack serious literary, artistic, political, or scientific value"—critically limits the uncertain sweep of the obscenity definition. The second requirement is particularly important because, unlike the "patently offensive" and "prurient interest" criteria, it is not judged by contemporary community standards. See *Pope v. Illinois*, 481 U.S. 497, 500 (1987). This "societal value" requirement, absent in the CDA, allows appellate courts to impose some limitations and regularity on the definition by setting, as a matter of law, a national floor for socially redeeming value. The Government's contention that courts will be able to give such legal limitations to the CDA's standards is belied by *Miller*'s own rationale for having juries determine whether material is "patently offensive" according to community standards: that such questions are essentially ones of *fact*.

In contrast to *Miller* and our other previous cases, the CDA thus presents a greater threat of censoring speech that, in fact, falls outside the statute's scope. Given the vague contours of the coverage of the statute, it unquestionably silences some speakers whose messages would be entitled to constitutional protection. That danger provides further reason for insisting that the statute not be overly broad. The CDA's burden on protected speech cannot be justified if it could be avoided by a more carefully drafted statute.

VII.

We are persuaded that the CDA lacks the precision that the First Amendment requires when a statute regulates the content of speech. In order to deny minors access to potentially harmful speech, the CDA effectively suppresses a large amount of speech that adults have a constitutional right to receive and to address to one another. That burden on adult speech is unacceptable if less restrictive alternatives would be at least as effective in achieving the legitimate purpose that the statute was enacted to serve.

In evaluating the free speech rights of adults, we have made it perfectly clear that "sexual expression which is indecent but not obscene is protected by the First Amendment." *Sable*, 492 U.S. at 126. See also *Carey v. Population Services Int'l*, 431 U.S. 678, 701 (1977) ("Where obscenity is not involved, we have consistently held that the fact that protected speech may be offensive to some does not justify its suppression"). Indeed, *Pacifica* itself admonished that "the fact that society may find speech offensive is not a sufficient reason for suppressing it." 438 U.S. at 745.

It is true that we have repeatedly recognized the governmental interest in protecting children from harmful materials. See *Ginsberg*, 390 U.S. at 639; *Pacifica*, 438 U.S. at 749. But that interest does not justify an unnecessarily broad suppression of speech addressed to adults. As we have explained, the Government may not "reduce the adult population . . . to . . . only what is fit for children." *Denver*, 518 U.S., at 759. . . .

The District Court found that at the time of trial existing technology did not include any effective method for a sender to prevent minors from obtaining access to its communications on the Internet without also denying access to adults. The Court found no effective way to determine the age of a user who is accessing material through e-mail, mail exploders, newsgroups, or chat rooms. 929 F. Supp. at 845 (findings 90-94). As a practical matter, the Court also found that it would be prohibitively expensive for noncommercial—as well as some commercial—speakers who have Web sites to verify that their users are adults. *Id.*, at 845-848 (findings 95-116). These limitations must inevitably curtail a significant amount of adult communication on the Internet. By contrast, the District Court found that "despite its limitations, currently available *user-based* software suggests that a reasonably effective method by which *parents* can prevent their children from accessing sexually explicit and other material which *parents* may believe is inappropriate for their children will soon be widely available." *Id.*, at 842 (finding 73) (emphases added).

The breadth of the CDA's coverage is wholly unprecedented. Unlike the regulations upheld in *Ginsberg* and *Pacifica*, the scope of the CDA is not limited to commercial speech or commercial entities. Its open-ended prohibitions embrace all nonprofit entities and individuals posting indecent messages or displaying them on their own computers in the presence of minors. The general, undefined terms "indecent" and "patently offensive" cover large amounts of nonpornographic material with serious educational or other value. Moreover, the "community standards" criterion as applied to the Internet means that any communication available to a nation-wide audience will be judged by the standards of the community most likely to be offended by the message. The regulated subject matter includes any of the seven "dirty words" used in the Pacifica monologue, the use of which the Government's expert acknowledged could constitute a felony. See Olsen Test., Tr. Vol. V, 53:16-54:10. It may also extend to discussions about prison rape or safe sexual practices, artistic images that include nude subjects, and arguably the card catalogue of the Carnegie Library.

For the purposes of our decision, we need neither accept nor reject the Government's submission that the First Amendment does not forbid a blanket prohibition on all "indecent" and "patently offensive" messages communicated to a 17-year old—no matter how much value the message may contain and regardless of parental approval. It is at least clear that the strength of the Government's interest in protecting minors is not equally strong throughout the coverage of this broad statute. Under the CDA, a parent allowing her 17-year-old to use the family computer to obtain information on the Internet that she, in her parental judgment, deems appropriate could face a lengthy prison term. See 47 U.S.C. § 223(a)(2) (Supp. 1997). Similarly, a parent who sent his 17-year-old college freshman information on birth control via e-mail could be incarcerated even though neither he, his child, nor anyone in their home community, found the material "indecent" or "patently offensive," if the college town's community thought otherwise.

The breadth of this content-based restriction of speech imposes an especially heavy burden on the Government to explain why a less restrictive provision would not be as effective as the CDA. It has not done so. The arguments in this Court have referred to possible alternatives such as requiring that indecent material be "tagged" in a way that facilitates parental control of material coming into their homes, making exceptions for messages with artistic or educational value, providing some tolerance for parental choice, and regulating some portions of the Internet—such as commercial web sites—differently than others, such as chat rooms. Particularly in the light of the absence of any detailed findings by the Congress, or even hearings addressing the special problems of the CDA, we are persuaded that the CDA is not narrowly tailored if that requirement has any meaning at all.

VIII.

In an attempt to curtail the CDA's facial overbreadth, the Government advances three additional arguments for sustaining the Act's affirmative prohibitions: (1) that the CDA is constitutional because it leaves open ample "alternative channels" of communication; (2) that the plain meaning of the Act's "knowledge" and "specific person" requirement significantly restricts its permissible applications; and (3) that the Act's prohibitions are "almost always" limited to material lacking redeeming social value.

The Government first contends that, even though the CDA effectively censors discourse on many of the Internet's modalities—such as chat groups, newsgroups, and mail exploders—it is nonetheless constitutional because it provides a "reasonable opportunity" for speakers to engage in the restricted speech on the World Wide Web. Brief for Appellants 39. This argument is unpersuasive because the CDA regulates speech on the basis of its content. A "time, place, and manner" analysis is therefore inapplicable. See *Consolidated Edison Co. of N.Y. v. Public Serv. Comm'n of N.Y.*, 447 U.S. 530, 536 (1980). It is thus immaterial whether such speech would be feasible on the Web (which, as the Government's own expert acknowledged, would cost up to $ 10,000 if the speaker's interests were not accommodated by an existing Web site, not including costs for database management and age verification). The Government's position is equivalent to arguing that a statute could ban leaflets on certain subjects as long as individuals are free to publish books. In invalidating a number of laws that banned leafleting on the streets *regardless of* their content—we explained that "one is not to have the exercise of his liberty of expression in appropriate places abridged on the plea that it may be exercised in some other place." *Schneider v. State (Town of Irvington)*, 308 U.S. 147, 163 (1939).

The Government also asserts that the "knowledge" requirement of both §§ 223(a) and (d), especially when coupled with the "specific child" element found in § 223(d), saves the CDA from overbreadth. Because both sections prohibit the dissemination of indecent messages only to persons known to be under 18, the Government argues, it does not require transmitters to "refrain from communicating indecent material to adults; they need only refrain from disseminating such materials to persons they know to be under 18." Brief for Appellants 24. This argument ignores the fact that most Internet fora—including chat rooms, newsgroups, mail exploders, and the Web—are open to all comers. The Government's assertion that the knowledge requirement somehow protects the communications of adults is therefore untenable. Even the strongest reading of the "specific person" requirement of § 223(d) cannot save the statute. It would confer broad powers of censorship, in the form of a "heckler's veto," upon any opponent of indecent speech who might simply log on and inform the would-be discoursers that his 17-year-old child—a "specific person . . . under 18 years of age," 47 U.S.C.A. § 223(d)(1)(A) (Supp. 1997)—would be present.

Finally, we find no textual support for the Government's submission that material having scientific, educational, or other redeeming social value will necessarily fall outside the CDA's "patently offensive" and "indecent" prohibitions. See also n. 37, *supra.*

IX.

The Government's three remaining arguments focus on the defenses provided in § 223(e)(5). First, relying on the "good faith, reasonable, effective, and appropriate actions" provision, the Government suggests that "tagging" provides a defense that saves the constitutionality of the Act. The suggestion assumes that transmitters may encode their indecent communications in a way that would indicate their contents, thus permitting recipients to block their reception with appropriate software. It is the requirement that the good faith action must be "effective" that makes this defense illusory. The Government recognizes that its proposed screening software does not currently exist. Even if it did, there is no way to know whether a potential recipient will actually block the encoded material. Without the impossible knowledge that every guardian in America is screening for the "tag," the transmitter could not reasonably rely on its action to be "effective."

For its second and third arguments concerning defenses—which we can consider together—the Government relies on the latter half of § 223(e)(5), which applies when the transmitter has restricted access by requiring use of a verified credit card or adult identification. Such verification is not only technologically available but actually is used by commercial providers of sexually explicit material. These providers, therefore, would be protected by the defense. Under the findings of the District Court, however, it is not economically feasible for most noncommercial speakers to employ such verification. Accordingly, this defense would not significantly narrow the statute's burden on noncommercial speech. Even with respect to the commercial pornographers that would be protected by the defense, the Government failed to adduce any evidence that these verification techniques actually preclude minors from posing as adults. Given that the risk of criminal sanctions "hovers over each content provider, like the proverbial sword of Damocles," the District Court correctly refused to rely on unproven future technology to save the statute. The

Government thus failed to prove that the proffered defense would significantly reduce the heavy burden on adult speech produced by the prohibition on offensive displays.

We agree with the District Court's conclusion that the CDA places an unacceptably heavy burden on protected speech, and that the defenses do not constitute the sort of "narrow tailoring" that will save an otherwise patently invalid unconstitutional provision. In *Sable*, 492 U.S. at 127, we remarked that the speech restriction at issue there amounted to "'burning the house to roast the pig.'" The CDA, casting a far darker shadow over free speech, threatens to torch a large segment of the Internet community.

ASHCROFT V. AMERICAN CIVIL LIBERTIES UNION
535 U.S. 564 (2002)

JUSTICE THOMAS announced the judgment of the Court and delivered the opinion of the Court with respect to Parts I, II, and IV, an opinion with respect to Parts III-A, III-C, and III-D, in which THE CHIEF JUSTICE and JUSTICE SCALIA join, and an opinion with respect to Part III-B, in which THE CHIEF JUSTICE, JUSTICE O'CONNOR, and JUSTICE SCALIA join.

This case presents the narrow question whether the Child Online Protection Act's (COPA or Act) use of "community standards" to identify "material that is harmful to minors" violates the First Amendment. We hold that this aspect of COPA does not render the statute facially unconstitutional.

I.

After our decision in *Reno* v. *American Civil Liberties Union*, Congress explored other avenues for restricting minors' access to pornographic material on the Internet. In particular, Congress passed and the President signed into law the Child Online Protection Act, 112 Stat. 2681-736 (codified in 47 U.S.C. § 231 (1994 ed., Supp. V)). COPA prohibits any person from "knowingly and with knowledge of the character of the material, in interstate or foreign commerce by means of the World Wide Web, making any communication for commercial purposes that is available to any minor and that includes any material that is harmful to minors." 47 U.S.C. § 231 (a)(1).

Apparently responding to our objections to the breadth of the CDA's coverage, Congress limited the scope of COPA's coverage in at least three ways. First, while the CDA applied to communications over the Internet as a whole, including, for example, e-mail messages, COPA applies only to material displayed on the World Wide Web. Second, unlike the CDA, COPA covers only communications made "for commercial purposes." *Ibid.* And third, while the CDA prohibited "indecent" and "patently offensive" communications, COPA restricts only the narrower category of "material that is harmful to minors." *Ibid.*

Drawing on the three-part test for obscenity set forth in *Miller v. California*, 413 U.S. 15 (1973), COPA defines "material that is harmful to minors" as

> "any communication, picture, image, graphic image file, article, recording, writing, or other matter of any kind that is obscene or that—
>
> "(A) the average person, applying contemporary community standards, would find, taking the material as a whole and with respect to minors, is designed to appeal to, or is designed to pander to, the prurient interest;
>
> "(B) depicts, describes, or represents, in a manner patently offensive with respect to minors, an actual or simulated sexual act or sexual contact, an actual or simulated normal or perverted sexual act, or a lewd exhibition of the genitals or post-pubescent female breast; and
>
> "(C) taken as a whole, lacks serious literary, artistic, political, or scientific value for minors."

Like the CDA, COPA also provides affirmative defenses to those subject to prosecution under the statute. An individual may qualify for a defense if he, "in good faith, has restricted access by minors to material that is harmful to minors—(A) by requiring the use of a credit card, debit account, adult access code, or adult personal identification number; (B) by accepting a digital certificate that verifies age; or (C) by any other reasonable measures that are feasible under available technology." § 231(c)(1). Persons violating COPA are subject to both civil and criminal sanctions. A civil penalty of up to $ 50,000 may be imposed for each violation of the statute. Criminal penalties consist of up to six months in prison and/or a maximum fine of $ 50,000. An additional fine of $ 50,000 may be imposed for any intentional violation of the statute. § 231(a).

. . .

COPA . . . applies to significantly less material than did the CDA and defines the harmful-to-minors material restricted by the statute in a manner parallel to the *Miller* definition of obscenity. See *supra,* at 5-6, 10. To fall within the scope of COPA, works must not only "depict, describe, or represent, in a manner patently offensive with respect to minors," particular sexual acts or parts of the anatomy, they must also be designed to appeal to the prurient interest of minors and "taken as a whole, lack serious literary, artistic, political, or scientific value for minors." 47 U.S.C. § 231 (e)(6).

These additional two restrictions substantially limit the amount of material covered by the statute. Material appeals to the prurient interest, for instance, only if it is in some sense erotic. Cf. *Erznoznik v. Jacksonville,* 422 U.S. 205, 213 (1975). Of even more significance, however, is COPA's exclusion of material with serious value for minors. See 47 U.S.C. § 231(e)(6)(C). In *Reno,* we emphasized that the serious value "requirement is particularly important because, unlike the 'patently offensive' and 'prurient interest' criteria, it is not judged by contemporary community standards." 521 U.S. at 873 (citing *Pope v. Illinois,* 481 U.S. 497, 500 (1987)). This is because "the value of [a] work [does not] vary from community to community based on the degree of local acceptance it has won." *Id.,* at 500. Rather, the relevant question is "whether a reasonable person would find . . . value in the material, taken as a whole." *Id.,* at 501. Thus, the serious value requirement "allows appellate courts to impose some limitations and regularity on the definition by setting, *as a matter of law,* a national floor for socially redeeming value." *Reno,* supra, at 873 (emphasis added), a safeguard nowhere present in the CDA.

...

When the scope of an obscenity statute's coverage is sufficiently narrowed by a "serious value" prong and a "prurient interest" prong, we have held that requiring a speaker disseminating material to a national audience to observe varying community standards does not violate the First Amendment. In *Hamling v. United States,* 418 U.S. 87 (1974), this Court considered the constitutionality of applying community standards to the determination of whether material is obscene under 18 U.S.C. § 1461, the federal statute prohibiting the mailing of obscene material. . . .

Fifteen years later, *Hamling's* holding was reaffirmed in *Sable Communications of Cal., Inc. v. FCC,* 492 U.S. 115 (1989). *Sable* addressed the constitutionality of 47 U.S.C. § 223 (b) (1982 ed., Supp. V), a statutory provision prohibiting the use of telephones to make obscene or indecent communications for commercial purposes. The petitioner in that case, a "dial-a-porn" operator, challenged, in part, that portion of the statute banning obscene phone messages. Like respondents here, the "dial-a-porn" operator argued that reliance on community standards to identify obscene material impermissibly compelled "message senders . . . to tailor all their messages to the least tolerant community." 492 U.S. at 124. Relying on *Hamling,* however, this Court once again rebuffed this attack on the use of community standards in a federal statute of national scope: "There is no constitutional barrier under *Miller* to prohibiting communications that are obscene in some communities under local standards even though they are not obscene in others. *If Sable's audience is comprised* of *different communities with different local standards, Sable ultimately bears the burden of complying with the prohibition on obscene messages."* 492 U.S. at 125-126 (emphasis added).

...

Respondents argue that COPA is "unconstitutionally overbroad" because it will require Web publishers to shield some material behind age verification screens that could be displayed openly in many communities across the Nation if Web speakers were able to limit access to their sites on a geographic basis. Brief for Respondents 33-34. "To prevail in a facial challenge," however, "it is not enough for a plaintiff to show 'some' overbreadth." *Reno, supra,* at 896 (O'CONNOR, J., concurring in judgment in part and dissenting in part). Rather, "the overbreadth of a statute must not only be real, but substantial as well." *Broadrick v. Oklahoma,* 413 U.S. 601, 615 (1973). At this stage of the litigation, respondents have failed to satisfy this burden, at least solely as a result of COPA's reliance on community standards. Because Congress has narrowed the range of content restricted by COPA in a manner analogous to *Miller's* definition of obscenity, we conclude, consistent with our holdings in *Hamling* and *Sable,* that any variance caused by the statute's reliance on community standards is not substantial enough to violate the First Amendment.

IV.

The scope of our decision today is quite limited. We hold only that COPA's reliance on community standards to identify "material that is harmful to minors" does not *by itself* render the statute substantially overbroad for purposes of the First Amendment. We do not express any view as to whether COPA suffers from substantial overbreadth for other reasons, whether the statute is unconstitutionally vague, or whether the District Court correctly concluded that the statute likely will not survive strict scrutiny analysis once adjudication of the case is completed below. While respondents urge us to resolve these questions at this time, prudence dictates allowing the Court of Appeals to first examine these difficult issues.

Petitioner does not ask us to vacate the preliminary injunction entered by the District Court, and in any event, we could not do so without addressing matters yet to be considered by the Court of Appeals. As a result, the Government remains enjoined from enforcing COPA absent further action by the Court of Appeals or the District Court.

For the foregoing reasons, we vacate the judgment of the Court of Appeals and remand the case for further proceedings.

It is so ordered.

JUSTICE O'CONNOR, concurring in part and concurring in the judgment.

I agree with the plurality that even if obscenity on the Internet is defined in terms of local community standards, respondents have not shown that the Child Online Protection Act (COPA) is overbroad solely on the basis of the variation in the standards of different communities. See *ante,* at 13 15. Like JUSTICE BREYER, however, see *post,* at 1 (opinion concurring in part and concurring in judgment), I write separately to express my views on the constitutionality and desirability of adopting a national standard for obscenity for regulation of the Internet.

The plurality's opinion argues that, even under local community standards, the variation between the most and least restrictive communities is not so great with respect to the narrow category of speech covered by COPA as to, alone, render the statute substantially overbroad. See *ante,* at 13-15. I agree, given respondents' failure to provide examples of materials that lack literary, artistic, political, and scientific value for minors, which would nonetheless result in variation among communities judging the other elements of the test. Respondents' examples of material for which community standards would vary include such things as the appropriateness of sex education and the desirability of adoption by same-sex couples. Brief for Respondents 43. Material addressing the latter topic, however, seems highly unlikely to be seen to appeal to the prurient interest in any community, and educational material like the former must, on any objective inquiry, see *ante,* at 15, have scientific value for minors.

But respondents' failure to prove substantial overbreadth on a facial challenge in this case still leaves open the possibility that the use of local community standards will cause problems for regulation of obscenity on the Internet, for adults as well as children, in future cases. In an as-applied challenge, for instance, individual litigants may still dispute that the standards of a community more restrictive than theirs should apply to them. And in future facial challenges to regulation of obscenity on the Internet, litigants may make a more convincing case for substantial overbreadth. Where adult speech is concerned, for instance, there may in fact be a greater degree of disagreement about what is patently offensive or appeals to the prurient interest.

Nor do I think such future cases can be resolved by application of the approach we took in *Hamling v. United States*, 418 U.S. 87 (1974), and *Sable Communications of Cal., Inc. v. FCC*, 492 U.S. 115 (1989). I agree with JUSTICE KENNEDY that, given Internet speakers' inability to control the geographic location of their audience, expecting them to bear the burden of controlling the recipients of their speech, as we did in *Hamling* and *Sable*, may be entirely too much to ask, and would potentially suppress an inordinate amount of expression. See *post*, at 5-6 (opinion concurring in judgment); contra, *ante*, at 15-19. For these reasons, adoption of a national standard is necessary in my view for any reasonable regulation of Internet obscenity.

Our precedents do not forbid adoption of a national standard. Local community-based standards originated with *Miller v. California*, 413 U.S. 15 (1973). In that case, we approved jury instructions that based the relevant "community standards" on those of the State of California rather than on the Nation as a whole. In doing so, we held that "nothing in the First Amendment requires" that a jury consider national standards when determining if something is obscene as a matter of fact. *Id.*, at 31. The First Amendment, we held, did not require that "the people of Maine or Mississippi accept public depiction of conduct found tolerable in Las Vegas, or New York City." *Id., at 32.* But we said nothing about the constitutionality of jury instructions that would contemplate a national standard—i.e., requiring that the people who live in all of these places hold themselves to what the nationwide community of adults would find was patently offensive and appealed to the prurient interest.

Later, in *Jenkins v. Georgia*, 418 U.S. 153, 157 (1974), we confirmed that "*Miller* approved the use of [instructions based on local standards]; it did not mandate their use." The instructions we approved in that case charged the jury with applying "community standards" without designating any particular "community." In holding that a State may define the obscenity standard by stating the *Miller* standard without further specification, 418 U.S. at 157, *Jenkins* left open the possibility that jurors would apply any number of standards, including a national standard, in evaluating material's obscenity.

To be sure, the Court in *Miller* also stated that a national standard might be "unascertainable," 413 U.S. at 31, and "unrealistic," *id.*, at 32. But where speech on the Internet is concerned, I do not share that skepticism. It is true that our Nation is diverse, but many local communities encompass a similar diversity. For instance, in *Miller* itself, the jury was instructed to consider the standards of the entire State of California, a large (today, it has a population of greater than 33 million people, see U.S. Dept. of Commerce, Bureau of Census, Statistical Abstract of the United States 23 (120th ed. 2000) (Table 20)) and diverse State that includes both Berkeley and Bakersfield. If the *Miller* Court believed generalizations about the standards of the people of California were possible, and that jurors would be capable of assessing them, it is difficult to believe that similar generalizations are not also possible for the Nation as a whole. Moreover, the existence of the Internet, and its facilitation of national dialogue, has itself made jurors more aware of the views of adults in other parts of the United States. Although jurors asked to evaluate the obscenity of speech based on a national standard will inevitably base their assessments to some extent on their experience of their local communities, I agree with JUSTICE BREYER that the lesser degree of variation that would result is inherent in the jury system and does not necessarily pose a First Amendment problem. See *post*, at 2. In my view, a national standard is not only constitutionally permissible, but also reasonable.

While I would prefer that the Court resolve the issue before it by explicitly adopting a national standard for defining obscenity on the Internet, given respondents' failure to demonstrate substantial overbreadth due solely to the variation between local communities, I join Parts I, II, III-B, and IV of JUSTICE THOMAS' opinion and the judgment.

Internet Defamation

ZERAN V. AMERICA ONLINE, INC.
129 F.3d 327 (4th Cir. 1997)

WILKINSON, Chief Judge.

Kenneth Zeran brought this action against America Online, Inc. ("AOL"), arguing that AOL unreasonably delayed in removing defamatory messages posted by an unidentified third party, refused to post retractions of those messages, and failed to screen for similar postings thereafter. The district court granted judgment for AOL on the grounds that the Communications Decency Act of 1996 ("CDA")—47 U.S.C. § 230—bars Zeran's claims. Zeran appeals, arguing that § 230 leaves intact liability for interactive computer service providers who possess notice of defamatory material posted through their services. He also contends that § 230 does not apply here because his claims arise from AOL's alleged negligence prior to the CDA's enactment. Section 230, however, plainly immunizes computer service providers like AOL from liability for information that originates with third parties. Furthermore, Congress clearly expressed its intent that § 230 apply to lawsuits, like Zeran's, instituted after the CDA's enactment. Accordingly, we affirm the judgment of the district court.

I.

"The Internet is an international network of interconnected computers," currently used by approximately 40 million people worldwide. *Reno v. ACLU,* 521 U.S. 844, ---- (1997). One of the many means by which individuals access the Internet is through an interactive computer service. These services offer not only a connection to the Internet as a whole, but also allow their subscribers to access information communicated and stored only on each computer service's individual proprietary network. *Id.* AOL is just such an interactive computer service. Much of the information transmitted over its network originates with the company's millions of subscribers. They may transmit information privately via electronic mail, or they may communicate publicly by posting messages on AOL bulletin boards, where the messages may be read by any AOL subscriber.

The instant case comes before us on a motion for judgment on the pleadings, see Fed.R.Civ.P. 12(c), so we accept the facts alleged in the complaint as true. *Bruce v. Riddle,* 631 F.2d 272, 273 (4th Cir. 1980). On April 25, 1995, an unidentified person posted a message on an AOL bulletin board advertising "Naughty Oklahoma T-Shirts." The posting described the sale of shirts featuring offensive and tasteless slogans related to the April 19, 1995, bombing of the Alfred P. Murrah Federal Building in Oklahoma City. Those interested in purchasing the shirts were instructed to call "Ken" at Zeran's home phone number in Seattle, Washington. As a result of this anonymously perpetrated prank, Zeran received a high volume of calls, comprised primarily of angry and derogatory messages, but also including death threats. Zeran could not change his phone number because he relied on its availability to the public in running his business out of his home. Later that day, Zeran called AOL and informed a company representative of his predicament. The employee assured Zeran that the posting would be removed from AOL's bulletin board but explained that as a matter of policy AOL would not post a retraction. The parties dispute the date that AOL removed this original posting from its bulletin board.

On April 26, the next day, an unknown person posted another message advertising additional shirts with new tasteless slogans related to the Oklahoma City bombing. Again, interested buyers were told to call Zeran's phone number, to ask for "Ken," and to "please call back if busy" due to high demand. The angry, threatening phone calls intensified. Over the next four days, an unidentified party continued to post messages on AOL's bulletin board, advertising additional items including bumper stickers and key chains with still more offensive slogans. During this time period, Zeran called AOL repeatedly and was told by company representatives that the individual account from which the messages were posted would soon be closed. Zeran also reported his case to Seattle FBI agents. By April 30, Zeran was receiving an abusive phone call approximately every two minutes.

Meanwhile, an announcer for Oklahoma City radio station KRXO received a copy of the first AOL posting. On May 1, the announcer related the message's contents on the air, attributed them to "Ken" at Zeran's phone number, and urged the listening audience to call the number. After this radio broadcast, Zeran was inundated with death threats and other violent calls from Oklahoma City residents. Over the next few days, Zeran talked to both KRXO and AOL representatives. He also spoke to his local police, who subsequently surveilled his home to protect his safety. By May 14, after an Oklahoma City newspaper published a story exposing the shirt advertisements as a hoax and after KRXO made an on-air apology, the number of calls to Zeran's residence finally subsided to fifteen per day.

Zeran first filed suit on January 4, 1996, against radio station KRXO in the United States District Court for the Western District of Oklahoma. On April 23, 1996, he filed this separate suit against AOL in the same court. Zeran did not bring any action against the party who posted the offensive messages. After Zeran's suit against AOL was transferred to the Eastern District of Virginia pursuant to 28 U.S.C. § 1404(a), AOL answered Zeran's complaint and interposed 47 U.S.C. § 230 as an affirmative defense. AOL then moved for judgment on the pleadings pursuant to Fed.R.Civ.P. 12(c). The district court granted AOL's motion, and Zeran filed this appeal.

II.

A.

Because § 230 was successfully advanced by AOL in the district court as a defense to Zeran's claims, we shall briefly examine its operation here. Zeran seeks to hold AOL liable for defamatory speech initiated by a third party. He argued to the district court that once he notified AOL of the unidentified third party's hoax, AOL had a duty to remove the defamatory posting promptly, to notify its subscribers of the message's false nature, and to effectively screen future defamatory material. Section 230 entered this litigation as an affirmative defense pled by AOL. The company claimed that Congress immunized interactive computer service providers from claims based on information posted by a third party.

The relevant portion of § 230 states: "No provider or user of an interactive computer service shall be treated as the publisher or speaker of any information provided by another information content provider." 47 U.S.C. § 230(c)(1). By its plain language, § 230 creates a federal immunity to any cause of action that would make service providers liable for information originating with a third-party user of the service. Specifically, § 230 precludes courts from entertaining claims that would place a computer service provider in a publisher's role. Thus, lawsuits seeking to hold a service provider liable for its exercise of a publisher's traditional editorial functions—such as deciding whether to publish, withdraw, postpone or alter content—are barred.

The purpose of this statutory immunity is not difficult to discern. Congress recognized the threat that tort-based lawsuits pose to freedom of speech in the new and burgeoning Internet medium. The imposition of tort liability on service providers for the communications of others represented, for Congress, simply another form of intrusive government regulation of speech. Section 230 was enacted, in part, to maintain the robust nature of Internet communication and, accordingly, to keep government interference in the medium to a minimum. In specific statutory findings, Congress recognized the Internet and interactive computer services as offering "a forum for a true diversity of political discourse, unique opportunities for cultural development, and myriad avenues for intellectual activity." *Id.* § 230(a)(3). It also found that the Internet and interactive computer services "have flourished, to the benefit of all Americans, *with a minimum of government regulation.*" *Id.* § 230(a)(4) (emphasis added). Congress further stated that it is "the policy of the United States . . . to preserve the vibrant and competitive free market that presently exists for the Internet and other interactive computer services, *unfettered by Federal or State regulation.*" *Id.* § 230(b)(2) (emphasis added).

None of this means, of course, that the original culpable party who posts defamatory messages would escape accountability. While Congress acted to keep government regulation of the Internet to a minimum, it also found it to be the policy of the United States "to ensure vigorous enforcement of Federal criminal laws to deter and punish trafficking in obscenity, stalking, and harassment by means of computer." *Id.* § 230(b)(5). Congress made a policy choice, however, not to deter harmful online speech through the separate route of imposing tort liability on companies that serve as intermediaries for other parties' potentially injurious messages.

Congress' purpose in providing the § 230 immunity was thus evident. Interactive computer services have millions of users. *See Reno v. ACLU*, 521 U.S. at ---- (noting that at time of district court trial, "commercial online services had almost 12 million individual subscribers"). The amount of information communicated via interactive computer services is therefore staggering. The specter of tort liability in an area of such prolific speech would have an obvious chilling effect. It would be impossible for service providers to screen each of their millions of postings for possible problems. Faced with potential liability for each message republished by their services, interactive computer service providers might choose to severely restrict the number and type of messages posted. Congress considered the weight of the speech interests implicated and chose to immunize service providers to avoid any such restrictive effect.

Another important purpose of § 230 was to encourage service providers to self-regulate the dissemination of offensive material over their services. In this respect, § 230 responded to a New York state court decision, *Stratton Oakmont, Inc. v. Prodigy Servs. Co.*, 1995 WL 323710 (N.Y. Sup. Ct. May 24, 1995). There, the plaintiffs sued Prodigy—an interactive computer service like AOL—for defamatory comments made by an unidentified party on one of Prodigy's bulletin boards. The court held Prodigy to the strict liability standard normally applied to original publishers of defamatory statements, rejecting Prodigy's claims that it should be held only to the lower "knowledge" standard usually reserved for distributors. The court reasoned that Prodigy acted more like an original publisher than a distributor both because it advertised its practice of controlling content on its service and because it actively screened and edited messages posted on its bulletin boards.

Congress enacted § 230 to remove the disincentives to self regulation created by the *Stratton Oakmont* decision. Under that court's holding, computer service providers who regulated the dissemination of offensive material on their services risked subjecting themselves to liability, because such regulation cast the service provider in the role of a publisher. Fearing that the specter of liability would therefore deter service providers from blocking and screening offensive material, Congress enacted § 230's broad immunity "to remove disincentives for the development and utilization of blocking and filtering technologies that empower parents to restrict their children's access to objectionable or inappropriate online material." 47 U.S.C. § 230(b)(4). In line with this purpose, § 230 forbids the imposition of publisher liability on a service provider for the exercise of its editorial and self-regulatory functions.

B.

. . .

The terms "publisher" and "distributor" derive their legal significance from the context of defamation law. Although Zeran attempts to artfully plead his claims as ones of negligence, they are indistinguishable from a garden variety defamation action. Because the publication of a statement is a necessary element in a defamation action, only one who publishes can be subject to this form of tort liability. Restatement (Second) of Torts § 558(b) (1977); Keeton et al., *supra,* § 113, at 802. Publication does not only describe the choice by an author to include certain information. In addition, both the negligent communication of a defamatory statement and the failure to remove such a statement when first communicated by another party—each alleged by Zeran here under a negligence label—constitute publication. Restatement (Second) of Torts § 577; *see also Tacket v. General Motors Corp.,* 836 F.2d 1042, 1046-47 (7th Cir. 1987). In fact, every repetition of a defamatory statement is considered a publication. Keeton et al., *supra,* § 113, at 799.

In this case, AOL is legally considered to be a publisher. "[E]very one who takes part in the publication . . . is charged with publication." *Id.* Even distributors are considered to be publishers for purposes of defamation law:

> Those who are in the business of making their facilities available to disseminate the writings composed, the

> speeches made, and the information gathered by others may also be regarded as participating to such an extent in making the books, newspapers, magazines, and information available to others as to be regarded as publishers. They are intentionally making the contents available to others, sometimes without knowing all of the contents—including the defamatory content—and sometimes without any opportunity to ascertain, in advance, that any defamatory matter was to be included in the matter published. *Id.* at 803. AOL falls squarely within this traditional definition of a publisher and, therefore, is clearly protected by § 230's immunity.

. . .

It is undoubtedly true that mere conduits, or distributors, are subject to a different standard of liability. As explained above, distributors must at a minimum have knowledge of the existence of a defamatory statement as a prerequisite to liability. But this distinction signifies only that different standards of liability may be applied *within* the larger publisher category, depending on the specific type of publisher concerned. *See* Keeton et al., *supra,* § 113, at 799-800 (explaining that every party involved is charged with publication, although degrees of legal responsibility differ). To the extent that decisions like *Stratton* and *Cubby* utilize the terms "publisher" and "distributor" separately, the decisions correctly describe two different standards of liability. *Stratton* and *Cubby* do not, however, suggest that distributors are not also a type of publisher for purposes of defamation law.

. . .

The simple fact of notice surely cannot transform one from an original publisher to a distributor in the eyes of the law. To the contrary, once a computer service provider receives notice of a potentially defamatory posting, it is thrust into the role of a traditional publisher. The computer service provider must decide whether to publish, edit, or withdraw the posting. In this respect, Zeran seeks to impose liability on AOL for assuming the role for which § 230 specifically proscribes liability—the publisher role.

Our view that Zeran's complaint treats AOL as a publisher is reinforced because AOL is cast in the same position as the party who originally posted the offensive messages. According to Zeran's logic, AOL is legally at fault because it communicated to third parties an allegedly defamatory statement. This is precisely the theory under which the original poster of the offensive messages would be found liable. If the original party is considered a publisher of the offensive messages, Zeran certainly cannot attach liability to AOL under the same theory without conceding that AOL too must be treated as a publisher of the statements.

. . .

If computer service providers were subject to distributor liability, they would face potential liability each time they receive notice of a potentially defamatory statement—from any party, concerning any message. Each notification would require a careful yet rapid investigation of the circumstances surrounding the posted information, a legal judgment concerning the information's defamatory character, and an on-the-spot editorial decision whether to risk liability by allowing the continued publication of that information. Although this might be feasible for the traditional print publisher, the sheer number of postings on interactive computer services would create an impossible burden in the Internet context. *Cf. Auvil v. CBS 60 Minutes,* 800 F.Supp. 928, 931 (E.D.Wash.1992) (recognizing that it is unrealistic for network affiliates to "monitor incoming transmissions and exercise on-the-spot discretionary calls"). Because service providers would be subject to liability only for the publication of information, and not for its removal, they would have a natural incentive simply to remove messages upon notification, whether the contents were defamatory or not. *See Philadelphia Newspapers, Inc. v. Hepps,* 475 U.S. 767, 777 (1986) (recognizing that fears of unjustified liability produce a chilling effect antithetical to First Amendment's protection of speech). Thus, like strict liability, liability upon notice has a chilling effect on the freedom of Internet speech.

Similarly, notice-based liability would deter service providers from regulating the dissemination of offensive material over their own services. Any efforts by a service provider to investigate and screen material posted on its service would only lead to notice of potentially defamatory material more frequently and thereby create a stronger basis for liability. Instead of subjecting themselves to further possible lawsuits, service providers would likely eschew any attempts at self-regulation.

More generally, notice-based liability for interactive computer service providers would provide third parties with a no-cost means to create the basis for future lawsuits. Whenever one was displeased with the speech of another party conducted over an interactive computer service, the offended party could simply "notify" the relevant service provider, claiming the information to be legally defamatory. In light of the vast amount of speech communicated through interactive computer services, these notices could produce an impossible burden for service providers, who would be faced with ceaseless choices of suppressing controversial speech or sustaining prohibitive liability. Because the probable effects of distributor liability on the vigor of Internet speech and on service provider self-regulation are directly contrary to § 230's statutory purposes, we will not assume that Congress intended to leave liability upon notice intact. . . .

Section 230 represents the approach of Congress to a problem of national and international dimension. The Supreme Court underscored this point in *Reno v. ACLU,* finding that the Internet allows "tens of millions of people to communicate with one another and to access vast amounts of information from around the world.[It] is 'a unique and wholly new medium of worldwide human communication.'" 521 U.S. at ----. Application of the canon invoked by Zeran here would significantly lessen Congress' power, derived from the Commerce Clause, to act in a field whose international character is apparent. While Congress allowed for the enforcement of "any State law that is consistent with [§ 230]," 47 U.S.C. § 230(d)(3), it is equally plain that Congress' desire to promote unfettered speech on the Internet must supersede conflicting common law causes of action. Section 230(d)(3) continues: "No cause of action may be brought and no liability may be imposed under any State or local law that is inconsistent with this section." With respect to federal-state preemption, the Court has advised: "[W]hen Congress has 'unmistakably . . . ordained,' that its enactments alone are to regulate a part of commerce, state laws regulating that aspect of commerce must fall. The result is compelled whether Congress' command is explicitly stated in the statute's language or implicitly contained in its structure and purpose." *Jones v. Rath Packing Co.,* 430 U.S. 519, 525 (1977). Here, Congress' command is explicitly stated. Its exercise of its commerce power is clear and counteracts the caution counseled by the interpretive canon favoring retention of common law principles.

IV.
For the foregoing reasons, we affirm the judgment of the district court.

AFFIRMED.

Net Neutrality

For the vast majority of us, the notion of a "free and open" Internet is sacrosanct. Since the early 1990s, we have grown accustomed—some would say reliant—on the World Wide Web to do our banking, file taxes, book flights and hotels, and buy merchandise. We also increasingly turn to the Internet for a wide range of entertainment, including live streaming of programming on Hulu, Netflix and HBO Go, and social networking on Facebook, Pinterest, and Twitter. These many Internet "destinations" reside in what is known as the "cloud"—the rapidly expanding array of information and applications that can only be accessed through an Internet user's remote connection. Many users have come to expect that they can surf the Web freely, accessing cloud applications without being blocked or slowed by their Internet service providers (ISPs). These users believe that they should be able to go to any site in the cloud, even if that site uses huge amounts of data or competes with an ISP's preferred site.

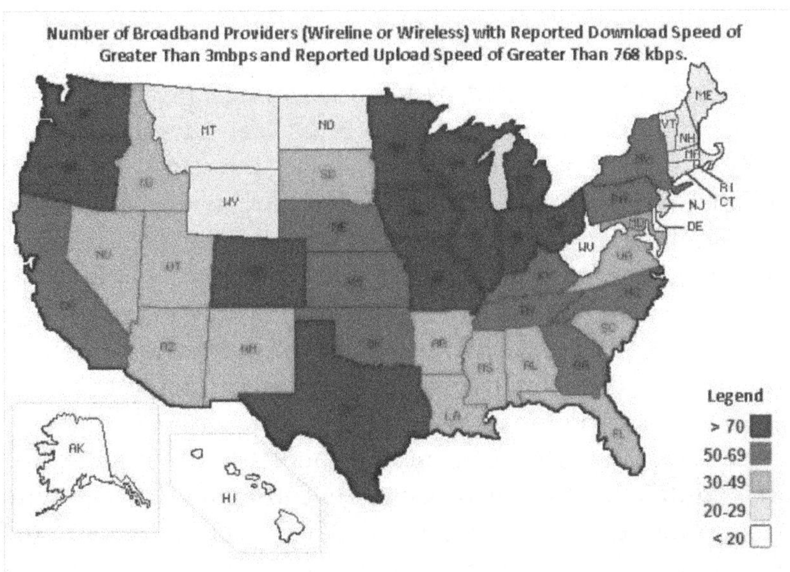

Net neutrality is about access speed and competition. This map illustrates the number of providers (in 2013) offering a download speed of greater than three megabits per second (Mbps) and an upload speed of greater than 768 kilobytes per second (Kbps). U.S. Broadband Statistics Report, 2014.

The ISPs, however, see the issue from a very different perspective. Most ISPs, like AT&T and Comcast, are private companies that offer Internet connections for a fee. Unlike a public utility, these companies paid to build their connection infrastructure, and they believe they have the right to recoup their investment by charging cloud applications for access to their customers or for a faster connection. For the ISPs, net neutrality costs them money because "data-hogging" streaming sites like Netflix or Facebook benefit from improved "broadband" connections but do not pay for those improvements. ISPs, in short, believe streaming sites should pay for their access to the connection pipeline, just as consumers pay. ISPs also believe that they should have the right to contract with a cloud application for preferred service, which would allow for the prospect that a bookseller like barnesandnoble.com could pay to direct consumers to its own site instead of amazon.com.

After a Comcast customer discovered that his broadband connection to a BitTorrent streaming site was being slowed deliberately, the issue of net neutrality blossomed into a major policy debate among ISPs, application Web sites, politicians, and consumers. The FCC's early efforts to regulate Internet traffic were rebuffed in the DC Circuit on jurisdictional grounds, since the FCC had not, at that point, classified Internet access as a "telecommunications service," which would have allowed ISPs to be regulated as common carriers under the Communications Act. Comcast Corp. v. FCC, 600 F.3d 642 (D.C. Cir. 2010). In December 2010, the FCC released its Open Internet Order, which, among other things, prohibited ISPs from blocking or otherwise discriminating against Web sites and cloud applications, including, for mobile phone ISPs, interfaces like Skype or FaceTime that compete with phone service. Preserving the Open Internet, Report and Order, 25 FCC Rcd. 17905 (2010). The DC Circuit largely struck down these rules in January 2014, citing the FCC's lack of statutory authority to impose common carrier regulations on entities not classified as common carriers. The Court, however, left open the possibility that, with proper reclassification, the FCC could develop Internet regulations. The opinion also settled the jurisdictional issue in the FCC's favor, ruling that section 706 of the 1996 Telecommunications Act "vests the FCC with affirmative authority to enact measures encouraging the deployment of broadband infrastructure." Verizon v. FCC, 740 F.3d 623 (D.C. Cir. 2014). Empowered by judicial support, the FCC quickly undertook to revisit the issue of net neutrality, proposing—and seeking comment on—a middle ground that would prohibit blocking but allow ISPs to negotiate "commercially reasonable" agreements to charge Web sites for faster connection speeds.

In May 2014, the FCC released a Notice of Proposed Rule Making, which used this commercially reasonable approach to implement tiered speeds for Internet users. Faced with a deluge of concern from consumers and cloud applications, and at the specific urging of President Obama, the

FCC, in early 2015, signaled that it was ready to abandon its 2014 Open Internet proposal. On February 26, 2015, the FCC adopted a new Report and Order with bright line rules that rejected the commercially reasonable approach and defined broadband as a "telecommunications service," making it subject to common carrier regulation under Title II of the Communications Act. In this "Title II Order," mobile and home broadband providers were prohibited from selectively slowing or blocking connections to websites and from entering into "paid prioritization" contracts that increase ISP traffic to favored sites. At the same time, the FCC, exercising its forbearance authority, exempted broadband providers from pricing regulations that would otherwise apply under Title II. Broadband providers could charge what they want, but their services could not be discriminatory. These new rules were upheld in U.S. Telecom Assoc. v. FCC, 825 F.3d 674 (D.C. Cir. 2016).

With the start of the Trump presidency in 2017, a Republican-controlled FCC announced its intention to roll back the Title II Order. In May 2017, the FCC issued a new Notice of Proposed Rule Making that would restore the regulatory landscape to where it had been in 2010, before the FCC began to take its interim steps toward non-discriminatory web access.

BEFORE THE FCC
WASHINGTON, D.C. 20554

	)	
In the Matter of	)	
Restoring Internet Freedom	)	WC Docket No. 17-108
	)	
	)	

NOTICE OF PROPOSED RULEMAKING

Adopted: May 18, 2017 **Released: May 23, 2017**

Comment Date: July 17, 2017

Reply Comment Date: August 16, 2017

1. Americans cherish a free and open Internet. And for almost twenty years, the Internet flourished under a light-touch regulatory approach. It was a framework that our nation's elected leaders put in place on a bipartisan basis. President Clinton and a Republican Congress passed the Telecommunications Act of 1996, which established the policy of the United States "to preserve the vibrant and competitive free market that presently exists for the Internet . . . unfettered by Federal or State regulation."

2. During this time, the Internet underwent rapid, and unprecedented, growth. Internet service providers (ISPs) invested over $1.5 trillion in the Internet ecosystem and American consumers enthusiastically responded. Businesses developed in ways that the policy makers could not have fathomed even a decade ago. Google, Facebook, Netflix, and countless other online businesses launched in this country and became worldwide success stories. The Internet became an ever-increasing part of the American economy, offering new and innovative changes in how we work, learn, receive medical care, and entertain ourselves.

3. But two years ago, the FCC changed course. It decided to apply utility-style regulation to the Internet. This decision represented a massive and unprecedented shift in favor of government control of the Internet.

4. The Commission's *Title II Order* has put at risk online investment and innovation, threatening the very open Internet it purported to preserve. Investment in broadband networks declined. Internet service providers have pulled back on plans to deploy new and upgraded infrastructure and services to consumers...

22. [In February 2015] the Commission adopted the *Title II Order*, reclassifying broadband Internet access services from information services to telecommunications services. In doing so, the Commission found it necessary to forbear from enforcing the "vast majority of rules adopted under Title II," including "30 statutory provisions[,]" and to render "over 700 codified rules inapplicable." The Commission adopted no-blocking, no-throttling, and no-paid-prioritization rules, as well as a general Internet conduct standard and "enhancements" to the transparency rule. In 2016, a divided panel of the D.C. Circuit Court of Appeals upheld the *Title II Order* in *United States Telecom Ass'n v. FCC*, with the D.C. Circuit denying petitions for rehearing of the case *en banc*.

. . . .

24. Today, we propose to reinstate the information service classification of broadband Internet access service and return to the light-touch regulatory framework first established on a bipartisan basis during the Clinton Administration. We also propose to reinstate the determination that mobile broadband Internet access service is not a commercial mobile service.

....

[I. Ending Regulation of Broadband as a Public Utility]

25. Our proposal to classify broadband Internet access service as an information service is based on a number of factors. First, we examine the text, structure, and history of the Communications Act and the Telecommunications Act, combined with the technical details of how the Internet works. Second, we examine Commission precedent. Third, we examine public policy and our goal of benefiting consumers through greater innovation, investment, and competition. We seek comment on our proposals and these analyses....

26. We start with the text of the Act itself. Section 3 of the Act defines an "information service" as "the offering of a capability for generating, acquiring, storing, transforming, processing, retrieving, utilizing, or making available information via telecommunications, and includes electronic publishing, but does not include any use of any such capability for the management, control, or operation of a telecommunications system or the management of a telecommunications service." Section 3 defines a "telecommunications service" as "the offering of telecommunications for a fee directly to the public, or to such classes of users as to be effectively available directly to the public, regardless of the facilities used." Section 3 also defines "telecommunications," used in each of the prior two definitions, as "the transmission, between or among points specified by the user, of information of the user's choosing, without change in the form or content of the information as sent and received.

27. We believe that Internet service providers offer the "capability for generating, acquiring, storing, transforming, processing, retrieving, utilizing, or making available information via telecommunications." Whether posting on social media or drafting a blog, a broadband Internet user is able to generate and make available information online. Whether reading a newspaper's website or browsing the results from a search engine, a broadband Internet user is able to acquire and retrieve infor-

mation online. Whether it's an address book or a grocery list, a broadband Internet user is able to store and utilize information online. Whether uploading filtered photographs or translating text into a foreign language, a broadband Internet user is able to transform and process information online. In short, broadband Internet access service appears to offer its users the "capability" to perform each and every one of the functions listed in the definition—and accordingly appears to be an information service by definition. We seek comment on this analysis. Can broadband Internet users indeed access these capabilities? Are there other capabilities that a broadband Internet user may receive with service? If broadband Internet access service does not afford one of the listed capabilities to users, what effect would that have on our statutory analysis? More fundamentally, we seek comment on how the Commission should assess whether a broadband provider is "offering" a capability. Should we assess this from the perspective of the user, from the provider, or through some other lens?

28. … The definition of "information service" speaks to the "capability" to perform certain functions. Is a consumer capable of accessing these online services without Internet access service? Could a consumer access these online services using traditional telecommunications services like telephone service or point-to-point special access? Or are we correct that offering Internet access is precisely what makes the service capable of "generating, acquiring, storing, transforming, processing, retrieving, utilizing, or making available information" to consumers?

29. In contrast, Internet service providers do not appear to offer "telecommunications," i.e., "the transmission, between or among points specified by the user, of information of the user's choosing, without change in the form or content of the information as sent and received," to their users. *For one*, broadband Internet users do not typically specify the "points" between and among which information is sent online. Instead, routing decisions are based on the architecture of the network, not on consumers' instructions, and consumers are often unaware of where online content is stored. Domain names must be translated into IP addresses (and there is no one-to-one correspondence between the two). Even IP addresses may not specify where information is transmitted to or from because caching servers store and serve popular information to reduce network loads. In short, broadband Internet users are paying for the access to information "with no knowledge of the physical location of the server where that information resides."….

33. The structure of Title II appears to be a poor fit for broadband Internet access service. In the *Title II Order*, the Commission, on its own motion, forbore either in whole or in part on a permanent or temporary basis from 30 separate sections of Title II as well as from other provisions of the Act and Commission rules. The significant forbearance the Commission granted in the *Title II Order* suggests the highly prescriptive regulatory framework of Title II is unsuited for the dynamic broadband Internet access service marketplace. We seek comment on this analysis, and on what weight we should give this analysis in examining the future of this model of regulation.

34. The purposes of the Telecommunications Act appear to be better served by classifying broadband Internet access service as an information service. Congress passed the Telecommunications Act to "promote competition and reduce regulation" and "[n]othing in the 1996 Act or its legislative history suggests that Congress intended to alter the current classification of Internet and other information services or to expand traditional telephone regulation to new and advanced services."....

39. We believe the Commission under Democratic and Republican leadership alike was correct in these decisions to classify broadband Internet access service as an information service and that, 20 years after the passage of the Telecommunications Act, we should be reluctant to second-guess the interpretations of those more likely to understand the contemporary meaning of the terms of the Telecommunications Act. We seek comment on our assessment. Did the Commission's historical information service classification better enable flexibility in marketplace offerings? Did the regulatory certainty of maintaining the same regulatory environment for approximately three decades (since the *Computer Inquiries*) foster additional investment or innovative business models to benefit consumers? How should we evaluate the prior Commissions' predictions of intermodal competition given the 4,559 Internet service providers now in the market? How many providers would likely have entered the market if traditional Title II regulation had been the norm? What actual harms, if any, resulted from light-touch regulation?

[II. Public Policy Concerns]

44. The Commission's decision to reclassify broadband Internet access service as a telecommunications service subject to Title II regulation has resulted in negative consequences for American consumers—including depressed broadband investment and reduced innovation because of

increased regulatory burdens and regulatory uncertainty stemming from the rules adopted under Title II. As providers have devoted more resources to complying with new regulations, the threat of regulatory enforcement of vague rules and standards has dampened providers' incentive to invest and innovate. Additionally, although reclassifying broadband Internet access service as a telecommunications service has led to significant regulatory burdens, it has not solved any discrete, identifiable problems. Restoring broadband Internet access service to its previous status as an information service subject to Title I is in the public interest because it will alleviate the harms caused by Title II reclassification....

47. We also seek specific comment on how the classification of broadband Internet access service as a telecommunications service has impacted smaller broadband Internet access service providers, many of whom lack the dedicated compliance staffs and financial resources of the nation's largest providers. Before the Commission adopted the *Title II Order*, many small providers made it clear that reclassification would harm their businesses and the customers they serve. Since reclassification, small providers—including non-profit, municipal ISPs—have been forced to reduce their investment and halt the expansion of their networks, and slow, if not delay, the development and deployment of innovative new offerings. For example, one small ISP had planned to "triple the number of new base stations" that would be deployed each month to provide fixed wireless broadband service to new customers, but put those plans on hold as a result of the Commission's reclassification. Other small providers have had to modify or abandon altogether past business models to account for increased compliance costs and depressed investment from outside investors. This depressed investment has had particularly strong impacts on the deployment of broadband to previously unserved and rural areas. What other impacts have small providers felt as a result of reclassification? Have there been any corresponding benefits for small providers?

48. In addition to imposing significant regulatory costs on Internet service providers, Title II reclassification created significant regulatory uncertainty. USTelecom specifically identified "regulatory uncertainty" as one of the causes of reduced investment. Regulatory uncertainty may have particularly significant effects on small Internet service providers, which may be poorly equipped to address the legal, technical, and financial burdens associated with an uncertain regulatory environment. That

uncertainty has directly led to reduced investment, which has harmed consumers....

[III. Administrative Authority]

53. An agency also is free to change its approach to interpreting and implementing a statute so long as it acknowledges that it is doing so and justifies the new approach. Evaluating the change in regulatory approach in the *Title II Order*, the D.C. Circuit majority in *USTelecom* applied a "highly deferential standard" to the agency's predictive judgments regarding the investment effects of reclassification, and deferred to the Commission's "'evaluat[ion of] complex market conditions'" underlying its rejection of providers' reliance interests in the prior classification. D.C. Circuit precedent also recognizes, however, that should the Commission's predictions "prove erroneous, the Commission will need to reconsider" the associated regulatory actions "in accordance with its continuing obligation to practice reasoned decision-making." We believe that the Commission's predictions and expectations regarding broadband investment and the nature and effects of reclassification on the operation of the marketplace were mistaken and have not been borne out by subsequent events. Moreover, we believe that a restoration of the information service classification for broadband Internet access service is likely to increase infrastructure investment. In such a case, principles of administrative law give us more than ample latitude to revisit our approach....

[IV. Deregulatory Framework]

70. ... To determine how to best honor our commitment to restoring the free and open Internet, we propose re-evaluating the Commission's existing rules and enforcement regime to analyze whether *ex ante* regulatory intervention in the market is necessary....

71. Below, we explore the best method to restore the long-standing consensus under both Democratic and Republican-led Commissions, represented by the four Internet Freedoms, that consumers should have access to the content, applications, and devices of their choosing as well as meaningful information about their service, all without deterring the investment and innovation that has allowed the Internet to flourish. We examine these freedoms and the Commission's current rules related to them, and for each, ask whether we should keep, modify, or eliminate them.

72. *[Eliminating the Internet Conduct Standard.]* In the *Title II Order*, the Commission created a catch-all standard intended to prohibit "current or future practices that cause the type of harms [the Commission's] rules are intended to address." This standard allows the Commission to prohibit practices that it determines unreasonably interfere with or unreasonably disadvantage the ability of consumers to reach the Internet content, services, and applications of their choosing or of online content, applications, and service providers to access consumers. This standard also gives the Commission discretion to prohibit any Internet service provider practice that it believes violates any one of the non-exhaustive list of factors adopted in the *Title II Order*....

74. Because the Internet conduct standard is premised on theoretical problems that will be adjudicated on an individual, case-by-case basis, Internet service providers must guess at what they are permitted and not permitted to do. The now-retracted so-called Zero Rating Report issued by the Wireless Telecommunications Bureau illustrates the dilemma providers experience under a Title II regulatory regime. After a thirteen-month investigation, the Report did not specifically call for an end to any provider's practices or identify any particular harm from offering consumers free data. Instead, it stated that the free-data plans "may raise" economic and public policy issues that "may harm consumers and competition." It then reiterated that any determination about the harm from free data offerings would be made by the Commission on a "case-by-case" basis, using a "non-exhaustive list of factors." Instead of giving providers clear rules of the road to govern future conduct, this report put a provider on notice that an enforcement action could be just around the corner. The Report, and the investigation that preceded it, left Internet service providers with two options: either wait for a regulatory enforcement action that could arrive at some unspecified future point or stop providing consumers with innovative offerings. We seek comment on whether this roving mandate has impacted innovation, and what impact that has had on consumers. We seek comment on whether eliminating this vague standard will spur innovation and benefit consumers.

75. We propose not to adopt any alternatives to the Internet conduct rule, and we seek comment on this proposal. Is there a need for any general non-discrimination standard in today's Internet marketplace? If so, what would that general non-discrimination standard be? The *2014 Notice* proposed prohibiting "commercially unreasonable practices." Should we consider that alternative? Or should we consider another general rule

and framework (such as Commission adjudication of non-discrimination complaints)? If we adopt our proposals to eliminate the Internet conduct standard and not to adopt any alternative general requirement, we seek comment on how we can encourage innovative business models that give consumers more choices and lower prices while also promoting consumer freedom on the Internet....

81. We seek comment on the continuing need for a no-blocking rule. The no-blocking rule, originally adopted in 2010, invalidated by the *Verizon* court, and re-adopted in the *Title II Order*, prohibits Internet service providers from blocking competitors' content by mandating that a customer has a right to access lawful content, applications, services, and to use non-harmful devices, subject to reasonable network management.

82. If we determine that a no-blocking rule is indeed necessary to ensure a free, open, and dynamic Internet, what are the best means to achieve this outcome consistent with the goals of maintaining Internet freedom and maximizing investment? Should we consider modifying the existing no-blocking rule to better align with our proposed legal classification of broadband Internet access service as an information service? The *Verizon* court made clear that the Commission's 2010 no-blocking rule impermissibly subjected Internet service providers to common-carriage regulation. We seek comment on whether there are other formulations of a no-blocking rule that are consistent with our proposed legal classification of broadband Internet access service as an information service and for which we would have legal authority.

83. *Need for the No-Throttling Rule.* In the *Title II Order*, the Commission concluded that throttling was a sufficiently severe and distinct threat that it required its own, separate, codified rule. The no-throttling rule mirrors the no-blocking rule and bans the impairment or degradation of lawful Internet traffic or use of a non-harmful device, subject to reasonable network management practices. We seek comment on whether this rule is still necessary, particularly for smaller providers. How does the rule benefit consumers, and what are its costs? When is "throttling" harmful to consumers? Does the no-throttling rule prevent providers from offering broadband Internet access service with differentiated prioritization that benefits consumers? Does the no-throttling rule harm latency-sensitive applications and content? Does it prevent product differentiation among ISPs? If we eliminate the no-blocking rule, should we also eliminate the no-throttling rule? If we determine that a no-throttling rule is indeed necessary to ensure a free, open, and dynamic Internet, are

there ways in which we could modify the no-throttling rule so it aligns with our proposed legal classification of broadband Internet access service as an information service and for which we would have legal authority?

84. The Commission justified the separate, codified no-throttling rule on the theory of preventing anti-competitive behavior for broadband Internet access providers' affiliated content. With the existence of antitrust and other regulations aimed at curbing collusion, we seek comment on whether a no-throttling rule is duplicative of these other regulatory regimes. Could the continued existence of this rule negatively impact future innovative, pro-competitive business deals that would not by themselves run afoul of merger conditions or established antitrust law?

85. *Need for the No Paid Prioritization Rule.* The Commission concluded in the *Title II Order* that "fast lanes" or "paid prioritization" practices "harm consumers, competition, and innovation, as well as create disincentives to promote broadband deployment." The Commission adopted this *ex ante* flat ban on individual negotiations to address an apparently nonexistent problem. The ban on paid prioritization did not exist prior to the *Title II Order* and even then the record evidence confirmed that no such rule was needed since several large Internet service providers made it clear that that they did not engage in paid prioritization and had no plans to do so. We seek comment on the continued need for such a rule and our authority to retain it.

86. What are the trade-offs in banning business models dependent on paid prioritization versus allowing them to occur when overseen by a regulator or industry actors? Is there a risk that banning paid prioritization suppresses pro-competitive activity? For example, could allowing paid prioritization give Internet service providers a supplemental revenue stream that would enable them to offer lower-priced broadband Internet access service to end-users? What would be the impacts on new startups and innovation? Does a no-paid-prioritization rule harm the development of real-time or interactive services? Could allowing paid prioritization enable certain critical information, such as consumers' health care vital signs that are being monitored remotely, to be transmitted more efficiently or reliably?...

123. Accordingly, IT IS ORDERED that, pursuant to sections 3, 10, 201(b), 230, 254(e), 303(r), and 332 of the Communications Act of 1934, as amended, and section 706 of the Telecommunications Act of 1996, as amended,

47 U.S.C. §§ 153, 160, 201(b), 254(e), 303(r), 332, 1302, this Notice of Proposed Rulemaking IS ADOPTED.

124. IT IS FURTHER ORDERED that pursuant to applicable procedures set forth in Sections 1.415 and 1.419 of the Commission's Rules, 47 CFR §§ 1.415, 1.419, interested parties may file comments on this Notice of Proposed Rulemaking on or before July 17, 2017 and reply comments on or before August 16, 2017.

NOTES AND QUESTIONS

1. In Blumenthal v. Drudge, 992 F. Supp. 44, 49-53 (D.D.C. 1998), a federal district court ruled that America Online (AOL) was immune from liability for a defamatory posting authored by muckraker Matt Drudge. Though Drudge was working under contract with AOL, the court ruled that he was nonetheless a third-party poster under section 230. The court did not consider theories of agency liability in reaching its decision. Should it have?
2. In the years since the *Zeran* decision, courts have expanded section 230 to provide blanket immunity for liability to Web sites for any injury caused by third-party postings, including uploads of child pornography, Doe v. America Online, 783 So. 2d 1010 (Fl. 2001); escort solicitations, Dart v. Craigslist, Inc., 665 F. Supp. 2d 961 (N.D. Ill. 2009); and an employee's threatening posts, Delfino v. Agilent Technologies, 52 Cal. Rptr. 3d 376 (2006). Do you think this is what Congress intended when it passed section 230?
3. Recently, a few courts have begun to limit section 230's applicability. In Fair Housing Council of San Fernando Valley v. Roommates.com, 521 F.3d 1157 (9th Cir. 2008), the court, en banc, ruled that a roommate-matching Web site could be held liable for housing discrimination under the Fair Housing Act since its drop-down search menu and results fields contained options that discriminated on the basis of gender and sexual orientation. Craigslist, however, was found to be immune from liability under section 230 for discriminatory roommate ads posted by third parties on its Web site. Chicago Lawyers' Committee for Civil Rights Under Law, Inc. v. Craigslist, Inc. 519 F.3d 666 (7th Cir. 2008).
4. Section 230(e)(2) expressly excludes immunity for postings that infringe intellectual property rights. Indeed, under the 1998 Digital Millennium Copyright Act, 17 U.S.C. § 512(c), Web sites, upon notice

by a copyright holder, must take down infringing posts to avoid potential liability for infringement. Thus, today, if a third-party poster had violated Zeran's copyright, AOL would likely take down the posts quickly once they were given notice. Is it fair that Congress allows copyright holders to enforce their rights online but prevents tort victims from suing for their injuries?

5. In the *Reno* case supra, Justice Stevens concludes that "the Internet is not 'invasive' as radio or television," since users would be unlikely to see sexually explicit images by accident. Do you agree? Which is more intrusive to the home, an Internet-connected computer in a child's bedroom or a bedside radio?
6. Since Internet speech cannot be narrowly tailored through time-channeling, even a carefully devised indecency statute may fail strict scrutiny. Justice O'Connor, in her *Reno* concurrence, suggests that "cyber-zoning," the virtual segregation of adult content sites, might be the answer. Is this a workable solution? In 2011, the Internet Corporation for Assigned Names and Numbers (ICANN), which is the organization that oversees Web domain names, rolled out ".xxx" as a top-level domain alternative to ".com." However, it has not been widely adopted by adult entertainment providers. If you operated an adult Web site, would you want to move your business to ".xxx"? Would it better to zone children's sites to ".kids," as some propose?
7. **The Future of the Internet.** In May 2017, comedian John Oliver used his platform as host of HBO's *Last Week Tonight* to criticize the FCC's circulation of its tentative "Restoring Internet Freedom" NPRM. In addition to rebutting many of the underlying assumptions of the NPRM, Oliver sought to mobilize the public in opposition to the Net Neutality roll-back. Oliver's website, www.gofccyourself.com, directed so many anti-roll-back commenters to the FCC's official comment site, the agency's server had to shut down temporarily.

CHAPTER 14

COMMERCIAL SPEECH & ADVERTISING

Commercial Speech Generally

Speech is generally considered to be commercial when it is directed at inducing a business transaction such as the sale of a product or service. Even so, the contours of what is considered commercial speech by the courts can be nebulous—is, for example, a corporation's ad to defend itself from sweatshop allegations commercial or non-commercial? This threshold question is important because commercial speech is treated differently from non-commercial speech under the First Amendment. In 1942, the U.S. Supreme Court, in Valentine v. Chrestensen ruled that advertising did not merit First Amendment protection. Justice William O. Douglas, writing for the majority, declared that it is "clear that the Constitution imposes no such restraint on government as respects purely commercial advertising."

Beginning in the 1970s, the Supreme Court has retreated from its absolute disavowal of First Amendment protection for commercial speech. In Virginia State Board of Pharmacy v. Virginia Citizens Consumers Council, the Court determined that a Virginia law that prevented pharmacists from advertising drug prices was unconstitutional. In 1980, the Court developed a four-part test to determine if a commercial speech regulation runs afoul of the First Amendment. This test, in the *Central Hudson* case infra, is still in use today, although it has substantially evolved over the last three decades. Much of commercial speech jurisprudence focuses on so-called vices, including liquor sales, casino gambling, and lotteries and contests, the latter two of which are of particular interest to broadcasters.

Lotteries and Contests

For decades, the FCC strictly prohibited broadcasting lotteries on radio and television. The origin of this ban dates to the 1930s, when crime syndicates regularly operated "numbers rackets"—schemes in which people placed bets in the (often false) hope of winning a prize. In part to prevent numbers racketeers from accessing the airwaves, Congress passed 18 U.S.C.A §1304 infra, making it a crime to broadcast advertisements concerning a lottery. Communications Act sections 312(a)(6), 312(b), and 503(b)(1)(E) of 1934 also direct the FCC to revoke licenses or fine broadcasters who violate §1304.

To be a lottery, there must be "chance, consideration, and a prize." All three must be present for a broadcaster to violate §1304. If all three are not present, then the game is considered a contest. Contests are commonly undertaken by broadcasters, although they are subject to strict disclosure and accuracy requirements under FCC regulations, also infra. In most cases, broadcast licensees and sponsors comply with §1304's ban by removing the consideration element. This is the reason that the phrase "no purchase necessary" almost always appears in a sweepstakes' terms and conditions. If there is an entry fee for a competition, some sponsors will devise it as a game of skill, although combinations of skill and luck (like, for example, a Scrabble or poker tournament) are subject to review by the FCC.

18 U.S.C.A. § 1304: Broadcasting lottery information

Whoever broadcasts by means of any radio or television station for which a license is required by any law of the United States, or whoever, operating any such station, knowingly permits the broadcasting of, any advertisement of or information concerning any lottery, gift enterprise, or similar scheme, offering prizes dependent in whole or in part upon lot or chance, or any list of the prizes drawn or awarded by means of any such lottery, gift enterprise, or scheme, whether said list contains any part or all of such prizes, shall be fined under this title or imprisoned not more than one year, or both.

Each day's broadcasting shall constitute a separate offense.

47 C.F.R. § 73.1216: Licensee-conducted contests

A licensee that broadcasts or advertises information about a contest it conducts shall fully and accurately disclose the material terms of the contest, and shall conduct the contest substantially as announced or advertised. No contest description shall be false, misleading or deceptive with respect to any material term.
Note 1: For the purposes of this rule:

(a) A contest is a scheme in which a prize is offered or awarded, based upon chance, diligence, knowledge or skill, to members of the public.

(b) Material terms include those factors which define the operation of the contest and which affect participation therein. Although the material terms may vary widely depending upon the exact nature of the contest, they will generally include: how to enter or participate; eligibility restrictions; entry deadline dates; whether prizes can be won; when prizes can be won; the extent, nature and value of prizes; basis for valuation of prizes; time and means of selection of winners; and/or tie-breaking procedures.

Note 2: In general, the time and manner of disclosure of the material terms of a contest are within the licensee's discretion. However, the obligation to disclose the material terms arises at the time the audience is first told how to enter or participate and continues thereafter. The material terms should be disclosed periodically by announcements broadcast on the station conducting the contest, but need not be enumerated each time an announcement promoting the contest is broadcast. Disclosure of material terms in a reasonable number of announcements is sufficient. In addition to the required broadcast announcements, disclosure of the material terms may be made in a non-broadcast manner.

Note 3: This rule is not applicable to licensee-conducted contests not broadcast or advertised to the general public or to a substantial segment thereof, to contests in which the general public is not requested or permitted to participate, to the commercial advertisement of non-licensee-conducted contests, or to a contest conducted by a non-broadcast division of the licensee or by a non-broadcast company related to the licensee.

Commercial Speech and Advertising

In 1988, Congress passed the Charity Games Advertising Clarification Act, allowing the broadcast of lotteries sponsored by nonprofit organizations. Congress has since relaxed the ban for state-sponsored lotteries and for American Indian casino gambling. These federal exceptions to the § 1304 ban, and others, were an issue for the U.S. Supreme Court in the *Greater New Orleans Broadcasting* case infra. States remain free to regulate lottery ads, as this is one of the few content-related areas not preempted by federal law. The preemption issue is relevant to the Supreme Court's holding in U.S. v. Edge, also infra.

Both the *Greater New Orleans* and *Edge* cases apply the four-part commercial speech test devised by the Supreme Court in Central Hudson v. Public Service Commission of New York (1980). *Central Hudson* is not about gambling or other vices, although it is now also invoked in cases involving vice-related advertisements. As a general matter, *Central Hudson's* test is used by courts to determine if a government commercial-speech regulation violates a speaker's First Amendment rights. Note that the test's fourth prong, originally a "least restrictive" standard, was modified to a "reasonable fit" standard in Board of Trustees of State University of New York v. Fox, 492 U.S. 469 (1989). The *Fox* decision, which made it easier for the government to prevail, is discussed at length in the *Edge* case infra.

CENTRAL HUDSON GAS & ELECTRIC CORP. V. PUBLIC SERVICE COMMISSION OF NEW YORK
447 U.S. 557 (1980)

Mr. Justice POWELL delivered the opinion of the Court.
This case presents the question whether a regulation of the Public Service Commission of the State of New York violates the First and Fourteenth Amendments because it completely bans promotional advertising by an electrical utility.

I.
In December 1973, the Commission, appellee here, ordered electric utilities in New York State to cease all advertising that "promot[es] the use of electricity." App. to Juris. Statement 31a. The order was based on the Commission's finding that "the interconnected utility system in New York State does not have sufficient fuel stocks or sources of supply to continue furnishing all customer demands for the 1973-1974 winter." *Id.*, at 26a.

Three years later, when the fuel shortage had eased, the Commission requested comments from the public on its proposal to continue the ban on promotional advertising. Central Hudson Gas & Electric Corp., the appellant in this case, opposed the ban on First Amendment grounds. App. A10. After reviewing the public comments, the Commission extended the prohibition in a Policy Statement issued on February 25, 1977

The Policy Statement divided advertising expenses "into two broad categories: promotional—advertising intended to stimulate the purchase of utility services—and institutional and informational, a broad category inclusive of all advertising not clearly intended to promote sales." App. to Juris. Statement 35a. The Commission declared all promotional advertising contrary to the national policy of conserving energy. It acknowledged that the ban is not a perfect vehicle for conserving energy. For example, the Commission's order prohibits promotional advertising to develop consumption during periods when demand for electricity is low. By limiting growth in "off-peak" consumption, the ban limits the "beneficial side effects" of such growth in terms of more efficient use of existing power-plants. *Id.*, at 37a. And since oil dealers are not under the Commission's jurisdiction and thus remain free to advertise, it was recognized that the ban can achieve only "piecemeal conservationism." Still, the Commission adopted the restriction because it was deemed likely to "result in some dampening of unnecessary growth" in energy consumption. *Ibid.*

The Commission's order explicitly permitted "informational" advertising designed to encourage "*shifts* of consumption" from peak demand times to periods of low electricity demand. Informational advertising would not seek to increase aggregate consumption, but would invite a leveling of demand throughout any given 24-hour period. The agency offered to review "specific proposals by the companies for specifically described [advertising] programs that meet these criteria." *Id.*, at 38a.

. . .

Appellant challenged the order in state court, arguing that the Commission had restrained commercial speech in violation of the First and Fourteenth Amendments. The Commission's order was upheld by the trial court and at the intermediate appellate level. The New York Court of Appeals affirmed. It found little value to advertising in "the noncompetitive market in which electric corporations operate." *Consolidated Edison Co. v. Public Service Comm'n*, 390 N.E.2d 749, 757 ([N.Y.] 1979). Since consumers "have no choice regarding the source of their electric power," the court denied that "promotional advertising of electricity might contribute to society's interest in 'informed and reliable' economic decisionmaking." *Ibid.* The court also observed that by encouraging consumption, promotional advertising would only exacerbate the current energy situation. *Id.*, at 758. The court concluded that the governmental interest in the prohibition outweighed the limited constitutional value of the commercial speech at issue. We noted probable jurisdiction, 444 U.S. 962 (1979), and now reverse.

II.

The Commission's order restricts only commercial speech, that is, expression related solely to the economic interests of the speaker and its audience. *Virginia Pharmacy Board v. Virginia Citizens Consumer Council*, 425 U.S. 748, 762 (1976); *Bates v. State Bar of Arizona*, 433 U.S. 350, 363-364 (1977); *Friedman v. Rogers*, 440 U.S. 1 (1979). The First Amendment, as applied to the States through the Fourteenth Amendment, protects commercial speech from unwarranted governmental regulation. *Virginia Pharmacy Board*, 425 U.S., at 761-762. Commercial expression not only serves the economic interest of the speaker, but also assists consumers and furthers the societal interest in the fullest possible dissemination of information. In applying the First Amendment to this area, we have rejected the "highly paternalistic" view that government has complete power to suppress or regulate commercial speech. "[P]eople will perceive their own best interests if only they are well enough informed, and . . . the best means to that end is to open the channels of communication rather than to close them. . . ." *Id.*, at 770, see *Linmark Associates, Inc. v. Willingboro*, 431 U.S. 85, 92 (1977). Even when advertising communicates only an incomplete version of the relevant facts, the First Amendment presumes that some accurate information is better than no information at all. *Bates v. State Bar of Arizona, supra*, at 374.

Nevertheless, our decisions have recognized "the 'commonsense' distinction between speech proposing a commercial transaction, which occurs in an area traditionally subject to government regulation, and other varieties of speech." . . . The Constitution therefore accords a lesser protection to commercial speech than to other constitutionally guaranteed expression. 436 U.S., at 456, 457. The protection available for particular commercial expression turns on the nature both of the expression and of the governmental interests served by its regulation.

The First Amendment's concern for commercial speech is based on the informational function of advertising. See *First National Bank of Boston v. Bellotti*, 435 U.S. 765, 783 (1978). Consequently, there can be no constitutional objection to the suppression of commercial messages that do not accurately inform the public about lawful activity. The government may ban forms of communication more likely to deceive the public than to inform it, or commercial speech related to illegal activity . . . .

If the communication is neither misleading nor related to unlawful activity, the government's power is more circumscribed. The State must assert a substantial interest to be achieved by restrictions on commercial speech. Moreover, the regulatory technique must be in proportion to that interest. The limitation on expression must be designed carefully to achieve the State's goal. Compliance with this requirement may be measured by two criteria. First, the restriction must directly advance the state interest involved; the regulation may not be sustained if it provides only ineffective or remote support for the government's purpose. Second, if the governmental interest could be served as well by a more limited restriction on commercial speech, the excessive restrictions cannot survive.

Under the first criterion, the Court has declined to uphold regulations that only indirectly advance the state interest involved. In both *Bates* and *Virginia Pharmacy Board,* the Court concluded that an advertising ban could not be imposed to protect the ethical or performance standards of a profession. The Court noted in *Virginia Pharmacy Board* that "[t]he advertising ban does not directly affect professional standards one way or the other." 425 U.S., at 769. In *Bates,* the Court overturned an advertising prohibition that was designed to protect the "quality" of a lawyer's work. "Restraints on advertising . . . are an ineffective way of deterring shoddy work." . . .

The second criterion recognizes that the First Amendment mandates that speech restrictions be "narrowly drawn." *In re Primus,* 436 U.S. 412, 438 (1978). The regulatory technique may extend only as far as the interest it serves. The State cannot regulate speech that poses no danger to the asserted state interest, see *First National Bank of Boston v. Bellotti, supra,* at 794-795, nor can it completely suppress information when narrower restrictions on expression would serve its interest as well. For example, in *Bates* the Court explicitly did not "foreclose the possibility that some limited supplementation, by way of warning or disclaimer or the like, might be required" in promotional materials. 433 U.S., at 384. See *Virginia Pharmacy Board, supra,* at 773. And in *Carey v. Population Services International,* 431 U.S. 678, 701-702 (1977), we held that the State's "arguments . . . do not justify the total suppression of advertising concerning contraceptives." This holding left open the possibility that the State could implement more carefully drawn restrictions. See *id.,* at 712 (POWELL, J., concurring in part and in judgment); *id.,* at 716-717 (STEVENS, J., concurring in part and in judgment).

In commercial speech cases, then, a four-part analysis has developed. At the outset, we must determine whether the expression is protected by the First Amendment. For commercial speech to come within that provision, it at least must concern lawful activity and not be misleading. Next, we ask whether the asserted governmental interest is substantial. If both inquiries yield positive answers, we must determine whether the regulation directly advances the governmental interest asserted, and whether it is not more extensive than is necessary to serve that interest.

III.

We now apply this four-step analysis for commercial speech to the Commission's arguments in support of its ban on promotional advertising.

A.

The Commission does not claim that the expression at issue either is inaccurate or relates to unlawful activity. Yet the New York Court of Appeals questioned whether Central Hudson's advertising is protected commercial speech. Because appellant holds a monopoly over the sale of electricity in its service area, the state court suggested that the Commission's order restricts no commercial speech of any worth. The court stated that advertising in a "noncompetitive market" could not improve the decisionmaking of consumers. 390 N.E.2d, at 757. The court saw no constitutional problem with barring commercial speech that it viewed as conveying little useful information.

This reasoning falls short of establishing that appellant's advertising is not commercial speech protected by the First Amendment. Monopoly over the supply of a product provides no protection from competition with substitutes for that product. Electric utilities compete with suppliers of fuel oil and natural gas in several markets, such as those for home heating and industrial power. This Court noted the existence of interfuel competition 45 years ago, see *West Ohio Gas Co. v. Public Utilities Comm'n*, 294 U.S. 63, 72 (1935). Each energy source continues to offer peculiar advantages and disadvantages that may influence consumer choice. For consumers in those competitive markets, advertising by utilities is just as valuable as advertising by unregulated firms.

Even in monopoly markets, the suppression of advertising reduces the information available for consumer decisions and thereby defeats the purpose of the First Amendment. The New York court's argument appears to assume that the providers of a monopoly service or product are willing to pay for wholly ineffective advertising. Most businesses—even regulated monopolies—are unlikely to underwrite promotional advertising that is of no interest or use to consumers. Indeed, a monopoly enterprise legitimately may wish to inform the public that it has developed new services or terms of doing business. A consumer may need information to aid his decision whether or not to use the monopoly service at all, or how much of the service he should purchase. In the absence of factors that would distort the decision to advertise, we may assume that the willingness of a business to promote its products reflects a belief that consumers are interested in the advertising. Since no such extraordinary conditions have been identified in this case, appellant's monopoly position does not alter the First Amendment's protection for its commercial speech.

B.

The Commission offers two state interests as justifications for the ban on promotional advertising. The first concerns energy conservation. Any increase in demand for electricity—during peak or off-peak periods—means greater consumption of energy. The Commission argues, and the New York court agreed, that the State's interest in conserving energy is sufficient to support suppression of advertising designed to increase consumption of electricity. In view of our country's dependence on energy resources beyond our control, no one can doubt the importance of energy conservation. Plainly, therefore, the state interest asserted is substantial.

The Commission also argues that promotional advertising will aggravate inequities caused by the failure to base the utilities' rates on marginal cost. The utilities argued to the Commission that if they could promote the use of electricity in periods of low demand, they would improve their utilization of generating capacity. The Commission responded that promotion of off-peak consumption also would increase consumption during peak periods. If peak demand were to rise, the absence of marginal cost rates would mean that the rates charged for the additional power would not reflect the true costs of expanding production. Instead, the extra costs would be borne by all consumers through higher overall rates. Without promotional advertising, the Commission stated, this inequitable turn of events would be less likely to occur. The choice among rate structures involves difficult and important questions of economic supply and distributional fairness. The State's concern that rates be fair and efficient represents a clear and substantial governmental interest.

C.

Next, we focus on the relationship between the State's interests and the advertising ban. Under this criterion, the Commission's laudable concern over the equity and efficiency of appellant's rates does not provide a constitutionally adequate reason for restricting protected speech. The link between the advertising prohibition and appellant's rate structure is, at most, tenuous. The impact of promotional advertising on the equity of appellant's rates is highly speculative. Advertising to increase off-peak usage would have to increase peak usage, while other factors that directly affect the fairness and efficiency of appellant's rates remained constant. Such conditional and remote eventualities simply cannot justify silencing appellant's promotional advertising.

In contrast, the State's interest in energy conservation is directly advanced by the Commission order at issue here. There is an immediate connection between advertising and demand for electricity. Central Hudson would not contest the advertising ban unless it believed that promotion would increase its sales. Thus, we find a direct link between the state interest in conservation and the Commission's order.

D.

We come finally to the critical inquiry in this case: whether the Commission's complete suppression of speech ordinarily protected by the First Amendment is no more extensive than necessary to further the State's interest in energy conservation. The Commission's order reaches all promotional advertising, regardless of the impact of the touted service on overall energy use. But the energy conservation rationale, as important as it is, cannot justify suppressing information about electric devices or services that would cause no net increase in total energy use. In addition, no showing has been made that a more limited restriction on the content of promotional advertising would not serve adequately the State's interests.

. . .

The Commission's order prevents appellant from promoting electric services that would reduce energy use by diverting demand from less efficient sources, or that would consume roughly the same amount of energy as do alternative sources. In neither situation would the utility's advertising endanger conservation or mislead the public. To the extent that the Commission's order suppresses speech that in no way impairs the State's interest in energy conservation, the Commission's order violates the First and Fourteenth Amendments and must be invalidated. . . .

The Commission also has not demonstrated that its interest in conservation cannot be protected adequately by more limited regulation of appellant's commercial expression. To further its policy of conservation, the Commission could attempt to restrict the format and content of Central

Hudson's advertising. It might, for example, require that the advertisements include information about the relative efficiency and expense of the offered service, both under current conditions and for the foreseeable future. Cf. *Banzhaf v. FCC,* 405 F.2d 1082 (1968), cert. denied *sub nom. Tobacco Institute, Inc. v. FCC,* 396 U.S. 842 (1969). In the absence of a showing that more limited speech regulation would be ineffective, we cannot approve the complete suppression of Central Hudson's advertising.

IV.

Our decision today in no way disparages the national interest in energy conservation. We accept without reservation the argument that conservation, as well as the development of alternative energy sources, is an imperative national goal. Administrative bodies empowered to regulate electric utilities have the authority—and indeed the duty—to take appropriate action to further this goal. When, however, such action involves the suppression of speech, the First and Fourteenth Amendments require that the restriction be no more extensive than is necessary to serve the state interest. In this case, the record before us fails to show that the total ban on promotional advertising meets this requirement.

Accordingly, the judgment of the New York Court of Appeals is

Reversed.

Mr. Justice BRENNAN, concurring in the judgment.

One of the major difficulties in this case is the proper characterization of the Commission's Policy Statement. I find it impossible to determine on the present record whether the Commission's ban on all "promotional" advertising, in contrast to "institutional and informational" advertising, see *ante,* at 2347, is intended to encompass more than "commercial speech." I am inclined to think that Mr. Justice STEVENS is correct that the Commission's order prohibits more than mere proposals to engage in certain kinds of commercial transactions, and therefore I agree with his conclusion that the ban surely violates the First and Fourteenth Amendments. But even on the assumption that the Court is correct that the Commission's order reaches only commercial speech, I agree with Mr. Justice BLACKMUN that "[n]o differences between commercial speech and other protected speech justify suppression of commercial speech in order to influence public conduct through manipulation of the availability of information." *Post,* at 2357.

Mr. Justice BLACKMUN, with whom Mr. Justice BRENNAN joins, concurring in the judgment.

I agree with the Court that the Public Service Commission's ban on promotional advertising of electricity by public utilities is inconsistent with the First and Fourteenth Amendments. I concur only in the Court's judgment, however, because I believe the test now evolved and applied by the Court is not consistent with our prior cases and does not provide adequate protection for truthful, nonmisleading, noncoercive commercial speech.

The Court asserts, *ante*, at 2351, that "a four-part analysis has developed" from our decisions concerning commercial speech. Under this four-part test a restraint on commercial "communication [that] is neither misleading nor related to unlawful activity" is subject to an intermediate level of scrutiny, and suppression is permitted whenever it "directly advances" a "substantial" governmental interest and is "not more extensive than is necessary to serve that interest." *Ante*, at 2350 and 2351. I agree with the Court that this level of intermediate scrutiny is appropriate for a restraint on commercial speech designed to protect consumers from misleading or coercive speech, or a regulation related to the time, place, or manner of commercial speech. I do not agree, however, that the Court's four-part test is the proper one to be applied when a State seeks to suppress information about a product in order to manipulate a private economic decision that the State cannot or has not regulated or outlawed directly.

. . .

The Court recognizes that we have never held that commercial speech may be suppressed in order to further the State's interest in discouraging purchases of the underlying product that is advertised. *Ante*, at 2351, n. 9. Permissible restraints on commercial speech have been limited to measures designed to protect consumers from fraudulent, misleading, or coercive sales techniques. Those designed to deprive consumers of information about products or services that are legally offered for sale consistently have been invalidated.

I seriously doubt whether suppression of information concerning the availability and price of a legally offered product is ever a permissible way for the State to "dampen" demand for or use of the product. Even though "commercial" speech is involved, such a regulatory measure strikes at the heart of the First Amendment. This is because it is a covert attempt by the State to manipulate the choices of its citizens, not by persuasion or direct regulation, but by depriving the public of the information needed to make a free choice. As the Court recognizes, the State's policy choices are insulated from the visibility and scrutiny that direct regulation would entail and the conduct of citizens is molded by the information that government chooses to give them. . . .

If the First Amendment guarantee means anything, it means that, absent clear and present danger, government has no power to restrict expression because of the effect its message is likely to have on the public. . . .

Mr. Justice STEVENS, with whom Mr. Justice BRENNAN joins, concurring in the judgment.

Because "commercial speech" is afforded less constitutional protection than other forms of speech, it is important that the commercial speech concept not be defined too broadly lest speech deserving of greater constitutional protection be inadvertently suppressed. The issue in this case is whether New York's prohibition on the promotion of the use of electricity through advertising is a ban on nothing but commercial speech.

In my judgment one of the two definitions the Court uses in addressing that issue is too broad and the other may be somewhat too narrow. The Court first describes commercial speech as "expression related solely to the economic interests of the speaker and its audience." *Ante*, at 2349. Although it is not entirely clear whether this definition uses the subject matter of the speech or the motivation of the speaker as the limiting factor, it seems clear to me that it encompasses speech that is entitled to the maximum protection afforded by the First Amendment. Neither a labor leader's exhortation to strike, nor an economist's dissertation on the money supply, should receive any lesser protection because the subject matter concerns only the economic interests of the audience. Nor should the economic motivation of a speaker qualify his constitutional protection; even Shakespeare may have been motivated by the prospect of pecuniary reward. Thus, the Court's first definition of commercial speech is unquestionably too broad.

The Court's second definition refers to "'speech proposing a commercial transaction.'" *Ante*, at 2349. A salesman's solicitation, a broker's offer, and a manufacturer's publication of a price list or the terms of his standard warranty would unquestionably fit within this concept. Presumably, the definition is intended to encompass advertising that advises possible buyers of the availability of specific products at specific prices and describes the advantages of purchasing such items. Perhaps it also extends to other communications that do little more than make the name of a product or a service more familiar to the general public. Whatever the precise contours of the concept, and perhaps it is too early to enunciate an exact formulation, I am persuaded that it should not include the entire range of communication that is embraced within the term "promotional advertising."

This case involves a governmental regulation that completely bans promotional advertising by an electric utility. This ban encompasses a great deal more than mere proposals to engage in certain kinds of commercial transactions. It prohibits all advocacy of the immediate or future use of electricity. It curtails expression by an informed and interested group of persons of their point of view on questions relating to the production and consumption of electrical energy—questions frequently discussed and debated by our political leaders. For example, an electric company's advocacy of the use of electric heat for environmental reasons, as opposed to wood-burning stoves, would seem to fall squarely within New York's promotional advertising ban and also within the bounds of maximum First Amendment protection. The breadth of the ban thus exceeds the boundaries of the commercial speech concept, however that concept may be defined.

The justification for the regulation is nothing more than the expressed fear that the audience may find the utility's message persuasive. Without the aid of any coercion, deception, or misinformation, truthful communication may persuade some citizens to consume more electricity than they otherwise would. I assume that such a consequence would be undesirable and that government may therefore prohibit and punish the unnecessary or excessive use of electricity. But if the perceived harm associated with greater electrical usage is not sufficiently serious to justify direct regulation, surely it does not constitute the kind of clear and present danger that can justify the suppression of speech. . . . In sum, I concur in the result because I do not consider this to be a "commercial speech" case. Accordingly, I see no need to decide whether the Court's four-part analysis, *ante*, at 2351, adequately protects commercial speech—as properly defined—in the face of a blanket ban of the sort involved in this case.

Mr. Justice REHNQUIST, dissenting.

The Court's analysis in my view is wrong in several respects. Initially, I disagree with the Court's conclusion that the speech of a state-created monopoly, which is the subject of a comprehensive regulatory scheme, is entitled to protection under the First Amendment. I also think that the Court errs here in failing to recognize that the state law is most accurately viewed as an economic regulation and that the speech involved (if it falls within the scope of the First Amendment at all) occupies a significantly more subordinate position in the hierarchy of First Amendment values than the Court gives it today. Finally, the Court in reaching its decision improperly substitutes its own judgment for that of the State in deciding how a proper ban on promotional advertising should be drafted. With regard to this latter point, the Court adopts as its final part of a four-part test a "no more extensive than necessary" analysis that will unduly impair a state legislature's ability to adopt legislation reasonably designed to promote interests that have always been rightly thought to be of great importance to the State. . . .

U.S. v. Edge Broadcasting Co.
509 U.S. 418 (1993)

Justice WHITE delivered the opinion of the Court.
In this case we must decide whether federal statutes that prohibit the broadcast of lottery advertising by a broadcaster licensed to a State that does not allow lotteries, while allowing such broadcasting by a broadcaster licensed to a State that sponsors a lottery, are, as applied to respondent, consistent with the First Amendment.

. . .

In 1975, Congress amended the statutory scheme to allow newspapers and broadcasters to advertise state-run lotteries if the newspaper is published in or the broadcast station is licensed to a State which conducts a state-run lottery. See 18 U.S.C. § 1307 (1988 ed., Supp. III). This exemption was enacted "to accommodate the operation of legally authorized State-run lotteries consistent with continued Federal protection to the policies of non-lottery States." S.Rep. No. 93-1404, p. 2 (1974). See also H.R.Rep. No. 93-1517, p. 5 (1974), U.S. Code Cong. & Admin. News 1974, p. 7007.

. . .

North Carolina does not sponsor a lottery, and participating in or advertising nonexempt raffles and lotteries is a crime under its statutes. N.C. Gen. Stat. §§ 14-289 and 14-291 (1986 and Supp.1992). Virginia, on the other hand, has chosen to legalize lotteries under a state monopoly and has entered the marketplace vigorously.

Respondent, Edge Broadcasting Company (Edge), owns and operates a radio station licensed by the Federal Communications Commission (FCC) to Elizabeth City, North Carolina. This station, known as "Power 94," has the call letters WMYK-FM and broadcasts from Moyock, North Carolina, which is approximately three miles from the border between Virginia and North Carolina and considerably closer to Virginia than is Elizabeth City. Power 94 is one of 24 radio stations serving the Hampton Roads, Virginia, metropolitan area; 92.2% of its listening audience are Virginians; the rest, 7.8%, reside in the nine North Carolina counties served by Power 94. Because Edge is licensed to serve a North Carolina community, the federal statute prohibits it from broadcasting advertisements for the Virginia lottery. Edge derives 95% of its advertising revenue from Virginia sources, and claims that it has lost large sums of money from its inability to carry Virginia lottery advertisements. . . .

II.

The Government argues first that gambling implicates no constitutionally protected right, but rather falls within a category of activities normally considered to be "vices," and that the greater power to prohibit gambling necessarily includes the lesser power to ban its advertisement; it argues that we therefore need not proceed with a *Central Hudson* analysis. The Court of Appeals did not address this issue and neither do we, for the statutes are not unconstitutional under the standards of *Central Hudson* applied by the courts below.

. . .

III.

. . .

B.

Left unresolved, of course, is the validity of applying the statutory restriction to Edge, an issue that we now address under the fourth *Central Hudson* factor, *i.e.,* whether the regulation is more extensive than is necessary to serve the governmental interest. We revisited that aspect of *Central Hudson* in *Board of Trustees of State Univ. of N.Y. v. Fox,* 492 U.S. 469 (1989), and concluded that the validity of restrictions on commercial speech should not be judged by standards more stringent than those applied to expressive conduct entitled to full First Amendment protection or to relevant time, place, or manner restrictions. *Id.,* at 477-478. We made clear in *Fox* that our commercial speech cases require a fit between the restriction and the government interest that is not necessarily perfect, but reasonable. *Id.,* at 480. This was also the approach in *Posadas,* 478 U.S., at 344.

We have no doubt that the fit in this case was a reasonable one. Although Edge was licensed to serve the Elizabeth City area, it chose to broadcast from a more northerly position, which allowed its signal to reach into the Hampton Roads, Virginia, metropolitan area. Allowing it to carry lottery ads reaching over 90% of its listeners, all in Virginia, would surely enhance its revenues. But just as surely, because Edge's signals with lottery ads would be heard in the nine counties in North Carolina that its broadcasts reached, this would be in derogation of the substantial federal interest in supporting North Carolina's laws making lotteries illegal. In this posture, to prevent Virginia's lottery policy from dictating what stations in a neighboring State may air, it is reasonable to require Edge to comply with the restriction against carrying lottery advertising. In other words, applying the restriction to a broadcaster such as Edge directly advances the governmental interest in enforcing the restriction in nonlottery States, while not interfering with the policy of lottery States like Virginia. We think this would be the case even if it were true, which it is not, that applying the general statutory restriction to Edge, in isolation, would no more than marginally insulate the North Carolinians in the North Carolina counties served by Edge from hearing lottery ads.

. . .

IV.

Because the statutes challenged here regulate commercial speech in a manner that does not violate the First Amendment, the judgment of the Court of Appeals is *Reversed.*

GREATER NEW ORLEANS BROADCASTING ASS'N V. U.S.
527 U.S. 173 (1999)

Justice STEVENS delivered the opinion of the Court.
Federal law prohibits some, but by no means all, broadcast advertising of lotteries and casino gambling. In *United States v. Edge Broadcasting Co.,* 509 U.S. 418 (1993), we upheld the constitutionality of 18 U.S.C. § 1304 as applied to broadcast advertising of Virginia's lottery by a radio station located in North Carolina, where no such lottery was authorized. Today we hold that § 1304 may not be applied to advertisements of private casino gambling that are broadcast by radio or television stations located in Louisiana, where such gambling is legal.

I.

Through most of the 19th and the first half of the 20th centuries, Congress adhered to a policy that not only discouraged the operation of lotteries and similar schemes, but forbade the dissemination of information concerning such enterprises by use of the mails, even when the lottery in question was chartered by a state legislature. Consistent with this Court's earlier view that commercial advertising was unprotected by the First Amendment, see *Valentine v. Chrestensen,* 316 U.S. 52, 54 (1942), we found that the notion that "lotteries . . . are supposed to have a demoralizing influence upon the people" provided sufficient justification for excluding circulars concerning such enterprises from the federal postal system, *Ex parte Jackson,* 96 U.S. 727, 736-737 (1878). We likewise deferred to congressional judgment in upholding the similar exclusion for newspapers that contained either lottery advertisements or prize lists. *In re Rapier,* 143 U.S. 110, 134-135 (1892); see generally *Edge,* 509 U.S., at 421-422; *Champion v. Ames,* 188 U.S. 321 (1903). The current versions of these early antilottery statutes are now codified at 18 U.S.C. §§ 1301-1303.

Congress extended its restrictions on lottery-related information to broadcasting as communications technology made that practice both possible and profitable. It enacted the statute at issue in this case as § 316 of the Communications Act of 1934, 48 Stat. 1088. Now codified at 18 U.S.C. § 1304 ("Broadcasting lottery information"), the statute prohibits radio and television broadcasting, by any station for which a license is required, of

> "any advertisement of or information concerning any lottery, gift enterprise, or similar scheme, offering prizes dependent in whole or in part upon lot or chance, or any list of the prizes drawn or awarded by means of any such lottery, gift enterprise, or scheme, whether said list contains any part or all of such prizes."

. . .

During the second half of this century, Congress dramatically narrowed the scope of the broadcast prohibition in § 1304. The first inroad was minor: In 1950, certain not-for-profit fishing contests were exempted as "innocent pastimes . . . far removed from the reprehensible type of gambling activity which it was paramount in the congressional mind to forbid." S.Rep. No. 2243, 81st Cong., 2d Sess., 2 (1950); see Act of Aug. 16, 1950, ch. 722, 64 Stat. 451, 18 U.S.C. § 1305.

Subsequent exemptions were more substantial. Responding to the growing popularity of state-run lotteries, in 1975 Congress enacted the provision that gave rise to our decision in *Edge* . . . With subsequent modifications, that amendment now exempts advertisements of state-conducted lotteries from the nationwide postal restrictions in §§ 1301 and 1302, and from the broadcast restriction in § 1304, when "broadcast by a radio or television station licensed to a location in . . . a State which conducts such a lottery." . . .

In 1988, Congress enacted two additional statutes that significantly curtailed the coverage of § 1304. First, the Indian Gaming Regulatory Act (IGRA), 102 Stat. 2467, 25 U.S.C. § 2701 *et seq.,* authorized Native American tribes to conduct various forms of gambling-including casino gambling-pursuant to tribal-state compacts if the State permits such gambling "for any purpose by any person, organization, or entity." . . . Second, the Charity Games Advertising Clarification Act of 1988, 18 U.S.C. § 1307(a)(2), extended the exemption from §§ 1301-1304 for state-run lotteries to include any other lottery, gift enterprise, or similar scheme-not prohibited by the law of the State in which it operates-when conducted by: (i) any governmental organization; (ii) any not-for-profit organization; or (iii) a commercial organization as a promotional activity "clearly occasional and ancillary to the primary business of that organization." There is no dispute that the exemption in § 1307(a)(2) applies to casinos conducted by state and local governments. And, unlike the 1975 broadcast exemption for advertisements of and information concerning state-conducted lotteries, the exemptions in both of these 1988 statutes are not geographically limited; they shield messages from § 1304's reach in States that do not authorize such gambling as well as those that do.

. . .

Thus, unlike the uniform federal antigambling policy that prevailed in 1934 when 18 U.S.C. § 1304 was enacted, federal statutes now accommodate both progambling and antigambling segments of the national polity.

II.

Petitioners are an association of Louisiana broadcasters and its members who operate FCC-licensed radio and television stations in the New Orleans metropolitan area. But for the threat of sanctions pursuant to § 1304 and the FCC's companion regulation, petitioners would broadcast promotional advertisements for gaming available at private, for-profit casinos that are lawful and regulated in both Louisiana and neighboring Mississippi. According to an FCC official, however, "[u]nder appropriate conditions, some broadcast signals from Louisiana broadcasting stations may be heard in neighboring states including Texas and Arkansas," 3 Record 628, where private casino gambling is unlawful.

. . .

III.

In a number of cases involving restrictions on speech that is "commercial" in nature, we have employed *Central Hudson's* four-part test to resolve First Amendment challenges:

> "At the outset, we must determine whether the expression is protected by the First Amendment. For commercial speech to come within that provision, it at least must concern lawful activity and not be misleading. Next, we ask whether the asserted governmental interest is substantial. If both inquiries yield positive answers, we must determine whether the regulation directly advances the governmental interest asserted, and whether it is not more extensive than is necessary to serve that interest." 447 U.S., at 566.

In this analysis, the Government bears the burden of identifying a substantial interest and justifying the challenged restriction. *Edenfield v. Fane*, 507 U.S. 761, 770 (1993); *Board of Trustees of State Univ. of N.Y. v. Fox*, 492 U.S. 469, 480 (1989); *Bolger v. Youngs Drug Products Corp.*, 463 U.S. 60, 71, and n. 20 (1983).

The four parts of the *Central Hudson* test are not entirely discrete. All are important and, to a certain extent, interrelated: Each raises a relevant question that may not be dispositive to the First Amendment inquiry, but the answer to which may inform a judgment concerning the other three. Partly because of these intricacies, petitioners as well as certain judges, scholars, and *amici curiae* have advocated repudiation of the *Central Hudson* standard and implementation of a more straightforward and stringent test for assessing the validity of governmental restrictions on commercial speech. . . . In this case, there is no need to break new ground. *Central Hudson*, as applied in our more recent commercial speech cases, provides an adequate basis for decision.

IV.

All parties to this case agree that the messages petitioners wish to broadcast constitute commercial speech, and that these broadcasts would satisfy the first part of the *Central Hudson* test: Their content is not misleading and concerns lawful activities, *i.e.*, private casino gambling in Louisiana and Mississippi.

. . .

The second part of the *Central Hudson* test asks whether the asserted governmental interest served by the speech restriction is substantial. The Solicitor General identifies two such interests: (1) reducing the social costs associated with "gambling" or "casino gambling," and (2) assisting States that "restrict gambling" or "prohibit casino gambling" within their own borders. Underlying Congress' statutory scheme, the Solicitor General contends, is the judgment that gambling contributes to corruption and organized crime; underwrites bribery, narcotics trafficking, and other illegal conduct; imposes a regressive tax on the poor; and "offers a false but sometimes irresistible hope of financial advancement." With respect to casino gambling, the Solicitor General states that many of the associated social costs stem from "pathological" or "compulsive" gambling by approximately 3 million Americans, whose behavior is primarily associated with "continuous play" games, such as slot machines. He also observes that compulsive gambling has grown along with the expansion of legalized gambling nationwide, leading to billions of dollars in economic costs; injury and loss to these gamblers as well as their families, communities, and government; and street, white-collar, and organized crime.

We can accept the characterization of these two interests as "substantial," but that conclusion is by no means self-evident. No one seriously doubts that the Federal Government may assert a legitimate and substantial interest in alleviating the societal ills recited above, or in assisting like-minded States to do the same. Cf. *Edge,* 509 U.S., at 428. But in the judgment of both the Congress and many state legislatures, the social costs that support the suppression of gambling are offset, and sometimes outweighed, by countervailing policy considerations, primarily in the form of economic benefits. Despite its awareness of the potential social costs, Congress has not only sanctioned casino gambling for Indian tribes through tribal-state compacts, but has enacted other statutes that reflect approval of state legislation that authorizes a host of public and private gambling activities. . . . Whatever its character in 1934 when § 1304 was adopted, the federal policy of discouraging gambling in general, and casino gambling in particular, is now decidedly equivocal.

. . .

V.

The third part of the *Central Hudson* test asks whether the speech restriction directly and materially advances the asserted governmental interest. "This burden is not satisfied by mere speculation or conjecture; rather, a governmental body seeking to sustain a restriction on commercial speech must demonstrate that the harms it recites are real and that its restriction will in fact alleviate them to a material degree." *Edenfield,* 507 U.S., at 770-771. Consequently, "the regulation may not be sustained if it provides only ineffective or remote support for the government's purpose." *Central Hudson,* 447 U.S., at 564. We have observed that "this requirement is critical; otherwise, "a State could with ease restrict commercial speech in the service of other objectives that could not themselves justify a burden on commercial expression."

The fourth part of the test complements the direct-advancement inquiry of the third, asking whether the speech restriction is not more extensive than necessary to serve the interests that support it. The Government is not required to employ the least restrictive means conceivable, but it must demonstrate narrow tailoring of the challenged regulation to the asserted interest-"a fit that is not necessarily perfect, but reasonable; that represents not necessarily the single best disposition but one whose scope is in proportion to the interest served." *Fox . . .*

As applied to petitioners' case, § 1304 cannot satisfy these standards. With regard to the first asserted interest alleviating the social costs of casino gambling by limiting demand the Government contends that its broadcasting restrictions directly advance that interest because "promotional" broadcast advertising concerning casino gambling increases demand for such gambling, which in turn increases the amount of casino gambling that produces those social costs. Additionally, the Government believes that compulsive gamblers are especially susceptible to the pervasiveness and potency of broadcast advertising. Brief for Respondents 33-36. Assuming the accuracy of this causal chain, it does not necessarily follow that the Government's speech ban has directly and materially furthered the asserted interest. While it is no doubt fair to assume that more advertising would have some impact on overall demand for gambling, it is also reasonable to assume that much of that advertising would merely channel gamblers to one casino rather than another. More important, any measure of the effectiveness of the Government's attempt to minimize the social costs of gambling cannot ignore Congress' simultaneous encouragement of tribal casino gambling, which may well be growing at a rate exceeding any increase in gambling or compulsive gambling that private casino advertising could produce. See

n. 5, *supra.* And, as the Court of Appeals recognized, the Government fails to "connect casino gambling and compulsive gambling with broadcast advertising for casinos"-let alone broadcast advertising for non-Indian commercial casinos. 149 F.3d, at 339.

We need not resolve the question whether any lack of evidence in the record fails to satisfy the standard of proof under *Central Hudson,* however, because the flaw in the Government's case is more fundamental: The operation of § 1304 and its attendant regulatory regime is so pierced by exemptions and inconsistencies that the Government cannot hope to exonerate it. See *Rubin,* 514 U.S., at 488. Under current law, a broadcaster may not carry advertising about privately operated commercial casino gambling, regardless of the location of the station or the casino. 18 U.S.C. § 1304; 47 CFR § 73.1211(a) (1998). On the other hand, advertisements for tribal casino gambling authorized by state compacts-whether operated by the tribe or by a private party pursuant to a management contract-are subject to no such broadcast ban, even if the broadcaster is located in, or broadcasts to, a jurisdiction with the strictest of antigambling policies. 25 U.S.C. § 2720. Government-operated, nonprofit, and "occasional and ancillary" commercial casinos are likewise exempt. 18 U.S.C. § 1307(a)(2).

The FCC's interpretation and application of §§ 1304 and 1307 underscore the statute's infirmity. Attempting to enforce the underlying purposes and policy of the statute, the FCC has permitted broadcasters to tempt viewers with claims of "Vegas-style excitement" at a commercial "casino," if "casino" is part of the establishment's proper name and the advertisement can be taken to refer to the casino's amenities, rather than directly promote its gaming aspects. While we can hardly fault the FCC in view of the statute's focus on the suppression of certain types of information, the agency's practice is squarely at odds with the governmental interests asserted in this case.

. . .

From what we can gather, the Government is committed to prohibiting accurate product information, not commercial enticements of all kinds, and then only when conveyed over certain forms of media and for certain types of gambling-indeed, for only certain brands of *casino* gambling-and despite the fact that messages about the availability of such gambling are being conveyed over the airwaves by other speakers.

Even putting aside the broadcast exemptions for arguably distinguishable sorts of gambling that might also give rise to social costs about which the Federal Government is concerned-such as state lotteries and parimutuel betting on horse and dog races, § 1307(a)(1)(B); 28 U.S.C. § 3704(a)-the Government presents no convincing reason for pegging its speech ban to the identity of the owners or operators of the advertised casinos. The Government cites revenue needs of States and tribes that conduct casino gambling, and notes that net revenues generated by the tribal casinos are dedicated to the welfare of the tribes and their members.... Yet the Government admits that tribal casinos offer precisely the same types of gambling as private casinos. Further, the Solicitor General does not maintain that government-operated casino gaming is any different, that States cannot derive revenue from taxing private casinos, or that any one class of casino operators is likely to advertise in a meaningfully distinct manner from the others. The Government's suggestion that Indian casinos are too isolated to warrant attention is belied by a quick review of tribal geography and the Government's own evidence regarding the financial success of tribal gaming. See n. 5, *supra.* If distance were determinative, Las Vegas might have remained a relatively small community, or simply disappeared like a desert mirage.

Ironically, the most significant difference identified by the Government between tribal and other classes of casino gambling is that the former is "heavily regulated." Brief for Respondents 38. If such direct regulation provides a basis for believing that the social costs of gambling in tribal casinos are sufficiently mitigated to make their advertising tolerable, one would have thought that Congress might have at least experimented with comparable regulation before abridging the speech rights of federally *un*regulated casinos. While Congress' failure to institute such direct regulation of private casino gambling does not necessarily compromise the constitutionality of § 1304, it does undermine the asserted justifications for the restriction before us. See *Rubin,* 514 U.S., at 490-491. There surely are practical and nonspeech-related forms of regulation-including a prohibition or supervision of gambling on credit; limitations on the use of cash machines on casino premises; controls on admissions; pot or betting limits; location restrictions; and licensing requirements-that could more directly and effectively alleviate some of the social costs of casino gambling.

We reached a similar conclusion in *Rubin.* There, we considered the effect of conflicting federal policies on the Government's claim that a speech restriction materially advanced its interest in preventing so-called "strength wars" among competing sellers of certain alcoholic beverages.

We concluded that the effect of the challenged restriction on commercial speech had to be evaluated in the context of the entire regulatory scheme, rather than in isolation, and we invalidated the restriction based on the "overall irrationality of the Government's regulatory scheme." *Id.,* at 488. As in this case, there was "little chance" that the speech restriction could have directly and materially advanced its aim, "while other provisions of the same Act directly undermine[d] and counteract[ed] its effects." *Id.,* at 489. Coupled with the availability of other regulatory options which could advance the asserted interests "in a manner less intrusive to [petitioners'] First Amendment rights," we found that the Government could not satisfy the *Central Hudson* test. *Id.,* at 490-491.

Given the special federal interest in protecting the welfare of Native Americans, see *California v. Cabazon Band of Mission Indians,* 480 U.S. 202, 216-217 (1987), we recognize that there may be valid reasons for imposing commercial regulations on non-Indian businesses that differ from those imposed on tribal enterprises. It does not follow, however, that those differences also justify abridging non-Indians' freedom of speech more severely than the freedom of their tribal competitors. For the power to prohibit or to regulate particular conduct does not necessarily include the power to prohibit or regulate speech about that conduct. *44 Liquormart. . . .*

Furthermore, even assuming that the state policies on which the Federal Government seeks to embellish are more coherent and pressing than their federal counterpart, § 1304 sacrifices an intolerable amount of truthful speech about lawful conduct when compared to all of the policies at stake and the social ills that one could reasonably hope such a ban to eliminate. The Government argues that petitioners' speech about private casino gambling should be prohibited in Louisiana because, "under appropriate conditions," 3 Record 628, citizens in neighboring States like Arkansas and Texas (which hosts tribal, but not private, commercial casino gambling) might hear it and make rash or costly decisions. To be sure, in order to achieve a broader objective such regulations may incidentally, even deliberately, restrict a certain amount of speech not thought to contribute significantly to the dangers with which the Government is concerned. See *Fox,* 492 U.S., at 480; cf. *Edge,* 509 U.S., at 429-430. But Congress' choice here was neither a rough approximation of efficacy, nor a reasonable accommodation of competing state and private interests. Rather, the regulation distinguishes among the indistinct, permitting a variety of speech that poses the same risks the Government purports to fear, while banning messages unlikely to cause any harm at all. Considering the manner in which § 1304 and its exceptions operate and the scope of the speech it proscribes, the Government's second asserted interest provides no more convincing basis for upholding the regulation than the first.

. . .

VI.

Accordingly, respondents cannot overcome the presumption that the speaker and the audience, not the Government, should be left to assess the value of accurate and nonmisleading information about lawful conduct. *Edenfield,* 507 U.S., at 767. Had the Federal Government adopted a more coherent policy, or accommodated the rights of speakers in States that have legalized the underlying conduct, see *Edge,* 509 U.S., at 428, this might be a different case. But under current federal law, as applied to petitioners and the messages that they wish to convey, the broadcast prohibition in 18 U.S.C. § 1304 and 47 CFR § 73.1211 (1998) violates the First Amendment. The judgment of the Court of Appeals is therefore

Reversed.

Chief Justice REHNQUIST, concurring.

Title 18 U.S.C. § 1304 regulates broadcast advertising of lotteries and casino gambling. I agree with the Court that "[t]he operation of § 1304 and its attendant regulatory regime is so pierced by exemptions and inconsistencies," *ante,* at 1933, that it violates the First Amendment. But, as the Court observes:

> "There surely are practical and nonspeech-related forms of regulation-including a prohibition or supervision of gambling on credit; limitations on the use of cash machines on casino premises; controls on admissions; pot or betting limits; location restrictions; and licensing requirements-that could more directly and effectively alleviate some of the social costs of casino gambling." *Ante,* at 1934.

Were Congress to undertake substantive regulation of the gambling industry, rather than simply the manner in which it may broadcast advertisements, "exemptions and inconsistencies" such as those in § 1304 might well prove constitutionally tolerable. "The problem of legislative classification is a perennial one, admitting of no doctrinaire definition. Evils in the same field may be of different dimensions and proportions, requiring different remedies. Or so the legislature may think. Or the reform may take one step at a time, addressing itself to the phase of the problem which seems most acute to the legislative mind. The legislature may select one phase of one field and apply a remedy there, neglecting the others." *Williamson v. Lee Optical of Okla., Inc.*, 348 U.S. 483, 489 (1955).

But when Congress regulates commercial speech, the *Central Hudson* test imposes a more demanding standard of review. I agree with the Court that that standard has not been met here, and I join its opinion.

Justice THOMAS, concurring in the judgment.
I continue to adhere to my view that "[i]n cases such as this, in which the government's asserted interest is to keep legal users of a product or service ignorant in order to manipulate their choices in the marketplace," the *Central Hudson* test should not be applied because "such an 'interest' is *per se* illegitimate and can no more justify regulation of 'commercial speech' than it can justify regulation of 'noncommercial' speech." *44 Liquormart, Inc. v. Rhode Island*, 517 U.S. 484, 518 (1996) (opinion concurring in part and concurring in judgment). Accordingly, I concur only in the judgment.

Deceptive Advertising

The hardest cases for the *Central Hudson* test involve truthful, non-misleading speech. Deceptive advertising practices, however, have long been regulated by the Federal Trade Commission (FTC), under the Federal Trade Commission Act of 1915, codified as 15 U.S.C.A. § 41 et seq. Under section 5 of the FTC Act, deceptive advertising is defined as commercial speech that

> is misleading in a material respect; . . . tak[ing] into account (among other things) not only representations made or suggested by statement, word, design, device, sound, or any combination thereof, but also the extent to which the adver-

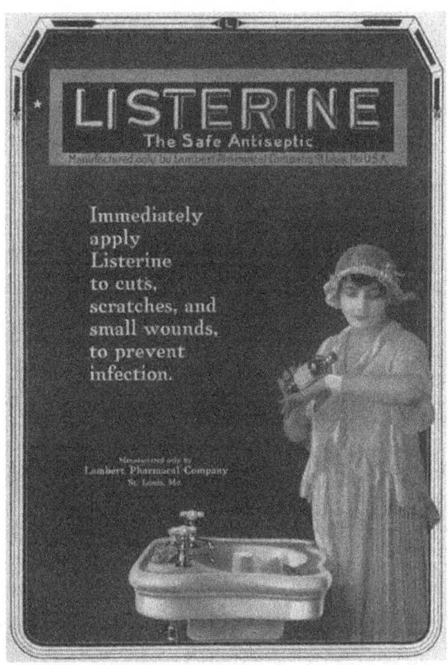

Listerine ad, 1917. In 1975, the FTC ruled that marketing the mouthwash as a treatment for colds and sore throats was misleading.

> tisement fails to reveal facts material in the light of such representations or material with respect to consequences which may result from the use of the commodity to which the advertisement relates under the conditions prescribed in said advertisement, or under such conditions as are customary or usual. . . .

In *Matter of Cliffdale Associates* infra, the FTC set forth its specific standard of review for deceptive advertising. The *National Bakers* case, also infra, is a classic example of how courts can find even a technically true advertisement deceptive.

FEDERAL TRADE COMMISSION
IN THE MATTER OF CLIFFDALE ASSOCIATES, INC.
103 F.T.C. 110 (1984)

Respondents are now and for sometime last past have been engaged in the advertising, offering for sale, sale, and distribution of a product variously known as the Ball-Matic, the Ball-Matic Gas Saver Valve and the Gas Saver Valve (hereinafter sometimes referred to as "Ball-Matic" or "product"), which product is advertised as a means of improving fuel economy in automobiles. Said product is an automobile retrofit device as "automobile retrofit device" is defined in section 511 of the Motor Vehicle Information and Cost Savings Act, 15 U.S.C. 2011. Respondents, in connection with the marketing of said product, have disseminated, published and distributed, and now disseminate, publish and distribute advertisements and promotional materials for the purpose of promoting the sale of said product.

In the course and conduct of their business, the respondents have disseminated and caused the dissemination of certain advertisements for the product through the United States mail and by various means in or affecting commerce, as "commerce" is defined in the Federal Trade Commission Act, including, but not limited to, the insertion of advertisements in magazines and newspapers with national circulations for the purpose of inducing, and which have induced, directly or indirectly, the purchase of said product in commerce.

Among the advertisements and other sales promotional materials disseminated by respondents are the materials identified as Exhibits A-F which are attached hereto.

Through the use of the advertisements referred to in Paragraph Four, and other advertisements and sales promotional materials, respondents represented and now represent, directly or by implication, that

a. the Ball-Matic is an important, significant, and unique new invention;

b. The Ball-Matic is needed on every motor vehicle except Volkswagens, diesel vehicles, or fuel injection vehicles;

c. the Ball-Matic when installed in a typical automobile and used under normal driving conditions will significantly improve fuel economy;

d. under normal driving conditions, a typical driver can usually obtain a fuel economy improvement of 20% (or more) or an improvement that will approximate or equal four miles per gallon when the Ball-Matic is installed in his/her automobile;

e. competent scientific tests prove the fuel economy claims made for the Ball-Matic;

f. results of consumer usage, as evidenced by consumer endorsements, prove that the Ball-Matic significantly improves fuel economy;

g. the consumer endorsements that appear in advertisements and sales promotional materials for the Ball-Matic are statements of persons who have used the Ball-Matic in the recent past or are currently using the Ball-Matic and who have given permission for the publication of these statements;

h. all consumer endorsements which appear in advertisements and sales promotional materials for the Ball-Matic were obtained from individuals or other entities who, at the time of providing their endorsements, were independent from all of the individuals and entities that have marketed the Ball-Matic;

i. the consumer endorsements that appear in advertisements and sales promotional materials for the Ball-Matic reflect the typical or ordinary experience of members of the public who have used the Ball-Matic.

. . .

With some minor language differences and different headlines, the advertisements are substantially similar. For example some of the headlines state:

> SAVE MONEY SAVE MONEY SAVE MONEY SAVE MONEY Without the Ball-Matic you're wasting up to $200 or more on gasoline EVERY CAR NEEDS ONE! (CX 1; *see* CX 5).
>
> STRIKE BACK AT RISING GAS PRICES! GET UP TO 4 EXTRA MILES PER GALLON-100 EXTRA MILES BETWEEN FILL-UPS-SAVE UP TO $200 A YEAR ON GAS OR DOUBLE YOUR MONEY BACK (CX 2; *see* CXs 3, 4).
>
> GET UP TO 4 EXTRA MILES PER GALLON-100 EXTRA MILES BETWEEN FILL-UPS-SAVE UP TO $200 A YEAR ON GAS (CXs 7, 8; *see* CXs 10, 11).

In most of the advertisements language similar to the following paragraphs appears somewhere in the text:

> Think of it! Thanks to an important automobile invention, every single car owner, every fleet operator, every truck or camper owner . . . everyone who operates a gas-powered combustion engine, may now be able to save up to 20% and more on their gasoline bills! (CX 8; *see* CXs 2, 3, 4, 6, 7, 10, 11, 12).
>
> The BALL-MATIC fits all American and foreign cars except Volkswagens. Do not use on diesel or fuel injection models (CX 8; *see* CXs 1, 2, 3, 4, 5, 6, 7, 9, 10, 11, 12).
>
> . . . [T]he carburetor is pre-set at the factory for idle conditions. This means that it is most efficient in regulating the gas-to-air mixture when the car is standing still and up to speeds of 35 mph. When you drive over that speed . . . or start up from a dead stop . . . or negotiate grades and steep hills . . . or pull a trailer or camper . . . or carry a full load of passengers, too much gas feeds into the carburetor and you get incomplete combustion. Every time that happens, it's just like pouring money down the drain (CX 10; *see* CXs 1, 2, 3, 4, 5, 6, 7, 8, 11, 12).

GUARANTEED SAVINGS

We firmly believe the Ball-Matic to be one of the best investments you can make to save money this year. The exact saving you will receive may vary significantly depending on the kind of car you drive, the condition of your engine, weather, your driving habits and the amount of driving you do; however we guarantee that you MUST SAVE AT LEAST FIVE TIMES the amount you paid for your BALL-MATIC in the first year or you may return it for a full refund (CX 5; *see* CX 6, 7, 8, 9, 10, 11, 12; *see also* CXs 2, 3, 4 ("double your money back")).

Test the BALL-MATIC yourself entirely at our risk. Install it in your own family or company car and if it doesn't deliver everything we say it will-starting with the first tankful, just return it and we'll refund your purchase price (CX 7; *see* CXs 1, 5, 6, 8, 11, 12; *see also* CXs 2, 3, 4, 10 ("double your money")).

CONTROLLED TESTS CONFIRM BIG DOLLAR SAVING

In the Spring of 1978, we arranged for a local Shell Service Station to conduct a controlled, supervised, test using seven different cars owned and driven by non-professional drivers. Each car was fitted with a locked gas cap and the keys kept in the possession of the testers.

After establishing base mileage consumption data for the various cars, the BALL-MATIC was installed and miles-per-gallon figures were re-checked. Every single car in the test showed meaningful improvement.

. . .

Yes, you can actually get up to 70 . . . 80 . . . 90 . . . even 100 extra miles from every single tankful. No matter how old or rundown your car may be . . . no matter how many gallons of gas it now devours each week . . . FROM THE VERY INSTANT YOU INSTALL THE BALL-MATIC GAS SAVER VALVE IN YOUR CAR, YOU MUST EXPERIENCE A DRAMATIC DECREASE IN GAS CONSUMPTION (CX 6; *see* CXs 2, 3, 4, 7, 8, 10, 11, 12).

READ THE RESULTS FOR YOURSELF!

The BALL-MATIC (gas saver) that I purchased has proven itself. I drive a 1970 Oldsmobile, now I get four miles more per gallon.

C.T.—Orange, California

Just a short note to inform you of the performance of your BALL-MATIC unit that I have installed in my 1972 Ford station wagon. Prior to using your device, I averaged 12 to 13 MPG, now that I have installed your unit my mileage has gone up to 16 MPG around town.

A. Coutts
Sherriff, Orange County, California

Before it was installed on my 1973 Ford L.T.D. I was getting 9 miles to the gallon, since installation of the BALL-MATIC I am getting almost 15 miles to the gallon.

R.B.—Hickman, Nebraska

After installing the BALL-MATIC on my 1972 Oldsmobile Toronado I increased from 7.5 to 10.5 miles to the gallon. Seeing this I took my station on as a BALL-MATIC dealer and within the first week sold over 100 valves.

This kind of extra income producer that other service stations should consider during this energy crisis to service their customers.

Louis Michaud
Mobile Service, New Britain, Connecticut

I want to express my thanks for the BALL-MATIC. Since it has been installed in my car, my gas mileage has not been under 18 miles per gallon. This is an increase of 5.5 miles per gallon.

Rev. R.N. Claremont, California

(CX 4; *see* CXs 2, 3, 6, 10; see also CXs 1, 5, 7, 8, 11, 12).

In addition to the statements quoted above in Finding 13, *supra*, respondents' advertisements and promotional materials contain a statement that consumers can save fuel "thanks to an amazing automobile discovery" (CXs 2-6, 10; 13-15). Other advertisements describe the Ball-Matic as an "important automobile invention" (CX 7). Many of the advertisements and promotional materials also contain bold type headlines in the text stating that the Ball-Matic is "the Most Significant Automotive Breakthrough of the Last Ten Years" (CXs 2-6, 10, 13-15). Some advertisements liken the Ball-Matic to a "minicomputer brain" (CXs 2-4, 6, 8, 10-12), and in one instance the Ball-Matic is referred to as a "unique, patented" valve (CX 9).

In truth and in fact, contrary to respondents' representations set forth in Paragraph Five:

a. the Ball-Matic is not an important, significant, or unique new invention;

b. the Ball-Matic is not needed on every motor vehicle except Volkswagens, diesel vehicles, or fuel injection vehicles.

c. the Ball-Matic when installed in a typical automobile will not significantly improve fuel economy;

d. under normal conditions, a typical driver cannot usually obtain a fuel economy improvement that will approximate or equal 20% or four miles per gallon when the Ball-Matic is installed in his/her automobile;

e. no competent scientific tests prove the fuel economy claims for the Ball-Matic;

f. results of consumer usage, as evidenced by consumer endorsements, do not prove that the Ball-Matic significantly improves fuel economy;

g. some individuals whose endorsements appeared in advertisements and sales promotional materials for the Ball-Matic did not give prior permission for the use of their endorsements, did not use the Ball-Matic at the time of the publication of their endorsements, and had not used the device in the recent past;

h. some consumer endorsements that appeared in advertisements and sales promotional materials for the Ball-Matic were obtained from individuals who, at the time they provided the endorsements, were not independent of all individuals and entities that have marketed the Ball-Matic.

i. the consumer endorsements and sales promotional materials do not reflect the typical or ordinary experience of members of the public who have used the Ball-Matic.

Therefore, said advertisements and sales promotional materials are deceptive or unfair.

At the time respondents made the representations alleged in Paragraph Five of the complaint, they did not possess and rely upon a reasonable basis for such representations. Therefore, said advertisements and sales promotional materials are deceptive or unfair.

The advertisements referred to in Paragraph Four and other advertisements and sales promotional materials represent, directly and by implication, that respondents had a reasonable basis for making, at the time they were made, the representations alleged in Paragraph Five. In truth and in fact, respondents had no reasonable basis for such representations. Therefore, said advertisements and sales promotional materials are deceptive or unfair.

In the course and conduct of their business, and at all times mentioned herein, respondents have been, and now are, insubstantial competition in or affecting commerce with corporations, firms and individuals engaged in the sale of automobile retrofit devices.

The use by respondents of the aforesaid unfair or deceptive statements, representations, acts and practices, directly or by implication, has had and now has the capacity and tendency to mislead members of the public into the erroneous and mistaken belief that said statements and representations were and are true and complete, and into the purchase of substantial quantities of respondents' product by reason of said erroneous and mistaken belief.

The acts and practices of respondents, as herein alleged, including the dissemination of the aforesaid false advertisements, were and are all to the prejudice and injury of the public and of respondents' competitors, and constituted and now constitute unfair methods of competition in or affecting commerce and unfair or deceptive acts or practices in or affecting commerce in violation of Section 5 of the Federal Trade Commission Act. The acts and practices of respondents, as herein alleged, are continuing and will continue in the absence of the relief herein requested.

. . . [Appended Statement of Policy]

Section 5 of the FTC Act declares unfair or deceptive acts or practices unlawful. Section 12 specifically prohibits false ads likely to induce the purchase of food, drugs, devices or cosmetics. Section 15 defines a false ad for purposes of Section 12 as one which is "misleading in a material respect." Numerous Commission and judicial decisions have defined and elaborated on the phrase "deceptive acts or practices" under both Sections 5 and 12. Nowhere, however, is there a single definitive statement of the Commission's view of its authority. The Commission believes that such a statement would be useful to the public, as well as the Committee in its continuing review of our jurisdiction.

We have therefore reviewed the decided cases to synthesize the most important principles of general applicability. We have attempted to provide a concrete indication of the manner in which the Commission will enforce its deception mandate. In so doing, we intend to address the concerns that have been raised about the meaning of deception, and thereby attempt to provide a greater sense of certainty as to how the concept will be applied.

I. SUMMARY

Certain elements undergird all deception cases. *First*, there must be a representation, omission or practice that is likely to mislead the consumer. Practices that have been found misleading or deceptive in specific cases include false oral or written representations, misleading price claims, sales of hazardous or systematically defective products or services without adequate disclosures, failure to disclose information regarding pyramid sales, use of bait and switch techniques, failure to perform promised services, and failure to meet warranty obligations.

Second, we examine the practice from the perspective of a consumer acting reasonably in the circumstances. If the representation or practice affects or is directed primarily to a particular group, the Commission examines reasonableness from the perspective of that group.

Third, the representation, omission, or practice must be a "material" one. The basic question is whether the act or practice is likely to affect the consumer's conduct or decision with regard to a product or service. If so, the practice is material, and consumer injury is likely, because consumers are likely to have chosen differently but for the deception. In many instances, materiality, and hence injury, can be presumed from the nature of the practice. In other instances, evidence of materiality may be necessary.

Thus, the Commission will find deception if there is a representation, omission or practice that is likely to mislead the consumer acting reasonably in the circumstances, to the consumer's detriment. We discuss each of these elements below.

II. THERE MUST BE A REPRESENTATION, OMISSION, OR PRACTICE THAT IS LIKELY TO MISLEAD THE CONSUMER

Most deception involves written or oral misrepresentations, or omissions of material information. Deception may also occur in other forms of conduct associated with a sales transaction. The entire advertisement, transaction or course of dealing will be considered. The issue is whether the act or practice is likely to mislead, rather than whether it causes actual deception.

Of course, the Commission must find that a representation, omission, or practice occurred. In cases of express claims, the representation itself establishes the meaning. In cases of implied claims, the Commission will often be able to determine meaning through an examination of the representation itself, including an evaluation of such factors as the entire document, the juxtaposition of various phrases in the document, the nature of the claim, and the nature of the transaction. In other situations, the Commission will require extrinsic evidence that reasonable consumers reach the implied claims. In all instances, the Commission will carefully consider any extrinsic evidence that is introduced.

Some cases involve omission of material information, the disclosure of which is necessary to prevent the claim, practice, or sale from being misleading. Information may be omitted from written or oral representations or from the commercial transaction.

In some circumstances, the Commission can presume that consumers are likely to reach false beliefs about the product or service because of an omission. At other times, however, the Commission may require evidence on consumers' expectations.

Marketing and point-of-sales practices that are likely to mislead consumers are also deceptive. For instance, in bait and switch cases, a violation occurs when the offer to sell the product is not a bona fide offer. The Commission has also found deception where a sales representative misrepresented the purpose of the initial contact with customers. When a product is sold, there is an implied representation that the product is fit for the purposes for which it is sold. When it is not, deception occurs. There may be a concern about the way a product or service is marketed, such as where inaccurate or incomplete information is provided. A failure to perform services promised under a warranty or by contract can also be deceptive.

III. THE ACT OR PRACTICE MUST BE CONSIDERED FROM THE PERSPECTIVE OF THE REASONABLE CONSUMER

The Commission believes that to be deceptive the representation, omission or practice must be likely to mislead reasonable consumers under the circumstances. The test is whether the consumer's interpretation or reaction is reasonable. When representations or sales practices are targeted to a specific audience, the Commission determines the effect of the practice on a reasonable member of that group. In evaluating a particular practice, the Commission considers the totality of the practice in determining how reasonable consumers are likely to respond.

A company is not liable for every interpretation or action by a consumer. In an advertising context, this principle has been well-stated:

> An advertiser cannot be charged with liability with respect to every conceivable misconception, however outlandish, to which his representations might be subject among the foolish or feeble-minded. Some people, because of ignorance or incomprehension, may be misled by even a scrupulously honest claim. Perhaps a few misguided souls believe, for example, that all "Danish pastry" is made in Denmark. Is it therefore an actionable deception to advertise "Danish pastry" when it is made in this country? Of

> course not. A representation does not become "false and deceptive" merely because it will be unreasonably misunderstood by an insignificant and unrepresentative segment of the class of persons to whom the representation is addressed. *Heinz W. Kirchner*, 63 F.T.C. 1282, 1290 (1963).

To be considered reasonable, the interpretation or reaction does not have to be the only one. When a seller's representation conveys more than one meaning to reasonable consumers, one of which is false, the seller is liable for the misleading interpretation. An interpretation will be presumed reasonable if it is the one the respondent intended to convey.

The Commission has used this standard in its past decisions. ". . . The test applied by the Commission is whether the interpretation is reasonable in light of the claim." In the Listerine case, the Commission evaluated the claim from the perspective of the "average listener." In a case involving the sale of encyclopedias, the Commission observed "[i]n determining the meaning of an advertisement, a piece of promotional material or a sales presentation, the important criterion is the net impression that it is likely to make on the general populace." The decisions in *American Home Products, Bristol Myers*, and *Sterling Drug* are replete with references to reasonable consumer interpretations. In a land sales case, the Commission evaluated the oral statements and written representations "in light of the sophistication and understanding of the persons to whom they were directed." Omission cases are no different: the Commission examines the failure to disclose in light of expectations and understandings of the typical buyer regarding the claims made.

When representations or sales practices are targeted to a specific audience, such as children, the elderly, or the terminally ill, the Commission determines the effect of the practice on a reasonable member of that group. For instance, if a company markets a cure to the terminally ill, the practice will be evaluated from the perspective of how it affects the ordinary member of that group. Thus, terminally ill consumers might be particularly susceptible to exaggerated cure claims. By the same token, a practice or representation directed to a well-educated group, such as a prescription drug advertisement to doctors, would be judged in light of the knowledge and sophistication of that group.

As it has in the past, the Commission will evaluate the entire advertisement, transaction, or course of dealing in determining how reasonable consumers are likely to respond. Thus, in advertising the Commission will examine "the entire mosaic, rather than each title separately." As explained by a court of appeals in a recent case:

> The Commission's right to scrutinize the visual and aural imagery of advertisements follows from the principle that the Commission looks to the impression made by the advertisements as a whole. Without this mode of examination, the Commission would have limited recourse against crafty advertisers whose deceptive messages were conveyed by means other than, or in addition to, spoken words. *American Home Products*, 695 F.2d 681, 688 (3d Cir. Dec. 3, 1982).

Commission cases reveal specific guidelines. Depending on the circumstances, accurate information in the text may not remedy a false headline because reasonable consumers may glance only at the headline. Written disclosures or fine print may be insufficient to correct a misleading representation. Other practices of the company may direct consumers' attention away from the qualifying disclosures. Oral statements, label disclosures or point-of-sale material will not necessarily correct a deceptive representation or omission. Thus, when the first contact between a seller and a buyer occurs through a deceptive practice, the law may be violated even if the truth is subsequently made known to the purchaser. *Pro forma* statements or disclaimers may not cure otherwise deceptive messages or practices.

Qualifying disclosures must be legible and understandable. In evaluating such disclosures, the Commission recognizes that in many circumstances, reasonable consumers do not read the entirety of an ad or are directed away from the importance of the qualifying phrase by the acts or statements of the seller. Disclosures that conform to the Commission's Statement of Enforcement Policy regarding clear and conspicuous disclosures, which applies to television advertising, are generally adequate, CCH *Trade Regulation Reporter*, ¶ 7569.09 (Oct. 21, 1970). Less elaborate disclosures may also suffice.

Certain practices, however, are unlikely to deceive consumers acting reasonably. Thus, the Commission generally will not bring advertising cases based on subjective claims (taste, feel, appearance, smell) or on correctly stated opinion claims if consumers understand the source and limitations of the opinion. Claims phrased as opinions are actionable, however, if they are not honestly held, if they misrepresent the qualifications of the holder or the basis of his opinion or if the recipient reasonably interprets them as implied statements of fact.

The Commission generally will not pursue cases involving obviously exaggerated or puffing representations, *i.e.*, those that the ordinary consumers do not take seriously. Some exaggerated claims, however, may be taken seriously by consumers and are actionable. For instance, in rejecting a respondent's argument that use of the words "electronic miracle" to describe a television antenna was puffery, the Commission stated:

> Although not insensitive to respondent's concern that the term miracle is commonly used in situations short of changing water into wine, we must conclude that the use of "electronic miracle" in the context of respondent's grossly exaggerated claims would lead consumers to give added credence to the overall suggestion that this device is superior to other types of antennae. *Jay Norris*, 91 F.T.C. 751, 847 n.20 (1978), *aff'd*, 598 F.2d 1244 (2d Cir.), *cent. denied*, 444 U.S. 980 (1979).

Finally, as a matter of policy, when consumers can easily evaluate the product or service, it is inexpensive, and it is frequently purchased, the Commission will examine the practice closely before issuing a complaint based on deception. There is little incentive for sellers to misrepresent (either by an explicit false statement or a deliberate false implied statement) in these circumstances since they normally would seek to encourage repeat purchases. Where, as here, market incentives place strong constraints on the likelihood of deception, the Commission will examine a practice closely before proceeding.

In sum, the Commission will consider many factors in determining the reaction of the ordinary consumer to a claim or practice. As would any trier of fact, the Commission will evaluate the totality of the ad or the practice and ask questions such as: how clear is the representation? how conspicuous is any qualifying information? how important is the omitted information? do other sources for the omitted information exist? how familiar is the public with the product or service?

IV. THE REPRESENTATION, OMISSION OR PRACTICE MUST BE MATERIAL

The third element of deception is materiality. That is, a representation, omission or practice must be a material one for deception to occur. A "material" misrepresentation or practice is one which is likely to affect a consumer's choice of or conduct regarding a product. In other words, it is information that is important to consumers. If inaccurate or omitted information is material, injury is likely.

The Commission considers certain categories of information presumptively material. First, the Commission presumes that express claims are material. As the Supreme Court stated recently, "[i]n the absence of factors that would distort the decision to advertise, we may assume that the willingness of a business to promote its products reflects a belief that consumers are interested in the advertising." Where the seller knew, or should have known, that an ordinary consumer would need omitted information to evaluate the product or service, or that the claim was false, materiality will be presumed because the manufacturer intended the information or omission to have an effect. Similarly, when evidence exists that a seller intended to make an implied claim, the Commission will infer materiality.

The Commission also considers claims or omissions material if they significantly involve health, safety, or other areas with which the reasonable consumer would be concerned. Depending on the facts, information pertaining to the central characteristics of the product or service will be presumed material. Information has been found material where it concerns the purpose, safety, efficacy, or cost of the product or service. Information is also likely to be material if it concerns durability, performance, warranties or quality. Information pertaining to a finding by another agency regarding the product may also be material.

Where the Commission cannot find materiality based on the above analysis, the Commission may require evidence that the claim or omission is likely to be considered important by consumers. This evidence can be the fact the product or service with the feature represented costs more than an otherwise comparable product without the feature, a reliable survey of consumers, or credible testimony.

A finding of materiality is also a finding that injury is likely to exist because of the representation, omission, sales practice, or marketing technique. Injury to consumers can take many forms. Injury exists if consumers would have chosen differently but for the deception. If different choices are likely, the claim is material, and injury is likely as well. Thus, injury and materiality are different names for the same concept.

V. CONCLUSION
The Commission will find an act or practice deceptive if there is a misrepresentation, omission, or other practice, that misleads the consumer acting reasonably in the circumstances, to the consumer's detriment. The Commission will not generally require extrinsic evidence concerning the representations understood by reasonable consumers or the materiality of a challenged claim, but in some instances extrinsic evidence will be necessary.

The Commission intends to enforce the FTC Act vigorously. We will investigate, and prosecute where appropriate, acts or practices that are deceptive. We hope this letter will help provide you and the public with a greater sense of certainty concerning how the Commission will exercise its jurisdiction over deception. Please do not hesitate to call if we can be of any further assistance.

. . .

ORDER

PART I.
It is ordered, That respondents Cliffdale Associates, Inc., a corporation, its successors and assigns, Jean-Claude Koven, individually and as an officer of Cliffdale Associates, Inc., and Arthur N. Sussman, an individual, and respondents' agents, representatives, and employees, directly or through any corporation, subsidiary, division, or other device, in connection with the advertising, offering for sale, sale or distribution of the automobile retrofit device variously known as the Ball-Matic, the Ball-Matic Valve, the Ball-Matic Gas Saver Valve and the Gas Saver Valve, or any other automobile retrofit device (as "automobile retrofit device" is defined in Section 511 of the Motor Vehicle Information and Cost Savings Act, 15 U.S.C. 2011) having substantially similar properties, in or affecting commerce as "commerce" is defined in the Federal Trade Commission Act, do forthwith cease and desist from:

a. representing, directly or by implication, that such device is a unique product or new invention; and

b. representing, directly or by implication, that such device is needed on every vehicle except Volkswagens, diesel vehicles and fuel injection vehicles.

PART II.

It is further ordered, That respondents Cliffdale Associates, Inc, a corporation, its successors and assigns, and its officers, and Jean-Claude Koven, individually and as an officer of Cliffdale Associates, Inc., and Arthur N. Sussman, an individual, and respondents' agents, representatives, and employees, directly or through any corporation, subsidiary, division, or other device, in connection with the advertising, offering for sale, sale or distribution of any automobile gasoline additive, engine oil additive, or automobile retrofit device (as "automobile retrofit device" is defined in Section 511 of the Motor Vehicle Information and Cost Savings Act, 15 U.S.C. 2011), in or affecting commerce as "commerce" is defined in the Federal Trade Commission Act, do forthwith cease and desist from representing, directly or by implication, that such device will or may result in fuel economy improvement when installed in an automobile, truck, recreational vehicle, or other motor vehicle unless, and only to the extent, respondents possess and rely upon a reasonable basis which substantiates such representation at the time of its initial and each subsequent dissemination. This reasonable basis shall consist of competent and reliable tests, such as:

a. chassis dynamometer tests done according to procedures that simulate typical urban and highway driving patterns, such as the then current urban and highway driving test schedules established by the Environmental Protection Agency; or

b. track or road tests done according to procedures that simulate urban and highway driving patterns, such as the them current procedures established in the Society of Automobile Engineers' J1082b test protocol.

A competent and reliable test means one in which persons qualified to do so conduct the test and evaluate its results in an objective manner using procedures that insure accurate and reliable results.

Respondents shall, when using the results of any tests required by this Part, clearly and conspicuously disclose the limitations upon the applicability of the results to any automobile, truck, recreational vehicle, or other motor vehicle. Where the results of such tests are used in connection with a representation of fuel economy improvement expressed in miles per gallon (or liter), miles per tankful, or percentage, or where the representation of the benefit is expressed as a monetary saving in dollars or percentages, all advertising and other sales promotional materials that contain the representation must also clearly and conspicuously disclose the following disclaimer: "REMINDER: Your actual saving may vary. It depends on the kind of driving you do, how you drive and the condition of your car."

PART III.

It is further ordered, That respondents Cliffdale Associates, Inc., a corporation, its successors and assigns, and its officers, Jean-Claude Koven, individually and as an officer of Cliffdale Associates, Inc., and Arthur N. Sussman, an individual, and respondents' agents, representatives, and employees, directly or through any corporation, subsidiary, division, or other device, in connection with the advertising, offering for sale, sale or distribution of any product or service in or affecting commerce as "commerce" is defined in the Federal Trade Commission Act, do forthwith cease and desist from:

a. using, publishing, or referring to any endorsement unless respondents have good reason to believe that at the time of such use, publication, or reference, the person or organization named subscribes to the facts and opinions therein contained;

b. failing to disclose a material connection, where one exists, between an endorser of any product or service and any of the respondents. A "material connection" shall mean, for purpose of this order, any relationship between an endorser of any product or service and any individual or other entity marketing such product or service which relationship might materially affect the weight or credibility of the endorsement and which relationship would not reasonably be expected by consumers.

c. representing, directly or by implication, any energy savings or energy consumption characteristics of any product, other than any gasoline additive, engine oil additive, or automobile retrofit device (as "automobile retrofit device" is defined in the Automobile Information and Cost Savings Act, 15 U.S.C. 2011), unless, at the time of making the representation, respondents possess and reasonably rely upon competent and reliable evidence that substantiates such representation;

d. representing, directly or by implication, that any consumer endorsement of a product or service represents the typical or ordinary experience of members of the public who use the product unless this is the case;

e. misrepresenting, in any manner, the purpose, procedure, results, or conclusion of any test or survey pertaining to the energy saving or energy consumption characteristics of any product.

PART IV.
It is further ordered, That respondents Cliffdale Associates, Inc., a corporation, its successors and assigns, and its officers, and Jean-Claude Koven, individually and as an officer of Cliffdale Associates, Inc., and Arthur N. Sussman, an individual, and respondents' agents, representatives, and employees, directly or through any corporation, subsidiary, division, or other device, in connection with the advertising, offering for sale, sale or distribution of any fuel saving product in or affecting commerce as "commerce" is defined in the Federal Trade Commission Act, do forthwith cease and desist from failing to maintain accurately the following records which may be inspected by Commission staff members upon fifteen (15) days' notice: copies of and dissemination schedules for all advertisements, sales promotional materials, and post-purchase materials; documents relating to the use of or publication of endorsements; records of the number of pieces of direct mail advertising sent in each direct mail advertisement dissemination; documents which substantiate, contradict, or otherwise relate to any claim which is a part of the advertising, sales promotional materials, or post-purchase materials disseminated by respondents directly or through any business entity. Such documentation shall be retained by respondents for a period of three (3) years from the last date any such advertising, sale promotional materials, or post-purchase material is disseminated.

PART V.
It is further ordered, That the corporate respondent shall forthwith distribute a copy of this order to all operating divisions of said corporation, and to all present and future personnel, agents, or representatives having sales, advertising or policy responsibilities with respect to the subject matter of this order and that the corporate respondent shall secure from each such person a signed statement acknowledging receipt of the order.

PART VI.
It is further ordered, That the corporate respondent notify the Commission at least thirty (30) days prior to any proposed change in the corporate respondent such as dissolution, assignment, or sale resulting in the emergence of a successor corporation, the creation or dissolution of subsidiaries or any other change in the corporation which may affect compliance obligations arising out of the order.

PART VII.
It is further ordered, That the individual respondents named herein promptly notify the Commission of the discontinuance of their present business or employment and of their affiliation with each new business or

employment for a period of ten years from the effective date of this order. Each such notice shall include the respondents' new business address and a statement of the nature of the business or employment in which the respondent is newly engaged as well as a description of respondent's duties and responsibilities in connection with the business or employment. The expiration of the notice provision of this paragraph shall not affect any other obligation arising under this order.

PART VIII.
It is further ordered, That the respondents shall, within sixty (60) days after service upon them of this order, and also one (1) year thereafter, file with the Commission a report, in writing, setting forth in detail the manner and form in which they have complied with this order.

It is so ordered.

NATIONAL BAKERS SERVICES, INC. V. FEDERAL TRADE COMMISSION
329 F.2d 365 (7th Cir. 1964)

DUFFY, Circuit Judge.
This is a petition for a review of an order of the Federal Trade Commission (Commission). The petitioner, National Bakers Services, Inc. (National), is an Illinois corporation. Its business is the licensing of bakers to produce "Hollywood Bread" under its formula and trademark. It has 182 baker-licensees throughout the United States.

In a complaint, the Commission charged National had disseminated certain advertisements in which it represented directly or by implication that its bread was a low calorie food; that its bread was "lower in calories than and, therefore, substantially different in caloric value from ordinary breads," and that eating said bread would cause the consumer to lose weight or prevent the consumer from gaining weight. The complaint charged that National's bread was not a low calorie food; that it was not substantially different in caloric value from ordinary bread, and that eating said bread would not cause the consumer to lose weight and would not prevent the consumer from gaining weight.

The complaint charged National's advertisements were "false advertisements" and that the dissemination thereof constituted unfair and deceptive acts and practices in violation of the Federal Trade Commission Act (Act). (Section 5 of the Federal Trade Commission Act, 15 U.S.C. § 45, 66 Stat. 632).

National's advertisements often contained a picture of a beautiful motion picture star; in some instances in a slender full length pose. The advertisements contain a picture of a loaf of bread bearing the label "Hollywood" and prominently displaying such words as "reducing diets," "figure-wise mothers," "dieting," "panther slim," "sweet, slim, trim lines," "stay slender," "leopard lithe," "tigress trim" and "diet wisely." Practically all of the advertisements contained a legend stating that there are "only about 46 calories in an 18 gram slice" of Hollywood bread.

Typical of the representations in National's advertisements is the following excerpt from Commission's Exhibit 4: "When a woman's Panther Slim * * * she's vital as well as slender. A good figure is more than luck when a lady watches her weight the famous Hollywood way. Hollywood Bread is high in protein, vitamins and minerals, yet has only 46 calories per 18 gram slice. Choice of Golden Light or Nut-like Dark Hollywood."

The Commission found that by means of its advertisements, National had represented that Hollywood bread was lower in calories than ordinary commercial bread, and that substitution of "Hollywood" bread for standard bread in a normal diet would effect a weight loss or prevent a gain in weight.

The Commission also found that the consuming public has no conception of the gram weight or caloric content of standard commercial bread, and that the use of the legend "only about 46 calories per 18 gram slice" was intended to and did convey the impression that "Hollywood" bread was lower in calories than standard bread, and that a consumer could eat an equal amount of it as other breads and yet effect a weight loss.

It is without dispute that there is no significant difference in the caloric content of "Hollywood" bread and other commercial white bread. Both contain approximately 276 calories per 100 grams. However, standard brands of bread are normally sold sliced into twenty 23 gram slices per one-pound loaf, while "Hollywood" bread is sliced into twenty-five 18 gram slices per one-pound loaf. The only reason that "Hollywood" bread contains approximately 46 calories per slice instead of approximately 63 Calories, is because "Hollywood" bread is more thinly sliced.

The Commission observed that National's bread was as suitable for use in a normal diet as well as a reducing diet as any other thinly sliced enriched bread which offers a consumer the opportunity to consume or serve the bread in smaller individual pieces. Accordingly, the Commission limited its prohibition against any representation as to the usefulness of "Hollywood" bread in such diets to those that do not clearly disclose that National's bread has "no less calories than other commercial breads" and that its "only usefulness in a reducing or weight control diet derives from the fact that its thinner slices enable the consumer to conveniently serve and consume smaller individual portions."

National asserts that its bread, due to a special formula, contains more protein than ordinary bread. National claims that because of this more favorable ratio between calories and essential protein, as well as because the thinner slice contains less calories per portion, "Hollywood" bread is more suitable in weight reducing diets than ordinary bread.
Several of National's advertisments [sic] contained "About 46 calories in an 18 gram slice. Up to 42% Extra protein." This statement would be true only if "Hollywood" bread and other breads were compared on the basis of identically sized slices. As actually sold, a slice of "Hollywood" bread contained approximately the same amount of protein as a standard slice of ordinary bread.

As noted by the Commission, the consumers were not informed by National's advertising that the calorie comparison implied is between units of unequal weight, while the protein comparison is between units of the same weight. The advertisements sought to leave the impression upon the consumer that National's bread is both lower in calories and higher in protein.

Deception may be by innuendo rather than outright false statements. Rhodes Pharmacal Co. v. Federal Trade Commission, 7 Cir., 208 F.2d 382, 387.

Although National urges that it did not violate the Act and that there is no substantial evidence that its advertisements were misleading in any material respect, it levels its heaviest attack upon the form of the Commission's order. National claims the order unreasonably restricts its freedom to truthfully advertise its product, and that restrictions in the order are not reasonably related to the facts of record in this proceeding.

We think the record as a whole supports the findings of the Commission, and that National, in its advertisements, falsely represented its bread to be lower in calories and more effective in controlling body weight than ordinary bread. These findings are supported by substantial evidence on the record considered as a whole. Waltham Precision Instrument Company, Inc. v. Federal Trade Commission, 7 Cir., 327 F.2d 427, 431.

The meaning of an advertisement is a question of fact. Kalwajtys v. Federal Trade Commission, 7 Cir., 237 F.2d 654, 656; Aronberg v. Federal Trade Commission, 7 Cir., 132 F.2d 165, 167. The important criterion in determining the meaning of an advertisement is the net impression that it is likely to make on the general populace. Aronberg. v. Federal Trade Commission, supra.

As to the order, the Commission has wide discretion in its choice of a remedy and the courts will not interfere if the Commission has made an allowable judgment in its choice of a remedy. Federal Trade Commission v. Ruberoid Co., 343 U.S. 470, 473; Federal Trade Commission v. Mandel Brothers, Inc., 359 U.S. 385, 392; Waltham Watch Company v. Federal Trade Commission, 7 Cir., 318 F.2d 28, 32.

This Court has held that the Commission's choice of a remedy as reflected in its order will be interfered with by the courts only if the remedy selected bears no reasonable relationship to the unlawful practices found to exist. Niresk Industries, Inc. v. Federal Trade Commission, 7 Cir., 278 F.2d 337, 343.

The Commission's order herein is affirmed. Enforcement ordered.

Prescription Drug Advertising

The United States, unlike nearly every other nation, permits drug companies to advertise prescription drugs directly to consumers on television and radio. While the FTC oversees ads for over-the-counter medications, prescription drug ads are regulated and reviewed by the Office of Prescription Drug Promotion (OPDP) of the Food and Drug Administration (FDA), an agency within the Department of Health and Human Services. The following FDA Web release outlines the specific requirements for prescription drug ads under FDA regulations.

Product Claim Advertisements

Product claim ads are the only type of ads that name a drug and discuss its benefits and risks. However, these ads must not be false or misleading in any way. We encourage companies to use understandable language throughout product claim ads that are directed to consumers.

All product claim ads, regardless of the media in which they appear, must include certain key components within the main part of the ad:

- The name of the drug (brand and generic)
- At least one FDA-approved use for the drug
- The most significant risks of the drug

Product claim ads must present the benefits and risks of a prescription drug in a balanced fashion.

Print product claim ads also must include a "brief summary" about the drug that generally includes all the risks listed in its approved "prescribing information."

- Under the Food and Drug Administration Amendments Act of 2007, print advertisements need to include the following statement: "You are encouraged to report negative side effects of prescription drugs to the FDA. Visit Medwatch or call 1-800-FDA-1088."

Broadcast product claim ads (TV, radio, telephone) must include the following:

- The drug's most important risks ("major statement") presented in the audio (that is, spoken) **AND**
- ***Either*** all the risks listed in the drug's prescribing information ***or*** a variety of sources for viewers to find the prescribing information for the drug

This means that drug companies do not have to include all of a drug's risk information in a broadcast ad. Instead, the FDA-approved prescribing-information portion of the ad may tell viewers or listeners where they can find more information about the drug. This is called the "adequate provision" requirement. For broadcast ads, we have said that including a variety of sources of prescribing information fulfills this requirement.

We have suggested that broadcast ads give the following sources for finding a drug's prescribing information:

- A healthcare provider (for example, a doctor)
- A toll-free telephone number
- The current issue of a magazine that contains a print ad
- A website address

Source: fda.gov (2014)

21 U.S.C.A. § 352: MISBRANDED DRUGS AND DEVICES

A drug or device shall be deemed to be misbranded—

. . .

(n) Prescription drug advertisements: established name; quantitative formula; side effects, contraindications, and effectiveness; prior approval; false advertising; labeling; construction of the Convention on Psychotropic Substances. In the case of any prescription drug distributed or offered for sale in any State, unless the manufacturer, packer, or distributor thereof includes in all advertisements and other descriptive printed matter issued or caused to be issued by the manufacturer, packer, or distributor with respect to that drug a true statement of (1) the established name as defined in section 502(e) 4 [subsec. (e) of this section], printed prominently and in type at least half as large as that used for any trade or brand name thereof, (2) the formula showing quantitatively each ingredient of such drug to the extent required for labels under section 502(e) [subsec. (e) of this section] 6, and (3) such other information in brief summary relating to side effects, contraindications, and effectiveness as shall be required in regulations which shall be issued by the Secretary in accordance with the procedure specified in section 701(e) of this Act. . . .

21 U.S.C.A. § 353B: PREREVIEW OF TELEVISION ADVERTISEMENTS

(a) In general. The Secretary may require the submission of any television advertisement for a drug (including any script, story board, rough, or a completed video production of the television advertisement) to the Secretary for review under this section not later than 45 days before dissemination of the television advertisement.

(b) Review. In conducting a review of a television advertisement under this section, the Secretary may make recommendations with respect to information included in the label of the drug—

(1) on changes that are—

(A) necessary to protect the consumer good and well-being; or

(B) consistent with prescribing information for the product under review; and

(2) if appropriate and if information exists, on statements for inclusion in the advertisement to address the specific efficacy of the drug as it relates to specific population groups, including elderly populations, children, and racial and ethnic minorities.

(c) No authority to require changes. Except as provided by subsection (e), this section does not authorize the Secretary to make or direct changes in any material submitted pursuant to subsection (a).

(d) Elderly populations, children, racially and ethnically diverse communities. In formulating recommendations under subsection (b), the Secretary shall take into consideration the impact of the advertised drug on elderly populations, children, and racially and ethnically diverse communities.

(e) Specific disclosures.

(1) Serious risk; safety protocol. In conducting a review of a television advertisement under this section, if the Secretary determines that the advertisement would be false or misleading without a specific disclosure about a serious risk listed in the labeling of the drug involved, the Secretary may require inclusion of such disclosure in the advertisement.

(2) Date of approval. In conducting a review of a television advertisement under this section, the Secretary may require the advertisement to include, for a period not to exceed 2 years from the date of the approval of the drug under section 505 or section 351 of the Public Health Service Act [42 USC § 262], a specific disclosure of such date of approval if the Secretary determines that the advertisement would otherwise be false or misleading.

NOTES AND QUESTIONS

1. In Bolger v. Youngs Drug Products Corp., 463 U.S. 60 (1983), the U.S. Supreme Court devised a test to define commercial speech: speech that is an advertisement, refers to a specific product, and has an economic motivation. The Court ruled that a drug company's mailings promoting its contraceptive products met this test, notwithstanding the significant informational value of the mailings. Is this a useful definition in an age of integrated sponsored content like product

placements, video news releases, and online native advertising formatted to appear non-commercial?

2. In 44 Liquormart, Inc. v. Rhode Island, 517 U.S. 484 (1995), the Supreme Court unanimously struck down a blanket ban on ads for spirits that displayed retail prices. Justice Stevens, joined by Justices Kennedy and Ginsburg, argued that a state ban on truthful, nonmisleading commercial speech that is useful to consumers may require greater First Amendment scrutiny than the *Central Hudson* test. Justice Thomas went further, concluding that commercial speech should be treated no differently than noncommercial speech under the First Amendment. The other justices concurred in the judgment. Should laws regulating truthful commercial content that helps consumers make informed decisions be subject to strict scrutiny by the courts?
3. On January 2, 1971, commercials for cigarettes were banned from television by law. In 1998, tobacco companies settled a civil suit for Medicaid reimbursement brought by forty-six states, agreeing to cease character-driven marketing like "Joe Camel," ban billboard ads, and end sports event sponsorships. In Lorillard Tobacco Co. v. Reilly, 533 U.S. 525 (2001), the Supreme Court applied the *Central Hudson* test to a Massachusetts law that restricted all tobacco product ads in locations accessible to children, including displays near schools, playgrounds, and parks. The Court overturned the law as overbroad, ruling that it was "nearly a complete ban on the communication of truthful information about smokeless tobacco and cigars to adult customers."
4. In April 2014, the Food and Drug Administration (FDA) proposed new regulations for electronic cigarettes, requiring disclosure of ingredients used to make fluid e-cigarette inhalants, proof that the inhalants are safe, and regulating inhalant delivery devices. Notably absent from the proposed regulations were any restrictions on e-cigarette advertising. Regulations on the Sale and Distribution of Tobacco Products, 79 FR 23141 (April 25, 2014).
5. One exception to liability for deceptive advertising is puffery. Puffery is when an advertiser uses an over-the-top superlative to promote a product. Puffery is the reason that your local pizzeria can advertise "world's best pizza" with impunity. The unsupported claim is simply not believable. On the other hand, if a store claims that its burgers were "voted best, three years straight," that could be materially deceptive.
6. **Product disparagement.** A number of states have enacted laws allowing food interests to sue the media and others for making false claims about the health or safety of agricultural or seafood products.

The most famous cases involve the news program "60 Minutes" and Oprah Winfrey. Apple growers sued "60 Minutes" for claiming that Alar, a chemical used to regulate apples' growth and enhance their color, was a carcinogen, while Texas cattle ranchers sued Oprah Winfrey after she aired a show that claimed that American beef industry practices could spread a fatal human brain disease that had been linked to mad cow disease. In the "60 Minutes" case, the claim was later determined to be false; in Oprah's case, the claim was later discovered to be true. Though both defendants avoided liability, media advocates are concerned that these statutes may chill news organizations from investigating the health and safety of our food supply. Indeed, in June 2017, a South Dakota meat supplier went to court in a $5.7 billion product disparagement suit against ABC, alleging "fake news" in the network's depiction of a beef product as "pink slime."

CHAPTER 15

MEDIA OWNERSHIP & DIVERSITY

Diversity. Most would agree that media benefits from diversity. But how should one define diversity? And can media measure it? For over forty years, the Congress, the FCC, and the Courts have grappled with these issues in earnest. This chapter looks at diversity from a number of perspectives. A key aspect of diversity, as both the *Comcast* and *Prometheus Radio Project* cases address infra, relates to market power, and the efforts of government to promote robust competition among media owners.

Cable Television Diversity

The 2009 case of Comcast v. FCC is the latest chapter in what has been a decade-long battle between the FCC and the DC Circuit to limit the market power of cable providers. In the 1992 Cable Act, Congress directed the FCC to issue "horizontal" and "vertical" caps on the cable industry. The horizontal caps limited "the number of cable subscribers a person is authorized to reach through cable systems owned by such person, or in which such person has an attributable interest." 47 U.S.C. § 533(f)(1)(A). This cap was designed to prevent a large "multiple system operator" (MSO), like Comcast or Time Warner Cable, from buying too many local cable systems across the country. The vertical cap limited the number of channels on a cable system that can be occupied by a video programmer in which a cable operator has an attributable interest." 47 U.S.C. § 533(f)(1)(B). This cap was meant to stop an MSO from using its market power to own (or have a stake in) too many channels on the cable box.

With caps in place, Congress hoped to foster healthy competition among cable providers in different markets and increase outlet diversity on local cable systems, since independent cable channels would have a chance to be included in the MSO's channel line-up. The Cable Act, however, directed the FCC to determine the quantitative limits for both caps. In Time Warner Entertainment v. United States, in 2000, the DC Circuit upheld the constitutionality of the caps. In 2001, the court rejected the percentages that the FCC ordered—a thirty percent horizontal cap and a forty percent vertical cap—on administrative law grounds, arguing that the quantitative limits were "arbitrary and capricious." In the wake of this 2001 case, Time Warner Entertainment v. FCC, the FCC went back to the drawing board, commissioning economic analyses and inviting comments and suggestions from industry and the public. After considerable deliberation, the FCC decided that the thirty percent horizontal cap was justifiable, a finding that Comcast quickly challenged in the DC Circuit.

COMCAST CORP. V. FCC
579 F.3d 1 (D.C. Cir. 2009)

GINSBURG, Circuit Judge:
Comcast Corporation and several intervenors involved in the cable television industry petition for review of a rule in which the Federal Communications Commission capped at 30% of all subscribers the market share any single cable television operator may serve. We agree with Comcast that the 30% subscriber limit is arbitrary and capricious. We therefore grant the petition and vacate the Rule.

I. Background
The Cable Television Consumer Protection and Competition Act of 1992 directed the FCC, "[i]n order to enhance effective competition," 47 U.S.C. § 533(f)(1), to aprescrib[e] rules and regulations . . .

> [to] ensure that no cable operator or group of cable operators can unfairly impede, either because of the size of any individual operator or because of joint actions by a group of operators of sufficient size, the flow of video programming from the video programmer to the consumer.

Id. § 533(f)(2)(A). The Commission is to "make such rules and regulations reflect the dynamic nature of the communications marketplace." Id. § 533(f)(2)(E).

Several cable operators immediately challenged certain provisions of the Act, in particular arguing the subscriber limit provision was facially unconstitutional as a content-based restriction of speech. See Daniels Cablevision, Inc. v. United States, 835 F.Supp. 1 (D.D.C. 1993), rev'd in part sub nom. Time Warner Entm't Co. v. United States (Time Warner I), 211 F.3d 1313 (D.C. Cir. 2000). We "conclude[d] that the subscriber limits provision is not content-based." Time Warner I, 211 F.3d at 1318. Applying "intermediate, rather than strict scrutiny," id., we upheld the relevant provision of the Act because the plaintiff "ha[d] not demonstrated that the subscriber limits provision is on its face either unnecessary or unnecessarily overburdensome" to speech protected by the First Amendment to the Constitution of the United States, id. at 1320.

In 1993 the Commission first exercised its rulemaking authority and set the subscriber limit at 30%. Much has changed in the subscription television industry since 1993: The number of networks has increased five-fold and satellite television companies, which were bit players in the early '90s, now serve one-third of all subscribers. Meanwhile, the FCC has twice changed the formula it uses to determine the maximum number of subscribers a cable operator may serve, but the subscriber limit has always remained at 30%.

In 2001 we considered a petition for review of a then newly revised version of the 30% subscriber limit. Time Warner Entm't Co. v. FCC (Time Warner II), 240 F.3d 1126 (2001). Then, as now, the Commission established the subscriber limit through an "open field" analysis, in which the agency "determines whether a programming network would have access to alternative [video programming distributors] of sufficient size to allow it to successfully enter the market, if it were denied carriage by one or more of the largest cable operators." Fourth Report and Order and Further Notice of Proposed Rulemaking, 23 F.C.C.R. 2134, 2143, 73 Fed.Reg. 11,048 (2008) (Fourth Report). In Time Warner II we described the formula then used by the FCC:

> [T]he FCC determines that the average cable network needs to reach 15 million subscribers to be economically viable. This is 18.56% of the roughly 80 million . . . subscribers, and the FCC rounds it up to 20% of such subscribers. The FCC then divines that the average cable programmer will succeed in reaching only about 50% of the subscribers linked to cable companies that agree to carry its programming, because of channel capacity, programming tastes of particular cable operators, or other factors. The average programmer therefore requires an open field of 40% of the market to be viable (.20/.50 = .40).
>
> Finally, to support the 30% limit that it says is necessary to assure this minimum, the Commission reasons as follows: With a 30% limit, a programmer has an open field of 40%

> of the market even if the two largest cable companies deny carriage, acting individually or collusively.

240 F.3d at 1131 (internal citations and quotation marks omitted). As is apparent from this description, in order to use the open field approach, the Commission must assign values to three variables: (1) The "minimum viable scale," which is the number of viewers a network must reach to be economically viable; (2) the relevant market, which is the total number of subscribers; and (3) the "penetration rate," which is the percentage of viewers the average cable network reaches once a cable operator decides to carry it.

In establishing the subscriber limit we reviewed in Time Warner II, the Commission had sought to ensure a minimum open field of 40% and reasoned that a 30% cap, rather than the seemingly obvious 60% cap, was necessary because the Commission was concerned about the viability of a video programming network if the two largest cable operators denied it carriage. Id. at 1132. We granted the petition because the record contained no evidence of cable operators' colluding to deny a video programmer carriage and "the legitimate, independent editorial choices" of two or more cable operators, id. at 1135, could not be said to "unfairly impede, either because of the size of any individual operator or because of joint actions by a group of operators of sufficient size, the flow of video programming from the video programmer to the consumer," 47 U.S.C. § 533(f)(2)(A). We directed the agency on remand to consider how the increasing market share of direct broadcast satellite (DBS) companies, such as DirecTV and Dish Network, diminished cable operators' ability to determine the economic fate of programming networks. Time Warner II, 240 F.3d at 1134.

On remand, the Commission adopted the current version of the 30% subscriber limit. The Rule here under review was designed to ensure that no single cable operator "can, by simply refusing to carry a programming network, cause it to fail." Fourth Report, 23 F.C.C.R. at 2154. Based upon the record before the court in Time Warner II, the subscriber limit under this standard could not have been lower than 60%. 240 F.3d at 1136. Based upon the present record, however, the Commission concluded no cable operator could safely be allowed to serve—mirabile dictu—more than 30% of all subscribers. Plus ça change, plus c'est la même chose?

In re-calculating the minimum viable scale, the Commission relied upon a study's finding regarding the number of viewers a cable network needed to reach in order to have a 70% chance of survival after five years, using data on the survival of cable networks between 1984 and 2001. Fourth Report, 23 F.C.C.R. at 2162. Based upon the study, the FCC found the minimum viable scale was 19.03 million subscribers, about four million more than the agency had found were necessary in 1999.

To determine the total number of subscribers, the FCC counted all cable subscribers and DBS customers, totaling approximately 96 million (up from 80 million in 1999). Id. at 2166–67. In re-calculating the penetration rate, the Commission observed, "many, if not most, new cable networks are placed on a digital tier. A consequence of being placed on a digital tier versus one of the basic levels of service . . . is a much lower penetration rate." Id. at 2163. Using an in-house study of the tiering and subscribership data for a sample of cable operators and a linear regression model, the Commission determined the penetration rate of the average network was 27.42%, or slightly more than half the 50% penetration rate it found in 1999. Id. at 2164.

From these data, the Commission calculated that a video programming network, to be viable, required an open field of 70% (up from 40% in 1999). Therefore, no cable operator could serve more than 30% of all subscribers.

Although the Commission recognized "that competition in the downstream market [especially from DBS companies] may affect the ability of a large cable operator to prevent successful entry by a programming network, and that [the] open field analysis does not directly measure this," it decided not to adjust the subscriber limit to account for such competition because doing so would be "quite difficult." Id. at 2167–68. The FCC then gave four reasons it did not regard competition from DBS companies as significant: Customers are reluctant to switch from cable service to DBS because (1) switching is costly; and (2) cable operators offer non-video services, such as telephone and internet access, that are not available with DBS; and (3) "video programming is a product, the quality of which cannot be known with certainty until it is consumed." Additionally, (4) "[c]ompetitive pressures from DBS will not provide any assistance to networks that," not having a contract with the largest cable operator, are unable to "launch due to a lack of financing." Id. at 2168–69.

Comcast now petitions for review of the Commission's latest version of the 30% subscriber limit. The National Cable & Telecommunications Association, Bright House Networks, the Cable Television & Communications Association of Illinois, Cablevision Systems Corporation, the Indiana, Michigan, Minnesota, and Missouri Cable Telecommunications

Associations, and Time Warner have intervened in support of Comcast's petition. The CCTV Center for Media & Democracy, United Church of Christ, and the Center for Creative Community (collectively CCTV Intervenors) have intervened in support of the FCC.

II. Analysis

Comcast suggests the CCTV Intervenors lack standing and argues the 30% subscriber limit is unconstitutional, outside the scope of the FCC's statutory authority, and arbitrary, capricious, and unsupported by substantial evidence. The Commission suggests Comcast lacks standing and, of course, defends the 30% limit on all fronts.

A. Standing

. . .

The Commission argues we must dismiss the petition because Comcast has failed to show it has suffered a concrete injury in fact that is "actual or imminent, not conjectural or hypothetical." . . . Similarly, Comcast claims the CCTV Intervenors cannot point to an actual or imminent injury they would suffer if the 30% subscriber limit were lifted.

Comcast argues it is injured because the 30% subscriber limit "unduly restrict[s] its opportunity to grow internally and make economically efficient acquisitions." . . . In support of the latter point, the Company invokes the Declaration of a Senior Vice President, who states that "[h]ad the horizontal ownership cap not been imposed by the FCC, Comcast would have seriously pursued further negotiations and due diligence with respect to" a specific but unidentified transaction. *Pick Decl.* at 2. This declaration is sufficient to support Comcast's standing . . . .

The CCTV Intervenors argue they will be harmed if a cable operator is allowed to serve more than 30% of all subscribers because such an operator could use its market position to restrict consumers' access to some cable networks. We need not decide whether this alleged harm is too "conjectural or hypothetical" to support standing, however, because "if one party has standing in an action, a court need not reach the issue of the standing of other parties when it makes no difference to the merits of the case." . . .

B. The 30% Subscriber Limit

We may set aside the Commission's decision "only if [it] was 'arbitrary, capricious, an abuse of discretion, or otherwise not in accordance with law.'" Mission Broad. Corp. v. FCC, 113 F.3d 254, 259-60 (D.C. Cir. 1997) (quoting 5 U.S.C. § 706(2)(A)). We will not do so if the agency "examined the relevant data and articulated a satisfactory explanation for its action." Fresno Mobile Radio, Inc. v. FCC, 165 F.3d 965, 968 (D.C. Cir. 1999) (internal quotation marks omitted).

Whether a cable operator serving more than 30% of subscribers can exercise "bottleneck monopoly power," Turner Broad. Sys. v. FCC (Turner I), 512 U.S. 622, 661 (1994), depends, as we observed in Time Warner II, "not only on its share of the market, but also on the elasticities of supply and demand, which in turn are determined by the availability of competition." 240 F.3d at 1134. A cable operator faces competition primarily from non-cable companies, such as those providing DBS service and, increasingly, telephone companies providing fiber optic service. As Comcast points out, DBS companies alone now serve approximately 33% of all subscribers. Recognizing the growing importance particularly of DBS, in Time Warner II we said in no uncertain terms that "in revisiting the horizontal rules the Commission will have to take account of the impact of DBS on [cable operators'] market power." Id.

Of the three aspects of the Commission's open field model—minimum viable scale, total number of subscribers, and penetration rate—only the total subscribers measure fully takes account of the competition from DBS companies and companies offering fiber optic services. As Comcast points out, the measure of minimum viable scale relies upon data from 1984-2001 and, as a result, fails to consider the impact of DBS companies' growing market share (from 18% to 33%) over the six years immediately preceding issuance of the Rule, as well as the growth of fiber optic companies. The penetration rate calculation, by the Commission's own admission, leaves out data regarding DBS penetration—an omission the FCC attempts to justify with the question-begging assertion that such data would not have materially changed the penetration rate.

Comcast argues the Commission has offered no plausible reason for its failure to heed our explicit direction in Time Warner II to consider the competitive impact of DBS companies. Instead the Commission made the four non-empirical observations we enumerated above. As for the first, transaction costs undoubtedly do deter some cable customers from switching to satellite services, but Comcast points to record evidence that almost 50% of all DBS customers formerly subscribed to cable; in the face of that evidence, the Commission's observation that cost may deter some customers from switching to DBS is feeble indeed. With regard to the second—that some cable consumers may be reluctant to switch to a satellite television service because, unlike cable companies, DBS companies do not offer internet and telephone services—the Commission does not point to any evidence tending to show these inframarginal customers are numerous enough to confer upon cable operators their supposed bottleneck power over programming. Moreover, as Comcast points out, both DirecTV and Dish Network have partnered with telephone companies to offer bundled DBS and telephone services. The Commission's third justification—that consumers will not switch providers to access new programming because they cannot know the quality of the programming before consuming it—warrants little discussion. As Comcast points out, there is no record support for this conjecture. In any event, it is common knowledge that new video programming is advertised on other television stations and in other media, and can be previewed over the internet, thus providing consumers with information about the quality of competing services. The FCC's fourth reason—that without its subscriber cap an upstart network will have trouble securing financing unless it has a contract with a cable company serving more than 30% of the market—is no more convincing than the other three when one recalls DBS companies already serve more than 30% of the market.

Finally, we note the Commission's observation that assessing competition from DBS companies is difficult—possibly true even if unexplained—does not justify the agency's failure to consider competition from DBS companies in important aspects of its model. That a problem is difficult may indicate a need to make some simplifying assumptions, see Chem. Mfrs. Ass'n v. EPA, 28 F.3d 1259, 1264 (D.C. Cir. 1994), but it does not justify ignoring altogether a variable so clearly relevant and likely to affect the calculation of a subscriber limit—not to mention one the court had directed the agency to consider.

Comcast, on the other hand, points beyond DBS companies' growing market share to their exclusive arrangements with certain highly sought after programmers as evidence that competition has led and will likely continue to lead subscribers to switch services. Indeed, Commissioner McDowell pointed out in dissent that, as of the date of the Fourth Report, DirecTV and Dish Network each served more customers than any cable company save Comcast itself. Fourth Report, 23 F.C.C.R. at 2228. Comcast also points to evidence that the number of cable networks has increased by almost 500% since 1992 and has grown at an ever faster rate since 2000, and that a much lower percentage of cable networks are vertically integrated with cable operators than was the case when the Congress passed the 1992 Act. There can be no doubt that consumers are now able to receive far more channels than they could in 1999, let alone 1992.

In sum, the Commission has failed to demonstrate that allowing a cable operator to serve more than 30% of all cable subscribers would threaten to reduce either competition or diversity in programming. First, the record is replete with evidence of ever increasing competition among video providers: Satellite and fiber optic video providers have entered the market and grown in market share since the Congress passed the 1992 Act, and particularly in recent years. Cable operators, therefore, no longer have the bottleneck power over programming that concerned the Congress in 1992. Second, over the same period there has been a dramatic increase both in the number of cable networks and in the programming available to subscribers.

In view of the overwhelming evidence concerning "the dynamic nature of the communications marketplace," 47 U.S.C § 533(f)(2)(E), and the entry of new competitors at both the programming and the distribution levels, it was arbitrary and capricious for the Commission to conclude that a cable operator serving more than 30% of the market poses a threat either to competition or to diversity in programming. Considering the marketplace as it is today and the many significant changes that have occurred since 1992, the FCC has not identified a sufficient basis for imposing upon cable operators the "special obligations," Turner I, 512 U.S. at 641, represented by the 30% subscriber limit. We conclude the Commission has failed to "examine[ ] the relevant data and articulate[ ] a satisfactory explanation for its action," Fresno Mobile, 165 F.3d at 968, and hold the 30% subscriber cap is arbitrary and capricious.

C. Remedy

Comcast asks us to vacate the 30% subscriber limit. "An inadequately supported rule . . . need not necessarily be vacated." Allied-Signal, Inc. v. U.S. Nuclear Regulatory Comm'n, 988 F.2d 146, 150 (D.C. Cir. 1993). Rather, "[t]he decision whether to vacate depends on the seriousness of the [rule's] deficiencies (and thus the extent of doubt whether the agency chose correctly) and the disruptive consequences of an interim change that may itself be changed." Id. at 150-51 (internal quotation marks omitted). In the past we have not hesitated to vacate a rule when the agency has not responded to empirical data or to an argument inconsistent with its conclusion. . . .

The Commission's dereliction in this case is particularly egregious. In the previous round of this litigation we expressly instructed the agency on remand to consider fully the competition that cable operators face from DBS companies. Time Warner II, 240 F.3d at 1134. The omission of this consideration was a major failing of the FCC's prior attempt to justify the 30% cap. The Commission nonetheless failed to heed our direction and we are again faced with the same objections to the rationale for the cap. It is apparent that the Commission either cannot or will not fully incorporate the competitive impact of DBS and fiber optic companies into its open field model. We have no trouble concluding, therefore, that vacatur is indicated by the first factor in Allied-Signal, "the seriousness of the [Rule's] deficiencies," 988 F.2d at 150. . . .

Vacatur is also indicated by the second Allied-Signal factor, viz., whether vacatur is likely to be unduly disruptive of the agency's regulatory program. 988 F.2d at 150–51. Although vacatur will eliminate the subscriber limit, cable operators will remain subject to, and competition will be safeguarded by, the generally applicable antitrust laws. . . .

The 30% subscriber cap has limited the ability of cable operators to communicate with the public for some 16 years despite our determination eight years ago that a prior version of the Rule was unconstitutional. See Time Warner II, 240 F.3d at 1128 ("the FCC has not met its burden under the First Amendment"). In light of the changed marketplace, the Government's justification for the 30% cap is even weaker now than in 2001 when we held the 30% cap unconstitutional. As the Supreme Court has observed, "the broadcast industry is dynamic in terms of technological change; solutions adequate a decade ago are not necessarily so now, and those acceptable today may well be outmoded 10 years hence." Columbia Broad. Sys. v. Democratic Nat'l Comm., 412 U.S. 94, 102 . . . (1973). To leave the Rule in place while the Commission tries yet again to justify it would be to . . . ignore this crucial fact about the nature of the video industry.

III. Conclusion

We hold the 30% subscriber limit is arbitrary and capricious because the Commission failed adequately to take account of the substantial competition cable operators face from non-cable video programming distributors. The petition for review is therefore granted and the subscriber limit is, accordingly,

Vacated.

RANDOLPH, Senior Circuit Judge, concurring . . . .

Broadcast Diversity

Section 202(h) of the Telecommunications Act of 1996 requires the FCC to review "all of its ownership rules biennially . . . and . . . determine whether any of such rules are necessary in the public interest as the result of competition." After completing this review, which is now done every four years, the FCC is required to "repeal or modify any regulation it determines to be no longer in the public interest." For many years, the FCC has been concerned about media diversity—especially broadcasting diversity. In the 2002 proposed rulemaking infra, the FCC formally identified four different types of diversity that merited FCC consideration: source diversity, outlet diversity, program diversity, and viewpoint diversity. In addition to defining each, the FCC concluded that viewpoint diversity—a classification that connects well to the "marketplace of ideas"—should be the primary concern of government policymakers. This decision to focus on viewpoint diversity lies at the heart of the FCC's deregulatory position in the *Prometheus Radio Project* case infra. In that case, public interest media access advocates successfully challenged a broad rollback of broadcast ownership restrictions proposed by the FCC under section 202(h). The *Prometheus* case also underscored the difficulty of measuring diversity, including the FCC's use of a much-maligned Diversity Index, which the 3rd Circuit Court of Appeals struck down.

As you review the diversity concepts in the FCC's 2002 proposed rulemaking, you may note that there is little discussion of ownership based on race or ethnicity. As the *Metro Broadcasting* case infra makes clear, ethnic and racial minorities have been historically underrepresented among broadcast license owners. In the 1980s, the FCC developed two programs for minority license applicants that would give them a preference over non-minority applicants. The crux of the debate in the *Metro Broadcasting* case revolves around the type of judicial scrutiny that should be applied to these programs, and whether there is a connection between who owns a station and the programs that air on it.

FCC NOTICE OF PROPOSED RULEMAKING

REVIEW OF THE COMMISSION'S BROADCAST OWNERSHIP RULES ADOPTED PURSUANT TO SECTION 202 OF THE TELECOMMUNICATIONS ACT OF 1996

17 F.C.C.R. 18503 (2002)

. . .

33. Diversity is one of the guiding principles of the Commission's multiple ownership rules. It advances the values of the First Amendment, which, as the Supreme Court stated, "rests on the assumption that the widest possible dissemination of information from diverse and antagonistic sources is essential to the welfare of the public." The Commission has elaborated on the Supreme Court's view, positing that "the greater the diversity of ownership in a particular area, the less chance there is that a single person or group can have an inordinate effect, in a political, editorial, or similar programming sense, on public opinion at the regional level."

34. The Commission has considered four aspects of diversity: viewpoint diversity, outlet diversity, source diversity, and program diversity. Viewpoint diversity ensures that the public has access to "a wide range of diverse and antagonistic opinions and interpretations." It attempts to increase the diversity of viewpoints ultimately received by the public by providing opportunities for varied groups, entities and individuals to participate in the different phases of the broadcast industry. Outlet diversity is the control of media outlets by a variety of independent owners. Source diversity ensures that the public has access to information and programming from multiple content providers, while program diversity refers to a variety of programming formats and content. Each of these components of diversity is described below.

35. Viewpoint Diversity. Viewpoint diversity has been the touchstone of the Commission's ownership rules and policies. We remain fully committed to preserving citizens' access to a diversity of viewpoints through the media. The Supreme Court has stated that "it has long been a basic tenet of national communications policy that the widest possible dissemination of information from diverse and antagonistic sources is essential to the welfare of the public." The diversity of viewpoints, by promoting an informed citizenry, is essential to a well-functioning democracy. The principal means by which the Commission has fostered diversity of viewpoints is through the imposition of ownership restrictions. In Sinclair, the Court of Appeals noted that ownership limits encourage diversity in the ownership of broadcast stations, which can in turn encourage a diversity of viewpoints in the material presented over the airwaves. The court added that diversity of ownership as a means to achieving viewpoint diversity has been found to serve a legitimate government interest, and has, in the past, been upheld under rational-basis review.

36. Outlet Diversity. The control of media outlets by a variety of independent owners is referred to as "outlet diversity." Outlet diversity ensures that the public has access to multiple, independently-owned distribution channels (e.g., radio, broadcast television, and newspapers) from which it can access information and programming. We have long assumed that diffusing ownership of outlets promotes a wide array of viewpoints. Thus outlet diversity was a key mechanism for promoting viewpoint diversity. In attempting to foster viewpoint diversity through structural regulation, our content-neutral method does not seek to evaluate the substance of any station's editorial decisions. Indeed, a major benefit of content-neutral structural regulation is that we avoid making inescapably subjective judgments about editorial decisions, viewpoints and content. Rather, we attempt only to preserve a sufficient number of independently owned outlets to increase the likelihood that independent viewpoints will be available in local markets. The Supreme Court has upheld the Commission's judgment that diversification of ownership enhances the possibility of achieving greater diversity of viewpoints.

37. Source Diversity. A related concept is "source diversity," which refers to the availability of content to consumers from a variety of content producers. Source diversity ensures that the public has access to information and programming from multiple content providers and producers. A wide array of content producers can contribute both to viewpoint diversity (particularly where the content is news and public affairs programming) and program diversity. A number of government efforts, both past and present, have been aimed at promoting source diversity on mass media distribution platforms. Our efforts centered initially on broadcast television, but have broadened in scope more recently to focus on MVPDs such as cable operators and DBS service.

38. Program Diversity. Program diversity refers to a variety of programming formats and content. Examples of program categories include formats such as dramas, situation comedies, reality television shows, and newsmagazines, as well as content, such as health, nature, foreign language/ethnic, and cooking. In 1960, when broadcast television was a more dominant mass communications medium in this country, we sought to promote program diversity through direct means.

. . .

41. Viewpoint diversity has been a central policy objective of the Commission's ownership rules. We seek comment on whether viewpoint diversity should continue to be a primary goal of the Commission's decision-making. The Commission has not viewed source and outlet diversity as policy goals in and of themselves, but as proxies for viewpoint diversity. Should the Commission continue to use source and outlet diversity as proxies to protect and advance viewpoint diversity? Or should each type of diversity be an explicit goal of the Commission's policymaking? Parties advocating that source and/or outlet diversity should be a goal of Commission ownership policies should address how priorities would be set among these types of diversity.

42. Once we define our diversity goal, we must then ask whether the marketplace will protect and advance diversity without regulatory requirements. As set forth in Section III, the current media marketplace appears robust in terms of the aggregate number of media outlets. Consumers generally have access to news, public affairs, and entertainment programming from a variety of media outlets—broadcast, cable, satellite, newspapers and the Internet. What has been the effect of this proliferation of new media outlets on the Commission's diversity goals? What effects, if any, do these outlets have on our objective of promoting diversity and the means by which we can best achieve those goals? How should these or other outlets be considered for the purposes of analyzing viewpoint diversity? Are there unique attributes of broadcasting that should lead us to define and measure diversity without reference to other media? Commenters should provide empirical data on consumer substitutability among the various media outlets or programs.

. . .

46. What other measures of diversity, quantitative or qualitative, should we consider, and what tools do we have to measure diversity with a reasonable degree of accuracy? Are audience demographics an appropriate measure of diversity? Is competition an appropriate proxy for diversity, such that the presence of a competitive local market will assuage our concerns about diversity? Should we take ratings figures or other measures of consumer usage into account in measuring diversity, and if so, how? In considering the various potential ways to measure diversity, we seek comment on how their use comports with the values and principles embodied in the First Amendment.

47. We also must consider the appropriate geographic area over which to measure diversity. Although radio ownership restrictions are limited to

the local market, television ownership is restricted both on the local level and nationally. Does the appropriate geographic area for measuring diversity differ based on whether the programming is local or national in nature? Should the appropriate geographic area for measuring diversity be the same as the relevant geographic market for competition purposes?

48. We also seek comment on whether the level of diversity that the public enjoys varies among different demographic or income groups. Although access to broadcasting services is available to all individuals in a community with the appropriate receiving equipment, access to other forms of media typically requires the user to incur a recurring charge, generally in the form of a subscription fee. Does this or any other differences between broadcasting and other media reduce the level of diversity that certain demographic or income groups enjoy? Does the fact that 86% of American households pay for television impact this analysis? What is the extent of any disparity in access to diversity, and how should we factor in that disparity in our diversity analysis?

49. Would one or more kinds of diversity be better promoted by alternatives to structural regulation, such as behavioral requirements? We invite comment on whether we should promulgate behavioral regulations. What, if any, behavioral requirements should be imposed and how should they be administered? How is diversity served, if at all, by existing behavioral rules such as those that require broadcasters to provide political candidates access to their facilities under certain conditions, or those that require cable systems to set aside channel capacity for certain uses (e.g., PEG, leased access)? What kind of programs and content contribute to viewpoint diversity?

50. In addition to seeking to foster the policy goals discussed above, the Commission has historically used the ownership rules to foster ownership by diverse groups, such as minorities, women and small businesses. The context of this comprehensive review of our ownership rules, we invite comment on whether we should consider such diverse ownership as a goal in this proceeding. If so, how should we accommodate or seek to foster that goal? In addition, we invite comment as to our legal authority to adopt measures to foster that goal. . . .

METRO BROADCASTING, INC. v. FCC

497 U.S. 547 (1990)

Justice BRENNAN delivered the opinion of the Court.

The issue in these cases, consolidated for decision today, is whether certain minority preference policies of the Federal Communications Commission violate the equal protection component of the Fifth Amendment. The policies in question are (1) a program awarding an enhancement for minority ownership in comparative proceedings for new licenses, and (2) the minority "distress sale" program, which permits a limited category of existing radio and television broadcast stations to be transferred only to minority-controlled firms. We hold that these policies do not violate equal protection principles.

I.

A.

. . . First, the Commission pledged to consider minority ownership as one factor in comparative proceedings for new licenses. When the Commission compares mutually exclusive applications for new radio or television broadcast stations, looks principally at six factors: diversification of control of mass media communications, full-time participation in station operation by owners (commonly referred to as the "integration" of ownership and management), proposed program service, past broadcast record, efficient use of the frequency, and the character of the applicants. . . . In the Policy Statement on Minority Ownership, the FCC announced that minority ownership and participation in management would be considered in a comparative hearing as a "plus" to be weighed together with all other relevant factors. See *WPIX, Inc.,* 68 F.C.C.2d 381, 411-412 (1978). The "plus" is awarded only to the extent that a minority owner actively participates in the day-to-day management of the station.

Second, the FCC outlined a plan to increase minority opportunities to receive reassigned and transferred licenses through the so-called "distress sale" policy. See 68 F.C.C.2d, at 983. As a general rule, a licensee whose qualifications to hold a broadcast license come into question may not assign or transfer that license until the FCC has resolved its doubts in a noncomparative hearing. The distress sale policy is an exception to that practice, allowing a broadcaster whose license has been designated for a revocation hearing, or whose renewal application has been designated for hearing, to assign the license to an FCC-approved minority enterprise. See *ibid.; Commission Policy Regarding the Advancement of Minority Ownership in Broadcasting,* 92 F.C.C.2d 849, 851 (1982). The assignee must meet the FCC's basic qualifications, and the minority ownership must exceed 50 percent or be controlling. The buyer must purchase the license before the start of the revocation or renewal hearing, and the price must not exceed 75 percent of fair market value. These two Commission minority ownership policies are at issue today.

B.

1.

In No. 89-453, petitioner Metro Broadcasting, Inc. (Metro), challenges the Commission's policy awarding preferences to minority owners in comparative licensing proceedings. Several applicants, including Metro and Rainbow Broadcasting (Rainbow), were involved in a comparative proceeding to select among three mutually exclusive proposals to construct and operate a new UHF television station in the Orlando, Florida, metropolitan area. After an evidentiary hearing, an Administrative Law Judge (ALJ) granted Metro's application. *Metro Broadcasting, Inc.*, 96 F.C.C.2d 1073 (1983). The ALJ disqualified Rainbow from consideration because of "misrepresentations" in its application. *Id.*, at 1087. On review of the ALJ's decision, however, the Commission's Review Board disagreed with the ALJ's finding regarding Rainbow's candor and concluded that Rainbow was qualified. *Metro Broadcasting, Inc.*, 99 F.C.C.2d 688 (1984). The Board proceeded to consider Rainbow's comparative showing and found it superior to Metro's. In so doing, the Review Board awarded Rainbow a substantial enhancement on the ground that it was 90 percent Hispanic owned, whereas Metro had only one minority partner who owned 19.8 percent of the enterprise. The Review Board found that Rainbow's minority credit outweighed Metro's local residence and civic participation advantage. *Id.*, at 704. The Commission denied review of the Board's decision largely without discussion, stating merely that it "agree[d] with the Board's resolution of this case."

Metro sought review of the Commission's order in the United States Court of Appeals for the District of Columbia Circuit, but the appeal's disposition was delayed; at the Commission's request, the court granted a remand of the record for further consideration in light of a separate ongoing inquiry at the Commission regarding the validity of its minority and female ownership policies, including the minority enhancement credit. The Commission determined that the outcome in the licensing proceeding between Rainbow and Metro might depend on whatever the Commission concluded in its general evaluation of minority ownership policies, and accordingly it held the licensing proceeding in abeyance pending further developments in the Docket 86-484 review.

The case returned to the Court of Appeals, and a divided panel affirmed the Commission's order awarding the license to Rainbow. The court concluded that its decision was controlled by prior Circuit precedent and noted that the Commission's action was supported by "'highly relevant congressional action that showed clear recognition of the extreme underrepresentation of minorities and their perspectives in the broadcast mass media.'" After petitions for rehearing and suggestions for rehearing en banc were denied, we granted certiorari. 493 U.S. 1017 (1990).

2.

The dispute in No. 89-700 emerged from a series of attempts by Faith Center, Inc., the licensee of a Hartford, Connecticut, television station, to execute a minority distress sale. In December 1980, the FCC designated for a hearing Faith Center's application for renewal of its license. See *Faith Center, Inc.*, FCC 80-680 (Dec. 21, 1980). In February 1981, Faith Center filed with the FCC a petition for special relief seeking permission to transfer its license under the distress sale policy. The Commission granted the request, see *Faith Center, Inc.*, 88 F.C.C.2d 788 (1981), but the proposed sale was not completed, apparently due to the purchaser's inability to obtain adequate financing. In September 1983, the Commission granted a second request by Faith Center to pursue a distress sale to another minority-controlled buyer. The FCC rejected objections to the distress sale raised by Alan Shurberg, who at that time was acting in his individual capacity. This second distress sale also was not consummated, apparently because of similar financial difficulties on the buyer's part.

In December 1983, respondent Shurberg Broadcasting of Hartford, Inc. (Shurberg), applied to the Commission for a permit to build a television station in Hartford. The application was mutually exclusive with Faith Center's renewal application, then still pending. In June 1984, Faith Center again sought the FCC's approval for a distress sale, requesting permission to sell the station to Astroline Communications Company Limited Partnership (Astroline), a minority applicant. Shurberg opposed the sale to Astroline on a number of grounds, including that the FCC's distress sale program violated Shurberg's right to equal protection. Shurberg therefore urged the Commission to deny the distress sale request and to schedule a comparative hearing to examine the application Shurberg had tendered alongside Faith Center's renewal request. In December 1984, the FCC approved Faith Center's petition for permission to assign its broadcast license to Astroline pursuant to the distress sale policy. See *Faith Center, Inc.*, 99 F.C.C.2d 1164 (1984). The FCC rejected Shurberg's equal protection challenge to the policy as "without merit."

Shurberg appealed the Commission's order to the United States Court of Appeals for the District of Columbia Circuit, but disposition of the appeal was delayed pending completion of the Commission's Docket 86-484 inquiry into the minority ownership policies. See *supra,* at 3006. After Congress enacted and the President signed into law the appropriations legislation prohibiting the FCC from continuing the Docket 86-484 proceeding, see *supra,* at 3006, the Commission reaffirmed its order granting Faith Center's request to assign its Hartford license to Astroline pursuant to the minority distress sale policy. See *Faith Center, Inc.,* 3 F.C.C.Rcd 868 (1988).

A divided Court of Appeals invalidated the Commission's minority distress sale policy. *Shurberg Broadcasting of Hartford, Inc. v. FCC,* 876 F.2d 902 (1989). In a *per curiam* opinion, the panel majority held that the policy "unconstitutionally deprives Alan Shurberg and Shurberg Broadcasting of their equal protection rights under the Fifth Amendment because the program is not narrowly tailored to remedy past discrimination or to promote programming diversity" and that "the program unduly burdens Shurberg, an innocent nonminority, and is not reasonably related to the interests it seeks to vindicate." *Id.,* at 902-903. Petitions for rehearing and suggestions for rehearing en banc were denied, and we granted certiorari.

II.

It is of overriding significance in these cases that the FCC's minority ownership programs have been specifically approved—indeed, mandated—by Congress. In *Fullilove v. Klutznick,* 448 U.S. 448 (1980), Chief Justice Burger, writing for himself and two other Justices, observed that although "[a] program that employs racial or ethnic criteria . . . calls for close examination," when a program employing a benign racial classification is adopted by an administrative agency at the explicit direction of Congress, we are "bound to approach our task with appropriate deference to the Congress, a co-equal branch charged by the Constitution with the power to 'provide for the . . . general Welfare of the United States' and 'to enforce, by appropriate legislation,' the equal protection guarantees of the Fourteenth Amendment." . . .

We hold that benign race-conscious measures mandated by Congress — even if those measures are not "remedial" in the sense of being designed to compensate victims of past governmental or societal discrimination—are constitutionally permissible to the extent that they serve important governmental objectives within the power of Congress and are substantially related to achievement of those objectives.

. . .

We hold that the FCC minority ownership policies pass muster under the test we announce today. First, we find that they serve the important governmental objective of broadcast diversity. Second, we conclude that they are substantially related to the achievement of that objective.

A.

Congress found that "the effects of past inequities stemming from racial and ethnic discrimination have resulted in a severe underrepresentation of minorities in the media of mass communications." H.R.Conf.Rep. No. 97-765, p. 43 (1982), U.S.Code Cong. & Admin.News 1982, 2237, 2261, 2287. Congress and the Commission do not justify the minority ownership policies strictly as remedies for victims of this discrimination, however. Rather, Congress and the FCC have selected the minority ownership policies primarily to promote programming diversity, and they urge that such diversity is an important governmental objective that can serve as a constitutional basis for the preference policies. We agree.

We have long recognized that "[b]ecause of the scarcity of [electromagnetic] frequencies, the Government is permitted to put restraints on licensees in favor of others whose views should be expressed on this unique medium." *Red Lion Broadcasting Co. v. FCC,* 395 U.S. 367, 390 (1969). The Government's role in distributing the limited number of broadcast licenses is not merely that of a "traffic officer," *National Broadcasting Co. v. United States,* 319 U.S. 190, 215 (1943); rather, it is axiomatic that broadcasting may be regulated in light of the rights of the viewing and listening audience and that "the wildest possible dissemination of information from diverse and antagonistic sources is essential to the welfare of the public." *Associated Press v. United States,* 326 U.S. 1, 20 (1945). Safeguarding the public's right to receive a diversity of views and information over the airwaves is therefore an integral component of the FCC's mission. We have observed that "'the "public interest" standard necessarily invites reference to First Amendment principles,'" *FCC v. National Citizens Committee for Broadcasting,* 436 U.S. 775, 795 (1978), quoting *Columbia Broadcasting System, Inc. v. Democratic National Committee,* 412 U.S. 94, 122 (1973), and that the Communications Act of 1934 has designated broadcasters as "fiduciaries for the public." *FCC v. League of Women Voters of Cal.,* 468 U.S. 364, 377 (1984). "[T]he people as a whole retain their interest in free speech by radio [and other forms of broadcast] and their collective right to have the medium function consistently with the ends and purposes of the First Amendment," and "[i]t is the right of the viewers and listeners, not the right of the broadcasters, which is paramount." *Red Lion, supra,* 395 U.S., at 390. "Congress may . . . seek to assure that the public receives through this medium a balanced presentation of information on issues of public importance that otherwise might not be addressed if control of the medium were left entirely in the hands of those who own and operate broadcasting stations." *League of Women Voters, supra,* 468 U.S., at 377.

Against this background, we conclude that the interest in enhancing broadcast diversity is, at the very least, an important governmental objective and is therefore a sufficient basis for the Commission's minority ownership policies. Just as a "diverse student body" contributing to a "'robust exchange of ideas'" is a "constitutionally permissible goal" on which a race-conscious university admissions program may be predicated, *Regents of University of California v. Bakke,* 438 U.S. 265, 311-313 (1978) (opinion of Powell, J.), the diversity of views and information on the airwaves serves important First Amendment values. Cf. *Wygant v. Jackson Board of Education,* 476 U.S. 267, 314-315 (1986) (STEVENS, J., dissenting). The benefits of such diversity are not limited to the members of minority groups who gain access to the broadcasting industry by virtue of the ownership policies; rather, the benefits redound to all members of the viewing and listening audience. As Congress found, "the American public will benefit by having access to a wider diversity of information sources." H.R.Conf.Rep. No. 97-765, *supra,* at 45, U.S.Code Cong. & Admin.News 1982, 2289.

B.

We also find that the minority ownership policies are substantially related to the achievement of the Government's interest. One component of this inquiry concerns the relationship between expanded minority ownership and greater broadcast diversity; both the FCC and Congress have determined that such a relationship exists. Although we do not "'defer' to the judgment of the Congress and the Commission on a constitutional question," and would not "hesitate to invoke the Constitution should we determine that the Commission has not fulfilled its task with appropriate sensitivity" to equal protection principles, *Columbia Broadcasting System, Inc. v. Democratic National Committee,* 412 U.S., at 103, we must pay close attention to the expertise of the Commission and the factfinding of Congress when analyzing the nexus between minority ownership and programming diversity. With respect to this "complex" empirical question, *ibid.,* we are required to give "great weight to the decisions of Congress and the experience of the Commission." *Id.,* at 102.

1.

The FCC has determined that increased minority participation in broadcasting promotes programming diversity. As the Commission observed in its 1978 *Statement of Policy on Minority Ownership of Broadcasting Facilities,* "ownership of broadcast facilities by minorities is [a] significant way of fostering the inclusion of minority views in the area of programming," and "[f]ull minority participation in the ownership and management of broadcast facilities results in a more diverse selection of programming." 68 F.C.C.2d, at 981. Four years later, the FCC explained that it had taken "steps to enhance the ownership and participation of minorities in the media" in order to "increas[e] the diversity in the control of the media and thus diversity in the selection of available programming, benefitting the public and serving the principle of the First Amendment." *Minority Ownership in Broadcasting*, 92 F.C.C.2d, at 849-850. See also *Radio Jonesboro, Inc.*, 100 F.C.C.2d 941, 945, n. 9 (1985) ("'[T]here is a critical underrepresentation of minorities in broadcast ownership, and full minority participation in the ownership and management of broadcast facilities is essential to realize the fundamental goals of programming diversity and diversification of ownership'") (citation omitted). The FCC's conclusion that there is an empirical nexus between minority ownership and broadcasting diversity is a product of its expertise, and we accord its judgment deference.

Furthermore, the FCC's reasoning with respect to the minority ownership policies is consistent with longstanding practice under the Communications Act. From its inception, public regulation of broadcasting has been premised on the assumption that diversification of ownership will broaden the range of programming available to the broadcast audience. Thus, "it is upon *ownership* that public policy places primary reliance with respect to diversification of content, and that historically has proved to be significantly influential with respect to editorial comment and the presentation of news." *TV 9, Inc.*, 495 F.2d, at 938 (emphasis added). The Commission has never relied on the market alone to ensure that the needs of the audience are met. Indeed, one of the FCC's elementary regulatory assumptions is that broadcast content is not purely market driven; if it were, there would be little need for consideration in licensing decisions of such factors as integration of ownership and management, local residence, and civic participation. In this vein, the FCC has compared minority preferences to local residence and other integration credits:

> "[B]oth local residence and minority ownership are fundamental considerations in our licensing scheme. Both policies complement our concern with diversification of control of broadcast ownership. Moreover, similar assumptions underlie both policies. We award enhancement credit for local residence because . . . [i]t is expected that [an] increased knowledge of the community of license will be reflected in a station's programming. Likewise, credit

> for minority ownership and participation is awarded in a comparative proceeding [because] 'minority ownership is likely to increase diversity of content, especially of opinion and viewpoint.'" . . .

2.

Congress also has made clear its view that the minority ownership policies advance the goal of diverse programming. In recent years, Congress has specifically required the Commission, through appropriations legislation, to maintain the minority ownership policies without alteration. See n. 9, *supra.* We would be remiss, however, if we ignored the long history of congressional support for those policies prior to the passage of the appropriations Acts because, for the past two decades, Congress has consistently recognized the barriers encountered by minorities in entering the broadcast industry and has expressed emphatic support for the Commission's attempts to promote programming diversity by increasing minority ownership. Limiting our analysis to the immediate legislative history of the appropriations Acts in question "would erect an artificial barrier to [a] full understanding of the legislative process." *Fullilove v. Klutznick,* 448 U.S., at 502 (Powell, J., concurring). The "special attribute [of Congress] as a legislative body lies in its broader mission to investigate and consider all facts and opinions that may be relevant to the resolution of an issue. One appropriate source is the information and expertise that Congress acquires in the consideration and enactment of earlier legislation. After Congress has legislated repeatedly in an area of national concern, its Members gain experience that may reduce the need for fresh hearings or prolonged debate when Congress again considers action in that area." *Id.,* at 502-503; see also *id.,* at 478 (opinion of Burger, C.J.) ("Congress, of course, may legislate without compiling the kind of 'record' appropriate with respect to judicial or administrative proceedings").

. . .

As revealed by the historical evolution of current federal policy, both Congress and the Commission have concluded that the minority ownership programs are critical means of promoting broadcast diversity. We must give great weight to their joint determination.

C.

The judgment that there is a link between expanded minority ownership and broadcast diversity does not rest on impermissible stereotyping. Congressional policy does not assume that in every case minority ownership and management will lead to more minority-oriented programming or to the expression of a discrete "minority viewpoint" on the airwaves. Neither does it pretend that all programming that appeals to minority audiences can be labeled "minority programming" or that programming that might be described as "minority" does not appeal to nonminorities. Rather, both Congress and the FCC maintain simply that expanded minority ownership of broadcast outlets will, in the aggregate, result in greater broadcast diversity. A broadcasting industry with representative minority participation will produce more variation and diversity than will one whose ownership is drawn from a single racially and ethnically homogeneous group. The predictive judgment about the overall result of minority entry into broadcasting is not a rigid assumption about how minority owners will behave in every case but rather is akin to Justice Powell's conclusion in *Bakke* that greater admission of minorities would contribute, on average, "to the 'robust exchange of ideas.'" 438 U.S., at 313. To be sure, there is no ironclad guarantee that each minority owner will contribute to diversity. But neither was there an assurance in *Bakke* that minority students would interact with nonminority students or that the particular minority students admitted would have typical or distinct "minority" viewpoints. See *id.*, at 312 (opinion of Powell, J.) (noting only that educational excellence is "*widely believed* to be promoted by a diverse student body") (emphasis added); *id.*, at 313, n. 48 ("'In the nature of things, it is hard to know how, and when, and even if, this informal "learning through diversity" actually occurs'") (citation omitted).

Although all station owners are guided to some extent by market demand in their programming decisions, Congress and the Commission have determined that there may be important differences between the broadcasting practices of minority owners and those of their nonminority counterparts. This judgment—and the conclusion that there is a nexus between minority ownership and broadcasting diversity—is corroborated by a host of empirical evidence. Evidence suggests that an owner's minority status influences the selection of topics for news coverage and the presentation of editorial viewpoint, especially on matters of particular concern to minorities. "[M]inority ownership does appear to have specific impact on the presentation of minority images in local news," inasmuch as minority-owned stations tend to devote more news time to topics of minority interest and to avoid racial and ethnic stereotypes in portraying minorities. In addition, studies show that a minority owner is more likely to employ minorities in managerial and other important roles where they can have an impact on station policies. If the FCC's equal employment policies "ensure that . . . licensees' programming fairly reflects the tastes and viewpoints of minority groups," *NAACP v. FPC,*

425 U.S., at 670, n. 7, it is difficult to deny that minority-owned stations that follow such employment policies on their own will also contribute to diversity. While we are under no illusion that members of a particular minority group share some cohesive, collective viewpoint, we believe it a legitimate inference for Congress and the Commission to draw that as more minorities gain ownership and policymaking roles in the media, varying perspectives will be more fairly represented on the airwaves. The policies are thus a product of "'analysis'" rather than a "'stereotyped reaction'" based on "'[h]abit.'" *Fullilove,* 448 U.S., at 534, n. 4 (STEVENS, J., dissenting) (citation omitted) . . .

D.

We find that the minority ownership policies are in other relevant respects substantially related to the goal of promoting broadcast diversity. First, the Commission adopted and Congress endorsed minority ownership preferences only after long study and painstaking consideration of all available alternatives. . . .

The minority ownership policies, furthermore, are aimed directly at the barriers that minorities face in entering the broadcasting industry. The Commission's task force identified as key factors hampering the growth of minority ownership a lack of adequate financing, paucity of information regarding license availability, and broadcast inexperience. The Commission assigned a preference to minority status in the comparative licensing proceeding, reasoning that such an enhancement might help to compensate for a dearth of broadcasting experience. Most license acquisitions, however, are by necessity purchases of existing stations, because only a limited number of new stations are available, and those are often in less desirable markets or on less profitable portions of spectrum, such as the UHF band. Congress and the FCC therefore found a need for the minority distress sale policy, which helps to overcome the problem of inadequate access to capital by lowering the sale price and the problem of lack of information by providing existing licensees with an incentive to seek out minority buyers. The Commission's choice of minority ownership policies thus addressed the very factors it had isolated as being responsible for minority underrepresentation in the broadcast industry.

. . .

In the context of broadcasting licenses, the burden on nonminorities is slight. The FCC's responsibility is to grant licenses in the "public interest, convenience, or necessity," 47 U.S.C. §§ 307, 309 (1982 ed.), and the limited number of frequencies on the electromagnetic spectrum means that "[n]o one has a First Amendment right to a license." *Red Lion,* 395 U.S., at 389. Applicants have no settled expectation that their applications will be granted without consideration of public interest factors such as minority ownership. Award of a preference in a comparative hearing or transfer of a station in a distress sale thus contravenes "no legitimate firmly rooted expectation[s]" of competing applicants. *Johnson, supra,* 480 U.S., at 638.

Respondent Shurberg insists that because the minority distress sale policy operates to exclude nonminority firms completely from consideration in the transfer of certain stations, it is a greater burden than the comparative hearing preference for minorities, which is simply a "plus" factor considered together with other characteristics of the applicants. Cf. *Bakke,* 438 U.S., at 317-318; *Johnson, supra,* at 638. We disagree that the distress sale policy imposes an undue burden on nonminorities. By its terms, the policy may be invoked at the Commission's discretion only with respect to a small fraction of broadcast licenses—those designated for revocation or renewal hearings to examine basic qualification issues—and only when the licensee chooses to sell out at a distress price rather than to go through with the hearing. The distress sale policy is not a quota or fixed quantity set-aside. Indeed, the nonminority firm exercises control over whether a distress sale will ever occur at all, because the policy operates only where the qualifications of an existing licensee to continue broadcasting have been designated for hearing and no other applications for the station in question have been filed with the Commission at the time of the designation. See *Clarification of Distress Sale Policy,* 44 Radio Reg.2d (P & F) 479 (1978). Thus, a nonminority can prevent the distress sale procedures from ever being invoked by filing a competing application in a timely manner.

In practice, distress sales have represented a tiny fraction—less than 0.4 percent—of all broadcast sales since 1979 . . . This means that, on average, only about 0.2 percent of renewal applications filed each year have resulted in distress sales since the policy was commenced in 1978. See 54 FCC Ann.Rep. 33 (1988). Nonminority firms are free to compete for the vast remainder of license opportunities available in a market that contains over 11,000 broadcast properties. Nonminorities can apply for a new station, buy an existing station, file a competing application against a renewal application of an existing station, or seek financial participation in enterprises that qualify for distress sale treatment. See Task Force Report 9-10. The burden on nonminority firms is at least as "relatively light" as that created by the program at issue in *Fullilove,* which set aside for minorities 10 percent of federal funds granted for local public works projects. . . .

III.

The Commission's minority ownership policies bear the *imprimatur* of longstanding congressional support and direction and are substantially related to the achievement of the important governmental objective of broadcast diversity. The judgment in No. 89-453 is affirmed, the judgment in No. 89-700 is reversed, and the cases are remanded for proceedings consistent with this opinion.

It is so ordered.

Justice STEVENS, concurring.

Today the Court squarely rejects the proposition that a governmental decision that rests on a racial classification is never permissible except as a remedy for a past wrong. *Ante,* at 3008. I endorse this focus on the future benefit, rather than the remedial justification, of such decisions.

I remain convinced, of course, that racial or ethnic characteristics provide a relevant basis for disparate treatment only in extremely rare situations and that it is therefore "especially important that the reasons for any such classification be clearly identified and unquestionably legitimate." *Fullilove v. Klutznick,* 448 U.S. 448, 534-535 (1980) (dissenting opinion). The Court's opinion explains how both elements of that standard are satisfied. Specifically, the reason for the classification—the recognized interest in broadcast diversity—is clearly identified and does not imply any judgment concerning the abilities of owners of different races or the merits of different kinds of programming. Neither the favored nor the disfavored class is stigmatized in any way. In addition, the Court demonstrates that these cases fall within the extremely narrow category of governmental decisions for which racial or ethnic heritage may provide a rational basis for differential treatment. The public interest in broadcast diversity like the interest in an integrated police force, diversity in the composition of a public school faculty or diversity in the student body of a professional school—is in my view unquestionably legitimate.

Therefore, I join both the opinion and the judgment of the Court.

Justice O'CONNOR, with whom The Chief Justice, Justice SCALIA, and Justice KENNEDY join, dissenting.

At the heart of the Constitution's guarantee of equal protection lies the simple command that the Government must treat citizens "as *individuals,* not 'as simply components of a racial, religious, sexual or national class.'" *Arizona Governing Comm. for Tax Deferred Annuity and Deferred Compensation Plans v. Norris,* 463 U.S. 1073, 1083 (1983). Social scientists may debate how peoples' thoughts and behavior reflect their background, but the Constitution provides that the Government may not allocate benefits and burdens among individuals based on the assumption that race or ethnicity determines how they act or think. To uphold the challenged programs, the Court departs from these fundamental principles and from our traditional requirement that racial classifications are permissible only if necessary and narrowly tailored to achieve a compelling interest. This departure marks a renewed toleration of racial classifications and a repudiation of our recent affirmation that the Constitution's equal protection guarantees extend equally to all citizens. The Court's application of a lessened equal protection standard to congressional actions finds no support in our cases or in the Constitution. I respectfully dissent.

I.

As we recognized last Term, the Constitution requires that the Court apply a strict standard of scrutiny to evaluate racial classifications such as those contained in the challenged FCC distress sale and comparative licensing policies. See *Richmond v. J.A. Croson Co.,* 488 U.S. 469 (1989); see also *Bolling v. Sharpe,* 347 U.S. 497 (1954). "Strict scrutiny" requires that, to be upheld, racial classifications must be determined to be necessary and narrowly tailored to achieve a compelling state interest. The Court abandons this traditional safeguard against discrimination for a lower standard of review, and in practice applies a standard like that applicable to routine legislation. Yet the Government's different treatment of citizens according to race is no routine concern. This Court's precedents in no way justify the Court's marked departure from our traditional treatment of race classifications and its conclusion that different equal protection principles apply to these federal actions.

In both the challenged policies, the Federal Communications Commission (FCC) provides benefits to some members of our society and denies benefits to others based on race or ethnicity. Except in the narrowest of circumstances, the Constitution bars such racial classifications as a denial to particular individuals, of any race or ethnicity, of "the equal protection of the laws." U.S. Const., Amdt. 14, § 1; cf. *Croson, supra,* at 493-494. The dangers of such classifications are clear. They endorse race-based reasoning and the conception of a Nation divided into racial blocs, thus contributing to an escalation of racial hostility and conflict. See *Croson, supra,* at 493-494. *Korematsu v. United States,* 323 U.S. 214, 240 (1944) (Murphy, J., dissenting) (upholding treatment of individual based on inference from race is "to destroy the dignity of the individual and to encourage and open the door to discriminatory actions against other minority groups in the passions of tomorrow"). Such policies may embody stereotypes that treat individuals as the product of their race, evaluating their thoughts and efforts—their very worth as citizens—according to a criterion barred to the Government by history and the Constitution. Accord, *Mississippi University for Women v. Hogan*, 458 U.S. 718, 725-726 (1982). Racial classifications, whether providing benefits to or burdening particular racial or ethnic groups, may stigmatize those groups singled out for different treatment and may create considerable tension with the Nation's widely shared commitment to evaluating individuals upon their individual merit. . . .

Nor does the congressional role in prolonging the FCC's policies justify any lower level of scrutiny. As with all instances of judicial review of federal legislation, the Court does not lightly set aside the considered judgment of a coordinate branch. Nonetheless, the respect due a coordinate branch yields neither less vigilance in defense of equal protection principles nor any corresponding diminution of the standard of review. . . .

Congress has considerable latitude, presenting special concerns for judicial review, when it exercises its "unique remedial powers . . . under § 5 of the Fourteenth Amendment," see *Croson, supra,* at 488 (opinion of O'CONNOR, J.), but this case does not implicate those powers. Section 5 empowers Congress to act respecting the States, and of course this case concerns only the administration of federal programs by federal officials. Section 5 provides to Congress the "power to enforce, by appropriate legislation, the provisions of this article," which in part provides that "[n]o State shall . . . deny to any person within its jurisdiction the equal protection of the laws." U.S. Const., Amdt. 14, § 1. Reflecting the Fourteenth Amendment's "dramatic change in the balance between congressional and state power over matters of race," *Croson,* 488 U.S., at 490 (opinion of O'CONNOR, J.), that section provides to Congress a particular, structural role in the oversight of certain of the States' actions. . . .

The Court's reliance on "benign racial classifications," *ante,* at 3008, is particularly troubling. "'Benign' racial classification" is a contradiction in terms. Governmental distinctions among citizens based on race or ethnicity, even in the rare circumstances permitted by our cases, exact costs and carry with them substantial dangers. To the person denied an opportunity or right based on race, the classification is hardly benign. The right to equal protection of the laws is a personal right. . . .

This dispute regarding the appropriate standard of review may strike some as a lawyers' quibble over words, but it is not. The standard of review establishes whether and when the Court and Constitution allow the Government to employ racial classifications. A lower standard signals that the Government may resort to racial distinctions more readily. The Court's departure from our cases is disturbing enough, but more disturbing still is the renewed toleration of racial classifications that its new standard of review embodies.

II.

For these reasons, and despite the harms that may attend the Government's use of racial classifications, we have repeatedly recognized that the Government possesses a compelling interest in remedying the effects of identified race discrimination. We subject even racial classifications claimed to be remedial to strict scrutiny, however, to ensure that the Government in fact employs any race-conscious measures to further this remedial interest and employs them only when, and no more broadly than, the interest demands... The FCC or Congress may yet conclude after suitable examination that narrowly tailored race-conscious measures are required to remedy discrimination that may be identified in the allocation of broadcasting licenses. Such measures are clearly within the Government's power.

Yet it is equally clear that the policies challenged in these cases were not designed as remedial measures and are in no sense narrowly tailored to remedy identified discrimination. . . .

III.

Under the appropriate standard, strict scrutiny, only a compelling interest may support the Government's use of racial classifications. Modern equal protection doctrine has recognized only one such interest: remedying the effects of racial discrimination. The interest in increasing the diversity of broadcast viewpoints is clearly not a compelling interest. It is simply too amorphous, too insubstantial, and too unrelated to any legitimate basis for employing racial classifications. The Court does not claim otherwise. Rather, it employs its novel standard and claims that this asserted interest need only be, and is, "important." This conclusion twice compounds the Court's initial error of reducing its level of scrutiny of a racial classification. First, it too casually extends the justifications that might support racial classifications, beyond that of remedying past discrimination. We have recognized that racial classifications are so harmful that "[u]nless they are strictly reserved for remedial settings, they may in fact promote notions of racial inferiority and lead to a politics of racial hostility." *Croson,* 488 U.S., at 493. . . . Second, it has initiated this departure by endorsing an insubstantial interest, one that is certainly insufficiently weighty to justify tolerance of the Government's distinctions among citizens based on race and ethnicity. This endorsement trivializes the constitutional command to guard against such discrimination and has loosed a potentially far-reaching principle disturbingly at odds with our traditional equal protection doctrine.

An interest capable of justifying race-conscious measures must be sufficiently specific and verifiable, such that it supports only limited and carefully defined uses of racial classifications. . . .

Even considered as other than a justification for using race classifications, the asserted interest in viewpoint diversity falls short of being weighty enough. The Court has recognized an interest in obtaining diverse broadcasting viewpoints as a legitimate basis for the FCC, acting pursuant to its "public interest" statutory mandate, to adopt limited measures to increase the number of competing licensees and to encourage licensees to present varied views on issues of public concern. . . . We have also concluded that these measures do not run afoul of the First Amendment's usual prohibition of Government regulation of the marketplace of ideas, in part because First Amendment concerns support limited but inevitable Government regulation of the peculiarly constrained broadcasting spectrum. See, *e.g., Red Lion, supra,* at 389-390. But the conclusion that measures adopted to further the interest in diversity of broadcasting viewpoints are neither beyond the FCC's statutory authority nor contrary to the First Amendment hardly establishes the interest as important for equal protection purposes.

The FCC's extension of the asserted interest in diversity of views in these cases presents, at the very least, an unsettled First Amendment issue. The FCC has concluded that the American broadcasting public receives the incorrect mix of ideas and claims to have adopted the challenged policies to supplement programming content with a particular set of views. Although we have approved limited measures designed to increase information and views generally, the Court has never upheld a broadcasting measure designed to amplify a distinct set of views or the views of a particular class of speakers. Indeed, the Court has suggested that the First Amendment prohibits allocating licenses to further such ends. See *National Broadcasting Co. v. United States, supra,* at 226 ("But Congress did not authorize the Commission to choose among [license] applicants upon the basis of their political, economic or social views, or upon any other capricious basis. If it did, or if the Commission by these Regulations proposed a choice among applicants upon some such basis, the [First Amendment] issue before us would be wholly different"). Even if an interest is determined to be legitimate in one context, it does not suddenly become important enough to justify distinctions based on race.

IV.

Our traditional equal protection doctrine requires, in addition to a compelling state interest, that the Government's chosen means be necessary to accomplish, and narrowly tailored to further, the asserted interest. See *Wygant,* 476 U.S., at 274 (plurality opinion); *Palmore v. Sidoti,* 466 U.S. 429, 432-433 (1984). This element of strict scrutiny is designed to "ensur[e] that the means chosen 'fit' [the] compelling goal so closely that there is little or no possibility that the motive for the classification was illegitimate racial prejudice or stereotype." *Croson,* 488 U.S., at 493 (opinion of O'CONNOR, J.). The chosen means, resting as they do on stereotyping and so indirectly furthering the asserted end, could not plausibly be deemed narrowly tailored. The Court instead finds the racial classifications to be "substantially related" to achieving the Government's interest, *ante,* at 3011, a far less rigorous fit requirement. The FCC's policies fail even this requirement.

A.

The FCC claims to advance its asserted interest in diverse viewpoints by singling out race and ethnicity as peculiarly linked to distinct views that require enhancement. The FCC's choice to employ a racial criterion embodies the related notions that a particular and distinct viewpoint inheres in certain racial groups, and that a particular applicant, by virtue of race or ethnicity alone, is more valued than other applicants because "likely to provide [that] distinct perspective." . . .

The FCC assumes a particularly strong correlation of race and behavior. The FCC justifies its conclusion that insufficiently diverse viewpoints are broadcast by reference to the percentage of minority-owned stations. This assumption is correct only to the extent that minority-owned stations provide the desired additional views, and that stations owned by individuals not favored by the preferences cannot, or at least do not, broadcast underrepresented programming. Additionally, the FCC's focus on ownership to improve programming assumes that preferences linked to race are so strong that they will dictate the owner's behavior in operating the station, overcoming the owner's personal inclinations and regard for the market. This strong link between race and behavior, especially when mediated by market forces, is the assumption that Justice Powell rejected in his discussion of health care service in *Bakke.* See 438 U.S., at 310-

311. . . .

B.

Moreover, the FCC's selective focus on viewpoints associated with race illustrates a particular tailoring difficulty. The asserted interest is in advancing the Nation's different "social, political, esthetic, moral, and other ideas and experiences," *Red Lion,* 395 U.S., at 390, yet of all the varied traditions and ideas shared among our citizens, the FCC has sought to amplify only those particular views it identifies through the classifications most suspect under equal protection doctrine. Even if distinct views could be associated with particular ethnic and racial groups, focusing on this particular aspect of the Nation's views calls into question the Government's genuine commitment to its asserted interest. . . .

Our equal protection doctrine governing intermediate review indicates that the Government may not use race and ethnicity as "a 'proxy for other, more germane bases of classification.'" *Hogan,* 458 U.S., at 726, quoting *Craig v. Boren,* 429 U.S. 190, 198 (1976). The FCC has used race as a proxy for whatever views it believes to be underrepresented in the broadcasting spectrum. This reflexive or unthinking use of a suspect classification is the hallmark of an unconstitutional policy. . . .

Moreover, the FCC's programs cannot survive even intermediate scrutiny because race-neutral and untried means of directly accomplishing the governmental interest are readily available. The FCC could directly advance its interest by requiring licensees to provide programming that the FCC believes would add to diversity. The interest the FCC asserts is in programming diversity, yet in adopting the challenged policies, the FCC expressly disclaimed having attempted *any* direct efforts to achieve its asserted goal. . . .

Other race-neutral means also exist, and all are at least as direct as the FCC's racial classifications. The FCC could evaluate applicants upon their ability to provide, and commitment to offer, whatever programming the FCC believes would reflect underrepresented viewpoints. . . .

The FCC has posited a relative absence of "minority viewpoints," yet it has never suggested what those views might be or what other viewpoints might be absent from the broadcasting spectrum. It has never identified any particular deficiency in programming diversity that should be the subject of greater programming or that necessitates racial classifications. . . .

The FCC seeks to avoid the tailoring difficulties by focusing on minority ownership rather than the asserted interest in diversity of broadcast viewpoints. The Constitution clearly prohibits allocating valuable goods such as broadcast licenses simply on the basis of race. See *Bakke,* 438 U.S., at 307 (opinion of Powell, J.). Yet the FCC refers to the lack of minority ownership of stations to support the existence of a lack of diversity of viewpoints, and has fitted its programs to increase ownership. See *1978 Policy Statement, supra; Commission Policy Regarding Advancement of Minority Ownership in Broadcasting,* 92 F.C.C.2d 849 (1982). This repeated focus on ownership supports the inference that the FCC seeks to allocate licenses based on race, an impermissible end, rather than to increase diversity of viewpoints, the asserted interest. And this justification that links the use of race preferences to minority ownership rather than to diversity of viewpoints ensures that the FCC's programs, like that at issue in *Croson,* "cannot be said to be narrowly tailored to any goal, except perhaps outright racial balancing." *Croson,* 488 U.S., at 507.

C.

Even apart from these tailoring defects in the FCC's policies, one particular flaw underscores the Government's ill fit of means to ends. The FCC's policies assume, and rely upon, the existence of a tightly bound "nexus" between the owners' race and the resulting programming. . . .

Three difficulties suggest that the nexus between owners' race and programming is considerably less than substantial. First, the market shapes programming to a tremendous extent. Members of minority groups who own licenses might be thought, like other owners, to seek to broadcast programs that will attract and retain audiences, rather than programs that reflect the owner's tastes and preferences. See *Winter Park Communications, Inc. v. FCC,* 873 F.2d 347, 358-361 (D.C. Cir. 1989) (case below) (Williams, J., concurring in part and dissenting in part) (surveying evidence suggesting programming geared to audience taste). Second, station owners have only limited control over the content of programming. The distress sale presents a particularly acute difficulty of this sort. Unlike the comparative licensing program, the distress sale policy provides preferences to minority owners who neither intend nor desire to manage the station in any respect. See *ante,* at 3005; *Commission Policy Regarding Advancement of Minority Ownership in Broadcasting, supra.* Whatever distinct programming may attend the race of an owner actively involved in managing the station, an absentee owner would have far less effect on programming.

Third, the FCC had absolutely no factual basis for the nexus when it adopted the policies and has since established none to support its existence.

D.

Finally, the Government cannot employ race classifications that unduly burden individuals who are not members of the favored racial and ethnic groups. See, *e.g., Wygant,* 476 U.S., at 280-281 (plurality opinion). The challenged policies fail this independent requirement, as well as the other constitutional requirements. The comparative licensing and distress sale programs provide the eventual licensee with an exceptionally valuable property and with a rare and unique opportunity to serve the local community. The distress sale imposes a particularly significant burden. The FCC has at base created a specialized market reserved exclusively for minority controlled applicants. There is no more rigid quota than a 100% set-aside. This fact is not altered by the observation, see *ante,* at 3027, that the FCC and the seller have some discretion over whether stations may be sold through the distress program. For the would-be purchaser or person who seeks to compete for the station, that opportunity depends entirely upon race or ethnicity. The Court's argument that the distress sale allocates only a small percentage of all license sales, *ante,* at 3027, also misses the mark. This argument readily supports complete preferences and avoids scrutiny of particular programs: It is no response to a person denied admission at one school, or discharged from one job, solely on the basis of race, that other schools or employers do not discriminate.

The comparative licensing program, too, imposes a significant burden. The Court's emphasis on the multifactor process should not be confused with the claim that the preference is in some sense a minor one. It is not. The basic nonrace criteria are not difficult to meet, and, given the sums at stake, applicants have every incentive to structure their ownership arrangement to prevail in the comparative process. . . .

In sum, the FCC has not met its burden even under the Court's test that approves of racial classifications that are substantially related to an important governmental objective. Of course, the programs even more clearly fail the strict scrutiny that should be applied. The Court has determined, in essence, that Congress and all federal agencies are exempted, to some ill-defined but significant degree, from the Constitution's equal protection requirements. This break with our precedents greatly undermines equal protection guarantees and permits distinctions among citizens based on race and ethnicity which the Constitution clearly forbids. I respectfully dissent.

Justice KENNEDY, with whom Justice SCALIA joins, dissenting.
Today the Court grants Congress latitude to employ "benign race-conscious measures . . . [that] are not . . . designed to compensate victims of past governmental or societal discrimination," but that "serve important governmental objectives . . . and are substantially related to achievement of those objectives." *Ante,* at 3008-3009. The interest the Court accepts to uphold the race-conscious measures of the Federal Communications Commission (Commission or FCC) is "broadcast diversity." Furthering that interest, we are told, is worth the cost of discriminating among citizens on the basis of race because it will increase the listening pleasure of media audiences. In upholding this preference, the majority exhumes *Plessy*'s deferential approach to racial classifications. The Court abandons even the broad societal remedial justification for racial preferences once advocated by Justice MARSHALL, *e.g., Regents of University of California v. Bakke,* 438 U.S. 265, 396 (1978) (separate opinion), and now will allow the use of racial classifications by Congress untied to any goal of addressing the effects of past race discrimination. All that need be shown under the new approach, which until now only Justice STEVENS had advanced, *Richmond v. J.A. Croson Co.,* 488 U.S. 469, 511 (1989) (opinion concurring in part and concurring in judgment); *Wygant v. Jackson Board of Education,* 476 U.S. 267, 313 (1986) (dissenting opinion), is that the future effect of discriminating among citizens on the basis of race will advance some "important" governmental interest.

I cannot agree with the Court that the Constitution permits the Government to discriminate among its citizens on the basis of race in order to serve interests so trivial as "broadcast diversity." In abandoning strict scrutiny to endorse this interest the Court turns back the clock on the level of scrutiny applicable to federal race-conscious measures. Even strict scrutiny may not have sufficed to invalidate early racebased laws of most doubtful validity, as we learned in *Korematsu v. United States,* 323 U.S. 214 (1944). But the relaxed standard of review embraced today would validate that case, and any number of future racial classifications the Government may find useful. Strict scrutiny is the surest test the Court has yet devised for holding true to the constitutional command of racial equality. Under our modern precedents, as Justice O'CONNOR explains, strict scrutiny must be applied to this statute. The approach taken to congressional measures under § 5 of the Fourteenth Amendment in *Fullilove v. Klutznick,* 448 U.S. 448 (1980), even assuming its validity, see

Croson, supra, at 518 (opinion of KENNEDY, J.), is not applicable to this case.

Postscript to Metro Broadcasting

ADARAND CONSTRUCTORS, INC. V. PENA
515 U.S. 200 (1995)

Justice O'Connor.
"[A] free people whose institutions are founded upon the doctrine of equality," ibid., should tolerate no retreat from the principle that government may treat people differently because of their race only for the most compelling reasons. Accordingly, we hold today that all racial classifications, imposed by whatever federal, state, or local governmental actor, must be analyzed by a reviewing court under strict scrutiny. In other words, such classifications are constitutional only if they are narrowly tailored measures that further compelling governmental interests. To the extent that Metro Broadcasting is inconsistent with that holding, it is overruled. . . .

PROMETHEUS RADIO PROJECT V. FCC
373 F.3d 372 (3d Cir. 2004)

AMBRO, Circuit Judge.
In these consolidated appeals we consider revisions by the Federal Communications Commission to its regulations governing broadcast media ownership that the Commission promulgated following its 2002 biennial review. On July 2, 2003, the Commission announced a comprehensive overhaul of its broadcast media ownership rules. It increased the number of television stations a single entity may own, both locally and nationally; revised various provisions of the regulations governing common ownership of radio stations in the same community; and replaced two existing rules limiting common ownership among newspapers and broadcast stations (the newspaper/broadcast cross-ownership rule and the radio/television cross-ownership rule) with a single set of "Cross-Media Limits." *See Report and Order and Notice of Proposed Rulemaking,* 18 F.C.C.R. 13,620, 2003 WL 21511828 (2003) (the "Order").

Several public interest and consumer advocacy groups (collectively, the "Citizen Petitioners") petitioned for judicial review of the Order in various courts of appeals, contending that its deregulatory provisions contravened the Commission's statutory mandates as well as the Administrative Procedure Act, 5 U.S.C. §§ 551 *et seq.* (the "APA"). Associations of networks, broadcasters, and newspaper owners also challenged the Order, arguing that pro-regulatory revisions as well as the absence of further deregulation violate the Telecommunications Act of 1996, Pub. L. No. 104-104, 110 Stat. 56 (1996) (the "1996 Act"), the APA, and the United States Constitution. The Judicial Panel on Multidistrict Litigation, acting pursuant to the random selection procedures of 28 U.S.C. § 2112(a), consolidated the petitions in this Court. On September 3, 2003, we stayed implementation of the rules pending our review.

For the reasons stated below, we affirm the power of the Commission to regulate media ownership. In doing so, we reject the contention that the Constitution or § 202(h) of the 1996 Act somehow provides rigid limits on the Commission's ability to regulate in the public interest. But we must remand certain aspects of the Commission's Order that are not adequately supported by the record. Most importantly, the Commission has not sufficiently justified its particular chosen numerical limits for local television ownership, local radio ownership, and cross-ownership of media within local markets. Accordingly, we partially remand the Order for the Commission's additional justification or modification, and we partially affirm the Order. The stay will continue pending our review of the Commission's action on remand.

I. Background

A. The 1934 Communications Act and Early Broadcast Ownership Regulation

In 1934 Congress authorized the Commission to grant licenses for private parties' exclusive use of broadcast frequencies. Recognizing that the finite radio frequency spectrum inherently limits the number of broadcast stations that can operate without interfering with one another, Congress required that broadcast licensees serve the public interest, convenience, and necessity. Communications Act of 1934, 47 U.S.C. § 309(a); *see also id.* §§ 307(a), 310(d), 312.

"In setting its licensing policies, the Commission has long acted on the theory that diversification of mass media ownership serves the public interest by promoting diversity of program and service viewpoints, as well as by preventing undue concentration of economic power." *FCC v. Nat'l Citizens Comm. for Broad.*, 436 U.S. 775, 780 (1978) ("*NCCB*"). The Commission's early regulations reflected its presumption that a single entity holding more than one broadcast license in the same community contravened public interest. *See Genesee Radio Corp.*, 5 F.C.C. 183, 186-87 (1938). In 1941, the Commission announced that it would not license more than one station in the same area to a single network organization. *See Nat'l Broad. Co. v. United States*, 319 U.S. 190, 206-08, 224-27 (1943) (upholding the rule). At the same time, the Commission prohibited common ownership of stations within the same broadcast service (AM radio, FM radio, and television) in the same community. *See Rules Governing Standard and High Frequency Broadcast Stations*, 5 Fed. Reg. 2382, 2384 (June 26, 1940) (FM radio); *Rules Governing Standard and High Frequency Broadcast Stations*, 6 Fed. Reg. 2282, 2284-85 (May 6, 1941) (television); *Rules Governing Standard and High Frequency Broadcast Stations*, 8 Fed. Reg. 16065 (Nov. 27, 1943) (AM radio). Regulations limiting an entity to the common ownership of seven AM radio stations, seven FM radio stations, and seven television stations survived judicial scrutiny in 1956. *See United States v. Storer Broad. Co.*, 351 U.S. 192 (1956). In the 1970s the Commission adopted its first cross-ownership bans, which prohibited, on a prospective basis, the common ownership of television and radio stations serving the same market, as well as combinations of radio or broadcast stations with a daily newspaper in the same community. *Amendment of Sections 73.35, 73.240 and 73.636 of the Commission Rules Relating to Multiple Ownership of Standard, FM and Television Broadcast Stations*, 22 F.C.C.2d 306, ¶ 5, 1970 WL 18044 (1970); *Amendment of Sections 73.34, 73.240 and 73.636 of the Commission's Rules Relating to Multiple Ownership of Standard, FM, and Television Broadcast Stations*, 50 F.C.C.2d 1046, 1975 WL 30457 (1975). The Supreme Court upheld the newspaper/broadcast cross-ownership ban as a "reasonable means of promoting the public interest in diversified mass communications." *NCCB*, 436 U.S. at 802, 98 S.Ct. 2096.

B. Deregulation Initiatives

The 1980s saw a deregulatory trend for media ownership. The Commission raised its national ownership limits to permit common ownership of 12 stations in each broadcast service (though still prohibiting station combinations that would reach more than 25% of the national audience). *Amendment of Section 73.3555 (formerly 73.35, 73.240, and 73.636) of the Commission's Rules Relating to Multiple Ownership of AM, FM, and Television Broadcast Stations*, 100 F.C.C.2d 74 ¶¶ 38, 39, 1985 WL 260060 (1985). The Commission also determined that UHF television stations should not be deemed to have the same audience reach as VHF stations, due to "the inherent physical limitations of [the UHF] medium," and therefore applied a 50% "discount" to UHF audiences as counted under the national audience limitation. *Id.* ¶¶ 42-44. In other words, UHF stations count only half of their audiences in determining compliance with the national television ownership rule.

In 1989 the Commission eased its "one to a market" radio/television cross-ownership rules by allowing waiver requests for radio/television cross-ownership in the 25 largest television markets. The Commission stated that it would look favorably upon requests for waivers where there would be 30 independently owned broadcast "voices" remaining in the market after consolidation. *Amendment of Section 73.3555 of the Commission's Rules, the Broadcast Multiple Ownership Rules,* 4 F.C.C.R. 1741, ¶ 1, 1989 WL 510875 (1989). In 1992, the Commission relaxed local and national radio ownership restrictions and adopted a tiered approach to radio concentration that allowed a single entity to own more radio stations in the largest markets (up to three AM and three FM stations, subject to a local audience reach limitation of 25% and a national cap of 30 AM stations and 30 FM stations) and fewer in the smallest markets. *Revision of Radio Rules and Policies,* 7 F.C.C.R. 6387, ¶ 27, 1992 WL 690638 (1992).

C. The Telecommunications Act of 1996

In 1996 Congress overhauled the Communications Act by enacting the Telecommunications Act of 1996. The 1996 Act contemplated a "pro-competitive, deregulatory national policy framework designed to accelerate rapidly private sector development of advanced telecommunications and information technologies and services to all Americans by opening all telecommunications markets to competition." S.Rep. No. 104-230, at 1-2 (1996). The 1996 Act eliminated all limits on national radio ownership and raised the national television audience reach cap from 25% to 35%. 1996 Act §§ 202(a), (c)(1)(B), 110 Stat. at 110-11. Congress also eased local radio ownership limits, establishing a four-tier sliding scale limit of numerical caps that allowed for as many as eight co-owned radio stations in the largest markets. *Id.* § 202(b)(1), 110 Stat. at 110.

The 1996 Act did not contain a new local television rule, but it directed the Commission to "conduct a rulemaking proceeding to determine whether to retain, modify, or eliminate" its existing local television ownership limitations. *Id.* § 202(c)(2), 110 Stat. at 111. It also expanded the applicability of the one-to-a-market radio/television cross-ownership restriction waiver to the fifty largest markets. *Id.* § 202(d), 110 Stat. at 111.

Finally, the 1996 Act instructed the Commission to review biennially its broadcast ownership rules "to determine whether any of such rules are necessary in the public interest as the result of competition." *Id.* § 202(h), 110 Stat. at 111-12. Section 202(h) also required the Commission to "repeal or modify any regulation it determines to be no longer in the public interest." *Id.*

D. Regulatory Review Since 1996

In 1999 the Commission responded to Congress's directive under § 202(c) of the 1996 Act to review its local television rule and announced that it would relax its prohibition on the common ownership of television stations with overlapping signals. The Commission's new rule would allow two commonly owned television stations (a television station "duopoly") in the same Designated Market Area ("DMA" or "market") as long as (1) neither station was ranked among the four largest ("top-four") stations in the market and (2) eight independently owned stations remained in the market post-merger. *Review of the Commission's Regulations Governing Television Broadcasting,* 14 F.C.C.R. 12,903, ¶ 8, 1999 WL 591820 (1999) (*"1999 Television Rule Review"*). In the same rulemaking, the Commission also relaxed the one-to-a-market radio/television cross-ownership restriction and allowed radio/television station combinations to exist within three-tiered limits that depend on the size of the market. *Id.* ¶ 9.

Meanwhile, in 1998 the Commission began the first biennial review of its broadcast ownership regulations as required under § 202(h). In 2000 it announced that it would retain the national television ownership rule (the 35% limit provided in the 1996 Act) and its cable/broadcast cross-ownership rule after determining that both rules remained "necessary in the public interest." *1998 Biennial Regulatory Review-Review of the Commission's Broadcast Ownership Rules and Other Rules Adopted Pursuant to Section 202 of the Telecommunications Act of 1996,* 15 F.C.C.R. 11,058, ¶ 4, 2000 WL 791562 (2000) (*"1998 Biennial Regulatory Review"*). On appeal, however, the United States Court of Appeals for the D.C. Circuit held that the Commission had not sufficiently explained its reasons for retaining either of these rules. *Fox Television Stations v. FCC,* 280 F.3d 1027, 1043-44, 1051-52 (D.C. Cir. 2002) (*"Fox I"*), *modified on reh'g,* 293 F.3d 537 (D.C. Cir. 2002) (*"Fox II"*). As for the national television ownership rule, the Court determined that the agency had taken a "wait and see" approach in evaluating its competition and diversity effects, which was impermissible in light of § 202(h)'s mandate to repeal or modify rules found no longer necessary in the public interest. *Id.* at 1042. It remanded the rule to the Commission for additional justification. *Id.* at 1049. The Court vacated the cable/broadcast cross-ownership rule, however, finding that the Commission's decision to retain it was arbitrary and capricious and contrary to § 202(h). *Id.* at 1053.

A few months later, the same Court reviewed the local television multiple-ownership rule. *Sinclair Broad. Group, Inc. v. FCC*, 284 F.3d 148 (D.C. Cir. 2002). The petitioner challenged the "eight independent voices" exception, contending that it lacked foundation or connection to the Commission's goal of promoting diversity in local markets. *Id.* at 152. The Court determined that the Commission had adequately justified its decision to retain the local television rule under the APA and § 202(h), but that it had not provided a rational basis for the exclusion of non-broadcast media from the eight voices exception. *Id.* at 165. It remanded the rule for the Commission's further justification. *Id.* at 169.

E. The Commission's 2003 Report and Order

In September 2002 a Notice of Proposed Rulemaking (the "Notice") announced that the Commission would review four of its broadcast ownership rules pursuant to § 202(h): the 35% national audience reach limit remanded in *Fox;* the local television rule remanded in *Sinclair;* the radio/television cross-ownership rule; and the dual network rule. *2002 Biennial Regulatory Review Notice of Proposed Rulemaking,* 17 F.C.C.R. 18,503, ¶ 6, 2002 WL 31108252 (2002). The Notice also advised that the Commission was incorporating into its biennial review pending proceedings on two additional rules: its rule limiting radio station ownership in local markets and its rule prohibiting newspaper/broadcast cross-ownership. *Id.* ¶ 7.

The Commission established a Media Ownership Working Group ("MOWG"), which commissioned twelve studies ranging from consumer surveys to economic analyses of media markets. These reports were released for public comment in October 2002. Interested parties filed thousands of pages of comments, consisting of legal, social, and economic analyses, empirical and anecdotal evidence, and industry and consumer data to respond to the issues identified in the Commission's Notice. Notably, nearly two million people weighed in by letters, postcards, e-mails, and petitions to oppose further relaxation of the rules. *Statement of Commissioner Jonathan S. Adelstein, Dissenting,* 18 F.C.C.R. 13,974, 13,977, 2003 WL 21251887 (July 2, 2003). The Commission also heard public comment at a February 2003 "field hearing" in Richmond, Virginia.

On June 2, 2003, the Commission adopted the Order modifying its ownership rules to provide a "new, comprehensive framework for broadcast ownership regulation" by a vote of 3-2. *Order* ¶ 3. The Order was released on July 2, 2003.

F. The Order's Modification of Broadcast Media Ownership Rules

After reaffirming the Commission's three traditional policy objectives in promoting the public interest-competition, diversity, and localism-*Order* ¶ 8, the Commission considered whether each of the six rules remained in the public interest and proposed modifications where it believed necessary. With respect to each of the rules, the Commission determined as follows.

1. Local Television Ownership

The existing local television ownership rule allowed television station duopolies, so long as at least one of the stations was not ranked among the market's four largest stations and so long as at least eight independently owned and operated full-power television stations would remain in the market post-merger. 47 C.F.R. § 73.3555(b). The Order modified this rule to permit television station triopolies in markets with 18 or more television stations and television station duopolies in markets with 17 or fewer television stations. *Order* ¶ 134. These limits are subject to the restriction (effectively a ban subject to a waiver provision) that a single firm may not own more than one top-four station in a market. This restriction forecloses common station ownership in markets with fewer than five television stations. *Id.* ¶ 186. The existing rule effectively precludes duopolies in most markets; only the largest 70 markets of the nation's 210 DMAs could comply with the "eight voices" test. *Adelstein Dissenting,* 18 F.C.C.R. at 13,998. The new rule would allow triopolies in the nine largest DMAs, which represent 25.2% of the population. Duopolies could exist under the new rule in the largest 162 markets, representing 95.4% of the nation's population. *Id.* at 13,997-98.

2. Local Radio Ownership

Although the Order retained the existing numerical limits on radio ownership that Congress established in § 202(b) of the 1996 Act, it modified other aspects of the rule. First, it changed the method for determining radio markets by replacing the "contour-overlap" method (described in detail in Part VI.B *infra*) with the geography-based market delineations created by Arbitron, a company that generates market data for radio advertisers. *Order* ¶ 239. Additionally, the Commission would now include noncommercial stations in the station count for each market. *Id.* The Commission grandfathered any existing radio station combinations rendered noncompliant under the newly defined markets, *id.* ¶ 484, but generally restricted transfer of these combinations, *id.* ¶ 487. The Commission also changed the local radio ownership rule by deciding to attribute "Joint Sales Agreements" (agreements under which a licensee sells advertising time on its station to a broker station for a fee) toward the brokering entity's numerical limit. *Id.* ¶ 239.

3 & 4. Newspaper/Broadcast and Radio/Television Cross-Ownership
The Commission has prohibited common ownership of a full-service television broadcast station and a daily public newspaper in the same community since 1975. *Amendment of Sections 73.35, 73.240, and 73.636 of the Commission's Rules Relating to Multiple Ownership of Standard, FM, and Television Broadcast Stations,* 50 F.C.C.2d 1046, 1975 WL 30457 (1975). Additionally, the Commission regulates the number of television and radio stations that may be commonly owned with limits that vary with the size of the market. 47 C.F.R. § 73.3555(c).

The Order announced the Commission's decision to repeal both cross-ownership rules (television/newspaper, radio/television) and replace them with a single set of Cross-Media Limits. The Commission determined that neither cross-ownership prohibition remained necessary in the public interest to ensure competition, diversity, or localism. *Order* ¶¶ 330, 371. The new Cross-Media Limits prohibit newspaper/broadcast combinations and radio/television combinations in the smallest DMAs, *i.e.*, those with three or fewer full-power commercial or noncommercial television stations. *Id.* ¶ 454. In contrast, in the largest markets-those with more than eight television stations-common ownership among newspapers and broadcast stations is unrestricted. *Id.* ¶ 473. In medium-sized markets-those with between four and eight television stations-one entity may own a newspaper and either (a) one television station and up to 50% of the radio stations that may be commonly owned in that market under the local radio rule or (b) up to 100% of the radio stations allowed under the local radio rule. *Id.* ¶ 466.

In structuring its Cross-Media Limits, the Commission drew upon a methodological tool named the "Diversity Index," which the Commission developed as a measure of viewpoint diversity in local markets to identify those "at-risk" markets where consolidation would have a deleterious effect. *Id.* ¶¶ 391, 442. The Diversity Index, explained more fully in Part IV.D.1 below, is a highly modified version of the formula for measuring market concentration—the Herfindahl-Hirschman Index—applied by the Department of Justice and Federal Trade Commission to analyze mergers. *Id.* ¶ 428.

5. National Television Ownership

The national television ownership rule prohibits entities from owning television stations that in the aggregate reach a certain percentage of our country's households. 47 C.F.R. § 73.3555(e)(1). Section 202(c) of the 1996 Act directed the Commission to delete the then-existing twelve-station cap and raise the audience reach limit from 25% to 35%. After the D.C. Circuit Court remanded the Commission's decision in the 1998 biennial review to retain the limit at 35%, *Fox I*, 280 F.3d at 1049, the Commission decided to increase the audience reach limit to 45%. *Order* ¶ 499. The Commission also declined to repeal or modify its existing 50% discount for UHF stations' audiences as counted toward the audience reach limit. *Id.* ¶ 500.

6. Dual Network Rule

Under the dual network rule, a television station may affiliate with more than one network except that it may not affiliate with more than one of the four largest networks, ABC, CBS, Fox, and NBC. 47 C.F.R. § 73.658(g). The rule effectively permits common ownership of networks to the exclusion of the top four. *Order* ¶ 592. The Commission determined that the dual network rule remained necessary in the public interest, and thus did not repeal or modify it. *Id.*

G. Procedural History of the Current Appeals

Within days of the publication of the Order, several organizations filed petitions for review of the Commission's revised rules in various courts of appeals, some contending that the Commission had gone too far in revising the rules, and others asserting that the Commission had not gone far enough. Some of these organizations, including the Prometheus Radio Project, filed their petitions in this Court. Under 28 U.S.C. § 2112(a), petitions to review administrative orders filed in different circuit courts within the first ten days of the appeal period trigger a lottery conducted by the Judicial Panel on Multidistrict Litigation. On August 19, 2003, the Panel announced that our Court had been selected in the lottery and consolidated the appeals here. We entered a stay of the effective date of the proposed rules after a hearing on September 3, 2003. *Prometheus Radio Project v. FCC*, No. 03-3388, 2003 WL 22052896 (3d Cir. Sept. 3, 2003). We then denied the Deregulatory Petitioners' motion, joined by the Commission, to transfer venue to the D.C. Circuit Court on September 16, 2003. *Prometheus Radio Project v. FCC*, No. 03-3388 (3d Cir. Sept. 16, 2003) (order denying motion to transfer). After pushing back briefing and oral argument at the request of the parties, on February 11, 2004, we heard approximately eight hours of oral argument addressing the merits of Petitioners' claims.

H. Subsequent Legislation
In January 2004, while the petitions to review the Order were pending in this Court, Congress amended the 1996 Act by increasing from 35% to 39% the national television ownership rule's audience reach cap in § 202(c). Consolidated Appropriations Act, 2004, Pub. L. No. 108-199, § 629, 118 Stat. 3, 99 (2004). The legislation also amended § 202(h) in two ways: (1) making the Commission's biennial review obligation quadrennial; and (2) insulating from § 202(h) review "rules relating to the 39 percent national audience reach limitation." 118 Stat. at 100. Prior to oral argument, Petitioners filed letter briefs addressing the effect of these amendments on their challenges to the Order.

II. Jurisdiction and Standard of Review
This is an appeal of an agency decision under the Communications Act of 1934, 47 U.S.C. §§ 151 *et seq.* Our jurisdiction is based on 47 U.S.C. § 402(a) and 28 U.S.C. § 2342(1). Our standard of review is governed by the APA and the 1996 Act provision authorizing the Commission's periodic regulatory review.

A. Standard of Review Under the Administrative Procedure Act

. . .

B. Standard of Review Considerations Under Section 202(h)
The Order was promulgated as part of the periodic review requirements of § 202(h) of the 1996 Act. Consequently, our review standard is informed by that provision, which, at the time of the Order's release, read:
(h) Further Commission Review. The Commission shall review its rules adopted pursuant to this section and all of its ownership rules biennially as part of its regulatory reform review under section 11 of the Communications Act of 1934 and shall determine whether any of such rules are necessary in the public interest as the result of competition. The Commission shall repeal or modify any regulation it determines to be no longer in the public interest.

110 Stat. 111-12. Section 11 of the Communications Act, to which § 202(h) refers, was also added by the 1996 Act to ensure that the Commission review periodically its regulations governing telecommunications services to "determine whether any such regulation is no longer necessary in the public interest as a result of meaningful economic competition between providers of such service" and "repeal or modify any regulation it determines to be no longer necessary in the public interest." 47 U.S.C. § 161.

The text and legislative history of the 1996 Act indicate that Congress intended periodic reviews to operate as an "ongoing mechanism to ensure that the Commission's regulatory framework would keep pace with the competitive changes in the marketplace" resulting from that Act's relaxation of the Commission's regulations, including the broadcast media ownership regulations. *2002 Biennial Regulatory Review*, 18 F.C.C.R. 4726, ¶¶ 16, 17 (2003) (citing preamble to the 1996 Act; H.R. Conf. Rep. No. 104-458 (1996)). Put another way, the periodic review provisions require the Commission to "monitor the effect of . . . competition . . . and make appropriate adjustments" to its regulations. *Id.* ¶ 5.

As noted, the first sentence of § 202(h) requires the Commission to "determine" whether media concentration rules are "necessary in the public interest as the result of competition." The second sentence contains a separate instruction to the Commission: to "repeal or modify" those rules "no longer in the public interest." . . .

III. Mootness and the National Television Ownership Rule

The national television ownership rule caps the number of television stations that a single entity may own on a national basis. In the 1996 Act, Congress limited the number of commonly owned stations to those reaching no more than 35% of the national audience. 1996 Act § 202(c)(1)(B), 110 Stat. 111. In its first biennial review, the Commission retained the 35% cap as "necessary in the public interest," but the D.C. Circuit Court held that the Commission had not adequately justified this decision. *Fox I*, 280 F.3d at 1048. On remand and in connection with its 2002 biennial review proceeding, the Commission increased the cap from 35% to 45%. *Order* ¶ 583. The Commission also decided to retain its method of discounting by 50% the audiences of UHF stations toward the cap. *Id.* ¶ 586.

Subsequently, however, Congress enacted a new national television ownership cap. In its 2004 Consolidated Appropriations Act, it modified § 202(c)(1)(B) of the 1996 Act to provide that "[t]he Commission shall modify its rules for multiple ownership . . . by increasing the national audience reach limitation for television stations to 39%." *See* Pub. L. No. 108-199, § 629, 118 Stat. 3, 99 (2004). Because the Commission is under a statutory directive to modify the national television ownership cap to 39%, challenges to the Commission's decision to raise the cap to 45% cap are moot. *Cf. PLMRS Narrowband Corp. v. FCC*, 182 F.3d 995, 1002 (D.C. Cir. 1999) (challenges to Commission's later-modified order are moot).

Although the 2004 Consolidated Appropriations Act did not expressly mention the UHF discount, challenges to the Commission's decision to retain it are likewise moot. Congress instructed the Commission to "increase the national audience reach limitation for television stations to 39%." 118 Stat. at 99. Since 1985 the Commission has defined "national audience reach" to mean "the total number of television households" reached by an entity's stations, except that "UHF stations shall be attributed with 50 percent of the television households" reached. 47 C.F.R. § 73.3555(e)(2)(i); *Multiple Ownership of AM, FM and Television Broadcast Stations*, 50 Fed. Reg. 4666, 4676, 1985 WL 260060 (Feb. 1, 1985). We assume that when Congress uses an administratively defined term, it intended its words to have the defined meaning. *See, e.g., Bragdon v. Abbott*, 524 U.S. 624, 631 (1998). Furthermore, because reducing or eliminating the discount for UHF station audiences would effectively raise the audience reach limit, we cannot entertain challenges to the Commission's decision to retain the 50% UHF discount. Any relief we granted on these claims would undermine Congress's specification of a precise 39% cap.

As additional evidence of the mootness of challenges to the UHF discount, we note that the 2004 Consolidated Appropriations Act also added a sentence to § 202(h): "This subsection does not apply to any rules relating to the 39% national audience limitation." 118 Stat. at 100. The UHF discount is a rule "relating to" the national audience limitation. *See* 47 C.F.R. § 73.3555(e)(2) (providing for the UHF discount in a section qualified "for the purposes of this paragraph (e)," the national television ownership rule paragraph). Congress apparently intended to insulate the UHF discount from periodic review, a position that is consistent with our reading of the legislation as endorsing the almost 20-year-old regulatory definition of "national audience reach" that provides for the UHF discount.

Although we find that the UHF discount is insulated from this and future periodic review requirements, we do not intend our decision to foreclose the Commission's consideration of its regulation defining the UHF discount in a rulemaking outside the context of Section 202(h). The Commission is now considering its authority going forward to modify or eliminate the UHF discount and recently accepted public comment on this issue. 69 Fed. Reg. 9216-17 (Feb. 27, 2004). Barring congressional intervention, *see, e.g.*, S. 1264, 108th Cong. § 12 (2003) (proposing phase-out and 2008 sunset of the UHF), the Commission may decide, in the first instance, the scope of its authority to modify or eliminate the UHF discount outside the context of § 202(h).

IV. Cross-Ownership Rules

The Commission's decision to repeal its newspaper/broadcast cross-ownership rules in favor of new Cross-Media Limits has been attacked on all fronts. Some petitioners support the repeal but argue that the Cross-Media Limits are too restrictive. Others challenge the repeal decision and argue that the new limits are too lenient. We conclude that the Commission's decision to replace its cross-ownership rules with the Cross-Media Limits is not of itself constitutionally flawed and does not violate § 202(h). But we cannot uphold the Cross-Media Limits themselves because the Commission does not provide a reasoned analysis to support the limits that it chose.

A. Regulatory Background and the 2002 Biennial Review

Since the 1970s, the Commission has enforced two separate limits on the common ownership of different-type media outlets in local markets. One cross-ownership rule prohibits the common ownership of a full-service television broadcast station and a daily public newspaper in the same community. 47 C.F.R. § 73.3555(d). The other limits the number of television and radio stations to the following combinations: (1) in markets where at least 20 independently owned media voices would remain post-merger, two television stations and six radio stations or one television station and seven radio stations; (2) in markets where at least 10 independent voices would remain, two television stations and four radio stations; and (3) in other markets, two television stations (subject to the local television ownership rule) and one radio station. *Id.* § 73.3555(c).

The Commission considered both cross-ownership rules during its 2002 biennial review under § 202(h). In the Order, the Commission announced that because neither rule remained necessary in the public interest, it was repealing them and replacing them with a single set of Cross-Media Limits. The three-tiered Cross-Media Limits regulate common ownership depending on the size of the market: small (those with three or fewer full-power commercial or noncommercial television stations), mid-sized (between four and eight television stations), and large (more than eight television stations). In small markets, newspaper/broadcast combinations and radio/television combinations are prohibited. *Order* ¶ 454. In medium-sized markets, an entity may own a newspaper and either (a) one television station and up to 50% of the radio stations that may be commonly owned in that market under the local radio rule or (b) up to

100% of the radio stations allowed under the local rule. *Id.* ¶ 466. In large markets, cross-ownership is unrestricted. *Id.* ¶ 473.

B. The Commission's decision not to retain a ban on newspaper/broadcast cross-ownership is justified under § 202(h) and is supported by record evidence.

The Commission determined that the rule prohibiting newspaper/broadcast cross-ownership was no longer necessary in the public interest for three primary reasons: (1) the ban is not necessary to promote competition in local markets because most advertisers do not view newspapers and television stations as close substitutes, *Order* ¶ 332; (2) the ban undermines localism by preventing efficient combinations that would allow for the production of high-quality local news, *id.* ¶ 343; and (3) there is not enough evidence to conclude that ownership influences viewpoint to warrant a blanket cross-ownership ban, thus making it unjustifiable on diversity grounds, *id.* at ¶ 364, (and moreover, the presence of other media sources-such as the Internet and cable-compensate for the viewpoint diversity lost to consolidation, *id.* ¶ 365). The Citizen Petitioners object to the localism and diversity components of the Commission's rationale. We conclude differently, as reasoned analysis supports the Commission's determination that the blanket ban on newspaper/broadcast cross-ownership was no longer in the public interest. Part II.C *supra.*

1. Newspaper/broadcast combinations can promote localism.

The Commission measured the promotion of localism by considering "the selection of programming responsive to local needs and interests, and local news quantity and quality." *Order* ¶ 78. Evidence that existing (grandfathered) newspaper-owned broadcast stations produced local news in higher quantity with better quality than other stations convinced the Commission that the ban on newspaper/broadcast combinations undermined its localism interest. The Commission principally relied on the findings of its MOWG study that newspaper-owned television stations provide almost 50% more local news and public affairs programming than other stations, an average of 21.9 hours per week. *Id.* ¶ 344 (citing Thomas C. Spavins *et al., The Measurement of Local Television News and Public Affairs Programs* (MOWG Study No. 7) at 3 (Sept.2002)). The Commission also found corresponding advantages in quality of local coverage provided by newspaper-owned stations, as shown by ratings (measuring consumer approval) and industry awards (measuring critical approval). *Id.* ¶ 344-45 (citing, among other things, findings by the Project for Excellence in Journalism that newspaper-owned stations "were more likely to do stories focusing on important community issues and to provide a wide mix of opinions, and they were less likely to do celebrity and human interest features").

The Citizen Petitioners argue that the MOWG study was flawed because it examined *all* newspaper/broadcast station combinations, including "intermarket" combinations (entities that own a newspaper and broadcast stations in different cities), as well as "intramarket" combinations (entities that own a newspaper and a broadcast station in the same city). But the Citizens Petitioners do not suggest that a study entirely focused on intramarket combinations would have different results. The six intramarket combinations that were included in the study (grandfathered exceptions to the cross-ownership ban) averaged more local news and public affairs programming as compared to the overall average (26 weekly hours compared to 21.9) and higher ratings for their 5:30 p.m. and 6:00 p.m. news programs (9.8 and 11 compared to 7.8 and 8.2). *MOWG Study No. 7* app. A; *Comments of Newspaper Association of America,* MB Docket No. 02-277 at 15 (Jan. 2, 2003).

The Citizen Petitioners also protest the Commission's reliance on anecdotal evidence of pro-localism combinations and its disregard of anecdotal evidence to the contrary. Significantly, however, the Commission used anecdotal evidence merely to illustrate its statistical findings-it did not rely on anecdote as the sole basis for its conclusions about localism. Moreover, the Commission properly discounted anecdotal evidence of a Canadian newspaper conglomerate's detrimental effect on localism. Can West, which controls 30% of Canada's daily newspaper circulation, requires its newspaper editors to publish editorials from headquarters, which it forbids local editorials to contradict. But the Commission explained that the Can West example shows the peril of national ownership and corporate centralization of media services, which is not relevant to the Commission's regulations on local combinations. *Order* ¶ 352. In summary, the Citizen Petitioners' arguments do not unsettle the Commission's conclusion that the newspaper/broadcast cross-ownership ban undermined localism.

2. A blanket prohibition on newspaper/broadcast combinations is not necessary to protect diversity.

The Commission offered two rationales for its conclusion that a blanket prohibition on newspaper/broadcast combinations is no longer necessary to ensure diversity in local markets. First, it found that "[c]ommonly-owned newspapers and broadcast stations do not necessarily speak with a single, monolithic voice." *Id.* ¶ 361. Given conflicting evidence in the record on whether ownership influences viewpoint, the Commission reasonably concluded that it did not have enough confidence in the proposition that commonly owned outlets have a uniform bias to warrant sustaining the cross-ownership ban. *Id.* ¶ 364.

Second, the Commission found that diverse viewpoints from other media sources in local markets (such as cable and the Internet) compensate for viewpoints lost to newspaper/broadcast consolidations. *Id.* ¶ 366. We agree record evidence suggests that cable and the Internet supplement the viewpoint diversity provided by broadcast and newspaper outlets in local markets. As discussed more fully below, we believe that the Commission gave too much weight to the Internet in deriving the Cross-Media Limits. But separate from the question of degree, we conclude that it was acceptable for the Commission to find that cable and the Internet contribute to viewpoint diversity.

C. The Commission's decision to retain some limits on common ownership of different-type media outlets was constitutional and did not violate § 202(h).

The Deregulatory Petitioners support the Commission's repeal of the newspaper/broadcast cross-ownership ban but object to its decision to retain any restriction on the common ownership of newspaper and broadcast media outlets. First they argue that any limits on newspaper/broadcast cross-ownership violate § 202(h), because, as the Commission acknowledges, the evidence suggests that the cross-ownership restrictions are not in the public interest. They also argue that the Cross-Media Limits violate the First and Fifth Amendments of the United States Constitution. We disagree on all counts.

1. Continuing to regulate cross-media ownership is in the public interest.

The Commission's finding that a blanket prohibition on newspaper/broadcast cross-ownership is no longer in the public interest does not compel the conclusion that no regulation is necessary. *See Order* ¶ 364. As described above, the Commission found evidence to undermine the premise that ownership always influences viewpoint, but it did not find the opposite to be true. And while the Commission found that other media sources contributed to viewpoint diversity in local markets, it could not have found that the Internet and cable were complete substitutes for the viewpoints provided by newspapers and broadcast stations. *See MOWG Study No. 3* (finding that the Internet and cable rank as sources of local news, but they do not outrank newspapers and broadcast television). Given the Commission's goal of balancing the public's interests in competition, localism, and diversity, it reasonably concluded that repealing the cross-ownership ban was necessary to promote competition and localism, while retaining some limits was necessary to ensure diversity.

2. Continuing to regulate cross-media ownership does not violate the Fifth Amendment.

The Deregulatory Petitioners argue that the Cross-Media Limits violate the Equal Protection Clause of the Fifth Amendment because they single out newspaper owners for special restrictions that do not apply to other media outlets. This argument is foreclosed, however, by the Supreme Court's decision in *NCCB* that endorsed the constitutionality of the 1975 newspaper/television cross-ownership ban. 436 U.S. at 801-02. Rather than concluding that newspaper owners were singled out for different treatment, the Court determined that "the regulations treat newspaper owners in essentially the same fashion as other owners of the major media of mass communication" by imposing limits on them as well as owners of television and radio stations. *Id.* at 801. We decline the Deregulatory Petitioners' invitation to disregard Supreme Court precedent because of changing times. Surely there are more media outlets today (such as cable, the Internet, and satellite broadcast) than there were in 1978 when *NCCB* was decided. But it cannot be assumed that these media outlets contribute significantly to viewpoint diversity as sources of *local* news and information. *See* Part IV.D.2 *infra.* Even if it could, it is the Supreme Court's prerogative to change its own precedent. *See State Oil Co. v. Khan,* 522 U.S. 3, 20 (1997) (stating that only the Supreme Court can overrule its own precedent); *Am. Civil Liberties Union of N.J. v. Black Horse Pike Reg'l Bd. of Educ.,* 84 F.3d 1471, 1484 (3d Cir. 1996) (stating that we are obliged to follow Supreme Court precedent "until instructed otherwise by a majority of the Supreme Court").

3. Continuing to regulate cross-media ownership does not violate the First Amendment.

The Deregulatory Petitioners argue that the Commission's decision to retain restrictions on the common ownership of newspapers and broadcast stations contravenes the First Amendment because it limits the speech opportunities of newspaper owners and broadcast station owners, and hence limits the public's access to information. Yet again their challenge is foreclosed by *NCCB,* where the Supreme Court affirmed the Commission's authority, despite a First Amendment challenge, to regulate broadcast/newspaper cross-ownership in the public interest. Due to the "physical scarcity" of the broadcast spectrum, the Court scrutinized the regulation to discern a rational basis. 436 U.S. at 799. The Commission's action, it held, was "a reasonable means of promoting the public interest in diversified mass communications." *Id.* at 802.

The Deregulatory Petitioners suggest, as they did in mounting their Fifth Amendment challenge, that the expansion of media outlets since *NCCB*'s day requires a rethinking of the scarcity rationale and the lower level of constitutional review it entails. Again we decline their invitation to disregard precedent, and we are not alone. *See FCC v. League of Women Voters of Cal.,* 468 U.S. 364, 376 & n. 11 (1984) (upholding the scarcity rationale until Congress speaks to the issue); *Fox I,* 280 F.3d at 1046 ("First, contrary to the implication of the networks' argument, this court is not in a position to reject the scarcity rationale even if we agree that it no longer makes sense. The Supreme Court has already heard the empirical case against that rationale and still 'declined to question its continuing validity.'" (citing *Turner v. FCC,* 512 U.S. 622, 638 (1994))).

Even were we not constrained by Supreme Court precedent, we would not accept the Deregulatory Petitioners' contention that the expansion of media outlets has rendered the broadcast spectrum less scarce. In *NCCB,* the Court referred to the "physical scarcity" of the spectrum-the fact that many more people would like access to it than can be accommodated. 436 U.S. at 799. The abundance of non-broadcast media does not render the broadcast spectrum any less scarce. *See, e.g., Ruggiero v. FCC,* 278 F.3d 1323, 1325 (D.C. Cir. 2002), *rev'd en banc,* 317 F.3d 239 (D.C. Cir. 2003) (citing the Commission's statement that "[n]ow . . . radio service is widely available throughout the country and very little spectrum remains available for new full-powered stations.").

In this context, we will apply a rational basis standard to the Commission's restrictions on the common ownership between newspaper and broadcast stations, and uphold them if they are rationally related to a substantial government interest. *See NCCB,* 436 U.S. at 799-800; *see also Am. Family Ass'n v. FCC,* 365 F.3d 1156, 1168 (D.C. Cir. 2004). In *NCCB,* the Supreme Court endorsed a substantial government interest in promoting diversified mass communications. *Id.* at 795, 802. The Supreme Court held that the Commission had "acted rationally in finding that diversification of ownership would enhance the possibility of achieving greater diversity of viewpoints." *Id.* at 796. Here, as in *NCCB,* the Commission justified its continued restrictions on common ownership of newspapers and broadcast stations as promoting the public interest in viewpoint diversity. *Order* ¶ 355. The Court has said that limiting common ownership is a reasonable means of promoting the public interest in viewpoint diversity. *NCCB,* 436 U.S. at 796, 436 U.S. 775. Therefore, applying *NCCB,* we hold that the Commission's continued regulation of the common ownership of newspapers and broadcasters does not violate the First Amendment rights of either.

D. The Commission did not provide reasoned analysis to support the specific Cross-Media Limits that it chose.

The Commission concluded that cross-ownership limits were necessary in specific situations to guard against "an elevated risk of harm to the range and breadth of viewpoints that may be available to the public." *Order* ¶ 442. But recognizing that ownership limits impede the speech opportunities for both broadcasters and newspapers, the Commission endeavored to craft new limits "as narrowly as possible." *Id.* ¶ 441. In that vein, the Commission sought to identify "at risk" local markets-those with high levels of viewpoint concentration-where continued regulation was necessary. By focusing its regulation on those markets, the Commission hoped to avoid needlessly overregulating markets with already ample viewpoint diversity.

But for all of its efforts, the Commission's Cross-Media Limits employ several irrational assumptions and inconsistencies. We do not object in principle to the Commission's reliance on the Department of Justice and Federal Trade Commission's antitrust formula, the Herfindahl-Hirschmann Index ("HHI"), as its starting point for measuring diversity in local markets. In converting the HHI to a measure for diversity in local markets, however, the Commission gave too much weight to the Internet as a media outlet, irrationally assigned outlets of the same media type equal market shares, and inconsistently derived the Cross-Media Limits from its Diversity Index results. For these reasons, detailed below, we remand for the Commission to justify or modify further its Cross-Media Limits.

1. Overview of the Commission's Diversity Index Methodology

The Commission designed a methodology called the Diversity Index to identify "at risk" markets where limits on cross-media ownership should be retained. . . .

First, the Commission selected which media outlets to include in its analysis of viewpoint diversity in local markets based on consumers' reported preferences for sources of local news and information. The Commission determined that broadcast television, daily and weekly newspapers, radio, and Internet (via cable connection and DSL, dial-up, or other connections) are the relevant contributors to viewpoint diversity in local markets. . . . Based on the popularity of each media source, the Commission assigned each a relative weight: broadcast TV 33.8%, daily newspapers 20.2%, weekly newspapers 8.6%, radio 24.9%, Internet (cable) 2.3% and Internet (DSL, dial-up, or other connection) 10.2%. *Order* ¶¶ 412, 415, 427.

Next, the Commission selected many sample markets for which it would determine a Diversity Index score. In each of those markets, it counted the number of outlets within each media type and assigned each outlet an equal market share. (For example, the New York City market has 23 television stations, so each one was attributed an equal 4.3% market share.) The Commission calculated the ownership share by multiplying the number of outlets owned by an entity by the market share. (Univision owns three television stations in New York, so its ownership share was 3 x 4.3% = 13.0%.) Each ownership share was then given its relative weight by media type. (Univision's 13.0% share was thus subject to the 33.8% multiplier for television stations. . . .

After the Commission calculated Diversity Index scores for markets of different sizes, it determined how those scores would change in several different consolidation "scenarios." To illustrate, the Commission determined that markets with five television stations had an average Diversity Index score of 911. If a newspaper and television station combined in a market of that size, that score would increase by 223, to 1134. The other combination scenarios were: (1) one television station and all of the radio stations allowed to be commonly owned under the local radio rule; (2) one newspaper and all of the radio stations allowed to be commonly owned under the local radio rule; (3) one newspaper, one television station, and half of the number of radio stations allowed to be commonly owned under the local radio rule; (4) two television stations; (5) one newspaper and two television stations; and (6) one newspaper, two television stations, and all of the radio stations allowed under the local radio rule. *Order* app. D.

Finding that all of the consolidation scenarios resulted in relatively high increases to the average Diversity Index scores for the smallest markets (those with three or fewer television stations), the Commission prohibited newspaper/television, newspaper/radio, and radio/television combinations in those markets. *Order* ¶¶ 456, 459, 460. In the large markets (nine or more stations), all of the consolidation scenarios resulted in acceptable increases to the average Diversity Index scores, so the Commission imposed no limits on cross-media ownership in those markets. In the mid-sized markets (between four and eight television stations), the Commission found that all of the scenarios, except the two involving a newspaper and television duopoly, should be allowed, based on their modest increases to the average Diversity Index scores for those markets. *Id.* ¶ 466.

2. The Commission did not justify its choice and weight of specific media outlets.

Petitioners from both sides of the regulatory spectrum attack the Commission's selection of media outlets for inclusion in the Diversity Index formula. The Citizen Petitioners argue that the Commission gave too much weight to the Internet at the expense of television and daily newspapers, thereby understating the level of concentration and overstating the level of diversity in a market. The Deregulatory Petitioners, on the other hand, argue that the Diversity Index understates the actual amount of diversity in a market by ignoring important media outlets, primarily cable television. As explained below, we affirm the Commission's reasoned decision to discount cable. But we think that the same rationale also applies to the Internet. Therefore, its decision to count the Internet as a source of viewpoint diversity, while discounting cable, was not rational.

The Commission properly excluded cable because of serious doubts as to the extent that cable provided independent local news-the Commission's recognized indicator of viewpoint diversity in local markets. . . .

The Commission suggests that "the virtual universe of information sources" on the Internet qualifies it as a source of viewpoint diversity. *Order* ¶ 427. But to accept this rationale we would have to distort the Commission's own premise that *local news* is an indicator of viewpoint diversity. *E.g., id.* ¶ 391 (Diversity Index measures "the relative importance of these media as a source of local news"). Search-engine sponsored pages such as Yahoo! Local and about.com, which were suggested by commenters as sources of local news and information, may be useful for finding restaurant reviews and concert schedules, but this is not the type of "news and public affairs programming" that the Commission said was "the clearest example of programming that can provide viewpoint diversity." *Id.* ¶ 394.

. . .

To accept its "universe of information" characterization of the Internet's viewpoint diversity, we would also have to disregard the Commission's professed intent to focus its consideration of viewpoint diversity on *media* outlets. . . . We agree that the Internet "helps citizens discharge the obligations of citizenship in a democracy," *Order* ¶ 393, when someone can go cityofglenfalls.com to find the city council's next agenda or use sfgov.org to learn how to get a marriage license in San Francisco. *See Comments of the Hearst Corporation,* MM Docket No. 01-235 at 11 & n. 36, apps. A & C (Dec. 3, 2001) (*"Hearst Comments"*) (listing these website addresses, among others, as examples of local government websites). But local governments are not, themselves, "media outlets" for viewpoint-diversity purposes. Like many entities, they just happen to use a particular media outlet-the Internet-to disseminate information.

Similarly, advertiser-driven websites such as hvnet.com and sfadvertiser.com, *see Hearst Comments* at apps. A & C, hardly contribute to viewpoint diversity. Like local governments, the sponsors of these websites are not "media outlets" just because they have "local information" that they want the public to have-if they were, their advertisements in telephone directories would also have to count toward viewpoint diversity. . . .

The Commission attempts to justify different treatment for cable and the Internet by suggesting that local cable news channels are only available in select markets, while the Internet is available everywhere. Not only is this distinction demonstrably false (as even the Commission acknowledged that almost 30% of Americans do not have Internet access, *Order* ¶ 365), it is irrelevant. That the Internet is more available than local cable news channels does not mean that it is providing independent local news. . . .

3. The Commission did not justify its assumption of equal market shares.

Both the Citizen Petitioners and the Deregulatory Petitioners object to the Commission's decision to assign all outlets within the same media type (that is, television stations, daily papers, or radio stations) an equal market share. . . .

The Commission's decision to assign equal market shares to outlets within a media type does not jibe with the Commission's decision to assign relative weights to the different media types themselves, about which it said "we have no reason to believe that all media are of equal importance." *Order* ¶ 409; *see also id.* ¶ 445 ("Not all voices, however, speak with the same volume."). It also negates the Commission's proffered rationale for using the HHI formula in the first place-to allow it to measure the actual loss of diversity from consolidation by taking into account the actual "diversity importance" of the merging parties, something it could not do with a simple "voices" test. *Id.* ¶ 396. Finally, assigning equal market shares to outlets that provide no local news almost certainly presents an understated view of concentration in several markets, thus contravening the Commission's goal of making "the most conservative assumption possible" about viewpoint diversity. *Id.* ¶ 400.

Additionally, there is no dispute that the assignment of equal market shares generates absurd results. For example, in New York City, the Dutchess Community College television station and the stations owned by ABC each receive an equal 4.3% market share. Or compare the Dutchess Community College station's weighted share of 1.5% (4.3% times the 33.8% multiplier for television) to a mere 1.4% weighted, combined share assigned to the New York Times Company's co-owned daily newspaper and radio station. *Order* app. C. A Diversity Index that requires us to accept that a community college television station makes a greater contribution to viewpoint diversity than a conglomerate that includes the third-largest newspaper in America also requires us to abandon both logic and reality. . . .

. . .

V. Local Television Ownership Rule

Both the Citizen Petitioners and the Deregulatory Petitioners challenge the Commission's modification to the local television ownership rule, which would allow triopolies in markets of 18 stations or more and duopolies in other markets, subject to a restriction on combinations of the four largest stations in any market. We uphold the top-four restriction but remand the numerical limits for the Commission to harmonize certain inconsistencies and better support its assumptions and rationale. We also remand for the Commission to reconsider or justify its decision to expand the rule's waiver provision-applicable to sales of failed, failing, or unbuilt television stations-by eliminating the requirement that waiver applicants notice the station's availability to out-of-market buyers.

. . .

In response to Congress's directive, the Commission promulgated a . . . rule that would permit common ownership of two commercial stations in markets that have 17 or fewer full-power commercial and noncommercial stations, and common ownership of three commercial stations in markets that have 18 or more stations. Both limits are subject to a restriction on the common ownership of stations ranked among the market's largest four based on audience share. *Order* ¶ 186. The Commission also decided to expand its criteria for waiving the rule's ownership restrictions for proposed combinations that involve failed, failing, or unbuilt stations by eliminating the requirement that waiver applicants provide notice of the sale to out-of-market buyers. *Id.* ¶ 225.

B. We uphold several threshold challenges to the Commission's overall regulatory approach.

Before we consider the specific modifications to the local television rule, we address some threshold challenges to the Commission's regulatory approach.

1. Limiting local television station ownership is not duplicative of antitrust regulation

. . .

2. Media other than broadcast television may contribute to viewpoint diversity in local markets.

. . .

We note that the record contains only weak evidence that cable can substitute for broadcast television as a source of viewpoint diversity. For example, the Commission found that among cable subscribers (a class that already omits one-third of American households) only 30% have access to local cable news channels. *See Order* ¶ 414 n. 924; *see also supra* Part IV.D.2 (describing why the Commission concluded that a majority of survey respondents' purported reliance on cable as a source of local news was probably based on confusion with broadcast news); *Reply Comments of the UCC*, MM Docket No. 01-235 at 5 (Feb. 15, 2002), *UCC Comments* at 30-31. With respect to the Internet, while record evidence indicates a negative correlation between respondents' reliance on broadcast television and the Internet as news sources (suggesting that people who use the Internet for local news do so at the expense of television), the Internet is also limited in its availability and as a source of local news. *Compare MOWG Study No. 3* at 3, 34; *with UCC Reply Comments* at 10 and *MOWG Study No. 8* tbl. 097. Therefore, it seems that the degree to which the Commission can rely on cable or the Internet to mitigate the threat that local station consolidations pose to viewpoint diversity is limited.

3. Consolidation can improve local programming.

The Commission supported its decision to relax the existing "eight voices" rule with findings that common ownership of television stations in local markets can result in "consumer welfare enhancing efficiencies" by eliminating redundant expenses and increasing opportunities for cross-promotion and related programming. *Order* ¶ 147. To promote localism, the Commission found that these efficiencies translated into improved local news and public interest programming. *Id.* ¶ 164. Evidence supporting this conclusion included findings that commonly owned television stations are more likely to carry local news than other stations and air a similar quality and quantity of local news as other stations. . . . In light of this evidence, we reject the Citizen Petitioners' contention that the Commission's finding of localism benefits from consolidation was unsupported.

4. The Commission adequately noticed its decision to allow triopolies. We also reject the Citizen Petitioners' contention that the Commission failed to provide adequate notice that it was considering a rule that would allow triopolies. The APA requires agencies to publish a notice of proposed rulemaking . . .

C. We uphold the Commission's decision to retain the top-four restriction.

. . .

The Deregulatory Petitioners assert that the top-four restriction prevents small-market stations from yielding any of the benefits of consolidation. They argue that by effectively precluding any consolidation in markets with fewer than five stations, the Commission deprives the benefit of consolidation from stations-those in small markets-who need it most. But the Commission's local television rule is protective of small-market stations. The numerical limits already allowed, in effect, extra concentration to ensure that small-market stations would realize the efficiency benefits of consolidation. As for the smallest markets with fewer than five stations-where the top-four restriction operates to preclude any consolidation-it was not unreasonable for the Commission to conclude, as it did, that the detriment of concentrated market power-*e.g.*, reduced incentive to improve programming of mass appeal-outweighed the efficiency benefits. . . .

D. We remand the specific numerical limits for the Commission's further consideration.

. . .

The Commission defends its equal market shares approach with the suggestion that market share, which varies with each season's new programs, is too "fluid" to be the basis for its regulations. *Id.* ¶ 193. But elsewhere in the local television ownership rule the Commission found that the market share was stable enough to rely on for support of its top-four restriction. *Id.* ¶ 195. And not only is the Commission's "market share is too fluid" rationale inconsistent with other aspects of the rule, it is unsupported. The Order cites no evidence to support its assumption that market share fluctuates more in television broadcasting than in other industries. Nor does it refute the Citizen Petitioners' suggestion that this is unlikely to be the case because, unlike most other industries, television station owners face a barrier to market entry (requirement of a license) and the number of market participants (television station owners) is in decline.

The Citizen Petitioners also object to the numerical limits because they allow markets that are already highly concentrated to become even more concentrated. For example, Philadelphia is a market with more than 18 stations, so the modified rule would allow the duopolist Viacom to acquire a third station and potentially increase its audience share from 25% to 34%. . . . No evidence supports the Commission's equal market share assumption, and no reasonable explanation underlies its decision to disregard actual market share. The modified rule is similarly unreasonable in allowing levels of concentration to exceed further its own benchmark for competition (1800)-a glaring inconsistency between rationale and result. We remand the numerical limits for the Commission to support and harmonize its rationale.

E. We remand the Commission's repeal of the Failed Station Solicitation Rule.

The Citizen Petitioners also challenge the Commission's repeal of the Failed Station Solicitation Rule ("FSSR"), 47 C.F.R. 73.3555 n.7, which required a waiver applicant to provide notice of the sale to potential out-of-market buyers before it could sell the failed, failing, or unbuilt television station to an in-market buyer. ...To alleviate concerns that its decision to allow duopolies would undermine television station ownership by minorities, the Commission created the FSSR to ensure that qualified minority broadcasters had a fair chance to learn that certain financially troubled-and consequently more affordable-stations were for sale. . . .

In repealing the FSSR without any discussion of the effect of its decision on minority television station ownership (and without ever acknowledging the decline in minority station ownership notwithstanding the FSSR), the Commission "entirely failed to consider an important aspect of the problem," and this amounts to arbitrary and capricious rulemaking. . . .

VI. Local Radio Ownership Rule

Petitioners challenge the Commission's decision to modify its local radio ownership rule, which limits the number of commercial radio stations that a party may own in local markets of different sizes, 47 C.F.R. § 73.3555(a), by, among other changes, adopting a new method for determining the size of local markets. They also argue that the Commission failed to justify its decision to retain the rule's specific numerical limits. We affirm the Commission's decision to modify the rule (including modifying its method for determining local market size), but we agree that its decision to retain the numerical limits was arbitrary and capricious, and hence remand for the Commission's further consideration.

. . .

In applying its local ownership rules, the Commission decided to grandfather existing radio, television, and radio/television combinations, and did "not require entities to divest their current interests in stations in order to come into compliance with the new ownership rules." Under past Commission rules, radio stations created in compliance with the rules were freely transferable under the Commission's policy that maintaining the status quo did not create new harm to public interest goals. . . . We reject the Deregulatory Petitioners' arguments that this modification to the local radio ownership rule contravenes § 202(h), constitutes arbitrary and capricious rulemaking, and violates the United States Constitution.

. . .

The Commission successfully demonstrates that the transfer restriction is "in the public interest" as required under § 202(h). The Commission notes that forcing divestitures at the time of transfer "could afford new entrants the opportunity to enter the media marketplace" and "could give smaller station owners already in the market the opportunity to acquire more stations," which would promote the public interest in having competitive and diverse radio markets. . . .

. . .

VII. Conclusion

Though we affirm much of the Commission's Order, we have identified several provisions in which the Commission falls short of its obligation to justify its decisions to retain, repeal, or modify its media ownership regulations with reasoned analysis. The Commission's derivation of new Cross-Media Limits, and its modification of the numerical limits on both television and radio station ownership in local markets, all have the same essential flaw: an unjustified assumption that media outlets of the same type make an equal contribution to diversity and competition in local markets. We thus remand for the Commission to justify or modify its approach to setting numerical limits. . . .

NOTES AND QUESTIONS

1. In its 2014 Quadrennial Regulatory Review, the FCC proposed revenue-based broadcast ownership privileges, "whether or not the standard is effective in promoting ownership of broadcast stations by women and minorities." The FCC stated that a "revenue-based standard would serve the public interest by promoting small-business participation," which would "encourage innovation and expand ownership and viewpoint diversity." 79 FR 29010-01 (2014). Would a distress-sale privilege for small business applicants require strict scrutiny?
2. **Cable consolidation.** In May 2016, federal regulators approved the acquisition of cable giant Time Warner Cable ("TWC") by Charter Communications, in a $67.1 billion merger that also included Bright House Networks. As with all media mergers, it was subject to review by both the FCC and the antitrust division of the Department of Justice. As of 2017, the new entity, controlled by Charter, reached 16.8 million pay TV subscribers and 21.4 million customers in the home broadband market. Note that TWC was spun off in 2009 from multi-platform content owner Time Warner, the plaintiff in earlier cable ownership litigation discussed in the *Comcast* case supra.
3. **More media mergers.** In July 2015, the FCC approved AT&T's $49 billion acquisition of satellite provider DirecTV, making the phone company one of the biggest players in both pay TV and mobile broadband. In October 2016, AT&T announced that it would seek approval to acquire Time Warner for $85 billion. With a green light from the Trump Administration, the deal will vertically integrate Time Warner content like CNN, Warner Bros. movies, Looney Tunes, and HBO into AT&T's mobile and pay TV distribution platforms. It remains to be seen if these AT&T mergers will put content producers like Discovery, Scripps, and Viacom in play for potential acquisition by a content distributor such as Verizon, Comcast, or even Facebook. What impact would these mergers have on media diversity?
4. **Fin-Syn.** In 1970, when three television networks effectively controlled broadcast television, the FCC issued the Financial Interest and Syndication Rules ("Fin-Syn"). Fin-Syn (in tandem with a Department of Justice [DOJ] consent decree) prohibited networks from owning the entertainment shows that aired on their networks and barred them from licensing network shows in the lucrative syndication market. The concern was that networks would use their market power to extract ownership rights from third-party producers. By the 1990s,

with the media landscape changed by competition from cable and independent production, the Fin-Syn rules were determined to be an arbitrary exercise of the FCC's administrative authority. The opinion, by Judge Richard Posner, concluded that allowing networks back into these markets increases diversity, which helps independent producers. Schurz Communications v. FCC, 982 F.2d 1043 (7th Cir. 1992). By 2006, only two independent producers remained, and both were affiliated with movie studios.

5. Which do you think has a greater impact on media diversity, national caps that limit ownership of broadcast stations, or local caps that limit the number of stations that one entity can own in a single market? Before you answer, look to see how many stations are controlled by the same entity in your local market. In Los Angeles, for example, CBS controls channels 2 and 9, and co-owns the network on channel 5. Fox and NBC also own more than one station. What impact does that have on diversity in Los Angeles?
6. While the *Prometheus* case was pending, Congress passed the Consolidated Appropriations Act, 2004, which increased the national television ownership cap to 39 percent of the national audience. The effect of this enactment was to render moot the Third Circuit's review of the FCC's proposal to increase the cap to 45 percent. The court, however, issued a stay on some key deregulatory initiatives, ruling that the FCC did not meet its administrative burden to explain and justify specific limits on cross-media ownership in a market with three or fewer television stations, and a reduction of limits on local television and radio station ownership. According to the court, the Diversity Index, a quantitative metric that the FCC used to support some of its deregulatory proposals, irrationally equated outlets across different media platforms as making equal contributions to a market's diversity and overemphasized the source diversity of the Internet. In 2010, the Third Circuit finally lifted its stay on the FCC's remaining deregulatory initiatives, but, by that time, the composition of the FCC, and many of the issues, had changed.
7. In the *Prometheus* case supra, the FCC argued that there was an "abundance of media," especially in light of the Internet's explosive growth. But is an abundance of Web sites the same as an abundance of diverse news sources? Many popular news Web sites are controlled by traditional media outlets like newspapers and cable news channels, and other sites simply aggregate news stories from other news outlets. From how many independent sources do you get your news?

SELECTED PROVISIONS FROM THE COMMUNICATIONS ACT OF 1934, AS AMENDED

47 U.S.C.A. § 151 et seq.

Title I: General Provisions

§ 151. Purposes of chapter; Federal Communications Commission created

For the purpose of regulating interstate and foreign commerce in communication by wire and radio so as to make available, so far as possible, to all the people of the United States, without discrimination on the basis of race, color, religion, national origin, or sex, a rapid, efficient, Nation-wide, and world-wide wire and radio communication service with adequate facilities at reasonable charges, for the purpose of the national defense, for the purpose of promoting safety of life and property through the use of wire and radio communications, and for the purpose of securing a more effective execution of this policy by centralizing authority heretofore granted by law to several agencies and by granting additional authority with respect to interstate and foreign commerce in wire and radio communication, there is created a commission to be known as the "Federal Communications Commission", which shall be constituted as hereinafter provided, and which shall execute and enforce the provisions of this chapter.

§ 152. Application of chapter

(a) The provisions of this chapter shall apply to all interstate and foreign communication by wire or radio and all interstate and foreign transmission of energy by radio, which originates and/or is received within the United States, and to all persons engaged within the United States in such communication or such transmission of energy by radio, and to the licensing and regulating of all radio stations as hereinafter provided; but it shall not apply to persons engaged in wire or radio communication or transmission in the Canal Zone, or to wire or radio communication or transmission wholly within the Canal Zone. The provisions of this chapter shall apply with respect to cable service, to all persons engaged within the United States in providing such service, and to the facilities of cable operators which relate to such service, as provided in subchapter V-A.

(b) Exceptions to Federal Communications Commission jurisdiction

Except as provided in sections 223 through 227 of this title, inclusive, and section 332 of this title, and subject to the provisions of section 301 of this title and subchapter V-A of this chapter, nothing in this chapter shall be construed to apply or to give the Commission jurisdiction with respect to (1) charges, classifications, practices, services, facilities, or regulations for or in connection with intrastate communication service by wire or radio of any carrier, or (2) any carrier engaged in interstate or foreign communication solely through physical connection with the facilities of another carrier not directly or indirectly controlling or controlled by, or under direct or indirect common control with such carrier, or (3) any carrier engaged in interstate or foreign communication solely through connection by radio, or by wire and radio, with facilities, located in an adjoining State or in Canada or Mexico (where they adjoin the State in which the carrier is doing business), of another carrier not directly or indirectly controlling or controlled by, or under direct or indirect common control with such carrier, or (4) any carrier to which clause (2) or clause (3) of this subsection would be applicable except for furnishing interstate mobile radio communication service or radio communication service to mobile stations on land vehicles in Canada or Mexico; except that sections 201 to 205 of this title shall, except as otherwise provided therein, apply to carriers described in clauses (2), (3), and (4) of this subsection.

§ 153. Definitions

For the purposes of this chapter, unless the context otherwise requires—

. . .

(2) Affiliate
The term "affiliate" means a person that (directly or indirectly) owns or controls, is owned or controlled by, or is under common ownership or control with, another person. For purposes of this paragraph, the term "own" means to own an equity interest (or the equivalent thereof) of more than 10 percent.

(3) Amateur station
The term "amateur station" means a radio station operated by a duly authorized person interested in radio technique solely with a personal aim and without pecuniary interest.

. . .

(6) Broadcast station

The term "broadcast station", "broadcasting station", or "radio broadcast station" means a radio station equipped to engage in broadcasting as herein defined.

(7) Broadcasting
The term "broadcasting" means the dissemination of radio communications intended to be received by the public, directly or by the intermediary of relay stations.

(8) Cable service
The term "cable service" has the meaning given such term in section 522 of this title.

(9) Cable system
The term "cable system" has the meaning given such term in section 522 of this title.

(10) Chain broadcasting
The term "chain broadcasting" means simultaneous broadcasting of an identical program by two or more connected stations.

(11) Common carrier
The term "common carrier" or "carrier" means any person engaged as a common carrier for hire, in interstate or foreign communication by wire or radio or interstate or foreign radio transmission of energy, except where reference is made to common carriers not subject to this chapter; but a person engaged in radio broadcasting shall not, insofar as such person is so engaged, be deemed a common carrier.

(12) Connecting carrier
The term "connecting carrier" means a carrier described in clauses (2), (3), or (4) of section 152(b) of this title.

(13) Construction permit
The term "construction permit" or "permit for construction" means that instrument of authorization required by this chapter or the rules and regulations of the Commission made pursuant to this chapter for the construction of a station, or the installation of apparatus, for the transmission of energy, or communications, or signals by radio, by whatever name the instrument may be designated by the Commission.

. . .

(28) Interstate communication
The term "interstate communication" or "interstate transmission" means communication or transmission (A) from any State, Territory, or possession of the United States (other than the Canal Zone), or the District of Columbia, to any other State, Territory, or possession of the United States (other than the Canal Zone), or the District of Columbia, (B) from or to the United States to or from the Canal Zone, insofar as such communication or transmission takes place within the United States, or (C) between points within the United States but through a foreign country; but shall not, with respect to the provisions of subchapter II of this chapter (other than section 223 of this title), include wire or radio communication between points in the same State, Territory, or possession of the United States, or the District of Columbia, through any place outside thereof, if such communication is regulated by a State commission.

. . .

(30) Licensee
The term "licensee" means the holder of a radio station license granted or continued in force under authority of this chapter.

. . .

(40) Radio communication
The term "radio communication" or "communication by radio" means the transmission by radio of writing, signs, signals, pictures, and sounds of all kinds, including all instrumentalities, facilities, apparatus, and services (among other things, the receipt, forwarding, and delivery of communications) incidental to such transmission.

. . .

(42) Radio station
The term "radio station" or "station" means a station equipped to engage in radio communication or radio transmission of energy.

. . .

(49) Station license
The term "station license", "radio station license", or "license" means that instrument of authorization required by this chapter or the rules

and regulations of the Commission made pursuant to this chapter, for the use or operation of apparatus for transmission of energy, or communications, or signals by radio, by whatever name the instrument may be designated by the Commission.

(50) Telecommunications
The term "telecommunications" means the transmission, between or among points specified by the user, of information of the user's choosing, without change in the form or content of the information as sent and received.

. . .

(59) Wire communication
The term "wire communication" or "communication by wire" means the transmission of writing, signs, signals, pictures, and sounds of all kinds by aid of wire, cable, or other like connection between the points of origin and reception of such transmission, including all instrumentalities, facilities, apparatus, and services (among other things, the receipt, forwarding, and delivery of communications) incidental to such transmission.

§ 154. Federal Communications Commission

(a) Number of commissioners; appointment
The Federal Communications Commission (in this chapter referred to as the "Commission") shall be composed of five commissioners appointed by the President, by and with the advice and consent of the Senate, one of whom the President shall designate as chairman.

(b) Qualifications

(1) Each member of the Commission shall be a citizen of the United States.

(2)(A) No member of the Commission or person employed by the Commission shall—

(i) be financially interested in any company or other entity engaged in the manufacture or sale of telecommunications equipment which is subject to regulation by the Commission;

(ii) be financially interested in any company or other entity engaged in the business of communication by wire or radio or in the use of the electromagnetic spectrum;

(iii) be financially interested in any company or other entity which controls any company or other entity specified in clause (i) or clause (ii), or which derives a significant portion of its total income from ownership of stocks, bonds, or other securities of any such company or other entity; or

(iv) be employed by, hold any official relation to, or own any stocks, bonds, or other securities of, any person significantly regulated by the Commission under this chapter; except that the prohibitions established in this subparagraph shall apply only to financial interests in any company or other entity which has a significant interest in communications, manufacturing, or sales activities which are subject to regulation by the Commission.

(B)

(i) The Commission shall have authority to waive, from time to time, the application of the prohibitions established in subparagraph (A) . . .

. . .

(5) The maximum number of commissioners who may be members of the same political party shall be a number equal to the least number of commissioners which constitutes a majority of the full membership of the Commission.

(c) Terms of office; vacancies.
[Commissioners] commissioners shall be appointed for terms of five years and until their successors are appointed and have been confirmed and taken the oath of office, except that they shall not continue to serve beyond the expiration of the next session of Congress subsequent to the expiration of said fixed term of office; except that any person chosen to fill a vacancy shall be appointed only for the unexpired term of the commissioner whom he succeeds. No vacancy in the Commission shall

impair the right of the remaining commissioners to exercise all the powers of the Commission.

§ 155. Commission

(a) Chairman; duties; vacancy
The member of the Commission designated by the President as chairman shall be the chief executive officer of the Commission. It shall be his duty to preside at all meetings and sessions of the Commission, to represent the Commission in all matters relating to legislation and legislative reports, except that any commissioner may present his own or minority views or supplemental reports, to represent the Commission in all matters requiring conferences or communications with other governmental officers, departments or agencies, and generally to coordinate and organize the work of the Commission in such manner as to promote prompt and efficient disposition of all matters within the jurisdiction of the Commission. In the case of a vacancy in the office of the chairman of the Commission, or the absence or inability of the chairman to serve, the Commission may temporarily designate one of its members to act as chairman until the cause or circumstance requiring such designation shall have been eliminated or corrected.

(b) Organization of staff
From time to time as the Commission may find necessary, the Commission shall organize its staff into (1) integrated bureaus, to function on the basis of the Commission's principal workload operations, and (2) such other divisional organizations as the Commission may deem necessary. Each such integrated bureau shall include such legal, engineering, accounting, administrative, clerical, and other personnel as the Commission may determine to be necessary to perform its functions . . .

§ 157. New technologies and services

(a) It shall be the policy of the United States to encourage the provision of new technologies and services to the public. Any person or party (other than the Commission) who opposes a new technology or service proposed to be permitted under this chapter shall have the burden to demonstrate that such proposal is inconsistent with the public interest.

(b) The Commission shall determine whether any new technology or service proposed in a petition or application is in the public interest within one year after such petition or application is filed. If the Commission initiates its own proceeding for a new technology or service, such proceeding shall be completed within 12 months after it is initiated. . . .

Title II: Common Carriers

47 U.S.C.A. § 202

§ 202. Discriminations and preferences

(a) Charges, services, etc.
It shall be unlawful for any common carrier to make any unjust or unreasonable discrimination in charges, practices, classifications, regulations, facilities, or services for or in connection with like communication service, directly or indirectly, by any means or device, or to make or give any undue or unreasonable preference or advantage to any particular person, class of persons, or locality, or to subject any particular person, class of persons, or locality to any undue or unreasonable prejudice or disadvantage. . . .

Title III: Broadcasting

47 U.S.C.A. § 301

§ 301. License for radio communication or transmission of energy

It is the purpose of this chapter, among other things, to maintain the control of the United States over all the channels of radio transmission; and to provide for the use of such channels, but not the ownership thereof, by persons for limited periods of time, under licenses granted by Federal authority, and no such license shall be construed to create any right, beyond the terms, conditions, and periods of the license. No person shall use or operate any apparatus for the transmission of energy or communications or signals by radio (a) from one place in any State, Territory, or possession of the United States or in the District of Columbia to another place in the same State, Territory, possession, or District; or (b) from any State, Territory, or possession of the United States, or from the District of Columbia to any other State, Territory, or possession of the United States; or (c) from any place in any State, Territory, or possession of the United States, or in the District of Columbia, to any place in any foreign country or to any vessel; or (d) within any State when the effects of such use extend beyond the borders of said State, or when interference is caused by such use or operation with the transmission of such energy, communications, or signals from within said State to any place beyond its borders, or from any place beyond its borders to any place within said State, or with the transmission or reception of such energy, communications, or signals from and/or to places beyond the borders of said State; or (e) upon any vessel or aircraft of the United States (except as provided in section 303(t) of this title); or (f) upon any other mobile stations within the jurisdiction of the United States, except under and in accordance with this chapter and with a license in that behalf granted under the provisions of this chapter.

. . .

§ 303. Powers and duties of Commission

Except as otherwise provided in this chapter, the Commission from time to time, as public convenience, interest, or necessity requires, shall—

(a) Classify radio stations;

(b) Prescribe the nature of the service to be rendered by each class of licensed stations and each station within any class;

(c) Assign bands of frequencies to the various classes of stations, and assign frequencies for each individual station and determine the power which each station shall use and the time during which it may operate;

(d) Determine the location of classes of stations or individual stations;

(e) Regulate the kind of apparatus to be used with respect to its external effects and the purity and sharpness of the emissions from each station and from the apparatus therein;

(f) Make such regulations not inconsistent with law as it may deem necessary to prevent interference between stations and to carry out the provisions of this chapter: Provided, however, That changes in the frequencies, authorized power, or in the times of operation of any station, shall not be made without the consent of the station licensee unless the Commission shall determine that such changes will promote public convenience or interest or will serve public necessity, or the provisions of this chapter will be more fully complied with;

(g) Study new uses for radio, provide for experimental uses of frequencies, and generally encourage the larger and more effective use of radio in the public interest;

(h) Have authority to establish areas or zones to be served by any station;

(i) Have authority to make special regulations applicable to radio stations engaged in chain broadcasting;

(j) Have authority to make general rules and regulations requiring stations to keep such records of programs, transmissions of energy, communications, or signals as it may deem desirable;

(k) Have authority to exclude from the requirements of any regulations in whole or in part any radio station upon railroad rolling stock, or to modify such regulations in its discretion;

(l)

> (1) Have authority to prescribe the qualifications of station operators, to classify them according to the duties to be performed, to fix the forms of such licenses, and to issue them to persons who are found to be qualified by the Commission and who otherwise are legally eligible for employment in the United States, except that such requirement relating to eligibility for employment in the United States shall not apply in the case of licenses issued by the Commission to (A) persons holding United States pilot certificates; or (B) persons holding foreign aircraft pilot certificates which are valid in the United States, if the foreign government involved has entered into a reciprocal agreement under which such foreign government does not impose any similar requirement relating to eligibility for employment upon citizens of the United States;
>
> (2) Notwithstanding paragraph (1) of this subsection, an individual to whom a radio station is licensed under the provisions of this chapter may be issued an operator's license to operate that station.
>
> (3) In addition to amateur operator licenses which the Commission may issue to aliens pursuant to paragraph (2) of this subsection, and notwithstanding section 301 of this title and paragraph (1) of this subsection, the Commission may issue authorizations,

under such conditions and terms as it may prescribe, to permit an alien licensed by his government as an amateur radio operator to operate his amateur radio station licensed by his government in the United States, its possessions, and the Commonwealth of Puerto Rico provided there is in effect a multilateral or bilateral agreement. . . .

§ 303a. Standards for children's television programming

(a) Establishment
The Commission shall, within 30 days after October 18, 1990, initiate a rulemaking proceeding to prescribe standards applicable to commercial television broadcast licensees with respect to the time devoted to commercial matter in conjunction with children's television programming. The Commission shall, within 180 days after October 18, 1990, complete the rulemaking proceeding and prescribe final standards that meet the requirements of subsection (b) of this section.

(b) Advertising duration limitations
Except as provided in subsection (c) of this section, the standards prescribed under subsection (a) of this section shall include the requirement that each commercial television broadcast licensee shall limit the duration of advertising in children's television programming to not more than 10.5 minutes per hour on weekends and not more than 12 minutes per hour on weekdays.

(c) Review of advertising duration limitations; modification
After January 1, 1993, the Commission—

(1) may review and evaluate the advertising duration limitations required by subsection

(b) of this section; and

(2) may, after notice and public comment and a demonstration of the need for modification of such limitations, modify such limitations in accordance with the public interest.

(d) "Commercial television broadcast licensee" defined
As used in this section, the term "commercial television broadcast licensee" includes a cable operator, as defined in section 522 of this title.

§ 303b. Consideration of children's television service in broadcast license renewal

(a) After the standards required by section 303a of this title are in effect, the Commission shall, in its review of any application for renewal of a commercial or noncommercial television broadcast license, consider the extent to which the licensee—

(1) has complied with such standards; and

(2) has served the educational and informational needs of children through the licensee's overall programming, including programming specifically designed to serve such needs.

(b) In addition to consideration of the licensee's programming as required under subsection (a) of this section, the Commission may consider—

(1) any special nonbroadcast efforts by the licensee which enhance the educational and informational value of such programming to children; and

(2) any special efforts by the licensee to produce or support programming broadcast by another station in the licensee's marketplace which is specifically designed to serve the educational and informational needs of children.

. . .

§ 307. Licenses

(a) Grant
The Commission, if public convenience, interest, or necessity will be served thereby, subject to the limitations of this chapter, shall grant to any applicant therefor a station license provided for by this chapter.

(b) Allocation of facilities
In considering applications for licenses, and modifications and renewals thereof, when and insofar as there is demand for the same, the Commission shall make such distribution of licenses, frequencies, hours of operation, and of power among the several States and communities as to provide a fair, efficient, and equitable distribution of radio service to each of the same.

(c) Terms of licenses

(1) Initial and renewal licenses
Each license granted for the operation of a broadcasting station shall be for a term of not to exceed 8 years. Upon application therefor, a renewal of such license may be granted from time to time for a term of not to exceed 8 years from the date of expiration of the preceding license, if the Commission finds that public interest, convenience, and necessity would be served thereby. Consistent with the foregoing provisions of this subsection, the Commission may by rule prescribe the period or periods for which licenses shall be granted and renewed for particular classes of stations, but the Commission may not adopt or follow any rule which would preclude it, in any case involving a station of a particular class, from granting or renewing a license for a shorter period than that prescribed for stations of such class if, in its judgment, the public interest, convenience, or necessity would be served by such action.

(2) Materials in application
In order to expedite action on applications for renewal of broadcasting station licenses and in order to avoid needless expense to applicants for such renewals, the Commission shall not require any such applicant to file any information which previously has been furnished to the Commission or which is not directly material to the considerations that affect the granting or denial of such application, but the Commission may require any new or additional facts it deems necessary to make its findings.

(3) Continuation pending decision
Pending any administrative or judicial hearing and final decision on such an application and the disposition of any petition for rehearing pursuant to section 405 or section 402 of this title, the Commission shall continue such license in effect.

(d) Renewals
No renewal of an existing station license in the broadcast or the common carrier services shall be granted more than thirty days prior to the expiration of the original license.

§ 308. Requirements for license

(a) Writing; exceptions
The Commission may grant construction permits and station licenses, or modifications or renewals thereof, only upon written application therefor received by it: Provided, That (1) in cases of emergency found by the Commission involving danger to life or property or due to damage to equipment, or (2) during a national emergency proclaimed by the President or declared by the Congress and during the continuance of any war. . . .

(b) Conditions
All applications for station licenses, or modifications or renewals thereof, shall set forth such facts as the Commission by regulation may prescribe as to the citizenship, character, and financial, technical, and other qualifications of the applicant to operate the station; the ownership and location of the proposed station and of the stations, if any, with which it is proposed to communicate; the frequencies and the power desired to be used; the hours of the day or other periods of time during which it is proposed to operate the station; the purposes for which the station is to be used; and such other information as it may require. The Commission, at any time after the filing of such original application and during the term of any such license, may require from an applicant or licensee further written statements of fact to enable it to determine whether such original application should be granted or denied or such license revoked. Such application and/or such statement of fact shall be signed by the applicant and/or licensee in any manner or form, including by electronic means, as the Commission may prescribe by regulation.

§ 309. Application for license

(a) Considerations in granting application
Subject to the provisions of this section, the Commission shall determine, in the case of each application filed with it to which section 308 of this title applies, whether the public interest, convenience, and necessity will be served by the granting of such application, and, if the Commission, upon examination of such application and upon consideration of such other matters as the Commission may officially notice, shall find that public interest, convenience, and necessity would be served by the granting thereof, it shall grant such application.

. . .

(d) Petition to deny application; time; contents; reply; findings

(1) Any party in interest may file with the Commission a petition to deny any application (whether as originally filed or as amended) to which subsection (b) of this section applies at any time prior to the day of Commission grant thereof without hearing or the day of formal designation thereof for hearing; except that with respect to any classification of applications, the Commission from time to time by rule may specify a shorter period (no less than thirty days following the issuance of public notice by the Commission of the acceptance for filing of such application or of any substantial amendment thereof), which shorter period shall be reasonably related to the time when the applications would normally be reached for processing. The petitioner shall serve a copy of such petition on the applicant. The petition shall contain specific allegations of fact sufficient to show that the petitioner is a party in interest and that a grant of the application would be prima facie inconsistent with subsection (a) of this section (or subsection (k) of this section in the case of renewal of any broadcast station license). Such allegations of fact shall, except for those of which official notice may be taken, be supported by affidavit of a person or persons with personal knowledge thereof. The applicant shall be given the opportunity to file a reply in which allegations of fact or denials thereof shall similarly be supported by affidavit.

(2) If the Commission finds on the basis of the application, the pleadings filed, or other matters which it may officially notice that there are no substantial and material questions of fact and that a grant of the application would be consistent with subsection (a) of this section (or subsection (k) of this section in the case of renewal of any broadcast station license), it shall make the grant, deny the petition, and issue a concise statement of the reasons for denying the petition, which statement shall dispose of all substantial issues raised by the petition. If a substantial and material question of fact is presented or if the Commission for any reason is unable to find that grant of the application would be consistent with subsection (a) of this section (or subsection (k) of this section in the case of renewal of any broadcast station license), it shall proceed as provided in subsection (e) of this section.

(j) Use of competitive bidding

(1) General authority

If, consistent with the obligations described in paragraph (6)(E), mutually exclusive applications are accepted for any initial license or construction permit, then, except as provided in paragraph (2), the Commission shall grant the license or permit to a qualified applicant through a system of competitive bidding that meets the requirements of this subsection.

(2) Exemptions
The competitive bidding authority granted by this subsection shall not apply to licenses or construction permits issued by the Commission—

(A) for public safety radio services, including private internal radio services used by State and local governments and non-government entities and including emergency road services provided by not-for-profit organizations, that—

(i) are used to protect the safety of life, health, or property; and

(ii) are not made commercially available to the public;

(B) for initial licenses or construction permits for digital television service given to existing terrestrial broadcast licensees to replace their analog television service licenses; or

(C) for stations described in section 397(6) of this title.

(3) Design of systems of competitive bidding
For each class of licenses or permits that the Commission grants through the use of a competitive bidding system, the Commission shall, by regulation, establish a competitive bidding methodology. The Commission shall seek to design and test multiple alternative methodologies under appropriate circumstances. The Commission shall, directly or by contract, provide for the design and conduct (for purposes of testing) of competitive bidding using a contingent combinatorial bidding system that permits prospective bidders to bid on combinations or groups of licenses in a single bid and to enter multiple alternative bids within a single bidding round. In identifying classes of licenses and permits to be issued by competitive bidding, in specifying eligibility and other characteristics of such licenses and permits, and in designing the meth-

odologies for use under this subsection, the Commission shall include safeguards to protect the public interest in the use of the spectrum and shall seek to promote the purposes specified in section 151 of this title and the following objectives:

(A) the development and rapid deployment of new technologies, products, and services for the benefit of the public, including those residing in rural areas, without administrative or judicial delays;

(B) promoting economic opportunity and competition and ensuring that new and innovative technologies are readily accessible to the American people by avoiding excessive concentration of licenses and by disseminating licenses among a wide variety of applicants, including small businesses, rural telephone companies, and businesses owned by members of minority groups and women;

(C) recovery for the public of a portion of the value of the public spectrum resource made available for commercial use and avoidance of unjust enrichment through the methods employed to award uses of that resource;

(D) efficient and intensive use of the electromagnetic spectrum;

(E) ensure that, in the scheduling of any competitive bidding under this subsection, an adequate period is allowed—

(i) before issuance of bidding rules, to permit notice and comment on proposed auction procedures; and
(ii) after issuance of bidding rules, to ensure that interested parties have a sufficient time to develop business plans, assess market conditions, and evaluate the availability of equipment for the relevant services. . . .

(k) Broadcast station renewal procedures

(1) Standards for renewal
If the licensee of a broadcast station submits an application to the Commission for renewal of such license, the Commission shall grant the application if it finds, with respect to that station, during the preceding term of its license—

(A) the station has served the public interest, convenience, and necessity;

(B) there have been no serious violations by the licensee of this chapter or the rules and regulations of the Commission; and

(C) there have been no other violations by the licensee of this chapter or the rules and regulations of the Commission which, taken together, would constitute a pattern of abuse.

(2) Consequence of failure to meet standard
If any licensee of a broadcast station fails to meet the requirements of this subsection, the Commission may deny the application for renewal in accordance with paragraph (3), or grant such application on terms and conditions as are appropriate, including renewal for a term less than the maximum otherwise permitted.

(3) Standards for denial
If the Commission determines, after notice and opportunity for a hearing as provided in subsection (e) of this section, that a licensee has failed to meet the requirements specified in paragraph (1) and that no mitigating factors justify the imposition of lesser sanctions, the Commission shall—

(A) issue an order denying the renewal application filed by such licensee under section 308 of this title; and

(B) only thereafter accept and consider such applications for a construction permit as may be filed under section 308 of this title specifying the channel or broadcasting facilities of the former licensee.

(4) Competitor consideration prohibited
In making the determinations specified in paragraph (1) or (2), the Commission shall not consider whether the public interest, convenience, and necessity might be served by the grant of a license to a person other than the renewal applicant.

. . .

§ 310. License ownership restrictions

(a) Grant to or holding by foreign government or representative
The station license required under this chapter shall not be granted to or held by any foreign government or the representative thereof.

(b) Grant to or holding by alien or representative, foreign corporation, etc.
No broadcast or common carrier or aeronautical en route or aeronautical fixed radio station license shall be granted to or held by—

(1) any alien or the representative of any alien;

(2) any corporation organized under the laws of any foreign government;

(3) any corporation of which more than one-fifth of the capital stock is owned of record or voted by aliens or their representatives or by a foreign government or representative thereof or by any corporation organized under the laws of a foreign country;

(4) any corporation directly or indirectly controlled by any other corporation of which more than one-fourth of the capital stock is owned of record or voted by aliens, their representatives, or by a foreign government or representative thereof, or by any corporation organized under the laws of a foreign country, if the Commission finds that the public interest will be served by the refusal or revocation of such license.

(c) Authorization for aliens licensed by foreign governments; multilateral or bilateral agreement to which United States and foreign country are parties as prerequisite. . . .

§ 312. Administrative sanctions

(a) Revocation of station license or construction permit
The Commission may revoke any station license or construction permit—

(1) for false statements knowingly made either in the application or in any statement of fact which may be required pursuant to section 308 of this title;

(2) because of conditions coming to the attention of the Commission which would warrant it in refusing to grant a license or permit on an original application;

(3) for willful or repeated failure to operate substantially as set forth in the license;

(4) for willful or repeated violation of, or willful or repeated failure to observe any provision of this chapter or any rule or regulation of the Commission authorized by this chapter or by a treaty ratified by the United States;

(5) for violation of or failure to observe any final cease and desist order issued by the Commission under this section;

(6) for violation of section 1304, 1343, or 1464 of Title 18; or

(7) for willful or repeated failure to allow reasonable access to or to permit purchase of reasonable amounts of time for the use of a broadcasting station, other than a non-commercial educational broadcast station, by a legally qualified candidate for Federal elective office on behalf of his candidacy.

. . .

§ 315. Candidates for public office

(a) Equal opportunities requirement; censorship prohibition; allowance of station use; news appearances exception; public interest; public issues discussion opportunities. If any licensee shall permit any person who is a legally qualified candidate for any public office to use a broadcasting station, he shall afford equal opportunities to all other such candidates for that office in the use of such broadcasting station: Provided, That such licensee shall have no power of censorship over the material broadcast under the provisions of this section. No obligation is imposed under this subsection upon any licensee to allow the use of its station by any such candidate. Appearance by a legally qualified candidate on any—

(1) bona fide newscast,

(2) bona fide news interview,

(3) bona fide news documentary (if the appearance of the candidate is incidental to the presentation of the subject or subjects covered by the news documentary), or

(4) on-the-spot coverage of bona fide news events (including but not limited to political conventions and activities incidental thereto), shall not be deemed to be use of a broadcasting station within the meaning of this subsection. Nothing in the foregoing sentence shall be construed as relieving broadcasters, in connection with the presentation of newscasts, news interviews, news documentaries, and on-the-spot coverage of news events, from the obligation imposed upon them under this chapter to operate in the public interest and to afford reasonable opportunity for the discussion of conflicting views on issues of public importance.

(b) Charges

(1) In general
The charges made for the use of any broadcasting station by any person who is a legally qualified candidate for any public office in connection with his campaign for nomination for election, or election, to such office shall not exceed—

(A) subject to paragraph (2), during the forty-five days preceding the date of a primary or primary runoff election and during the sixty days preceding the date of a general or special election in which such person is a candidate, the lowest unit charge of the station for the same class and amount of time for the same period; and

(B) at any other time, the charges made for comparable use of such station by other users thereof.

(2) Content of broadcasts

(A) In general
In the case of a candidate for Federal office, such candidate shall not be entitled to receive the rate under paragraph (1)(A) for the use of any broadcasting station unless the candidate provides written certification to the broadcast station that the candidate (and any authorized committee of the candidate)

shall not make any direct reference to another candidate for the same office, in any broadcast using the rights and conditions of access under this chapter, unless such reference meets the requirements of subparagraph (C) or (D).

(B) Limitation on charges
If a candidate for Federal office (or any authorized committee of such candidate) makes a reference described in subparagraph (A) in any broadcast that does not meet the requirements of subparagraph (C) or (D), such candidate shall not be entitled to receive the rate under paragraph (1)(A) for such broadcast or any other broadcast during any portion of the 45-day and 60-day periods described in paragraph (1)(A), that occur on or after the date of such broadcast, for election to such office.

(C) Television broadcasts
A candidate meets the requirements of this subparagraph if, in the case of a television broadcast, at the end of such broadcast there appears simultaneously, for a period no less than 4 seconds—

(i) a clearly identifiable photographic or similar image of the candidate; and

(ii) a clearly readable printed statement, identifying the candidate and stating that the candidate has approved the broadcast and that the candidate's authorized committee paid for the broadcast.

(D) Radio broadcasts
A candidate meets the requirements of this subparagraph if, in the case of a radio broadcast, the broadcast includes a personal audio statement by the candidate that identifies the candidate, the office the candidate is seeking, and indicates that the candidate has approved the broadcast.

. . .

§ 317. Announcement of payment for broadcast

(a) Disclosure of person furnishing

(1) All matter broadcast by any radio station for which any money, service or other valuable consideration is directly or indirectly paid, or promised to or charged or accepted by, the station so broadcasting, from any person, shall, at the time the same is so broadcast, be announced as paid for or furnished, as the case may be, by such person: Provided, That "service or other valuable consideration" shall not include any service or property furnished without charge or at a nominal charge for use on, or in connection with, a broadcast unless it is so furnished in consideration for an identification in a broadcast of any person, product, service, trademark, or brand name beyond an identification which is reasonably related to the use of such service or property on the broadcast.

(2) Nothing in this section shall preclude the Commission from requiring that an appropriate announcement shall be made at the time of the broadcast in the case of any political program or any program involving the discussion of any controversial issue for which any films, records, transcriptions, talent, scripts, or other material or service of any kind have been furnished, without charge or at a nominal charge, directly or indirectly, as an inducement to the broadcast of such program.

. . .

§ 326. Censorship

Nothing in this chapter shall be understood or construed to give the Commission the power of censorship over the radio communications or signals transmitted by any radio station, and no regulation or condition shall be promulgated or fixed by the Commission which shall interfere with the right of free speech by means of radio communication.

. . .

§ 333. Willful or malicious interference

No person shall willfully or maliciously interfere with or cause interference to any radio communications of any station licensed or authorized by or under this chapter or operated by the United States Government.

. . .

§ 335. Direct broadcast satellite service obligations

(a) Proceeding required to review DBS responsibilities
The Commission shall, within 180 days after October 5, 1992, initiate a rulemaking proceeding to impose, on providers of direct broadcast satellite service, public interest or other requirements for providing video programming. Any regulations prescribed pursuant to such rulemaking shall, at a minimum, apply the access to broadcast time requirement of section 312(a)(7) of this title and the use of facilities requirements of section 315 of this title to providers of direct broadcast satellite service providing video programming. Such proceeding also shall examine the opportunities that the establishment of direct broadcast satellite service provides for the principle of localism under this chapter, and the methods by which such principle may be served through technological and other developments in, or regulation of, such service.

(b) Carriage obligations for noncommercial, educational, state public affairs, and informational programming.

(1) Channel capacity required

(A) In general
Except as provided in subparagraph (B), the Commission shall require, as a condition of any provision, initial authorization, or authorization renewal for a provider of direct broadcast satellite service providing video programming, that the provider of such service reserve a portion of its channel capacity, equal to not less than 4 percent nor more than 7 percent, exclusively for noncommercial programming of an educational or informational nature.

(B) Requirement for qualified satellite provider

The Commission shall require, as a condition of any provision, initial authorization, or authorization renewal for a qualified satellite provider of direct broadcast satellite service providing video programming, that such provider reserve a portion of its channel capacity, equal to not less than 3.5 percent nor more than 7 percent, exclusively for noncommercial programming of an educational or informational nature.

(2) Use of unused channel capacity
A provider of such service may utilize for any purpose any unused channel capacity required to be reserved under this subsection pending the actual use of such channel capacity for noncommercial programming of an educational or informational nature.

(3) Prices, terms, and conditions; editorial control
A provider of direct broadcast satellite service shall meet the requirements of this subsection by making channel capacity available to national educational programming suppliers, upon reasonable prices, terms, and conditions, as determined by the Commission under paragraph (4). The provider of direct broadcast satellite service shall not exercise any editorial control over any video programming provided pursuant to this subsection. . . .

§ 338. Carriage of local television signals by satellite carriers

(a) Carriage obligations

(1) In general
Each satellite carrier providing, under section 122 of Title 17, secondary transmissions to subscribers located within the local market of a television broadcast station of a primary transmission made by that station shall carry upon request the signals of all television broadcast stations located within that local market, subject to section 325(b) of this title.

(2) Remedies for failure to carry
In addition to the remedies available to television broadcast stations under section 501(f) of Title 17, the Commission may use the Commission's authority under this chapter to assure compliance with the obligations of this subsection, but in no instance shall a Commission enforcement proceeding be required as a predicate to the pursuit of a remedy available under such section 501(f).

. . .

§ 396. Corporation for Public Broadcasting

. . .

(b) Establishment of Corporation; application of District of Columbia Nonprofit Corporation Act.

There is authorized to be established a nonprofit corporation, to be known as the "Corporation for Public Broadcasting", which will not be an agency or establishment of the United States Government. The Corporation shall be subject to the provisions of this section, and, to the extent consistent with this section, to the District of Columbia Nonprofit Corporation Act. . . .

§ 399. Support of political candidates prohibited

No noncommercial educational broadcasting station may support or oppose any candidate for political office.

Title V: Penalties

§ 501. General penalty

Any person who willfully and knowingly does or causes or suffers to be done any act, matter, or thing, in this chapter prohibited or declared to be unlawful, or who willfully and knowingly omits or fails to do any act, matter, or thing in this chapter required to be done, or willfully and knowingly causes or suffers such omission or failure, shall, upon conviction thereof, be punished for such offense, for which no penalty (other than a forfeiture) is provided in this chapter, by a fine of not more than $10,000 or by imprisonment for a term not exceeding one year, or both; except that any person, having been once convicted of an offense punishable under this section, who is subsequently convicted of violating any provision of this chapter punishable under this section, shall be punished by a fine of not more than $10,000 or by imprisonment for a term not exceeding two years, or both.

§ 503. Forfeitures

(a) Rebates and offsets
Any person who shall deliver messages for interstate or foreign transmission to any carrier, or for whom as sender or receiver, any such carrier shall transmit any interstate or foreign wire or radio communication, who shall knowingly by employee, agent, officer, or otherwise, directly or indirectly, by or through any means or device whatsoever, receive or accept from such common carrier any sum of money or any other valuable consideration as a rebate or offset against the regular charges for transmission of such messages as fixed by the schedules of charges provided for in this chapter, shall in addition to any other penalty provided by this chapter forfeit to the United States a sum of money three

times the amount of money so received or accepted and three times the value of any other consideration so received or accepted, to be ascertained by the trial court; and in the trial of said action all such rebates or other considerations so received or accepted for a period of six years prior to the commencement of the action, may be included therein, and the amount recovered shall be three times the total amount of money, or three times the total value of such consideration, so received or accepted, or both, as the case may be.

(b) Activities constituting violations authorizing imposition of forfeiture penalty; amount of penalty; procedures applicable; persons subject to penalty; liability exemption period.

(1) Any person who is determined by the Commission, in accordance with paragraph (3) or (4) of this subsection, to have—

(A) willfully or repeatedly failed to comply substantially with the terms and conditions of any license, permit, certificate, or other instrument or authorization issued by the Commission;

(B) willfully or repeatedly failed to comply with any of the provisions of this chapter or of any rule, regulation, or order issued by the Commission under this chapter or under any treaty, convention, or other agreement to which the United States is a party and which is binding upon the United States;

(C) violated any provision of section 317(c) or 509(a) of this title; or

(D) violated any provision of section 1304, 1343, 1464, or 2252 of Title 18; shall be liable to the United States for a forfeiture penalty. A forfeiture penalty under this subsection shall be in addition to any other penalty provided for by this chapter; except that this subsection shall not apply to any conduct which is subject to forfeiture under subchapter II of this chapter, part II or III of subchapter III of this chapter, or section 507 of this title.

§ 508. Disclosure of payments to individuals connected with broadcasts

(a) Payments to station employees

Subject to subsection (d) of this section, any employee of a radio station who accepts or agrees to accept from any person (other than such station), or any person (other than such station) who pays or agrees to pay such employee, any money, service or other valuable consideration for the broadcast of any matter over such station shall, in advance of such broadcast, disclose the fact of such acceptance or agreement to such station.

(b) Production or preparation of programs
Subject to subsection (d) of this section, any person who, in connection with the production or preparation of any program or program matter which is intended for broadcasting over any radio station, accepts or agrees to accept, or pays or agrees to pay, any money, service or other valuable consideration for the inclusion of any matter as a part of such program or program matter, shall, in advance of such broadcast, disclose the fact of such acceptance or payment or agreement to the payee's employer, or to the person for whom such program or program matter is being produced, or to the licensee of such station over which such program is broadcast.

(c) Supplying of program or program matter
Subject to subsection (d) of this section, any person who supplies to any other person any program or program matter which is intended for broadcasting over any radio station shall, in advance of such broadcast, disclose to such other person any information of which he has knowledge, or which has been disclosed to him, as to any money, service or other valuable consideration which any person has paid or accepted, or has agreed to pay or accept, for the inclusion of any matter as a part of such program or program matter.

(d) Waiver of announcements under section 317(d). . . .

§ 509. Prohibited practices in contests of knowledge, skill, or chance

(a) Influencing, prearranging, or predetermining outcome
It shall be unlawful for any person, with intent to deceive the listening or viewing public—

> (1) To supply to any contestant in a purportedly bona fide contest of intellectual knowledge or intellectual skill any special and secret assistance whereby the outcome of such contest will be in whole or in part prearranged or predetermined.

(2) By means of persuasion, bribery, intimidation, or otherwise, to induce or cause any contestant in a purportedly bona fide contest of intellectual knowledge or intellectual skill to refrain in any manner from using or displaying his knowledge or skill in such contest, whereby the outcome thereof will be in whole or in part prearranged or predetermined.

(3) To engage in any artifice or scheme for the purpose of prearranging or predetermining in whole or in part the outcome of a purportedly bona fide contest of intellectual knowledge, intellectual skill, or chance.

(4) To produce or participate in the production for broadcasting of, to broadcast or participate in the broadcasting of, to offer to a licensee for broadcasting, or to sponsor, any radio program, knowing or having reasonable ground for believing that, in connection with a purportedly bona fide contest of intellectual knowledge, intellectual skill, or chance constituting any part of such program, any person has done or is going to do any act or thing referred to in paragraph (1), (2), or (3) of this subsection.
(5) To conspire with any other person or persons to do any act or thing prohibited by paragraph (1), (2), (3), or (4) of this subsection, if one or more of such persons do any act to effect the object of such conspiracy.

(b) "Contest" and "the listening or viewing public" defined
For the purposes of this section—

(1) The term "contest" means any contest broadcast by a radio station in connection with which any money or any other thing of value is offered as a prize or prizes to be paid or presented by the program sponsor or by any other person or persons, as announced in the course of the broadcast.

(2) The term "the listening or viewing public" means those members of the public who, with the aid of radio receiving sets, listen to or view programs broadcast by radio stations.

(c) Penalties
Whoever violates subsection (a) of this section shall be fined not more than $10,000 or imprisoned not more than one year, or both.

Title VI: Cable (Statute § 601 et seq. Codified as § 520 et seq.)

§ 531. Cable channels for public, educational, or governmental use (§ 611)

(a) Authority to establish requirements with respect to designation or use of channel capacity
A franchising authority may establish requirements in a franchise with respect to the designation or use of channel capacity for public, educational, or governmental use only to the extent provided in this section.

(b) Authority to require designation for public, educational, or governmental use
A franchising authority may in its request for proposals require as part of a franchise, and may require as part of a cable operator's proposal for a franchise renewal, subject to section 546 of this title, that channel capacity be designated for public, educational, or governmental use, and channel capacity on institutional networks be designated for educational or governmental use, and may require rules and procedures for the use of the channel capacity designated pursuant to this section. . . .

§ 534. Carriage of local commercial television signals (§ 614)

(a) Carriage obligations
Each cable operator shall carry, on the cable system of that operator, the signals of local commercial television stations and qualified low power stations as provided by this section. Carriage of additional broadcast television signals on such system shall be at the discretion of such operator, subject to section 325(b) of this title.

(b) Signals required

(1) In general

(A) A cable operator of a cable system with 12 or fewer usable activated channels shall carry the signals of at least three local commercial television stations, except that if such a system has 300 or fewer subscribers, it shall not be subject to any requirements under this section so long as such system does not delete from carriage by that system any signal of a broadcast television station.

(B) A cable operator of a cable system with more than 12 usable activated channels shall carry the signals of local commercial television stations, up to one-third of the aggregate number of usable activated channels of such system.

(2) Selection of signals
Whenever the number of local commercial television stations exceeds the maximum number of signals a cable system is required to carry under paragraph (1), the cable operator shall have discretion in selecting which such stations shall be carried on its cable system, except that—

(A) under no circumstances shall a cable operator carry a qualified low power station in lieu of a local commercial television station; and

(B) if the cable operator elects to carry an affiliate of a broadcast network (as such term is defined by the Commission by regulation), such cable operator shall carry the affiliate of such broadcast network whose city of license reference point, as defined in section 76.56 of title 47, Code of Federal Regulations (in effect on January 1, 1991), or any successor regulation thereto, is closest to the principal headend of the cable system.

(3) Content to be carried

(A) A cable operator shall carry in its entirety, on the cable system of that operator, the primary video, accompanying audio, and line 21 closed caption transmission of each of the local commercial television stations carried on the cable system and, to the extent technically feasible, program-related material carried in the vertical blanking interval or on subcarriers. Retransmission of other material in the vertical blanking internal or other nonprogram-related material (including teletext and other subscription and advertiser-supported information services) shall be at the discretion of the cable operator. Where appropriate and feasible, operators may delete signal enhancements, such as ghost-canceling, from the broadcast signal and employ such enhancements at the system headend or headends.

(B) The cable operator shall carry the entirety of the program schedule of any television station carried on the cable system unless carriage of specific programming is prohibited, and other programming authorized to be substituted, under section 76.67 or subpart F of part 76 of title 47, Code of Federal Regulations (as in effect on January 1, 1991), or any successor regulations thereto.

(4) Signal quality

(A) Nondegradation; technical specifications
The signals of local commercial television stations that a cable operator carries shall be carried without material degradation. The Commission shall adopt carriage standards to ensure that, to the extent technically feasible, the quality of signal processing and carriage provided by a cable system for the car riage of local commercial television stations will be no less than that provided by the system for carriage of any other type of signal.

(B) Advanced television
At such time as the Commission prescribes modifications of the standards for television broadcast signals, the Commission shall initiate a proceeding to establish any changes in the signal carriage requirements of cable television systems necessary to ensure cable carriage of such broadcast signals of local commercial television stations which have been changed to conform with such modified standards.

(5) Duplication not required
Notwithstanding paragraph (1), a cable operator shall not be required to carry the signal of any local commercial television station that substantially duplicates the signal of another local commercial television station which is carried on its cable system, or to carry the signals of more than one local commercial television station affiliated with a particular broadcast network (as such term is defined by regulation). If a cable operator elects to carry on its cable system a signal which substantially duplicates the signal of another local commercial television station carried on the cable system, or to carry on its system the signals of more than one local commercial television station affiliated with a particular broadcast network, all such signals shall be counted toward the number of signals the operator is required to carry under paragraph (1).

(6) Channel positioning

Each signal carried in fulfillment of the carriage obligations of a cable operator under this section shall be carried on the cable system channel number on which the local commercial television station is broadcast over the air, or on the channel on which it was carried on July 19, 1985, or on the channel on which it was carried on January 1, 1992, at the election of the station, or on such other channel number as is mutually agreed upon by the station and the cable operator. Any dispute regarding the positioning of a local commercial television station shall be resolved by the Commission. . . .

§ 535. Carriage of noncommercial educational television (§ 615)

(a) Carriage obligations
In addition to the carriage requirements set forth in section 534 of this title, each cable operator of a cable system shall carry the signals of qualified noncommercial educational television stations in accordance with the provisions of this section.

(b) Requirements to carry qualified stations

(1) General requirement to carry each qualified station
Subject to paragraphs (2) and (3) and subsection (e) of this section, each cable operator shall carry, on the cable system of that cable operator, any qualified local noncommercial educational television station requesting carriage.

(2) Systems with 12 or fewer channels

(A) Notwithstanding paragraph (1), a cable operator of a cable system with 12 or fewer usable activated channels shall be required to carry the signal of one qualified local noncommercial educational television station; except that a cable operator of such a system shall comply with subsection (c) of this section and may, in its discretion, carry the signals of other qualified noncommercial educational television stations.

(B) In the case of a cable system described in subparagraph (A) which operates beyond the presence of any qualified local noncommercial educational television station –

(i) the cable operator shall import and carry on that system the signal of one qualified noncommercial educational television station;

(ii) the selection for carriage of such a signal shall be at the election of the cable operator; and

(iii) in order to satisfy the requirements for carriage specified in this subsection, the cable operator of the system shall not be required to remove any other programming service actually provided to subscribers on March 29, 1990; except that such cable operator shall use the first channel available to satisfy the requirements of this subparagraph.

(3) Systems with 13 to 36 channels

(A) Subject to subsection (c) of this section, a cable operator of a cable system with 13 to 36 usable activated channels –

(i) shall carry the signal of at least one qualified local noncommercial educational television station but shall not be required to carry the signals of more than three such stations, and

(ii) may, in its discretion, carry additional such stations.

(B) In the case of a cable system described in this paragraph which operates beyond the presence of any qualified local noncommercial educational television station, the cable operator shall import and carry on that system the signal of at least one qualified noncommercial educational television station to comply with subparagraph (A)(i). . . .

§ 553. Unauthorized reception of cable service (§ 633)

(a) Unauthorized interception or receipt or assistance in intercepting or receiving service; "assist in intercepting or receiving" defined

(1) No person shall intercept or receive or assist in intercepting or receiving any communications service offered over a cable system, unless specifically authorized to do so by a cable operator or as may otherwise be specifically authorized by law.

(2) For the purpose of this section, the term "assist in intercepting or receiving" shall include the manufacture or distribution of equipment intended by the manufacturer or distributor (as the case may be) for unauthorized reception of any communications service offered over a cable system in violation of subparagraph (1).

(b) Penalties for willful violation

(1) Any person who willfully violates subsection (a)(1) of this section shall be fined not more than $1,000 or imprisoned for not more than 6 months, or both.

(2) Any person who violates subsection (a)(1) of this section willfully and for purposes of commercial advantage or private financial gain shall be fined not more than $50,000 or imprisoned for not more than 2 years, or both, for the first such offense and shall be fined not more than $100,000 or imprisoned for not more than 5 years, or both, for any subsequent offense. . . .

CPSIA information can be obtained
at www.ICGtesting.com
Printed in the USA
BVHW061131030121
596789BV00006B/17